Techniques of Crime Scene Investigation

Also by Barry Fisher

with David Fisher and Jason Kolowski
Forensics Demystified (2007)

———————————

with William Tillstone and Catherine Woytowicz
Introduction to Criminalistics: The Foundation of Forensic Science (2009)

Techniques of Crime Scene Investigation

Ninth Edition

Barry A.J. Fisher and David R. Fisher

CRC Press
Taylor & Francis Group
Boca Raton London New York

CRC Press is an imprint of the
Taylor & Francis Group, an **informa** business

Cover image: wellphoto/Shutterstock

The views of the authors of this book are their own and are not necessarily those of the State of New Jersey, New Jersey Institute of Technology, or the US Dept of Health and Human Services. Commercial products mentioned in this book should not be considered as endorsements of such products by the authors.

Ninth edition published 2022
by CRC Press
6000 Broken Sound Parkway NW, Suite 300, Boca Raton, FL 33487-2742

and by CRC Press
4 Park Square, Milton Park, Abingdon, Oxon, OX14 4RN

CRC Press is an imprint of Taylor & Francis Group, LLC

© 2022 Taylor & Francis Group, LLC

First edition published by Elsevier 1949
Eighth edition published by CRC Press 2012

Reasonable efforts have been made to publish reliable data and information, but the author and publisher cannot assume responsibility for the validity of all materials or the consequences of their use. The authors and publishers have attempted to trace the copyright holders of all material reproduced in this publication and apologize to copyright holders if permission to publish in this form has not been obtained. If any copyright material has not been acknowledged please write and let us know so we may rectify in any future reprint.

Except as permitted under U.S. Copyright Law, no part of this book may be reprinted, reproduced, transmitted, or utilized in any form by any electronic, mechanical, or other means, now known or hereafter invented, including photocopying, microfilming, and recording, or in any information storage or retrieval system, without written permission from the publishers.

For permission to photocopy or use material electronically from this work, access www.copyright.com or contact the Copyright Clearance Center, Inc. (CCC), 222 Rosewood Drive, Danvers, MA 01923, 978-750-8400. For works that are not available on CCC please contact mpkbookspermissions@tandf.co.uk

Trademark notice: Product or corporate names may be trademarks or registered trademarks and are used only for identification and explanation without intent to infringe.

Library of Congress Cataloging-in-Publication Data

Names: Fisher, Barry A. J., author. | Fisher, David R., author.
Title: Techniques of crime scene investigation / Barry A. J. Fisher and David R. Fisher.
Identifiers: LCCN 2021055589 (print) | LCCN 2021055590 (ebook) | ISBN 9781498758130 (hbk) | ISBN 9780429272011 (ebk)
Subjects: LCSH: Crime scene searches. | Criminal investigation.
Classification: LCC HV8073 .F49 2022 (print) | LCC HV8073 (ebook) | DDC 363.25/2--dc23
LC record available at https://lccn.loc.gov/2021055589
LC ebook record available at https://lccn.loc.gov/2021055590

ISBN: 978-1-498-75813-0 (hbk)
ISBN: 978-0-429-27201-1 (ebk)

DOI: 10.4324/9780429272011

Typeset in Minion
by Deanta Global Publishing Services, Chennai, India

Access the Support Material: www.routledge.com/9781498758130

In memory of the victims of terrorism around the world…may God avenge their blood.

Contents

Foreword — xvii
Preface — xix
Acknowledgments — xxi
About the Authors — xxiii

PART I   The Crime Scene — 1

1   Introduction — 3
Classification and Individualization of Physical Evidence — 9
Important Considerations in Crime Scene Investigations — 10
Teamwork — 10
Professional Development — 11
ISO/IEC 17020 Accreditation — 12
ISO/IEC 17043 Accreditation — 12
Legal Cases Regarding Forensic Science — 12
Funding — 14
Mental Health — 14
Cognitive Bias — 15
The Future — 15
Further Reading — 15
Chapter Questions — 15

2   First on Scene and Crime Scene Personnel — 17
The First Officer at the Scene — 17
Crime Scene Dos and Don'ts — 20
Recording the Time — 20
When a Suspect is Found at the Scene — 20
Injured Person on the Scene — 21
Entering the Scene Proper — 21
Protecting the Integrity of the Scene — 22
Dead Person on the Scene — 23
Summoning the Medical Examiner — 23
Firearms and Ammunition at the Scene — 24
What to Do Until Investigating Personnel Arrive — 25
Continued Protection of the Scene — 25
Crime Scene Personnel — 26
Further Reading — 27
Chapter Questions — 27

3   Documenting the Crime Scene — 29
Preparation and Plan of Action — 29
Note-taking — 29
Crime Scene Photography — 30
  Types of Cameras — 31
  Number of Photographs — 32
  Photographing a Dead Body — 34
  Admissibility of Photographs — 36

vii

Videography	36
Drones	37
Sketching the Crime Scene	38
Information Included in Crime Scene Sketches	38
Equipment	38
Types of Sketches	39
Locating Objects in the Sketch	39
CAD Software	40
3D Scanning	40
Further Reading	41
Chapter Questions	41

4 Physical Evidence Collection — 43

Detailed Search	43
Collection of Evidence	43
Chain of Custody	48
Preservation	49
The Underwater Crime Scene	50
HAZMAT Crime Scenes	51
Final Survey	51
Releasing the Scene	51
Further Reading	51
Chapter Questions	51

5 Crime Scene Reconstruction — 53

Bloodstain Pattern Analysis (BPA)	59
Accident Reconstruction	62
Forensic Shooting Reconstructions	64
Further Reading	65
Chapter Questions	65

PART II Physical Evidence — 67

6 Fingerprint Evidence — 69

Fingerprints and Palm Prints	69
Where to Look for Fingerprints	69
Different Types of Fingerprints	70
Fingerprint Developing Techniques	71
Development with Powders	71
Lasers and Alternative Light Sources	75
Integrated Automated Fingerprint Identification System	75
Preservation by Photography	77
Preservation of Plastic Fingerprints	77
Preservation with Fingerprint-lifting Tape	77
How Long Does a Fingerprint Remain on an Object?	78
The Effect of Temperature Conditions on the Possibility of Developing Fingerprints	78
Examination of Developed Fingerprints	78
Palm Prints	78
Prints from the Sole of the Foot	80
Ear, Lip, and Other Prints	80
Transporting Objects with Fingerprints	80
Taking Fingerprints for Elimination	80
Prints of Gloves	80
Prints of Other Coverings	81

Latent Fingerprints on Human Skin	82
Taking Fingerprints from a Decedent	82
Fingerprint Enhancement using Adobe Photoshop®	84
Fingerprint Examiner Conclusions	84
ACE-V	86
IAI Certification	86
OSAC Friction Ridge Subcommittee	86
Fingerprints from Online Photos	87
Fake Fingerprints	87
Further Reading	87
Chapter Questions	88

7 Blood, Forensic Biology, and DNA — 89

A Word of Caution!	89
Contamination	89
ISO 18385—Forensic DNA Grade	90
Presumptive Tests for Blood	90
Searching for Bloodstains	91
Description and Recording of Bloodstains	93
Collection and Preservation of Bloodstains	94
Removal of Biological Stains	94
Bloodstained Objects	95
Species Testing	95
Forensic DNA Typing	97
PCR-based Technology	97
Mitochondrial DNA	99
Y-STRs	99
CODIS	99
Missing Persons	100
Massively Parallel Sequencing/Next Generation Sequencing	100
Rapid DNA	101
Forensic Genetic Genealogy	101
OSAC Human Forensic Biology Subcommittee	102
SWGDAM	102
The Future	102
Further Reading	102
Chapter Questions	103

8 Forensic Traces — 105

Sources of Traces	105
Clothing	105
Footwear	106
Evidence from the Body	106
Other Objects as Sources of Trace Evidence	107
Collection and Preservation of Trace Evidence	109
Examples of Trace Evidence	109
Building Materials	109
Asbestos	110
Safe Insulation	110
Paint	110
Rust	111
Metals	111
Textiles and Fibers	112

Buttons	114
Cordage and Rope	115
Cigarettes and Tobacco	115
Matches	115
Ash	116
Soil	116
Wood	116
Chips and Splinters of Wood	117
Sawdust, Wood Meal, or Particles of Finely Powdered Wood	117
Plant Material	118
Glass	118
Broken Panes of Glass	118
Glass Perforated by a Bullet	119
Cracked or Burst Panes of Glass	120
Glass Splinters	121
Objects Left at the Crime Scene	122
Paper	122
Articles of Clothing	122
Product Markings	122
Foodstuffs	123
Cosmetics	123
Hair	123
Feathers (Plumology)	124
Electrical Wire	124
Tape	125
Headlamps	125
Physical Fit	126
OSAC Trace Materials Subcommittee	126
SWGMAT	126
Further Reading	126
Chapter Questions	127

9 Impression Evidence — 129

Footprints	129
Value of Footprints	130
Preservation of Footwear and Tire Impressions	130
Footprints on Floors	130
Preservation of Footwear Evidence	131
Photographing Footwear Impressions	131
Casting with Dental Stone	132
Casting Water-Filled Impressions	133
Casting Impressions in Snow	133
Preservation of Footprints (Dust Prints)	133
Taking Comparison Footprints from a Suspect	134
Comparison of Footprints	134
Marks on Clothes and Parts of the Body	135
Fabric Marks	135
Tool Marks	135
Preservation of Tool Marks	137
Casting Tool Marks	137
Trace Evidence on Tools	137
Preserving a Tool	139
Fragments of Tools	139

	Tire Tread and Tire Track Evidence	140
	OSAC Footwear and Tire Subcommittee	140
	SWGTREAD	140
	Further Reading	141
	Chapter Questions	141
10	**Firearms Examination**	143
	Characteristics of Firearms	143
	Ammunition	145
	Firearms Evidence	147
	Gunshot Residue (GSR) Analysis	148
	Collecting Firearms Evidence	150
	Handling of Firearms	152
	Cartridge Cases	154
	Bullets	157
	Marking Bullets	157
	Small Shot	159
	Test Firing	160
	Powder Pattern Examination	161
	National Integrated Ballistic Information Network	162
	3D Printed "Ghost" Guns	163
	OSAC Firearms & Toolmarks Subcommittee	163
	SWGGUN	163
	Further Reading	163
	Chapter Questions	163
11	**Arson and Explosives**	165
	Introduction	165
	Physical Evidence	167
	Explosives	170
	Low Explosives	170
	High Explosives	171
	Blasting Agents	172
	Military Explosives	173
	Homemade Explosives (HME)	173
	Bomb Scene Investigation	174
	OSAC Fire & Explosion Investigation Subcommittee	176
	Further Reading	176
	Chapter Questions	176
12	**Illicit Drugs and Toxicology**	179
	U.S. DEA Drug Schedule Classification	179
	Schedule I	179
	Schedule II	179
	Schedule III	180
	Schedule IV	180
	Schedule V	180
	Psychoactive Drugs	180
	Narcotics	180
	Depressants	180
	Stimulants	181
	Hallucinogens	182
	Cannabis	182
	Designer Drugs	183

Steroids	183
Inhalants	184
Nonprescription Drugs	184
Crime Scene Search	184
Searching a Suspect	184
Searching a Dwelling	185
Searching a Vehicle	185
Clandestine Drug Laboratories	185
Collection and Preservation of Evidence	186
Field Testing	186
Forensic Toxicology	188
OSAC Seized Drugs Subcommittee	188
SWGDRUG	189
OSAC Forensic Toxicology Subcommittee	189
SWGTOX	189
Further Reading	189
Chapter Questions	189

13 Document Evidence — 191

Video Spectral Comparator	195
Graphology	195
OSAC Forensic Document Examination Subcommittee	195
SWGDOC	195
Forensic Linguistics	195
Further Reading	197
Chapter Questions	197

PART III The Investigation and Special Considerations — 199

14 Ethics in Crime Scene Investigation — 201

Further Reading	207
Chapter Questions	207

15 Sexual Assault Investigation — 209

Sexual Assault	209
The Interview	209
Medical Examination	210
Date-Rape Drugs	214
Sexual Child Molestation and Incest	214
Public Lewdness/Forcible Touching	215
Rape Kit Backlog	216
National Best Practices	216
Conclusion	216
Further Reading	216
Chapter Questions	216

16 Burglary Investigation — 219

Points of Entry	219
Entry through Windows	219
Entry through Doors	220
Entry through Basement Windows and Skylights	222
Entry through Roofs	222
Entry through Walls	223
Entry through Floors	223

    Simulated Burglaries   223
    Detailed Examination of the Scene   223
    Safe Burglaries   224
    Safe Burglaries using Explosives   226
    Forensic Locksmithing   228
    Further Reading   228
    Chapter Questions   228

17 Motor Vehicle Investigation   231

    Grand Theft Auto   231
    Abandoned Vehicles   232
    Homicide in a Vehicle   233
    Hit-and-run Investigation   234
    Marks from Vehicles   237
    Wheel Marks   237
    Skid marks   237
    Airbags   237
    Digital Automotive Image System (DAIS)   238
    Further Reading   238
    Chapter Questions   238

18 Death Investigation   239

    Murder, Suicide, or Accident?   240
        Cause of Death   240
    Suicide   240
    Signs of Struggle   243
    Location of Weapon   244
    Examination of a Dead Body at the Crime Scene   244
    Murder   246
    Detailed Examination of the Crime Scene   248
    Outdoor Crime Scenes   252
    Discovering a Body Hidden at another Location   254
    Investigation of a Greatly Altered Body or Skeleton   255
    The Scene of Discovery   257
    Outdoors   257
        Indoors   259
    Packing and Transporting   260
    Examining Remains of Clothing and Other Objects   260
    Clothing   260
    Boots and Shoes   261
    Estimating the Time of Death   261
    Postmortem Signs of Death   261
    Changes in the Eyes   261
    Temperature of the Body   261
    Rigidity of the Body   262
    Lividity   262
    Decomposition of the Body   263
    Action of Insects on a Dead Body   263
    Other Indications of Time of Death   264
    The Autopsy   265
    Abrasions   266
    Contusions or Bruises   266
    Crushing Wounds   267

Bone Injuries 267
Cutting Wounds 267
Stab Wounds 268
Chopping Wounds 269
    Marks or Damage to Clothing 270
Defense Injuries 270
Firearm Injuries 270
Bullet Injuries 270
Close and Distant Shots 271
Marks from Primers 272
Traces from Bullets 272
Traces from Cartridge Cases 272
Traces from the Barrel of the Weapon 273
Injuries from Small Shot 273
Damage to Clothes from Shooting 273
Modes of Death from Shooting 273
Explosion Injuries 274
Death by Suffocation 274
Hanging 275
Strangling 276
Blocking of the Mouth or Nose 278
Blocking of the Larynx and Air Passages 278
Squeezing to Death 278
Drowning 278
Death from Electric Current 279
Death from Fires 279
Death by Freezing 280
Death by Poisoning 280
Carbon Monoxide Poisoning 282
Rape-homicide and Sexual Assault-related Murders 283
Infanticide and Child Abuse 283
Trunk Murder, Dismemberment of the Body 285
Accidental Death 285
Serial Murders 285
Further Reading 287
Chapter Questions 287

19 Digital Evidence and the Electronic Crime Scene 289

Computer Seizure 290
Steps to Remember 290
Collecting Video Evidence 291
Determine if There Is a Video 292
Stop the Recorder 292
Confiscate the Recording Medium Immediately 292
Document the Video System's Physical Relationship to the Crime Scene 292
Seek Technical Assistance if Problems Occur 293
Mobile Device Forensics 293
Digital/Multimedia Scientific Area Committee 294
OSAC Digital Evidence Subcommittee 295
SWGDE 295
OSAC Facial Identification Subcommittee 295
FISWG 295
OSAC Speaker Recognition Subcommittee 295

	OSAC Video/Imaging Technology and Analysis Subcommittee	295
	SWGIT	295
	Further Reading	295
	Chapter Questions	296
20	**Report Writing, Courtroom Testimony, and the Future**	**297**
	Report Writing	297
	Courtroom Testimony	298
	Statistics	300
	Future Issues in Forensic Science	301
	The Human Biome and Microbial Forensics	301
	Robotics	302
	Artificial Intelligence	302
	Generative Adversarial Network (GAN)	302
	Virtual Reality/Augmented Reality	302
	Virtopsy	303
	Time-tracing Fingerprinting	303
	Further Reading	303

Appendix A: Equipment for Crime Scene Investigations	305
Appendix B: Forensic Science Websites	311
Forensic Science Lexicon	317
Bibliography	319
Index	331

Foreword

The challenges facing law enforcement investigators in the 21st century are enormous! Never before in history has the investigation process been as complex and multifaceted as it is today. Individual criminals, small criminal groups, street gangs, and highly organized domestic and international criminal enterprises utilize sophisticated techniques to engage in their particular brand of criminal conduct. Additionally, extremely tech-savvy terrorist organizations and "home grown" terrorists pose a grave threat to public safety and are no longer exclusively investigated by federal authorities. Law enforcement investigators must be capable of dealing with the plethora of threats to public safety caused by criminals and terrorists who utilize innovative tradecraft and state-of-the-art technology.

Additionally, investigators are increasingly called upon to assist in their department's crime prevention mission. Successful police executives understand that investigators can no longer exclusively function in a reactive mode. During my years as the NYPD's Chief of Detectives (and before that, as the Deputy Commissioner of Operations directing COMPSTAT), "preventing potential unlawful activity" was a critically important element of the Detective Bureau's mission and the overall NYPD crime reduction strategy.

At the same time as they face these daunting challenges, investigators must address significant potential problems associated with the reliability of traditional investigative techniques involving eyewitness identification, interrogation, informants, and forensic science. Serious legitimate questions regarding these techniques have been raised by the Innocence Project and similar organizations, and this has had a very significant impact on criminal investigations and the entire criminal justice system.

In the face of these unprecedented difficulties, forensic evidence has never been more crucial to the criminal investigation process than it is now! *All* law enforcement personnel including the first responding patrol officer, assigned detective, crime scene investigator, intelligence analyst, and criminalist (as well as supervisors and executives) should be knowledgeable regarding the correct procedures involving forensic evidence recognition, documentation, preservation, processing, collection, invoicing, analysis, and storage. In today's challenging environment, it is absolutely essential that law enforcement personnel thoroughly understand and meticulously comply with the forensic evidence procedures that are applicable to their function in the investigation process.

For the past 20 years, it has been a singular honor and privilege to work with Barry A.J. Fisher and to call him my friend. As a world-renowned forensic scientist and former Director of the Los Angeles County Sheriff's Department Scientific Services Bureau, Barry Fisher has been a remarkable innovator and exemplary leader within the forensic science community. I am extremely pleased that Barry has included new material regarding Crime Scene Unit accreditation, the electronic crime scene, and the latest in DNA technology in this ninth edition of his groundbreaking book *Techniques of Crime Scene Investigation*. This book continues to be both a scholarly forensic science textbook and practical crime scene guide for law enforcement responders. *Techniques of Crime Scene Investigation* is a must-read for all law enforcement personnel involved in the criminal investigation process who want to ensure that they are complying with the proper techniques regarding crime scene processing and forensic evidence analysis.

Phil Pulaski
Chief of Detectives (ret.), New York City Police Department

Preface

This is the ninth edition of this textbook. It seems like only yesterday when, in the late 1970s, I (Barry) was invited to revise a classic criminal justice textbook, *Techniques of Crime Scene Investigation*, which was first published in 1949 in Swedish under the title *Handbok i brottsplatsundersökning* and subsequently in English in 1964. The original authors were Arne Svensson and Otto Wendel, two police investigators from Sweden. In 1981, I revised the text in the third edition and since then have served as the principal author. My son, David, who is also a forensic scientist, joined me as co-author in the previous edition (eighth) and again in this latest ninth edition.

Readers may well ask why a new edition. The answer lies in the fact that there is an increased focus on forensic science due to several factors. One factor was the publication of the report by The National Academy of Sciences: *Strengthening Forensic Science in the United States: A Path Forward*.[*] Another factor has been the work done by the Organization of Scientific Area Committees (OSAC)[†] for Forensic Science. Finally, the debunking of a few forensic science disciplines that were long thought to have been based on sound science has increased the focus on forensic science in general, and crime scene investigation in particular, among the public. New practitioners and students of this field must be made aware of the increased scrutiny that they will face in the judicial system. Judges are taking a more involved role than ever before as far as the types of evidence and testimony that they allow into their courtrooms. No longer will substandard forensic science or crime scene investigation be acceptable.

Having said all this, criminal investigations remain as complex as ever and require professionals from many disciplines to work cooperatively toward one common goal: the delivery of justice in a fair and impartial manner. Police investigators, prosecutors, and defense attorneys must be able to use these resources to their fullest potential.

Science and technology applied to the solution of criminal acts solves crimes and potentially saves lives. Scientific crime scene investigation aids police investigators in identifying suspects and victims of crimes, clearing innocent persons of suspicion, and ultimately bringing the wrongdoers to justice. When the justice system is able to remove a criminal from society, innocent persons do not become new victims of criminal acts.

This book is about the proper and effective use of science and technology in support of justice. The ninth edition of *Techniques of Crime Scene Investigation* is written for students of crime scene investigation, police investigators, crime scene technicians, forensic scientists, and attorneys. The material presented in this text covers the proper ways to examine crime scenes and collect a wide variety of physical evidence that may be encountered at crime scenes. It is not possible to cover every imaginable situation, but this book is a guide that attempts to promote best practices and recommendations. The areas are discussed in general terms to give the reader some idea of the information that can be developed from physical evidence if it is collected properly. Few of the procedures mentioned in the book are not inviolable, meaning that readers should not presume that practices referenced in the text can never be modified. On the contrary, crime scene investigation requires a degree of common sense and innovation. It is not possible to conjure up every imaginable situation a crime scene investigator may encounter in a case.

We do not claim to be experts in each and every discipline presented herein. Neither will studying the contents of this text make you an expert in all types of crime scene investigations or forensic science. But we hope that it gives students, police investigators, and others engaged in or interested in the subject some insight into the field and helps interested readers to pursue further studies.

The use of forensic science in criminal investigations depends on a number of factors. Police investigators must be knowledgeable about the capabilities of the forensic science support services available to them and appreciate how to

---

[*] https://www.ojp.gov/pdffiles1/nij/grants/228091.pdf.
[†] https://www.nist.gov/osac.

use them effectively. Forensic practitioners must be familiar with police investigative procedures, the scientific theory that supports their own activities, and the legal aspects needed to convey the information from the crime scene to the members of a jury. Judges, prosecutors, and defense attorneys must understand the scientific and technological issues of the case and be able to work with the expert to admit expert testimony into court. Police agencies that run forensic science labs must fund them at an appropriate level to ensure quality, reliability, and timely service to the criminal justice system. All of these efforts require the cooperation and willingness of different professionals within the criminal justice system to work well together. Those of us who apply science and technology to the investigation of crimes have a duty to do our best for the criminal justice system we serve.

Acknowledgments

With each new edition, we write to our many friends and colleagues in the forensic science community throughout the world and ask them to share cases for a new edition while we continue to use interesting and informative cases from earlier editions. The following are those who graciously answered our request for cases, although we were unable to use all the material submitted.

The names are listed alphabetically:

Maj. Gen. Hassan Ahmed Al-Obaidly, Qatar Forensic Laboratory Dept., Doha, Qatar; Myriam Azoury, Division of Identification and Forensic Science, Jerusalem, Israel; Richard Bisbing LLC, Chicago, IL; Robert Blackledge, El Cajon, CA; Dr. John DeHaan, Fire-Ex Forensics, Inc., Vallejo, CA; Bridget Fleming, Forensic Science Ireland, Dublin, Ireland; Sandra Enslow, Los Angeles County Sheriff's Department, Los Angeles, CA; Ken Goddard, US Fish & Wildlife Forensics Laboratory, Ashland, OR; Tony Grissim, Leica Geosystems part of Hexagon, Monterey, CA; Mike Grubb, San Diego County Sheriff's Crime Laboratory, San Diego, CA; Dwane Hilderbrand, Forensic ITC Services, Scottsdale, AZ; Kimmo Himberg, Police University College, Tampere, Pirkanmaa, Finland; Edward Hueske, Forensic Training & Consulting, LLC, Palestine, TX; Ragnar Jónsson and Björgvin Sigurðsson, Reykjavik Metropolitan Police, Crime Scene and Forensic Unit, Reykjavik, Iceland; Major General Khamis, Dubai Police, Dubai, UAE; John Lentini, Scientific Fire Analysis, LLC, Islamorada, FL; Dr. Laura Liptai, Bio Medical Forensics, Moraga, California; Dr. Fuad Tarbah, Dubai Polic, Dubai, UAE; Tsadok Tsach, Division of Identification and Forensic Science, Jerusalem, Israel; Dr. Sheila Willis, Forensic Science Ireland, Dublin, Ireland; Wendy van Hilst, Forensic Crime Scene Dept., Politie Nederland, Amsterdam, The Netherlands; Ray Wickenheiser and Ronald Stanbro, New York State Police, Albany, NY; and Richard Wilabee (ret.), Los Angeles County Sheriff's Department, Los Angeles, CA.

Appreciation also goes to Dr. Kevin Parmelee, who reviewed portions of the manuscript and assisted in preparing companion PowerPoint slides and a test bank of questions to serve as teaching aids for educators who use the text.

We also wish to thank our editor, Mark Listewnik who was most patient with us in realizing the publication of this 9th edition. Vijay Bose from Deanta Global, our project manager, was instrumental in getting this book through the production process.

We cannot thank our wives enough, Susan and Deena, for their support and encouragement throughout this long project.

Finally, thank you to the Almighty for his continued blessings that He bestows on us and our families each and every day.

Barry A.J. Fisher
Indio, California
barry.a.j.fisher@gmail.com

David R. Fisher
Newark, New Jersey
davidfisher100@gmail.com

About the Authors

Barry A.J. Fisher served as the Crime Laboratory Director for the Los Angeles County Sheriff's Department, a position he held from 1987 until his retirement in 2009. He began his career in criminalistics with the Sheriff's crime lab in 1969 and worked in a wide variety of assignments.

Barry is a member of many professional organizations. He is a Distinguished Fellow and past president of the American Academy of Forensic Sciences and was awarded the Academy's highest award, the Gradwohl Medallion. He served as president of the International Association of Forensic Sciences, president of the American Society of Crime Laboratory Directors, and a past-chairman of the American Society of Crime Laboratory Directors—Laboratory Accreditation Board.

Fisher has served as a member of several editorial boards: the *Journal of Forensic Sciences*, the *Journal of Forensic Identification*, *Forensic Science Policy and Management*, and the *McGraw-Hill Encyclopedia of Science and Technology*. He is a co-author of two other books: *Forensics Demystified* and *Introduction to Criminalistics: The Foundation of Forensic Science*. He has lectured throughout the United States, Canada, England, Australia, Singapore, France, Israel, Japan, China, Turkey, Portugal, and the United Arab Emirates on forensic science laboratory practices, quality assurance, and related topics.

Since retiring in 2009, Fisher has consulted for the United Nations Office on Drugs and Crime, the United States Department of Justice, International Criminal Investigative Training Program (ICITAP), and Analytic Services Inc., a not-for-profit institute that provides studies and analyses to aid decision-makers in national security, homeland security, and public safety.

Barry is a native New Yorker and received his Bachelor of Science degree in chemistry from the City College of New York. He holds a Master of Science degree in chemistry from Purdue University and an MBA from California State University, Northridge. Barry and his wife, Susan, live in Indio, California. He has two married sons and eight grandchildren.

Barry can be reached by email at barry.a.j.fisher@gmail.com. He tweets at @barryajfisher.

David R. Fisher is currently Director of the Forensic Science program at the New Jersey Institute of Technology (NJIT). The program is the first undergraduate forensic science degree program in the State of New Jersey. Prior to joining NJIT, David was a criminalist for 17 years in the Department of Forensic Biology at the Office of Chief Medical Examiner (OCME) in New York City. In that position, he worked on thousands of criminal cases including homicides, sexual assaults, and property crimes. He has testified in court and in the grand jury as an expert witness in forensic biology and DNA on numerous occasions. After the events of 9/11, he aided in the identification of victims of the World Trade Center terrorist attack. He is also a Medical Investigator with the Disaster Mortuary Operational Response Team (DMORT) under the National Disaster Medical System (NDMS).

David is board certified in General Criminalistics by the American Board of Criminalistics and is a Fellow in the American Academy of Forensic Sciences. He is also a Special Member of the Vidocq Society which provides pro bono expert assistance to the law enforcement community on solving their cold case homicides. In addition, he is a member of the Council of Forensic Science Educators and the New Jersey Association of Forensic Scientists. He received his Bachelor of Science degree in biochemistry and cell biology from the University of California at San Diego (UCSD) and a Master of Science degree in Forensic Science from the John Jay College of Criminal Justice of the City University of New York (CUNY). David, his wife Deena, and their three children live in New Jersey.

David can be reached by email at davidfisher100@gmail.com.

Part I

The Crime Scene

CHAPTER 1

Introduction

Crime scene investigation and forensic science have taken a dramatic turn in the past two decades. The entertainment industry has capitalized on the public's interest in crime scene investigation-based entertainment that features a heavy dose of science and technology. In 2000, the TV show *CSI: Crime Scene Investigation* was launched, followed by two spinoffs and a host of other shows of the same genre, such as *Dexter, Bones, and NCIS*. In addition, numerous documentaries on Netflix, Amazon Prime Video, and Hulu about actual criminal cases involving forensic evidence have raised questions about crime scene investigation and forensic science, making the public aware of its strengths and limitations.

In 1992, the Innocence Project began to demonstrate that errors in some cases resulted in exonerations of innocent people and that forensic science played a role in some of these wrongful convictions. As a result of this media attention, public awareness of the profession's shortcomings, and several government reports, many policymakers are paying closer attention to crime scene investigation and forensic science than ever before. These factors including a significant amount of lobbying by the **Consortium of Forensic Science Organizations** (CFSO)* resulted in a study authorized by the United States Congress published in 2009 by the National Academy of Sciences (NAS), *Strengthening Forensic Science in the United States: A Path Forward*.†

The **NAS Report** made 13 recommendations which are summarized as follows:

1. Create an independent federal forensic agency—the National Institute of Forensic Science (NIFS).
2. Establish standard terminology to be used in lab reports and testimony, as well as the minimum information that should be included.
3. Support and fund peer-reviewed scientific research on forensic disciplines.
4. Maximize independence of forensic labs.
5. Encourage research to minimize bias and sources of human error.
6. Set standards for forensic best practices.
7. Require accreditation and certification.
8. Require quality assurance and quality control.
9. Establish a national code of ethics for all forensic science disciplines.
10. Students should be encouraged to pursue graduate studies to improve and develop applicable research methodologies in forensic science. Continuing legal education programs for law students, practitioners, and judges should also be established and supported.

---

* The CFSO (www.thecfso.org) is an association of forensic science professional organizations together representing over 20,000 members across the United States.
† The National Research Council of the National Academies issued the report "Strengthening Forensic Science in the United States: A Path Forward" (www.ojp.gov/pdffiles1/nij/grants/228091.pdf).

DOI: 10.4324/9780429272011-2

11. The coroner system should be eliminated, and funds should be provided to establish a medical examiner system. All medicolegal autopsies should be performed or supervised by a board-certified forensic pathologist.
12. The government should launch a new effort to achieve nationwide interoperability for fingerprint data.
13. Congress should provide funding to bring the Centers for Disease Control, FBI, forensic scientists, and crime scene investigators together to develop roles as first responders in counterterrorism preparedness.

NAS reports are advisory and have no force of law. While the report has been disseminated widely and has been cited in many court cases, only some of the recommendations made, however, have been adopted by the forensic science community.

Since the release of the NAS report, several states have established forensic science commissions, such as the ones in Virginia, Texas, Delaware, New York, and Arizona, for example.* These commissions were established to develop minimum standards for all public forensic laboratories within the respective states and to provide administrative oversight to the forensic laboratories in order to improve the quality and delivery of forensic services. They also monitor forensic laboratory compliance with accreditation standards and require lab representatives to appear regularly before the commissions to answer questions.

In 2013 the federal government created a partnership between the Department of Justice (DOJ) and the National Institute of Science and Technology (NIST) to create the National Commission on Forensic Science (NCFS).[†] In 2014, NIST created the **Organization of Scientific Area Committees** (OSAC),[‡]

> an initiative by NIST and the DOJ to strengthen forensic science in the United States. The organization is a collaborative body of more than 500 forensic science practitioners and other experts who represent local, state, and federal agencies; academia; and industry. NIST has established OSAC to support the development and promulgation of forensic science consensus documentary standards and guidelines, and to ensure that a sufficient scientific basis exists for each discipline (Figure 1.1)

OSAC maintains a repository of technically sound published standards for forensic science.[§] These written documents (some of which are existing standards published by Standards Development Organizations like ASTM, NIST, and ISO) define minimum requirements, best practices, standard protocols, and other guidance to help improve consistency within and across forensic science disciplines, ensure confidence in the accuracy, reliability, and reproducibility of lab results, and positively increase the impact of admissibility and expert testimony in courts of law. As of Feb 2022, the OSAC Registry contains 78 standards. The OSAC also maintains a comprehensive lexicon[¶] of forensic science terms and definitions to help establish consistency and understanding among stakeholders as to the way various terms are used. While OSAC is built on a consensus-based organizational structure, it has no authority to enforce standards. It does, however, promote the adoption of its Registry by accrediting bodies that audit participating forensic science service providers for compliance.

In 2016, under the Obama Administration, the **President's Council of Advisors on Science and Technology** (PCAST) issued a report that found a general lack of adequate scientific studies to establish the validity of many kinds of forensic science. PCAST made a variety of recommended actions to strengthen forensic science and promote its more rigorous use in the courtroom (Figure 1.2).** PCAST concluded that two gaps needed to be addressed: (1) greater clarity

---

* Although only ten states and the District of Columbia currently have statutorily created forensic science commissions, many more states have DNA commissions or informal advisory boards or are considering forming commissions. State commissions vary significantly in their functions. The following are some of the states with commissions or advisory boards: Forensic Science Board—VA Dept of Forensic Science (www.dfs.virginia.gov/about-dfs/forensic-science-board/), Texas Forensic Science Commission (www.txcourts.gov/fsc/), DE Forensic Science Commission (forensics.delaware.gov/resources/index.shtml?dc=forensic-science), New York State Commission on Forensic Science (www.criminaljustice.ny.gov/forensic/aboutofs.htm), and the Arizona Forensic Science Advisory Committee (www.azag.gov/criminal/azfsac).

† After three years of operation, the DOJ decided not to reauthorize the NCFS (www.justice.gov/archives/ncfs).

‡ The mission of The Organization of Scientific Area Committees for Forensic Science (www.nist.gov/osac) is to strengthen the nation's use of forensic science by facilitating the development of technically sound standards and encouraging their use throughout the forensic science community.

§ OSAC Registry (www.nist.gov/osac/osac-registry). The OSAC Registry serves as a trusted repository of high quality, science-based standards and guidelines for forensic practice.

¶ https://lexicon.forensicosac.org/.

** "Forensic Science in Criminal Courts: Ensuring Scientific Validity of Feature-Comparison Methods."

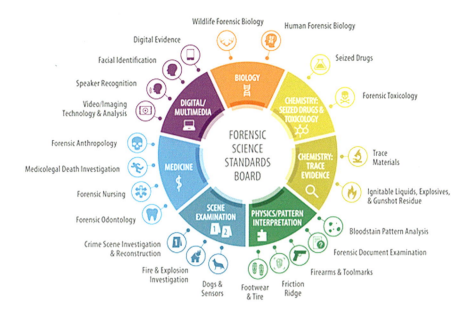

Figure 1.1 OSAC members and affiliates make up a multi-level organization consisting of a Forensic Science Standards Board, seven Scientific Area Committees (SAC), (The Scene Examination SAC consists of the following subcommittees: Crime Scene Investigation & Reconstruction, Fire & Explosion Investigation, and Dogs & Sensors.) and 22 discipline-specific subcommittees. These experts work together to draft and evaluate forensic science standards via a transparent, consensus-based process that allows for participation by all stakeholders. (*National Institute of Standards and Technology.*)

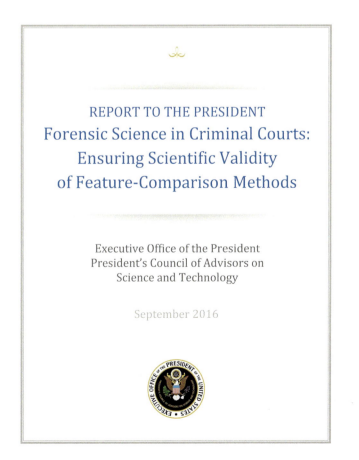

Figure 1.2 The PCAST report asserted that many forms of forensic pattern-matching evidence presently lack foundational validity.

about the scientific standards needed for the validity and reliability of forensic methods and (2) the need to evaluate forensic methods to determine whether or not they have been scientifically established to be valid and reliable.

As noted in these two major reports and by the OSACs, forensic science plays a critical role in the investigation and adjudication of crimes in our criminal justice system. But before science can be brought to bear on evidence, it must be recognized and collected in an appropriate manner at crime scenes. The crime scene investigator, therefore, plays a crucial role in any forensic science testing of evidence recovered from a crime scene.

Webster's Dictionary defines evidence as "something legally submitted to a tribunal to ascertain the truth of a matter." Police investigators deal with evidence on a daily basis. Their ability to recognize, collect, and use evidence in criminal investigations determines to a large degree their success as investigators as well as the outcome of the case.

Evidence can be divided into two broad types: (1) testimonial evidence and (2) real, or physical, evidence. **Testimonial evidence** is evidence given in the form of statements made under oath, or affirmation, usually in response to questioning. Physical evidence is any type of evidence with an objective existence, that is, anything with size, shape, and dimension.

Physical evidence can take any form. It can be as large as a house or as small as a fiber. It can be as fleeting as an odor or as obvious as the destructive results at the scene of an explosion. The variety of physical evidence that may be encountered in an investigation is infinite. Physical evidence may also be considered either direct evidence (evidence that supports a conclusion of fact without inference) or circumstantial evidence (evidence that requires an inference to connect it to a conclusion of fact).

What is the value of physical evidence and why should police investigators concern themselves with an understanding of the uses and ways to collect physical evidence?

Physical evidence can prove a crime has been committed or establish key elements of a crime.

    Proof of sexual assault requires showing nonconsensual sexual intercourse. In an alleged rape case, the victim's torn clothing, bruises, and vaginal tearing may be sufficient to prove nonconsensual intercourse.

    In another example, arson investigators dispatched to the scene of a suspicious fire collected some burned carpeting. Later analysis proved that gasoline was present in the carpet, proving that the fire was intentionally set.

Case Review

On October 18, 2013, at approximately 8 pm, the Santa Sophia Catholic Church, located in Spring Valley, California, was intentionally set on fire. The fire resulted in over $200,000 worth of damage. A forensic evidence technician was called to the scene to assist the Bomb/Arson Unit. Over 20 items of evidence were collected at the scene of the fire (Figure 1.3a-d).

Figure 1.3 (a) Photo of the church fire. (b) Of the most significant items of evidence was a boot print left by the suspect as he tried to kick in a glass window and (c) a latent handprint. That same day, the suspect was identified through a database match to a fingerprint (d) he left on the window. At arrest, the suspect was found to be wearing boots with a similar pattern to that found on the window. The boot impression would later be positively identified as having been caused by one of the boots the suspect was wearing at the time of the arrest. Multiple items from inside the church, believed to be used to set the fires, were processed for latent prints. The suspect was also identified through prints developed on those items. The suspect ultimately pled guilty and was sentenced to 28 years in state prison. (*Courtesy of Mike Grubb, San Diego County Sheriff's Crime Laboratory, San Diego, CA.*)

Physical evidence can place the suspect in contact with the victim or with the crime scene.

A suspect was apprehended shortly after an alleged murder in the victim's home. A bloody fingerprint at the crime scene after a search of the **Integrated Automated Fingerprint Identification System** (IAFIS) ended up matching the suspect. The suspect was at a loss to explain how his fingerprint made it inside the victim's house (Figure 1.4).

Physical evidence can establish the identity of persons associated with the crime.

Every cautious burglar knows not to leave fingerprints at the crime scene, so it was not surprising to find in the trash at the scene surgical gloves that were used when handling the safe. The identity of the burglar was established by developing latent fingerprints inside the latex gloves (Figure 1.5).

Physical evidence can exonerate the innocent.

An eight- and nine-year-old brother and sister accused an elderly neighbor of child molestation. They claimed that the man gave each of them pills that made them feel drowsy and then he molested them. The investigator had a physician examine the children, and blood and urine specimens were collected for a toxicology screen. The analyses of the blood and urine specimens were negative. When presented with this information, the children confessed that they had fabricated the entire story because they disliked their neighbor.

Physical evidence can corroborate the victim's testimony.

A motorist picked up a female hitchhiker. She claimed that he pulled a knife and attempted to rape her. During the struggle, the woman's thumb was cut before she managed to escape. She related her story to the police and the suspect was eventually arrested. During the interrogation, the suspect steadfastly proclaimed his innocence. The investigator noted a small quantity of dried blood on the suspect's left jacket lapel. He claimed the blood came from a shaving mishap. The investigator submitted the jacket along with blood samples from the suspect and the

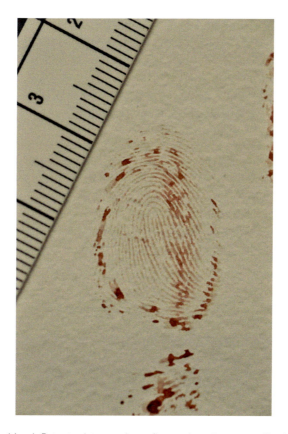

Figure 1.4 A patent fingerprint in blood. Patent prints are those fingerprints that are easily visible without the use of powders, alternate light sources, or chemicals.

Figure 1.5 Latex gloves left behind at the scene were cut open to develop the latent fingerprints inside the gloves. Latent prints are those fingerprints that are hidden or invisible and need powders, light, and/or chemicals in order to visualize them.

victim to the crime laboratory. The DNA results indicated that the blood on the jacket came from the victim. The physical evidence was instrumental in obtaining a conviction for attempted rape.

A suspect confronted with physical evidence may make admissions or even confess.

Dogfighting still occurs from time to time in parts of the United States. Blood found on a suspect's shirt was species tested and determined to be canine. The suspect, who first claimed the blood was his own, made a full admission when confronted by the evidence.

Physical evidence is more reliable than eyewitnesses to crimes.

Psychological experiments have shown that observations made by test subjects in simulated violent crimes are sometimes inaccurate after the event. Volunteers in a psychological test were witnesses to staged assaults. After the mock crimes, they were asked to detail their observations in writing. The study showed that the mind fills in gaps of physical features. If a portion of a physical characteristic was not seen or did not make sense, the subjects made up descriptions that seemed reasonable. This behavior occurs subconsciously; subjects are not aware that it is taking place. People simply report what they believe they have seen. This in turn has sometimes led to wrongful convictions due to mistaken identity.*

The CSI Effect

The so-called "CSI Effect" has prejudiced the public's notion of the role of physical evidence in criminal cases.

The CSI Effect refers to the phenomenon in which jurors hold unrealistic expectations of forensic evidence and investigation techniques, and have an increased interest in the discipline because of the influence of CSI-type television shows. This effect includes raising the state's burden of proof because of jury expectations that forensic evidence should always be discussed at trial, and the belief forensic evidence is never wrong.†

Moreover, forensic science is perceived by most of the public to be unbiased and not subject to manipulation. If scientific testing is used to evaluate and characterize physical evidence, jurors are often inclined to believe that the police

---

* The Innocence Project (www.innocenceproject.org) has worked towards the exonerations of many wrongfully convicted individuals from mistaken eyewitness testimony through the use of post-conviction DNA typing.
† Monica Robbers, 2008.

investigation was properly conducted.* In contrast to the "CSI Effect," a large percentage of the population also views forensic science skeptically as seen in cable news satire shows such as *Last Week Tonight with John Oliver*.†

Negative evidence—the absence of physical evidence—may provide useful information and even stop defense arguments at the time of trial.

> In an insurance fraud case, the victim claimed his home was burglarized. No evidence of forced entry could be found and eventually the fraud was discovered. It is important to remember, however, as Carl Sagan is purported to have said, "the absence of evidence, is not evidence of absence!"

CLASSIFICATION AND INDIVIDUALIZATION OF PHYSICAL EVIDENCE

Some investigators may think that every item of physical evidence can be directly associated with a specific person, place, or thing and believe that it is possible to link that evidence to a unique source. This is not the case. Although some may argue that certain types of physical evidence may come from one and only one source, physical evidence is mostly only associated with a class or group and rarely to a unique, sole source. Very few kinds of physical evidence can be individualized or said to be uniquely associated with another item of evidence.

Most physical evidence found at crime scenes can be classified. By classification, we mean that an item of evidence shares a common source. Such items can be placed into groups with all other items having the same properties or class characteristics. Examples of this type of physical evidence include fabric from a mass-produced item of clothing or automobile paint from a specific make and model.

The difference between **individualization** (or a statement explicitly stating uniqueness) and **classification** can be understood by using a hypothetical case. Consider a blue-colored cotton fiber found at the scene of a burglary. A suspect wearing a torn blue cotton shirt is apprehended. All the tests conducted at the crime laboratory on the evidence fiber and exemplar fibers from the shirt show that they cannot be differentiated. Can it be concluded that the blue cotton fiber found at the scene came from the torn blue cotton shirt worn by the suspect? No! The best that can be stated in this example is that the fiber could have come from the shirt in question or any other one manufactured with similar blue cotton fibers. The item has been classified as a blue cotton fiber and can only be placed into a class of all other similar blue cotton fibers.

A follow-up question for the expert testifying about the identification of the fibers (which is often not asked) is to inquire about the significance of finding this evidence. Can anything be stated about the fact that the evidence was found? Stating this another way, suppose that blue cotton fibers are routinely found on random people. How might this factor impact a jury versus fibers that are rarely found?

Contrast the fiber evidence with a pieced-together broken plastic comb. One can easily conclude the broken pieces originally came from one and only one source because of the pieces' unique shape and jigsaw puzzle fit (Figure 1.6a-c).

In the case of fingerprints or firearms evidence, such a simple calculation is not yet possible since we do not know the probability of each mark occurring or whether the marks are independent of one another. Intuitively, the examiner may conclude that finding so large a number of seemingly random events must make the comparison unique to a single source. Studies are underway to attempt to use statistics on pattern evidence which may allow the examiner to give numerical values with their conclusion. By attaching a statistical number to a conclusion, such as a likelihood ratio, juries will be in a better position to decide how much weight to give an item of evidence.‡

Physical evidence can corroborate testimony, place a subject at a scene, and be useful in a variety of ways as an interrogation tool. It also provides valuable information for juries to assist them in their deliberations.

---

* Recent high profile cases involving police misconduct with racial overtones as well as errors made in crime labs may have lessened the CSI Effect.
† An episode of *Last Week Tonight with John Oliver* (www.youtube.com/watch?v=ScmJvmzDcG0) highlights many of the problems with forensic science, including how forensic science can be surprisingly unscientific.
‡ The Center for Statistics and Applications in Forensic Evidence (CSAFE) (https://forensicstats.org) is a publicly funded research center that seeks to apply proven statistical and scientific methods to improve the accuracy of the analysis and interpretation of forensic evidence. They are working on developing best practices to apply statistical methods in the evaluation of pattern evidence.

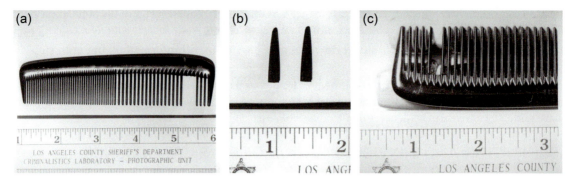

Figure 1.6 This case is an example of a physical match or jigsaw match. A comb (a) with three missing teeth was found in the suspect's possession. Two plastic teeth (b) found at the crime scene were (c) fitted exactly to the comb. (*Courtesy of Los Angeles County Sheriff's Department.*)

Historically, when sufficient markings are present on pattern evidence (e.g., fingerprints, firearms evidence, footwear evidence, tire impressions, and tool marks), practitioners would offer a conclusive opinion that the known and questioned item came from a common source to a reasonable degree of scientific certainty.* Use of the term *scientific certainty*, however, has been repudiated by the U.S. Department of Justice. The question ultimately comes down to how an expert witness might express a level of confidence that a known specimen and questioned item of evidence are connected.

IMPORTANT CONSIDERATIONS IN CRIME SCENE INVESTIGATIONS

In addition to the "how-to" elements of crime scene investigation, several other issues need to be discussed. These represent a philosophical approach to the subject and should be considered an integral part of forensic science and forensic identification.

Forensic scientists, crime scene specialists, and investigators are the individuals whose jobs apply science and technology to solving criminal acts. They hold an important place in the criminal justice system. Their skill and knowledge in the criminal investigation may establish the innocence or guilt of a defendant. Professional ethics and integrity are essential to their effort.

The National Academy of Science report "*Strengthening Forensic Science in the United States: A Path Forward*" contains a significant number of recommendations concerning practitioners and laboratory institutions. Among the recommendations is that public forensic science laboratories should be independent of or autonomous within law enforcement agencies and that a national code of ethics should be established.

At the present time, most forensic practitioners work primarily in law enforcement or prosecution agencies. Partly as a result of the NAS report, there has been some limited movement towards independence from police agencies. This change is not yet widely adopted. Some have argued that separating forensic science laboratories from law enforcement or prosecuting agencies would eliminate the perception of bias.

TEAMWORK

An essential element in crime scene investigation is teamwork. The investigation of criminal acts involves scores of people who often work for different agencies. This system was purposefully designed so that no one person or entity

---

* In 2016, the United States Attorney General issued a directive from the Department of Justice instructing forensic scientists working in federal laboratories and United States Attorneys to refrain from using the phrase "reasonable degree of scientific certainty" when testifying. The National Commission on Forensic Science (NCFS) also issued a statement that "it is the view of the NCFS that the scientific community should not promote the use of this terminology. Additionally, the legal community should recognize that medical professionals and other scientists do not routinely use 'to a reasonable scientific certainty' when expressing conclusions outside of the courts since there is no foundational scientific basis for its use. Therefore, legal professionals should not require that forensic testimony be admitted conditioned upon the expert witness testifying that a conclusion is held to a 'reasonable scientific certainty,' a 'reasonable degree of scientific certainty,' or a 'reasonable degree of [discipline] certainty,' as such terms have no scientific meaning and may mislead jurors or judges when deciding whether guilt has been proved beyond a reasonable doubt."

can operate independently. As such, turf issues will always arise, and it is important to remember to "stay in one's lane" as best as possible. In addition, as we move towards larger and more complex criminal justice systems, we are more likely to be dealing with people who are faceless voices at the other end of the phone.

For any complex system to work, teamwork is essential. Each element of the criminal investigation—uniformed officer, detective, crime scene specialist, forensic scientist, forensic pathologist, photographer, prosecutor, defense attorney, plus all the other vital players in the "system"—must work cooperatively with the other stakeholders to make the entire process work.

No one element or person is more important than any other person or element. Each person has a vital role to play, and each portion of the case must be accomplished in a responsible, professional, and timely manner to make every component function properly. Everyone working on a case should feel that he or she is essential to the successful resolution of an investigation. Each must feel empowered to do what needs to be done, if only for the sake of justice. Prima donnas have no place in this process!

PROFESSIONAL DEVELOPMENT

Crime scene investigation, forensic identification, and forensic science require continuing education and networking with other professionals. It is unthinkable, for example, that a physician, dentist, accountant, or lawyer would not maintain ongoing study through professional conferences and continuing education. This is equally true in the forensic science profession.

Law enforcement agencies employ most crime scene investigators and forensic science professionals. Many police agencies fund continuing education in their annual budgets. This economic commitment is essential to the ongoing professionalism of practitioners and is used for professional association dues, professional conferences, workshops, and other continuing education.

For those engaged in crime scene investigation work, it is worthwhile to join a professional organization. The **International Association for Identification** (IAI)* is one of the oldest professional associations of its kind. It was founded in 1915. For those pursuing a career in crime scene work, the IAI is an excellent organization to help maintain competency in this field. The IAI publishes the *Journal of Forensic Identification* and holds an annual conference that brings colleagues together to attend workshops and technical presentations and to exchange information. The IAI is worthy of consideration for membership for any serious practitioner. In addition, the IAI offers crime scene certification at four different levels: Crime Scene Investigator, Crime Scene Analyst, Crime Scene Reconstructionist, and Senior Crime Scene Analyst. Each certification requires a rigorous testing process with a minimum passing score of 75%. Certification can also be obtained in the following disciplines: bloodstain pattern analysis, footwear, forensic art, forensic photography and imaging, forensic video, latent print, and tenprint fingerprint. Obtaining certification is beneficial because it: 1) measures quality, 2) enhances credibility, 3) introduces a degree of peer standardization, and 4) enhances consumer confidence. However, not all certifying programs are to be trusted. Persons considering a board certifying program are encouraged to evaluate them critically. A program that does little more than require the payment of a fee should raise questions.

Another association for crime scene investigators to consider is the **Association for Crime Scene Reconstruction**.† The association was founded in 1991 with a group of professionals in Oklahoma and Texas who investigated crime scenes and performed forensic analyses and comparisons on evidence from crime scenes. They saw a need for an organization that would encompass an understanding of the whole crime scene and the necessity of reconstructing that scene in order to better understand the elements of the crime and to recognize and preserve evidence.

Training and continuing education are important for all practitioners within the criminal justice system: uniformed officers, detectives, crime scene investigators, forensic scientists, prosecutors, defense attorneys, and judges. Continuing education and attendance at professional association seminars and workshops are essential to professional competency and professional development. To demonstrate this point, one should ask themselves, "Would I consider going to a physician, dentist, accountant, lawyer, or another professional who does not periodically attend continuing

---

* www.theiai.org/.
† www.acsr.org/.

education classes to keep up his or her professional competency?" Funds for professional development should be considered a priority in all law enforcement organizations that conduct forensic science testing and crime scene investigation. It cannot be overstated enough that we all need to stay up to date with our field. Practitioners should also be willing to give back to the profession by teaching, giving papers or talks at conferences, or organizing a workshop.

ISO/IEC 17020 ACCREDITATION

While many crime laboratories in the United States are accredited, most Crime Scene Units that are not part of a crime lab lack accreditation. The leadership of law enforcement agencies needs to seek out and obtain accreditation for CSI units. The accreditation that is most appropriate for CSI falls under **ISO/IEC 17020—accreditation for forensic inspection services**. The **International Organization for Standardization** (ISO) specifies requirements for the operation of bodies performing forensic inspection under ISO/IEC 17020. (ISO is an independent, non-governmental international organization that brings together experts to develop voluntary, consensus-based relevant standards to ensure that products and services are reliable and of good quality.) An important difference between inspection agencies and testing laboratories is that many types of inspection involve professional judgment to determine acceptability against general requirements, which is why the inspection body needs to be competent to perform the task. ISO/IEC 17020 consists of eight sections: scope, normative references, terms and definitions, general requirements, structural requirements, resource requirements, process requirements, and management system requirements. The **ANSI National Accreditation Board** (ANAB) forensic accreditation program offers forensic-specific requirements in areas where ISO/IEC 17020 is general. ANAB is the longest established provider of accreditation based on ISO standards for forensic agencies in the United States. Any Crime Scene Unit or CSI service provider seeking ANAB accreditation must demonstrate conformance to the ISO/IEC 17020 conformity assessment, as well as the applicable ANAB accreditation requirements, additional requirements where applicable, and the CSU/CSI service provider's own documented management system.* It is recommended that all agencies performing crime scene investigations seek and maintain accreditation. Just like no one would undergo surgery in a non-accredited hospital, the public demands that their CSU/CSI service providers meet basic accreditation standards in order to assure the acceptability of results.

ISO/IEC 17043 ACCREDITATION

ISO/IEC 17043 specifies the requirements for the competence of providers of proficiency tests and for the development and operation of proficiency tests. When a forensic lab or crime scene unit administers proficiency tests to its laboratory analysts or investigators, they should ensure that the proficiency test provider is accredited under ISO/IEC 17043. ANAB also offers accreditation to ISO/IEC 17043 standards along with supplemental accreditation requirements for forensic science proficiency test providers.

LEGAL CASES REGARDING FORENSIC SCIENCE

Crime scene investigation and forensic science operate within a legal framework. Thus, it is not surprising that a number of cases or legal rulings define some of the aspects of forensic science and crime scene investigation. The goal of any criminal investigation is not only to figure out what happened and who did it but also to bring the wrongdoer to justice. Since the final stop in a criminal investigation is in the courts, regulations, rules, legal precedents, and case law must be taken into consideration throughout the investigation. The following is a review of some of the case law and rules of evidence that deal with forensic evidence:

- *Frye v. United States*, **293 F. 1013 (D.C. Cir. 1923)**. Frye is one of the earliest cases in the United States to address the notion of admissibility of expert testimony. Expert testimony is used to help jurors understand complex issues generally beyond a lay person's knowledge. The Frye case dealt with the polygraph and whether its results were

---

* The ANAB Directory of Accredited Organizations (http://search.anab.org/) shows the latest forensic inspection agencies and crime scene units that are accredited in crime scene investigation.

admissible. The court made the following statement in its opinion which sums up its ruling: "Just when a scientific principle or discovery crosses the line between the experimental and demonstrable stages is difficult to define. Somewhere in this twilight zone, the evidential force of the principle must be recognized, and while courts will go a long way in admitting expert testimony deduced from a well-recognized scientific principle or discovery, the thing from which the deduction is made must be sufficiently established to have gained general acceptance in the particular field in which it belongs." Polygraph evidence was held to be inadmissible in this case. The Frye Rule essentially lays out the notion of general acceptance within the *relevant scientific community*. Frye is still the standard in a number of States and has been modified in Federal cases by the Federal Rules of Evidence, specifically Rule 702.

- **Daubert v. Merrell Dow Pharmaceuticals, 509 U.S. 579 (1993).** In Daubert, the U.S. Supreme Court modified the way courts view expert testimony. The Court ruled that the trial judge serves in the capacity of gatekeeper and decides what expert evidence may be admissible. Daubert also expands the requirements for admissibility beyond general acceptance and adds the notion of reliability. (The Daubert standard, however, is not used in all states.)

- **Federal Rules of Evidence Rule 702** codifies Daubert and other later cases into the Federal Rules.

    If scientific, technical, or other specialized knowledge will assist the trier of fact to understand the evidence or to determine a fact in issue, a witness qualified as an expert by knowledge, skill, experience, training, or education, may testify thereto in the form of an opinion or otherwise, if (1) the testimony is based upon sufficient facts or data, (2) the testimony is the product of reliable principles and methods, and (3) the witness has applied the principles and methods reliably to the facts of the case.

Different states use one or more of the above standards to govern the admissibility of expert scientific testimony. Some have adopted the federal rules while others continue to follow Frye, and still others have adopted a hybrid version. These legal issues are of interest to lawyers and judges who must deal with them in evidentiary hearings.

- **Kumho Tire Co. v. Carmichael, 526 U.S. 137 (1999)** was a United States Supreme Court case that applied the Daubert standard to expert testimony from a non-scientist, specifically a tire failure expert. In a unanimous decision, the court determined that a federal trial judge's "gatekeeping" applies not only to "scientific" testimony but to all expert testimony.

- **Melendez-Diaz v. Massachusetts, 129 S.Ct. 2527 (2009)** is a decision by the U.S. Supreme Court that determined that a forensic analyst's lab report is prepared for use in criminal prosecution and is subject to the confrontation clause of the 6th Amendment. The 6th Amendment of the U.S. Constitution gives the defendant the right to confront his/her accuser. The question considered in Melendez-Diaz was whether lab reports constitute testimony and, therefore, require the analyst who wrote the report to testify in court about their findings. The court concluded that the expert who wrote the lab report must testify as the witness for the State against the defendant to give the defendant the ability to examine the witness concerning the work he did in the case.

- **Bullcoming v. New Mexico, 131 S. Ct. 62 (2010)** followed the *Melendez-Diaz* case. The question presented in *Bullcoming* was whether the confrontation clause permitted the prosecution to introduce a forensic laboratory report containing a testimonial certification—made to prove a particular fact—through the in-court testimony of another scientist who did not sign the certification or perform or observe the test reported in the certification. The Supreme Court held that surrogate testimony of that order does not meet the constitutional requirement. The accused's right is to be confronted with the analyst who made the certification, unless that analyst is unavailable at trial and the accused had an opportunity, pretrial, to cross-examine that particular scientist. This case has significant ramifications, particularly in cases where the original expert and the evidence are no longer available for re-examination. Consider an old serial murder case that occurred many years prior. The pathologist who performed the autopsy might no longer be available and the deceased's remains are buried. The question to be determined is how evidence in such a case might be presented. Whether the confrontation clause permits the prosecution to introduce the testimony of a forensic analyst through the in-court testimony of a supervisor remains to be seen.

- **Brady v. Maryland, 373 U.S. 83 (1963).** Brady requires the prosecution to provide material evidence to the defense which may exculpate the defendant. Brady material readily adapts itself to forensic evidence and may become an issue in criminal proceedings. What is required under Brady? Prosecutors are required to disclose to the defense evidence favorable to a defendant that is either exculpatory or impeaching and is material to either guilt or punishment. Evidence is "favorable" to the defendant if it either helps the defendant or hurts the prosecution. In *Strickler v. Greene* (1999) 527 U.S. 203, 280–281, the United States Supreme Court stated:

In Brady, this Court held "that the suppression by the prosecution of evidence favorable to an accused upon request violates due process where the evidence is material either to guilt or to punishment, irrespective of the good faith or bad faith of the prosecution." Brady v. Maryland, supra, 373 U.S. at 87. We have since held that the duty to disclose such evidence is applicable even though there has been no request by the accused, [*United States v. Agurs* (1976) 427 U.S. 97, 107] and that the duty encompasses impeachment evidence as well as exculpatory evidence, [*United States v. Bagley* (1985) 473 U.S. 667, 676]. Such evidence is material "if there is a reasonable probability that had the evidence been disclosed to the defense, the result of the proceeding would have been different." Id at 682; see also [*Kyles v. Whitley* (1995) 514 U.S. 419, 433–434].

Prosecutors must determine what Brady evidence there may be *before* trial. The definition of "material evidence" is generally provided in the context of an appeal from a conviction. Evidence is material if there is a reasonable probability that the result of the proceeding would have been different had the evidence been disclosed. A reasonable probability of a different outcome is shown where suppression undermines confidence in the outcome. Such evidence must have a specific, plausible connection to the case, and must demonstrate more than minor inaccuracies. Exculpatory evidence is evidence favorable to the defendant and material to the issue of guilt or punishment. Impeachment evidence is also included under Brady. Examples of possible impeachment evidence of a material witness include:

1. Pending criminal charges.
2. Parole or probation status of the witness.
3. Evidence contradicting a prosecution witness' statements or reports.
4. Evidence undermining a prosecution witness' expertise (e.g., inaccurate statements).
5. A finding of misconduct by a Board of Rights or Civil Service Commission, that reflects on the witness' truthfulness, bias, or moral turpitude.
6. Evidence that a witness has a reputation for untruthfulness.
7. Evidence that a witness has a racial, religious, or personal bias against the defendant individually or as a member of a group.
8. Promises, offers, or inducements to the witnesses, including a grant of immunity.

- ***Maryland v. King*, 569 U.S. (2013)** is a Supreme Court decision that ruled that requiring a forensic DNA sample for arrestees supported by probable cause does not violate the 4th Amendment against unreasonable searches and seizures. According to the majority opinion, DNA collection serves "a well-established, legitimate government interest: the need of law enforcement officers safely and accurately to process and identify persons taken into custody." Not all states, however, allow for the collection of DNA samples from arrestees; several states have legislation forbidding this.

FUNDING

CSI and forensic science funding needs are often ignored until some major problem comes to light. Often inadequate funding goes along with inadequate oversight from the local criminal justice establishment. Quality and timely work have a price tag; inadequate funding has consequences. Parent organizations must remember to fund staff and support operations in addition to line units. Failure to provide adequate funding to ensure quality work and timely lab service is indefensible. The damage done when failures in the forensic science delivery system occur can be horrific. The citizens of a democracy have a right to expect that justice is administered fairly, impartially, and in an expedient manner.

MENTAL HEALTH

A word on mental health and psychological first aid is in order. The nature of the work that CSIs do can take its toll on even the most experienced and seasoned investigator. Many CSI units have made it mandatory that all crime scene personnel speak to a counselor after processing a "difficult" scene. CSI leadership should make an effort to establish a culture where no one should feel embarrassed about seeking help from a therapist, counselor, or EAP program. Besides training in Crime Scene Investigation, unit heads should also offer training in psychological first aid so that team members can spot warning signs when a co-worker should be offered help. Many CSIs have been known to suffer from alcohol/drug abuse, post-traumatic stress disorder (PTSD), and a host of other mental health issues because they did not seek help early on. Investigators should be made aware of where they can seek help and that it will not have a negative effect on them professionally. It is also important that all CSIs take time off when needed and have enough time for rest and relaxation. Having CSIs that are overworked and stressed out can compromise the effective processing of a crime scene.

COGNITIVE BIAS

Psychologists have studied a problem that affects the reliability of conclusions in many fields, including forensic science. Cognitive bias concerns the ways in which perceptions and opinions can be modified by elements other than those applicable to the decision at hand. Cognitive bias includes "contextual bias," where individuals are influenced by irrelevant information; "confirmation bias," where examiners interpret information, or look for new evidence that conforms to pre-existing beliefs or opinions; and "avoidance of cognitive dissonance," where individuals will not accept new information that is inconsistent with their initial conclusion. A goal of forensic science is to minimize bias. One area that has been discussed in forensic science is linear sequential unmasking so the examiner has no or very limited extraneous information about the nature of the material being tested. Itiel Dror[*,†,‡] has been a leader in the effects of bias in forensic science. In one study, Dror showed how latent fingerprint examiners' conclusions can be influenced by knowledge about other forensic examiners' decisions (a form of confirmation bias). Dror has published extensively in this area, and forensic practitioners should be aware of his work.

THE FUTURE

Crime scene investigation and forensic science are complex processes that will continue to be essential components of the criminal justice system and public safety. All stakeholders must keep them strong and vibrant.

The following chapters will cover the most current and up-to-date techniques and methods of crime scene investigation. It is incumbent for all CSIs and investigators to ensure that the appropriate scientific techniques and principles are used to bring out the truth in criminal investigations. CSIs cannot settle for the status quo; they must continuously strive to use the most innovative and advanced methodologies to support the criminal justice system in its search for truth and justice.

Further Reading

Durnal, Evan W. "Crime scene investigation (as seen on TV)." *Forensic Science International* 199.1–3 (2010): 1–5.

Shelton, Donald E. "The 'CSI Effect': Does it really exist?." *National Institute of Justice Journal* 259 (2008).

Slack, Donia P. "Trauma and coping mechanisms exhibited by forensic science practitioners: a literature review." *Forensic Science International: Synergy* 3 (2020): 310–316.

Wallace, Edward, Michael Cunningham, and Daniel Boggiano. *Crime Scene Unit Management: A Path Forward*. Routledge, 2015.

Zapf, Patricia A., and Itiel E. Dror. "Understanding and mitigating bias in forensic evaluation: lessons from forensic science." *International Journal of Forensic Mental Health* 16.3 (2017): 227–238.

Chapter Questions

1. Define the term evidence.

---

[*] Kassin, Saul M., Itiel E. Dror, and Jeff Kukucka. "The forensic confirmation bias: Problems, perspectives, and proposed solutions." *Journal of Applied Research in Memory and Cognition* 2.1 (2013): 42–52.
[†] Dror, Itiel E., David Charlton, and Alisa E.Péron. "Contextual information renders experts vulnerable to making erroneous identifications." *Forensic Science International* 156.1 (2006): 74–78.
[‡] Dror, Itiel E., and Jeff Kukucka. "Linear sequential unmasking–expanded (LSU-E): A general approach for improving decision making as well as minimizing noise and bias." *Forensic Science International: Synergy*, 3 (2021).

2. Give examples of testimonial vs. real evidence.
3. Which of the following pieces of evidence would be more probative in associating the defendant to the victim in a murder trial?
   a) A fiber found on the defendant's jacket when he was arrested that is similar to those from the carpet at the crime scene.
   b) A bloodstain found on the defendant's jacket that subsequently matches the victim's DNA profile.
   c) A hair found on the defendant's jacket that is similar to those of the victim's dog.
   d) Eyewitness testimony of a neighbor who saw someone matching the defendant's build at the scene.
4. What two recommendations did the PCAST report address?
5. Name three things that physical evidence can accomplish.
6. What is the difference between classification and individualization?
7. All of the following can be part of a criminal investigation, except the:
   a) CSI.
   b) forensic scientist.
   c) Prosecutor.
   d) defense attorney.
   e) none of the above.
8. The forensic practitioner's sole obligation is to serve the aims of _____
   a) Justice.
   b) their agency.
   c) the victim.
   d) the prosecutor.
9. Name two professional organizations for Crime Scene Investigation.
10. The IAI certifies crime laboratories.
    a) True
    b) False

CHAPTER 2

First on Scene and Crime Scene Personnel

Wherever he steps, whatever he touches, whatever he leaves, even unconsciously, will serve as silent evidence against him. Not only his fingerprints or his footprints but his hair, the fibers from his clothes, the glass he breaks, the tool mark he leaves, the paint he scratches, the blood or semen he deposits or collects—all these and more bear mute witness against him. This is evidence that does not forget. It is not confused by the excitement of the moment. It is not absent because human witnesses are. It is factual evidence. Physical evidence cannot be wrong; it cannot perjure itself; it cannot be wholly absent. Only its interpretation can err. Only human failure to find it, study, and understand it, can diminish its value.

Paul L. Kirk* (Figure 2.1)

THE FIRST OFFICER AT THE SCENE

Crime scenes are dynamic, rapidly changing environments. The first officers to arrive on the scene must be concerned with countless details. Their major tasks are to protect the crime scene. To a great extent, the success of the investigation and, perhaps, any chance for a successful resolution of the case hinges on actions and steps taken by the first officers to arrive at the crime scene.

Consider the crime scene as a snapshot of what occurred in the final moments of a crime. The scene is the place from which much of the physical evidence associated with the crime is obtained. It provides investigators with a starting point for the inquiry to determine the identities of the suspect and victim and to piece together the circumstances of what happened during the crime. Physical evidence found at the scene can be the key to the solution of the crime. The first officer's most important task at the scene is to prevent the destruction or diminished value of potential evidence that may lead to the apprehension of the suspect and the ultimate resolution of the crime. The responsibility of the first uniformed officers at the scene can never be minimized. What these officers do or don't do, whether innocent or intentional, may have serious ramifications in the course of the investigation.

Some police agencies have very specific policies for uniformed personnel concerning their duties and responsibilities at the crime scene. First responders should be familiar with their duties and responsibilities and execute these

---

* Paul L. Kirk, 1902–1970, was a microchemist and a leader in the field of criminalistics. He was a professor at the University of California, Berkeley for 43 years. Through his work at Berkeley, Kirk began to develop a more structured and scientific approach to criminalistics and in 1937, was selected to head the criminology program at Berkeley. Eight years later, he established a major in technical criminology. Kirk wrote the groundbreaking textbook *Crime Investigation*. In addition, he consulted on many criminal cases, including the well-known murder trial of Sam Sheppard.

Figure 2.1 Professor Paul L. Kirk. The highest honor in the criminalistics section of the American Academy of Forensic Sciences is the Paul L. Kirk Award. (*Photograph from https://en.wikipedia.org/wiki/Paul_L._Kirk.*)

tasks to the best of their ability. Superior officers and training officers should monitor the performance of both new and experienced uniformed personnel. Police agencies should understand the importance of ongoing training and continuing education, not only for investigative and technical personnel but also for first responder personnel as well. The duties of the first officer to arrive at the crime scene are the same, no matter what his/her rank, and remain the same regardless of the seriousness of the crime. The first responder at the scene must assume that the suspect left clues or physical evidence behind. The first responder's actions or inactions must not be allowed to destroy or change anything at the scene. Information developed from evidence left at the scene may help to reconstruct the crime or reveal the identity of the suspect.

Common sense strongly suggests that a crime scene will yield useful information. No one can enter a location without changing it in some way, either by bringing something into it or by removing something from it. The notion of an individual coming in contact with a scene and changing it in some way is known as the **Locard Exchange Principle**, named after the French forensic scientist, Edmond Locard (1877–1966). A popular restatement of this principle may be summarized as: *every contact leaves a trace*. Although changes to a crime scene may be extremely small, the course of an investigation may well hinge on their detection. Therefore, the first officer's action or inaction may affect the future of the investigation (Figure 2.2).

Naturally, the general rule of protecting the crime scene cannot be applied in every case. The resources of the crime scene unit as well as the nature of the crime must be taken into account. Petty thefts and other misdemeanors will not receive the same in-depth investigation as a homicide case or a major terrorist incident. Some police agencies may arbitrarily set a lower limit to the property value lost in a burglary as a way to determine the scope of their investigation. Some police agencies, for example, employ small Evidence Collection Teams for property crimes and full Crime Scene Units for larger, violent crimes against people.

Figure 2.2 Edmond Locard, French forensic scientist (1877–1966). (*Photograph from https://locardslab.com/2014/11/18/scientist-spotlight-edmond-locard/.*)

At first glance, the actions to be taken by the first officer on the scene may seem simple and not well beyond the scope of routine police duties. Some further examination of these duties will show that this is not the case.

First responders should not approach the scene in haste. All movements should be calm and deliberate. Officers should expect the worst and take the position that it is better to be overly cautious and remember the popular adage: *if something can go wrong, it will!* Approaching the assignment with an open mind helps an officer avoid carelessness and false moves that may prove to be disastrous.

Some errors committed in the protection and examination of the crime scene may never be set right. The eventual success of the investigation may be dependent on the preventative and preliminary measures taken by the first officer to arrive at the crime scene. Unfortunately, there are too many examples of how an omission or a mistake on the part of the first responder proved fatal to the investigation. It is often the small things that cause these problems. For example, using a toilet at the scene and then flushing it may wipe away an important fingerprint, or using a drinking glass on a kitchen counter or smoking at a scene are simple, unintended examples that may result in important evidence being contaminated or destroyed.

In a difficult situation, the officer may be faced with a dilemma that requires quick analysis of the circumstances and the taking of appropriate steps. However, if the basic rule of always anticipating the worst and taking extensive rather than minimal precautions is followed, the most serious errors can usually be avoided. Remember, it is always better to explain in court why you did do something, than why you didn't.

Because conditions and situations can vary greatly from one crime scene to another, it is not possible to set hard and fast rules to govern all situations. However, certain guidelines can be established. These are mainly applicable to homicide cases and other serious crimes because it is in these cases that the officer is faced with the most difficult tasks and the actions taken to have the most far-reaching consequences.

CRIME SCENE DOS AND DON'TS*

Do	Don't
• Limit access to the crime scene by using crime scene tape and a major incident log. • Attempt to identify possible routes used by the suspect. • Note original conditions at the crime scene. • Record changes in conditions especially concerning your activities (or EMTs/paramedics). • Protect evidence from adverse environmental conditions. • Conduct all non-CSI tasks outside the tape (coffee drinking, smoking, talking on a cell phone). • Record the location of the evidence before moving it. • Package trace evidence (paint, glass, etc.) first into bindles and then into individual larger envelopes. • Keep an open mind as to what might be evidence. • Be aware that you are a potential source of contamination. • Take photographs of items at 90° with and without L - scales (right angle scales). • Call expert personnel to crime scenes for detailed or difficult collection or documentation. • Take photographs of all aspects of crime scenes: perspective shots, mid-range shots, and close-ups. • Establish an area for garbage outside of the crime scene.	• Permit unnecessary personnel to enter the crime scene. • Use routes possibly used by the suspect. • Assume others will note original conditions, etc. • Fail to document any changes or contamination at the scene. • Allow evidence to be compromised by the elements. • Eat or use any facilities or the phone within the crime scene. • Remove items and package them without documentation. • Package trace evidence together in a bundle. • Ignore items that appear out of place or are difficult to explain. • Touch anything unnecessarily. • Photograph items without scales. • Assume that the expert can always answer the questions from non-expert collections or documentation. • Not change gloves in between handling different items of evidence. • Limit your photographs to overalls and item locations.

RECORDING THE TIME

Precise notations of the time are very important in an investigation. Noting the time is important when checking a suspect's story and can be helpful in other circumstances as well. Therefore, the first officer at the scene should write down arrival times and other times that may turn out to be significant. Notation should be made of the time that the crime was committed, the time that the officer was first called, the time of arrival at the scene, and so on. Such notations lend precision and credibility to the officer's statement if testifying in court becomes necessary. Keeping track of the time spent at the scene also maintains a chronological record of the way things were done during the crime scene investigation. These notes will prove invaluable when specific details about the investigation are needed as the case proceeds. This information can be recorded into case management software on a tablet or laptop at the crime scene, or in an officer's notebook.

WHEN A SUSPECT IS FOUND AT THE SCENE

The first thing an officer must do when entering a scene is to render it safe, as the suspect may still be on location. Officers should always remember that their safety is of paramount importance! The first officer to arrive at a crime scene may need to arrest or detain a suspect. The police officer must use common sense in taking whatever measures are necessary to protect the scene. If it is not possible to hold the suspect at the scene or in the police vehicle, and if a backup officer is unavailable, a possible alternative might be to find a reliable person to protect the scene until other officers arrive. The first officer must instruct such persons on how to guard the scene because he or she likely will be inexperienced in this.

The first officer should also be aware that the longer the suspect remains at the crime scene, the greater the possibility becomes for changing or contaminating the crime scene. The suspect could remove evidence, leave new evidence, or even gain information by observing details at the scene. The suspect (if known) should be searched and removed from the location as quickly as possible.

---

* This list was originally developed by Ron Linhart and Elizabeth Devine, LA County Sheriff's Crime Laboratory.

INJURED PERSON ON THE SCENE

Saving lives is the priority and takes precedence over all other considerations. If an injured person is on the scene, first aid should be administered immediately even if it means valuable evidence may be lost or destroyed. If first aid to the injured is not immediately essential, the officer should note the victim's position on a simple sketch, and with a photo. The officer should note how the victim is lying or sitting, the position of the hands, arms, and legs, the condition of clothes, and so on. It is also important to notice if the victim's hands have anything in them such as hairs, fibers, etc. Using a smartphone camera may help in this endeavor.

When paramedics or emergency medical personnel arrive, the officer should—without interfering in their work—instruct them how to enter the scene without disturbing it unnecessarily. Observing the movements of medical personnel and noting whether any objects were moved is also required. (Paramedics should be instructed to dispose of all medical equipment like gloves, gauze, etc. outside of the crime scene.)

If civilian emergency medical personnel transport the injured person, a police officer should accompany the victim. An alert investigator may hear an important word or accusation or what might be equivalent to a dying declaration that might be the key to the entire case. In one case, a dying woman uttered the name of her assailant. This vital information fell on the untrained, inattentive ears of the civilian emergency medical personnel, and no amount of interviewing could sharpen their recall.

The officer should arrange for proper removal and custody of the victim's clothing. Sometimes when the hospital is contacted to obtain the victim's garments, the clothing has been wadded into a hopeless mess after being cut from the body. Representatives of police agencies should make periodic visits to local hospitals to instruct medical personnel in the proper handling of evidence. The medical profession's lack of interest in and knowledge about evidence is challenging, considering the broad range of their training and the media's attention to criminal investigations.

ENTERING THE SCENE PROPER

After making sure the scene is safe and rendering aid to any victims, the officer should attempt to form a hypothesis of what happened as quickly as possible. This assessment will likely be the basis for subsequent actions. When entering the scene proper, or the focal point of events, the officer must proceed with extreme caution and concentrate his/her attention on possible evidence that may be found on doors, doorknobs, light switches, floors, ceiling, etc.

An effort must be made to observe details, particularly those that are fleeting, and to take contemporaneous written or electronic notes on such points as:

- Doors—open, closed, or locked? On which side was the key?
- Windows—open or closed? Were they locked?
- Lights—on or off? Which lights were on?
- Shades, shutters, or blinds—open or closed?
- Odors—cigarette smoke, gas, gun powder, perfume, decomposition, etc.?
- Signs of activity—meal preparation, dishes in the sink, house clean or dirty, etc.?
- Date and time indicators—mail, newspapers, dates on milk cartons, stopped clocks, spoiled foods, items that should have been hot or cold but were at room temperature.

Nothing at the crime scene should be moved unless necessary. The crime scene should remain as close as possible to its original state until the crime scene unit arrives. If it becomes necessary to remove any object because others may disturb it, the officer should consider the possibility that the item may have fingerprints or DNA present and act accordingly. Before any object is moved, its location should be recorded and photographed. The exact original position of an object at a scene may become important later on in the case.

Under no circumstances should anyone be allowed to wander about the crime scene simply to satisfy his or her curiosity. There have been many instances where first officers arrived at the scene and wandered about the scene leaving fingerprints, trace evidence, and DNA on a variety of surfaces. Such carelessness cannot be tolerated. These activities are all the more problematic when senior officers or department brass show up out of curiosity to see what is going on.

Those at the crime scene should refrain from using the toilet, avoid turning on water faucets, eating, drinking, smoking, or using towels at the scene. The suspect may have used these objects—i.e., a towel could have been used to wipe a bloodstained weapon. The rule is simple: the first officer at the crime scene should not touch anything unless necessary or unless she is charged with the responsibility of processing the scene for physical evidence. Any first officer to arrive at a scene should consider it an embarrassment if their fingerprints or DNA are found and identified at the crime scene due to their sloppiness.

First officers should realize that the lead investigator might call on them later to account for their movements at the crime scene. This may be necessary for the investigating officer to get a better idea of the original condition of the crime scene or to explain seemingly out-of-place items at the scene.

Sometimes, the victim or a relative may attempt to clean up the scene—perhaps to put everything in proper order for when the police arrive or perhaps to try to conceal something. Cleaning might serve as a psychological need to put things back in their proper place. If a cleanup is in progress when the officer arrives, it should be stopped. If the cleanup has been completed or the officer suspects that is the case, a detailed inquiry should be made to determine the original condition of the scene. It may be possible to recover material or undamaged items that were thrown out or discarded.*

PROTECTING THE INTEGRITY OF THE SCENE

As soon as possible after arriving, the officer should take steps to protect the scene from anyone not directly involved with the investigation, including other officers, supervisors, command personnel, the press, curiosity seekers, and family members. This is no easy task and sometimes requires some ingenuity because, initially, there may not be enough personnel to protect the crime scene.

Protecting the crime scene is an ongoing activity. Uniformed officers should remain posted at the scene. The victim's family, the public, and the press should be kept away from the crime scene proper (Figure 2.3). Fellow officers, especially command officers, who have no business visiting the crime scene, are a more serious problem. In highly publicized crimes, superior officers often exhibit a desire to see (or perhaps tour might be a better term) the scene. This should be avoided. A simple solution is to have a sign-in log so anyone who enters or leaves the crime scene is accounted for. An alternative is to set up a command post with a pot of coffee and donuts to help keep unnecessary persons away. A remote video camera could be set up inside the command post to allow superiors to have a visual inspection of the crime scene without actually entering it. Another possibility to discourage officers from visiting a scene is to let them know that there is a possibility they could be called to testify down the road. Sometimes it may be necessary to inform superiors politely that the scene is active and their presence might compromise findings and interfere with collecting physical evidence.

Simply locking a door or stringing rope or commercially available yellow crime scene tape around the perimeter can secure the crime scene. If these measures do not suffice, first responders may resort to using vehicles, boards, or furniture gathered from another area away from the scene to help keep curiosity seekers out. Even with devices such as police barricades, yellow crime scene tape, and ropes, officers may still need to take an active role in keeping unauthorized people away. In addition, with today's drone technology, another area of concern is the crime scene being filmed from above. In these instances, it might be necessary to set up a temporary tent to protect the outdoor crime scene from unauthorized drone photography. However, this might be difficult to do in a large outdoor area.

The extent of any protective measures must be decided on a case-by-case basis. As a general rule, if the scene is indoors, the barricade should include the central scene and, where possible, the probable entry and exit paths used by the suspect. In this regard, it is important to focus attention on potential evidence on the ground outside a window, in rooms through which the suspect had to pass, in stairways, and/or entrances.

---

* In some cases CSIs might need to contact the local garbage company to track down the approximate location where a garbage truck dumped its waste at the landfill in order to locate a probative piece of evidence such as a murder weapon.

Figure 2.3 The press may show up at crime scenes to report on a big story. As long as they do not interfere with the investigation or cross the police line, they should be allowed to stay as it is their 1st amendment right.

If the location is outdoors, an ample area should be roped off to include the paths taken by the suspect to and from the crime scene. Sometimes, critical evidence may be found on or near a route leading to or away from the scene. It is important to search paths carefully. In some cases, before the arrival of the police, onlookers trample the crime scene.

In open areas, barricades can be set up only if an officer is stationed outside the perimeter to guard them. The protection of the scene in open areas merely requires that the officer not walk around aimlessly inside or immediately outside the roped-off area. Limiting movements permits later accountability for the officer's tracks.

The first officer should remain at the scene whenever possible. Leaving the supervision of the crime scene to persons other than police officers should only be done in exceptional circumstances. Protective measures at the scene should be taken as early as possible to prevent valuable, often vital evidence from being destroyed. It is also important that barricades be sufficiently extensive from the beginning of the investigation. Sometimes, a sufficient area around the crime scene is not protected early enough in the investigation.

When large outdoor areas are to be protected, officers may use police cadets, police reserves, auxiliary police, or others who can be trusted to assume responsibility for protecting the scene.

DEAD PERSON ON THE SCENE

If the first officer on the scene can establish certain signs of death, such as clear rigor mortis, odor, lividity, beginning decomposition, and so forth, the body is not to be touched or removed until a detailed examination can be made. Once the first officer at the crime scene has established that the victim is dead and has made a cursory inspection of the crime scene, superiors must be notified regarding the nature of the case. The officer's cell phone should be used for this purpose rather than a police radio because it is not uncommon for the press and other news sources to monitor police radio frequencies using scanners. The phone at the scene should not be used.

SUMMONING THE MEDICAL EXAMINER

Whether the medical examiner should be contacted at this point of the investigation is often a matter of local custom. Some agencies, by agreement with the medical examiner's office, first wait for the investigating officers to arrive and begin their investigation. Notification of death may be made at this time, with an estimate of the time the medical examiner or **Medicolegal Death Investigator** (MLI)* should arrive. This can save the medical examiner's staff time by not having to wait needlessly at the scene until the police have completed their portion of the investigation. Policies should be arranged with the medical examiner's office on such callout matters.

The medical examiner's office has legal jurisdiction over the body at the crime scene. Therefore, the body should not be moved or searched without the consent of the medical examiner or MLI. (In cases of suicide, any suicide note or letter belongs to the jurisdiction of the medical examiner, as well.)

On rare occasions, the first officer must take immediate steps to remove the body from the scene. In these situations, the officer must ensure that the deceased is placed on the stretcher in the same position in which the body was discovered, provided that circumstances permit. Limbs rigidly fixed in a certain position should not be straightened. If the victim is found face down, the body should remain in that position because lividity may change position and appearance, and trickles of blood may change direction.

If the rigidity of **rigor mortis**† must be broken to transport the body, the officer must make note of it, preferably with sketches and photographs showing the original position. Before the body is moved, its position should be documented, sketched, and photographed. The position of the head, arms, hands, knees, and feet must be shown on the sketch. The officer should also note the condition of the clothes and any bloody tracks that may be present. This can be extremely important in answering the question of whether the body had previously been moved. Blood may run while the body is being removed. A question may later arise about the source of this secondary flow of blood.

Postmortem lividity or **livor mortis** is another sign of death. It is caused by the settling of the blood in the lower portion of the body, causing a purplish red discoloration of the skin due to the action of gravity. The discoloration does not occur in the areas of the body that are in contact with the ground or another object. The presence of livor mortis can be used by forensic investigators to determine whether or not a body has been moved (for instance, if the body is found lying face down but the pooling is present on the deceased's back, investigators can determine that the body was originally positioned face up).

In cases of strangulation or hanging where unmistakable signs of death are observed, the first officer at the scene should do nothing to the body. If there is a danger that the rope might break, the officer may attempt to support the corpse, but it should not be cut down. If obvious signs of life are present, the officer must try to save the person.

Knots in ropes should not be untied, if possible. The knot may be typical of a certain occupation or skill level. The noose may be cut and the loose ends labeled appropriately. An alternative to labeling is to tie the ends back together with string or thread. If these materials are not available, the noose or rope should be placed so that the officer can later recall which ends belong together. In emergencies, the knot may be loosened somewhat and the noose pulled over the victim's head. It is also important to remember which end of the rope was anchored to a fixed object or pulled over a branch or beam. The direction of distorted surface fibers on the rope may indicate whether the victim was pulled up because it is always possible that hanging was staged to cover up a murder. It is important to consider that the suspect's DNA could be on any knots or areas of the ligature surrounding the knots.

FIREARMS AND AMMUNITION AT THE SCENE

The general rule is that any firearms or ammunition should be left until investigating personnel arrives. However, the recovery of weapons and ammunition may become necessary. If they may be inadvertently moved or lost during the removal of an injured person, or if the conditions are such that they cannot be properly protected, then they may be removed.

---

* The medicolegal death investigator is responsible for the dead person, whereas law enforcement jurisdiction is responsible for the scene. The medicolegal death investigator performs scene investigations emphasizing information developed from the decedent and determines the extent to which further investigation is necessary.

† Rigor mortis is a recognizable sign of death that is caused by a chemical change in the muscles after death. The limbs of the corpse become stiff and difficult to move or manipulate. It begins after about three hours of death, reaches maximum stiffness after 12 hours, and gradually dissipates after about 72 hours.

When picking up pistols and revolvers, a pen or pencil should never be inserted into the barrel to lift the weapon as seen on TV. Dust, blood, particles of tissue, and other debris in the barrel may become dislodged. To move a gun, grasp the checkered surface of the grips with two gloved fingers or use the trigger guard. Before the weapon is moved, however, its position should be marked on a sketch and photographed. The position of bullets and cartridge casings may reveal the direction of the shot and possibly the location of the assailant. The positions of hammers and safeties should also be noted. Care should be taken not to disturb potential trace DNA evidence, or transfer DNA from another item.

If a weapon is found, it should be in the same condition in which it was recovered when delivered to a firearms examiner for examination. When the firearm is packaged for submission as evidence, a detailed description of what was done to it should be prepared and sent to the crime laboratory. The only acceptable change to the weapon would be to unload it. An investigator with firearms experience should render the weapon safe while wearing gloves before sending it to the crime lab.

WHAT TO DO UNTIL INVESTIGATING PERSONNEL ARRIVE

While waiting for investigators to arrive, the first officer on the scene should attend to the following:

- **Write down the names of witnesses and other persons who entered the scene.** This is important for the subsequent sorting of fingerprints and DNA and other clues found at the scene.
- **Note who was at the scene when the officer arrived.** This information can become particularly important if the crime had just occurred.
- **Establish basic facts.** A factual account of what happened is of great assistance to the detectives when they arrive because it helps them to decide on their next moves. However, the first officer should never undertake lengthy and detailed interrogations of witnesses, suspects, or victims that may damage later questioning or give rise to misleading suggestions in later statements. Furthermore, the officer cannot properly guard the scene if occupied with interrogations.
- **Keep the suspect and witnesses separated when possible.** Allowing the suspect and witnesses to talk may interfere with later questioning. Family members may be left in the care of neighbors when necessary, taking care that no alcoholic drinks or sedatives are administered. Remember that the dramatically grieving relative may be the prime suspect.
- **Instruct witnesses not to discuss the events.** This can prevent distortion or bias by suggestion. If possible, the principal witnesses should be separated. In relating events to one another, witnesses may distort each other's impressions to a point at which they believe that they saw things that they did not see or that never happened.
- **Do not discuss the crime with witnesses or bystanders.** This is also intended to prevent suggestion and distortion. Furthermore, circulating details of the crime may hinder the investigation.
- **Listen attentively, but unobtrusively.** An alert officer can often pick up information of vital importance to the investigation simply by being a good listener.
- **Protect evidence that is in danger of being destroyed.** During inclement weather such as rain or snow, divert water and cover tracks with boxes, cardboard, tents, etc. If the crowd of onlookers becomes large, it may become necessary to expand the protective measures at a given location to prevent the trampling of the evidence.

When the investigating officers arrive, the first officer should report all that has been learned and observed and the actions that were taken. This is very important to the evaluation and planning of the crime scene investigation. It is particularly important that reports be given to the extent to which the scene has been altered and whether objects have been disturbed or moved.

CONTINUED PROTECTION OF THE SCENE

When protecting the scene after the investigators have arrived, the officers detailed to protect it should act only on orders from the detective in charge. During the technical examination of the scene, it is the crime scene investigator who is in charge of the officers on security duty as well as of the scene proper.

No one should be allowed access to the crime scene without the lead investigator's permission, not even other investigators or superior officers. Command officers would render a fine service to their investigators if they would preserve the integrity of the crime scene with a passion and set an example for other officers by keeping out of the scene. Unfortunately, there are numerous instances of police officers on sightseeing tours through crime scenes. Sometimes they destroy more evidence than any group of laypeople could accomplish. Even experienced investigators are guilty of allowing these tours, especially in murder cases and other serious crimes.

News reporters sometimes arrive at the scene before investigators. People in the neighborhood usually call them or they may have heard a call on the police scanner. The first officers on the scene should not, under any circumstances, give information about the case to reporters. To inform the press is the responsibility of the police chief, sheriff, or public information officers designated by them. Officers should not favor one reporter or news agency by giving out information that may not be available to the competitors through prescribed channels. In dealing with reporters, officers should be neither curt nor nonchalant, but they should be firm, even when reporters are persistent. The officer should remember that reporters often give invaluable assistance in the investigation of major crimes by soliciting the public's help when needed.

CRIME SCENE PERSONNEL

Ideally, a crime scene unit should have the following personnel: a team leader, a photographer (who also keeps the photolog), sketch preparer, evidence custodian, and recovery personnel (searchers). In smaller agencies, or depending on the time of day/day of the week, it may not be possible to have all of these individuals respond to every crime scene. To this end, most crime scene units will cross-train all personnel in each of these areas so that each CSI can perform more than one of these functions when needed.

In addition, the crime scene unit should also have a list of specialty personnel who may need to be called upon on less frequent occasions: a forensic entomologist, botanist, forensic anthropologist, geologist, bomb technician, forensic engineer, cadaver dog handler, divers, HAZMAT team, and a locksmith. Agencies can sign intermittent contracts or have memorandums of understanding (MOUs) with these professionals since they are usually not full-time employees.

Case Review

In one of California's most notorious serial murder cases, an individual dubbed the "Night Stalker" by the press terrorized the Los Angeles area in the mid-1980s. Before his reign of terror ended, at least 13 people were viciously murdered and numerous others were assaulted. His murder spree ranged from San Francisco to Orange County. A regional task force was led by detectives from the Los Angeles County Sheriff's Department Homicide Bureau. Evidence of a satanic link—upside-down pentagrams were noted at early crime scenes and attributed to the assailant (Figure 2.4a and b). After his capture and during his trial, upside-down pentagrams were found on the dashboard of his car and in his holding cell.

The crime scene attributed to the "Night Stalker" started to show a grisly pattern: restraints (i.e., cords, belts, handcuffs, and thumb-cuffs) were found at many scenes as well as various tools that were used to bludgeon his victims. A characteristic shoe impression was linked to several crime scenes. The unusual shoe pattern was preserved through the use of photography, plaster casting, and tape lifts (Figure 2.4c and 2.4d). The shoe impressions were compared and found to have similar class characteristics to the Avia Aerobic, size 11½. After consultation with the owners of the Avia Company, it was determined that only one pair of size 11½ shoes was distributed in the Los Angeles area, of 97 pairs in the entire state. After a public official mentioned the existence of the shoe prints at a press conference, those prints stopped showing up at subsequent crime scenes, and the shoes were never recovered.

The Firearms and Latent Print sections of the Los Angeles County Sheriff's Department, Scientific Services Bureau, played an important part in the perpetrator's conviction. Rifling marks from bullets recovered at different scenes were compared. It was established that they were fired from the same handgun. This substantiated the initial hypothesis that the same individual committed these crimes. On the day of his arrest, items belonging to Richard Ramirez were seized from a local bus depot locker (Figure 2.4e). Among these items were a yellow

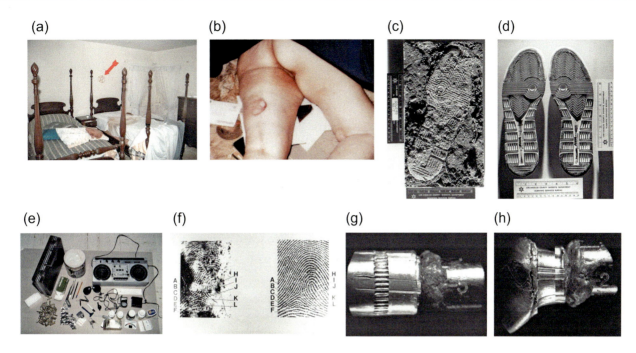

Figure 2.4 (a, b) Photos from murders attributed to the "Night Stalker" serial killer show evidence of a satanic link. (c, d) A characteristic shoe print was found at several of the crime scenes, but the shoes were never recovered. (e, f) Fingerprinting linked items found in a bus depot locker to Richard Ramirez. (g, h) Live ammunition from the bus locker matched expended cartridges found at four of the crime scenes. (*Courtesy Los Angeles County Sheriff's Department Scientific Services Bureau.*)

flashlight and live rounds of ammunition. A latent fingerprint (Figure 2.4f) on the flashlight was identified as belonging to Ramirez, thereby linking him to the recovered property. More importantly, the live rounds exhibited a magazine signature identical to markings on expended cartridges found at four of the crime scenes (Figure 2.4g and 2.4h).

Based on a latent fingerprint from a vehicle the Night Stalker had used in an assault in Orange County, California, he was identified as Richard Ramirez. A mug shot photograph was released to the press the following morning. That same morning, as newspapers were being distributed, Ramirez was on a bus returning to Los Angeles from Arizona. Within hours he was spotted and captured by citizens in East Los Angeles. Once in custody, he was positively identified as Richard Ramirez, alias the Night Stalker. Four years elapsed before Richard Ramirez was found guilty of all counts brought against him, which included 13 murders and 30 other felonies. He was sentenced to death and died in prison from lymphoma in 2013. In 2021, Netflix released the docuseries *Night Stalker: The Hunt for a Serial Killer*, detailing Ramirez's crimes and how he was ultimately captured.

Further Reading

Dutelle, Aric W. *An Introduction to Crime Scene Investigation.* Jones & Bartlett Learning, 2020.

LeMay, Jan. *CSI for the First Responder: A Concise Guide.* CRC Press, 2017.

Chapter Questions

1. Which of the following is a major task that the first responder must be concerned with?
    a. Calling for backup.
    b. Contacting their supervisor to apprise them of the situation.

c. Protecting the crime scene.
   d. Arresting the suspect.
2. Which of the following principles is associated with processing crime scenes and is often summarized as "every contact leaves a trace"?
   a. Locard's Exchange Principle.
   b. Trace Evidence Principle.
   c. Kirk's Principle.
   d. First Officer's Principle.
3. Describe why it is important for the first responder to record the times associated with a crime scene investigation.
4. When entering a crime scene, the first responder should proceed with extreme caution and concentrate their attention to possible evidence at which locations?
5. What is the very first thing the first responding officer should do when arriving at a crime scene?
6. When is it appropriate for the first responding officer to move a piece of evidence?
   a. When the evidence is a gun.
   b. When he is charged with the responsibility of processing the scene for physical evidence.
   c. Only when the scene is secured.
   d. If the crime is serious such as a homicide.
7. You are called to the scene of a sexual assault that took place at a park. Describe how you would secure the scene.
8. What should be done until investigating personnel arrive at the crime scene?
9. Describe the proper procedure when dealing with multiple witnesses at the scene of a crime.
10. List five crime scene "dos" and five crime scene "don'ts."

CHAPTER 3

Documenting the Crime Scene

It is simply impossible to recall everything one observes at a crime scene. Documentation, therefore, is an essential component of effective crime scene investigation and is a must for subsequent legal proceedings.

Documenting the crime scene consists of several systematic steps: preparation & plan of action, note-taking, photography & videography, sketching, and 3-D scanning. The remaining steps of crime scene processing: detailed search, collection of evidence, final survey, and releasing of the scene will be discussed in the next chapter. Since it is impossible to recall all of the details observed while processing a crime scene, it is critical to memorialize what was done at the scene to refer back to at a later date. Information about who was at the scene, where the evidence was collected from, when did the first officer respond, and a host of other facts needs to be recorded. This chapter covers some of the best practices to follow when documenting and processing crime scenes.

PREPARATION AND PLAN OF ACTION

Crime scenes should be approached in a systematic, methodical way. Certain steps must be performed before others. Considerations about legal and scientific matters must be made when searching a crime scene. These details must be included in an action plan or method of approach before processing can begin.

General action plans should be readily available to crime scene investigators and should be included in written departmental procedures which define crime scene responsibilities. Standard Operating Procedures (SOPs) should detail what tasks are to be done, in what order, and by whom. It is impossible to anticipate every detail in a crime scene investigation; however, certain rules should dictate the responsibilities of uniformed officers, detectives, criminalists, and CSIs. In addition to the general SOPs that each Crime Scene Unit should have, case-specific requirements might require supplemental plans of action to address unique facts or circumstances about a particular case. This can be determined during the initial walk-through of the crime scene.

NOTE-TAKING

Of all the duties and responsibilities of crime scene investigation, perhaps the most important is contemporaneous note-taking. Note-taking is important for several reasons. It forces investigators to commit observations to writing and to keep a detailed, sequential record of everything observed and accomplished. Often, seemingly insignificant items found in an investigator's notebook turn out to be critical to an investigation later.

Some general points about notes and note-taking are:

1. Notes should be made as events unfold, i.e., in chronological order.
2. Notes should detail step-by-step actions.

3. Notes should be complete and thorough.
4. Notes should be clearly and legibly written. Sloppy notes or those that do not clearly state the investigator's meaning will be subject to misinterpretation and/or cross-examination during trial.
5. Negative or unexpected conditions, e.g., the absence of bloodstains or a light that is found on should be noted.
6. The note-taker should be as specific as possible. If an item of evidence is to be located, a description such as "on the living room floor, 6 inches east of the west wall and 3 feet south of the north wall" should be used. Vague statements such as "near" or "to the left of" should be avoided.
7. Case notes, sketches, tape recordings, or photos should never be discarded or deleted, even if poor quality or unintended. They should be placed into a case folder or computer file and retained for as long as the department's policy requires.
8. The initial investigating officer should remember that some investigations may go on for years and future detectives will have to rely on the case notes made at the start of the investigation.

Digital audio recorders make it easy to take down information that can be transcribed later on; some investigators also use audio recording apps on their smartphones for this purpose. Investigators should remember that impromptu remarks from other officers at the scene, however, might later prove embarrassing.

Any notes taken at crime scenes should include the following information:

- Date and time the crime was first reported and type of crime.
- Location of the crime scene and a description of the area.
- Description of the crime or event leading up to the investigation.
- Name of the person who requested the crime scene investigation.
- Names of all officers, witnesses, investigators, and specialized personnel at the crime scene.
- Names of the persons who will be conducting the crime scene search, taking photographs, 3-D scans, sketches, and collecting evidence.
- Weather and lighting conditions at the time of the investigation.
- Description of the primary crime scene, including the location of the body and accompanying details.
- Description of the location, the surrounding houses, streets, community, and other landmarks.
- Description of the interior and exterior of the crime scene, including the type of residence, number of rooms, and windows.
- Description of the outside of the scene including the terrain, type of plants, soil, GPS coordinates, etc.
- The date and time the crime scene investigation was concluded.
- Any additional information required by department directives or SOPs.

These details represent only some of the many pieces of information that may be included in the investigator's notes. They do not represent all the possible information. Each CSU should have its own checklist. Meticulous note-taking is one of the keys to good police work and competent crime scene investigation.

CRIME SCENE PHOTOGRAPHY

The well-worn saying "a picture is worth a thousand words" certainly holds true with crime scene photography. No matter how well an investigator can verbally describe a crime scene, photographs can give the viewer a wealth of information about a scene that cannot easily be expressed in words.

Before a detailed examination of the crime scene is made or before any items are moved or even touched, the crime scene should be photographed. The photographs should be taken to clearly and accurately depict the scene as it was found, the paths taken by the suspect(s) to the scene, the point of entry, and the escape route taken. Detailed photographs should be taken of physical evidence in the condition in which it was found before any removal for "bagging and tagging."

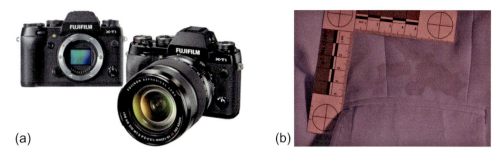

Figure 3.1 (a) The FujiFilm X-T1 Forensic IR Kit (This mirrorless camera is only offered to law enforcement/military entities and medical/scientific professionals that intend to use the camera for scientific purposes.) is one such camera. It offers technology to see light from the ultraviolet (UV), visible, and infrared (IR) portions of the light spectrum (380nm-1000nm). (b) The camera has the capability to capture bloodstains on black fabric, something that is usually difficult to see under normal lighting conditions.

Figure 3.2 (a) The Forenscope® mobile multispectral UV-VIS-IR forensic tablet is designed for CSI documentation. It has a 13 megapixel camera with macro and micro lenses. (b) Bloodstains viewed on a shirt under normal camera vs. ForenScope Camera. (*www.ForenScope.com*.)

Types of Cameras

The digital camera used most often by CSI's is the **digital single lens reflex** (DSLR) **camera**. Cameras today come in many makes and models with very high resolutions. The high-resolution capability allows pictures to be made into high-quality enlargements with little distortion or pixelation and allows examiners to resolve very fine details within the photograph. Photographic resolution is measured in pixels. Digital cameras with a resolution in the 12 megapixel and higher range yield excellent results. (If you want the best possible image quality, then a bigger sensor is more important than huge megapixel counts.) Proper forensic photography equipment minimally requires a DSLR camera with an interchangeable "normal" lens, barrier & bandpass filters, off-camera flash and sync cord, tripod, scale(s), protective case, storage media, 18% gray card, alternate light source (ALS), and spare batteries.[*] For some forensic applications, the ability to capture light from the ultraviolet (UV) and infrared (IR) portions of the light spectrum allows for outstanding detailed images of blood spatter, bruising, document forgery, tattoo identification, bone fragments, and gunshot residue (GSR) (Figure 3.1a and b). In addition, most high-quality cameras include GPS capability to indicate the location the photograph was taken. Many low-end digital "point and shoot" cameras also have good-quality resolution and are useful for many situations, however investigators who regularly photograph crime scenes typically use DSLR cameras. Smartphone cameras are useful when photos are necessary and professional digital photographic equipment is unavailable. Finally, there are mobile multispectral forensic tablets[†] that can produce high-quality images that are on par with digital photos from DSLR cameras (Figure 3.2a and b).

---

[*] B&H Photo (www.bhphotovideo.com/) is an online store that sells most forensic photographic equipment.
[†] The Forenscope® Tablet (https://forenscope.com/) can be used to capture body fluids, GSR, and other forensic evidence without filters and goggles.

While digital photography provides excellent results, its use has created a new set of challenges for law enforcement users. Cameras are able to store hundreds of photos on a single digital storage card. Each agency needs to create its own policies on how it is going to save and store these images in such a way that allows them to be admissible as evidence. Additionally, the large volume of digital photographs creates storage issues with each agency's IT department. Files need to be backed up routinely either off-site or in a secure file in the cloud. Devices must be available to view and print a variety of different digital formats, e.g., TIFF, GIF, JPG, as well as any newly developed formats.

It is also easy to distribute photos over the internet from the crime scene to other locations (i.e., police headquarters, crime lab, district attorney's office, etc.). One must be careful, however, of sensitive photographs "leaking" out. Security of digital images must be appropriately maintained. If a digital photo goes "viral" on the internet, it can never be retrieved and may result in unanticipated consequences in the future. Therefore, secure networks must be set up by the agency's IT Dept prior to sending crime scene photos over the internet.

Number of Photographs

How many photographs should be taken? There is no simple answer, but generally, it is better to overshoot a crime scene (take more photographs than is necessary) than to economize and take too few. Another consideration, however, is that the more photos taken, the more which have to be stored. Time may also be a concern; certain types of cases must be processed quickly. In the final analysis, the experience of the crime scene photographer will best answer the question of the number of photos to take.

Photographs serve several purposes. They aid in refreshing the memories of witnesses and investigators and show the relationships of items of evidence at the crime scene. A very important purpose of crime scene photographs is that they help to convey an image of the crime scene and the circumstances of the crime to the jury. With these purposes in mind, several important photographs should be made in almost every crime scene, including:

- **Location**. Photographs of the location of the crime scene should be taken. In the case of a residence, for example, the exterior of the dwelling should be shot, including the locations of doors and windows. Photographs of surrounding areas of the house should be included, such as the front and backyards and views in each direction. Drone or aerial photographs are also often useful to depict the location of the principal site and other areas of interest in proximity to the crime scene. Pictures from Google Maps and/or Google Earth can also provide useful perspectives.

- **Witness photographs**. Witness photographs are overall photos of the crime scene. They depict the scene as observed by a witness. In the case of a murder crime scene in a house, such photographs might depict the victim lying on the floor as viewed from several locations in the room. These photographs are designed to tell a story, to relate what the location looked like to someone who was not present. To accomplish this task, several overlapping photographs should be made. In addition, long- and intermediate-range photographs should be taken to show perspective and the relative positions of different items found at the crime scene.

- **Bystander photographs**. Photographs of bystanders or crowds that have gathered outside the crime scene should be taken. Sometimes the suspect will appear in these groups of people to watch the aftermath of their crime.

- **Close-up photographs**. In addition to long- and intermediate-range photos, close-up pictures should also be taken to further clarify the scene. Two photographs should be routinely taken: (1) one showing the item as it appears and (2) a photograph of the same item with a ruler included. The film plane must be parallel to the plane of the object. The ruler and the parallel film plane ensure the ability later to produce good-quality enlargements or 1:1 photographs of the evidence (Figure 3.3).

- **Evidence photographs**. Photographs of all items of evidence should be made prior to their removal or changing their location or position in any way. Photographs should be made of shoe imprints, fingerprints, bloodstains, weapons, defense wounds, serial numbers, and other such items. Additional photographs should be taken during the crime scene search as new items of evidence are discovered when items at the crime scene are moved.

- **Examination quality photographs** should ideally be taken back in the lab. Use the camera's native ISO to ensure the best color, contrast, saturation, and minimize artifacts from noise. Images should be captured in RAW file format and saved with the least compression available.

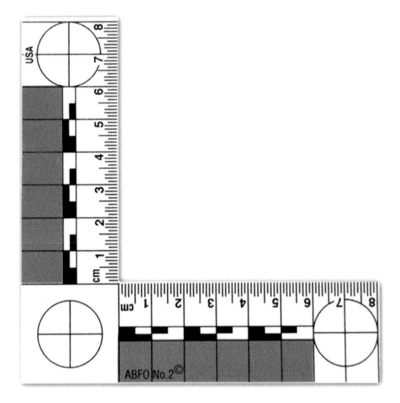

Figure 3.3 An "L" shaped ruler, originally developed by the American Board of Forensic Odontology (www.abfo.org), is typically used for crime scene photos. Rulers are available through law enforcement supply outlets and Amazon.com.

When taking photographs, a photo log should be kept. Some police agencies use preprinted forms and others keep track of photographs by some other means, such as a crime scene app on a tablet.* A typical log might include the case number, date, time, photographer's name, type of camera, lens, and a listing of each photograph. The list might include a very brief description of the location of the evidence. Normally, photographs should be taken at eye level to give the proper perspective of the scene. If the photo is taken from a different perspective, it should be noted in the log. Digital cameras will also mark other photo data in the picture's file when it is saved.

The type of lens used also affects the perspective of the scene. A normal lens should be used, such as a 50-mm lens. If the crime scene is indoors with cramped quarters, medium-wide-angle lenses may be used; however, the lens change should be noted in the photo log.

When using a flash, in most cases it should not be mounted on the top of the camera, but should be held off at an angle when shooting. This is to prevent a reflection in the photo from flash bounce. In low-light situations, flash photography is recommended even though software is available to deal with low-light situations. Most shooting is done with a hand-held camera, but for exposures less than 1/60th of a second, a tripod should be used to ensure sharp photographs. Extraneous subjects and items at the scene do not belong in the photographs such as crime scene equipment or personnel.

Posed photographs that locate where a witness stood when first entering the crime scene may be taken. A photograph should then be taken from that location to show the appearance of the crime scene from that point of observation.

Finally, 360-degree photographs are a great way to capture the scene in its entirety. L-Tron Corporation's OSCR360 Capture Kit (www.l-tron.com/oscr360) can capture a 360-degree photograph in under 4 seconds allowing command

---

* Many Crime Scene Units have implemented software programs to record and document pertinent information, such as photo logs, evidence logs, access logs, sketches, interviews, and other relevant crime scene information. An example of such a program is CrimePad® by Visionations (www.visionations.com). CrimePad is a mobile investigation management system designed for all members involved in an investigation, including first responders, CSI's, detectives, and command staff.

staff, juries, prosecutors, and witnesses to take a virtual tour of the scene. Individual photographs taken with a DSLR camera can then be linked to the 360-degree image.

Photographing a Dead Body

In photographing an unknown body, full-face and right-profile face photos are always taken. If necessary, further pictures should be taken, including a whole view, left profile—especially with a view to identification from the ear—and detailed photos of scars, injuries, teeth, tattoos, clothes, etc. It is good practice to ensure that an unidentified body is not buried before it is photographed; however, it is important to photograph the body before putrefaction sets in and swells or discolors the features. With regard to a body that has undergone some degree of change, although a photograph of the face may be considered quite meaningless, it should still be done. It should also be remembered that the individual may be identified after burial and that the relatives may ask to see the photograph of the face. In taking a full-face picture, the body should be laid on its back with the face turned upward.

For identification photographs, when the body is in a mortuary, the stand or other structure that is generally placed under the head should be removed for the photograph. The lower jaw tends to drop, causing the mouth to open, so it is recommended to prop the chin up with a peg or other object that will not be too conspicuous in the photograph. The camera is placed vertically above the face. The color of the background material should be chosen so that the outer contour of the head is well defined against it. Often the simplest way is to spread a towel under the head. When profile portraits are taken, the body should be raised so that the camera can be placed at the side of the head. A suitable background is also required for this exposure so that the profile shows up distinctly. The head should not be turned to one side to make it easier to photograph because this might cause considerable alteration in appearance owing to the position of the camera.

In photographing whole-face pictures, the camera is placed high above the body. If this is not possible because of a low roof, then the body can be turned a little to one side, but the procedure must be well-thought-out to avoid the possibility of blood running down or other conditions of the body being altered. Under no circumstances should the body be tied or suspended in a leaning position. In photographing scars, injuries, tattoos, piercings, and details of clothing, a ruler should always be placed on or by the side of the object to provide scale. A ring flash can also be used for closeups.

Photographs are best taken in color. However, in certain instances in which tattoos or other marks present on the body are poorly contrasted, appropriate filters, black and white photography, or IR photography may be helpful.

Even at such an early stage when the changes in the body are limited to rigidity and lividity stains, it may be difficult to distinguish scars, and other birthmarks from lividity stains, discolorations of the skin, and wrinkles. With the greater deterioration of the remains, due to decomposition, the greater the difficulties in obtaining good-quality photographs. Tattooing can be barely perceptible when the skin becomes dark-colored and blistered. Under such conditions, the investigator must not rely on personal judgment but should consult the pathologist. Any special characteristics are described in essentially the same way as for living persons, except in one respect. In the case of a description of a living person with many tattoos, only those that are characteristic or unusual (names, dates, emblems, etc.) are described.* With unknown bodies, however, all tattoos should be described, including the most common types. It is very important that these and other special characteristics be described accurately in a recognized manner with respect to kind, form, size, and position (Figure 3.4).

Ultraviolet (UV) and infrared (IR) photography imaging techniques are useful methods for studying and recording injuries on human skin, such as bite marks, ligature marks, and other injuries (Figure 3.5).

Many people are x-rayed to diagnose medical conditions or for detecting dental cavities. These films are often retained in doctors' offices for many years. Before an unknown body is autopsied or buried, dental and body x-rays should be taken. They not only provide a means of identification, but might also provide information as to the cause of death (Figure 3.6a and b).

---

* Gang members often have elaborate tattooing. Such tattooing may suggest specific gang membership. The most comprehensive textbook of tattoos is *Forensic Analysis of Tattoos and Tattoo Inks* by Dr. Michelle Miranda.

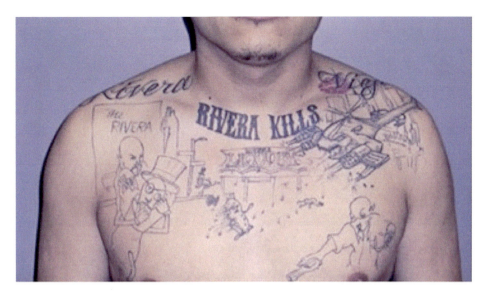

Figure 3.4 Tattoos may help identify victims as well as suspects. A detective was looking through photos of a homicide victim when one caught his eye. The tattoo depicted an unsolved murder crime scene he had investigated. It seems the gang member tattooed a depiction of the crime on his chest. (*Courtesy of the Los Angeles County Sheriff's Department.*)

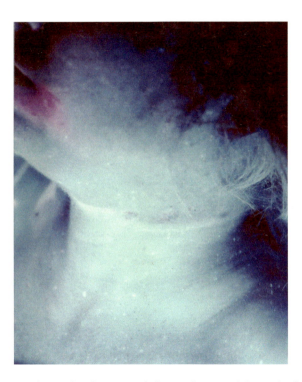

Figure 3.5 Using ultraviolet photography to visualize strangulation marks around the neck of one of the victims in the 1970s Hillside Strangler serial murder case in Los Angeles. (*Courtesy of the Los Angeles County Department of Coroner.*)

This section is not meant to be an all-encompassing guide to crime scene photography and photogrammetry, but rather to present some important points to consider. Several worthwhile classes in general photography that give the beginning crime scene photographer the basics about photography are offered in colleges and adult education programs. Universities and junior colleges with police science programs may also offer classes on crime scene photography. Professional organizations like the International Association for Identification have presentations on crime scene photography at their annual seminars. The IAI also offers certification in Forensic Photography and Imaging.

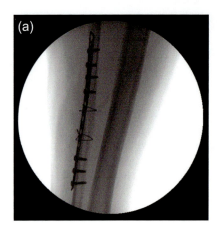 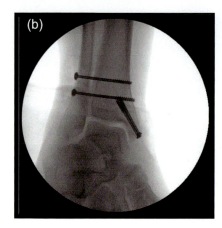

Figure 3.6 (a) These antemortem x-rays of a metal rod placement after a trimalleolar fracture of the right fibula along with (b) ankle screws to repair a broken ankle can be compared to postmortem x-rays to make a positive identification.

Investigators need to feel comfortable using their camera equipment and should not first learn how to use their camera at the crime scene! Knowing the correct exposure, bracketing, lighting, f-stop, and other settings is crucial to producing high-quality photographs. Practice in using one's camera and understanding the proper use of one's equipment is essential.

Admissibility of Photographs

For a photograph to be admissible in court, the investigator must be able to testify that it accurately depicts the area shown. To be accurate, it must represent the subject matter properly in terms of color, scale, and form. Photographs must be in focus and should show the relationships and distances between objects.

All digital files from the crime scene photographs should be retained. They are important to demonstrate that the picture has not been altered. These are also important if enlargements or enhancements of certain areas of the photo are needed to better depict parts of the crime scene. Under no circumstances should photos be deleted. If a mistake is made, retake the photo, but do not delete the photo with the error. Digital evidence software (such as Veripic®, www.veripic.com/digitalevidencemanager) can manage all digital images; it uses an audit trail that can show if images were manipulated, can fulfill electronic discovery requests, and can maintain chain of custody.

Other software, such as Amped software (www.ampedsoftware.com) can detect photo tampering, identify the processing history of the image, verify the camera model used to take the photo, and verify if an image is an unmodified original file.

VIDEOGRAPHY

Video recording is another method of documenting a crime scene. Lightweight, portable, low-light video cameras are ideally suited for gathering a video rendition of a crime scene. Videography does not replace the need for still photographs but has the advantage of more graphically depicting the scene. Smartphones also have video recording capabilities and may be used to record a crime scene in the absence of a professional video camera.

When videotaping a scene, the investigator should walk the video operator through the location. The video should begin outside of an indoor crime scene or with an overall view of the outdoor location. The detective should narrate the video by recording the audio portion as the video is shot. The narration should include the name of the speaker, time, date, location, case number, and other pertinent identifying information.

If digital recordings are to be used as evidence, they should not be edited or erased. The entire recording must be in its original condition if it is to be admissible as evidence. Some agencies use edited videos solely to refresh the investigator's memory. Courts may or may not admit these recordings for the jury's consideration. As with most generalizations on the legal aspects of crime scenes, it is prudent to check with local authorities to determine what will be

Figure 3.7 This Unmanned Aerial Vehicle (UAV) is an example of one of the many drones available which may be adapted for aerial crime scene coverage.

acceptable to the prosecution and to the court. It is better to find out in advance rather than to assume the practice is acceptable and then find out that a key piece of evidence is excluded for some legal reason that was not considered.

While the scene is being recorded, other personnel at the location should be silent because their voices can be picked up. Such conversations may prove distracting and sometimes embarrassing if recorded.

As with photographs, close-up video recordings of small items of evidence should contain a scale to show the actual size of the item. Additionally, panning the area and zooming in on the item should show the relative location.

It is also worthwhile to video the crowd of onlookers and spectators that gather around the crime scene. Suspects have been known to stay at the scene and blend in with the crowd to observe the response of law enforcement. This video can be examined later on once a suspect is developed to see if he was in the crowd of onlookers. The video can also be shown to any victims and/or witnesses to see if they recognize the perpetrator in the crowd behind the crime scene tape.

Drones

One of the newer approaches to crime scene documentation by law enforcement is the use of drones (Figure 3.7). Often referred to as **Unmanned Aerial Vehicles** (UAVs), these are small, remote-controlled, unmanned devices fitted with digital cameras. They can take accurate photos of crime scenes and accidents and are far more cost-effective than using manned helicopters for the same purpose. Drones can also be fitted with laser scanning systems for survey-grade measurement accuracy for large outdoor crime scenes or accident investigations.* Most measuring systems in drones utilize **Light Detection and Ranging** (LiDAR). This technology is used for measuring ranges by targeting an object with a laser and measuring the time for the reflected light to return to the receiver.

Agencies considering using UAVs should consider state restrictions for law enforcement to fly UAVs and whether they are approved for police use by the Federal Aviation Administration (FAA). There are legal considerations too, such as search warrants, that might be required for certain types of aerial searches.

---

* One such system is Riegl Laser Measurement systems (www.riegl.com/).

Before beginning a new UAV program, police agencies should research the issues. There are many UAV models and portable cameras to be considered. Cost, including personal training costs, along with the sophistication of these devices will dictate the use of law enforcement drones.*

The public may express concerns about "mission creep," using drones for surveillance purposes such as following suspects around or peering into homes and over property. Such a perception may be seen as "big brother" watching citizens. Considerations for public engagement before starting up a new UAV program may be worthwhile.

SKETCHING THE CRIME SCENE

Photographs alone are not sufficient for recording a crime scene adequately. A crime scene sketch should also be routinely made. Sketches and photographs complement each other to depict the crime scene sufficiently and properly. Sketches clarify the appearance of the crime scene and make it easier to comprehend. It is, therefore, important for investigators to develop the ability to make good crime scene sketches.

A crime scene sketch is not considered an architectural drawing, such as one drawn by an artist or forensic surveyor. It is simply an illustrative diagram or drawing that depicts the appearance of the crime scene. Nevertheless, sketching the crime scene requires some skill on the part of the investigator. Generally, it is easier if two people work on producing the sketch: one person to draw and the other to take measurements.

Sketches sometimes leave out important information or contain errors. Yet despite these drawbacks and problems in making crime scene sketches, they do provide important information and, when done properly, are very helpful. Sketches help investigators recall details of the crime scene. They also aid prosecutors, courts, and juries to better understand the crime scene.

Sketches offer a permanent record of the relationship of evidence at the scene to other items and help to supplement photographs. They depict the overall layout of the location more easily than can be accomplished by photographs. Sketches also allow for selectivity. A sketch may be drawn purposely to leave out extraneous or confusing details that are recorded in a photograph.

Crime scene sketches can provide a record of conditions that are not readily recorded by other means. Distances can be shown over large areas and topography can be easily illustrated. Paths taken by subjects or vehicles can be shown on drawings more easily than on photographs. Drawings may be used to aid in questioning suspects and witnesses of crimes and to authenticate the testimony of witnesses. Sketches combine the best features of photographs and crime scene notes.

Information Included in Crime Scene Sketches

What information should be present on a sketch? Information placed on a sketch is used to make the drawing understandable and admissible into evidence. Like all evidence, sketches should contain case-identifying information: case number, name of the suspect, victim, and investigator, the person drawing the diagram, and date and time the sketch was made. They should contain a scale and distance measurements between items present on the sketch. The location depicted in the drawing should be included as well as reference points to located items. A legend or key may be helpful to identify and clarify portions of the drawing and the direction of north.

Equipment

Writing materials are needed. Although pens may be used, lead pencils are easier to work with, especially if erasures are needed. Colored pencils are also useful to outline important items. Graph paper is the easiest to use, although blank paper will also do. Graph paper simplifies scale drawings and provides guidelines for line measurements. A drawing surface, such as a clipboard, is also helpful.

Measuring devices such as rulers and tapes are required. A 50- or 100-foot surveyor's tape is useful to measure longer distances. Laser and infrared-measuring devices used by realtors and contractors make measuring interiors easy. A compass is also useful to determine direction. A **total station** can also be used to take measurements of outdoor

---

* *Precision Products* (www.yourprecision.com) is one such company that sells forensic drone packages.

scenes. (A total station is an optical instrument commonly used in construction, surveying, and civil engineering) (Figure 3.8a and b).

Types of Sketches

Different types of indoor and outdoor crime scene locations present distinct problems in sketching. To best represent the crime scene, it may be necessary to rely upon different types of sketches. The type of sketch chosen by an investigator is not especially important. What is important is that the resulting drawing best depicts the crime scene and most easily illustrates the event to the viewer.

The overview, floor plan, or bird's-eye-view sketch is the simplest and most common one used in diagramming crime scenes. It may be used in nearly all crime scene situations where the items of interest are in one plane. In addition to its simplicity, it is also the easiest for laypeople, such as jury members, to grasp.

Another type of crime scene sketch is the elevation drawing. This type of sketch is used when the vertical plane, rather than the horizontal, is of interest. Thus, if blood stains or bullet impact marks/holes were present on a wall of a house, the elevation drawing of the wall would be used to depict this scene.

The cross-projection, or exploded, view is a combination of the preceding two types. It is similar to the floor plan sketch except the walls have been folded down into the same plane as the floor. The ceiling should also be included in this type of sketch.

The perspective drawing is another type of sketch that depicts a three-dimensional drawing of the scene. Although the final drawing will be very clear if done properly, this type of sketch requires greater artistic skill and is generally not recommended.

Locating Objects in the Sketch

Once the drawing has been made and the relative locations of the items have been sketched, it is necessary to locate them in the sketch. Location is defined as the actual position where the object is located at the crime scene. A position on a plane or flat surface is defined by two measurements. A knife located on the floor of a room requires two measurements from two fixed points to accurately locate its position on the floor. A measurement to show location could be taken from the north wall and the east wall, e.g., 3 feet from the north wall and 6 feet 7 inches from the east wall.

Although perpendicular measurements are the easiest to use, they may be impossible in outdoor crime scenes. In those situations, it is necessary to find fixed points to locate the item in question. This can be done by using telephone

Figure 3.8 (a) A total station is an electronic/optical instrument used for surveying that can measure distance and angles of crime scenes. (b) Individual points are measured by an infrared carrier signal that is generated by an emitter within the total station's optical path and reflected by a prism reflector. A typical total station can measure distances with an accuracy of about 1.5mm.

Figure 3.9 Computer-aided drawings (referred to as CAD) have gained wide use for crime scene documentation. They provide the investigator and juries a visual way to better understand the crime scene. (*3D Eyewitness*, https://3deyewitness.com/.)

poles, fire hydrants, trees, the exterior corner of a building, and so on. Whatever the item of reference used, it must be permanent and identifiable. The number on a telephone pole, a street address, or a roadside marker may be used as a point of reference to locate an object.

GPS, or global positioning system devices, are used in a variety of industries and have become useful in locating the position of evidence in remote outdoor crime scenes. Locations are given using latitude and longitude coordinates.

CAD Software

Commercial computer software is available to render images of crime scenes in traditional 2D diagrams or 3D animation (Figure 3.9).

In addition to the ability to draw crime scenes to scale, computer programs have specialized measurement tools for analysis of 3D data like bullet trajectories in shooting scenes, determining the point of origin of blood spatter, and measuring the height of witnesses/suspects. Most of the software can depict the scene in three dimensions on a video monitor and take the viewer through the scene utilizing computer-animated graphics in a "fly-through" mode. In the courtroom, these systems have been used to project the video image onto a screen to explain to a jury the sequence of events in a crime scene. The software can be used to depict the crime scene in 3D pictorial form as seen from the perspective of the victim or the suspect.

3D SCANNING

Increasingly, 3D scanning has become quite popular to accurately visualize crime scenes, buildings, automobile accident scenes, and arson investigations. These types of scanners provide the thorough, data-driven documentation that investigators require. By storing information from a scene digitally, investigators can review even the most minute details, share that information with other investigators, and return to the virtual scene of the crime over and over to evaluate probative pieces of evidence. CSIs can also use 3D laser scanners to document and reconstruct shootings, automobile accidents, and blood spatter events. This technology gathers the evidence quickly and efficiently by creating 3D point clouds of on-scene information that can be uploaded immediately and shared among

Figure 3.10 The FARO 3D digital scanner is easy to use and can quickly and accurately capture millions of data points in this accident scene. (*Photo credit: FARO, www.faro.com.*)

other investigators working the case.* Software attached to these scanners can transform scans into courtroom presentations (Figure 3.10).

Further Reading

Galvin, Robert S. *Crime Scene Documentation: Preserving the Evidence and the Growing Role of 3D Laser Scanning.* CRC Press, 2020.

Gardner, Ross M., and Donna Krouskup. *Practical Crime Scene Processing and Investigation.* CRC Press, 2018.

Mancini, Keith, and John Sidoriak. *Fundamentals of Forensic Photography: Practical Techniques for Evidence Documentation on Location and in the Laboratory.* Taylor & Francis, 2017.

Marin, Norman, and Jeffrey Buszka. *Alternate Light Source Imaging: Forensic Photography Techniques.* Routledge, 2014.

Marsh, Nick. *Forensic Photography: A Practitioner's Guide.* Wiley, 2014.

Robinson, Edward M. *Crime Scene Photography.* Academic Press, 2016.

Shaler, Robert C. Crime Scene Forensics: A Scientific Method Approach. Taylor & Francis, 2011.

Chapter Questions

1. List at least three steps used when documenting a crime scene.
2. When taking notes at the crime scene, which of the following is true:
    a. Make notes as events unfold, i.e., in chronological order.
    b. Be sure to note negative or unexpected conditions.
    c. Make notes complete and thorough.

---

* FARO (www.faro.com) is one such manufacturer of 3D scanners for crime scene investigation.

d. Make notes clear and legibly written.
   e. All of the above.
3. (True or false) The first officer at the scene should immediately collect physical evidence associated with the crime.
4. What is a total station?
5. Why are crime scene sketches needed if you have photographs?
6. (True or false) If a bad photograph is taken, it can be deleted.
7. Name two crime scene search patterns that can be used in outdoor searches.
8. (True or false) If possible, put off searching nighttime crime scenes until daylight hours.
9. List three pieces of information that should be included in photos and sketches.
10. What photography techniques can be used to document wounds?

Chapter 4

Physical Evidence Collection

A major theme of this text concerns the proper handling of physical evidence. Two of the main areas that must be considered in any discussion of the proper techniques of collection and preservation of physical evidence are the legal and scientific issues surrounding these actions.

Although laws regarding physical evidence vary from state to state, there is one common denominator. The Constitution, through the 4th Amendment, protects people from unreasonable searches and seizures by the government. The 4th Amendment states:

> The right of the people to be secure in their persons, houses, papers, and effects, against unreasonable searches and seizures, shall not be violated, and no Warrants shall issue, but upon probable cause, supported by Oath or affirmation, and particularly describing the place to be searched, and the persons or things to be seized.

The 4th Amendment, however, is not a guarantee against all searches and seizures, but only those that are deemed unreasonable under the law. Before any search commences or evidence is seized, a warrant must be obtained. The prosecutor's office should be consulted if there is any doubt. There are several exceptions to the warrant requirement: (1) search incident to a lawful arrest, where the search is permissible as a protective measure for police safety and to secure evidence that might be destroyed; (2) plain view exception, where if on the premises legally to serve a duly issued warrant, the police may seize other contraband if in plain view; (3) consent, where if given, the police may conduct a warrantless search; (4) vehicle search, where police may conduct a warrantless search of an automobile if they have probable cause of a crime or illegal contraband; and (5) emergency or hot pursuit exception, where evidence that can be destroyed or made to disappear before a warrant can be issued may be seized without a warrant.

Failure to secure a search warrant outside of these exceptions may result in legal sanctions by the court. In some cases, the physical evidence seized at a crime scene may be inadmissible in court. The legal doctrine called the ***fruit of the poisonous tree*** provides that any subsequent information derived from illegally seized physical evidence is inadmissible in court and cannot be used.

DETAILED SEARCH

Once the crime scene is thoroughly documented, a detailed search for evidence can begin. Documentation is not entirely completed at this point. As evidence is located, additional documentation is required for each item that is collected.

COLLECTION OF EVIDENCE

Sufficient evidence should be collected for laboratory processing and examination. Evaluating the amount of specimens to gather is largely a matter of experience. As a general rule, however, as much material as is reasonably possible to collect should be collected. It is usually impractical and sometimes impossible to return to a crime scene at a later time to collect more material if more should be needed. Generally speaking, more is better than less. It is also easier to explain why one did collect something, instead of why one didn't collect something. As a crime scene investigator or detective gains experience and understands the requirements of the crime laboratory, the amount of material will become less over time. Additionally, evidence storage facilities only have a finite amount of space available, so a degree of reasonableness must be exercised. In complex and challenging crime scenes, it can also be desirable to have the criminalist or forensic scientist come to the crime scene to assist in collecting and packaging the evidence.

Forensic science laboratory examinations compare known specimens with questioned specimens (Ks vs Qs). Known samples, or **exemplars**, are needed for comparative laboratory analyses. For example, if a blood-stained shirt is submitted to a crime laboratory, the DNA typing results must be compared with something to provide useful information. Blood samples or **buccal** (cheek) swabs from the victim and suspect should, therefore, be submitted separately in the case of DNA evidence. In addition, people who may have had legitimate access to a burglary scene must also submit DNA samples for testing to the crime laboratory. Similarly, if an automobile paint specimen is submitted for laboratory analysis, a known sample of paint from the suspected vehicle must be submitted for comparison.

Blank samples may also be important. Consider an arson investigation. An issue can be raised that heat from a fire may cause wood or carpeting to give off certain by-products, which might be confused with accelerant material. Unburned samples of wood or carpet can be collected for testing to clarify this argument. Blank samples, or substrate controls, are used to verify that the uncontaminated samples do not interfere with the analysis. Most DNA labs, however, no longer test substrate controls because they do not act as adequate negative controls.

Physical evidence should be handled as little as possible. Too much handling may obliterate fingerprints; dislodge minute trace evidence such as hairs, fibers, and debris; break apart brittle evidence, or contaminate evidence. Forceps, latex gloves, masks, special containers, and a clean work area are required for handling physical evidence.

Crime scene investigators should have an assortment of envelopes, containers, evidence tape, and assorted packaging material on hand to properly collect and preserve physical evidence (Figure 4.1). Plastic bags should be avoided for biological materials. Biological evidence such as moist, blood-stained clothing if stored for a few days in sealed plastic bags will cause the evidence to deteriorate and grow mold. If it is necessary to transport blood-soaked articles that cannot be air-dried at the crime scene directly to the laboratory for processing, plastic containers are appropriate

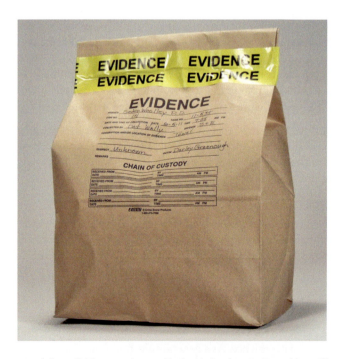

Figure 4.1 An example of commercially available paper bags with the chain of custody markings. These are available from a variety of law enforcement product supply houses, such as Sirchie© or Armour Forensics©.

Figure 4.2 Clean paint cans are excellent containers for collecting arson debris evidence. They will contain the volatile components for testing for the presence of ignitable liquids or accelerants.

for such purposes but only for short periods. Wet clothes should be dried in an evidence drying cabinet as soon as possible.

Airtight containers are used for volatile evidence such as gasoline-soaked debris (Figure 4.2). Clean metal paint cans with wide mouth openings make excellent containers for arson evidence. Burned debris that is to be checked for accelerants should never be packaged in plastic bags or plastic jars because volatile evidence will escape through most plastic containers.

It is good practice to double-wrap very small objects such as hair, fibers, or glass fragments. These items should first be folded up in a sheet of paper, such as in a **druggist's fold*** or gelatin lifter, and then placed in an envelope. Careful packaging of minute items of evidence will ensure that they are not lost.

It is also important to safely package evidence. Evidence should be labeled, indicating any potential hazards, by using biohazard stickers before submitting these items to the laboratory. Sharp objects including knives, blades, or needles should not be placed in a paper bag. These items should be packaged in strong cardboard boxes which are clearly marked and secured with zip-ties to prevent the analysts from accidentally cutting themselves. Firearms should be packaged unloaded and rendered safe. Boxes especially made for these types of evidence can be purchased from commercial crime scene equipment suppliers (Figure 4.3).

Contamination is a concern for all types of evidence. Items of evidence should be packaged separately in individual containers. Each piece of evidence should be completely segregated from other evidence, especially known samples from questioned items. If evidence was found commingled when it was collected, then a notation should be made if submitting more than one item together.

Microscopic or trace evidence presents unique collection problems. A number of techniques are available to collect this type of evidence. Vacuum cleaners specially equipped with traps have been used to collect trace evidence such as hairs, fibers, glass fragments, and debris. Evidence collection vacuums are available commercially; however, vacuums pick up considerable debris, which is time consuming to sort out.

Preferable methods for collecting trace evidence consist of shaking, sweeping, or picking trace evidence off clothing or other large surfaces and allowing the trace materials to fall onto a clean sheet of paper. Some prefer to use

---

* A druggist's fold is a folding pattern used on a sheet of paper that can enclose small amounts of physical evidence such as powder, hairs, or fibers.

Figure 4.3 Clear storage cases such as this one sold by Arrowhead Forensics (arrowheadforensics.com) are made for firearms submissions and allow the weapon to be secured with cable ties. The clear window allows for easy viewing of the serial number and verifying that the gun has been cleared and rendered safe.

specialized clear plastic adhesive tape. A four-inch length of tape, or tape-lift, may be pressed onto suspected areas and then placed, sticky side down, on an appropriate backing for microscopic examination and further treatment.

Each of these techniques has advantages and disadvantages. Before one technique is chosen over another, it is recommended that the crime laboratory be consulted because the laboratory may prefer one practice to another.

Case Review

An alleged sexual assault of an elderly woman occurred in her bedroom during the early morning hours. The assailant broke into her house while she was washing and dressing. She was wearing a green jacket at the time of the assault.

During the struggle between the woman and her assailant, she was pushed onto the floor and onto her bed. Initially, the assailant had his clothes on but later was partly dressed.

The victim's green jacket was taken into evidence on the day of the assault. It and her clothes were brought to the forensic science laboratory, tape-lifted, and examined for trace evidence.

The suspect denied being involved although he lived nearby. Several weeks after the incident, the suspect's blue hooded sweatshirt was taken to the laboratory for examination (Figure 4.4). He had stated he wore it on the night of the incident. The laboratory found no evidence of sexual assault; however, the suspect's DNA was detected on the green jacket.

The suspect stated he had not been in the woman's house in several years. Fibers do not usually persist over time and are lost quickly due to wear, activity, and washing. An examination for the presence of fibers was conducted, and fibers were found on the suspect's blue hooded sweatshirt similar to the victim's green jacket. This suggested recent contact between the assailant and victim.

His blue sweatshirt had a knitted outer surface made of a mix of blue cotton fibers and blue polyester fibers. The inner surface had a non-woven finish and was also made of blue cotton fibers and blue polyester fibers. It was well worn. It shed individual fibers and also shed some "pills" of fibers.

A search of the tape-lifts of her green jacket for fibers matching the blue sweatshirt was conducted. Blue cotton fibers and blue polyester fibers found were compared by microscopy (color, morphology, and fluorescence) and found to be the same (Figures 4.5a and b; Figure 4.6).

Figure 4.4 Front of suspect's sweatshirt.

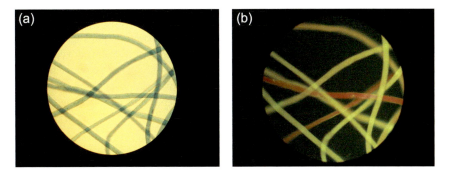

Figure 4.5 (a) Blue polyester fibers from inside of suspect's sweatshirt viewed with high power microscopy using transmitted light and (b) blue polyester fibers from inside of suspect's sweatshirt viewed with high power microscopy using fluorescent light. Some fibers had green fluorescence and some had orange fluorescence.

Fibers on the victim's jacket matched the fibers of the suspect's sweatshirt and provided support that the suspect had been in contact with the victim rather than his contention that he had had no contact with her.

As a result of the trace evidence, the suspect pleaded guilty when the case came to court.
Had the green jacket and blue sweatshirt been submitted in the same bag to the crime lab, however, this evidence would have been worthless.

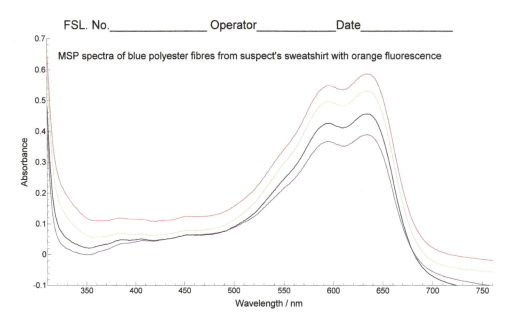

Figure 4.6 Fiber match confirmatory tests were carried out including microspectrophotometry analysis covering both the visible and ultraviolet region.

(Courtesy of Bridget Fleming, Forensic Science Laboratory, Ireland.)

Following the detailed search, physical evidence is collected. It is useful to set priorities as to which evidence will be collected first. This strategy is based on the type of case and circumstances surrounding the evidence. While there is no set rule as to what order evidence should be collected, the most fragile evidence such as fingerprints, trace DNA, arson evidence (because of its volatility), and trace evidence should be given precedence. Once all the relevant evidence has been collected, the scene should be searched again for thoroughness. It is a good idea for a second CSI team to search the scene again to make certain that potential evidence was not overlooked.

Evidence to be sent to the forensic science laboratory should be packaged to prevent breakage, spoilage, or contamination that could destroy its value. Evidence containers should be sealed and be sturdy enough so that they will not break in transit. When evidence consists of several objects, these should be packaged in separate containers or wrapped individually. Each package should be marked as to its contents and then packed in a shipping container. Bottles and glass containers containing liquid should not be packaged with other evidence because they might break and contaminate the other exhibits. If Styrofoam or other packing material is used for cushioning, any objects that might be altered by contact with such packing material should be separated and wrapped. The evidence should be sealed with tamper-proof evidence tape and initialed across the tape.*

Chain of Custody

The concept of a **chain of custody** is important to understand. The courts require proof that evidence collected during an investigation and the evidence ultimately submitted to the court are one and the same. To prove that the integrity of the physical evidence has been maintained, a chain of custody must be established. The chain shows who had contact with the evidence, at what date and time, under what circumstances, and what changes, if any, were made to the evidence. The chain of custody can also be used to help locate evidence years later if additional testing is required (e.g., post-conviction adjudications).

Typically, evidence is placed in a container with a label or is tagged. Identifying information about the case is written on the container or tag as well as in reports and logs to establish the chain. Police department policy may dictate

---

* The **International Association for Property and Evidence (IAPE)** (https://home.iape.org/) is a non-profit organization created by and for law enforcement professionals to help establish standards for all property and evidence departments. The IAPE provides education and training in all aspects of evidence handling, storage, maintenance, and disposal of law enforcement held evidence.

which information is required, but generally the following types of information are needed to establish the chain of custody:

- Name and/or initials of the individual collecting the evidence and each person subsequently having custody of it.
- Dates the item was collected and transferred.
- Agency, case number, and type of crime.
- Voucher or property clerk number.
- Victim's or suspect's name.
- Storage location.
- Brief description of the item.

Barcode systems are routinely used to capture this information for Laboratory Information Management Systems (LIMS). This information serves to prove the chain of custody to the court and assists in admitting the items into evidence.

Preservation

Storage of physical evidence has legal implications. Evidence must be held in a secured area after it is collected and before transportation to court. Evidence reasonably presumed to have been tampered with by unauthorized persons because it had been kept in an unsecured area may be inadmissible in court. Evidence should be maintained in a specific secured area, with limited access by only authorized personnel.

Even if objects have been individually identified, they should also be marked with the recovering officer's initials and the date collected so that the identity of a given object cannot be questioned. Identification markings may be placed directly on the object or on a tag attached directly to the object. When this is not practical, markings are placed onto the sealed container housing the evidence.

A voucher with a complete inventory of all items submitted and a request for laboratory examination should be included with each packaging container. An inventory enables lab personnel to check the contents so that small objects among the many items are not misplaced or overlooked. The request for specific examinations allows the forensic science laboratory to determine what needs to be done and what questions are being asked.

The written request to the laboratory about the case should be as complete as possible, listing the sequence of events and statements of the suspect, the victim, witnesses, etc. This information can assist the examiner's evaluation of which laboratory tests are required and in what order. The information may also provide answers to questions that come up as a result of the laboratory's findings. It may be helpful to include copies of pertinent police reports. It is also beneficial for the investigator and forensic scientist to communicate to determine the best sequence of examinations to be done on the items of evidence submitted when in doubt.*

The following is a brief description of packaging instructions for certain items of evidence:

- Objects with fingerprints or glove prints should be packed so that they do not come in contact with each other or the package sides.
- Tool marks on objects should be protected from contamination and moisture.
- Clothing containing dry biological stains (blood, semen, or saliva) should be packaged separately in brown paper bags in such a way that the stains are not broken or rubbed off.
- Victim's clothing must not be packaged or come in contact with the suspect's.
- Strands of hair on garments should not be allowed to come in contact with other garments that may contain hair. Trace evidence such as hair can be secured in a coin envelope, gel lifter, or post-it note.

---

* It's appropriate to mention the issue of contextual bias. Some have argued that too much information about the case may cause an examiner to make conclusions not based on laboratory tests alone. Some labs use an intermediary—a case officer who in turn passes the evidence on to examiners and keeps non-relevant information away from the laboratory criminalist. When information is needed, then sequential unmasking can be done. It is important to note that even if one has the highest ethical standards, bias still exists (Dror, 2021).

- Firearms which have been rendered safe should be rigidly fixed inside a container unloaded without further wrapping. It is best to hand deliver firearms evidence to the lab in person.
- Cartridge cases and bullets should be packed separately with soft cushioning material. Federal regulations should be consulted before shipping.
- Live-cartridges should be packed in cushioning material to protect fingerprints and shipped by a parcel carrier clearly labeled.
- Stomach contents and organs for toxicological examination should be placed in tightly sealed glass jars and packed in cushioning material. The containers should be of a size proportionate to the amount of fluid so that volatile agents do not evaporate.
- Controlled substances should be tightly cushioned in vials or pillboxes so that they will not break. Absorbent cotton can be used.
- Arson evidence should be placed inside a new metal paint can to prevent evaporation of any volatile compounds and sealed.
- DNA swabs should be dried and placed in an envelope or cardboard swab container and sealed. Commercial tubes with a desiccant can also be used, such as Bode® SecurSwab DNA Collection Systems. Depending on the type of swab, the extraction and recovery efficiency can differ.*
- Sharp objects, such as knives or needles, should be secured in a cardboard or plastic container to prevent them from poking through the packaging material.
- Charred paper should be packed in sturdy boxes and supported on all sides with absorbent cotton. The container should preferably not be shipped but hand-carried to the laboratory. It is also possible to place the charred paper in a large plastic bag that is inflated and sealed tightly.
- For entomological evidence, representative samples of BOTH live and preserved samples from the same areas should be submitted. Preserved samples (fly eggs, maggots, pupae, and adult flies) can be placed into 80% ethyl alcohol. Live specimens should be placed in a container with a ventilated lid with very small holes and a food medium. In addition, always record the ambient temperature at the crime scene, maggot mass, and the microhabitat where the deceased is found.

Evidence gathering procedures should be regularly reevaluated and, if necessary, rewritten. All law enforcement personnel involved in the investigation must follow their agency's policies and SOPs. The reasons for this are evident. Defense attorneys will attempt to show that the written policies and procedures were not followed or, if policies and procedures do not exist, that the practices employed were not generally acceptable or personnel lacked appropriate training. The results are the same: even if forensic tests point to the defendant, improper or inadequate evidence collection and preservation techniques will render the evidence inadmissible, or its value will be diminished.

After each item of evidence is collected, it should be recorded in an evidence log. Case management software used at the crime scene is a great way to keep track of evidence, assign tasks, centralize all photos, track progress, and print customized reports.

The Underwater Crime Scene

Some unique crime scene environments require specialized processing. The aquatic crime scene presents such a challenge. As with crime scenes on land, underwater investigations require the same level of meticulousness. The underwater CSI has to be first and foremost a well-trained diver. After becoming an advanced open water diver, CSIs require additional training in underwater photography and sketching, underwater communications, mapping techniques, metal preservation, body recovery in water, light and heavy salvage, vehicle recovery, and more. These conditions can be very hazardous and usually have zero visibility. In order to locate evidence, a scuba diver might be required to scour the bottom of a lake or river by hand, searching through the silt, mud, trash, and foliage for a discarded gun. For a body or an automobile, side-scan sonar can be used to create an image of the target before divers are sent down. This makes locating the target easier. The Professional Association of Diving Instructors (PADI), as well as other diving schools, offers professional courses in underwater crime scene investigation.

---

* Bruijns, Brigitte, et al. "The extraction and recovery efficiency of pure DNA for different types of swabs." *Journal of Forensic Sciences* 63.5 (2018): 1492–1499.

HAZMAT Crime Scenes

Sometimes a particularly serious case may warrant outside assistance, such as hazardous material specialists in the case of clandestine drug laboratory cases or when investigating mass disasters, terrorist acts, bombings, or major fires. These types of crime scenes require unique expertise, which is sometimes not considered by police professionals.

Because the threat of chemical and biological (as well as radiological and nuclear) terrorism is a reality, police and crime scene personnel may become involved. It is important to have a plan with written protocols when faced with a HAZMAT crime scene. Ultimately, federal agencies, such as the Federal Bureau of Investigation, the Department of Homeland Security, the Department of Defense, Centers for Disease Control and Prevention, and other organizations will be brought into a situation. However, local public safety agencies may be the first responders on the scene and first to assess the situation.

The subject matter concerning terrorist incident response and biological and chemical devices is beyond the scope of this book.* Many law enforcement agencies are engaged in pre-incident planning, preparation, and tabletop exercises in order to know how to respond to such an event. Having an understanding of Chemical, Biological, Radiological, Nuclear, and Explosive (CBRNE) hazards is vital for personal safety.

Crime scenes present potential safety risks to personnel. An understanding and appreciation of the potential risks coupled with appropriate safety precautions will minimize these risks.

FINAL SURVEY

Once the detailed search has been concluded and all of the evidence collected, a final survey of the crime scene is conducted. This is where the CSIs go back over the crime scene to make sure nothing was missed. It is good practice to have a checklist during the final survey to ensure that nothing has been overlooked. This checklist can serve as a record and can prove quite useful later on if ever questioned about whether something was or wasn't done at the scene. A different CSI other than the team leader should conduct the final survey.

RELEASING THE SCENE

Once processing is complete, the crime scene may be released. Once a scene has been released, however, the integrity of the scene can no longer be guaranteed. If there is ever doubt that more work needs to be done, it is perfectly acceptable to come back the next day as long as the scene is guarded overnight by a uniformed officer. It is better to be thorough and work longer than to release a scene too early. Once a scene is released, CSIs and detectives rarely have an opportunity to revisit a scene for a second search. And even if they do, it is very likely that the scene will have been altered.

Further Reading

Lee, Henry C., and Elaine M. Pagliaro. *Crime Scene Guidebook*. US Department of Justice, Office of Justice Programs, National Institute of Justice, 2011. https://www.ojp.gov/ncjrs/virtual-library/abstracts/crime-scene-guidebook

Technical Working Group on Crime Scene Investigation (US). *Crime Scene Investigation: A Guide for Law Enforcement*. US Department of Justice, Office of Justice Programs, National Institute of Justice, 2013. https://shop.nfstc.org/product-tag/csi-guide/

Chapter Questions

1. What does the term "fruit of the poison tree" mean in the context of evidence collection?
2. Give at least five items of information that should be present on evidence packaging to maintain a chain of custody.

---

* For a comprehensive guide to HAZMAT crime scene investigations see Fish, Jacqueline T., et al. *Practical Crime Scene Investigations for Hot Zones*. CRC Press, 2010.

3. Evidence may be stored
    a. In the trunk of a police vehicle.
    b. In your office desk.
    c. In the police evidence storage locker.
    d. None of the above.
4. What are reference samples and how are they used?
5. How should wet, bloody evidence be packaged for transportation to the crime lab or evidence storage facility?
6. (True or false) Arson evidence may be safely stored in zip-lock plastic bags to prevent loss of volatile evidence.
7. How should firearms be sent to the crime lab?
8. Why should plastic bags be avoided for biological evidence?
9. How should sharp objects be packaged?
10. (True or false) A hair from a crime scene can be secured in a druggist's fold or a gel lifter.

CHAPTER 5

Crime Scene Reconstruction

Crime scene reconstruction can be considered as "advanced crime scene investigation." In addition to the collection, documentation, and preservation of evidence found at a scene, forensic scientists, CSI's, and detectives have to determine the significance of physical evidence to a case—in other words, what does it all mean? Crime scene reconstruction is a process by which the evidence that is collected at a crime scene is used to determine how the crime was committed, the sequence of events that occurred, and what could or could not have transpired during the commission of the crime. The task involves interpreting all the available evidence and logically constructing a scenario of events to explain how the pieces fit together. It is the process of determining the sequence of events before, during, and after a crime. To be successful, the practitioner requires a knowledge of science and especially, logic. An open mind is essential because the examiner must be willing to revise a hypothesis that no longer fits with the evidence as it develops.

Readers who wish to gain more information about Crime Scene Reconstruction are urged to become involved with professional organizations such as the **International Association for Identification** (www.theiai.org), the **Association for Crime Scene Reconstruction** (www.acsr.org), and the **International Association of Bloodstain Pattern Analysts** (www.iabpa.org).

Case Review

A Lebanese singer who rose to fame in the Arab world after winning the top prize in a TV show in 1996 was brutally murdered in Dubai in July 2008. The victim was rumored to have a troubled private life and was married three times. She fled from Beirut to Egypt and was living in Dubai at the time of her death.

On July 28, 2008, at 8:15 pm the Dubai Police received a call from the building's watchman who discovered the victim's body in her apartment. The watchman stated that her door was slightly open which raised his suspicion.

The first officer chronicled the crime scene. The victim was found in her apartment. Her throat was deeply slashed, and she lay in a pool of blood. Her clothes were on and there was no evidence of forced entry into her apartment. A bloody shoe print was visible next to the body. The first officer also found an envelope from a real estate development company next to the body (Figures 5.1a–d).

A team of crime scene investigators from the Dubai Police arrived to collect and preserve the physical evidence including trace evidence for further testing. During the search, officers found clothing inside a red fire extinguisher emergency cabinet. It contained a pair of charcoal-colored bloody trousers and a brown colored striped t-shirt. A letter from the same Real Estate Development Company was recovered along with the clothing (Figures 5.2a and b).

All evidence was documented, collected, and submitted to the Dubai forensic laboratory for examination. Surveillance tapes from the building's CCTV cameras were also obtained.

The digital forensics department was able to extract video from the surveillance cameras, which showed a suspect dressed in sportswear and a cap (Figure 5.3).

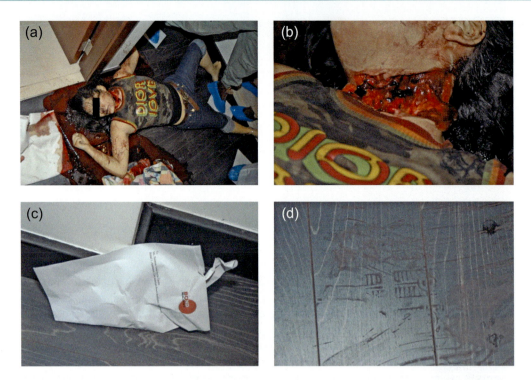

Figure 5.1 Original pictures taken by the Dubai Crime Scene Investigation team show the (a) location of the victim at the time her body was discovered, (b) the incised wound to the victim's throat, (c) an envelope next to the body, (d) and a bloody shoe print.

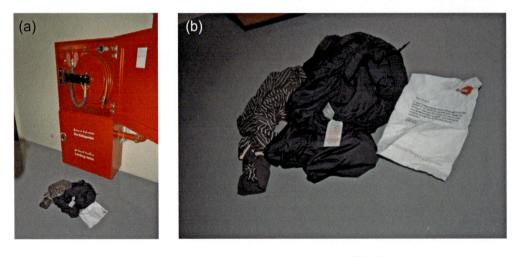

Figure 5.2 Original pictures of the evidence taken by crime scene photographers. (a) The fire extinguisher emergency cabinet and (b) a pair of charcoal bloody pants, a t-shirt, and a letter from the same company as in Figure 5.1c were found in the fire cabinet.

The surveillance camera footage from the 22nd floor confirmed the suspect being present on the floor of the victim's apartment (Figure 5.4).

Investigators were also able to track down the route taken by the suspect to commute to and from the crime scene by analyzing various street cameras in the vicinity (Figure 5.5).

Next, a team of investigators was assigned to search for the clothing and shoes with the same manufacturer markings and labels that were found on the evidence from the crime scene. One sportswear store was found that sold athletic clothing and merchandise. Investigators were able to obtain receipts and credit card records for the purchase of the items in question from the store (Figure 5.6).

The receipts and credit card information confirmed that the suspect purchased a pair of pants and a pair of Nike shoes. The transaction was made using a Mastercard. The card number along with the name of the card

Figure 5.3 Still photos of surveillance videotapes from the building's CCTV cameras. From right to left: The suspect held a plastic bag while walking towards the parking lot. In the next frame, he is seen with another man who was pointing at something. In the third frame, the image showed the suspect continuing into the building's parking lot.

Figure 5.4 More surveillance camera footage from the 22nd floor (the floor of the victim's apartment) again showed the suspect. These timestamps were a few minutes after the timestamps from the photos above.

owner, date and time of purchase, the expiration date of the card used, as well as the signature all pointed to the suspect (Figure 5.7).

The receipts indicated the purchase was made on July 27, 2008, at 8:38 pm.

Additional purchases were made on July 27, 2008, using the same credit card used earlier that day at another shop. Another receipt was recovered from that shop; the suspect purchased a t-shirt and a "BUCK" brand pocket knife. Both receipts were signed by the suspect and were submitted for handwriting identification. Credit card information and other personal data lead them to the identity of the accused.

Further information determined that the suspect entered the United Arab Emirates (UAE) on a visa sponsorship of a trade agency and was staying at the Oasis Beach Hotel, a distance of about 500 meters from the crime scene. Dubai airport and immigration details showed the suspect left the UAE abruptly on July 28, 2008, at approximately 3:15 pm. The hotel registration system confirmed he had a reservation until the end of the month.

The Dubai police crime scene reconstruction team determined that the suspect visited the victim on July 28, 2008, impersonating a real estate bond agent. When the victim failed to open the door, the suspect slid an envelope printed with the real estate company's name addressed to her under the door, assuring his identity and gaining the victim's trust. He was able to trick her into opening the apartment gate and letting him in.

The DNA evidence from the suspect's clothing was tested. Swabs were taken from his pants and areas of the t-shirt such as inside the collar and underarms for DNA testing. Samples were also taken from the respective envelope and letter found at the crime scene for the presence of DNA.

Figure 5.5 The red line is the path used by the suspect from his hotel to the crime scene and the green line is the path taken by him after exiting the crime scene and back to his hotel.

Figure 5.6 Some of the items shown on receipts purchased by the suspect at two stores near the crime scene.

Footwear impression experts determined that the bloody footwear impression found next to the deceased was similar to the shoes the suspect purchased, showing the same tread design and sole print. In addition, fingerprint examiners were able to retrieve fingerprints of the suspect on the letter and the envelope from the crime scene.

Handwriting experts determined that the signatures from both receipts belonged to the suspect and concluded that the envelope and the letter found at the crime scene were forged by the suspect and were not from the real estate company.

Telecommunication analysis led to findings that initiated a link between the suspect and a person named "HT." "HT" and the suspect knew one another based on existing communication records. It was confirmed that contact had been made between "HT" and the suspect quite often; the last was recorded just seven hours prior to the murder.

It turns out that "HT" was on the Board of Directors at the "EU" trading agency—the same company that sponsored the entry of the suspect into UAE. "HT" was rumored to be a former lover of the victim. "HT" sent a series of threatening text messages to the victim's mother which were also recovered.

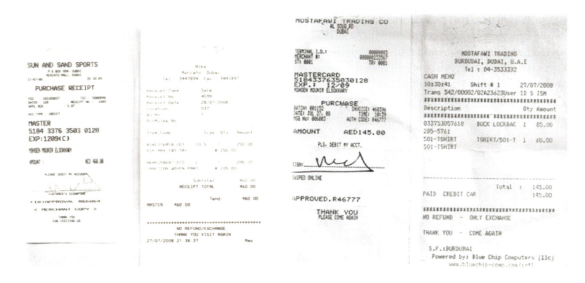

Figure 5.7 Store receipts and credit card receipts purchased by the suspect at two shops.

In the messages "HT" harassed the victim's mother, calling her names and using foul language. The suspect accused her of leaving the victim in Dubai for prostitution.

After assembling this case information, investigators traveled to Egypt to brief authorities there.

Charges were discussed with the Egyptian authorities leading to the arrest of the suspect in Cairo. The suspect confessed to murdering the victim for $2 million.

Recordings between the suspect and "HT" confirmed the case to be a murder for hire.

After several trips to Cairo, Dubai investigators and forensic experts provided evidence to the Egyptian prosecutor and testified in court.

In court, the suspect confessed to being paid $2 million to carry out the murder and was found guilty of all charges. "HT" was also convicted of capital murder.

The motive of the case was determined to be a one-sided failed love story. "HT," a former lover of the victim, whose failed attempts to draw her back to him fueled his anger. It was rumored he tried to lure the victim who was then married and lived with her husband, by offering her money but she declined. The victim's rejection of his proposal sent him into a rage that led the suspect into sending threatening text messages to the victim's mother. The victim had fled the country for a fresh start but "HT" knew of her whereabouts and hired a hitman to murder her.

(*Courtesy of Major General Khamis Matar Al Muzainah, Commander in Chief, Dubai Police, United Arab Emirates.*)

There have been several people in the past who practiced versions of crime scene reconstruction. Edmund Locard was one such individual. With the simple and intuitive statement attributed to Locard, "every contact leaves a trace" modern forensic science had an important practitioner. Locard became known as the Sherlock Holmes of France and his oft-quoted statement became known as **Locard's Exchange Principle**.

But Locard was not the first to recognize the importance of science in the investigation of crime. Hans Gross (1847–1915) was an Austrian criminal jurist and an examining magistrate. He is believed to be the creator of the field of criminalistics and is to this day seen as the father of criminal investigation. Gross was a professor at several Austrian Universities and his book *Criminal Investigation: A Practical Handbook for Magistrates, Police Officers, and Lawyers* was written to cover different aspects of criminology. The book consolidated into one system fields of knowledge that had not previously been integrated, such as psychology and science, which could be successfully used against crime. Gross adapted some fields to the needs of criminal investigation, such as crime scene photography. In 1912, he founded the Institute of Criminalistics (later: Institute of Criminology).

Edward Oscar Heinrich (1881–1953) was an American forensic scientist who was known as the "Wizard of Berkeley." He received his bachelor's degree in chemistry at the University of California, Berkeley in 1908 and combined his training in chemistry with criminal investigations. Heinrich is quoted as stating that "Crime analysis is an orderly procedure. It's precise and it always follows the same questions that I ask myself: precisely what happened, when, where, why, and who did it?" His efforts resulted in solving many of the notable cases of his day.

Case Review

During a convenience store armed robbery, a deputy sheriff fired at the assailant, wounding him and sadly killing an innocent shopper in the market. The family of the decedent filed a civil lawsuit against the Sheriff's Department and the deputy sheriff alleging that the officer was improperly trained which caused the victim's death. The bullet was recovered from the victim during an autopsy. The hollow-point ammunition had tiny pieces of fabric in the nose cavity of the bullet. The top fabric cut out was from the victim's blouse and the bottom was from the robber. The sequence of events clearly showed that the deputy's fired bullet first struck the criminal and subsequently hit the victim. This was an example of crime scene reconstruction proving the sequence of events during a gun battle (Figure 5.8).

The process of reconstruction begins when the investigator arrives at the scene and conducts an initial walkthrough of where the crime took place. At this early stage, one might begin to formulate a rough idea of how the crime occurred. This initial hypothesis will likely change many times as more information is developed and pieces begin to fall into place. Eventually, once all the information and supporting documentation come together, the examiner will formulate the theory of how the crime took place.

Crime scene reconstruction is usually the last step in an investigation. All of the other analyses must come together to allow the examiner to form a hypothesis of the crime. The process requires the assistance of many persons associated with the crime and the crime scene investigation: police detectives, crime scene investigators, forensic specialists,

Figure 5.8 The order of clothing fragments caught in the hollow-point round fired by a deputy sheriff helped to reconstruct the sequence of events in an officer-involved shooting. An innocent bystander and an armed robber were killed by the shot and it was up to the laboratory to determine who was struck first. The order of the fragments of clothing proved that the bullet first hit the robber and then the bystander. (*Courtesy of the Los Angeles County Sheriff's Department.*)

Figure 5.9 (a) The blood in this photograph traveled from top to bottom in a downward direction based on the directionality of the tails of the bloodstains. In this area of convergence analysis (b) two areas of convergence (seen in circled areas) have been determined from this bloodstain pattern.

criminalists, and medical examiners. The person doing the reconstruction should wait until they have had a chance to review all of the other reports of analyses by the other experts involved in the case.

As new information is developed, it must be examined to determine if it fits with the hypothesis and whether or not it is necessary to re-evaluate the hypothesis. The completed reconstruction will be the presentation of the sequence of events before, during, and after the crime. It will consist of all the known factors including the locations and positions of everyone involved. The examiner will be required to show how the crime occurred. The investigators will be challenged in court to try to show that alternative theories are possible. While investigators can never be absolutely certain of what occurred at the scene of the crime, they can offer important information for the jury based on scientific principles, logic, and their experience in reconstruction.

BLOODSTAIN PATTERN ANALYSIS (BPA)

Bloodstain pattern analysis (BPA) is the interpretation of bloodstains at a crime scene to recreate the mechanism that produced the bloodstain pattern. Analysts examine the size, shape, distribution, and location of the bloodstains to form opinions about what happened. The directionality of a bloodstain is determined by the pointed or tail end of a stain. The tail indicates the direction of travel. The angle of impact can also be determined by using the following formula:

$$\text{Angle of impact } (\theta) = \arcsin\left[\left(\frac{\text{width of}}{\text{blood stain}}\right) \Big/ \left(\frac{\text{length of}}{\text{blood stain}}\right)\right]$$

Bloodstain pattern evidence is often present at crimes of violence. Because blood behaves in well-understood mechanisms, the shape, grouping, and distribution of bloodstains can assist the investigator in reconstructing what took place at the crime scene. In addition to determining to whom the blood belongs through DNA, it is often necessary to determine the movement and direction of persons, the sequence of events, the area of convergence and area of origin* of a pattern, the number of impacts during an incident, and the object used to create a specific pattern. These determinations can be used to corroborate or contradict the statement(s) made by victim(s), suspect(s), and/or witness(es). Being able to identify the type of bloodstain present and how it was created can also aid an investigator in deciding what stains are the most probative to collect for DNA typing. Bloodstain patterns often tell a story of what took place at a crime scene; it is up to the investigator to read that story and interpret it (see Figure 5.9).

---

* This video by the National Forensic Science Technology Center (www.youtube.com/watch?v=3jFKZaSeNjg) shows the proper way to calculate the area of convergence and area of origin. These can also be calculated by using BPA software such as HemoSpat (www.hemospat.com).

There are three basic types of bloodstains: spatter (blood that travels through the air from a mechanism), passive stains (transfer, drop, flow and large volume stains), and altered stains (clotted, diluted, diffused, insects, and voids). Determining how a stain was made will oftentimes be a critical piece of information in a case.

Case Review

Police responded to a 911 call of a husband who said that he had come home after a night of playing cards with the guys and discovered his wife on the floor covered in blood and his house ransacked. When questioned by police about the blood on his clothes he said that he got the bloodstains on his shirt and pants when he leaned over his wife's body to administer cardiopulmonary resuscitation (CPR). After examining his clothes, investigators determined that the majority of blood on the suspect's clothes was from a spatter-producing event and were not transfer stains. After being presented with this evidence, the suspect confessed to beating his wife with a baseball bat and turning his house upside down to make it look like a break-in.

In describing bloodstains at a crime scene, some of the terms generally used are swipe, wipe, spatter, drip stain, expired blood, parent stain, satellite stain, insect stain, and several others. The AAFS Standards Board (ASB) has published Terms and Definitions in Bloodstain Pattern Analysis* based on recommended terminology along with definitions to standardize the terms used in this field. This standardized terminology allows investigators to be on the same page when discussing, writing, reporting, or testifying about these stains. In addition, the ASB and the American National Standards Institute (ANSI) have also published: Standard for a Quality Assurance Program in Bloodstain Pattern Analysis;† Standard for Report Writing in Bloodstain Pattern Analysis;‡ Standards for a Bloodstain Pattern Analyst's Training Program;§ and Standard for the Validation of Procedures in Bloodstain Pattern Analysis.¶

Bloodstain pattern analysis (BPA) is a field in and of itself, and an in-depth discussion of it is beyond the scope of this book. BPA requires much experience and training to correctly make interpretations about bloodstain patterns. Beginning and advanced bloodstain pattern interpretation courses are available, and it is highly recommended that such courses of study be taken prior to performing crime scene reconstruction on actual cases. Continuing education and experience will allow the investigator to draw the most accurate conclusions. Crime scene reconstruction through the use of bloodstain pattern interpretation is a useful technique but only for those who are properly trained. All too often, unfortunately, investigators overstate their conclusions based on a limited understanding of BPA and crime scene reconstruction.

Case Review

On a Sunday afternoon, October 7, 2007, police arrived at an apartment building in the western part of Reykjavík, Iceland. A man stated that he had found his neighbor seriously injured in an apartment on the second floor. Police found a male, lying unconscious in his bed. His head was covered in blood and bloodstain spatter was seen on nearby walls. A pool of blood along with smaller stains was noted on the pillow and bed, with a thin layer of bluish powder around it. On the kitchen floor, police found a fire extinguisher, covered in blue powder and blood (Figures 5.10a–c).

After paramedics arrived and took care of the victim, the scene was sealed off and detectives and a CSI unit were called to the scene. The victim died later that same day due to massive head trauma.

The suspect who made the call to the emergency dispatch was arrested at the scene. Police officers and detectives did not believe his explanation about finding his friend covered in blood. The suspect had fresh wounds on

---

* https://www.aafs.org/asb-standard/terms-and-definitions-bloodstain-pattern-analysis.
† https://www.aafs.org/asb-standard/standard-quality-assurance-program-bloodstain-pattern-analysis.
‡ https://www.aafs.org/asb-standard/standard-report-writing-bloodstain-pattern-analysis.
§ https://www.aafs.org/asb-standard/standards-bloodstain-pattern-analysts-training-program.
¶ https://www.aafs.org/asb-standard/standard-validation-procedures-bloodstain-pattern-analysis.

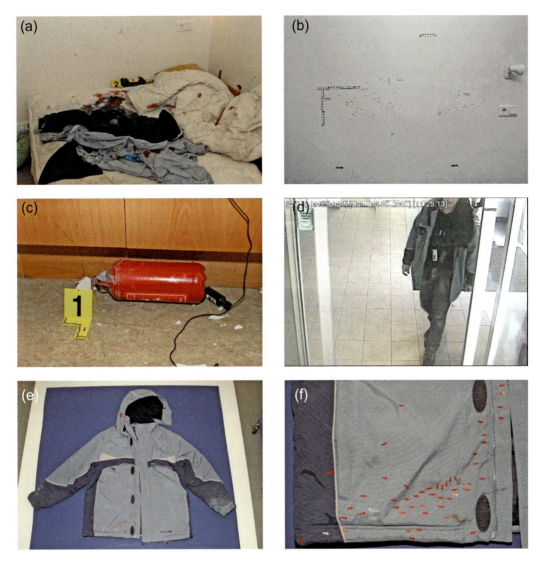

Figure 5.10 (a) A pool of blood along with smaller stains were noted on the pillow and bed, along with (b) nearby walls. A (c) fire extinguisher was found on the kitchen floor covered in blood and a blue powder. In the captured CCTV footage, the suspect (d) was wearing a gray/blue jacket. Back in the lab, it was revealed that the (e) jacket had many small reddish-brown stains and (f) an unknown bluish powder on the lower front and sleeves.

his hands and red stains on his jeans. The suspect was taken to the police station for questioning, but before leaving he gave the police permission to search his apartment.

The victim was a male 44-year-old, the suspect, a 38-year-old male. They lived in the same apartment building, on the same floor, next door to each other. Both were known to the police for various offenses.

The incoming call to the police came at 13:34 and the first police officers arrived on the scene at 13:39. The suspect and victim were together in a supermarket, next door to their apartment building, and CCTV in the supermarket showed them leaving together. CCTV at the entrance of their apartment building showed them entering the building together at 11:33, and CCTV footage showed no one entering or leaving the apartment building until police arrived. In the CCTV footage, the suspect was wearing a blue jacket. When he was arrested at the scene, he was not wearing the jacket; it was found in the suspect's bedroom. The jacket had many small reddish stains on the front side and an unknown bluish powder on the lower front side and sleeves (Figures 5.10d–f).

On observing the BPA evidence at the scene, investigators concluded that the shape and distribution of bloodstains were consistent with the attack taking place while the victim was on his bed. There appeared to be an impact pattern on the wall above the topside of the bed and cast-off stains on the nearby wall and closet. The fire extinguisher (see Figure 5.10c) was used as the weapon.

Investigators took pictures showing the position of the suspect and the victim and where they believed the suspect stood and how he held the weapon. There was a void in bloodstain distribution on a closet behind the suspect's position and bloodstains on the suspect's clothing were all above knee height.

The fire extinguisher at the scene was 33 cm high and weighed 3,569 grams. Most of the bloodstains on the extinguisher were on the bottom half, but the top half was covered with a thin layer of blue powder. When compared to an unused extinguisher, it was about 44 grams lighter. Fingerprint examination did not yield any results. The blood matched the victim. The bluish powder, seen on the extinguisher, on the bed, and the suspect's clothing, originated from the extinguisher. It is believed that the suspect pressed the handle of the extinguisher at some point during the assault and released some of the powder.

Bloodstain patterns were noted on the suspect's jacket and jeans. The stains were a combination of impact spatter and cast-off stains. Bluish dust, believed to have originated from the fire extinguisher, was observed on the sleeves as well. DNA results from blood on the suspect's clothing were from the victim.

In court, the suspect's defense stated that bloodstains on his clothing were due to the suspect having touched the victim's head while calling for emergency services, thus resulting in bloody transfer patterns on the jacket.

The court was shown the difference between impact patterns and transfer patterns, and also the difference between cast-off stains and transfer patterns. Listening to testimony in court, the defense stated to the court that the suspect now remembered that the victim had coughed up blood on him while he was making the call. The jacket was examined, but no stains characteristic of expired blood were found. The forensic pathologist further stated that the victim would not have been able to cough up blood due to the massive head trauma and unconscious state.

The court dismissed the suspect´s explanation of the bloodstains on his clothes. The court, in its verdict, stated that the defendant assaulted the victim consistent in the manner demonstrated by the blood spatter pattern and crime scene reconstruction reports and backed up by DNA results and the autopsy report. The suspect received a sentence of 16 years in prison for murder.

(Courtesy of Ragnar Jónsson, Detective Chief Inspector and BPA Specialist; and Björgvin Sigurðsson, MSFS, Forensic Specialist, Reykjavík Metropolitan Police, Crime Scene & Forensic Unit, Reykjavík, Iceland.)

ACCIDENT RECONSTRUCTION

CSIs and forensic engineers* are often called upon to examine accident scenes ranging from vehicle fatalities involving other vehicles or pedestrians; hit and runs; structural failures; and other accidents. Forensic engineering brings the application of engineering to the investigation of failures or other performance problems. In a vehicle crash, for example, the investigator would examine the speedometers of the vehicles involved, measure the length of skid marks on the road, collect evidence, interview witnesses, examine the maintenance records of the vehicles, and more in order to reconstruct the accident. Accident reconstruction is most often used in civil cases, however, it is also used in a fair amount of criminal cases.

Case Review

A 19-year-old female was a passenger on a motorcycle. The rider was going uphill on a left-hand curve, struck a guardrail on the right, which ejected the young woman from the back of the motorcycle. Her face was struck, consistent with the facial trauma which included open fractures of the nasal complex, maxilla, frontal sinus and mandible as well as extensive facial lacerations most prominently to the upper right lip. Prior to the forensic engineering analysis, the striking object was unknown and the narrow-most issue in the case. The plaintiff alleged

---

* The American Society of Civil Engineers has a Forensic Engineering Division (https://www.asce.org/communities/institutes-and-technical-groups/forensic-engineering-division/committees/forensic-engineering-division) which develops practices and procedures for the application of engineering principles to the investigation of accidents and failures.

she struck one of five nails sticking out 4" on the stop sign post to cause the extensive lacerations and trauma to the face. The scope of the forensic engineer in this case was to determine the likely cause of the facial trauma.

Evidence included inspection of the accident scene as well as overall and microscopic inspection of the helmet. Photos of the motorcycle were evaluated since the subject motorcycle was no longer available. In the helmet inspection, no evidence of forceful impact to the helmet was found internally, specifically to the expanded polystyrene (EPS) (a rigid closed-cell foam comprising the interior of the helmet). Evidence found on the helmet included:

1. Blood evidence at the bottom of the helmet.
2. A flat surface scrape on the right side (parietal aspect) of the helmet.
3. Signs of blood and tissue proximal to the helmet opening.
4. Scrapes and gouges above the face shield, including a focal gouge with a polymer curl, were found on the exterior forehead area of the helmet.

There was no evidence of signposts and/or guardrail intrusions that breached the facial perimeter of the helmet. Most of the helmet damage was localized on the right temporal/parietal area and the left mandibular area, which is consistent with impact to the left chin bar and glancing shear to the right parietal/forehead. A focal gouge with curled polymer was found on the exterior forehead area of the helmet. A microscopic analysis found

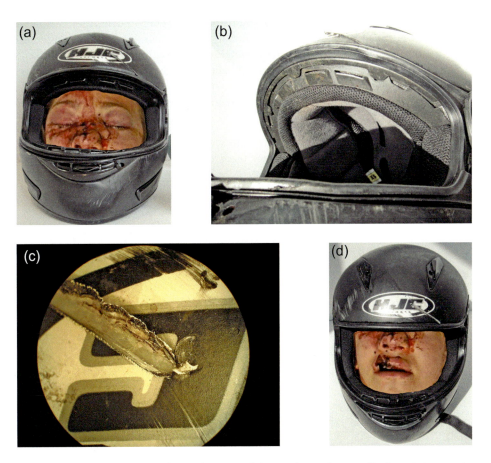

Figure 5.11 (a) Facial trauma to victim included open fractures of the nasal complex, maxilla, frontal sinus, and mandible as well as extensive facial lacerations. (b) The helmet inspection revealed no evidence of forceful impact to the helmet internally, however, there was blood evidence at the bottom of the helmet, a surface scrape on the right side, signs of blood and tissue proximal to the helmet opening, and scrapes and gouges above the face shield. (c) Microscopic analysis found that there was blood inside the peeled and curled-up shell of the helmet proving that bleeding occurred and was deposited to the outside of the helmet before contact with the straight non-yielding surface that caused the gouge (consistent with a guard rail at the side of the road.) It was determined that the victim's (d) loosely worn helmet likely rotated forward to impact her face during impact and ejection from the motorcycle resulting in blood/tissue evidence on the superior interior opening of the helmet as well as the exterior.

that there was blood inside the peeled and curled-up shell of the helmet. Therefore, extensive bleeding occurred and was deposited to the outside of the helmet prior to contact with the straight non-yielding surface that caused the gouge. This surface was determined from the scene investigation to be consistent with a barrier at the side of the road.

Anatomically, the motorcycle operator (who was also the manager of the online motorcycle shop) noted that her helmet was worn large and loose which corroborated the physical evidence. It was determined that the plaintiff's loosely worn helmet likely rotated forward to impact her face during impact and ejection from the motorcycle, resulting in blood/tissue-like evidence on the superior interior opening of the helmet as well as exterior to the helmet.

In conclusion, the physical evidence on the helmet, scene inspection, and testimony were consistent with the injuries sustained from a loose-fitting helmet. The careful microscopic inspection was imperative to a full interpretation of the physical evidence and proper causation determination (Figures 5.11a–d).

(Courtesy of Laura L. Liptai, Ph.D., Biomedical Forensics, Moraga, California.)

FORENSIC SHOOTING RECONSTRUCTIONS

Shooting reconstructions often use trajectory analysis and ballistics in order to determine the point from which a bullet was fired. Ballistics is defined as the science of the motion of projectiles. It takes into consideration the type of weapon, nature of the ammunition, distance to the target, angle of entrance and exit holes, and other factors (Figure 5.12). A skilled CSI doing a shooting reconstruction conducts examinations with specific training in trajectory analysis. Wooden dowels and laser pointers are often employed to determine angles of impact and trajectories (Figure 5.13a and b). Like bloodstain pattern analysis, trajectory analysis requires training as well as experimentation in order to master the subject.

The person who is responsible for preparing a report on crime scene reconstruction should query all individuals who have expertise that may shed light on how the crime took place and synthesize the information into a report.

This chapter is meant to give readers a brief overview of the elements of crime scene reconstruction. It is very important to remember not to overstate one's conclusions when doing reconstructions.

Figure 5.12 Entrance holes of three bullets. The unsmooth quarter panel of this car makes determining the angle of entry difficult.

Figure 5.13 (a) Stringing can also be used to determine the angle of trajectory. (b) Additional tools seen here, including protractors, lasers, and dowels, are often used in a shooting reconstruction.

Further Reading

Bevel, Tom. "Bloodstain pattern analysis in homicide cold case investigations." *Cold Case Homicides*. CRC Press, 2017. 477–490.

Choromanski, Kacper. *Bloodstain Pattern Analysis in Crime Scenarios*. Springer, 2020.

DeForest, Peter R., et al. *Blood Traces: Interpretation of Deposition and Distribution*. Wiley, 2021.

James, Stuart, et al. *Principles of Bloodstain Pattern Analysis: Theory and Practice*. CRC Press, 2005.

Wonder, A. Y. *Blood Dynamics*. Academic Press, 2001.

Chapter Questions

1. Define crime scene reconstruction.
2. How does crime scene reconstruction differ from crime scene investigation?
3. What is BPA or bloodstain pattern analysis?
4. Trajectory analysis cannot determine:
    a. The location of the shooter.
    b. The distance the weapon was fired.
    c. The make of the weapon.
    d. The force of the trigger pull.
5. What is ballistics?
6. Calculate the angle of impact for an elliptical stain having a width of 1mm and a length of 3mm.
7. What is the difference between a blood swipe and a blood wipe?
8. Describe how a cast-off bloodstain pattern is created.
9. What is the significance of a void within a pattern?
10. Describe the difference between point of convergence and point of origin. How is each calculated?

Part II

Physical Evidence

CHAPTER 6

Fingerprint Evidence

Establishing the identity of a suspect or victim can be crucial in solving a case. Identification is possible through a variety of methods. Fingerprints are usually thought of first when considering methods of identifying individuals. Other ways of establishing identity, including forensic anthropology, forensic odontology, DNA, and facial recognition are also important and will be addressed in separate chapters.

FINGERPRINTS AND PALM PRINTS*

Some of the most valuable clues at the crime scene are fingerprints and palm prints (bare footprints are sometimes discovered as well and may also identify a person, provided there are known reference prints). In this section, the term "fingerprints" includes all types of prints of friction ridge skin. Prints of the palms or soles of the foot are made under the same conditions as fingerprints and are preserved in the same manner. It is, therefore, sometimes difficult to decide whether a print has been left by a finger, a palm, or the sole of a foot.

There are three basic principles of why fingerprints are useful in CSI: a fingerprint is an individual characteristic, a fingerprint will remain unchanged during a person's lifetime, and prints have ridge patterns that allow them to be systematically classified.

WHERE TO LOOK FOR FINGERPRINTS

In burglary investigations, the perpetrator's point of entry is the usual place to begin a search for prints. It may be possible at this point to determine if the burglar worked with or without gloves. If a door was broken open, prints (including shoe prints) may be located on the lock, the immediate surroundings, or other places on the door where the entry had been forced. With broken windows, particular attention should be given to pieces of broken glass that may contain prints or blood. The common method to break a window is to knock a small hole in a windowpane. A burglar can then break away pieces of glass with her fingers until she has succeeded in making an opening large enough to be able to reach the window latch. Often, fingerprints or glove prints will be found on broken pieces of glass. Broken glass does not always lie just inside the window because burglars sometimes dispose of the broken glass shards to conceal an entry. Fingerprints may be left on the inside of window sills, window frames, and door jambs when the burglar climbs through the window and grips these parts of the window frame.

Searches for fingerprints should also be made in areas where the burglar is suspected to have eaten or drunk. Prints on glass or china are often of good quality. If the criminal became intoxicated at the scene, probative results can often be expected from the print search. In some cases, the burglar wore gloves at the start, began drinking alcohol, and gradually became intoxicated. Forgetting caution, the gloves might be removed. (In addition to fingerprint evidence, investigators should note that DNA testing is widely used in property crimes. Investigators should consider

---

* An excellent interactive website (https://sites.rutgers.edu/fingerprinting/) maintained by Professor Daniel Asen (Rutgers University, Newark, NJ) highlights the history and present-day circumstances of fingerprinting through modules and video lectures.

the possibility of obtaining DNA samples from foodstuffs and evidence containing saliva (drinking containers and cigarettes) in addition to fingerprint evidence.)

Case Review

A suspect entered a convenience store in Kodiak, Alaska, where he robbed the clerk, hit her in the head with a gun, and forced her into a back room, where he tied her up with an electrical extension cord and attempted to rape her. The police developed a good suspect, but the clerk was unable to identify him. Inked finger and palm prints were submitted and identification was made from the latent prints developed on the plug of the extension cord (Figure 6.1a and b).

Light switches, circuit breakers, and fuses should always be examined, as well as any light bulbs that were loosened or removed. If the suspect wore gloves, special care should be taken at places where the activity was of a type in which gloves would have been a hindrance. For example, opening a case or drawers with difficult locks or searching in the drawers of a bureau may be difficult with gloves. Burglars sometimes will remove gloves during the crime and leave fingerprints at the scene. If the thief used the toilet, he might have removed his gloves. Prints should be searched for on the toilet flush lever, on the door lock, and on any paper that may have been used.

Burglars sometimes bring tools or other objects to the scene and leave them behind. Fingerprints may be detected on papers used to wrap tools, on flashlights (do not forget to examine the batteries), and other items including the *inside* of gloves. All smooth surfaces on which prints could have been left should be examined. Good prints are often found on glass, china, polished, painted, or otherwise smooth surfaces, smooth cardboard cartons, and paper. In some cases, prints have been recovered on rough surfaces, starched collars, cuffs, and newspapers. When examining furniture, do not omit places the criminal may have touched when pulling out drawers or moving the furniture. Even if the thief worked with gloved hands, prints may have been left when a heavy piece of furniture was moved because the gloves may have slipped and a part of the wrist or palm left a print.

A flashlight is a good tool for searching for latent prints. Fingerprints can be observed by holding the flashlight at low angles so that the surface is observed under **oblique illumination**. However, flashlights may not work on all surfaces. If prints are expected in a particular place and they are not observed, the area should be examined by other methods, including alternate light sources, chemical developers, or powders.

DIFFERENT TYPES OF FINGERPRINTS

Fingerprints can be divided into three main groups: (1) plastic fingerprints, (2) patent prints containing some foreign matter or "visible prints," and (3) latent fingerprints.

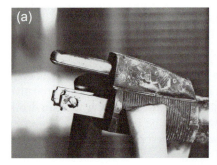 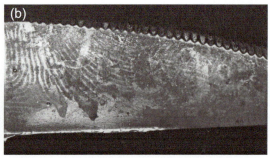

Figure 6.1 Though only a partial print, identification of the suspect was made from the latent prints developed on the plug (a, b) of the extension cord. (*Courtesy of Alaska Department of Public Safety, Scientific Crime Detection Laboratory, Latent Print Section.*)

- **Plastic fingerprints** occur when a finger touches or presses against soft material and creates a negative impression of its friction ridge pattern. These prints are found on such materials as fresh paint, on substances that melt easily or soften when held in the hand (e.g., chocolate), on adhesive tape, in thick layers of dust, plastic explosives, putty that has not hardened, candle wax, fats, flour, soap, thick and sticky oily films, grease, pitch, tar, resin, and clay, to name a few.
- **Patent fingerprints** from fingers contaminated with foreign matter are common. Dust prints occur when a finger is pressed in a thin layer of dust and some of the dust sticks on the friction ridges. When the finger is then placed on a clean surface, a fingerprint results. In some cases, a dust print may be fully identifiable and may be clear enough to search in a single fingerprint file. Prints can be left when fingers are contaminated with other substances like pigments, ink, soot, flour, face powder, oils, safe insulation, or blood.
- **Latent fingerprints** result from small amounts of grease, sweat, and dirt deposited on a surface. The skin on the hands and soles of the feet have no oil glands. Grease found on fingers comes from other parts of the body that the hands touched. Secretion from friction skin contains 98.5 to 99.5% water; the balance is organic and inorganic components. If the hands are cold, practically no liquid is secreted; when they become warm, secretion returns to normal. Latent prints are most often found on objects with polished or smooth surfaces and on paper. However, under some conditions, they may also be detected on rough surfaces, and even on smooth fabrics. "Latent prints" include those invisible to the unaided eye plus all others that are visible but only properly examined after development.

FINGERPRINT DEVELOPING TECHNIQUES

There have been many advances in fingerprint technology, specifically in techniques for visualizing prints. Most of these techniques involve chemical reagents that react with materials present in the components that make up the print. Collaboration between forensic chemists and forensic identification specialists has made these techniques possible and continued effort is to be encouraged. Forensic chemists and criminalists should be assigned to identification units within laboratories to work with fingerprint and identification specialists to develop and use chemical-based fingerprint visualization techniques.

Many procedures are available to develop latent fingerprints.* Those listed in the next sections are some of the standard procedures in use; however, new ones are developed regularly. *It is important to understand that practical experience with these procedures is needed to use them effectively.* Certain methods work better than others for different materials. The sequence of using these procedures is also important because it is possible to use multiple procedures, one following the other, for print development. Some procedures have an adverse effect on other types of evidence, e.g., certain solvents can cause inks to run on documents or render biological evidence unsuitable for DNA typing. Latent fingerprint examiners are cautioned that they should understand if any of these techniques might adversely interact with other classes of evidence before trying them on casework. Latent print examiners should work closely with other forensic scientists to develop procedures for using chemical developing methods with safeguards to avoid the destruction of other types of physical evidence. They should also consider forming regional users or study groups to help keep up with rapidly changing technology. Such groups are made up of local practitioners who meet regularly and share technical experiences with other practitioners. These regional groups are especially helpful in small identification units with only one or two examiners, who may be unable to attend technical conferences.

DEVELOPMENT WITH POWDERS

Brushing fingerprint powder over a latent print makes the print visible. The substances that form the print show up and the print becomes fully visible. The choice of the powder depends partly on the kind of surface on which the print is found and partly on how it is to be preserved. If the latent print is of high quality, the choice of powder for development is not especially important. Several types of fingerprint powders are commercially available: black, white, colored, aluminum, copper, fluorescent, and magnetic. The type used is determined by the color of the background and the nature of the surface.

---

* The *Fingerprint Sourcebook* by the National Institute of Justice aims to be the definitive resource on the science of fingerprint identification.

Safety Data Sheets (SDSs) (formerly Material Safety Data Sheets) for fingerprint powders are available from suppliers and online. Common sense suggests that long-term exposure to fine particulate matter may cause respiratory problems over time. Persons who routinely use fingerprint powders should wear dust masks or specially designed chemical hoods to minimize the amount of powder inhaled.

Fiberglass, animal hair, synthetic, or natural fiber brushes may be used to develop fingerprints. The brush should not be damp or oily. It is first lightly dipped in the powder and then tapped with the finger so that only a small amount of the powder is left on the brush. The object is then lightly brushed in circular motions. Powder particles will adhere to all places where there is oil or dirt. If fingerprints are present on the object, they show up more or less clearly.

Fingerprint brushes may be a source of DNA contamination or secondary transfer. DNA technology has become highly sensitive and there have been documented instances where DNA has been transferred from one crime scene to another. This of course could result in DNA having nothing to do with one item of evidence being discovered in an unrelated item. At a minimum, crime scene investigators should use clean, single-use fingerprint brushes between dusting different items.

The powder should not be sprinkled over or tapped onto the object while brushing. Prints from sweaty or dirty fingers or produced by a firm grip may cause the friction ridges to spread out, filling up the spaces between the ridges. Too much powder can destroy these prints. If too much powder is used, it can be "washed" by pressing a fingerprint lifter against the print. The lifter will remove the excess and the spaces between the ridges may be nearly free of powder. If necessary, the latent print can be reprocessed to get usable results.

Some fingerprint examiners use black fingerprint powder as a universal developer on smooth nonporous surfaces. On dark surfaces, such as furniture and firearms, aluminum or copper powders also give good results. These powders are useful if the print is to be photographed before being lifted.

Another aid to fingerprint development, the Magna-Brush, utilizes magnetic powders and a magnetic applicator. Streamers of magnetized powder are brought in contact with the suspected surface. The powder adheres to the latent print, while the magnet removes the excess. This method has the advantage of not leaving excess powder on the object and the surrounding area. Because of the nature of the process, it can be used effectively only on nonmagnetic surfaces (Figure 6.2). Fluorescent powders are yet another type that may be used in some special cases. Available in

Figure 6.2 Magnetic fingerprint powders consist of black powder with iron shavings mixed in. Here a Magna-brush is able to dust for prints and then remove the excess powder using its magnet. (*Courtesy of the Los Angeles County Sheriff's Department.*)

powder and aerosol forms, these powders are used to dust paper currency and documents and are sprayed in areas where recurring thefts take place. They are technically not fingerprint powders because they are used prior to the prints being deposited. It is important to remember not to return any excess powder to the main container--any excess powder should be discarded.

The following are different development techniques that have been widely used in the CSI community and by latent print examiners. It is important to become familiar with these techniques using mock casework before using them in actual casework.

Amido Black. This stain turns proteins present in blood blue-black. It does not react with any of the normal components of fingerprints and should be used in conjunction with other developing techniques. Amido Black works well on tile, PVC, drywall, and posterboard.

DFO (1,8-diazafluoren-9-one). DFO is a ninhydrin-like analogue. It reacts with proteins to give a highly fluorescent, red-colored product that is more sensitive than ninhydrin. Although some prints developed using DFO will be visible to the naked eye, illumination with high-intensity light improves the sensitivity; however, interference may become a problem from certain colored inks and papers that fluoresce. Longer wavelength light sources, such as mercury vapor lamps at 546 nm lessen the interference. Ninhydrin may be used in conjunction with DFO; however, DFO must be used first.

Gentian violet or crystal violet. These dyes, which produce a purple color, stain fatty components of latent prints and are especially effective when used on the sticky side of adhesive tape. It also works great on untreated wood. The material is toxic and appropriate laboratory precautions must be taken. Using a laser increases the sensitivity of the procedure. A yellow-orange light source yields the best results, e.g., a copper vapor laser at the 578-nm line. An alternative dye, Basic Fuchsin, yields good results with green excitation and has an absorption maximum at about 500 nm.

Iodine. Iodine is one of the oldest methods of visualizing latent prints on porous and nonporous substrates. The technique is simple to use; however, iodine vapors are toxic and corrosive and the reaction is not permanent. Methods have been introduced for fixing prints developed by iodine fuming, e.g., 7,8-benzoflavone, which also increases sensitivity.

Ninhydrin solution. Ninhydrin is another technique for use with porous surfaces, e.g., paper, cardboard, wallboard, and raw wood. Ninhydrin reacts with amino acids to form a purple-colored compound called "Ruhemann's Purple." The reaction is speeded up by means of humidity and elevated temperatures. Treating with zinc chloride solution and viewing with a laser improve the sensitivity of the techniques. Background fluorescence may be overcome by using cadmium nitrate solution cooled to liquid nitrogen temperatures and viewed with a laser. Modifications to the chemical structure of ninhydrin have been synthesized and show usefulness under certain conditions. The importance of these analogues is that they fluoresce at different wavelengths and provide a way to overcome background interference from certain substrates (Figure 6.3).

Physical developer (PD; also called stabilized physical developer, or SPD). PD is a silver-based solution used as a substitute for the conventional latent print silver nitrate procedure. PD is useful in detecting latent prints on porous surfaces that are wet or have been wet, e.g., paper, cardboard, and raw wood. The technique may be used following ninhydrin. PD reacts with components of sweat and appears in shades from gray to almost black. PD-developed prints are preserved by photography.

Silver nitrate. Silver nitrate solution reacts with chlorides in prints, but with the advent of physical developer, it is not in widespread use. It may have some application on raw wood, however, the background staining of the substrate may cause problems in photography.

Small particle reagent (SPR). This is a wet process for developing latent prints on wet surfaces. The reagent is a suspension of molybdenum disulfide particles prepared in a detergent solution. Molybdenum adheres to lipids found in prints as a gray deposit. The process works well on nonporous surfaces, e.g., plastic bags, wax paper, glass, and painted surfaces, and may be used effectively on water-soaked firearms. Visible prints may be lifted and/or photographed.

Sudan black. This process is used on nonporous articles, e.g., glass, plastics, and metal. Usually less sensitive than SPR, it may be the method of choice if the substrate is oily or greasy. Sudan black reacts with the lipid components of prints and stains them blue-black. It is messy to use and not effective on dark-colored objects.

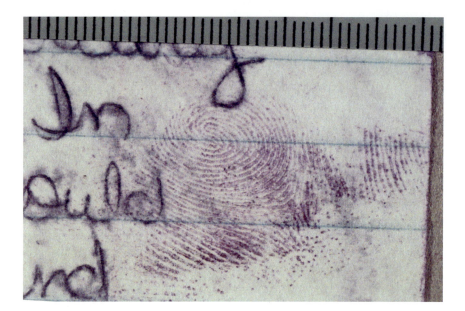

Figure 6.3 A latent partial print developed from a letter on lined paper using ninhydrin.

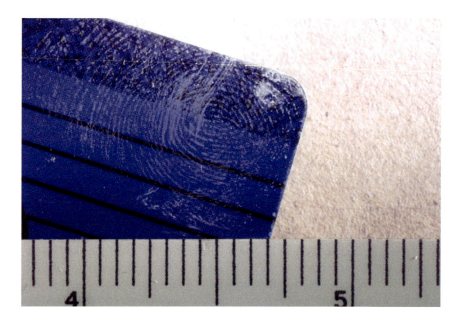

Figure 6.4 Cyanoacrylate fuming of a credit card.

Superglue or cyanoacrylate fuming. Superglue is used on nonporous surfaces to produce visible prints that are white. The visible prints may be dusted with powder, photographed and lifted, or washed with laser-sensitive dyes such as Rhodamine 6G and others, and viewed with lasers or alternative light sources. Superglue is one of the easier procedures to use; however, in some instances, other latent print visualization techniques may yield superior results (Figure 6.4).

Vacuum metal deposition (VMD). VMD is an effective technique for nonporous, semi-porous, and porous surfaces, e.g., plastic bags, plastic packaging material, banknotes, fabrics, and other surfaces. The standard process employs the sequential vacuum deposition of a very thin layer of gold in a vacuum chamber followed by a thin layer of zinc. Fingerprints developed by VMD are of much higher definition (often to 3rd level detail) and have excellent contrast than prints developed using cyanoacrylate. VMD can also be used for targeted DNA swabbing in cases of grabbing on clothing. The major drawback to vacuum metal deposition is that the equipment is expensive and the sample chamber of the vacuum coater is not very large.

LASERS AND ALTERNATIVE LIGHT SOURCES

The word "laser" is an acronym for **L**ight **A**mplification by **S**timulated **E**mission of **R**adiation. The use of lasers and other alternative light sources are quite effective in locating and visualizing latent prints, as well as other types of physical evidence such as trace evidence and certain types of biological evidence at the crime scene and in the crime lab.

Several types of alternate light sources are widely used in CSI. No single wavelength of light will work best in all forensic applications. Several factors need to be considered in choosing the type of high-intensity light most suitable for use in a forensic laboratory or field applications. Some of the factors that must be considered are cost, the color of light or wavelengths available, light intensity or power output, portability, voltage requirements, safety, available service on an emergency basis, and the ability to use the unit in other forensic applications. Technology has moved light sources along greatly and a wide variety of units are available; some are very portable and look like handheld flashlights.

Naturally, the more sophisticated the unit, the more cost becomes a factor. Some units used in laboratory settings may require special setups and workspace remodeling, e.g., darkened work areas to take photographs, laboratory sinks and fume hoods to handle light-sensitive dyes, power requirements, plumbed in water to cool the unit or additional units to recirculate coolant to the laser, liquid nitrogen for use in certain laser procedures—the list can be formidable and must be considered when budgeting for certain units. Other costs include maintenance and purchase of parts that must be replaced from time to time.

Safety is a concern with high-intensity light sources. The intensity of the light can cause eye fatigue and eye damage. Persons working with these tools should be required to wear appropriate eye protection to minimize any damage.

Reflective Ultra Violet Imaging Systems (RUVIS) can also detect untreated prints on smooth, nonporous surfaces. RUVIS devices enable fingerprint collection to be performed on plastic bags, sticky sides of tape, glossy magazines, linoleum tiles, and credit cards. Naturally occurring chemicals and contaminants present in latent prints fluoresce under the RUVIS without any treatment.

INTEGRATED AUTOMATED FINGERPRINT IDENTIFICATION SYSTEM*

The Integrated Automated Fingerprint Identification Systems (IAFIS) represents the single biggest advance in fingerprint identification technology. It allows for the ability to compare a latent fingerprint discovered at the crime scene to a national fingerprint database. The amount of human effort to conduct a manual search for a latent print against millions of inked prints is extremely high and prior to IAFIS was a huge undertaking (Figure 6.5a and b).

Today, searching a database of several million prints is a daily occurrence. Even more staggering, the search of prints on file in the IAFIS database takes only minutes.

IAFIS has revolutionized the way police departments search latent prints for matches. At one time, it was not uncommon for some crime scene investigators to dust low property value crime scenes to placate crime victims who wanted

---

* In July 1999, the fingerprint identification function was automated. This national, computerized system for storing, comparing, and exchanging fingerprint data in a digital format permits comparisons of fingerprints in a faster and more accurate manner. It is located in, and operated by, the Criminal Justice Information Services (CJIS) Division of the FBI in Clarksburg, West Virginia. IAFIS provides three major services to its customers. First, it is a repository of criminal history information, fingerprints, criminal subject photographs, as well as information regarding military and civilian federal employees and other individuals as authorized by Congress. Second, it provides positive identification of individuals based on fingerprint submissions (both through ten-print fingerprint cards and latent fingerprints). Third, it provides tentative identification of individuals based on descriptive information such as a name, date of birth, distinctive body markings, and identification numbers. IAFIS's primary function is to provide the FBI a fully automated fingerprint identification and criminal history reporting system. Additionally, IAFIS has made several other accomplishments. It has improved latent fingerprint identification services to the law enforcement community and it has also helped to develop uniform biometric standards. These improvements have eliminated the need to process and retain paper fingerprint cards and has, thereby, accelerated the identification process. Another benefit has been the development of improved digital image quality (U.S. Department of Justice, Federal Bureau of Investigation).

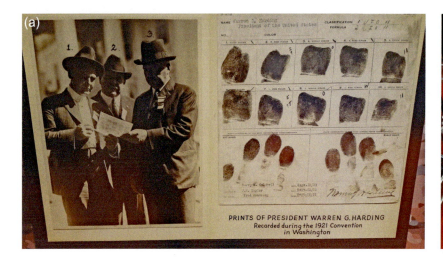 

Figure 6.5 Prior to the advent of computers and databases, manual searches were conducted of tenprint cards. (a) Pictured here are the fingerprints of US President Warren Harding which were recorded during the IAI's 1921 convention in Washington DC. (b) Tenprint cards like the ones shown here along with millions of others were stored in large filing cabinets at the FBI. Historic photographs from the FBI's Colossal Fingerprint Factory can be found at https://rarehistoricalphotos.com/fbi-fingerprint-files-facility-1944/. By 1943, more than 20,000 employees were sorting through 70 million fingerprints.

the police to do something. The effort put into dusting a scene seemed to give victims a feeling that the police were doing something. In only a small percentage of cases would latent prints be matched to those of a suspect. Some police administrators even questioned the value of going through the effort of trying to locate fingerprints in low property value residential burglaries and automobile burglaries.

IAFIS has completely changed that way of thinking. Simply stated, the more quality latent prints collected at crime scenes and searched against IAFIS, the greater is the chance of identifying criminals.

The quality of fingerprints used to create the IAFIS database is critical. Poorly taken fingerprint cards uploaded into the IAFIS database eliminate the possibility of making a correct identification when conducting a latent print search. Because a surprisingly high number of crimes may be associated with one perpetrator, the quality of the inked fingerprints and the IAFIS data entry process becomes very important.

An alternative to taking inked prints is an electronic scan whose generic name is Livescan. Livescan technology produces high-quality print cards without the need to take inked prints. Each hand is inserted into a reader and fingerprints from each finger are captured. At the end of the process, a standard print card is produced. The next step of the process is to input the print card into the IAFIS database. A shortcoming of the system is that IAFIS systems are proprietary and Livescan systems cannot transfer electronic data directly into IAFIS.

The FBI has been at the forefront in recognizing the importance of new identification technology and biometrics. Of particular note is the effort to integrate many forms of biometrics of people besides fingerprints. This includes criminal histories; mug shots; scars and tattoo photos; physical characteristics like height, weight, hair color, eye color; and aliases.

In 2011, the FBI developed and incrementally integrated a new system to replace IAFIS. This new system, **Next Generation Identification** (NGI)* provides the world's largest electronic repository of biometric and criminal history information. The NGI system's capabilities include Advanced Fingerprint Identification Technology (AFIT); facial recognition search, which allows law enforcement to search criminal photos using a probe photo; Iris Service, which uses an iris image repository that is linked to tenprint fingerprint records, in addition to other capabilities. NGI also contains civil identities (photos submitted for licensing, employment, security clearances, military service,

---

* NGI Fact Sheet (www.fbi.gov/file-repository/ngi-monthly-fact-sheet/view).

volunteer service, and immigration benefits). Over 80 percent of the photos are of criminals. The NGI system provides a platform for multimodal functionality that will continue to evolve with new technologies.*

PRESERVATION BY PHOTOGRAPHY

Fingerprints found at the scene of a crime should be preserved by photography when possible. This procedure has many advantages. Photography leaves the objects intact so that further photos can be taken if the first are unusable. It also makes it easier to show the evidence in court because the object on which the latents were discovered can be seen in the picture. The photography of fingerprints differs from ordinary picture-taking. The photographer must be skilled in photographic techniques and understand how to obtain a reproduction of a fingerprint as accurate and true to the original as possible. Additionally, knowledge of the principles of fingerprint comparison is helpful to appreciate what the person making the print identification requires. The finished photograph should be white on a black background or black on a white background. It should be 1:1, the actual size, and a ruler should be included in the photograph to allow for the printing to be 1:1. The person taking the photograph should advise the person making the fingerprint comparison whether the print is a direct or mirror image or a positive or negative image. Expert examiners can use the pattern type and minutiae of a partial print to help determine which finger it came from and how to orient the print in its proper orientation

If the print is visible without fingerprint powder development, it should be photographed as found, in view of the possibility that any measures taken for development might destroy it. This can generally be done by a suitable arrangement of lighting. An attempt can then be made to make the print clearer, for example, by treatment with powders, after which more photographs are taken. Fingerprints should be photographed with a scale in the photo.

PRESERVATION OF PLASTIC FINGERPRINTS

When a fingerprint has been left in material that has hardened or is able to withstand transport and when it is on a small, easily transportable object, it may be sent directly to the crime laboratory. If removing the plastic print poses some special problem, it should be photographed using oblique lighting to bring out as much detail as possible. An appropriate casting material may then preserve the fingerprint impression.

Frequently, curved surfaces with latent fingerprints present, such as doorknobs, are difficult to photograph or do not lend themselves to the use of lifting tape. For such surfaces, elastic or rubber material works well. Rubber lifters are commercially available items made of a thin, rubbery material coated with an adhesive. A transparent celluloid material removed prior to use and replaced after use protects the adhesive. The color of the lifter is either black or white for use with different fingerprint powders depending on contrast.

To use this technique, the latent fingerprint is first dusted with an appropriately colored fingerprint powder. The protective covering of the lifter is pulled away and the sticky surface is pressed against the print and then pulled away. Part of the powder sticks to the lifter and gives the mirror image of the print. After the print is collected, the protective covering is carefully replaced on the lifter.

The lifter comes in different sizes and can be cut for a specific use. It is also useful for picking up footprints in the dust. The lifting method is simple and easy to master. It requires no knowledge of photography and no photographic equipment. Its use, however, requires greater accuracy in specifying the position of the print.

PRESERVATION WITH FINGERPRINT-LIFTING TAPE

The most common method of collecting latent fingerprint evidence today is by special transparent lifting tape. The material is supplied in rolls and is usually 1 or 2 inches wide. After the surface is dusted with fingerprint powder, the tape is placed over the print. Care must be taken to prevent any air pockets. The tape is smoothed down over the print with the aid of a finger and then drawn off. Particles of fingerprint powder adhere to the sticky surface of the tape and thereby transfer the fingerprint pattern. The tape is finally placed on a card whose color contrasts with the color of

---

* www.fbi.gov/services/cjis/fingerprints-and-other-biometrics/ngi.

the powder used. If insufficient ridge detail is present for any useful comparison, the epithelial cells on the tape can be used for DNA typing (however, as mentioned earlier, contamination is a concern).

HOW LONG DOES A FINGERPRINT REMAIN ON AN OBJECT?

Plastic prints remain for any length of time provided that the object on which they are left or the substance in which they are formed is stable. In investigations, it sometimes happens that police officers find fingerprints that give the impression of having been made in dust, but on closer examination are found to be dust-filled plastic prints in oil paint made years earlier.

Prints that have resulted from contamination of the fingers with soot, flour, face powder, or safe filling material are soon destroyed. Prints of fingers contaminated with blood, pigments, ink, and oil are more resistant and can be kept for a long time under favorable conditions.

Latent prints on glass, china, and other smooth objects can remain for years if they are in a well-protected location. On objects in the open air, a print can be developed several months after it is made. Fingerprints on paper are very stable and will last for years, provided the paper does not become wet and deteriorate.

THE EFFECT OF TEMPERATURE CONDITIONS ON THE POSSIBILITY OF DEVELOPING FINGERPRINTS

When objects that may contain fingerprints are found outdoors in ice or snow, they must be thawed slowly and placed so that the thawed water does not run over and destroy the prints. A suitable method of treatment is to scrape away as much snow and ice as possible, with the greatest care, before the object is brought to a warm place. Only when the object is dry should the print be developed.

When plastic fingerprints are present in oil or grease, the thawing must be allowed to proceed slowly and under close scrutiny because the print may easily be destroyed by heat. Such prints should be photographed when they appear.

Damp objects should be dried indoors at ordinary room temperature. As a general rule, never examine cold objects, especially metal, until they have been kept for at least some hours at room temperature. In indoor investigations in a cold house, the rooms should first be heated. The heating should be done slowly so that water from thawing does not run off frosted objects or places.

EXAMINATION OF DEVELOPED FINGERPRINTS

The officer who investigates the crime scene should only search for, develop, and preserve the fingerprints. Unless specially qualified in the identification of fingerprints, the officer cannot be expected to carry out the continued examination of the developed prints.

A detailed account of fingerprint identification is not included here, partly because it lies outside the scope of crime scene investigation, and partly because it is a vast and specialized subject. Several comprehensive works on this subject are available at the end of this chapter under "Further Reading."

The officer examining the scene should preserve all developed fingerprints. Even small, fragmentary prints that might seem insignificant to a nonspecialist may turn out to be very valuable when examined by an expert. Large fingerprints are not necessarily more valuable than small ones.

PALM PRINTS

Patterns of friction ridge skin appear on the palm just as they are found on the fingers. When part of a palm print is found, the area involved can often be deduced from the position of the print, or other parts of the hand and possibly fingers having left marks in the form of smears or portions of print. If the position of the hand represented by the fragment can be determined, this will greatly facilitate the expert's work. Ron Smith & Associates (www.forensictraining.online/) offers an excellent online training course on palm prints that meets IAI continuing education

Figure 6.6 A palm print developed on a car door window.

credits (Figure 6.6). In 2013, the FBI established the National Palm Print System (NPPS).* This system contains more than 15 million unique palm print identities and more than 29 million individual palm prints tied to those identities, all of which are searchable to law enforcement across the United States.

Case Review

In June 2012, a 44-year-old man's body was discovered in his driveway in Moore, Oklahoma. Investigators found a pair of palm prints on a truck near the body. A senior criminalist searched the palm prints through the Oklahoma State Bureau of Identification (OSBI) Automated Fingerprint Identification System. However, no national palm print database search could be conducted in 2012, so she was unable to identify the prints.

Shortly after the NPPS' deployment in May 2013, the OSBI began a special project to review cold cases for unidentified latent prints suitable for a search through the FBI's Next Generation Identification (NGI) System. In February 2014, the OSBI searched the two latent palm prints from the 2012 Moore case through NGI. After finding no matches, the OSBI added the palm prints to the NGI's Unsolved Latent File.

In March 2016, a criminalist from the OSBI's Latent Evidence Unit received an unsolved latent match notification on the submitted latent palm prints, so she requested palm prints from the FBI's Criminal Justice Information Services Division. A senior criminalist identified the palm prints taken from the crime scene by comparing them to those stored in the NPPS.

According to court documents, the subject admitted to police that he drove his roommate to the victim's house, where the roommate and the victim got into a fight. The subject told investigators his roommate repeatedly kicked and stomped the victim while the victim was on the ground. The medical examiner determined that the victim died from blunt force trauma injuries and possible asphyxia due to an assault. However, the subject refused to testify against his roommate, and prosecutors had only the forensic evidence—the palm prints of the subject.

---

* www.fbi.gov/services/cjis/cjis-link/national-palm-print-system.

In January 2018, the subject was formally charged and found guilty of one count of first-degree manslaughter for his role in the victim's death.

(Retrieved from FBI.gov, www.fbi.gov/services/cjis/cjis-link/national-palm-print-system.)

PRINTS FROM THE SOLE OF THE FOOT

Friction ridges on the soles of the feet have the same evidentiary value as fingerprints and are developed and preserved in the same way as other prints. Cases sometimes occur in which burglars lacking gloves for their hands have taken off their socks and put them on their hands to avoid leaving fingerprints. The thought of leaving footprints never entered their minds!

EAR, LIP, AND OTHER PRINTS

Occasionally, ear prints (**auricle morphometry**) and lip prints (**cheiloscopy**) are found at a crime scene. A suspect might have put his ear up to a door or wall to listen to what was being said on the other side. Lip prints have also been found in lipstick on letters, envelopes, or coffee cups placed by female suspects. Another method used by criminals is to hold an object between the index and middle fingers like a pair of scissors to prevent leaving fingerprints. The sides of the fingers also have friction ridge detail that can be used for useful comparisons. Research in these atypical prints is ongoing. The main hurdle for using these prints is that no database exists that contains these types of prints. Examiners are, therefore, left to perform direct comparisons which require known exemplars. While not typically done in most cases, this type of evidence would likely provide useful information in certain circumstances.

TRANSPORTING OBJECTS WITH FINGERPRINTS

The crime scene investigator must decide the best way to transport objects that are to be examined for fingerprints. Wrapping such items directly in paper, cloth, or plastic bags should be avoided because prints may be destroyed. If possible, the object should be wedged firmly in a strong box so that the packing does not touch the surface. Because a rigid suspension can cause breakage or other damage to an object in transit, the box must be wrapped in a sufficient quantity of soft material such as cotton, corrugated paper, crumpled newspaper, etc. If nails are used to fix the object in the box or for the lid, they should not be hammered completely in; the heads should be left free so that they can be pulled out without using much force.

TAKING FINGERPRINTS FOR ELIMINATION

As a rule, persons who have legitimate access to the premises leave the majority of fingerprints found and developed at the crime scene; thus, it is important to eliminate these fingerprints so that the continuing examination may concentrate upon the remaining foreign prints—presumably those of the perpetrator. The investigating officer should, therefore, always take elimination prints of all persons that have legitimate access to the premises. These should be submitted to the fingerprint examiner together with the crime scene prints. Because the identification of legitimate fingerprints is as critical as the identification of the criminal's prints, the elimination prints should be as clear as a suspect's prints recorded for filing purposes.

A large proportion of latent prints developed at a crime scene are palm prints; therefore, elimination palm prints should also be taken. Inked palm prints require special care in order to be useful for comparison purposes. The palm should be inked with a roller to ensure that all parts of the palm are inked. The prints should be made on a sheet of white paper. Place the inked palm flat on the paper and press on the center of the top of the hand.

PRINTS OF GLOVES

The general knowledge of the value of fingerprint evidence has resulted in criminals using gloves as their most usual protective measure. In many cases, when an investigator is looking for fingerprints, glove smears are found. All too often, little attention is paid to them. The search is focused on places where the perpetrator might have preferred to work bare-handed. If the perpetrator exerted a good deal of force while wearing the gloves they might slip, permitting an area on the wrist or a portion of the palm near the wrist to be exposed, leaving an identifiable latent print from the palm area.

Prints of gloves, however, may be valuable so it is advisable always to examine and preserve them for closer investigation as long as they are not just smears formed by the glove-covered hand slipping against a surface. The leather of a glove may show a surface pattern that is characteristic. The glove print may show furrows in a more or less definitive pattern or it may be perforated. It is much the same with fabric gloves. The surface pattern varies according to the method of manufacture and the yarn or material used. It is the wrinkled or textured surface pattern of leather gloves that can make identification possible.

In contrast, the surface pattern of fabric gloves is regular for each type so identification is not generally possible. Characteristic and, from the point of view of identification, very valuable formations in the seams may be present, especially at the tips of the fingers. After they have been worn for some time, leather or fabric gloves become shaped to the hands, and typical wrinkle formations often are produced in the leather of the fingers, at the seams, or at places where the gloves do not fit the fingers properly. These wrinkle formations and injuries in the form of tears or holes or, in the case of leather gloves, cracks in the surface of the skin generally show in the print and are most valuable. In rare cases, it is even possible to find fragments of a fingerprint within a glove print. This can occur when the gloves have such large holes that some part of a finger is exposed and leaves a print at the same time as that of the glove.

If prints of gloves and friction ridges appear together, it may be difficult to distinguish the differences without close examination. At first glance, the print gives the impression of being blurred or composed of two glove prints within each other. On closer examination, however, its regular lines, which lack the detailed pattern of the friction ridges, distinguish the glove print. Glove prints are formed best on smooth surfaces. Their development requires great care because the prints are not as persistent as fingerprints and therefore may easily be destroyed if too much powder is used. To ensure not destroying any such prints that may be present at the scene of the crime, the area should not be painted in an unstructured way. A systematic search may be made with the aid of a lamp and then cautiously brushed. There is also the prospect of finding glove prints on conspicuous and easily accessible places because the culprit might abandon all caution and believe that he is fully protected by his gloves and so use his hands freely.

In developing prints, white or black powder may be used. A fingerprint lifter can lift the developed print, but sometimes it is better to take possession of the object on which the print is found so that it can be compared directly with prints from the gloves of a suspect. Leather or fabric gloves can produce a print. With the former, the leather contains some fat, while both leather and fabric gloves become contaminated with dirt, and oil from the skin after being worn for some time. In addition, the warm and moist secretion from the skin of the hands plays an important part, at least with fabric gloves.

Comparison prints from the suspect's gloves are best made on glass, which is generally most convenient even when the original prints are on furniture. In certain cases, it may be necessary to form a print on the same kind of material as that at the scene. Where possible, such material should be packaged separately when a print and gloves from a suspect are sent for examination. Comparison prints should be made in a manner similar to that used for the original ones. For example, if it is possible to decide how the hand of the suspect gripped the object, this information should be communicated to the fingerprint examiner so that the same grip can be applied for the comparison print. Consideration must also be given to the degree of pressure that may have been used in forming the original print and this should be noted. It is important that neither too much nor too little pressure be used in making the comparison prints because the appearance is greatly affected by pressure.

It is often difficult to make clear prints with a glove, but exhaling on the finger of the glove may help. In certain instances, it may be treated with powder, however, this technique risks destroying any characteristic details.

PRINTS OF OTHER COVERINGS

In addition to gloves, other items such as socks, towels, and handkerchiefs are sometimes used as protection for the hands. Individuals have occasionally protected the insides of their hands with adhesive tape to prevent the formation of fingerprints. In most cases, when using the above-mentioned procedures, prints might be left if the material is thin, dirty, or damp. Prints left from hand coverings rarely have any value for identification. Identification is possible only in cases in which the material used has a characteristic surface pattern and shows typical injuries, unusual seams, or characteristic crease formations that are reproduced in the print. In such a case, the investigation is tedious because the extent of the edges of the protective medium is not definitely fixed as it would be in the case of a glove; therefore, it must be searched for before a direct comparison can be undertaken.

Although the possibility of identification of hand coverings in such cases is not great, the print should still be given some attention because the method of operation may be typical for a particular individual or gang who has perhaps carried out other crimes in the same or another area.

LATENT FINGERPRINTS ON HUMAN SKIN*

Several techniques have been reported for developing latent prints on human skin. These show some value, but success has been limited. One technique is the Kromekote® Lift Technique. The equipment needed includes a fiberglass filament brush, fingerprint powder, and Kromekote cards. Kromekote cards are approximately 5- × 7-inch, high-gloss, 80-lb paper similar in appearance to photographic paper. Kromekote is generally available from local paper suppliers or online. The Kromekote card is used to lift the print from the skin surface by placing the card over the skin in the suspected area and applying pressure for about 3 seconds. The card is carefully removed and then dusted with black fingerprint powder to develop the print transferred onto the card. The fingerprint obtained is the mirror image of a normal print and can be reversed through photography.

After the Kromekote technique is used, fingerprint powder can be applied directly to the skin to develop prints. The literature reports that the Magna-Brush gives results superior to a fiberglass filament brush. If a print is developed by this method, it must be photographed and then may be lifted using lifting tape. Fingerprints on skin surfaces appear to last about 1.5 hours on living victims. Deceased victims should be examined for latent prints on the skin as soon as possible.

TAKING FINGERPRINTS FROM A DECEDENT

Even when a decedent's fingerprints are not in a criminal fingerprint file, there is still the possibility of identifying the body through other fingerprint records. In many cases, there is reason to assume that a body is of a certain missing person, but even relatives are unable to identify the body because it has undergone so many changes. Under these conditions, fingerprints are taken in order to compare them with latent prints in the home of the decedent or their place of employment. This type of investigation often gives a positive result.

There is no special difficulty in taking fingerprints from a body after the rigidity has relaxed or when rigidity has only developed to a small extent and the body has not undergone any considerable change. If fingers are rigid, the joints should be bent several times until they are sufficiently flexible. The tips of the fingers are then inked, using a rubber roller and printing ink or commercially available inking materials, and the prints are taken on small pieces of thin card that are pressed against the papillary pattern on the tip of the finger. The finger should not be rolled against the card because the print will inevitably suffer from slipping. With some practice, the card may instead be rolled around the fingertip for satisfactory results.

A number of prints of the same finger are taken so that the best results can be selected. When a sufficient number of prints have been taken from one finger, each piece of card is marked to show to which finger it corresponds. When prints have been taken from all the fingers, the best are selected from each and stuck onto the respective sections of a fingerprint card. It is important to be careful not to get the fingers mixed up when sticking on the prints; if prints of two fingers do happen to get interchanged, then a search in the register will probably be fruitless. It is best to make up two cards, one to be sent to the state or federal file and the other filed with the records. If suitable thin cards cannot be obtained, ordinary glazed writing paper can be used. In such a case, using a piece of wood or sheet metal that fits the finger facilitates taking the prints. The pieces of paper are placed on this and fixed or held fast on it when the prints are taken.

Difficulty is often experienced when the body is considerably decomposed. The changes in the fingers consist either of their drying up and becoming hard or of the tissues becoming loose and filled with liquid and the epidermis

---

* The FBI has published research in the area of collecting fingerprints off of skin, www.iowaiai.org/hidden-evidence-latent-prints-on-human-skin/.

becoming fragile and puckered ("dishpan" hands). The first generally occurs when the body has been in a dry place and the second when it has been in the water.

When the fingers have shriveled and dried up, fingerprints cannot be taken by the methods just described. Other methods must be employed. The prints may be read directly from the fingers and classified without taking impressions. A selection is then made of the finger or fingers most suitable for recording with ink. Only persons with considerable experience in fingerprint classification can use this method. When reading a pattern directly from a finger it must be remembered that the print is seen reversed, as in a mirror.

Another method to record fingerprints from deceased persons is by photography. This method is rather tedious and difficult to carry out. If the fingers are stiff and bent, it is necessary to photograph each finger separately.

Frequently, fingertips are so dried out and wrinkled that the friction ridge pattern cannot be read because important parts are concealed in hard folds of the skin. The pattern may be read by amputating the fingers from the hand and softening the skin. The pathologist should have an opportunity to view the deceased before this step is taken. The fingers should be cut at the second or middle joint and placed in individually labeled bottles, each bottle noting the hand and finger. Only the pathologist or other competent person should perform this operation. The investigator should be present to verify that the fingers do not get mixed up.

One method for softening dried fingers is to let them soak in a solution of diluted liquid fabric softener for 1 or 2 days, after which they are carefully kneaded until they are sufficiently soft for a print to be taken with the aid of printing ink. If difficulties are still encountered, the fingers must be photographed.

Taking fingerprints from a corpse removed from water is difficult because of changes in the body. In general, changes may be divided into three stages: (1) the epidermis of the fingertips becomes loose and coarsely ridged; (2) the epidermis is loose everywhere and can be removed; and (3) the epidermis is completely missing.

In the first stage, the fingertips must be washed and dried, preferably with cotton or a soft towel. This operation must be done with care and without rubbing so that the skin is not torn off. Fingerprints are then taken in the usual way.

When the skin is wrinkled and granulated, water must first be injected into the upper joint of the finger so that the creases and granulations are smoothed out. For this purpose, a 10-ml hypodermic syringe with a fine needle is used. The needle is inserted approximately at the center of the inside of the middle joint and brought close to the bone in the upper joint, after which water is injected until the skin appears hard and tense. The needle must not be allowed to come too near the skin because the pressure might be sufficient to break the skin, nor should it be put in or too near the outer joint—the return path would be so short that the water would run out again. After the needle has been removed, the print is taken in the usual way. In earlier technical literature, an injection of glycerin, paraffin, or even melted tallow was recommended. However, a properly performed injection with water gives better results and is easier to perform.

In the second stage, when the epidermis has loosened, it is easier to take fingerprints. The loose skin (finger stalls) of the tip is pulled or cut off from the fingertips; the skin from each finger is placed in a labeled test tube filled with water. The finger stalls should not be put in an envelope or other paper wrapping because after a time they will dry up and stick to the paper. When they have been removed this way, the finger stalls may be sent to the fingerprint unit for examination.

For easier handling and photographing, the best procedure is to place the skin from each finger separately between two glass slides. To do this, the fingerprint pattern is cut out of the finger stalls. Because the cutout pieces of skin are then convex, they easily split when flattened between the glass slides. This splitting is unavoidable; therefore it is necessary to make cuts in the edges so that the splits do not occur in parts of the fingerprint pattern needed for the purpose of classification. When placing them between the glass slides, a small piece of paper or card with the name of the finger is placed near the top of the sample to indicate that the print is being viewed from the correct side. There is not much risk of any such piece of skin being the wrong side because the inside is lighter, smoother, and glossier than the outside. If, however, in a particular case some doubt exists as to which is the inside, taking the piece of skin out and viewing it can determine which side is concave. The glass slides should be taped together. The fingerprint patterns should be photographed by transmitted light; the lines will show up very distinctly.

Prints may also be taken with the aid of printing ink. After careful cleaning and drying, the pattern area is coated with printing ink in the usual way and pressed against a piece of paper. This method is difficult to carry out because the skin is generally so fragile that the print can be destroyed by the slightest carelessness. Occasionally, the finger stalls are so strong that they can be picked up on a finger and the print can be taken as it would be from a living person. However, only in rare cases is the skin on all ten digits in such good condition that this method can be used.

It often happens that large portions of the epidermis become loose, but small parts remain so firmly attached that the finger stalls cannot be removed whole. Careful scraping of the attached tissues may loosen the tips in a comparatively whole condition. If this is impossible, the part of the underlying tissues to which the finger stalls are attached is cut off, and the whole piece is mounted on a piece of plasticine. The fingerprint can then be taken with printing ink or photographed.

It is far more difficult to take a fingerprint from a dead person when the epidermis of the fingers has fallen away and cannot be found. This occurs generally with bodies that have been in the water for a long period of time. Sometimes it is possible to make out the fingerprint pattern in the remaining underskin. Only rarely is it possible to take these fingerprints with printing ink, due to very low ridges in the pattern. The only possible method is to photograph the pattern. In general, however, it can be assumed that the fingerprint pattern will have disappeared entirely because of the loosening of the skin.

It is difficult to take a palm print from a dead body, even in a case where the body has undergone little or no change. There is hardly any hope of taking a complete palm print and it is, therefore, necessary to take portions of the print on small pieces of paper or card. To simplify the identification of these prints, each piece of paper should have outlined on it a hand on which the part corresponding to the palm print is marked. In taking finger and palm prints from bodies, printing ink is the best medium because the impressions can be mounted directly onto a fingerprint card or other suitable form. These forms can later be filed with other cards. However, an alternate method may be used that employs black fingerprint powder. In some cases, the results of this method may be superior to those with printing ink. The finger or palm is lightly coated with the black powder, using a brush. The impression is obtained by lifting transparent fingerprint tape. The pieces of tape are then mounted directly onto a fingerprint card or on paper cut up into squares for attachment to the card.

In the case of palms, pieces of tape should be laid lengthwise over the whole palm area and removed one at a time. The pieces are then mounted onto a card or paper. This method is somewhat more difficult than the inking method, but it is superior in that a full impression is obtained. A condition for successful lifting is that two persons are available: one to hold the hand and one to manipulate the tape.

FINGERPRINT ENHANCEMENT USING ADOBE PHOTOSHOP®

Software such as Adobe Photoshop® and others, can be used to enhance and restore poor-quality images. While there are often good reasons to enhance photos, the process also allows for claims that the photo was manipulated. Such assertions might be used to render a photograph inadmissible in court. Therefore, it is important to retain original photos and keep a log of any digital enhancements made to the photo. The audit trail in the software itself is usually the best way to show what changes were made and what steps are necessary to recreate the original photo. It is important to clarify to the jury when testifying that the ridge detail on the print is not being manipulated when using Photoshop; it is only the background noise from the digital image that is being removed (Figure 6.7).

FINGERPRINT EXAMINER CONCLUSIONS

Over the last several years an effort has been made to improve the quality and consistency of friction ridge examination practices. The Friction Ridge Subcommittee of the Physics/Pattern Scientific Area Committee of the Organization of Scientific Area Committees (OSAC) has proposed the Standard for Friction Ridge Examination Conclusions. The following are the range of conclusions that an expert fingerprint examiner may reach in their report:

- **Source exclusion** is the conclusion that two friction ridge impressions did not originate from the same source. Source exclusion is reached when in the examiner's opinion, considering the observed data, the probability that the two impressions came from the same source is considered negligible.
- **Support for different sources** is the conclusion that the observations provide more support for the proposition that the impressions originated from different sources rather than the same source; however, there is insufficient

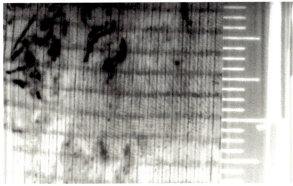

Figure 6.7 The fingerprint ridge detail in the top image was not visible. Adobe Photoshop® was used to enhance the fingerprint resulting in the bottom image which reveals the ridge detail of the latent fingerprint. Sometimes the background in a photo obscures the ridge detail. Removing or muting the background of an image can allow the ridge detail to be seen more clearly. An audit trail of all enhancements to the image was saved for future court admissibility.

support for a Source Exclusion. The degree of support may range from limited to strong or similar descriptors of the degree of support. Any use of this conclusion shall include a statement of the degree of support and the factor(s) limiting a stronger conclusion.

- ***Inconclusive/lacking support*** is the conclusion that the observations do not provide a sufficient degree of support for one proposition over the other. Any use of this conclusion shall include a statement of the factor(s) limiting a stronger conclusion.
- ***Support for same source*** is the conclusion that the observations provide more support for the proposition that the impressions originated from the same source rather than different sources; however, there is insufficient support for a Source Identification. The degree of support may range from limited to strong or similar descriptors of the degree of support. Any use of this conclusion shall include a statement of the degree of support and the factor(s) limiting a stronger conclusion.
- ***Source identification*** is the strongest degree of association between two friction ridge impressions. It is the conclusion that the observations provide extremely strong support for the proposition that the impressions originated from the same source and extremely weak support for the proposition that the impressions originated from different sources. Source Identification is reached when the friction ridge impressions have corresponding ridge detail and the examiner would not expect to see the same arrangement of details repeated in an impression that came from a different source.

When rendering one of the conclusions above, the examiner must also adhere to the following qualifications:

1. An examiner shall not assert that a source identification is the conclusion that two impressions were made by the same source or imply an individualization to the exclusion of all other sources.
2. An examiner shall not suggest that the offered conclusion is an expression of absolute certainty.

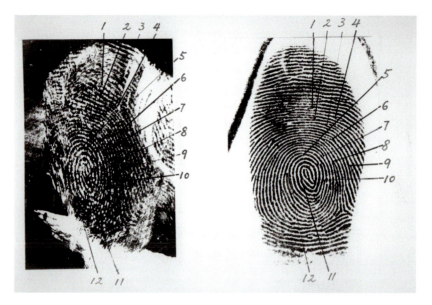

Figure 6.8 A Certified Latent Print Examiner oftentimes has to make courtroom exhibits to show members of the jury the different minutiae between the latent (left) and known (right) prints. Here the examiner used 12 unique points of comparison to conclude source identification between the latent and the known. (*Courtesy of the Institute of Forensic Science, Beijing, China.*)

3. An examiner shall not assert or imply that latent print examination is infallible or has a zero-error rate.
4. An examiner shall not cite the number of latent print comparisons performed in his or her career as a measure for the accuracy of a conclusion offered in the case at hand.
5. An examiner shall not use the expression "reasonable degree of scientific certainty" or similar assertions as a description of the confidence held in his or her conclusion.

ACE-V

ACE-V is the most common method of fingerprint examination worldwide. It is a four-step process to reach a determination on each print. The acronym stands for **A**nalysis (the examiner assesses the print to determine whether it is suitable for comparison), **C**omparison (the examiner analyses characteristics of the prints and identifies conformities between the latent and known prints), **E**valuation (the examiner reaches a conclusion by determining if a sufficient number of minutiae between the questioned and known print exist), and **V**erification (the examiner's conclusion is verified by a second examiner).

IAI CERTIFICATION

There is a great need for a practical and equitable method for identifying those fingerprint examiners who possess the required qualifications and competence to be considered qualified latent print examiners in our criminal justice system. As with other forensic disciplines, certification is based on the individual's record of qualifications as reviewed by their peers as well as on the results of a formal exam. The IAI offers a certification program in Latent Certification (www.theiai.org/latent_print.php) to become a Board Certified Latent Print Examiner (CLPE) (Figure 6.8). The IAI also offers certification in Tenprint Certification (https://theiai.org/tenprint_fingerprint.php). The Certified Tenprint Examiner compares friction ridge impressions of intentionally recorded comparisons and performs IAFIS searches (Figure 6.9).

OSAC FRICTION RIDGE SUBCOMMITTEE*

The OSAC Friction Ridge Subcommittee focuses on standards and guidelines related to the examination of friction ridge detail from the hands and feet. While there are currently no friction ridge standards published on the OSAC

---

* www.nist.gov/osac/friction-ridge-subcommittee.

Figure 6.9 Here a Tenprint examiner is comparing intentionally recorded prints of an unknown individual to a known individual.

Registry, the subcommittee has developed several standards and best practice recommendations that have been sent to Standards Development Organizations. Prior to the formation of the OSAC Friction Ridge Subcommittee, the Scientific Working Group on Friction Ridge Analysis, Study and Technology (SWGFAST) published a number of standards which are now available on the OSAC website (https://www.nist.gov/osac/friction-ridge-subcommittee).

FINGERPRINTS FROM ONLINE PHOTOS

With the proliferation of digital photos on the internet, there have been several instances of positive identifications made of individuals who posted pictures online where their hands and/or fingers are in the image with unusually high resolution views of ridge detail. Oftentimes people will post pictures to "brag" of illegal activity or even post crimes being committed in real time. While faces of perpetrators are usually left out of these photos, many times the image reveals the suspect's fingers holding drugs, stolen items, or money. These photos can sometimes be converted to IAFIS uploadable images in order to reveal the suspect's identity.

FAKE FINGERPRINTS

Over the past several years, it has been demonstrated that it is possible to create a counterfeit fingerprint using 3D print technology. These counterfeit fingerprints can be used to bypass fingerprint scanners on mobile devices as well as other biometric security systems. Although it is uncommon, it is also possible to plant a fake fingerprint at a crime scene. Investigators and attorneys need to be aware that the possibility exists that latent prints at a crime scene may be counterfeit and not from the actual suspect. There are many methods available on the internet to make artificial fingerprints in order to elude law enforcement. CSI's need to know that such a possibility exists and that analytical tests might need to be performed in order to authenticate the print.

Further Reading

Ashbaugh, David R. *Quantitative-qualitative Friction Ridge Analysis: An Introduction to Basic and Advanced Ridgeology.* CRC Press, 1999.

Daluz, Hillary Moses. *Fundamentals of Fingerprint Analysis*, 2nd edition. CRC Press, 2018.

Datta, Ashim K., et al. *Advances in Fingerprint Technology*, 3rd edition. CRC Press, 2013.

De Alcaraz-Fossoul, Josep, ed. *Technologies for Fingermark Age Estimations: A Step Forward*. Springer International Publishing, 2021.

The Fingerprint Sourcebook, U.S. Dept of Justice, National Institute of Justice by I.A.I. *Scientific Working Group on Friction Ridge Analysis, Study and Technology (SWGFAST)*. 2011.

Garrett, Brandon L. "The reliable application of fingerprint evidence." *UCLA Law Review Discourse* 66 (2018): 64.

"Latent print examination and human factors: improving the practice through a systems approach." *The Report of the Expert Working Group on Human Factors in Latent Print Analysis*, National Institute of Justice, February 2012.

Srihari, Sargur N., Harish Srinivasan, and Gang Fang. "Discriminability of fingerprints of twins." *Journal of Forensic Identification* 58.1 (2008): 109.

Ulery, Bradford T., et al. "Accuracy and reliability of forensic latent fingerprint decisions." *Proceedings of the National Academy of Sciences* 108.19 (2011): 7733–7738.

Ulery, Bradford T., et al. "Measuring what latent fingerprint examiners consider sufficient information for individualization determinations." *PloS One* 9.11 (2014): e110179.

Chapter Questions

1. Describe how fingerprints are formed at the scene of a crime.
2. You have been asked to search for fingerprints at the scene of a residential burglary. Describe where you would search for any fingerprints left behind.
3. List the three main groups of fingerprints that can be found.
4. Which of the following chemicals would be the most appropriate when attempting to locate fingerprints on the sticky side of tape?
    a) DFO.
    b) SPR.
    c) Gentian violet.
    d) Ninhydrin.
5. Which of the following is an alternative to taking inked fingerprints from suspects?
    a) CODIS.
    b) Livescan.
    c) IAFIS.
    d) NIBIN.
6. Describe the proper procedure for collecting and preserving a latent fingerprint.
7. You have been asked to collect a knife from the crime scene with a visible fingerprint in blood. Describe how you would package the item up.
8. Can fingerprints be lifted from human skin? If so, describe one of the techniques.
9. What are auricle morphometry and cheiloscopy?
10. What are the two types of certifications available to fingerprint examiners?

CHAPTER 7

Blood, Forensic Biology, and DNA

It can be said that of all the significant advances made in forensic science during the past few decades, forensic DNA has made the greatest strides. DNA (deoxyribonucleic acid) is present at most crime scenes. It can be used to determine the identity of unknown human remains, tie a suspect or victim to a crime scene, establish paternity, and identify the unknown perpetrator to a cold case. Today, forensic DNA typing plays a significant role in criminal investigations and has revolutionized the ability to prosecute criminals and exonerate the innocent.

A WORD OF CAUTION!

Before discussing any testing procedures concerning blood and other biological fluids, some remarks are appropriate about the dangers of blood-borne diseases, e.g., hepatitis B, hepatitis C, and HIV. Individuals working around wet or dried blood at crime scenes, autopsies, and in crime laboratories where whole blood or other biological specimens are present are advised to use universal precautions. These include personal protective equipment (PPE) such as Tyvek™ suits, lab coats, gloves, masks, and goggles/face shields. The important thing to remember is that the type of barrier protection should be appropriate for the type of exposure anticipated. Persons who routinely work with blood and blood products should receive hepatitis vaccinations.

Surgical gloves should be worn when working with any biological products: blood, saliva, semen, etc. (Nitrile gloves are available to those with latex allergies.) Cut-resistant gloves should also be worn when scraping an item for DNA evidence with a razor blade or using sharp tools. Smoking, eating, or drinking in areas that contain these items is not to be permitted. When specific questions arise about the proper handling of biological evidence, crime lab forensic biology personnel are good resources. Working around biological samples of unknown sources has a potential risk, however, with appropriate care and caution, those risks can be minimized.

Guidelines for handling biological materials should be posted and discussed with personnel who must handle these materials. Periodic briefing, or annual "Right to Know" training to remind personnel how to handle this type of evidence is important. Appropriate procedures must be taken for the disposal of biological evidence as well.

CONTAMINATION

Contamination is a big concern when it comes to DNA and biological evidence. Webster's dictionary defines contamination as the "act of making impure or unsuitable by contact or mixture with something unclean or foreign." When collecting evidence or processing a crime scene, it is critical to eliminate, or at least, minimize the accidental transfer of DNA as much as possible.

Contamination can occur between items of evidence; it is for this reason that collected items of evidence should be packaged separately. Commingled items that are packaged together run the risk of biological material being transferred from one item to the other. Known and questioned samples also should *never* be packaged together. One should ensure that any tools or equipment used to collect or process evidence don't become a source of contamination

DOI: 10.4324/9780429272011-9

as well. If disposables cannot be used, tools should be wiped down with a 10% bleach solution, followed by 70% ethanol.

Contamination can also occur when a crime scene investigator inadvertently deposits their DNA on an item of evidence. Without a mask, this can occur by coughing, sneezing, or talking at a crime scene (or in the lab). Handling or touching an item without gloves can also leave behind trace amounts of epithelial (skin) cells that could contaminate any DNA profiles that are subsequently developed. Any individual entering a crime scene (including police brass) should submit their DNA sample to the testing laboratory for quality assurance measures. Elimination samples, such as these, are NOT eligible to be uploaded to the DNA database (i.e., **CO**mbined **D**NA **I**ndex **S**ystem (CODIS)) but are used by the laboratory solely for in-house quality control. If elimination samples are not taken from police officers or crime scene personnel who may have inadvertently contaminated evidence, then any unknown DNA profiles developed could potentially be uploaded to CODIS.

ISO 18385—FORENSIC DNA GRADE

The prevention of contamination is one of the major challenges in forensic DNA analysis. ISO 18385 is an international standard that specifies requirements for the production of consumables and reagents used in the collection, storage, and analysis of biological material for forensic DNA purposes. This includes items such as swabs, containers, tubes, and plasticware. The "forensic DNA grade" standard was created for manufacturers of forensic products to produce verifiable DNA-free products to reduce inadvertent contamination. When purchasing forensic products for use at crime scenes, it is recommended to buy products under ISO 18385 certification to reduce human-to-product contamination.*

PRESUMPTIVE TESTS FOR BLOOD†

Scenes of violent crimes often contain minute quantities of blood that, because of their small size, may not be readily noticed. Presumptive blood tests (sometimes called catalytic tests) may be used to search for these small amounts of blood. These chemical tests are also useful at scenes where the suspect cleaned up the crime scene or to differentiate between blood and other stains (e.g., rust, lipstick, ketchup, etc.).

Historically, several chemicals have been used as presumptive tests to determine the presence of blood: leucomalachite green, phenolphthalin (also known as Kastle-Meyer reagent), ortho-tolidine, and tetramethylbenzidine. All are presumptive or screening tests. Another presumptive test, luminol, is described later.

Presumptive tests are color spot tests that react in the presence of hemoglobin (the oxygen-carrying molecule found in blood). They are extremely sensitive and can easily detect very small quantities of blood. The test results are easy to perform and lend themselves to use by crime scene technicians in the field. Interpretation of test results is critical because other materials can give false-positive results. A positive result can result from either the presence of human or animal blood, as well as a variety of other false positives such as plant materials that contain peroxidase.

Chemical kits used for presumptive tests are available through law enforcement supply companies, or bulk chemicals may be purchased at considerable savings from chemical supply houses. Of the above-mentioned tests, phenolphthalin and leucomalachite green are generally considered the most specific while ortho-tolidine and tetramethylbenzidine are the most sensitive. Generally, the phenolphthalin, or Kastle-Mayer test, is a good overall choice. The test may be conducted on filter paper or on cotton-tipped swabs. After collection of the sample, a drop of Kastle-Mayer reagent is added followed by a drop of 3% hydrogen peroxide. The presence of hemoglobin causes, or catalyzes, an oxidative reaction to occur resulting in a pink color change‡ (Figure 7.1).

The luminol test is easily used in the field and very useful for searching large areas for blood, particularly if the area has been cleaned up. A drawback of the test is that the room must be dark because blood reacts with luminol by giving off

---

* The "Phantom of Heilbronn" (www.iso.org/news/2016/07/Ref2094.html) is a story about a female "serial killer" who worked in a consumable manufacturing facility. She was inadvertently contaminating consumables being used at multiple crime scenes.
† For an excellent review of presumptive tests, see Cox, M. "A study of the sensitivity and specificity of four presumptive tests for blood." *Journal of Forensic Sciences* 36.5 (1991): 1503–1511.
‡ A video of the test can be found at www.youtube.com/watch?v=ZvhN9DDm9iI.

Figure 7.1 The Kastle-Mayer test showing a positive test for blood. (*Courtesy of the LA County Sheriff's Department.*)

light, a process called chemiluminescence.* The reagent is applied with a spray bottle and the glow given off is sometimes very faint; therefore, the area must be completely darkened in order to visualize the luminescence. The test works best on older stains. In some instances, outlines of shoes and even marks caused by mopping or wiping up an area can be visualized by means of this test. At times, pinpoint glowing is observed, which is not the result of bloodstains; with a positive test, whole areas are seen as glowing. Bleach can also yield false-positive results, so care must be taken in interpreting results. Bluestar® reagent is also an effective latent blood detection tool that can be used at crime scenes and does not have any deleterious effects on DNA testing.† Its advantages over luminol include that it is nontoxic, total darkness is not required, and it has stronger luminescence, longer lasting reactions, and higher sensitivity.

Searching for Bloodstains

A dried, but relatively fresh bloodstain is generally reddish-brown in color and glossy in contrast to, for example, rust stains. In a very thin layer, the color may be grayish-green. The gloss slowly disappears under the action of sunlight, heat, wind, or as the result of an attempt to wash it away. Bloodstains can assume other colors from red to brown or black, or they may appear green, blue, or grayish-white. The color and the time required for the change depend on the underlying material: the change is quicker on metal surfaces and slower on textiles. With some types of cloth the blood soaks into the threads; with others it lies on the pile. The surface gloss is often less marked on fabric. Bloodstains on wallpaper may show surprising colors because of the blood's taking up color from the paper. Certain other stains, composed of pigment, rust, tobacco, snuff, urine, feces, coffee, and other substances can easily be confused with bloodstains. In searching for bloodstains, stains should not be classified according to color because a stain that appears to deviate from the normal character of a bloodstain may be composed of blood, whereas one that resembles blood may be composed of some other substance. When searching for stains it is convenient to allow the light from a flashlight to fall obliquely against the surface under examination. Sometimes a stain shows up better against a surface when it is illuminated with colored light. Lasers are also very effective in locating biological stains and makes biological evidence easier to see than with an alternate light source‡ (Figure 7.2).

---

* Blood does *not* fluoresce, and adding a blue light to search for blood stains is unnecessary. Other biological fluids, however, such as semen, saliva, and urine do fluoresce under UV alternate light sources.
† Jakovich, Cathy J. "STR analysis following latent blood detection by luminol, fluorescein, and Bluestar." *Journal of Forensic Identification* 57.2 (2007): 193.
‡ The Dual77+ Forensic Laser allows for the bright visualization of bodily fluid stains and operates at a wavelength of 445nm or at 520nm.

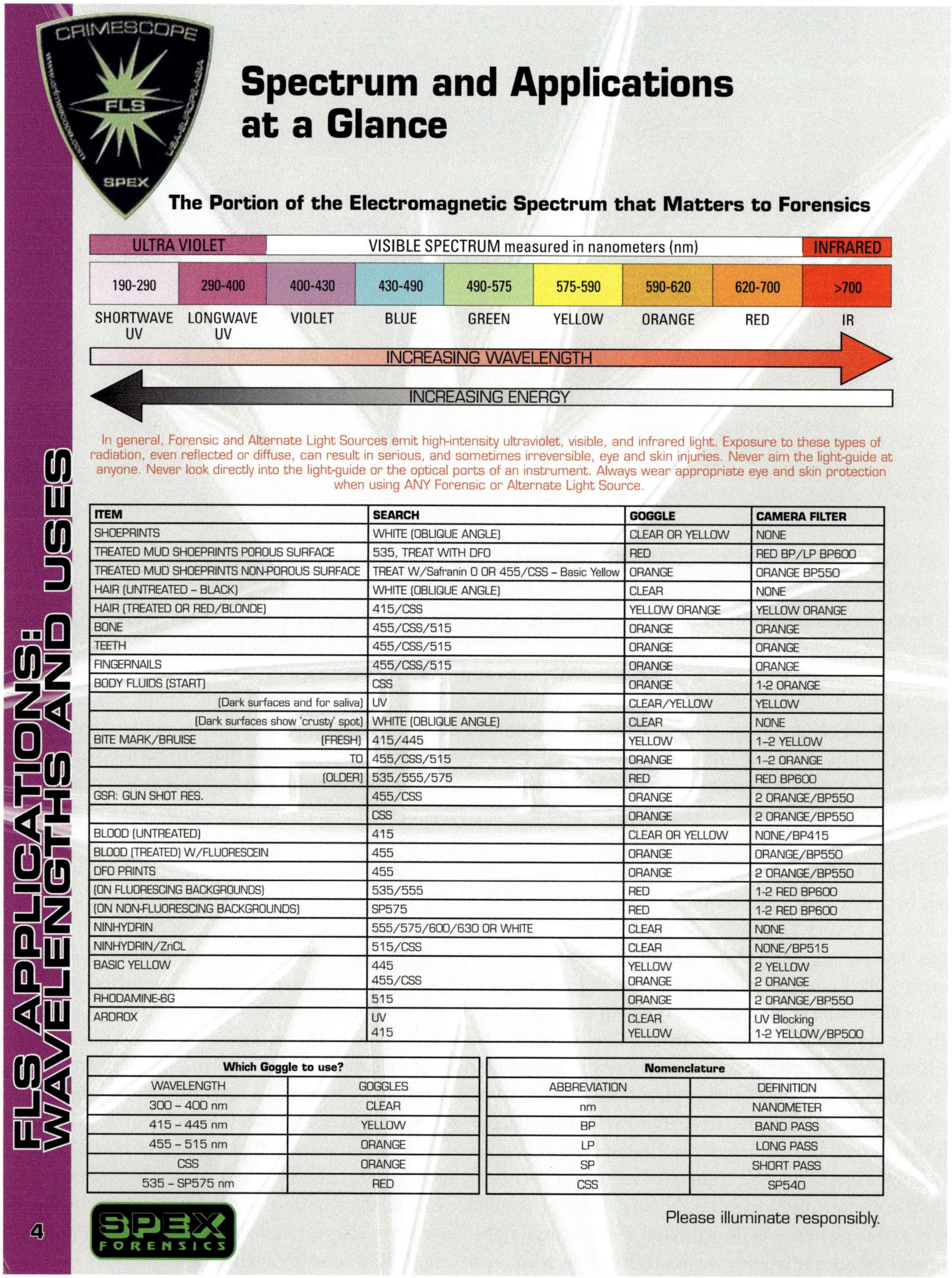

Spectrum and Applications at a Glance

The Portion of the Electromagnetic Spectrum that Matters to Forensics

ULTRA VIOLET		VISIBLE SPECTRUM measured in nanometers (nm)						INFRARED
190-290	290-400	400-430	430-490	490-575	575-590	590-620	620-700	>700
SHORTWAVE UV	LONGWAVE UV	VIOLET	BLUE	GREEN	YELLOW	ORANGE	RED	IR

INCREASING WAVELENGTH →
← INCREASING ENERGY

In general, Forensic and Alternate Light Sources emit high-intensity ultraviolet, visible, and infrared light. Exposure to these types of radiation, even reflected or diffuse, can result in serious, and sometimes irreversible, eye and skin injuries. Never aim the light-guide at anyone. Never look directly into the light-guide or the optical ports of an instrument. Always wear appropriate eye and skin protection when using ANY Forensic or Alternate Light Source.

FLS APPLICATIONS: WAVELENGTHS AND USES

ITEM	SEARCH	GOGGLE	CAMERA FILTER
SHOEPRINTS	WHITE (OBLIQUE ANGLE)	CLEAR OR YELLOW	NONE
TREATED MUD SHOEPRINTS POROUS SURFACE	535, TREAT WITH DFO	RED	RED BP/LP BP600
TREATED MUD SHOEPRINTS NON-POROUS SURFACE	TREAT W/Safranin O OR 455/CSS – Basic Yellow	ORANGE	ORANGE BP550
HAIR (UNTREATED – BLACK)	WHITE (OBLIQUE ANGLE)	CLEAR	NONE
HAIR (TREATED OR RED/BLONDE)	415/CSS	YELLOW ORANGE	YELLOW ORANGE
BONE	455/CSS/515	ORANGE	ORANGE
TEETH	455/CSS/515	ORANGE	ORANGE
FINGERNAILS	455/CSS/515	ORANGE	ORANGE
BODY FLUIDS (START)	CSS	ORANGE	1-2 ORANGE
(Dark surfaces and for saliva)	UV	CLEAR/YELLOW	YELLOW
(Dark surfaces show 'crusty' spot)	WHITE (OBLIQUE ANGLE)	CLEAR	NONE
BITE MARK/BRUISE (FRESH)	415/445	YELLOW	1-2 YELLOW
TO	455/CSS/515	ORANGE	1-2 ORANGE
(OLDER)	535/555/575	RED	RED BP600
GSR: GUN SHOT RES.	455/CSS	ORANGE	2 ORANGE/BP550
	CSS	ORANGE	2 ORANGE/BP550
BLOOD (UNTREATED)	415	CLEAR OR YELLOW	NONE/BP415
BLOOD (TREATED) W/FLUORESCEIN	455	ORANGE	ORANGE/BP550
DFO PRINTS	455	ORANGE	2 ORANGE/BP550
(ON FLUORESCING BACKGROUNDS)	535/555	RED	1-2 RED BP600
(ON NON-FLUORESCING BACKGROUNDS)	SP575	RED	1-2 RED BP600
NINHYDRIN	555/575/600/630 OR WHITE	CLEAR	NONE
NINHYDRIN/ZnCL	515/CSS	CLEAR	NONE/BP515
BASIC YELLOW	445	YELLOW	2 YELLOW
	455/CSS	ORANGE	2 ORANGE
RHODAMINE-6G	515	ORANGE	2 ORANGE/BP550
ARDROX	UV	CLEAR	UV Blocking
	415	YELLOW	1-2 YELLOW/BP500

Which Goggle to use?

WAVELENGTH	GOGGLES
300 – 400 nm	CLEAR
415 – 445 nm	YELLOW
455 – 515 nm	ORANGE
CSS	ORANGE
535 – SP575 nm	RED

Nomenclature

ABBREVIATION	DEFINITION
nm	NANOMETER
BP	BAND PASS
LP	LONG PASS
SP	SHORT PASS
CSS	SP540

Please illuminate responsibly.

Figure 7.2 This chart from SPEX Forensics shows various forensic items and appropriate Alternate Light Source (ALS) setting combinations. Also listed are the correct goggles and camera filters to view and photograph good quality images when using the ALS. (*Photo credit: SPEX Forensics.*)

Occasionally, the assailant will clean up the scene. Furniture is straightened, damage is concealed, and blood is washed off—all for the purpose of concealing the crime, delaying its discovery, and/or destroying evidence. The search of the scene should therefore also be extended to places that are not in direct view. A criminal with bloody fingers may, for example, have opened a drawer, leafed through papers, grasped a doorknob, or a handrail. Washbasins, garbage pails, and similar items should be given close attention. Towels, draperies, and other fabrics that may have served to wipe off blood should also be examined. If a floor has been washed to remove bloodstains, blood may possibly be found in its cracks, in joints between tiles, under the edges of linoleum, behind floorboards and electric socket plates, and in similar places. An item that is devoid of blood that is believed to have been touched or handled by a perpetrator should still be swabbed and submitted for DNA testing. The search for blood on clothes must be carried out carefully and systematically. Even if blood has been washed off the more conspicuous parts, stains may still be found on the seams, on the lining, inside the sleeves, in pockets, and so forth. Stains that have been diffused by washing may be concentrated in the laboratory. Suspects may also have bloodstains not only on their clothes but also on their bodies. Clothing can also be scraped with a razor blade to collect skin (i.e., epithelial) cells to determine who might have been wearing a particular garment (Figure 7.3). Another method for collecting skin cells from different items of evidence is through the use of the M-Vac® System. The M-Vac is a wet-vacuum DNA collection tool that collects DNA from porous and rough objects or surfaces (Figure 7.4).

In the open air, the search for bloodstains is often more difficult. Rain, snow, sun, and wind may have obliterated the stains of a blood trail. The blood trail may have changed its color in a very short time because of the character of the ground. If the ground gives an impression of dampness in certain areas, these parts should be given special attention, as should blades of grass, leaves, branches of trees, etc.

Objects on which the presence of bloodstains are suspected should be examined very carefully in cracks, joints, and seams because bloodstains can sometimes seep into such places, even after the object has been washed or cleaned. It should also be remembered that just because an item does not have blood on it, does not mean it is insignificant. Remember, the absence of evidence is not evidence of absence!

Description and Recording of Bloodstains

In the case of bloodstains, a description should be made of their form, color, size, position, and direction. The best way to preserve the appearance of bloodstains is through photography. Photographs depicting overall, medium-range, and close-up views should be made. A scale should be included for the close-up photographs.

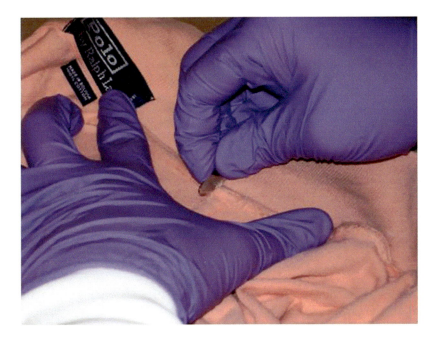

Figure 7.3 A sterile razor blade can be used to scrape an article of clothing for skin cells for DNA typing.

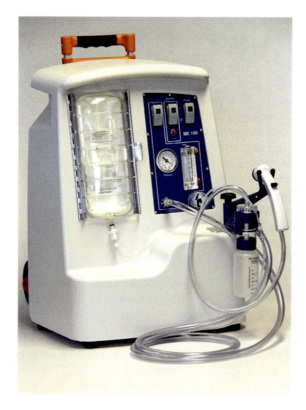

Figure 7.4 The M-Vac system is a wet-vacuum DNA collection tool that can collect DNA from many different types of surfaces, including a victim's water-soaked clothing. (*Photo Credit: M-Vac Systems, Inc.,* www.m-vac.com/.)

Besides photography, a rough sketch or worksheet is useful to show the general appearance of the stains as well as their relative position to other areas of the crime scene.

Collection and Preservation of Bloodstains

Of all the common types of evidence found at crime scenes, blood is an excellent source of DNA. It is a certainty, however, that wet bloodstains packaged in airtight containers such as plastic bags will yield poor DNA results after an extended period of time. Any type of preservation technique that hastens putrefaction or mold growth should be avoided. Thus, storing bloodstains that are still damp in airtight containers or warm environments should be avoided. Conversely, an air-dried sample stored in a paper bag at room temperature will retain its evidentiary usefulness for a significantly longer time. Once blood evidence has been found it must be collected and preserved in a manner to achieve maximum benefit. All too often improper collection and preservation of this type of evidence make the crime laboratory's work difficult and sometimes impossible.

Preservation of blood and other biological evidence may require special handling in jurisdictions with case law dealing with the preservation of such evidence. Biological evidence, i.e., blood, semen, saliva, and so forth, does deteriorate with time. Drying the specimens slows down this deterioration. Some courts have held that the police have an affirmative duty to preserve evidence for defendants that can prove their innocence. Failure to do this may result in the evidence being excluded and, in some instances, the entire case being dismissed.

Removal of Biological Stains

Biological stains may be present in a liquid, damp, or completely dry state. Depending on the circumstance, different procedures may be used. The easiest method of collection of wet biological fluid is to place an absorbent piece of material into the liquid. The recommended procedure is to use sterile cotton-tipped swabs that can be used to collect both wet and dried stains.

 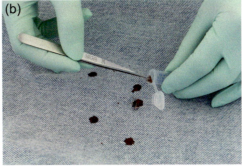

Figure 7.5 Different collection techniques of bloodstains in the crime lab. (a) Sterile cotton swabs can be moistened with a drop of sterile water to swab a dried bloodstain or (b) the bloodstain can be cut out for and placed in an 1.5mL Eppendorf tube for DNA extraction. (*Courtesy of LA County Sheriff's Department.*)

The cotton swab is placed in the liquid and allowed to become saturated. The swab can then be left to air-dry and then placed in a coin envelope or a container with a desiccant. The envelopes and containers should be marked to indicate where the specimen came from and who collected it. This is especially important when multiple blood samples are collected.[*] Most biological material found at crime scenes is dried. Collection of dried specimens may be accomplished in a variety of different methods. It may be collected on a cotton swab moistened with sterile distilled water. After the sample is collected and dried, the swab can be placed into an envelope and marked. For very small stains, it is best to concentrate the sample on one area of the swab, rather than spread it around the entire surface of the swab. Another method is to cut the entire stain out (Figure 7.5a and b).

Bloodstained Objects

Generally, it is best to submit the entire bloodstained object or item to the laboratory rather than remove the blood. The location of the object must be carefully noted and photographed. If blood on the object appears loose and likely to flake off, it should be collected and packaged separately before packaging the item of interest.

Often, it is not feasible to submit an entire large item of bloodstained evidence, for example, a bloodstained carpet or mattress, to the laboratory. There are two ways to collect blood in such instances. The first is to follow the already outlined procedure of using the moistened cotton swab. The second is simply to cut out a portion of the item containing the bloodstain. The cutting is then placed in an appropriate package and marked.

Species Testing

Species testing is used to determine what species a bloodstain came from. Approximately two dozen different animal antisera are commercially available for use in the species origin test. For criminal cases, the most often used antisera are human and domestic animal antisera such as dog, cat, cow, horse, deer, and so on. Differentiating closely related species of animals may sometimes be difficult. Species determination is also useful in animal poaching cases, animal cruelty cases, or trading in endangered species.[†]

Semen-stained Evidence Semen, or seminal fluid, stains are usually found on bedding, undergarments, clothing, tissues, condoms, and other evidence involved in sex-related crimes. An alternate light source (or laser) is often used to locate semen stains due to semen's fluorescent properties (Figure 7.6). Once a possible semen stain is located, a presumptive test is performed to determine if the stain is presumptively positive for semen. This is done by testing for the presence of acid phosphatase (AP), an enzyme secreted by the prostate gland and found in large amounts in semen. The AP test is a color spot test that changes from clear to purple (Figure 7.7).

---

[*] A simple practice is to label the item using your initials followed by a number, e.g., BF-1, BF-2, BF-3, etc. Field notes would indicate the location of each item.
[†] The U.S. Fish & Wildlife Service Forensics Laboratory (www.fws.gov/lab/) is the only lab in the world dedicated to crimes against wildlife. This lab is similar to other forensic labs, except that the victim is an animal.

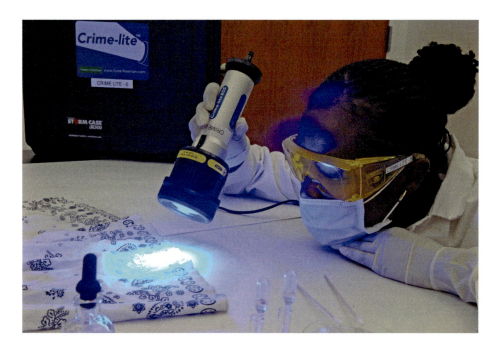

Figure 7.6 The Crime-lite 80s is an alternate light source (ALS) that can reveal semen stains by causing them to fluoresce. When light of a certain color and frequency strikes a semen stain, the stain returns light of a different color and frequency. To visualize the fluorescence, one must use a filter (i.e., orange goggles) to block the intense blue light and to visualize the fluorescence. (*Courtesy of LA County Sheriff's Department.*)

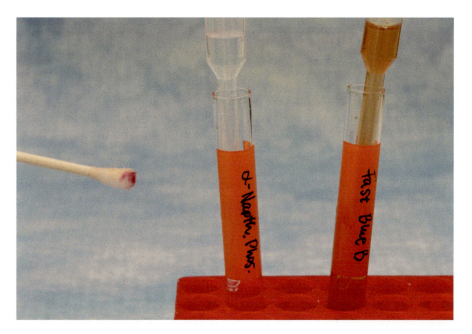

Figure 7.7 A positive presumptive test for the presence of acid phosphatase, an enzyme found in large concentrations in semen. (*Courtesy of LA County Sheriff's Department.*)

After an item of evidence is screened for the presence of AP, a confirmatory test is required to report the presence of semen. This can be done either by microscopic visualization of stained spermatozoa or an immuno-chromatographic lateral flow strip test which is specific for human semenogelin.*

---

* Independent Forensics (www.ifi-test.com/) manufactures a Rapid Stain Identification Series (RSID) for semen and other bodily fluids.

Forensic DNA Typing

DNA typing is capable of eliminating suspects as well as incriminating them. However, to give meaning to biological stains collected at a crime scene, DNA samples from victims and suspects must be routinely submitted to the crime laboratory along with the evidence. Elimination samples from consensual partners, people with legitimate access to crime scenes, crime scene investigators, EMS, and other individuals whose DNA might be present at a scene should also be submitted to the lab for testing. It is important to collect DNA specimens appropriately with the proper collection container. **Buccal swabs** (swabs from the inside of the cheek) are an excellent alternative to collecting blood samples. Commercial kits are available for this purpose.*

DNA typing is based on our genetic makeup. Anyone who has attended a sporting event or been in a large crowd of people recognizes the obvious: people look different. Differences are manifested by gender, race, stature, hair color, eye color, and shape of facial features, to name a few of the common features. The fact is that people can easily recognize others through some subjective mental process.

We can also recognize family traits among brothers and sisters, parents and children, and sometimes even more distant familial relationships. How often have people commented that a son looks just like his father or mother or that two siblings look alike? These family characteristics can be seen over and over in family lineage.

An individual's physical appearance and family traits are a manifestation of the biochemical blueprint and building blocks that make people unique. The notion of differences and similarities in individuals has its scientific basis in the study of genetics. Genetics' roots go back to the mid-19th century when Gregor Mendel suggested that genes controlled factors influencing heredity. During the next 150 years, major strides were made in the study of genetics, genes, chromosomes, and DNA.

DNA is the biochemical key to differentiating uniqueness among individuals (except for identical twins). It has been called the chemical messenger in that it conveys genetic information that is the basis of the way individual living things take shape, grow, and reproduce.

Pictorially, the DNA molecule resembles a twisted ladder or double helix. The steps within the ladder consist of four chemical subunits or bases: guanine (G), adenine (A), thymine (T), and cytosine (C). The bases pair in predictable ways—A always with T and G always with C—and form the steps or rungs of the double-stranded DNA helix. The combinations of the A-T and G-C are referred to as base pairs. Over three billion base pairs are contained in human DNA; however, only small portions of these base pairs determine unique traits between persons and are of forensic interest.

DNA is folded into microscopic bundles called chromosomes and exists in all cells that contain nuclei. DNA is not present in red blood cells because these cells have no nuclei; white blood cells, however, contain DNA. DNA is present in blood, semen, tissues, bone marrow, hair, saliva, urine, and tooth pulp. Each of these samples has the potential to yield DNA typing results.

Forensic biologists are able to unravel the DNA code and examine pieces of DNA to look for similarities and differences between individuals. For forensic DNA purposes, a PCR (polymerase chain reaction) procedure is used. The methodology is known as **short tandem repeat** (STR) analysis.

PCR-based Technology

The **polymerase chain reaction** (PCR) is a technology that copies short segments of DNA millions of times in a process that resembles how DNA duplicates itself naturally in the body. (Some have described this process as the equivalent of a biological Xerox machine.) PCR is a powerful technology because it can be applied to any tissue specimen, no matter how small, or old, and produces millions of copies within a few hours. After extracting the DNA from the cells, the PCR process consists of initially separating the DNA double helix into two strands by heating the sample. A PCR reaction mixture is then added containing DNA primers (short segments of DNA that flank the target sequence of DNA to be copied), DNA polymerase (an enzyme that catalyzes the reaction), and the four nucleotides

---

* See, for example, Bode Technology Group, Buccal DNA Collector (www.bodetech.com/pages/bode-buccal-dna-collection-systems). Investigators should consult with their forensic science laboratories to determine which sample collection method is acceptable to the crime lab.

A, C, T, and G. This mixture contains all the ingredients necessary to copy both of the original DNA strands that were separated. The procedure is performed in an instrument called a thermal cycler and is typically repeated for 26–30 cycles, doubling the amount of DNA after each cycle (Figure 7.8). After the PCR process, the mixture of DNA fragments is separated through a process called capillary electrophoresis (Figure 7.9a and b). A very thin capillary is used to perform DNA separation, allowing the mixture of DNA fragments to be separated based on size. A laser then "reads" the DNA fragments and software converts the electronic data into an electropherogram.

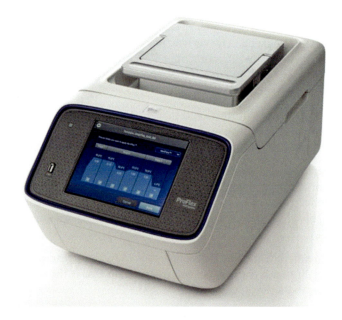

Figure 7.8 A thermal cycler heats and cools a sample for predefined set amounts of time allowing the PCR process to proceed. Each cycle roughly doubles the amount of DNA present. (*Photo Credit: ThermoFisher, ProFlex 96-well PCR thermal cycler.*)

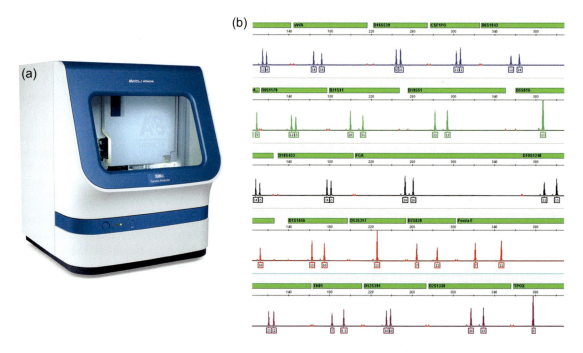

Figure 7.9 (a) This ThermoFisher 3500xl Genetic Analyzer contains multiple capillaries that allow for multiple samples to be typed in a single injection. (b) The data produced from the Genetic Analyzer results in an electropherogram, or DNA profile, that can be compared to other knowns and unknowns. (*Photo Credit: ThermoFisher.*)

MITOCHONDRIAL DNA

Another type of DNA typing is called mitochondrial DNA (mtDNA). Mitochondria are found in the cytoplasm of most cells. They play an essential part in generating the energy necessary for cell function. Mitochondrial DNA is contained within each mitochondrion. This distinct source of DNA differs from the DNA found in the nucleus of cells (nuclear DNA) in several respects:

- mtDNA is a much smaller molecule (and is circular).
- mtDNA is only inherited maternally.
- mtDNA is present within a cell in multiple copies because there are many mitochondria located in a particular cell and many copies of mtDNA within each mitochondrion. The actual copy number varies with cell type, depending on the energy requirements of the cell. For example, 20 to 25% of a liver cell is composed of mitochondria, whereas 50% of the volume of a cardiac cell comprises mitochondria. Nuclear DNA is only present in two copies per cell (one copy in the case of an egg or sperm cell).

Mitochondrial DNA typing has several applications in criminal investigations. It can be used as an investigative tool for the identification of missing persons because it is possible to use the mother, sibling, or any maternal relative as a reference source since they possess identical mtDNA types. In the case of nuclear DNA, this is only possible if a person has an identical twin or if multiple nuclear genetic profiles are typed from relatives in a process called kinship analysis. In certain cases, DNA is degraded due to environmental insults, aging, or some other factor limiting the quantity of DNA extracted. Thus, it is incapable of producing a typing result. The high copy number of mtDNA means a higher likelihood of survival of intact sequences and success with samples that have little or no nuclear DNA to begin with.

Y-STRS

Y-STRs are found in males because only males possess a Y chromosome (females have two X chromosomes.) Cases in which Y-STR testing might be used are those that involve very high levels of female DNA mixed with small amounts of male DNA or where the number of men involved in a gang rape is unknown. Although Y-STR testing can prove quite valuable in certain types of cases, the results are of a lower power of discrimination than autosomal STRs. Y-STR haplotype frequency estimates can be determined at www.yhrd.org by entering the Y-STR profile. Y-STRs can also be used in paternity testing, ancestry determinations, and genealogy research since paternal grandfathers, fathers, uncles, and sons of an unknown male all share the same Y-STRs.

CODIS*

CODIS is the acronym for the **COmbined DNA Index System**, an FBI-sponsored initiative similar in concept to the Integrated Automated Fingerprint Identification System. The DNA profile, which consists of one or two alleles at 24 CODIS Core loci, is stored in the database. CODIS generates investigative leads in cases in which biological evidence is recovered from the crime scene. Hits made among profiles in the forensic database can link crimes together. Based upon a hit confirmation, police from multiple jurisdictions can coordinate their investigations and share the leads they developed independently. Matches made between the forensic unknown and convicted offender databases, which contain DNA profiles of individuals convicted of certain crimes, provide investigators with the identity of the DNA source.

Before CODIS, forensic scientists could manually compare DNA results to determine if there was a match. Now, as a result of CODIS, there are an increasing number of "cold hits," that is matches of unknown forensic samples to known convicted offenders and case-to-case hits.

CODIS has several different indexes of DNA records, each with its own rules and requirements:

- **Forensic Unknown Index.** This index contains DNA profiles generated from crime scene evidence. To be classified as a forensic unknown, the DNA samples must be attributed to the putative perpetrator. Items taken directly from the suspect are not forensic unknowns and are not eligible for upload to the National DNA Index System (NDIS).

---

* http://www.fbi.gov/services/laboratory/biometric-analysis/codis/codis-and-ndis-fact-sheet.

The unknown index is searched against the Offender Indexes at high stringency (i.e., all alleles are required to match between two DNA profiles with only one mismatch).

- **Forensic Partial and Forensic Mixture Indexes**. DNA profiles obtained from crime scene evidence could be partially degraded and/or contain DNA from more than one person. These profiles may also contain less than the required CODIS Core Loci. These indexes are also searched against the offender indexes but at moderate stringency (i.e., the two DNA profiles can contain a different number of alleles).
- **Convicted Offender Index**. All states now have legislation that mandates convicted offenders provide DNA samples for DNA typing. DNA results are stored in each state's DNA offender index and in NDIS.
- **Arrestee Index.** States that are authorized to collect and enter DNA samples from arrestees can upload profiles into this index.
- **Detainee Index**. Consists of DNA profiles from non-US persons detained under the authority of the United States and required to provide a DNA sample.
- **Legal Index.** The Legal Index consists of DNA profiles of persons whose DNA samples are collected under applicable legal authority.
- **Missing Person Index.** This index consists of DNA records of missing persons.
- **Relatives of Missing Person Index.** Consists of DNA records from the biological relatives of individuals reported missing who may voluntarily provide DNA samples. Since DNA is passed from parents to children, the most beneficial sample is from a biological parent, sibling, or child.
- **Unidentified Human Remains Index.** Contains DNA records of recovered deceased persons/body parts whose identities are unknown.

Y-STR and mtDNA profiles are only searched with the missing person-related indexes.

MISSING PERSONS

Over 600,000 people go missing in the U.S. every year. 4400 unidentified bodies are recovered each year, with about 1000 of those bodies remaining unidentified after one year. The National Missing and Unidentified Persons System (NamUs)* is funded by the National Institute of Justice (NIJ) and is a clearinghouse for unidentified remains and missing person records. NamUs provides technology, forensic testing, and investigative support to resolve missing persons and unidentified remains cases. It includes links to medical examiner and coroner offices, law enforcement agencies, and victim assistance groups. The NamUs system consists of two different databases. The first database contains case reports of unidentified remains entered by medical examiners and coroners throughout the United States, Guam, and Puerto Rico. Unidentified persons are people who died and whose bodies have not been identified. Anyone can search this database using characteristics such as sex, race, distinct body features, and dental information. The second database contains case reports of missing persons entered by law enforcement and the public; before it appears as a case in NamUs, the information is verified. Relatives of missing persons can also submit case information directly to the NamUs website. When a new missing person or unidentified decedent case is entered into NamUs, the system automatically performs cross-matching comparisons between the databases, searching for matches or similarities between cases. NamUs also provides free DNA testing and other forensic services. Close relatives (i.e., parents, children, siblings) of the missing can submit DNA reference samples to aid in the identification of unknown human remains through kinship analysis.

MASSIVELY PARALLEL SEQUENCING/NEXT GENERATION SEQUENCING

Massively parallel sequencing, or next generation sequencing (NGS), provides more information-rich data than capillary electrophoresis-based DNA methods. NGS is a high throughput approach to Forensic DNA sequencing. This technology uses parallel platforms for sequencing 1 million to 43 billion short reads per run and can generate autosomal STR, Y-STR, and X-STR allele calls; identity markers; phenotypic markers; and biogeographical ancestry markers for each sample all at the same time. As more of the forensic DNA community adopt this new technology, all kinds of investigative leads for different types of cases can be generated. As the development of these predictive

* https://namus.nij.ojp.gov/.

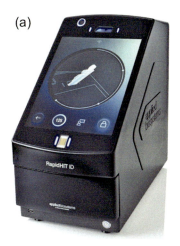 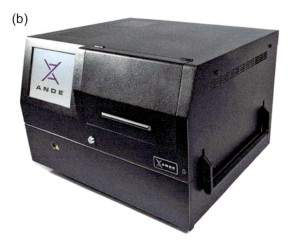

Figure 7.10 The two NDIS-approved Rapid DNA systems are (a) ThermoFisher's RapidHIT ID (www.thermofisher.com) system and (b) ANDE's 6C Rapid DNA Instrument (www.ande.com/).

methodologies continues, physical traits such as hair color, eye color, and biogeographical ancestry will become increasingly useful to help solve crime.*

RAPID DNA

Rapid DNA is a term used to describe the fully automated process of DNA typing from a reference sample. Rapid DNA instruments are capable of producing a CODIS DNA profile in under two hours and querying CODIS to search for unsolved crimes while a qualifying arrestee is in police custody during the booking process (Figure 7.10a and b). These Rapid DNA systems also help police expedite DNA testing and exonerate those who have been wrongfully arrested.

FORENSIC GENETIC GENEALOGY

Forensic Genetic Genealogy (FGG) is the use of DNA analysis combined with traditional genealogy research to generate investigative leads for unsolved crimes. FGG differs from STR DNA typing in both the type and technology that is used, as well as the database (i.e., GEDmatch) that is searched. FGG examines single nucleotide polymorphisms (SNPs) to identify shared blocks of DNA between a forensic sample and the sample donor's potential relatives. Closer relatives will have larger shared blocks of identical DNA than more distant ones. Due to predictive levels of recombination between generations, it is then possible to analyze these shared blocks of genetic information and make inferences regarding potential familial relationships. A genetic association to a shared common ancestor then requires traditional genealogy research and other investigative work to determine the true relationship of any genetic association. Once a suspect is generated based on this association, STR DNA typing must be performed to confirm that the forensic sample originated from the suspect.†

Case Review

Joseph James DeAngelo Jr., the infamous "Golden State Killer," was a former police officer who committed at least 13 murders, 50 rapes, and over 100 burglaries across California between 1973 and 1986. DeAngelo was responsible for at least three crime sprees, each of which was given a different nickname in the press, before it became known three decades later that they were all committed by the same person.

---

* Verogen's (www.verogen.com) MiSeq FGx Sequencing System is the first NGS system for forensic and human identity applications.
† U.S. Dept of Justice, www.justice.gov.

In 2001, DNA testing pointed to the fact that the "East Area Rapist" and the "Original Night Stalker" were the same person, however, authorities did not know his identity as his DNA was not present in CODIS. Years later in 2017, investigators and professional genealogists used SNP data from evidence samples to identify members of DeAngelo's family through FGG using the GEDmatch (www.gedmatch.com) database.[*]

In April of 2018, DeAngelo was charged with eight counts of first-degree murder based on DNA evidence including additional subsequent charges. On June 29, 2020, he pled guilty to multiple counts of murder and kidnapping and was sentenced to life in prison without the possibility of parole.[†]

OSAC Human Forensic Biology Subcommittee[‡]

The Human Forensic Biology Subcommittee focuses on standards and guidelines related to training, method development and validation, data analysis, interpretation, statistical analysis, reporting, and testimony for human forensic serological and DNA testing. Several standards published by the AAFS Standards Board (ASB) have been approved for the OSAC Registry including Standard for Validation of Probabilistic Genotyping Systems, Standard for Forensic DNA Interpretation and Comparison Protocols, and Standards for Training in Forensic Serological Methods.

SWGDAM[§]

The Scientific Working Group on DNA Analysis Methods (SWGDAM) is a group of forensic DNA analysts from local, state, and federal laboratories throughout the U.S. It serves as a forum to discuss, share, and evaluate forensic biology methods, protocols, and research to enhance forensic biology services. Most Scientific Working Groups (SWGs) in other forensic disciplines have transitioned over to the OSACs, however, NIST and the FBI have agreed that SWGDAM will remain operational since one of SWGDAM's key responsibilities is to provide recommendations to the FBI Director of revisions to the FBI's Quality Assurance Standards (QAS) for DNA analysis. Adherence to these QAS is required by Federal law as a condition of a lab's participation in NDIS. SWGDAM also publishes guidelines and recommendations for the Forensic DNA community such as Interpretation Guidelines, Training Guidelines, Validation Guidelines, Recommendations for the Efficient DNA Processing of Sexual Assault Evidence Kits, and others.

THE FUTURE

Forensic biology is among the fastest evolving technologies used in crime laboratories today. The revolution in the biotechnology industry makes it a near certainty that new DNA applications for forensic science will continue to develop for the foreseeable future.

Further Reading

Bright, J.-A., and M. Coble. *Forensic DNA Profiling: A Practical Guide to Assigning Likelihood Ratios*. CRC Press, 2019.

Buckleton, John S., Jo-Anne Bright, and Duncan Taylor, eds. *Forensic DNA Evidence Interpretation*. CRC Press, 2018.

Butler, John M. *Fundamentals of Forensic DNA Typing*. Academic Press, 2010.

Butler, John M. *Advanced Topics in Forensic DNA Typing: Methodology*. Academic Press, 2012.

Butler, John M. *Advanced Topics in Forensic DNA Typing: Interpretation*. Academic Press, 2015.

Gill, Peter. *Misleading DNA Evidence: Reasons for Miscarriages of Justice*. Academic Press, 2014.

Gill, P., et al. *Forensic Practitioner's Guide to the Interpretation of Complex DNA Profiles*. Elsevier Academic Press, 2020.

---

[*] GEDmatch is a website for genetic genealogy research. Anyone can upload their DNA file obtained from a direct-to-consumer testing company (such as 23andMe), analyze results, and compare DNA shared with others. Verogen purchased GEDmatch in 2019.
[†] https://en.wikipedia.org/wiki/Joseph_James_DeAngelo.
[‡] www.nist.gov/osac/human-forensic-biology-subcommittee.
[§] www.swgdam.org/.

Meakin Georgina E, et al. "Evaluating forensic DNA evidence: Connecting the dots." *Wiley Interdisciplinary Reviews: Forensic Science* 3.4 (2021): e1404.

Murphy, Erin E. *Inside the Cell: The Dark Side of Forensic DNA*. Bold Type Books, 2015.

Steensma, Kristy, et al. "An inter-laboratory comparison study on transfer, persistence and recovery of DNA from cable ties." *Forensic Science International: Genetics* 31 (2017): 95–104.

van Oorschot, Roland AH, et al. "DNA transfer in forensic science: a review." *Forensic Science International: Genetics* 38 (2019): 140–166.

van Oorschot, Roland AH, et al. "DNA Transfer in Forensic Science: Recent Progress towards Meeting Challenges." *Genes* 12.11 (2021): 1766.

Chapter Questions

1. You are about to enter the scene of a double homicide to begin your investigation and collect evidence. Please list the appropriate personal protective equipment (PPE) you would wear while processing the scene.
2. (True or false) When collecting clothing from the same person, you can bag these items together if they are properly labeled.
3. Which of the following is a presumptive test used for screening blood at a crime scene?
    a) PCR.
    b) STR.
    c) Acid phosphatase.
    d) p30.
    e) Kastle-Mayer test.
4. Describe the most appropriate way to collect a liquid bloodstain at the scene of a crime.
5. Which of the following is the correct pairing of bases with DNA?
    a) A-T, G-C.
    b) A-C, G-T.
    c) A-A, G-T.
    d) C-A, T-G.
6. Briefly describe the polymerase chain reaction (PCR) and how it is used in forensic DNA typing.
7. Which of the following is the forensic DNA database maintained by the FBI?
    a) NIBIN.
    b) IAFIS.
    c) CODIS.
    d) STR.
    e) DNABASE.
8. Which type of cells do not contain DNA?
    a) Cardiac cells.
    b) Muscle cells.
    c) Red blood cells.
    d) White blood cells.
    e) Sperm cells.
9. (True or false) mtDNA is inherited maternally.
10. (True or false) Y-STR profiles are generally more statistically significant than autosomal STRs.

CHAPTER 8

Forensic Traces

Trace evidence, trace materials, or traces are terms for small, often microscopic material. Such evidence may easily be overlooked in crime scene investigations unless proper care is exercised in the search. The variety of trace evidence is endless. The purpose of this chapter is to examine some of the more common types of trace materials frequently encountered in criminal investigations and to discuss concepts of collection, preservation, identification, and use of these materials.*

When an individual comes into contact with a person or location, certain small and seemingly insignificant changes occur. Small items such as fibers, hairs, and assorted microscopic debris may be left by the person or picked up from contact with the environment or another individual. In short, it is not possible to come in contact with an environment without changing it in some small way by adding to it or taking something away from it. This concept of transference is known as the ***Locard Exchange Principle*** and is the basis for studying trace evidence.[†]

The importance of transferred traces is that it links suspects to victims or locations. It is physical evidence of contact and, although microscopic, can become a significant part of an investigation. Traces can also corroborate statements and determine the sequence of events.

SOURCES OF TRACES

Clothing

Clothing is an excellent source of trace evidence. Microscopic and macroscopic substances cling to clothing by static electricity or become caught in the fabric itself. Useful evidence is most likely to be found if the clothes are collected from the suspect or victim as soon after the crime as possible. As time passes, small items of evidence no bigger than a fiber may easily become dislodged from the clothing and lost.

After the suspect is arrested, his or her clothes should be cursorily inspected for obvious physical evidence connected with the crime. If evidence is observed, its location and description should be noted.

If possible, the subject should be made to undress while standing on clean wrapping or butcher paper. The paper will catch any traces that might fall from the clothing. The clothing should then be collected, tagged, marked for chain of custody, and packaged in paper bags. Plastic bags should be avoided when packaging clothing because plastic promotes moisture and the clothes may develop mold or mildew. Care should be taken when placing the garments into paper bags; they should not be shaken because that might loosen or dislodge trace evidence. If the clothes are wet or bloodstained, they should first be allowed to air-dry before packaging.

---

* The Trace Materials Crime Scene Investigation Guide produced by OSAC is an excellent resource for CSIs in best practices for trace evidence collection and packaging.
† The American Society of Trace Evidence Examiners (ASTEE), www.asteetrace.org, is a professional organization of over 350 professionals in the field of trace evidence that encourages the exchange and dissemination of information within the field.

DOI: 10.4324/9780429272011-10

It is especially important to keep the suspect's clothing away from any sources of trace evidence located at the scene. If known samples from the scene have been collected as exemplars, they should never be packaged with the evidence to avoid cross-contamination.

Similarly, a suspect should not be brought to the crime scene while clothed in the same garments worn during the crime. This will prevent the argument that any trace evidence found on the clothes was from the visit to the scene while in police custody. Once clothing has been collected and packaged in paper bags, it should be submitted to the crime laboratory for careful examination.

Although some police agencies may have equipment to vacuum the garments and send the sweepings to the laboratory, it is preferable to allow the laboratory to conduct the collection. In instances when extremely small items of evidence such as a single hair or fiber might be lost, evidence should be carefully packaged in a paper fold or folded sticky note, and then inside an outer envelope. The location of the evidence should be noted along with a brief description of the item.

Clothes from murder and assault victims pose other problems for consideration. As on a suspect's clothing, trace evidence may be present on the victim's clothes as well. These garments, however, may have been removed by personnel other than law enforcement who usually are not knowledgeable about proper collection and preservation of evidence. Problems invariably arise when paramedics or hospital personnel remove clothing during life-threatening emergencies. It is not uncommon for clothing to be cut off the victim with the aim of initiating emergency procedures. Often, this results in cutting through bullet holes, tears caused by stabbing, and the like. Frequently, wet bloodstained garments are rolled up and packaged in a large plastic bag and tightly sealed.

In these instances of improper evidence handling by emergency medical personnel, police agencies can do little more than attempt to educate those professionals and hope that the potential value of the evidence is not too badly diminished. Crime laboratory personnel should be advised that the victim's clothing was cut off so that they can effectively interpret the information in their attempt to reconstruct the crime.

Clothing on deceased victims requires further considerations. Before the victim is undressed, the clothing should be carefully examined for trace evidence by the investigator, criminalist, and/or pathologist. An alternate light source is a useful tool in locating trace evidence. Each item of clothing should be carefully removed and placed into a separate paper bag. In most instances of violent death, the clothes will be wet from blood. The garments should be air-dried before packaging. Collecting tape-lifts of the decedent's clothing and/or body prior to transport will reduce the possibility of loss of traces.

Footwear

Shoes and other footwear are valuable items of evidence. They may have dust, soil, debris, vegetation, or bloodstains on them. In addition to the presence of trace evidence, shoes and other footwear are useful in pattern impression comparisons. Shoes should be individually packaged in paper bags to avoid cross-contamination. Particular care must be taken when packaging footwear evidence containing clumps of dried soil. Careful examination of the soil might lead to determining the path taken by a suspect based on the layer structure of the soil. This possibility would be greatly lessened if the soil became dislodged and pulverized in transit to the laboratory.

Evidence from the Body

Useful traces may be discovered by a careful examination of the suspect or victim's body. Injuries caused by a struggle between victim and suspect may be noted. Additionally, microscopic particles of gunshot residue (GSR) are often present on the hands of a shooter following the discharge of a firearm. A GSR collection kit with adhesive stubs should be used when collecting this type of evidence. Avoid having officers who have recently fired a gun collect GSR evidence.

Hair is sometimes found on the victim's body in rape cases. A close examination of the head, ears, and fingernails may yield traces of debris from a burglary, assault, or other crime in which there was contact between the suspect and another person or the crime scene. Visible hairs should be placed in a paper fold or inside a folded sticky note and then inside an envelope.

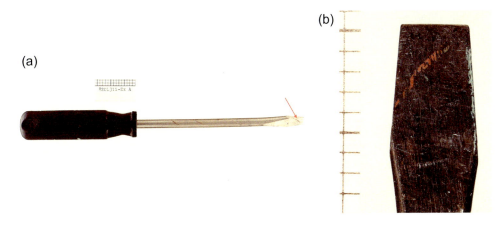

Figure 8.1 (a) A flathead screwdriver seized from a suspect in a burglary case. (b) Close-up of the tip of the screwdriver showing the presence of a small amount of red paint, which matched the paint at the breaking-and-entering location. (*Courtesy of the Royal Canadian Mounted Police, Forensic Laboratory Services.*)

OTHER OBJECTS AS SOURCES OF TRACE EVIDENCE

Trace evidence may also be present on tools and weapons. Items should be carefully packaged to protect the material on them. This may be done best by placing the tool in a cardboard box and securing it with zip ties. If the instrument bears larger particles that may be lost, the particles should be carefully removed and placed in appropriately labeled containers.

Tools used in burglaries may contain traces of building material, metal shavings, paint, and so forth. These items may be used to establish a connection between the tool and the location. Similarly, a weapon such as a knife may have hairs or fibers present that may prove to be useful evidence (Figure 8.1a and b).

Larger items may contain traces as well. For example, a vehicle from a hit-and-run accident. Naturally, objects of this size cannot be brought to the laboratory unless the laboratory has a vehicle garage. Careful examination in the field, however, can yield hairs, fibers, skin, blood, and the like.

To the trained trace examiner in the crime lab, tools such as stereo microscopes, polarized light microscopes, scanning electron microscopes, and analytical instruments make the examination and characterization of trace items of evidence possible. A far greater problem than size is quantity of material. Particles and material collected from vacuum sweepings and careful searches of evidence can yield thousands of microscopic items to be examined. Patience and the examiner's expertise can ultimately determine the nature and utility of these collected items.

Case Review

On March 27, 2003, in rural Darke County Ohio, a married couple was shot to death execution-style while asleep in their bed. The only other occupant in the house at the time was their four-year-old great-grandson who discovered the bodies. The boy attempted to call 911, however, the phone lines had been cut. Knowing that he needed help, he ran nearly a mile to a church where he attended preschool. He told the teacher that his grandparents were "melting." The victims had been shot at point-blank range with a 12-gauge shotgun.

It appeared to investigators that the murderer had intended the crime scene to look like a robbery; however, a deposit bag containing a large amount of cash remained undisturbed in the kitchen and no jewelry or other valuables appeared to be missing. A basement window had been forced open and partial footwear impressions were cast from adjacent soil. Recovered from the head of the bed was a makeshift silencer composed of a quilting material. This material was wrapped in a cone-shaped fashion and exhibited masking tape on one end and black powder on the other.

Over the course of the following week, investigators eliminated a number of suspects and began to focus on the son and stepson of the victims. The suspect's girlfriend informed investigators that the suspect had left for work exceptionally early the day of the murders. An acquaintance of the suspect had also come forward and claimed that the suspect had contacted him shortly before the murders about acquiring a non-registered firearm. Investigators compared the suspect's cell phone records with local ads listing firearms for sale. They located a man who claimed to have sold a 12-gauge shotgun to the suspect just days before the murders. This man still had the firearm box, which included the shotgun serial number. However, investigators did not have a murder weapon for comparison. Subsequent interviews and a search of the suspect's house failed to reveal a shotgun or any probative evidence.

Five days after the murders, an extensive search of nearly 30 miles of roads, bridges, and waterways between the crime scene and the suspect's place of employment was conducted. The search was unsuccessful until, on a hunch, one investigator and a Darke County Sheriff's deputy drove to a bridge over the Stillwater River. In the shallow water right off the side of the bridge, they recovered a 12-gauge shotgun with a piece of masking tape on the barrel. About one mile downstream snagged on a tree branch, a large black trash bag was recovered.

The shotgun and trash bag were immediately transported to the Miami Valley Regional Crime Laboratory for examination. Among the items recovered from the bag were two spent shotgun shells, a roll of masking tape, a pair of black athletic shoes, latex gloves, a package of quilting material, and clothing items.

Trace evidence examination of masking tape pieces recovered from the makeshift silencer at the scene, the barrel of the shotgun recovered from the river, and the roll of masking tape recovered from the trash bag revealed numerous jigsaw matches connecting the first nine feet of tape off a new roll (Figure 8.2a and b). It was conclusive that the tape from the silencer and the shotgun barrel originated from the roll of tape in the trash bag. Also, the quilting material recovered from the bag was the same composition as that used in the makeshift silencer.

The shotgun was processed by the Firearms and Tool Mark Section in an attempt to restore the obliterated serial number. Five of the eight digits in the serial number were successfully raised. These digits matched the corresponding numbers on the box obtained from the seller. Additionally, the spent shell casings from the bag were found to be of the same brand as those recovered from the victims at autopsy.

The athletic shoes recovered from the trash bag were compared to the partial footwear impressions recovered from the scene and were found to be of the same tread design. It was noted that these shoes were approximately two sizes smaller than those worn by the suspect.

At this point, many of the items from the bag could be linked to the crime scene but nothing could be directly linked to the suspect. That changed upon examination of the latex gloves by a latent print examiner. Remarkably, one of the gloves revealed a partial fingerprint under ultraviolet light. This partial print was intact despite the immersion of the evidence in water for nearly a week. This anomaly was likely due to the deposition of an oily residue on the suspect's hands before donning the glove. Comparison of this partial latent print revealed that it matched a portion of the suspect's right index finger—his trigger finger (Figure 8.2c).

The motive in this case was determined to be financial. The suspect was losing his home to foreclosure and he stood to inherit his father's property if his father and step-mother were deceased. The suspect, age 25, was convicted on all charges and was sentenced to life in prison without parole (Figure 8.2 a-c).

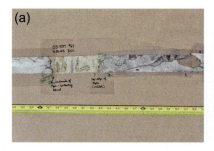
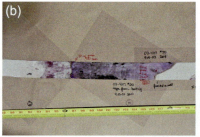
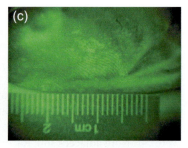

Figure 8.2 (a, b) Trace examination of masking tape pieces recovered from a makeshift silencer. The shotgun barrel and the roll of masking tape recovered from the trash bag showed numerous jigsaw matches connecting the first nine feet of tape off a new roll. (c) An initial photograph of the partial latent print on the glove fingertip as observed with the Reflected UV Imaging System (RUVIS) before processing. *(Courtesy of Suzanne Noffsinger, Trace Evidence Examiner, Miami Valley Regional Crime Laboratory, Dayton, Ohio.)*

COLLECTION AND PRESERVATION OF TRACE EVIDENCE

As with all evidence, the investigator or crime scene technician must be concerned with various legal and scientific aspects of collection and preservation of trace materials. Legally, issues of chain of custody and the need for a search warrant or court order must not be overlooked. When in doubt, the investigator should consult with the local district attorney or state attorney general's office for guidance.

Scientific requirements depend upon the nature of the evidence collected and the proximity of the laboratory conducting the examinations. It is obvious that if evidence needs to be mailed or sent by a parcel carrier, special care must be taken to preserve fragile substances properly.

A question sometimes asked is, "Is it better to remove an item of trace material from a larger item or leave it alone?" The answer is, "It depends." If a hair, fiber, loose paint chip, or another very small and easily lost item of evidence can become dislodged or lost from the item to which it is attached, that smaller item should be removed. On the other hand, if in the investigator's opinion the smaller substance is secure, then it should not be handled. It is preferable to submit the entire item with traces attached to it to the laboratory for an examination. Of course, in those instances in which the item is too large or inconvenient to transport, the trace material should be carefully removed, packaged, and sent to the laboratory for examination. Photographs depicting trace evidence in its original location should be taken. This is helpful to the laboratory as well as to jurors trying to understand the significance of the evidence.

Small items of evidence should always be double packaged. Double packaging means that the evidence should be first placed into an appropriate container and secured. The first container should then be inserted into a larger container. Both containers should be appropriately marked to document the person performing the packaging, the date and time, the case number, and a very brief description of the item. If the inner container should inadvertently open, the outer one will contain the evidence.

As an example of double packaging, consider a hypothetical case. Suppose an investigator has observed a small fiber on the bumper of a car suspected in a hit-and-run accident. Bringing the car to the laboratory or a location where the vehicle could be placed on a lift and raised for a thorough examination of the undercarriage would be the best way to conduct an examination. Assume this is not possible. The detective still wants to collect the fiber for comparison with the victim's clothing. The fiber should be carefully removed and placed in a paper fold or sticky note. This would then be marked with the initials, date, time, case number, and so on and would then be placed into a second or outer package. This outer package would also be appropriately marked.

Control or known trace samples should also be collected that best represent the color and condition of the questioned material. The investigator should make every attempt to collect a sufficient quantity of known material to be submitted with the items in question. The known exemplars must never be packaged with the questioned samples. This separation is necessary to avoid cross-contamination of the unknowns by known specimens.

Almost all types of trace evidence can be placed in a class or group, that is, identified. Only in rare cases is trace evidence of the type discussed in this chapter capable of conclusively indicating a specific source or origin. A single fiber cannot be shown to have come from a unique garment, nor a clump of dirt from a specific location. Does this mean that trace evidence is of no value? On the contrary, because of its prevalence, trace evidence may often be the sole means of corroborating testimonial evidence in a case.

EXAMPLES OF TRACE EVIDENCE

Building Materials

A wide variety of building materials may be encountered in burglary cases. Materials such as stucco, cement, brick, mortar, plaster, sheetrock, plasterboard, window glass, wood, and paint constitute evidence generally considered as building materials. These materials are most likely found on the clothing of burglary suspects, in their cuffs, pockets, and shoes. Another likely location for this type of debris is on tools used to break into a location.

Items suspected of containing building material debris should be carefully packaged and submitted along with appropriate exemplars to the crime laboratory.

The investigator should carefully examine the crime scene to determine the nature of the trace evidence. In breaking-and-entering cases, the point of entry or any other location indicating damage should be examined and known samples of building materials collected. If tool marks are present at the point of entry, samples of building materials should not be collected from the area of the tool mark, but rather adjacent to the mark. Furthermore, if an area is to be cut out, particular care must be taken not to cut through the tool mark.

In cases of building material that show indications of tampering at several locations, it is necessary to collect known specimens of the material in question from each of the damaged areas. This is important because the composition of the building material may vary from place to place. It is very important to package each item of evidence separately, properly marking the package and noting the location where the specimen was collected.

Tools may be useful sources of building material evidence. Bits of paint, plaster, wood, and even glass may become attached to the tool. In addition to the debris they may contain, tools are useful for tool mark comparisons and for physically matching broken pieces of the tool.

If building material is noticed at the end of a tool, the area should be wrapped carefully so as not to dislodge the evidence. If the item is too large to be transported, the trace material can be carefully removed with a clean razor blade onto a clean sheet of paper. The paper is then folded and placed in an envelope. Both paper and envelope should be properly marked.

The interior or the trunk of a suspect's vehicle should be searched for the presence of building materials. Vacuum sweeps or tape-lifts may be taken for a later search of debris. Clothing is an especially good place to find building materials. The clothes should be collected from the suspect as promptly as possible to minimize any loss of evidence.

Physical, chemical, and microscopic methods can characterize building materials. In most cases, building material traces can only demonstrate class characteristics and cannot be shown to be unique to a specific source. As with other evidence of this type, it is valuable as circumstantial evidence.

Asbestos

Although asbestos is no longer permitted for use as insulation because of its link to mesothelioma, it may be present in older buildings and some safes and can be positively identified microscopically.

Safe Insulation

Various types of materials are used in fire-resistant safes to prevent the contents from burning. Some common materials used in these safes are diatomaceous earth, vermiculite, and cement, to name a few. These materials may readily become deposited on a safe burglar in the course of opening the safe. Examination of a suspect's clothing, shoes, and tools may yield safe insulation, which can be identified microscopically and chemically. Expertise in recognizing the types of insulation used by various manufacturers may allow the analyst to give the case detective an investigative lead.

Paint

Paint evidence is frequently recovered in hit-and-run accidents, burglaries, and forced-entry cases. In some cases, it is possible to show conclusively that the paint came from a specific location if the chips are large enough and the edges can be fitted together in jigsaw puzzle fashion. Do not attempt to fit the paint chips together prior to submission to the crime lab as this may alter the edges or cause a transfer of materials.

Paint and other protective coatings such as lacquer, enamel, and varnish can be identified by physical and chemical properties. Physical characteristics such as color, layering, weathering, and texture are useful in characterizing this evidence. Chemical properties such as solubility and composition can indicate the type of paint and identify the pigmentation and fillers used in the manufacturing process.*

Even if a vehicle cannot be identified, known and questioned specimens can be compared by examining chemical and physical properties. The best that can be stated is that the paint from the control and questioned sources are

---

* The American Society for Testing and Materials (ASTM) maintains a variety of testing methods used for trace materials, including Forensic Paint Analysis and Comparison (www.astm.org/Standards/E1610.htm).

indistinguishable, that is, they could have come from the vehicle in question or any similarly painted vehicle. In some instances, vehicles and residences that have been painted and repainted many times may have so many layers of paint that upon examination, the probability is very high that the two specimens share a common source.

When standard specimens of paint from automobiles or a door or window in a forced-entry case are collected, the specimen should be taken as close to the area of damage as possible to lessen the possibility that an area further away from the location of interest was painted differently. In burglary cases, it is particularly important not to collect a standard or control paint sample from the pry area. The specific area of the jimmy or pry may contain a tool mark that may be compared with a pry bar or other tool found at a later time.

When collecting paint samples in a hit-and-run investigation involving two vehicles, a total of four paint samples should be collected and separately packaged. From vehicle A, collect a sample from the point of impact that contains a paint transfer from vehicle B. Also, collect a standard paint sample that shows no damage but is adjacent to the damaged area. Similarly, two samples should be collected from vehicle B, one from the damaged area and a second from the undamaged area to be used as a standard.

If dislodged paint chips are present in the damaged area of the vehicle, they should be carefully collected and packaged to avoid breaking. They may be able to be fitted with other, larger paint chips collected from the scene of the accident or the second vehicle.

To collect a known paint sample from a vehicle, hold a folded piece of paper and tap the side of the vehicle with a pocket knife or similar tool. This will dislodge some paint and allow it to fall into the paper. Care should be taken not to separate the outer layer of paint from the undercoating. Avoid using cellophane tape to collect the paint samples. It is best to place the paint sample into folded paper or a small box with a good seal. Small envelopes are not advised for this type of evidence because the seams of the envelope located in the bottom corners are generally not sealed. Paint chips placed in envelopes usually fall out through the small, unsealed space. Small plastic bags should also be avoided because they have a static electric charge that makes it extremely difficult to remove the chips once the evidence is received at the laboratory. The known paint sample should include the substrate (typically metal or plastic for a vehicle) to ensure all layers of the paint are collected. Multiple known samples may be required if there are multiple areas of damage. Often, different areas of vehicles can be painted differently.

Paint on tools should not be removed. It is preferable to wrap the end of the tool carefully so as not to dislodge the paint and submit the tool to the laboratory with the paint intact.

Rust

Rust stains may sometimes be confused with bloodstains. However, rust can easily be differentiated from blood by a simple chemical field test.

Metals

Filings, shavings, and other metal particles can easily be identified chemically or spectrographically. It is possible to make a comparative analysis of a known and questioned metal sample that can show class characteristics. Metal filings located in the jaws of pipe wrenches are fairly common sources of this type of evidence. The wrench is used as a burglary tool by placing it onto a doorknob. Metal filings present in the teeth can be compared to those from the doorknob. Metal shavings can also be found on hacksaw blades (Figure 8.3).

Case Review

A 13-year-old boy decided to poison his mother slowly with mercury. He collected enough mercury by breaking into a number of homes in the neighborhood with a 17-year-old friend and removing the mercury in their thermostat switches. He may have read that mercury salts are highly toxic and mistook this to mean that elemental mercury and table salt together are highly toxic. Whatever the reason, he placed the mercury in a glass salt shaker along with table salt, shook the contents to break the mercury into fine droplets, and left the shaker to be used by his mother.

The forensic science laboratory was requested to show that the shaker had been used to dispense the mercury. The lid of the shaker was examined using a scanning electron microscope (SEM) with an energy dispersive x-ray

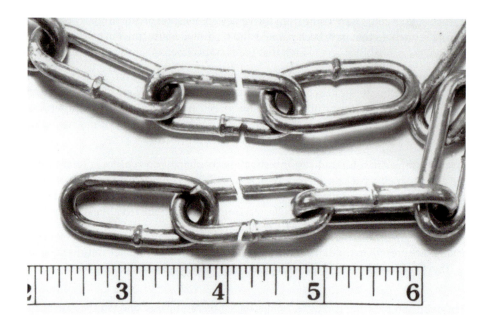

Figure 8.3 In the case of an alleged jailbreak attempt, the investigator wanted to know whether the inmate had used a hacksaw blade on his leg irons. When the escape attempt was reenacted, a magnet was able to pick up numerous metal particles from the clothing of the investigator, whose hand was also slightly injured from using the blade. None of this evidence was found on the inmate, calling into question the hypothesis he had tried to escape from jail on his own. (*Courtesy of the Los Angeles County Sheriff's Department.*)

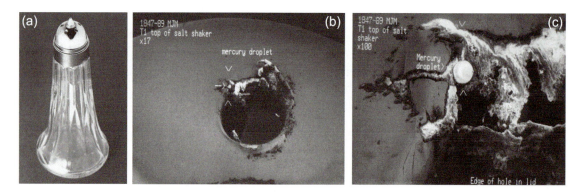

Figure 8.4 (a) A glass salt shaker used by a boy in an attempt to poison his mother. (b) One of the holes of the shaker was photographed using scanning electron microscopy. (c) The magnification clearly shows the droplet of mercury. (*Courtesy of the Centre of Forensic Sciences, Toronto, Canada.*)

detector (EDX). This combination allowed the operator to magnify an image of the object and determine its elemental composition. The lid of the salt shaker was made of plastic coated with nickel and chromium to give it a shiny appearance. The area around the holes in the shaker's lid was examined for traces of mercury and, using the SEM, one fine droplet of elemental mercury, clinging to the nickel plating at one of the holes, was found and identified as mercury by using EDX (Figure 8.4a-c).

Textiles and Fibers

Fragments of cloth may become evidence in a wide variety of cases. Torn fabrics have been examined in murder cases in which the victim was tied and gagged with torn fabric, in burglary cases in which a suspect left a small torn piece of clothing caught at the point of entry, and in hit-and-run cases in which torn clothing was left on the undercarriage of the suspect's vehicle.

Fragments of textile evidence may yield class as well as individual characteristics. A portion of fabric may be physically fitted into another piece of fabric, thereby showing a common source. A number of physical, chemical, and microscopic characteristics of textiles can be used for comparison purposes. Properties such as color, type of cloth, dye, direction of yarn twist, and thread count are useful in characterizing the evidence.

When a fragment of fabric is found during the course of a crime scene search, its location should be noted, indicated in a crime scene sketch, and photographed. As with other items of trace evidence, it is preferable not to remove the fabric from the object to which it is attached. If this is not possible, the fabric should be packaged in a clean container, properly labeled with the appropriate chain of custody information.

The location of the evidence at a point of entry or the physical appearance of the fabric may be useful as investigative leads. The detective may be able to theorize the location of a tear on an article of clothing or the type of cloth evidence that needs to be found for comparative purposes.

Investigators may overlook fiber evidence because of its extremely small size compared to fabric evidence. Five types of textile fibers can be encountered as evidence: animal fibers, such as wool; vegetable fibers, such as cotton or hemp; synthetic fibers, such as polyester, nylon, rayon, etc.; mineral fibers, such as glass wool; and blends of synthetic and natural fibers, the most common of which are polyester and cotton. Fiber evidence may be transferred by one person's clothing coming in contact with another's or from articles such as blankets, carpet, upholstery, and so forth. Fibers may be present on clothing, in fingernail scrapings, on hit-and-run vehicles, at points of entry, and on hair covered by knit hats. Be aware that secondary and tertiary transfers of fibers are also possible.

Removal of fibers from other objects is best done at the crime laboratory. If this is not possible, fiber evidence can be removed by using forceps, lifting tape or by vacuum sweeping. Of the three procedures, the tape method is probably the best. A length of tape about four inches long is taped end-to-end, forming a cylinder with the sticky side of the tape on the outside. The hand is inserted into the center of the tape and the sticky side of the tape is pressed on the item of interest. After sampling, the tape is placed sticky side down on a clean transparency sheet. The procedure has its advantage in that it only collects surface material, whereas vacuum sweeping collects huge quantities of debris and forceps may miss many items of trace evidence.

The laboratory can determine the type of fiber and whether it is similar to the known/control fiber specimen. It is not possible, with fiber evidence, to state that it came from one and only one source because most garments and textiles used today are mass produced. It is usually not possible to determine if a specific sample came from the garment in question or from another garment of similar manufacture.

Case Review

When Marie Guster arrived at her north-side home at 3:00 am, one cold January morning, her earlier apprehensions were proven right. She found her teenage babysitter, Linda Cole, dead on the living room floor. Marie's three-and-a-half-year old daughter was asleep, unharmed, but would later describe to her mother how Bill had hurt Linda. Marie's original alarm came from the knowledge that Bill Lovell, who had been a regular visitor of Marie's, had phoned her place of employment from the crime scene at 1:15 am, angrily demanding to know Marie's whereabouts.

The duty officer for the crime laboratory was called at 3:30 am by the police who had only 30 minutes earlier been summoned to the scene. Crime scene investigators from the crime laboratory arrived soon thereafter and found a teenage girl brutally raped and stabbed to death. As latent print specialists dusted for fingerprints, the forensic microscopist surveyed the scene and began collecting trace evidence. In the end, four latent prints from the house were identified as having been made by Linda Cole, and five latent prints from the house were identified as having been left by Marie Guster. No fingerprints were developed on bloody knives and forks used as murder weapons and no unidentified fingerprints were available for searching with an automated fingerprint identification system (AFIS). Bill was not saying a word. The means to solve the case was left with the microscopist.

The crime scene was littered with Linda's torn blue panties, her plaid skirt, a knife, and two forks. She was clad only in a white sweater and white socks. A torn bra was inside the sweater and a knife protruded from her throat. Semen seeped from her vagina. One foreign head hair was recovered from her left sock. An autopsy later the same

Figure 8.5 Typical alpaca fibers. Original magnification at 100x, and cross polars with first order compensator. (*Courtesy of Richard E. Bisbing LLC, Chicago, IL.*)

day revealed bruises on the sides of her face, and knife and puncture wounds in her chest. Less than two weeks later, initial trace evidence results were ready from the crime laboratory and presented at a preliminary hearing.

Lifting tape was used to collect foreign fibers from Linda's and Bill's clothing. Bill's coat lining supported an abundance of yellow wool (alpaca) fibers as did his red shirt. Similar alpaca fibers were found on Linda's sweater. As part of a cross transfer, several white acrylic fibers, similar to the white acrylic fibers composing Linda's white sweater, and a polyester fiber similar to polyester fibers composing the facing of her torn bra, were recovered from Bill's red shirt.

After finding the alpaca fibers, the police were told, "There must be a yellow sweater or blanket out there." The detectives went to Bill's wife and asked about it. His wife, Beverly, pointed to a yellow sweater over in the corner and said, "Bill wore that the night of the murder." Microscopical examination of the yellow fibers composing the cardigan sweater showed them to be similar to the fibers found on Bill's coat lining, on Bill's red shirt, and on Linda's white sweater. The color match was confirmed by microspectrophotometry (MSP). White acrylic fibers similar to the fibers composing Linda's sweater were found on the inside of Bill's yellow alpaca cardigan.

Later, police detectives arranged with Bill's wife to search her home for white acrylic fibers (alibi samples) which could be similar to the white acrylic fibers found on Bill's shirt and sweater. Since Beverly Lovell had requested the additional investigation, the detectives and forensic microscopist were admitted to the home and given permission to conduct the search. Fibers from nine items were obtained and returned to the laboratory. Only fibers from a white scarf found in the bottom drawer in the children's room were similar to the white acrylic fibers composing Linda's white sweater. There were no yellow alpaca fibers on the scarf. Later, the acrylic fibers from the scarf were distinguished from those of Linda's sweater by infrared microspectroscopy (FTIR).

The defendant claimed to have an alibi. Nevertheless, within six months William Lovell was convicted for murder. Upon appeal, based on a faulty search warrant for blood, saliva, and hair samples from the defendant, the court wrote: "We note that the cumulative effect of the various trace evidence identifications was very important to the prosecution's case. However, if we exclude the semen and pubic hair exemplars from evidence at trial, there is still overwhelming proof which links defendant to the crime; the evidence of forcible rape is still present without 'identification' of the donor of the sperm. The pubic hair comparison was damaging, but far more damaging were the yellow alpaca sweater fibers. Many other incriminating comparisons were presented, and this testimony complemented the evidence which established that the defendant was the last known person to be at the scene before the killing." (Figure 8.5).

Buttons

Buttons come in a very wide range of sizes and patterns; only in exceptional cases is it possible to match a button with the buttons of a particular garment. When a button is torn off, generally the thread and sometimes a piece of fabric may be present. If exemplars of the sewing thread and the garment are available for comparison, a more definitive conclusion about the source of the button may be made. If a piece of broken button is discovered, it is possible to match the broken piece physically with another portion of the button. This type of evidence can lead to a more conclusive statement about the source of the evidence.

Cordage and Rope

Pieces of string or rope are sometimes found at crime scenes. If they were used to tie up a victim, the knots should not be untied; rather, the rope should be cut and tied back together with string. The knots present in the rope may prove to be useful evidence.

Rope and cordage evidence can be compared with exemplars for similarities. Properties that can be examined include the material from which the cordage is manufactured, the number of strands, direction of the twist in the rope, color, diameter, weight per unit of length, etc. All these properties taken together will allow the examiner to determine whether the material is of a similar manufacture.

In some cases, rope and cordage evidence may have other trace evidence attached to it. In cases of strangulation, it may be possible to identify epithelial (skin) cells attached to the cordage.

Cigarettes and Tobacco

Cigarettes, cigarette butts, tobacco, and ash are sometimes found at crime scenes and may be overlooked as potentially useful evidence. Some laboratories maintain cigarette libraries from which they can often identify the brand from a cigarette butt. In some cases, information about the brand a subject smokes may be useful to the investigation. Similarly, the appearance of ash left at a location may indicate that a suspect smoked a pipe or cigar, which is useful in describing the habits of that individual.

Cigarette butts may be a useful source of other physical evidence. In some cases, latent fingerprints have been developed from cigarette butts by the ninhydrin process. It is also possible to determine the smoker's DNA from the saliva left on the butt. Although latent prints and DNA typing results may be negative, these procedures should be considered.

Empty cigarette packages may also be found along with cigarettes. Besides the brand and the possibility of determining fingerprints, it is sometimes possible to determine the general location of the sale of the cigarettes by the numbers on the package. The ability to determine the area of sale depends on whether the distributor kept records of these numbers (Figure 8.6a and b).

Matches

Matches found at a crime scene may be from smokers or from suspects who used them for other purposes. Several may commonly be found in burglary cases. The surface of a single match is usually too small to find sufficient detail to identify a latent fingerprint. However, other useful bits of information may be determined from matches.

Matches may be wood or paper. The type of wood, microscopic appearance of the cardboard, color, dimension, and shape are useful in comparing a burned match with some exemplars associated with the suspect. Paper matches from a matchbook are by far the most common kind at crime scenes and offer the best chance of directly incriminating a suspect. To show a connection, it is necessary to find the book of used matches on the suspect or at least at the location with this suspect's latent prints on it. Cardboard matches are made from waste paper; as such, there is wide variability

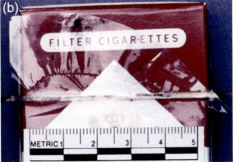

Figure 8.6 Sometimes seemingly insignificant items left at the scene are important. (a, b) The cellophane wrapping from a pack of Marlboro cigarettes was shown to have come from a pack of cigarettes found on a suspect. (*Courtesy of the Los Angeles County Sheriff's Department.*)

from book to book. It is possible to show a connection between the cardboard left in the matchbook and that of the match. In some instances, it is possible to fit the match into the book by the appearance of the torn end of the match and the remaining end in the book.

Matches are sometimes used as toothpicks. If the end of the match appears to be chewed, it may be possible to test the saliva on the match for DNA.

Ash

The composition of ash will vary greatly depending on the source. It can sometimes be identified microscopically, chemically, or by means of spectroscopy. However, the source of the ash may prove difficult to determine. One type of ash common in arson cases is the residue of burned highway flares. This ash contains a significant level of strontium, responsible for the bright red color of the flare.

Soil*

Soil evidence may be encountered in a wide variety of criminal investigations. It may be found on shoes, clothing, or the underside of motor vehicles and is useful in tying the suspect or victim to a location. A tire or footwear impression in soil makes it possible to prove that the subject was in fact present.

Soil is a mixture of decaying and weathered rock and decomposed organic material known as humus. It contains a wide variety of minerals such as quartz, feldspar, and mica as well as partially decomposed leaves, pine needles, pollen grains, and other plant fragments. Thus, it is easy to differentiate soils from various locations by microscopic examination of various components.

Known soil specimens from the crime scene are absolutely required for an analysis of the evidence sample. Samples should be collected from various regions at the specific location in question and several feet away from it, and at other locations, such as the subject's home and work, for elimination purposes.

Known samples can be placed in individual small glass jars. (Metal containers should be avoided since metal can be a component of soil, and can add metallic contaminants to the samples.) Two or three tablespoons of topsoil are all that is usually required for known specimens. It is important not to dig deeper than an inch or so when collecting these specimens. The subsoil may have a significantly different composition from the topsoil and lead to confusing results. Again, the containers should be appropriately labeled and the location of each sample noted. When taking soil samples, be aware that footwear impressions may be present.

Wood

As evidence, wood may be present as sawdust, splinters, chips, large pieces used as assault weapons (i.e., baseball bats), etc. Evidence may be present at the crime scene, on a suspect's clothing, or in a wound. Wood may also have tool marks.

Because of the wide variety of wood types and their use in building, furniture, and hand tools, this type of evidence is most valuable. It is possible to identify, compare, and match sources of wood evidence. Wood may be divided into two types: hard woods and soft woods. It is possible to determine the type of wood and often the type of tree from pieces the size of sawdust particles. The examination of wood is done microscopically.

If the question is to decide whether two pieces of stem from a tree originally belonged together, the original external contour of the stem is a good guide, if it is in good condition. Cracks in the bark, structures and formations on the surface of the bark, and the position of the sawed surface in relation to the longitudinal axis of the trunk, together with the placing and general appearance of any felling cut have their own significance for the task of identification, which is simply a matter of seeing how the different pieces fit together. By matching them against one another, it is possible to determine the correspondence between two pieces of wood separated from each other in the longitudinal direction of the tree.

---

* An excellent video (www.youtube.com/watch?v=o9dWZOj1U5A) produced by the FBI, OSAC, University of Kentucky, and the International Union of Geological Sciences (IUGS) demonstrates the proper way to collect forensic soil evidence.

The annual rings of a tree are very characteristic. By making a cross section of an object under investigation, it is often possible to obtain a picture just as characteristic of the tree, within a limited region of the stem. Bruises and decay in the wood are often characteristic in position and extent and may assist in identification.

If an object under investigation is made from wood that has been worked in some way with tools (knife, plane, saw) or has been painted or surface treated in any other way, the possibility of identification is increased. Imperfections in the edge of the knife or plane blade (including planing machines) leave characteristic marks that can possibly be found on both pieces of wood. Unplaned wood, when sawed in the direction of the grain, often shows marks of varying width and depth from the saw used. In the case of frame-sawed lumber, these marks arise during the upward and downward movements of the frame saw. The variations are caused by inequalities in the setting of the teeth and by variations in the pressure on the wood under the saw. The same conditions hold for wood cut with a circular saw; the marks are more or less curved, depending on the diameter of the saw, and differ from the marks of a frame saw, which are straight but may be more or less oblique with reference to the grain of the wood. These saw marks have special significance in the identification of pieces of wood separated from one another in the direction of the grain.

It can be more difficult to determine, solely with the aid of marks from the saw used, whether two cut off pieces originally belonged together. If the cutting was done with a hand saw, identification is sometimes possible because the marks of such a saw are often irregular and show characteristic formations. This is connected with the fact that changes in the position of the saw, in relation to the piece of wood, always occur on the forward and backward strokes of the sawing arm. Also, after a pause in sawing, the saw never takes up exactly the same position again when restarted. In cutting with a machine saw, the marks are generally regular and reproducible and therefore cannot generally be used for identification. A transverse section of wood has a poorer power of reproducing marks from a saw than a longitudinal section, owing to the difference in the structure.

If pieces of wood have been dyed or surface treated in any way, shades of color may be useful for identification and the pigment can be chemically and spectrographically examined to confirm the agreement or difference between the constituents. There may also be several coats of paint, and agreement or difference in this respect may be noted.

Any knots or cracks in pieces of wood, as well as drill holes, nail holes, or screw holes, are significant when it is necessary to decide whether or not pieces of wood originally were a unit. Based on nail or screw holes or remaining nails or screws, it is sometimes possible to determine whether a certain piece of wood was previously combined with another piece or formed part of a floor or wall.

If pieces of wood are separated from one another by a break running in the direction of the grain, identity can be determined by fitting the pieces to one another. Certain difficulties are associated with a break going across the grain because the broken surfaces are often badly splintered and a number of significant pieces may have fallen away and been lost.

Chips and Splinters of Wood

Considerable quantities of chips or splinters may be found at the scene of a forced entry. They are usually examined to find marks from the tool used to gain entry. Chips of wood can also be valuable in the identification of the tool in another way. Mixed in with chips from the forced doors or windows may be a chip that has broken off the handle of a chisel, a hammer, or another tool. A piece from a broken tool handle may be compared later with a tool recovered in the perpetrator's possession. Pieces of wood from the tool may be painted in the same way as the handle of the tool or make a physical match with the tool in jigsaw puzzle fashion.

Sawdust, Wood Meal, or Particles of Finely Powdered Wood

Particles of wood can sometimes be found in the pant cuffs, pockets, hat, or gloves of the suspect or detected on tape-lifts of the suspect's clothes. Clues consisting of these particles may also be left behind at the scene if the clothes of the suspect were contaminated with them and the trace material brought to the scene. In some cases, the species of tree can be determined simply by microscopic examination and the occurrence of any foreign bodies on or together with the particles can be confirmed.

Wood anatomy and identification is a narrow specialty not found in many crime labs. University and U.S. Government experts are available for assistance in such cases.*

---

* The Forest Products Laboratory of the U.S. Department of Agriculture is a good resource for forensic wood evidence (www.fpl.fs.fed.us/).

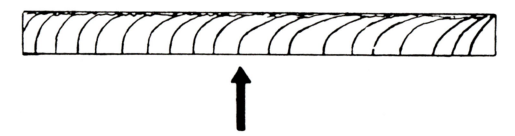

Figure 8.7 A diagram showing the curved lines in the edge of the glass in concentric fracture. They are almost perpendicular to the side from which force was applied. In radial fractures, the direction is reversed.

Plant Material

A wide variety of materials of plant origin may be useful sources of physical evidence. Leaves, seeds, bark, twigs, and pollen are sometimes collected as evidence. They may be attached to clothing, found in a vehicle, or present on a weapon. Fragments of plant material generally require a high degree of expertise to identify. Botanists employed at natural history museums or at a local arboretum may be willing to lend their expertise in the identification of such material.

Pollen (palynology) is a useful material for determining whether a subject was present in an area where flowering plants are located. Vacuum sweepings of a suspect's clothing may yield microscopic pollen grains whose species can be microscopically identified.*

Glass[†]

Glass may be useful evidence in a wide variety of cases. Hit-and-run cases often have headlamp glass or windshield glass present, burglaries frequently involve window glass, and bottle glass is sometimes found in assault cases. Broken glass may yield information about the direction and speed of a projectile and, in the case of multiple projectiles, the sequence of events.

Broken Panes of Glass

The police investigator often must decide whether a pane of glass was broken from the outside or the inside or if it was struck by a bullet or by a rock. Pieces from the broken pane or the hole often show marks characteristic of the type of injury and the direction of the force. If correctly interpreted, these indications give useful information.

Anyone who examines the edge of a piece of broken glass will note a series of curved lines that form right angles with one side of the pane and curve tangentially with the other side. These fracture lines are a result of force applied to the glass pane and are referred to as rib markings; they can be used to determine from which direction the force came that caused the glass to break (Figure 8.7).

When an object has been thrown through a glass pane, two types of fractures that form a pattern resembling a spider's web will be seen. These fractures are called radial and concentric fractures. Radial fractures are cracks that start at the center or point from which the object struck the glass and run radially outward or in a somewhat star-shaped pattern from the point at which the break starts. Concentric fractures form concentric circular cracks in the glass around the point of impact (Figure 8.8).

Determining the direction of force becomes a simple matter of examining rib markings along the edges of radial or concentric fractures. Before drawing any conclusions about the direction of force, the examiner must be certain whether a radial or a concentric fracture is being examined. It is also worthwhile to mark the pane of glass to show the inside and outside clearly.

---

* For more information on forensic botany, see Hall, David W., and Jason Byrd. *Forensic Botany: A Practical Guide*. John Wiley & Sons, 2012.
† The American Society of Testing and Materials (ASTM) has the following published standards for glass testing:
  ASTM E1967—*Standard Test Method for the Automated Determination of Refractive Index of Glass Samples Using the Oil Immersion Method and a Phase Contrast Microscope*
  ASTM E2330—*Standard Test Method for Determination of Concentrations of Elements in Glass Samples Using Inductively Coupled Plasma Mass Spectrometry (ICP-MS) for Forensic Comparisons*

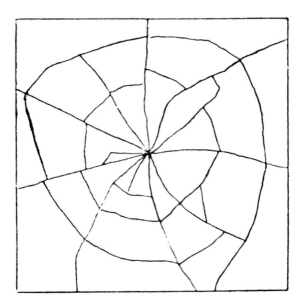

Figure 8.8 A sketch illustrating the radial and concentric fractures in a pane of glass. The radial fractures are analogous to the spokes of a bicycle wheel and radiate out from the center. The concentric fractures are more or less circular.

The determination of the direction of force is accomplished as follows: carefully remove a piece of broken glass, make note of which side faces which, locate an edge that corresponds to a radial fracture and examine it edgewise. Observe with which surface of the glass the rib markings make a right angle, because that side of the glass is not the side from which the force came; the force came from the opposite side.

The results of concentric fractures are opposite those of radial fractures. In examining the edge of a concentric fracture, the side of the glass forming the right angle with the rib markings is the side from which the force came. Because of this obvious chance of confusion, it is very important to be able to distinguish between radial and concentric fractures. It is also important to have made note of which side of the glass faced which direction.

With small pieces of glass, it is very important not to get the sides mixed up. It is advisable to collect all the pieces of glass and fit them together so that a complete picture is obtained of the broken pane where the force acted. In the case of window panes, a useful indication can be obtained from the layer of dirt often present on the outside of the glass.

Conclusions should be drawn from the curved lines of the edge surfaces only in the case of fractures that lie nearest to the point of attack. Solely with these closest fractures can one be sure that the fractures resulted from the break in question. Fractures at a greater distance from the point of attack may have been produced, for example, when the object used for breaking the glass was brought back or by projecting and interfering pieces of glass being broken off by hand.

When glass is transported to the laboratory for examination, the pieces should be carefully marked and individually wrapped in paper. The wrapped evidence may then be placed together in a box for easier transportation. Packaging should be done to minimize breakage.

Glass Perforated by a Bullet

If a bullet perforates a pane of glass, the hole is expanded in a crater on the side where the bullet exited the pane. The location at which the cone-shaped crater is narrowest indicates the direction from which the bullet was fired (Figure 8.9).

The appearance of the hole can indicate the velocity of the projectile. High-velocity bullets leave an almost circular hole in a pane of glass without noticeable cracking or with cracks merely starting. Lower velocity ammunition leaves an almost regular polygon with radial cracks running outward.

A shot at very close range more or less completely shatters the glass from the pressure of the muzzle gases; the extent depends on the power of the cartridge and the thickness of the glass. In such cases, it is impossible to obtain a clear

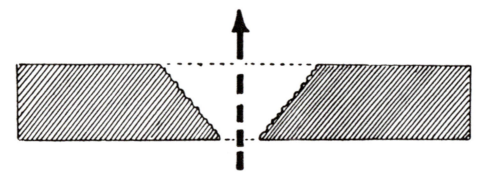

Figure 8.9 A diagram showing the formation of a bullet hole in a pane of glass; note the crater form of the hole. The arrow shows the direction of the projectile.

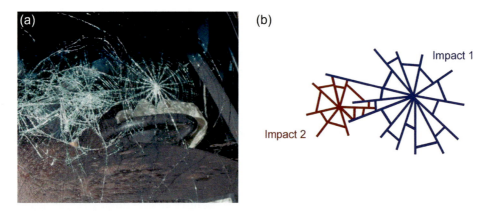

Figure 8.10 (a, b) The sequence of individual fractures can also be determined. In this example, impact 1 was created before impact 2 because the radial fractures from impact 1 block the radial fractures from impact 2 from extending.

idea of the appearance of the shot hole unless the shattered splinters of glass can be pieced together. In most cases, this is not possible because the splinters from the parts nearest the actual hole are too small. In a very favorable case, indications of the metal of the bullet on the edges around the hole may be detected spectrographically. A reliable indication that the glass was shattered by a shot at close range is the presence of gunshot residue particles on the glass.

It is sometimes difficult to determine whether a hole in a pane of glass was caused by a bullet or by a stone that was thrown. A small stone thrown at relatively high speed (such as one flung by the action of a tire of a passing car) can produce a hole very similar to that caused by a bullet. However, the crater-like expansion of a hole caused by a small stone may not show the same uniform fracture in the glass as a bullet hole would. Furthermore, holes caused by small stones generally do not show the same geometrical regularity in the radial and concentric cracks in the glass around the hole as that usually shown by a bullet hole. On the other hand, a large stone can shatter a pane of glass in a manner that nearly resembles the results of a close-range shot. Thus, a careful search for the projectile is necessary to determine the cause of the break.

If a number of breaks are in a pane of glass, it is sometimes possible to determine the order of events producing the holes. Radial cracks produced by the first incident stop by themselves or run to the edges of the glass. On the other hand, cracks from subsequent incidents stop when they meet a crack already present in the glass as a result of earlier fractures. Even when the damage is extensive and large portions of glass have fallen away, the order of the damage can often be established by fitting the pieces together (Figure 8.10a and b).

Cracked or Burst Panes of Glass

If a pane of glass has been cracked by the action of heat, it shows characteristic long wavy fractures. Pieces that have fallen out are generally found in the same direction as the source of heat. If a limited area of the glass has been exposed to a direct flame, a piece of glass corresponding to that area often breaks off.

Automobile safety glass breaks completely or partially into pieces or small rods of a regular form when subjected to a violent blow or shock. Automobile manufacturers use tempered glass intentionally because it lessens the chance of vehicle occupants being cut by flying glass.

A pane of tempered glass shattered by a bullet may still remain hanging in position on the vehicle. In a typical pattern, the crack formation extends over the whole pane, but close around the point of fracture, a large number of small pieces of glass usually come loose and fall away; thus a study of the crater formation in the glass is possible only in rare cases. If pieces that have fallen out are found, however, in favorable cases, they can be pieced together in their places near the point of impact and the appearance of the fracture can be reconstructed.

If a few small pieces believed to be tempered glass are found at the scene of an accident, a simple test can determine whether the glass is in fact tempered. Interference patterns caused by strain in the glass are easily observed by examining the glass with polarized light. A specimen of glass is placed over a light source with a polarizing filter. The glass is viewed with a second polarizing filter and a characteristic pattern is observed, indicating tempered glass.

Glass Splinters

At a scene where the suspect has obtained entry by breaking a window, the investigating officer should always remember to collect pieces of glass for comparison purposes. If a suspect is found at a later time, a careful examination of the clothing may show splinters of glass (Figure 8.11). Glass splinters may also be found in the handle of a tool used to force entry into a building.

When such splinters of glass are found on a suspect's clothing or tools from a burglary investigation, they will usually be too small to make a direct physical comparison against the pane of glass from which they possibly came. However, a number of other comparisons can be made to show a common source between the exemplar and questioned glass specimens.

Glass evidence may be examined for a number of physical and chemical properties. Density, refractive index, color, thickness, and chemical composition are some of the common characteristics examined to differentiate glass. Such tests will not result in a definite identification because glass is a mass-produced material with wide use.

When known samples of glass evidence are collected as exemplars, at least one square inch from each broken glass object should be collected. For multipane glass, samples should be collected from all layers and packaged separately

Figure 8.11 A burglar may be linked to a window he smashed by the tiny fragments of glass that fly backward onto his person and clothing. (*Courtesy of the Centre of Forensic Sciences, Toronto, Canada.*)

because there may be variations in glass properties. Always note the direction one or both of the sides of the glass face before taking the sample. Glass should be taken from the window frame rather from the ground. Finally, puncture-resistant packaging such as boxes or rigid plastic containers should be used. Tape may be placed on the glass to keep it intact during transport if a physical fit is possible.

OBJECTS LEFT AT THE CRIME SCENE

Criminals sometimes leave items behind at the crime scene that they believe have no further use. Items may be lost or forgotten by the suspect. He may have been surprised during the act and forced to leave abruptly without picking up personal effects. Items left behind can be extremely valuable to investigators; they may help connect the suspect to the crime in other ways or prove the suspect's identity if fingerprints or DNA are present.

Paper

Paper such as newspaper, wrapping paper, and paper bags are sometimes left at a crime scene. Traces, handwriting, latent fingerprints, and trace DNA may be present. If the paper at the scene is torn or cut, a search of the suspect's home or car may turn up a matching piece of paper that can be fitted together with the evidence. In some cases, watermarks or stains on a piece of paper may be used to show a connection to a particular paper manufacturer.

Articles of Clothing

Manufacturer's markings on clothing are occasionally of value. The presence of a foreign label in clothing may indicate the nationality of the wearer; however, because a huge number of clothes are imported, any conclusion is open to question. Size and laundry marks may be valuable. Size gives an indication of the physical characteristics of the subject and laundry marks may identify the suspect. Other marks such as initials and even names are sometimes found. One should always search for hair and other trace evidence. If secretions or dried blood are found on an article of clothing left at a crime scene, the subject's DNA type may be determined. Pockets should be searched as a matter of course. In some cases, useful evidence will be found. Torn pieces of clothing are valuable. If a matching piece of clothing can be found in the suspect's home or car, it can easily tie the suspect to the location.

Product Markings

Many commercial products bear manufacturer's marks on the label, package, or container. The markings are used to designate the date, lot number, location of manufacture, and other such details as a control to assist the manufacturer in checking on distribution, sales of the product, and quality control. The markings may also assist the investigator in determining the origin of products found at crime scenes. Because the markings are usually in code form, the manufacturer or distributor must be contacted to determine the meaning of the information.

Case Review

When a car wash in a large metropolitan area opened for business one morning, a restroom was found unlocked. Inside a deceased woman lying naked on the floor was found. Near her body were a used condom and an open empty condom packet. DNA analysis of the semen inside the used condom produced a good profile but was not a match for any entries in CODIS. The case remained cold until after more than a decade when a DNA hit was made. However, when the outside surface of the used condom was swabbed trying to obtain the victim's DNA from vaginal epithelial cells, only a partial match was obtained. Still in evidence was one vaginal cotton swab obtained at autopsy from the victim collected back in 1993. Could condom trace evidence on the swab be compared with any traces found on the used condom, and also with any residues on the inside surface of the empty condom packet?

All three items were positive for the same condom lubricant; all three showed numerous corn starch grains, and all three showed traces of the same antioxidant added to impede the degradation of the latex. The lubricant and cornstarch grains are found in a number of latex condoms from different manufacturers. Stamped on the outside of the empty condom packet were a lot number and the expiration date. From contact with the manufacturer it was learned that the entire lot had been purchased in the same metropolitan area as where the crime was committed. The used condom was also consistent with their brand in terms of shape, color, and texture

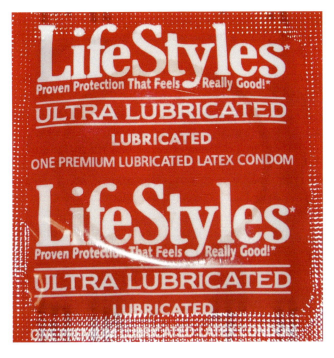

Figure 8.12 The brand of condom found at the crime scene.

(Figure 8.12). The clincher was that of the three major latex condom manufacturers they were the only ones back in 1993 that used that particular antioxidant. Apparently, this was sufficient to convince the jury that the traces from the vaginal cotton swab, the used condom, and the open empty condom packet were all connected. The defendant was found guilty and received a life sentence.

(*Case submitted courtesy of Robert D. Blackledge, El Cajon, CA.*)

Foodstuffs

Foodstuffs in the form of stains or debris are sometimes found as evidence and may be useful in determining the type of work in which a subject is engaged. For example, if vacuum sweepings are examined and a quantity of wheat starch is found, it could indicate that the suspect had been baking. Through careful examination, it is possible to determine the nature of very small samples of foodstuffs through microscopic and microchemical means.

Cosmetics

Cosmetics such as lipstick, nail polish, and various creams and lotions may sometimes be collected as evidence in cases. If exemplars are available, a laboratory can make a chemical comparison to determine whether the known and questioned specimens share a common source. Cosmetic firms are constantly reformulating their products, and so if the brand of the cosmetic can be determined, it may be possible to determine the approximate time a given specimen was on the market.

Hair

Hair evidence is generally associated with crimes involving physical contact such as murder, rape, assault, traffic accidents, and other similar crimes. Hair may be found at the crime scene, on the victim or suspect, or attached to a weapon, tool, vehicle, or article of clothing. Because of its small size, hair may be difficult to find. Care and patience are required to conduct a thorough search for this evidence.

Microscopic hair comparison is rarely done anymore today due in large part to errors found by the FBI during a Root Cause Analysis of Microscopic Hair Comparison Analysis.* The Innocence Project uncovered these cases in

---

* https://vault.fbi.gov/root-cause-analysis-of-microscopic-hair-comparison-analysis/root-cause-analysis-of-microscopic-hair-comparison-analysis-part-01-of-01/view.

which the interpretation of hair examinations has been in conflict with DNA test results. While microscopic hair comparisons are no longer done, DNA testing (both nuclear and mtDNA) can reveal the identity of the person who shed the hair.

Other useful information such as species, location of growth on the body, hair treatment, hair disease, and whether hairs fell out naturally or were forcibly pulled can also be determined.

When conducting a hair examination, the criminalist first attempts to determine whether the hair evidence is animal or synthetic in origin. Microscopic examination of a hair quickly determines whether the evidence is animal, synthetic, or simply a plant fiber. Furthermore, it is possible to determine whether the hair is human or animal in origin and, if animal, the species of the animal. Domestic animals such as dogs and cats are somewhat common. Hairs from wild animals are sometimes collected at crime scenes, for example, at the scene of skeletal remains. Although differentiating between human and animal hair is not difficult, determining the species of animal requires a greater degree of expertise from a hair examiner.

In addition to determining that a specimen of hair is human, it is usually possible to determine whether the hair is from the head or another part of the body. At one time, it was possible to draw a conclusion about the gender of an individual based on the length of a hair strand. Present hairstyles no longer make that deduction valid.

Examination of hair may indicate that it was chemically treated. Hairs that have been bleached, dyed, straightened, or otherwise treated can be compared with specimens from a subject to determine whether the subject's hair has been treated in the same way. Sometimes, hair shows the presence of lice or fleas, which can be useful as a means of comparison. Microscopic examination of the hair root may indicate that the hair was forcibly pulled out as opposed to falling out naturally. Such information may be used to indicate a struggle.

Searching for hair at the crime scene is a tedious process. Subjecting the floor, furniture, and other objects to a very thorough examination is necessary; a flashlight and pair of tweezers are suggested for this purpose. Hair found on an object or in a certain location should be placed in a paper fold or sticky note and then placed in a properly labeled envelope. Detailed notes should be made to indicate the date and time of collection, and location of the hair. A sketch or photograph of the area should be made. When a number of hair samples are collected from the same location at the crime scene, sorting the specimens is not recommended. They should be submitted to the crime laboratory for careful expert examination. If several hairs from different locations are collected, it is important not to package them together.

Hair evidence is frequently found on the body of a victim. Pulled-out strands of hair may be found clutched in the hands or under the fingernails of a murder victim. A rape victim sometimes has her assailant's pubic hair present on her body or the bed or location where she was lying.

Pubic hair combings in rape and rape-murder cases are a routine way of collecting hair evidence. It is advisable to collect hair as well as other types of evidence associated with these cases as soon as possible. Trace evidence such as hair is quickly lost unless gathered promptly.

Clothing belonging to the victim of a murder, rape, or assault should be examined for hair evidence. Hairs may become entangled among threads of the fabric. Generally, a very careful examination of the clothing is necessary to locate hairs.

Feathers (Plumology)

In rare instances, feathers may be collected as evidence in an investigation. Most crime laboratories have very little or no expertise in analyzing this type of material. Feathers may be identified by experts at museums or academic institutions.*

Electrical Wire

Insulated electrical wire is sometimes collected as evidence. The wire may have been used to tie up a victim of a crime or it is sometimes attached to a car stereo stolen from a vehicle. In both cases, it may be possible to show that one end of the wire was once part of another end.

---

* For an overview of plumology see https://academy.allaboutbirds.org/feathers-article/.

Generally, an electrical wire that has many strands does not lend itself to tool mark examination. The wires are so fine that sufficient markings are not imparted onto the wire from the tool. If the wire is of a thicker gauge, it may be possible to examine extrusion marks on both ends to determine if each of the pieces has the same class characteristics.

Extrusion marks will also be present on the wire insulation. Because the insulation has a greater surface area, it is easier to work with that portion of the evidence. The extrusion markings along with the cut edge, which sometimes can be made to fit the other piece of wire evidence, can lead to the conclusion that the wires were once from the same continuous piece.

If a positive fit cannot be made, physical characteristics such as the number of strands of wire, the gauge, the appearance of the break, and the color and markings on the insulation may be used at least to show that the wire was of a similar manufacture.

Tape

Electrical, adhesive, duct, masking, and packing tape are sometimes recovered at crime scenes. The tape may have been used to bind a victim, to tape two objects together, or to seal a threatening package. If a roll of tape is located in the suspect's belongings, it may be possible to piece together the portion of tape from the scene and that found in the suspect's possession through physical fit. Questioned tape pieces should be placed on clear plastic sheets (i.e., transparency sheets) to prevent wadding. In cases where a victim was bound, do not attempt to unwrap bindings. Instead, cut any binding away from the torn tape ends using pinking shears and label the cut ends clearly. The pinking shears will create edges that are easily differentiated from existing edges. If the tape is sticky, do not place the tape on paper or in a paper bag. Place the sticky tape on non-stick foil or on acetate sheets. Since tape is often torn with the teeth, DNA testing can also be done on the ends (Figure 8.13).

Headlamps

Headlamps from automobiles and other motor vehicles are sometimes submitted to crime laboratories in traffic accident investigations. A careful examination of the headlamp filament may help determine whether the lamp was on

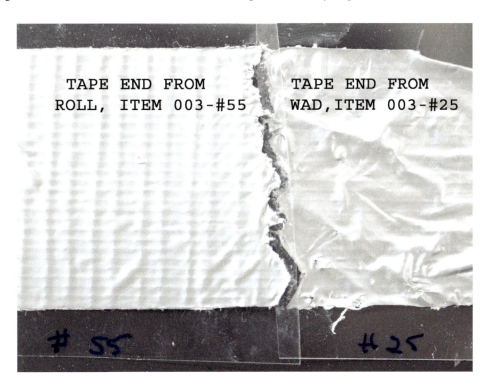

Figure 8.13 Duct tape is commonly used in a variety of different crimes. Often, it is possible to demonstrate that the tape found on the victim or at the crime scene and the tape found in possession of the suspect came from the same source by a careful examination of the cut or torn ends. (*Courtesy of Frederic A Tulleners, UC Davis, California.*)

or off at the time of the accident. Lighted filaments will behave differently from unlighted filaments when subjected to a sudden stop in a car crash. Many of today's cars no longer use filament type headlights. It is not possible to draw a conclusion for light-emitting diodes (LED), high intensity discharge, or fluorescent bulbs.

The entire lamp assembly with the lamp inside should be sent to the lab. A protective enclosure, such as nested styrofoam cups, should cover the lamps. Do not turn on lamps at the crime scene to see if they work.

Physical Fit

Physical fit evidence may be found at many different types of crime scenes. Examples include: stabbings where the knife tip left in the wound fits back to the blade; assaults where wood pieces fit to the baseball bat; hit-and-run where broken parts from the front bumper fit back to the car; and kidnapping where a torn ransom note fits back to the pad of paper.

Additionally, broken tools are frequently discovered at burglaries of safes and breaking-and-entering cases. Broken ends from screwdrivers, wrecking bars, and metal punches are important types of physical evidence. Refitting these materials with irregular edges together demonstrates that they were at one time joined as a single object.

In addition to the physical fit, a microscopic examination of the knife and the broken piece of blade usually shows fine scratches caused by wear and tear on the flat surface of the blade. These markings run continuously through the area of the break and can conclusively show that the broken piece and the blade were once a continuous piece.

OSAC TRACE MATERIALS SUBCOMMITTEE

The National Institute of Standards and Technology (NIST), Organization of Scientific Area Committees (OSAC) Trace Materials Subcommittee (www.nist.gov/osac/trace-materials-subcommittee) focuses on standards and guidelines related to examination and interpretation of physical evidence that may result from the transfer of small or minute quantities of materials (e.g., hairs, fibers, paint, tape, glass, geological materials). The OSAC Registry now has multiple Trace Materials standards published by the American Society for Testing Materials (ASTM) including, the *Standard Guide for Fourier Transform Infrared Spectroscopy in Forensic Tape Examinations*, *Standard Guide for Forensic Paint Analysis and Comparison*, and *Standard Test Method for the Automated Determination of Refractive Index of Glass Samples Using the Oil Immersion Method and a Phase Contrast Microscope*.

SWGMAT

Prior to the formation of the OSACs, the Scientific Working Group for Materials Analysis (SWGMAT*) was dedicated to improving the field of trace evidence analysis through development of guidelines and best practices for the analysis of trace evidence, the training of new examiners, and the interpretation of data. SWGMAT's efforts have now been absorbed by the OSAC Trace Materials Subcommittee.

Further Reading

Desiderio, Vincent J., Chris E. Taylor, and Niamh Nic Daéid, eds. *Handbook of Trace Evidence Analysis*. Wiley, 2020.

Fitzpatrick, Robert W., and Laurance J. Donnelly. "Introduction to Forensic Soil Science and Forensic Geology: A Synthesis," *Geological Society, London, Special Publications* 492, 2021.

Hall, David W., and Jason Byrd. *Forensic Botany: A Practical Guide*. Wiley, 2012.

Petraco, Nicholas, and Thomas Kubic. *Color Atlas and Manual of Microscopy for Criminalists, Chemists, and Conservators*. CRC Press, 2003.

Robertson, James, Claude Roux, and Kenneth G. Wiggins. *Forensic Examination of Fibres*. CRC Press, 2017.

---

* www.asteetrace.org/swgmat.

Chapter Questions

1. Which of the following items could be classified as trace evidence?
   a) Safe insulation.
   b) Glass shards.
   c) Soil.
   d) All of the above.
2. Describe how Locard's exchange principle occurs with regard to trace evidence left behind at a crime scene.
3. When dealing with a homicide victim's clothing, which of the following procedures is the best way to capture any trace evidence?
   a) Let the medical examiner collect the clothing at the autopsy.
   b) Examine the clothing for trace evidence before transporting the body for an autopsy and collect any items that you find.
   c) Remove the clothes at the scene and package together to minimize cross-contamination.
   d) Allow the clothes to fully dry on the body before transporting to the autopsy.
4. When is it better to remove an item of trace evidence from a larger object rather than collecting the whole item?
5. The _____ exemplars must never be packaged with the questioned samples.
   a) Known.
   b) Unknown.
   c) Crime scene.
   d) Standard.
6. Describe the proper procedure for collecting paint samples from a hit-and-run investigation involving two vehicles.
7. Which of the following techniques would be the best method for collecting fibers found on the floor at the point of entry at a homicide scene?
   a) Using forceps.
   b) Tape-lifts.
   c) Vacuum.
   d) All are acceptable.
8. (True or false) When trying to determine the direction of force in glass using a concentric edge, the side of the glass forming a right angle with the conchoidal fracture is the side the force came from.
9. What are some of the characteristics that a criminalist can provide when examining paint?
10. How is glass significant in a forensic context?

CHAPTER 9

Impression Evidence

Minute imperfections on a large variety of objects such as tools, footwear, and tires produce markings in their normal (and sometimes unusual) usage. These markings are often characteristic of the type of tool or object used. In many instances, microscopic unique markings are left that can be traced directly to the object or instrument in question.

Such marks caused by a tool are of two general types: compression marks and scraping marks. Compression marks are those left when an instrument is in some way pushed or forced into a material capable of picking up an impression of the tool. Examples include shoe impressions, tire impressions, fabric impressions, the mark left by a hammer hitting a piece of wood, the mark of a screwdriver used to jimmy a window, breech mark impressions on shell casings, etc. Scraping or striated marks are produced by a combination of pressure and sliding contact by the tool and result in microscopic striations imparted to the surface onto which the tool was worked. Examples of scraping marks are those found on fired bullets, left by a cutting tool such as a bolt cutter, from a wrench used on a doorknob, from an ax used to cut wood, and from a screwdriver blade dragged over a surface. In order for compression or scraping marks to be observed, the tool must be made of a harder material than the object on which it is used.

The random nature and microscopic imperfections found on tools are a result of their manufacture and usage. Casting, grinding, and polishing metal instruments, as well as using them, result in small but observable differences from one tool to the next. Such differences have even been demonstrated in consecutively manufactured items.

Comparative examination is the method by which impression-type evidence is studied. The marks left at the crime scene (or castings of the mark) are compared with test markings made by the tool or object in question. Through careful and often tedious examination of the known and questioned evidence, a determination can be made as to whether or not a particular item was responsible for a specific mark.*

FOOTPRINTS

Footprints are a common type of impression evidence found at or near crime scenes. In favorable situations, such evidence may demonstrate that the suspect was at the scene of the crime. A detailed examination of footprints is tedious and time-consuming work and may be overlooked by the investigator. Although this discussion concerns footwear impressions, the investigator should not overlook soil evidence that might later be discovered on the suspect's shoes.

When a cast is made of a footprint in soft ground, one would expect to obtain a faithful reproduction of the heel and sole of the shoe that made the print. As a rule, however, the result of casting is actually quite different—the cast has an arched form. The back of the heel and the point of the toe are considerably lower than the other parts of the cast because, in normal walking, the back of the heel is placed on the ground first. After that, each part of the heel and sole

---

* Assertions of uniqueness of pattern evidence examination have been hotly debated in the past few years. Proponents claim that given sufficient random or accidental markings on a tool, experts can proffer conclusive opinions on the source of a tool mark. Others argue that uniqueness may only be described statistically.

is pressed down on the ground in succession until the foot is lifted, with a final strong pressure of the point of the toe against the earth. The pressure that regulates the depth of the impression is the greatest at the back of the heel and at the point of the toe. When running, the footprints are less distinct, partly owing to slipping of the foot and partly to sand and earth thrown into the print. The form of the print depends on the individual's style of running; many people run on their toes, others set both heel and toe hard in the ground, and others set the whole foot down in the earth at once. In deciding whether an individual walked or ran, the length of the step is the best guide.

VALUE OF FOOTPRINTS

Individual footprints are generally preserved only if they contain details of value for identification. The most valuable details are signs of wear, characteristic fittings or marks of fittings that have come off, injuries, marks of nails and pegs, especially when these are irregularly placed, and repair marks. If they are particularly characteristic or occur in sufficient numbers, such details may form decisive evidence. In the interest of thoroughness, footprints should be preserved even if they do not show any details. Although the size and shape of the shoe or a pattern in the heel or sole is of lesser evidential value, a representative print should nonetheless be preserved for its value as an investigative lead.

If footprints are found in snow that has a frozen crust, it is a waste of time to attempt to take a cast of them. When the foot breaks through the hard surface of the snow, the surface snow goes with it and forms a hard bottom to the mark. The coarse grains of ice in the surface layer do not reproduce any details of the shoe—not even such large defects as a hole through the sole—and it is not possible to obtain any useful information of the size by measuring the footprint because the hard snow is broken and pressed down at points considerably outside the outer contour of the shoe.

A footwear print may be a foot impression or a footprint (dust print). Foot impressions occur when the foot treads in some moldable material such as earth, sand, clay, snow, etc. Footprints are formed on a hard base when the foot or the sole and heel of a shoe are contaminated with some foreign matter such as road dirt, dust, flour, blood, or moisture. Footprints may also be latent when naked or stocking-covered feet on a smooth surface having formed them.

Footwear impression evidence and information from the gait pattern may indicate that the subject was walking or running, had sustained an injury or walked with a limp, was possibly intoxicated, had a tendency to walk toe-in or toe-out, or was carrying a heavy object.*

PRESERVATION OF FOOTWEAR AND TIRE IMPRESSIONS

Although the focus here is on footprints, much of what follows concerning preservation and collecting this type of evidence applies equally well to tire impression evidence.

Foot impressions are generally found outdoors; the first precautionary measure is therefore to protect the impression from alteration or destruction, preferably by covering it with a box or cordoning off the area. Impressions in thawing snow are especially troublesome, so a box covered with snow to prevent thawing should protect them. If a foot impression is in such a position that it is possible for it to gradually fill up or be damaged by running water, it must be surrounded by a wall of earth, sand, or snow; alternatively, a hole may be dug close to the impression and the water drained toward the hole. However, these protective measures are only stopgaps and the actual preservation should be undertaken as soon as possible.

FOOTPRINTS ON FLOORS

Interior locations often have footprints present, especially on surfaces such as tiled floors, glass, desktops, countertops, and chair seats. A simple procedure to locate these indoor prints is to turn off all the interior lights and, by means of a high-intensity flashlight, search the surfaces by shining the light at a low angle. Often these impressions are dust prints and very easily destroyed. Once detected, care must be taken to make certain they are preserved (Figure 9.1).

---

* The field of forensic podiatry deals with pedal evidence, the use of podiatry in forensic cases and a person's gait. The American Society of Forensic Podiatry(www.theasfp.org) promotes utilizing the analysis and evaluation of evidence related to the human foot in forensic cases.

Impression Evidence   131

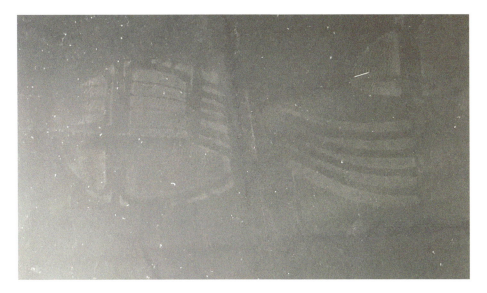

Figure 9.1 A dust print lifted by an electrostatic dust print lifter.

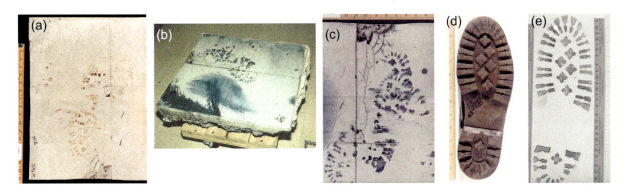

Figure 9.2 In 1992, a horrific murder of a young woman occurred in New York City in the rear of a retail store. The victim was bound and gagged in the rear office and stabbed multiple times with a screwdriver. At the scene, detectives noted bloody footprints on the cement floor. The piece of floor in question was cut out and transported to the FBI laboratory. The suspect's shoe shared agreement of class and randomly acquired characteristics of sufficient quality and quantity with the prints on the floor. Bloody footprints (a) are visible on a portion of the concrete floor. The actual portion of the floor (b) was stained with amido black by the examiner to make the prints more visible (c). The soles of the suspect's shoes (d) and a print of the shoes (e) were compared and in the opinion of the examiner the known footwear was the source of the questioned impression. (*Courtesy of William Bodziak, Bodziak Forensics, Florida and formerly with the FBI Laboratory.*)

PRESERVATION OF FOOTWEAR EVIDENCE

Preservation should be done by photographing and casting or, in the case of dust prints, by lifting.

PHOTOGRAPHING FOOTWEAR IMPRESSIONS

The most common errors made in crime scene photography involve taking photographs of shoe and tire impressions that result in poor-quality photographs. Reasons for this include the following: not using a tripod to support the camera, not shooting perpendicular to the impression, failing to use a scale or ruler in the photograph, and not using oblique lighting. Overall, taking quality photographs is relatively simple, but it requires practice (Figure 9.2a–e).

The camera should be placed vertically above the impression on a tripod with a scale placed next to the impression. The film plane should be parallel to the impression so as not to cause distortion in the photograph. It is good practice

Figure 9.3 Photograph of a shoe print in mud with the film plane parallel to the impression and illuminated with oblique lighting.

to place two scales in the photograph at right angles to each other. One ruler can be placed adjacent to the long axis of the foot impression and a second perpendicular to the first, in the region adjacent to the heel (Figure 9.3).*

If the bottom of the impression is appreciably deeper than the surface of the ground or snow, the scale should be brought down to the same level. Before photographing, any material that may have fallen into the impression after it was formed should be cleaned away. For this purpose, it is convenient to use tweezers, a piece of paper onto which lumps of earth are rolled, or other such objects that cannot be picked up by the tweezers. If it is not possible to carry out this cleaning without injuring details of the impression, it should be omitted. Materials trampled into the impression, such as leaves or grass, should not be removed because they form part of the impression and no details will be found under them. Careless removal of a trampled blade of grass can destroy large parts of the impression. Any water that may be present should be carefully removed by a hypodermic syringe or small pump. If a foot impression has been made in snow, it may be difficult to get a clear picture of it. Hard snow may be dusted with aluminum powder, which gives a clearer picture. With loose snow, aluminum powder can be dusted into the mark by tapping the brush.

Because the details in foot impressions are three dimensional, the photograph should be made under illumination that will bring out those details to the best advantage. Direct sunlight enhances the details by creating highlights and shadows. When the sky is cloudy and the daylight diffuse without shadow, artificial light must be used; photoflood or flash illumination is suitable. These considerations, of course, also apply to situations in which it is imperative that the pictures be taken at night. The important point to remember about the illumination is that the light must not be held at too low an angle because too much shadow will obscure rather than emphasize detail.

Casting footwear impressions is generally done with dental stone. Other materials include paraffin, sulfur, and silicone rubber,† which are less frequently used.

CASTING WITH DENTAL STONE

Dental stone is a type of gypsum or calcium sulfate that can be used to cast shoe and tire impressions. At one time, plaster of Paris was more widely used for this purpose, however, dental stone is superior and readily available from dental supply companies. Dental stone can be used for casting most impressions, even in snow.

---

* This video at (https://www.youtube.com/watch?v=1nB5SeZUhtA) from the National Forensic Academy shows the proper way to photograph footwear impression evidence.
† Casting impressions takes practice. It is recommended that one develop skills by working on non-evidentiary footmarks with dental stone or any of the other techniques.

Foot impressions in loose, dry sand and earth can be taken without any special preparation. Some literature suggests removing loose twigs and leaves, but this practice can damage the impression and is discouraged. Also, using fixatives such as spray lacquers or talc, practices generally recommended for use with plaster of Paris, are not necessary with dental stone.

CASTING WATER-FILLED IMPRESSIONS

Dental stone lends itself quite well to casting water-filled impressions. If an impression is very muddy or filled with water, no attempt should be made to remove the water because this may damage the impression.

A retaining wall or frame should be placed around the impression. The retainer should allow for a cast of at least two inches in thickness. Dental stone is lightly sprinkled or sifted directly into the water-filled impression to about an inch thickness, followed by normally prepared dental stone that has been prepared with a little less water and is slightly thicker. The cast should be poured to about two-inches thick and allowed to set in place for an hour.

To cast a footprint, about two pounds of dental stone in about 12 ounces of water is used. A clean rubber bowl can be used for mixing. Water should first be added to the bowl followed by sifting in the dental stone. The mixture should be stirred to remove any lumps and air bubbles. The final mix should be the consistency of pancake batter. An alternative method is to use a zippered plastic bag to carry about two pounds of dental stone and to mix the material right in the bag. This procedure is reported to be very convenient to use. (Note that when dental stone is mixed with water the solution heats up. This heating causes difficulties when casting impressions in snow. For this reason, a small amount of snow or ice should be added to the mixture to keep the temperature down, and the mixture should be made slightly more viscous than pancake-batter consistency.)

After the material is mixed, it should be gently poured onto an area adjacent to the impression and allowed to flow onto the impression. If it is necessary to pour the material into the impression, a baffle such as a flat stick or spoon can be used to lessen the impact of the material. Great care needs to be taken that the dental stone does not destroy any of the fine material in the impression. Before the cast hardens it should be marked, using a twig, scribe, or other sharp instrument, with information including the date, investigator's name or initials, case number, and location of the impression.

The material will harden sufficiently for removal in about 30 minutes. Clumps of soil and rocks clinging to the cast should not be disturbed and the cast should be allowed to air-dry thoroughly for about 48 hours. If the impression is deep and firmly seated, it should be carefully excavated so that it finally lies on a pillar that may then be cut off.*

CASTING IMPRESSIONS IN SNOW

When casting impressions in snow, the impression is prepared first by spraying a thin layer of Snow Print Wax (available from a number of law enforcement supply companies). The print should be photographed a second time after the application of the Snow Print Wax spray. After the spray has been applied to cover the print completely and then allowed to dry, the dental stone is carefully poured into the impression. The stone is prepared with cold water and snow and should be made slightly thicker than normal. The material should be allowed to set up for at least an hour before removal and should dry for about 48 hours.†

PRESERVATION OF FOOTPRINTS (DUST PRINTS)

Footprints are always preserved by photographing. After this is done, one of the following methods should be applied:

1. *Recovering the object on which the footprint is made.* Footprints are often found on objects stepped on by the suspect (entering in the dark through a window, for example). If the window is broken, all fragments of glass should be examined. This type of print is usually best detected by low-angle illumination from one side. Rubber heels and soles leave exceptionally good prints on glass. Detailed prints are often also found on paper or cardboard

---

* The video at www.youtube.com/watch?v=_WYU2f0anjU by the National Forensic Academy shows how to cast footwear impression evidence at a crime scene.
† The video at www.youtube.com/watch?v=60dLgWfDV8I demonstrates how to cast a footwear impression in snow.

Figure 9.4 A footwear examiner making an (a) exemplar print of a known shoe in order to compare to a (b) questioned impression. (*Courtesy of the Los Angeles County Sheriff's Department.*)

that may be strewn about the room during a safe burglary. All such loose objects bearing prints should be carefully preserved for transport to the laboratory. When the seriousness of the crime warrants it and when the print consists of a dried liquid such as blood or ink, it may be advisable to remove a portion of linoleum or floor tile that bears a clear impression.

2. *Lifting by a special lifter* is preferred whenever dust or a dust-like substance holds the print from the shoe. The lifter is a sheet of black rubber with a slightly sticky surface that is pressed against the print, picking up a replica of the whole print. Oblique light photography under laboratory conditions brings out this dust print to a contrast often better than that observed in the original print. If a sufficiently large fingerprint lifter is available, it may be used instead of the special lifter. Care must be taken not to stretch the rubber lifter because the dust image may become distorted.

3. *Lifting by photographic paper* may be employed when special lifters are not available. Black (exposed, developed, fixed, and washed) or white (fixed and washed) photographic paper is used, as determined by the color of the material in the print. The paper is dampened with water or dilute ammonia, laid emulsion side down over the print, and beaten against the print with a stiff brush or clapped with the palm. When the whole surface has been thoroughly beaten, the paper is removed and laid out to dry.

4. *Lifting by static electricity* is another technique. Companies selling evidence collection equipment also sell field kits called **electrostatic dust lifters**, which pick up dust prints onto Mylar-coated foil by means of static electricity. This procedure has applications in certain situations in which suspects walked on tile floors.[*]

TAKING COMPARISON FOOTPRINTS FROM A SUSPECT

When the original prints are from covered feet, for example, shoes or sneakers, the examiner who makes comparison shoe prints should wear them. When comparison footprints are taken, the soles are coated with water-based ink using a large inkpad. The inked shoes are then carefully stepped onto a sheet of tracing paper or acetate sheet (Figure 9.4a and b).

In taking prints of bare feet, the feet are blackened by pressing them against a thin layer of printing ink. To get a true picture of the formation of the sole of the foot in different positions, four different prints are taken: normal standing position, standing position with pressure against the outside of the foot and with pressure against the inside, and finally when walking. This also applies to stocking feet.

COMPARISON OF FOOTPRINTS

Comparison between footprints found at the scene of a crime and those of a suspect should be made by an expert.[†] Prints or impressions of shoe-covered feet are seldom the same size as the shoes; even when they are made, slipping and the movement of walking can damage prints. The mark of a naked foot in movement can be as much as one inch longer than the mark of the same foot in the standing position. A foot impression in wet earth can become

---

[*] This video at www.youtube.com/watch?v=LCh3k9CkXr4 shows the procedure for electrostatic dustprint lifting.
[†] The IAI offers footwear certification in order to become a recognized Certified Footwear Examiner.

appreciably smaller when the earth dries; in clay, the length can decrease by up to three-quarters of an inch. Thus, in establishing identity, too much significance should not be attached to dimensions. When examining the mark of a shoe-covered foot, the circumference characteristics should be checked. If the marks from the scene of the crime and from the suspect are similar in form, it is less important that they may differ somewhat in size.

Identification is based mainly on characteristic marks on the sole or heel. The examination is best done by direct comparison of the preserved footmark from the scene of the crime with the foot covering of the suspect. These are photographed side by side and characteristic points are marked. With footprints, however, it is generally convenient to take a print of the foot covering of the suspect and compare the prints. When it is a question of prints of bare feet, an examination is made first to see if there are any identifiable friction skin patterns and, if this is the case, the investigation is carried out just like for finger and palm prints.

In examining the foot covering of a suspect, dust, dirt, and earth should be kept and, if necessary, compared with similar materials at the scene of the crime. If a shoe is found at the crime scene, it may contain characteristic marks of wear from the owner's foot. Such marks can then be compared with the markings inside shoes and in some cases may be shown to have been worn by the suspect. The shoe and/or laces can also be swabbed for DNA to determine the wearer.

Case Review

A suspect unlawfully entered a dwelling committing a burglary in violation of a valid order of protection. The suspect broke a window to gain entry, committed burglary, and beat up the victim. The suspect had previously resided there at some point in time. Submitted to the Trace Evidence section of the laboratory were a pair of boots, a CD with two photos of partial footwear impressions from a window sill (point of entry), and various swabs from the crime scene (Figure 9.5).

MARKS ON CLOTHES AND PARTS OF THE BODY

If clothing is pressed against a smooth surface, a latent print may be produced. Such a print is developed in the same way as a fingerprint or glove print. Clothing contaminated with a foreign material such as blood can also form a print. When clothing comes in contact with a plastic substance (e.g., clay), an identifiable plastic impression may be formed in it.

FABRIC MARKS

When a mark from clothing is to be recorded, it must be photographed with the camera placed vertically above or centrally in front of the mark. A scale must be placed at the side of the mark. If the mark is sufficiently large, the scale may be placed in the center of it. In such cases, a number of pictures should be taken and the scale should be moved to either side for each exposure so that details are not concealed.

Marks of clothes are identified with the aid of the structure of the fabric, faults in the fabric, seams, patches and other repairs, damage, and the like.

Sometimes, a whole section of the body forms impression marks from a body print or impression. In one case, a burglar fell from a water spout onto the damp earth below, making an impression that clearly showed the face with a characteristic nose and both hands, one holding a crowbar and the other a pistol. When a hand has made a print or impression on a plastic medium, one should look for identifiable friction skin patterns. Other marks may also be found such as those of rings, injuries, characteristic skin wrinkles, hand coverings, and so on. The preservation of marks of parts of the body is done in the same way as for footprints.

TOOL MARKS

Marks of tools or of objects that have been used as tools are often found at the scene of a crime, especially in cases of burglary. Marks may have been left in wood, metal, putty, or paint. Among the tools that leave identifiable marks are axes, knives, screwdrivers, chisels, crowbars, pliers, cutters, and drill bits. Some of these tools may be homemade.

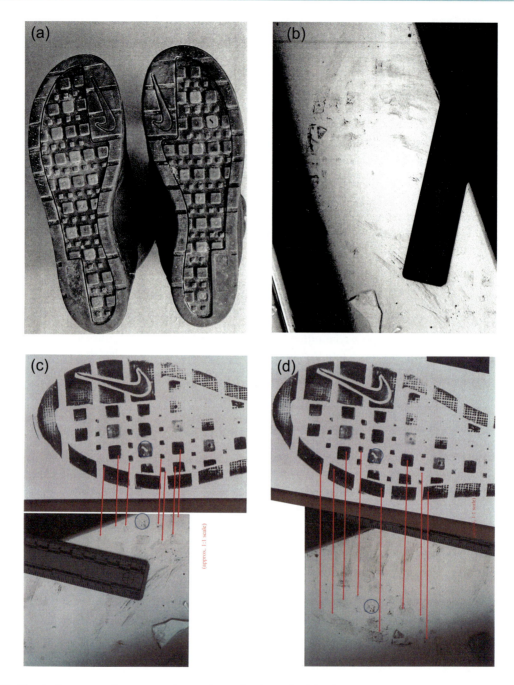

Figure 9.5 The footwear examiner prepared control samples from the (a) submitted boots for comparison to the (b) partial footwear impression seen on the CD. Comparative (c, d) examination led to a positive identification of the left boot as having been the source of both the partial footwear impressions at the point of entry. (*Case submitted by Ray Wickenheiser. Photo credits: Ronald Stanbro, New York State Police.*)

These marks are essentially of two types: those in which only the general form and size of the tool are apparent and those in which injuries, irregularities, and other peculiar characteristics are reproduced in the form of striations or indentations. Marks of the first type may not make a definite identification of the tool possible, but do serve as a guide when it is necessary to decide whether the tool of a suspect could have produced the marks. Tool marks that show striations, indentations, or similar details resulting from damage or other irregularities in the tool are the most valuable as evidence.

PRESERVATION OF TOOL MARKS

Whenever possible, tool marks should be kept in their original condition. This may be done by recovering the whole object or part of the object on which the marks appear. Sometimes, it can be arranged that the marks remain untouched at the scene of the crime but can be recovered later if this is required. This is permissible, however, only when the marks are in such a position that they are completely protected, for example, a small mark on the inside of a door or window frame. If a mark in metal is not immediately recovered, it should be covered with a thin film of oil to prevent oxidation. In recovering the mark, it is important that it be protected against dirt, moisture, and scratching during transport. Tissue or other soft paper should be placed over the tool mark in packaging.

CASTING TOOL MARKS

Casting or other methods of taking impressions of a tool mark should be used only as a last resort. No matter how good a cast is, it can never be equal to the original. This applies especially to marks made in soft materials such as wood, putty, and paint; many of the casting media most suited for these materials are unable to reproduce all the finer details important for identification. Experiments have shown that an impression or a cast cannot reproduce scratches in paint caused by extremely small irregularities in the edge of a tool. Consequently, a microscopic comparison of the cast with a mark made from the suspected tool may not lead to any positive results. If, however, the original mark is compared with one made directly by the tool, then a positive identification is possible.

In the casting of marks, however, very satisfactory results may be obtained with Mikrosil,* and the completed cast will show fine detail (Figure 9.6).

Difficulties and some expense may be involved in taking possession of the original tool mark. Therefore, it should be subjected to a close examination with the aid of a magnifier to make sure that it shows typical details from the tool before any further steps are taken. In each particular case, consideration must also be given to the type of crime, value of the object, whether a tool from a suspect is available or the probability that such a tool may be found, etc.

Whether the actual mark is recovered or a cast is made, the tool mark should be photographed whenever practical. The picture should show clearly the location of the mark in relation to the rest of the object. Close-up photographs are generally taken in cases in which the mark may be destroyed in the casting process or during removal. The photographs must be made with the film plane parallel to the mark and should include a scale. Oblique lighting is used to enhance details in the mark. Close-up photographs should be in actual size, if possible, or in the case of smaller marks, enlarged. It is generally not possible to identify the tool used from photographs.

TRACE EVIDENCE ON TOOLS

In connection with all tool marks and suspected tools, it should be remembered that the tool might also have deposited traces in the form of paint, oil, or other materials. In turn, clues in the form of wood fragments and paint from the object may be found on the tool. These traces are sometimes just as valuable as the tool mark. Samples should therefore always be taken from the area of the tool mark whenever the actual mark is not recovered. Valuable tool marks are also sometimes found on splinters of wood, loosened flakes of paint, and chunks of safe insulation.

During the examination of the crime scene, the possibility should always be kept in mind that any tool mark found might be compared with marks from previous crimes. It happens frequently that identity is established among tool marks from different burglaries long before the suspect is apprehended or the actual tool is found.

The investigating officer should always endeavor to imagine being in a similar position to the suspect when the tool marks were made to consider how the suspect held the tool, stood, or was supported when breaking in or prying open. A burglary may be faked with the object of concealing embezzlement or of defrauding an insurance company; therefore, the investigator should always examine the opposite part of a mark (e.g., in a door frame). The fake burglar often overlooks the fact that this other part of the mark must be present.

---

* This video at www.youtube.com/watch?v=ZD-KSGDFX_g from the CSI Network shows the casting of tool mark impressions with Mikrosil.

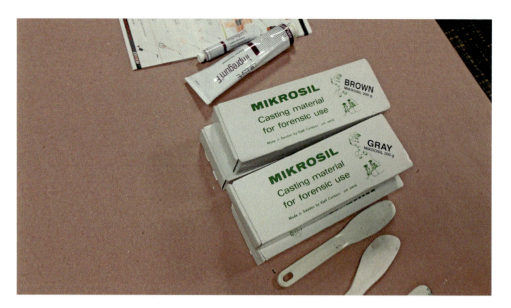

Figure 9.6 Mikrosil is a silicone based casting material. It is superior to other known silicone casting techniques because it increases the visibility of tool marks. It comes in brown, black, white, and gray.

Moreover, it is essential for the expert who is to carry out the comparative examination of the tool and the tool marks to understand how the criminal held the tool when making the marks. In most cases, if the examination is to have any prospect of leading to the identification of the tool, the expert must make a comparison mark in exactly the same way as the suspect has done. This applies especially to those tool marks that show scratches resulting from damage or other irregularities in the tool. The distance between the scratches varies according to whether a knife, for example, is held at right angles to its direction of movement or is held askew; the appearance of the scratches depends on the angle taken by the knife in relation to the plane of the cut. It is best if the position of a "fixed" mark and the conditions at the place are shown to the expert in a sketch or a comprehensive photograph. If known, a statement that the suspect is right- or left-handed should be added.

It is essential that the comparison mark be made in the same material as the mark at the scene of the crime (with the same paint or surface treatment, of the same degree of moisture, etc.) because the clarity of definition of the microscopic scratches varies with different materials. Thus, a quantity of material for use in producing comparison marks should be sent with the tool and tool mark—it may be necessary to make ten or more such marks with the suspected tool.

The police officer should not attempt to fit the tool into the mark or make a comparison mark with a suspected tool. In most cases, the officer does not have access to an instrument suitable for closer examination of the character of a tool mark, which may be necessary to decide how the comparison mark is to be made. Also, traces of paint or foreign metal on the tool, only observable with a microscope or powerful magnifying glass, may be lost or the tool may be damaged.

Casts or impressions of tool marks should be packed in such a way that they cannot be altered or destroyed during transport. Positive casts should never be made because this may cause fine details to become obscured. If the negative cast of the mark might be destroyed in transmission, it is best to make two and keep one in reserve.

Regarding boring marks, only wood bits and certain spiral bits generally leave identifiable marks. The bottom of the boring, if there is one, and boring chips are important. With other types of bits, identification is possible only in the most favorable cases and then as a rule only when the bottom of the boring is present.

At times, the CSI comes up against the problem of deciding, for example, from which side of a window frame (outside or inside) a hole has been bored. In most cases, this can be seen from the more or less loose wood fibers around the entrance and exit holes of the bit, but with some bits it may actually be difficult to decide the direction of boring. Reliable information is obtained by cutting through the surrounding wood in the longitudinal direction of the hole—by first sawing through the wood around the hole from each side up to about half an inch from the hole and then breaking the wood apart. It will then be found that the wood fibers are directed upward from the hole in one edge of each half and downward in the other edges. The wood fibers around the boring are displaced in the direction of rotation of the drill, so upon cutting the boring into two parts in this manner, they reveal clearly the direction of boring. The degree of orientation of the wood fibers varies for different types of bits and it is possible to obtain an idea of the type of bit used by carrying out test borings with different bits.

Saw marks usually do not offer any possibility of identifying the saw used. In a few cases, some idea may be obtained by noting the degree of set and possibly also the number of teeth per inch of the saw used, but this can be done only if sawing was stopped before the wood was sawn through. In some cases it is possible to find, in the base of the saw cut, impressions of the teeth of the saw made when the saw was at rest for an instant before it was withdrawn. It is also possible to obtain from the base of the saw cut a measure of the width of cut and therefore of the approximate amount of set.

Hacksaw marks offer little possibility of identification. However, with blades with different numbers of teeth per inch, if the blade did not go through the piece of metal, it may be possible to examine the bottom of the cut and observe the impression of the teeth to obtain an idea of the number of teeth per inch. This may also be observed at the sides of the actual cut where the saw jumped and left shallow marks of the teeth in the surface of the metal, especially when first started.

PRESERVING A TOOL

Once the tool has been found, care should be taken to preserve its evidentiary value. It should be carefully marked or tagged. If markings are made on the tool, they should not be placed in the area of the working surface. Similarly, minute items of trace evidence should be carefully preserved. The tool should be carefully packaged for transportation to the laboratory. It is important to remember that the handles of tools can be swabbed for trace DNA as well.

Tool marks made by cutting tools generally present little difficulty when the object cut is large enough to collect sufficient characteristics, such as the shackle of a padlock. Smaller items such as wire cable and multi-strand wire show identifiable markings only in exceptional cases.

If the wire has plastic insulation as a covering, a physical match may be made by an examination of the extrusion markings on the cable as well as the microscopic, jagged cut on the ends of the insulation. Generally, striations on the fine wire will be insufficient.

Manufacturing marks such as casting, extruding, grinding, and so on are important when attempting to match items together physically. These markings and random breaks that occur when tools or other materials break or tear are important means of identification.

Impression or casting media must be chosen for each particular case, taking into consideration the type of material in which the mark is formed and its orientation, that is, on the horizontal or vertical. Some impression materials such as plaster and plasticine have a tendency to shrink or expand after setting; they should not be used for casting. Dental impression creams have been found useful as casting materials. They generally come packaged in individual tubes, with one the catalyst and the other the setting agent, and are simply mixed and easy to apply. Other materials such as moulage, polysulfide rubber-based material, and silicone rubber are also useful.

A retaining wall should be built around the impression. Modeling clay or putty may be used for this purpose. The casting material should be thoroughly mixed according to the manufacturer's instructions and applied to the impression by means of a spatula. A tag with string attached may be used for identification purposes. The string may be inserted just below the surface of the casting material.

FRAGMENTS OF TOOLS

At crime scenes where doors, windows, or locked drawers show signs of forcible entry, the investigating officer must remember to examine the floor immediately adjacent to the point of entry carefully before examining the actual tool marks. It is not uncommon for burglary tools to break during forced entry; therefore, large or small fragments of the tool may be found at the scene and prove to be very valuable as evidence. Broken pieces of a tool might also be found inside a lock on which picking or prying has been attempted.

In many cases it is possible to establish that such broken fragments originally were parts of tools found in the possession of a suspect. The physical matching of two or more pieces that originally were one piece—a so-called fracture match—is the most convincing and easily demonstrable type of proof against an offender.

The converse situation should also be kept in mind. A broken tool left by the burglar at the crime scene can be matched with fragments of that tool that may be found in the suspect's clothing, home, or place of business. Pieces may also have been left at the scene of another burglary.

The search for such tool fragments is best done with a flashlight, the beam of which is directed over the search area at a very low angle. When the light strikes a metallic fragment, it will give off bright reflections that make the particles easy to find. Any suspected fragment should be recovered and placed in a vial or envelope that can be labeled as to the time and place of recovery.

A magnet or metal detector can also be used in searching for tool fragments. If a deliberate effort to look for such pieces of broken tools is not made, there is the risk of trampling them into the ground, embedding them in the officer's shoes, or kicking them aside while engaging in other routines of crime scene search.

Impression evidence is often encountered at crime scenes. Submitting that evidence to the laboratory along with the suspected tool can result in an identification.

TIRE TREAD AND TIRE TRACK EVIDENCE

Tire tread impressions show tread design and dimensional features of individual tires on a vehicle, whereas **tire tracks** show relational dimensions between two or more tires and can be used to determine the wheelbase of the vehicle.

There are several useful pieces of information that an examiner can learn from examining tire treads. These include: **tread design**, **noise treatment**, **tread wear features**, and **random individual characteristics** (i.e., plug marks, nails, cracks, or unique wear marks).

When looking at a known tire tread, it is important to ink the full circumference of the tire. Points of damage or a foreign object caught in the tread can serve as individual random characteristics that can be used during a comparison. During a comparison impressions are superimposed on known impressions over a cast or the original tire (Figure 9.7a and b).

OSAC FOOTWEAR AND TIRE SUBCOMMITTEE*

The OSAC footwear and tire subcommittee focuses on standards and guidelines related to the detection, documentation, recovery, examination, and comparison of footwear and tire evidence. Footwear and tire examiners provide expert opinions regarding source conclusions, determine the make, or model of the source of a questioned impression, and compare questioned impressions to those of an item of footwear or tire from an image or video.

Several standards have been published by ANSI/ASB in the field of footwear and tire impressions including *Best Practice Recommendation for Lifting of Footwear and Tire Impressions, Best Practices for Casting Footwear and Tire Impression Evidence at the Crime Scene,* and *Standard for Minimum Qualifications and Training for a Footwear/Tire Forensic Science Service Provider.*

SWGTREAD

Prior to the formation of the OSACs, the Scientific Working Group for Shoeprint and Tire Tread Evidence was created by the FBI to standardize and advance the forensic analysis of footwear and tire impression evidence. SWGTREAD standards can be found on the subcommittee's website.

---

* www.nist.gov/osac/footwear-tire-subcommittee.

Figure 9.7 (a) Tire cast with unique individual characteristics and the (b) the actual Kirkland tire that made the tire tread in (a). (This video at www.youtube.com/watch?v=kt9FUvpyn0Y shows how a tire tread cast is lifted.)

Further Reading

Bodziak, William J. *Tire Tread and Tire Track Evidence: Recovery and Forensic Examination*. CRC Press, 2008.

Bodziak, William J. *Footwear Impression Evidence: Detection, Recovery, and Examination*. CRC Press, 2017.

Petraco, Nicholas. *Color Atlas of Forensic Toolmark Identification*. CRC Press, 2010.

Pierce, David S. *Mechanics of Impression Evidence*. CRC Press, 2011.

Vernon, Denis Wesley, and John A. DiMaggio. *Forensic Podiatry: Principles and Methods*. CRC Press, 2017.

Chapter Questions

1. (True or false) Small and sometimes microscopically unique markings can be directly traced to the object or instrument in question.
2. Describe the differences between compression marks and scraping marks.
3. Which of the following could be an individual characteristic that might be found on a footwear impression at a crime scene?
    a) Size.
    b) Width.
    c) Marks of nails and pegs.
    d) Brand of the footwear.
4. Describe the proper procedure for photographing a footwear impression at the scene of a burglary.

5. How many pounds of dental stone would be needed for a typical footwear impression?
   a) Two.
   b) Four.
   c) Six.
   d) Ten.
6. Which of the following procedures must be done when casting a tire impression in snow?
   a) Mix the dental stone quickly so that it does not freeze.
   b) Use a baffle to pour in the mixture.
   c) Spray the impression first with Snow Print Wax.
   d) Use an electrostatic lifter before pouring in the mixture.
7. Describe the proper method when using sulfur casting on a footwear impression in snow.
8. You are called to the scene of a burglary and notice a footwear print in cooking oil on top of the kitchen cabinet near a broken window. Which of the following techniques would be the best way to collect this print?
   a) Dental stone casting.
   b) Rubber lifter.
   c) Sulfur casting.
   d) Photographing the print at an oblique angle.
9. List the two methods for collecting comparison footprints from a suspect.
10. What is the difference between tire treads and tire tracks?

CHAPTER 10

Firearms Examination

Crimes involving the use of firearms represent a major area of crime scene investigation and forensic science. Firearms evidence may be present in a variety of crimes such as murder, attempted murder, suicide, assault, rape, criminal possession of a firearm, robbery, and so on. A number of questions can be answered by the proper application of firearms evidence: What kind of weapon was used? Was the weapon in proper working order? How far away was the weapon fired? In what direction was the weapon fired? Did a specific weapon fire a bullet? Did a particular person fire the weapon?

Because of the importance of reconstructing the circumstances of the crime and corroborating accounts of the crime by witnesses, suspects, and victims, firearms evidence is particularly important. This chapter deals with the major areas of firearms examination.*

The field of firearms identification is sometimes improperly referred to as ballistics. This is an improper use of terminology. "Ballistics" refers to the trajectory taken by a projectile and relies on an understanding of physics. Firearms identification, on the other hand, refers to the study of firearms and includes the operation of firearms, cartridges, gunshot residue (GSR) analysis, bullet and cartridge case comparisons, powder pattern determination, and the like. Many date the beginnings of modern forensic firearms identification to the Saint Valentine's Day massacre on February 14, 1929, in Chicago (Figure 10.1). With the aid of a newly developed comparison microscope, Calvin Goddard was able to identify the two "Tommy" guns confiscated from Fred Burke's house that had been used in the infamous massacre (Figures 10.2 and 10.3).

CHARACTERISTICS OF FIREARMS

Today, there are literally thousands of types of firearms. They can be classified broadly into two groups: long arms such as rifles and shotguns, and handguns such as revolvers and semi-automatic pistols (bipod, tripod, and other exotic weapons may also sometimes be encountered). Of interest to law enforcement, handguns represent the firearm most used in crimes; shoulder arms are used less frequently. Obsolete weapons such as muskets, unusual firearms such as those disguised to appear as something other than a handgun, and homemade weapons such as "zip guns" and 3-D printed guns are used less frequently.

Firearms may also be characterized by whether they have smoothbore or rifled barrels, the former used in shotguns and the latter in most other firearms. Rifling found in gun barrels are spiral grooves cut into the barrel that impart a rotational spin to the bullet as it leaves the barrel, resulting in more stable flight.

Firearms may be single shot, revolver, automatic, and semi-automatic. The single-shot firearm is loaded manually, fired once, and unloaded manually. The revolver differs from the single-shot pistol, in that it has a rotating cylinder holding from 4 to 24 cartridges. Each time a cartridge is fired, the cylinder revolves by means of cocking the hammer

---

* The Association of Firearm and Tool Mark Examiners (www.afte.org) is an international professional organization for practitioners of firearm and toolmark identification. The AFTE glossary provides a common language for professionals in this field with standardized definitions.

Figure 10.1 The infamous St. Valentine's Day Massacre occurred on February 14, 1929, in Chicago. Two rival gangs were fighting over the illicit liquor market created after prohibition made selling alcohol illegal. One of the gangs dressed as police officers entered a warehouse and gunned down their competitors. The first officers on the scene probably did not realize the impact this case would have, but this case played a major role in the future of forensic science in the United States and marked one of the earliest uses of forensic firearms identification. (*Courtesy of the Chicago Police Department*.)

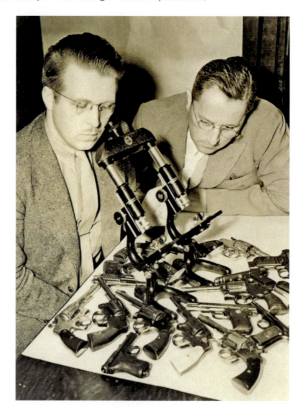

Figure 10.2 Dr. Calvin Goddard pictured in front of a comparison microscope. Goddard is credited with perfecting the comparison microscope for ballistics research. (*Photo credit: www.stvalentinemassacre.com*.)

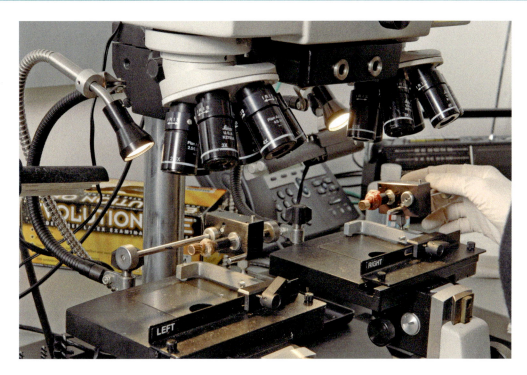

Figure 10.3 A modern day comparison microscope used to compare two bullets allegedly fired from the same gun. (*Courtesy of the Los Angeles County Sheriff's Department.*)

or pulling the trigger, which places the cartridge into position to be fired. The automatic firearm generally found in military weapons is a repeating type. Cartridges are fired in succession as long as the trigger is pressed and until the ammunition supply is exhausted. The semi-automatic pistol (often improperly referred to as an "automatic") functions similarly to the automatic, but fires only one shot each time the trigger is pulled.

In single shot- and revolver-type firearms, the cartridge casing generally remains in the weapon after firing, although single-shot weapons have been made that eject cases automatically. With automatic and semi-automatic firearms, the cartridge case is ejected from the weapon automatically.

Shotguns differ in two major ways from other firearms: shotgun barrels are not rifled and are smoothbore and fire a different type of ammunition consisting of many lead pellets, rifled slugs, sabots, or shot (Figure 10.4). (There are also some who load shotshells with various other materials like rock salt, flechettes, lead balls, piano wire, or less lethal materials: beanbags, rubber bullets, etc.) Shotguns are of the single- and double-barreled break action for reloading, pump action, semi-automatic, or bolt-action types.

The caliber designation of a firearm is a measure of the bore of the barrel and is measured in 1/100 or 1/1000 of an inch or in millimeters. The caliber designation is only an approximation of the bore diameter and is measured from land to opposing land (Figures 10.5 and 10.6). Shotgun bores are measured in gauges; the smaller the number, the larger the diameter. Thus, a 12-gauge shotgun has a larger diameter bore than a 20-gauge shotgun. The term "gauge" was originally the number of lead balls of that size weighing 1 pound.

AMMUNITION

Small arms cartridges or rounds are of two general types: rimfire and centerfire. Rim fire ammunition is almost exclusively .22-caliber (plus the .17-caliber), while larger calibers are center fire.

Some older firearms, other than .22-caliber, did use rimfire ammunition. The terms rim and center refer to the position of the primer located in the base of the cartridge. In a rimfire round, the primer is in the rim in an area around the circumference of the base while centerfire rounds have the primer in the center. The primer is a small shock-sensitive explosive charge in the base of the cartridge used to set off the propellant powder when struck by the firing pin.

Figure 10.4 The inside of a shotgun shell showing the gunpowder and shot. This type of cartridge is used for trap shooting. (*Courtesy of Lucian Haag, Forensic Science Services, Inc., Carefree, AZ.*)

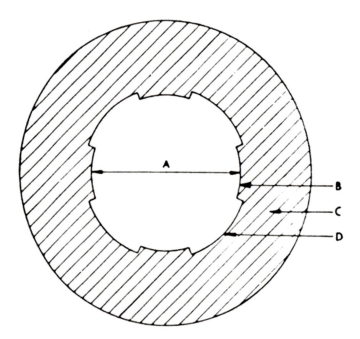

Figure 10.5 The caliber of a rifled weapon is generally determined from the diameter of a bore, measured between two opposite lands. (a) caliber, (b) land, (c) barrel, and (d) groove.)

The bullet is the projectile fired from the weapon. Bullets are generally a lead alloy and jacketed with a harder metal such as copper or brass or nonjacketed. The purpose of the jacket is to keep the bullet intact and from breaking up when it strikes a target, to prevent damage while in the weapon, and to control expansion.

Gunpowder or smokeless powder consists of tiny cylinders, balls, flakes, or discs of nitrocellulose or nitrocellulose and nitroglycerine in so-called double-based powder (Figure 10.7). When confined and ignited, the powder rapidly burns, giving off a large quantity of gas. The expanding gas is the means by which the bullet is propelled through the barrel and out of the weapon. Black powder is also used in certain ammunition.

Figure 10.6 The rifling, consisting of lands and grooves, can be seen in this gun barrel and is what imparts spin on the bullet. (*Courtesy of Lucian Haag.*)

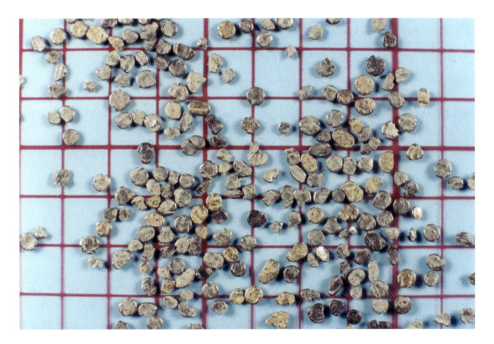

Figure 10.7 A photomicrograph example of gunpowder, in this case Winchester 231 propellant. (*Courtesy of Lucian Haag.*)

FIREARMS EVIDENCE

When a weapon is fired, the firing pin strikes the base of the cartridge detonating the primer, which in turn ignites the gunpowder. Expansion of gases forces the casing against the breech, which resists the rearward movement, and propels the bullet down the barrel. The bullet picks up the tiny imperfections of the rifling as it passes through. The scratches or striations are caused by the imperfections in the lands and grooves placed in the barrel at the time of manufacture and caused through use of the weapon. Characteristic markings from the mechanical action of loading, chambering,

Figure 10.8 Two bullets viewed under a comparison microscope show characteristic markings imparted by the barrel onto the bullet's surface. The firearms examiner uses these striations to determine whether an unknown bullet was fired from a particular firearm. (*Courtesy of the Los Angeles County Sheriff's Department.*)

and firing the round, as well as from extracting and ejecting the casing, will be present on the bullet, cartridge casing, and cartridge base. If compared against rounds fired from the same weapon, these marks will show similarities that the firearms identification expert can use to determine if the rounds were fired from the same gun (Figure 10.8).

Beyond determining whether two rounds were fired from the same weapon, a great deal of other information can be developed from evidence associated with firearms. The presence of cartridge cases may indicate an automatic, semi-automatic, bolt-action or slide-action firearm, or a single-shot firearm when more than one round was fired. The relative location of the casings to the shooter may sometimes suggest the type of weapon fired or that a revolver was emptied at the scene.

Bullets and even fragments of bullets may be used to determine the type of weapon used from the size and weight of the projectile and an examination of the striations on the outside surface. For example, the number, direction of twist, and measurements of land and groove markings can be useful in determining the type, make, model, and caliber of firearm. Examination of the area that the bullet struck will yield information about the path and distance from which the weapon was fired. This is also possible with shot fired from a shotgun.

Tests on the shooter's hands may determine if a weapon was recently fired. If the firearm is recovered, it can be tested to determine if it is in proper working order or if it could have been accidentally discharged. The owner of the firearm can possibly be determined by the serial number.

GUNSHOT RESIDUE (GSR) ANALYSIS

When the firing pin strikes the base of a cartridge, the shock causes the primer to detonate, in turn causing the ignition of the main gunpowder charge. The chemical reaction thus started causes a rapid expansion of gases, which propels the bullet out of the barrel of the gun. The by-products of the reaction are burned and unburned powder and the components of the primer mixture (Figure 10.9).

Primers use shock-sensitive compounds containing such materials as lead, barium, and antimony. Particles containing barium, antimony, and lead on a suspect's hands indicate that the suspect was in proximity to a gun being fired.

Upon discharging a weapon, microscopic particles of GSR are deposited on the hands of the shooter and the nearby area as an aerosol. These particles adhere to the hands but are removed by washing, wringing, or placing hands in the pockets. Handcuffing a suspect behind the back can also dislodge these particles. Studies show that GSR material will remain on a shooter's hands for up to 6 hours. The particles are in the highest concentration immediately after shooting and are gradually lost over time. Because of this time factor, GSR evidence must be collected as quickly as possible.

Scanning Electron Microscopy/Energy Dispersive X-ray (SEM/EDX) analysis is the most widely used method of testing for GSR. GSR evidence is collected with aluminum stubs with double-sided cellophane tape for SEM. The chemical components of the primer present on the shooter's hands are the substances tested for in the GSR procedure. In general, barium, lead, and antimony are characteristic of most ammunition.

GSR evidence collection kits are available commercially and through local crime laboratories. In all cases, the person collecting the evidence should wear gloves to prevent possible contamination of the evidence. Information concerning the subject's occupation and hobbies should be noted. This is important for interpretation of test results. Obtaining GSR results is straightforward, but its interpretation is another matter. Negative GSR results (no GSR detected) do not conclusively mean that a subject did not fire a handgun. Similarly, positive GSR results do not prove someone fired a gun because a person could have handled a gun or been in close proximity to a gun that was fired.

A shooting suspect's hands should be protected until evidence samples are collected. Handcuffing behind the back is likely to remove GSR. Hands may be bagged loosely with paper bags but not in plastic bags, which cause perspiration and hence a cleansing effect. In the case of a deceased subject, the 6-hour time limit is flexible but the hands should be protected until such time as the evidence can be collected.

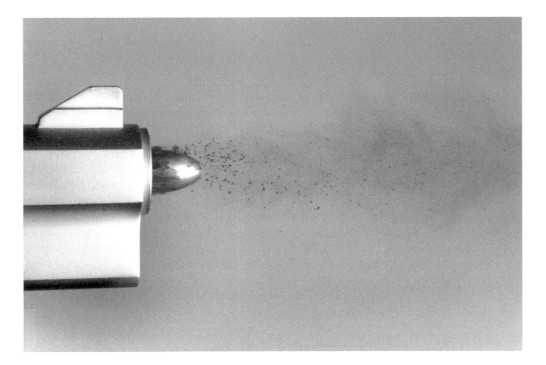

Figure 10.9 When a firearm is discharged, gases from the detonation of the primer and burning gunpowder escape from the barrel, and in the case of revolvers, from the gap between the frame and the cylinder. These gases along with burned and unburned particles of gunpowder and primer are referred to as gunshot residue (GSR). (*Courtesy of Lucian Haag.*)

Because of the ambiguity in conclusions about whether an individual fired a weapon using GSR, some forensic laboratories have opted to discontinue this service. Instead, some laboratories opt to swab the gun, including the trigger, trigger guard, backstrap, slide, grip, and/or unspent ammunition for DNA typing instead.

COLLECTING FIREARMS EVIDENCE

The crime scene in which a firearm was involved should be processed in much the same way as that discussed earlier in the text. In addition, a number of other considerations must be taken into account in these types of cases. (It goes without saying that in situations when a gun needs to be quickly rendered safe, some of the following may not apply. In these situations, the destruction of evidence should be minimized to the extent possible.)

When sketching and measuring the crime scene, it is particularly important to carefully note and measure the location of all cartridge casings, bullet holes, bullets and bullet fragments, and shotgun shot patterns that are found. This information is vital to the reconstruction of the crime and can be used to verify statements by witnesses and suspects. Special care must be taken when walking through the location so that casings or bullets are not stepped on or inadvertently kicked.

If a weapon is found at the scene, it should not be moved until its location is noted through measurement, sketches, photographs, and 3-D scans. The investigator should remember that fingerprints and/or DNA might be present, so when the weapon is moved, it must be handled in a way that will not destroy them. The floor below the weapon should be examined for a depression or other marks that would indicate that it was dropped from some height or fell from the shooter's hands. Traces of wood, fibers, paint, building material, blood, and hair should be looked for on the weapon and carefully preserved for transport if found.

If a decedent is holding a gun, it is important to note the exact grip and position of the weapon in the hand. The suspect may have placed it there while staging a homicide to look like a suicide. In such a case, the way in which a weapon is held in relation to the injuries on the body is decisive as to whether the dead person could have produced the injuries. In the case of an automatic pistol, the recoil of the slide may have caused a surface graze in the region of the thumb or the web of the hand, and the presence of such an injury is suggestive that the dead person had fired a shot with a semi-automatic pistol. A closer examination of the hand of the dead person may show marks of powder, especially if a revolver had been used. From these marks, the investigator may deduce that both hands were in the vicinity of the muzzle blast or the gap of the revolver. One hand may have been used as a guide while the other pressed the trigger or both hands may have been held up in defense.

In the case of long-barreled guns, rifles, and shotguns, special attention should be given to the possibility of the dead person having fired a suicide shot with the weapon. Special arrangements such as strings, belts, sticks, and the like may have been used, and these in turn may have left marks in the form of fibers, dirt, soot, or the like on the trigger or trigger guard. A shoe might have been removed in order to depress the trigger with a toe.

The position of cartridges, cartridge cases, and bullets is just as important as that of weapons. From their position it may be possible to estimate the position of firing, direction of the shot, and perhaps the path of the bullet. If a bullet has penetrated a tree, a piece of furniture, or a wall, the shot track may give information regarding the direction of the shot and also the path of the bullet. There is a much better opportunity of determining the exact course of a bullet when it has passed through a fixed object such as a windowpane and then struck a wall. With the aid of the path of the bullet and of shot wounds on the deceased, it may be possible to determine the deceased's position when shot. In calculating the distance of the shot, the depth to which a bullet had penetrated a wall, may be significant. The penetrating power is dependent on the distance of the shot. Allowance should be made for the loss of energy in passing through an object, such as a body. A more accurate determination of distance can be made with the aid of gunshot injuries on the clothes and body of the deceased.

The position of a bullet found at the scene of a crime should be recorded in the same way as for weapons. Bullets should be collected separately and packed so that there can be no confusion. If two or more weapons have been used, the bullets should not get mixed up so that the place where each one was found can be fixed exactly. Great care should also be taken in collecting and packing bullets to prevent the striations from being damaged or destroyed. If a bullet penetrated or was lodged in a wall, the bullet should not be probed for and dug out with a knife, chisel, or other metal

Figure 10.10 Example of different bullet fragments. (*Courtesy of Lucian Haag.*)

objects. Instead, a portion of the wall surrounding the bullet should be carefully removed in one piece and the bullet recovered by breaking away the supporting material. It may become important to ascertain other objects that came in contact with the projectile (Figure 10.10). Trace evidence should not be removed nor should the bullet be washed until a microscopic study is performed. Care should be taken that the investigator's marking of the bullet does not destroy this trace evidence. The firearms examiner should also consult with a forensic biologist if DNA typing is needed to determine the best order for the bullet to be examined.

The same considerations with respect to fixing the position and taking possession of weapons and bullets apply to cartridges and cartridge cases found at the scene of a crime. The position of a cartridge that misfired or of a cartridge case that was ejected from a semi-automatic pistol may indicate the type of pistol used and form a valuable supplement of the make of pistol from marks left by the weapon on the bullet and casing. Semi-automatic pistols differ with respect to the ejection of the casings; some throw them out to the left, some to the right, and some straight up. The casing is thrown out with a force that varies with different types of pistols. It may rebound against furniture, walls, wall coverings, and so on and change direction. The position may give an indication of the type of weapon; however, there is often variation from weapon to weapon. If a cartridge case has not bounced off an object or has not fallen and was prevented from rolling (i.e., a carpet, lawn, etc.), then its position can give a good indication of the type of weapon and place or direction of firing. Outdoors, it is necessary to take into account the direction and strength of the wind. In all cases the incline of the ground should be considered.

The position of shotgun wads, which often remain relatively undamaged, may also give information about the direction of shooting. These can generally be found about five–eight yards or more from the place of firing in the approximate direction of fire, but it is necessary to take into consideration the direction and strength of the wind (Figure 10.11).

A weapon that has been used in a case of murder, suicide, or assault may contain clues from the victim or suspect in the form of blood, hair, fragments of textiles, cloth fibers, and so on. Such information may appear to be of little value, but might prove that the weapon was actually used in a particular case. Loose hairs, dried blood, fibers, and other traces can also be used to help reconstruct the order in which a bullet penetrated multiple objects.

Firearms should be packed in such a way that DNA, fingerprints, or other clues are not destroyed. A cardboard box that suspends the weapon with the minimum number of bearing surfaces is preferred. If epithelial (skin) cells, fingerprints, and/or bloodstains are present on a weapon, they might be destroyed if the whole of the weapon is dusted with fingerprint powder. Latent print examiners should confer with the forensic biologist to determine whether the order of DNA or latent print evidence collection has a better chance of success. There is no hard and fast rule as to which type of evidence should be collected first; however, examiners should keep in mind that collection of one type of evidence could potentially prevent or inhibit the collection of a subsequent type of evidence.

Figure 10.11 Some examples of different shotgun wads. (*Courtesy of Lucian Haag.*)

Contamination in the form of oil, cement, paint, or similar material may also be significant in determining the way in which a suspect acquired a weapon or may give an indication of where a weapon was previously kept. It may possibly have been taken from the suspect's place of work or in an earlier burglary in which the suspect was less careful and left fingerprints or DNA that can be used as incriminating evidence.

If the weapon was concealed at the crime scene or in the vicinity or taken away by the suspect, it is important to know the type of weapon for which one is searching. The only means of determining that is from a study of the injuries on the victim or by removal of the bullet at autopsy. In practice, it is difficult to draw the correct conclusions from the appearance of the wounds because they are affected by the elasticity of the skin, underlying bones and muscles, angle of application, and other such factors. In these types of cases, however, a board certified forensic pathologist can give valuable assistance.

HANDLING OF FIREARMS

When picking up a firearm, great care must be taken not to destroy evidence. The best way to lift a pistol or revolver is to hold it with two gloved fingers on the checkered part of the butt or possibly by a ring on the butt, if present. Shotguns may conveniently be held around the checkered part of the neck of the butt. If necessary, the weapon can be lifted by a steady grip with the fingers on the trigger guard. Never lift a weapon by placing a stick or similar object in the trigger guard, even with a light weapon such as a revolver or pistol, because the weapon may be cocked and a shot might be fired if the trigger is touched. As a general rule never lift a weapon found at the crime scene before first making sure that no one is in the direction in which the muzzle is pointing. The weapon may actually be cocked so that even the slightest movement could cause a shot to be fired.

Picking up a gun by putting a pencil or stick in the barrel should never be done and is totally wrong. Doing so may destroy valuable clues in the barrel. In a contact shot (i.e., when the muzzle is in contact with a body) or close proximity shot, as with a suicide, blood or textile fibers might be found in the barrel from the vacuum caused by the gas pressure. This phenomenon is known as backspatter.

A layer of dust, spider webs, or loose rust particles found in the bore may suggest that no shot has been fired from a weapon for some time. The absence of a powder deposit or the presence of grease in the bore may also indicate that the weapon has not been used, while an examination of the powder layer in the bore may show that the fired cartridge was loaded with black powder or with smokeless powder. It is difficult to decide from the appearance of the powder deposit how much time has elapsed since the last shot was fired from a weapon. Therefore, if the bore of a weapon is to be examined for any such clues, introducing any object into it will interfere with its examination. For the same reason, cotton should not be put in the muzzle during transport of the weapon or when it is sent to an expert. To protect any deposit in the bore, a twist of paper, rubber cap, or muzzle protector can be placed over the muzzle. The layer of dust in the bore is always thickest near the muzzle and decreases in thickness toward the breech, assuming that it has resulted from a long period of storage. The confirmation of such a distribution of the deposit nearest the muzzle is of importance.

After the weapon has been picked up, any loose objects or particles such as hairs, fibers, dried blood, brain matter, and the like that might fall off in transport are removed and kept. With a near shot against a hair-covered part of the body, sometimes strands of hair or tissue can be found held fast between the slide and barrel of a semi-automatic pistol. Also, any traces on the weapon in the form of fibers of wood, paint, cement, or the like, which might indicate that the weapon had fallen on the floor, should be collected while at the scene of the crime.

When a weapon is taken into possession, it should be subjected to a preliminary examination. Fingerprint impressions in grease or blood can easily be seen. If fingerprints, bloodstains, fibers, and so on are found on the weapon, they all must be preserved. It is important for the firearms examiner to also be mindful of subsequent DNA examinations and the potential for their own DNA to contaminate the evidence. Therefore, the firearms examination must be conducted with gloves and a mask covering the mouth and nose at a minimum. If latent fingerprints are to be developed by powder, care must be taken to keep the powder from entering the barrel. Likewise, when a revolver is processed by powder dusting, the front of the cylinder must be protected so that the mouth of each chamber can be examined for flaring.

Everything found in the first examination of the weapon should be written down accurately; any objects, particles, or swabs collected should be placed in an envelope labeled accurately with the exact place of finding. Any manufacturer markings should also be noted, as well as the caliber marking and serial number. The investigator's initials should be inscribed on some major part of the weapon such as the barrel or frame, or the weapon may be tagged. It is most important to note the condition of the weapon when found, if the safety is on or not and whether the weapon is cocked and loaded. With some semi-automatic pistols, the latter cannot be observed by a superficial glance, but where it is shown by, for example, an indicating pin, it should be noted. In the most common types of weapon, this condition can easily be confirmed from the position of the rear part of the bolt. It should also be noted whether the bolt (breech block or slide) is closed, partly open, or fully open. A cartridge case jammed in the ejection port should be noted, together with a statement of the exact position of the cartridge, whether the base or neck of the case is turned outward, etc., and also whether the magazine is firm or loose (not pushed all the way in).

With a semi-automatic pistol, the magazine is loosened, after which the slide is moved to remove any cartridge in the chamber. In doing this, it should be remembered that fingerprints might be found in grease on the cartridge in the chamber and on the sides of the magazine, which should therefore be examined first before any further handling. The weapon should not be considered unloaded until an inspection is made by looking into the chamber through the ejection port of the gun and physically checking to confirm that the chamber is empty. A broken extractor, jammed cartridge, or other factor may cause a cartridge to remain in the chamber. It is a poor practice to assume that a weapon is unloaded simply because a cartridge was not ejected. The cartridge is placed in an envelope or container with a label attached; a label can also be tied on by a thread around the groove of the cartridge. Any cartridges in the magazine should not be "stripped" if the weapon is to be sent to an expert for examination. Cartridges may carry DNA, fingerprints, and also marks from the guiding surfaces of the magazine, and it may be of significance to confirm them (e.g., whether the cartridges have been charged into the magazine several times). Furthermore, the order of the cartridges in a magazine may be important in certain cases and should always be noted.

In the case of a revolver, nothing should be done with the cartridges in the cylinder if the weapon is to be examined further. The exact position of the cylinder at the moment when the weapon is found is significant and should be noted, for example, the position of the fired cartridge in relation to the hammer. The position of the cylinder can be marked provided that this does not destroy other clues. The cylinder should not be "rolled" because then irrelevant marks from the recoil plate or firing pin could be formed on the bases of the fired cases and the cartridges.

In the case of weapons of single-shot or repeating types, nothing should be done with the bolt unless the weapon is cocked or has the empty case in the chamber. If, however, the hammer is cocked, an unfired cartridge may be in the chamber and should be removed to prevent any accident. The cartridge is taken out and labeled as described

Figure 10.12 (a, b) Serial number restoration. (*Courtesy of the Los Angeles County Sheriff's Department.*)

earlier. Semi- or fully automatic weapons generally have a cartridge in the chamber unless the bolt is in the rearward position, so the slide should be moved while making sure that no fresh cartridge is introduced into the chamber. To prevent this, a detachable magazine is removed from the weapon; in the case of a fixed magazine, the uppermost cartridges are held back with a piece of wood or some other object that will not injure the cartridges or deposit any fresh marks on them.

All the precautions taken with a firearm must be noted accurately in the report. The investigating police officer may be required to describe these precautions in connection with legal proceedings at a later time. What may appear to be of secondary importance during the investigation of the crime may later be significant. When a weapon is sent to a firearms expert for examination, the only clues that need to be preserved are those that might be destroyed in transit. The only action taken is the one that cannot be omitted without risk of accident or that is essential in assisting the search for the suspect. Many traces on the weapon or significant facts in connection with the mechanism can be of such a character that special instruments or specially trained personnel are necessary to deal with them properly. Perhaps marks of colored lacquer from the sealing around the primer are on the breech face or recoil plate; a chemical examination may be required to confirm whether this could have come from a specific fired cartridge. The bore, lacquer pigments from the sealing between the bullet and case or metallic particles from the jacket of the bullet may be found. In grease and dirt on the breech face, an impression of the markings may also be on the base of the cartridge case; special arrangements will be required for photographing this impression.

As noted earlier, any marks indicating the manufacturer, type, and caliber should be recorded, along with the serial number. With many weapons, in particular certain pistols and revolvers, such markings are often lacking. The butt plates, however, are usually marked with the maker's or seller's initials, which may be a good guide.

Many weapons also carry proof marks. Several European countries strictly regulate the manufacture of firearms and require a special mark to be stamped on the weapon's barrel to indicate that it has been tested and found safe. Proof marks are also found on some American-made weapons sold in foreign countries. In cases of inexpensive firearms, the proof mark may be the only clue to the manufacturer of the weapon.

Occasionally, firearms are recovered from which serial numbers have been ground off for the purpose of concealing the ownership of the weapon. When numbers are stamped into the frame of the weapon, changes in the metal structure deep below the surface result. If the process that removed the stamp was not sufficiently deep, the serial numbers or markings can be restored. Depending on the nature of the metal, a number of techniques are possible: magnetic particle testing, chemical etching, electrochemical etching, and heating (Figure 10.12a and b).

CARTRIDGE CASES

If no cartridge cases are found at the scene of a shooting, it may be because a revolver, single-shot pistol, automatic pistol with cartridge case collector, rifle, or shotgun was used. One might expect that criminals would try to protect themselves by picking up the cartridge cases thrown out by an auto-loading weapon. In practice, this is not often done because it would take time and the suspect might run more risk of being discovered, especially if the shooting was heard by persons in the vicinity.

In collecting cartridge cases, one should not forget that valuable clues might be found on cartridge cases in the form of loose particles, fingerprints, and/or DNA. These may be collected by means of a clean swab and then placed into an envelope marked with the place of finding. The internal diameter of a cartridge case corresponds at the neck with the diameter of the bullet. From the size, form, and appearance of a cartridge case, it may be possible to predict the type of weapon used.

Revolver cartridge cases are almost always cylindrical, with a rim but no extractor groove (a groove for the extractor running around the case with the rim). They may be made for rim fire (smooth base) or center fire (with primer cap). Many manufacturers make revolvers to take automatic pistol cartridges. Thus, both Colt and Smith & Wesson make revolvers of .45-caliber so that automatic pistol cartridges of .45-caliber can be used in them. Similarly, semi-automatic pistol cartridges of 7.65 mm can be fired in .32-caliber revolvers and semi-automatic pistol cartridges of 6.35 mm can be fired in .25-caliber revolvers. Automatic pistol cartridges (with the exception of .45-rimless cartridges, 9-mm Parabellum cartridges, and bottleneck cartridges) have a rim that, although not much larger than the cylindrical surface of the cartridge, is quite sufficient to hold the cartridge fast in the chamber of a revolver cylinder when the internal diameter of the latter corresponds with the diameter of the cartridge. In many revolvers provided with one common extractor for all the cartridges, the rim also functions quite satisfactorily when pistol cartridges are used.

Revolver cartridges of .320-caliber can also be fired in certain semi-automatic pistols of 7.65-mm caliber. In some cases, such pistols have also repeated normally and even ejected revolver cartridge cases, but the ejected cases are often ruptured and sometimes jam the pistol.

Smaller caliber projectiles can be fired in larger bore weapons. An example of this is the ability of a .38-Special revolver to fire .32–20 cartridges. Desperate persons in need of ammunition wrap cartridges in paper to accommodate a larger chamber, reduce the diameter by filing and even perform the dangerous act of driving a cartridge into a chamber by means of a hammer. Only an expert can determine the type of gun that might have been used in a shooting by an examination of the fired bullets or cartridges. An investigator must be careful not to pass up a weapon because it does not seem to correspond to the ammunition at hand.

Caliber and manufacturer's marks generally are found on the base of the cartridge case and sometimes also the year of manufacture. Sometimes, the maker's marks are in code consisting of letters and figures.

Fired cartridge cases are especially valuable for identification because they show marks from the weapon that in most cases make it possible to decide whether they were fired from a particular weapon or not. It is therefore of special importance in an outdoor shooting that all possible efforts be made to determine the location of the shooting so that any cartridge cases left behind can be found. The most valuable marks on cartridge cases are those made by the firing pin on the primer and by the breech face on the primer and base of the case, but the marks produced by the extractor, ejector, and the edge of the breech may also be important (Figures 10.13 and 10.14). Flaws or damage in the chamber may also show on the metal case and make identification of the weapon possible. If, when the suspect is found, he or she has already thrown away the weapon where it cannot be recovered (e.g., in water), it is important to attempt to find out whether the suspect or some other person (e.g., the previous or legal owner) ever fired a test shot, and if so, where. It is possible that the cartridge case and the bullet may be found there. With cartridge cases, it is not particularly important whether the test shot was fired a long time before. The part of the weapon that leaves marks on the case may not have altered even though there was a long interval of time between the test shot and the crime. It is different in the case of bullets because sometimes the bore of a weapon may undergo such changes in a comparatively short time that comparison of a bullet with a test shot fired previously is useless. The nature of the place where the weapon has been kept and the number of shots that have been fired with it are important factors.

From the marks made by the extractor, ejector, and edge of the breech of a semi-automatic pistol on a cartridge case, it is also possible to determine the make of semi-automatic pistol from which the case was fired. Semi-automatic pistols of different types and makes are often constructed differently with respect to the position of the extractor and ejector; this in turn affects the formation of the breech. The combination of these factors forms what is known as a system, that is, the characteristics mentioned allow classification of the type of construction of the pistol. If both cartridge case and bullet are available for determination of the make, the possibilities are increased because the number of land

Figure 10.13 Primer face of cartridge showing impression made by firing pin. (*Courtesy of LASD.*)

Figure 10.14 Extractor marks on a cartridge casing. (*Courtesy of LASD.*)

Figure 10.15 Example of severely mutilated bullets after penetrating a hard object. (*Courtesy of Lucian Haag.*)

impressions on the bullet, their width, and the angle of twist can also be characteristic of the type of weapon and form a valuable contribution to the investigation.

Under no conditions should a cartridge case that is to be examined be tried in the chamber of a weapon; any marks made by the weapon on the case may be destroyed and other marks may be formed. It happens sometimes that at the scene of a crime in which a firearm has been used, a cartridge is found that has misfired and been thrown out by movement of the slide or bolt, or that has jammed between the breech-lock and the edge of the breech and been removed by hand. Even such an unfired cartridge may carry valuable marks that can make possible an identification or determination of the make of the weapon used.

BULLETS

Bullets that penetrate hard objects are often severely mutilated, sometimes to a degree that the weapon from which they were fired cannot be identified (Figure 10.15). Therefore, every effort must be made to preserve what little remains of the rifling impression when a bullet is lodged in a wall, tree, or bone.

In the latter case, the method of removal, if at all, will depend on whether the shooting victim is dead. If the victim is dead, the principles for bone, tree, or wall are alike. No projectile should be pried from its position. Instead, the supporting material and the bullet should be cut out as one piece. Then the surrounding bone, plaster, or wood can be broken away carefully, leaving the projectile in the best possible condition, considering all circumstances. If the investigator wishes, the bullet as embedded in supporting material may be sent to the laboratory. Bullets removed by probing show ample evidence of the destructive effect of improper technique. Before removal, some careful testing will indicate the direction of the bullet's track.

MARKING BULLETS

After removal, the bullet should be initialed on the base. No mark should be placed on the rifling impression or on areas of ricochet. If in doubt as to the proper area to mark, the investigator should place the bullet in an envelope, a plastic vial, or a small box, then seal and mark the container.

Bullets may be of different sizes and shapes and made in different ways. The most common types are entirely of lead, semi-jacketed, or fully jacketed; but there are also bullets with a hole in the point (hollow point), with the point covered with softer metal, lead bullets with a copper cone pressed into the point, and the like (Figure 10.16).

With fully jacketed (solid nose) bullets, the jacket encloses entirely the point of the bullet but is open at the rear end of it, exposing the lead core. With a semi-jacketed (soft nose) bullet, on the other hand, the jacket encloses the whole of the rear end of the bullet while the core is free at the point to a larger or smaller extent. The semi-jacketed bullet breaks up when it meets a bone or other hard part of the body, but if it passes merely through soft parts, it may remain relatively undamaged or it may expand. If it strikes the branch of a tree in its flight, it may actually be split or deformed before reaching its target. On the other hand, a fully jacketed bullet often remains undamaged or only slightly deformed on striking, for example, a body. Less scrupulous shooters sometimes file the point of a fully jacketed bullet to produce the same effect as that of a semi-jacketed one. This result is obtained if the bullet leaves the barrel whole; however, because the jacket is open at both ends, there is a risk of the lead core only being driven out

Figure 10.16 Examples of different types of bullets. (*Courtesy of Lucian Haag.*)

and the jacket remaining behind in the barrel. If this is not noticed, then when the next shot is fired, the weapon will burst or a bulge will be produced in the barrel.

Lead bullets may be of different degrees of hardness. Bullets of soft lead are often greatly deformed and sometimes break up when they strike a body, while those of hard lead may retain their regular shape to the same extent as a fully jacketed bullet.

Ammunition intended for automatic pistols usually has fully jacketed bullets, while revolver ammunition usually has lead bullets. There are, however, also automatic pistol cartridges with lead or semi-jacketed bullets and revolver cartridges with fully jacketed bullets. An intermediate position is taken by the previously mentioned cartridges of .22-caliber with lead bullets, which can be fired in certain automatic pistols, single-shot pistols, revolvers, and rifles. Also, as mentioned previously, revolver cartridges of .320-caliber, which are provided with lead bullets, can be fired in pistols of 7.65-mm caliber.

The type of jacket, if any, and the contour, weight, and composition of the bullet, and the number, size, and design of cannelures may give an indication of the maker of the cartridge. In American cartridges, lead bullets are sometimes copper plated. On a fired bullet, the bore of the weapon will have left marks from the lands and sometimes also from the bottom of the grooves. A microscopic examination of these land and groove marks sometimes shows characteristic details that make possible an identification of the weapon. The number, width, and direction of twist of the lands and grooves make possible a determination of the make of the weapon from which the bullet may have been fired. The angle or rate of twist can be determined, but this is difficult and inaccurate when the projectile is mutilated (Figure 10.17).

The number and width of the land and groove impressions, together with the direction and angle of the twist, vary for different manufacturers and types of weapons. Under no conditions should a bullet be tested in the bore of a weapon by pushing it into the muzzle. The microscopic marks on the bullet might be completely destroyed. If it is necessary to search for a weapon in connection with a bullet that has been found, the investigator can obtain a useful guide from a study of the land impressions on the bullet. The number of marks, their width, and the direction of the twist can

Figure 10.17 The direction of twist (R) and number of lands and grooves on this bullet reveal class characteristics as to the type of gun that could have fired this bullet. (*Courtesy of LASD.*)

be compared with a suspected weapon (Figure 10.18). If a long time has passed after the actual shooting, any deposit of dust or powder in the barrel would no longer be significant. If the barrel has evidently been cleaned or oiled, then silicone casting material can be introduced into the muzzle of the weapon to obtain an impression of the lands and grooves so that their number and width can be compared with the marks on the bullet. Otherwise, this information must be obtained from inspection of the muzzle of the weapon, with the aid of a flashlight.

Generally, the number of "suspect" guns in any investigation is not large. Therefore, it is better to let the laboratory sort these weapons by firing test shots. A number of factors affect the width of land impressions, so that an exact comparison between a cast of the barrel and the bullet cannot be made. Anything within a reasonable range of tolerance should be submitted for laboratory tests.

If a muzzle-loading weapon has been used, it is possible that the bullet may show marks from the ramrod. Homemade bullets may be identified with the mold used. In the case of muzzle-loaders, it is also necessary to search the scene for any paper wads that might have been used in loading the gun. These often remain undamaged and the paper might be identified from a torn piece of newspaper or from a scrap of paper in the suspect's possession. Although the rifled slugs and single balls of lead sometimes used in shotguns may give an opportunity for identification of the weapon, they can give information only as to the caliber. Homemade balls can possibly be identified with the molds in which they were made.

SMALL SHOT

At close range the charge of shot, which has not yet disbursed, makes a large wound in a body, but at longer range the shot spreads out, more or less depending on the degree of choke of the gun, barrel length and size, and amount of shot. The amount of spread gives an estimate of the distance of the shot. If scaled photographs of the wound or shot pattern are available, comparison shots can be fired using the suspect weapon and ammunition of the same make and vintage. These are usually fired at heavy poster board or blotting paper. Without scaled photographs or comparison tests, only very broad estimates are possible because the patterns produced by various combinations of guns and ammunition will vary over a considerable range.

Figure 10.18 A firearms reference library can be used to help narrow down the type of gun that was used by examining class characteristics on test shots. (*Courtesy of LASD.*)

By measuring the diameter of any shot found, it is possible to find the size of shot that would be marked on the cartridge. In this connection, it should be noted that there might be certain minor variations in size of shot in one and the same cartridge. It is important to collect as many pellets as possible so that the determination is more reliable. Often the shot is deformed to such an extent that it is impossible to measure its diameter with any accuracy. In this case, it is convenient to weigh as large a number of shot as possible, calculate the mean weight, then weigh the same number of shot from cartridges with the different sizes of shot that may be in question and calculate their mean weight for comparison.

If a weapon is sent to a firearms expert to determine whether a bullet or a cartridge case has been fired from it, a sufficient number of cartridges (five to six or more) of the same type as that used in the actual incident should be submitted along with it. This is necessary if powder or shot patterns are to be fired. All ammunition in the weapon and any partial boxes of unfired ammunition associated with the victim or suspect should be submitted with the weapon. Sufficient differences may exist between ammunition found in the gun and other ammunition available to the expert so that comparison tests are difficult, doubtful, or impossible.

If a number of tests must be fired for comparison and transmission to various laboratories, inquiries should be made as to the nature and make of test ammunition desired in each investigation. For best results, these test specimens should be obtained by a laboratory and not by the field investigator.

TEST FIRING

Test firings of a weapon must be done so that the bullet can be recovered undamaged. For all jacketed bullets and most types of lead bullets, a cotton wad box or water trap is used to stop the bullet. With a cotton wad box, as a consequence of its rotation, the bullet twists itself up in the cotton waste, which finally forms a ball around the bullet, and the velocity progressively decreases until the bullet is finally held in the cotton. Occasionally, long staple surgical cotton is placed in front of the cotton waste. This forms a ball around the bullet, further protecting the surface. Because of the mild damage to the bullet's surface due to the abrasive action of the cotton, water is frequently used as a collecting medium. For the collection of projectiles fired from handguns, five–six feet of water is ample

Figure 10.19   (a) Recovering a test shot from (b) a ballistics water tank. (*Courtesy LASD.*)

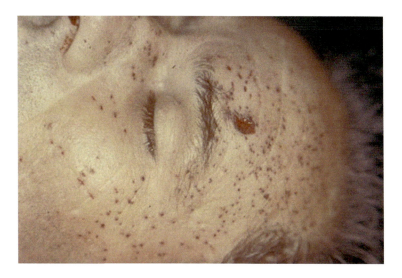

Figure 10.20   The distance of the gunshot can be estimated by the degree of stippling and how spread out it is. This wound pattern is from an intermediate gunshot wound. Photo Credit: http://library.med.utah.edu/WebPath/FORHTML/FOR038.html.)

(Figure 10.19a and b). Generally, it is undesirable for the expert to carry out test shots with the weapon personally because the microscopic imperfections in the bore of the weapon may be destroyed in the process. It is important to examine the weapon before any tests are fired.

POWDER PATTERN EXAMINATION

When a weapon is fired at close range (up to several feet), burned and sometimes unburned particles of gunpowder are discharged onto the target. This effect is referred to as a powder pattern deposit. The appearance of the powder pattern is sometimes helpful in establishing the distance from the fired weapon to the target. If the weapon was fired perpendicular to the target, the resulting powder pattern distribution will be circular around the bullet entry hole (Figure 10.20).

The diameter of the circle and the distribution of particles can be used to estimate the distance. Type of firearm, barrel length, and type of ammunition are all factors that affect the size and density of the powder pattern. If the muzzle of the weapon is in contact with the skin or within approximately 1/2 inch, the powder pattern is generally absent. This is due to the lack of space available for expansion of the powder, so that at close range it will penetrate the body through the entrance wound.

To make a distance determination, it is important to use the same firearm and ammunition used in the crime. A series of test firings are made into paper or cardboard at different distances and the test patterns are compared with the evidence. In most instances, it is also useful to make the tests on material the same as or similar to the evidence.

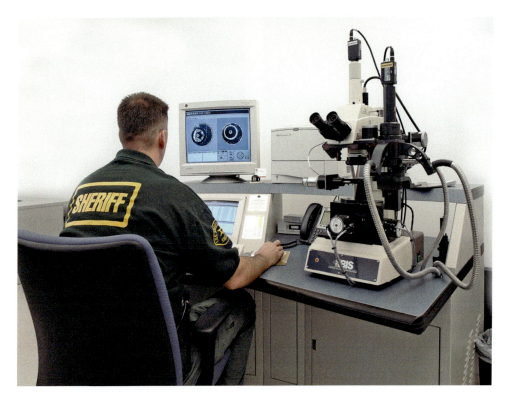

Figure 10.21 A National Integrated Ballistic Information Network (NIBIN) workstation. (*Courtesy of LASD.*)

In certain instances, the powder pattern is not easily visible. Bloodstained or dark-colored clothing causes these difficulties in visualization. Infrared photography is helpful in bloodstain cases on dark clothing. Chemical tests for nitrates present in the gunpowder, such as the Walker test or Griess test or, for lead and barium in the primer, the sodium rhodizonate test, are useful in developing the powder pattern.

NATIONAL INTEGRATED BALLISTIC INFORMATION NETWORK*

The National Integrated Ballistic Information Network (NIBIN) is a networked computer database maintained by the ATFE of fired cartridge casing and bullet images used by crime laboratories (Figure 10.21). The system was developed to link firearms evidence and to solve open cases by allowing firearms examiners to compare evidence with fired bullets, cartridge casings, shotgun shells, and firearms recovered in other jurisdictions. By means of a microscope attached to the system, images of bullets and cartridge casings are electronically scanned and stored for later retrieval and comparison with other case images. To use NIBIN, examiners enter cartridge information into the Integrated Ballistic Identification System (IBIS). The system has the ability to compare the new images rapidly with images in regional and national databases. The firearms examiner visually compares the images to determine if there is a hit.

The value of these systems is their ability to associate firearms evidence between unrelated crimes. Test firing of all confiscated firearms that come into the custody of the police becomes even more important because of the possibility of developing more information about cases that appear to be unrelated. Moreover, it is also important to recover projectiles and cartridge casings at ALL crime scenes and submit them for imaging.

Firearms evidence occurs in many crimes, such as assault, murder, and the like, and is particularly important because of the large amount of useful information it can provide. Because this type of evidence is encountered so frequently, investigators must be familiar with the proper methods of handling it and its value to the case.

---

* https://www.atf.gov/firearms/national-integrated-ballistic-information-network-nibin.

3D PRINTED "GHOST" GUNS

Ghost guns have become a recent problem. Individual components of these guns can be purchased over the internet and assembled into working firearms. The challenge for law enforcement is that these guns have no manufacturer's serial number and cannot be traced back to a seller or buyer. In addition to the serial number issue, these guns usually do not show up on x-ray machines and may be passed through security checkpoints without detection.

Many ghost guns are 3D printed out of plastic or other polymers with just a few metal parts. Many of these guns look and feel like factory made weapons, however, their operability is often poor with frequent jams. Other ghost guns look like toys, but in actuality they are real working firearms.

Ghost guns can be purchased online as kits and can be assembled with minimal effort. Depending on how the gun was assembled (i.e., those that use metal barrels), traditional striation marks will still be found on the bullet. In other ghost guns where the barrel is made of plastic, identifying a ghost gun as being the source of a fired projectile is not possible using current methods.

OSAC FIREARMS & TOOLMARKS SUBCOMMITTEE*

The Firearms & Toolmarks Subcommittee focuses on standards and guidelines related to the examination of firearm and toolmark evidence. This includes the comparison of microscopic toolmarks on bullets, cartridge cases, and other ammunition components and may also include firearm function testing, serial number restoration, muzzle-to-object determination, tools and toolmarks.

Published standards include *Safe Handling of Firearms and Ammunition* and *Standard Test Method for the Forensic Examination and Testing of Firearms*. This OSAC has also developed and proposed several standards for development by a Standards Development Organization.

SWGGUN

The Scientific Working Group for Firearms and Toolmarks (SWGGUN) was established by the FBI in 1998 as an international group of experts in the discipline of firearm and toolmark identification. SWGGUN guidelines are not endorsed by OSAC, but may be helpful to stakeholders.

Further Reading

Cizdziel, James, and Oscar Black. *Forensic Analysis of Gunshot Residue, 3D-Printed Firearms, and Gunshot Injuries: Current Research and Future Perspectives*. Nova Science Pub Inc., 2019.

Houck, Max M., ed. *Firearm and Toolmark Examination and Identification*. Elsevier, 2015.

Monturo, Chris. *Forensic Firearm Examination*. Academic Press, 2019.

Walker, Robert E. *Cartridges and Firearm Identification*. CRC Press, 2012.

Wallace, James Smyth. *Chemical Analysis of Firearms, Ammunition, and Gunshot Residue*. Crc Press, 2018.

Chapter Questions

1. (True or false) The field of firearms identification is referred to as forensic ballistics.
2. Which of the following are the two groups of firearms?
   a) Long arms and handguns.
   b) Rifles and shotguns.

---

* https://www.nist.gov/osac/firearms-toolmarks-subcommittee.

c) Revolvers and semi-automatic.
d) Single shot and multiple shot.

3. _____ is/are found in gun barrels and impart(s) a twisting motion on the bullet as it leaves the barrel.
   a) Ridges.
   b) Minutia.
   c) Rifling.
   d) Imperfections.
4. Describe how shotguns differ from other firearms.
5. Beyond determining that two rounds were fired from the same gun, what other information can be developed from firearms-related evidence?
6. Typically, how long will GSR remain on the shooter's hands?
   a) 1 hour.
   b) 3 hours.
   c) 6 hours.
   d) 24 hours.
7. (True or false) When a firearm is found at a scene, it must be rendered safe immediately and then documented.
8. Which of the following can be used to determine the approximate position of the shooter?
   a) Cartridge cases.
   b) Bullets.
   c) Cartridges.
   d) All of the above.
9. In a contact shot to a victim, there is often blood found within the barrel of the handgun. This is called:
   a) Backspatter.
   b) Forward spatter.
   c) Low velocity spatter.
   d) Spatter pressure.
10. Which of the following marks found on cartridge cases can be used to identify the make of the firearm?
    a) Striations.
    b) Lands.
    c) Grooves.
    d) Extractor.

CHAPTER 11

Arson and Explosives

INTRODUCTION

Fires and explosions account for a large number of property crimes but also may be the cause of serious bodily injury and death investigations. In addition to the requisite expertise needed in many other areas of crime scene investigations, fire scene and bomb scene investigators require added skills to properly investigate these types of crimes.* Personnel working in larger municipalities, state agencies, and the federal government possess such expertise. Prudence suggests that these individuals should be brought into the investigation at an early stage, if needed.

Arson is defined as the willful and malicious burning of another's property or the burning of one's own property for some illegal purpose such as defrauding an insurer. As a crime, arson ranks only behind traffic-related incidents in the highest losses of life and property. In dollars, property losses due to arson can be placed in the billions of dollars annually.

When a fire occurs, fire investigators are called to the scene to determine the cause of the fire and the potential for arson.

According to the National Academies of Sciences, more research is needed on the natural variability of burn patterns and damage characteristics and how they are affected by the presence of various accelerants. In fact, as FRONTLINE reported in the 2010 film *Death by Fire*, many of the supposed telltale signs of arson—the remnants of accelerant pour patterns, for example—can actually be caused by natural phenomena during accidental fires.

"The fire investigation community largely consists of people who are firemen. They're not scientists," arson expert John Lentini told FRONTLINE. "Extinguishing a fire and investigating a fire involve two different skill sets and two different mindsets."

Another scientific expert, Gerald Hurst, offered a startling "devil's advocate" opinion about the state of arson testimony in the courtroom: "I could take almost any fire and—if I were so inclined—convince a jury that it was arson. It's frighteningly simple, frighteningly easy."

Arson investigation can be complex. The consequences can be considerable as the following case study shows:

Cameron Todd Willingham Case

On December 23, 1991, a fire destroyed the Corsicana, TX, home of Cameron Todd Willingham that he shared with his wife and three daughters, killing the three girls. Willingham, who was asleep when the fire started, survived. His wife was at the Salvation Army buying Christmas presents for the girls. At Willingham's 1992 trial,

---

* Professional organizations focusing on fire investigation and bomb scene investigation are the International Association of Arson Investigators (www.firearson.com), the National Association of Fire Investigators (www.nafi.org), and the International Association of Bomb Technicians and Investigators (www.iabti.org/).

prosecutors claimed he intentionally set the fire to his home in order to kill his own children. Willingham said he was asleep in the home when the fire started and always maintained his innocence. He was convicted based on the testimony of forensic experts who said they had determined that the fire was intentionally set and a jailhouse informant who said Willingham had confessed to him. On October 29, 1992, he was sentenced to death. Thirteen years later, in the days leading up to Willingham's execution, his attorneys sent the governor and the Board of Pardon and Parole a report from Gerald Hurst, a nationally recognized arson expert, saying that Willingham's conviction was based on erroneous forensic analysis. Documents obtained by the Innocence Project show that state officials received that report but apparently did not act on it. Willingham was executed by lethal injection in Huntsville, TX on February 17, 2004.

Months after Willingham was executed, the Chicago Tribune published an investigative report that raised questions about the forensic analysis. The Innocence Project assembled five of the nation's leading independent arson experts to review the evidence in the case, and this prestigious group issued a 48-page report finding that none of the scientific analysis used to convict Willingham was valid. In 2006, the Innocence Project formally submitted the case to the Texas Forensic Science Commission, asking the empowered state entity to launch a full investigation. Along with the Willingham case, the Innocence Project submitted information about another arson case in Texas where identical evidence was used to send another man to death row. In that case, Ernest Willis was exonerated and freed from prison because the forensic evidence was not valid. In 2008, the Texas Forensic Science Commission (TFSC) agreed to investigate the case. In 2009, an arson expert hired by the commission issued a report finding that experts who testified at Willingham's trial should have known it was wrong at the time. Days before the expert was set to testify, however, Gov. Rick Perry replaced key members of the panel, delaying the investigation for months. An investigative report in the September 7, 2009, issue of *The New Yorker* magazine deconstructs every facet of the state's case against Willingham. The 16,000-word article by David Grann[*] shows that all of the evidence used against Willingham was invalid, including the forensic analysis, the informant's testimony, other witness testimony, and additional circumstantial evidence. On October 14, Texas Judge Charlie Baird held a hearing in the Willingham case to determine whether to hold a court of inquiry. And on October 15, the TFSC discussed the case in depth at its regular meeting. On April 15, 2011, the TFSC issued its final report in the Willingham/Willis case.[†]

Arson investigation requires a considerable amount of care, attention to detail, and skill on the part of the investigator. Arson scenes present a host of problems that are uncommon to most other crime scene investigations. In most criminal investigations, once the crime has been committed and the police notified, the scene may be secured in relatively the same condition in which it was found. This is anything but the case in fire investigation. By the time the arson investigator arrives on the scene, numerous individuals including firefighters, supervisory personnel, onlookers, and possibly the owner of the property will have visited the crime scene. The preservation of the crime scene is frequently the last thing to be considered by firefighters when "knocking down" a blaze.

The issue of criminal intent is another major difference in arson investigations compared with other investigations. With most other crimes, the investigator frequently knows on arrival or shortly thereafter that a crime has been committed. With arson cases, determining whether a fire was set accidentally or intentionally may require significantly more investigation.

Arson and explosion crime scenes are unique in the amount of destruction and devastation present. An item that normally is identifiable as important evidence in an investigation can be totally or partially destroyed by the fire or by firefighters. In spite of the difficulties inherent in arson investigation, a careful and thorough search of the fire scene can produce much useful information.

A number of motives are frequently associated with arson. Probably the most common motives are concealment of other crimes and defrauding an insurance company. A fire investigator frequently finds that the fire was set to cover up another crime such as murder, burglary, embezzlement, or fraud. The attempt in these cases is to destroy records and evidence of the crime that could make identifying the suspect or the victim of a murder impossible. In insurance

---

[*] The full text of the "Trial by Fire" article from *The New Yorker* can be found here: https://tinyurl.com/2hhxvyd4.
[†] http://www.fsc.state.tx.us/documents/FINAL.pdf.

fraud cases, the suspect may have suffered a business reversal or be heavily in debt. The fire is set to appear accidental with the intent of filing a false insurance claim. Other motives such as malicious mischief caused by juveniles, revenge, extortion, sabotage, terrorist acts, and pyromania all represent potential reasons for setting fires.

The arson investigator should focus the investigation to answer several questions:

1. *Where did the fire originate?* Information can be obtained by searching for V-shaped patterns, although this is not always indicative of a fire's origin. The most information will be gained by going through the scene and noting what areas suffered the most fire damage and exposure to heat. Be alert to multiple origins in some intentionally set fires.
2. *How was the fire started?* The investigator should look for faulty electrical wiring, the presence of igniters, matches, ignitable material, kindling, and other means of starting the fire. Ignitable fluids will run into cracks and under objects on the floor and cause burning in locations that would not normally burn.
3. *Was the cause of the fire an accident or was it intentionally set?* This is the key issue in determining whether the fire was arson. Evidence such as breaking into and entering the building, presence of ignitable fluids, and multiple points of origin may indicate a maliciously set fire. Also, the presence of "streamers" to spread the fire from one area to another is a sign of arson.

PHYSICAL EVIDENCE

The presence of ignitable fluids, or accelerants, is the most commonly sought physical evidence in arson investigations. Even in cases in which fire damage was particularly extensive or the scene was completely wetted down, there is still a good probability of detecting ignitable fluids when evidence is collected properly. The search for ignitable fluids should be concentrated at the point where the fire started. If charred rags or carpeting are noted, these should be collected and sent to the laboratory. Wood flooring, furniture, and carpet padding into which gasoline or kerosene may have been absorbed should also be collected as well as empty containers or broken glass jars found at the scene.

Ignitable fluids are highly volatile and evaporate easily. For this reason, appropriate packaging must be used to preserve these items for laboratory analysis. Packaging evidence in paper or plastic bags or containers will not preserve it. Such packages allow volatile liquids to dissipate completely. The best manner of packaging these items is in clean metal paint cans. Items should be placed into the cans, which should then be tightly sealed with metal lids. An alternative method of preserving evidence is to use glass jars with metal screw-cap lids. Metal and glass containers retain small amounts of liquids and vapors that can be analyzed by the crime laboratory. The quantity of material needed for chemical analysis of an ignitable substance is extremely small. Laboratory instruments are capable of readily identifying ignitable liquids in quantities of less than a fraction of a drop. In fact, if an odor of an ignitable liquid can be detected, there is a good chance that a forensic lab can identify the source (Figure 11.1).

Laboratory analysis can differentiate among the many types of accelerants used in arson cases. The common types are gasoline, kerosene, charcoal lighter fluid, paint thinner, and turpentine. In some cases, the dyes contained in

Figure 11.1 Ordinary clean metal paint cans make for easy collection and preservation of arson evidence.

gasoline can be used as a means of comparison with known samples. Highly sophisticated scientific instrumentation at some laboratories may be able to differentiate brands of gasoline; however, most crime labs do not conduct such examinations, and if only a residue of a sample is available, it is not possible to do such testing.

A careful search of all entrances and windows should be made to determine whether the building had been forcefully entered. If tool marks are observed, the area should be cut out or an impression made and submitted to the laboratory. Also, samples of building materials such as glass, paint, plaster, stucco, wallboard, cement, etc., that may have been deposited on the suspect's clothing should be collected for purposes of control or known samples. All evidence must be properly marked for identification and packaged properly. In some instances, an apparent forced entry might have been used to cover up arson, so such things as the side from which a window was broken, screen cut, etc., should be checked. The investigation should include the search for igniting materials. Burned matches and matchbooks should also be collected. Burned matches, in some cases, can be physically fitted into a matchbook found on a suspect, and matchbooks can be chemically processed for fingerprints. Occasionally, pieces of a timing device used to delay the ignition of a fire may be discovered.

Other types of igniters such as candles, black powder, smokeless powder, sodium and water, electrical devices, lit cigarettes, and similar items should be noted and collected. It is important that the manner in which the fire started be established. This can help determine the M.O. (modus operandi) of the arsonist (Figure 11.2a–c).

If the scene of the arson is a business establishment, the investigator may notice that file cabinets have been pulled open and papers strewn about. Burned papers should be carefully collected and placed into cardboard boxes, handling them as little as possible. Burned paper may be examined at the laboratory and useful information can be determined. For example, it may be very beneficial to know what files were burned or are missing.

If the fire was started outdoors, the area of the origin of the fire should be examined. Soil from that area should be collected and tested for the presence of ignitable materials. To accomplish this, a clean, gallon paint can should be filled with soil, sealed, and submitted to the laboratory along with a control sample.

Any items left at the scene by the arsonist should be preserved. Traces such as pieces of clothing, hair, blood, tools, broken tools, etc., may prove to be important as a means of establishing the identity of the suspect.

When a suspect is apprehended, a careful search of his property should be made to determine whether anything can be tied to the crime or the crime scene. Any accelerants such as gasoline or kerosene should be packaged and submitted to the laboratory for comparison with accelerants detected at the scene of the arson. Similarly, objects such as tools, matches, matchbooks, incendiary devices, and the like should be collected The suspect's clothing and shoes should be collected, packaged, and sent to the laboratory for examination for the presence of these materials.

The suspect's vehicle should be inspected for the presence of material removed from or transported to the scene of the arson. Any search of the suspect's vehicle or residence may require a search warrant. The local prosecutor should be contacted if there is any question.

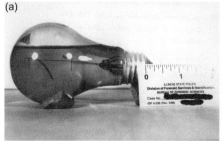 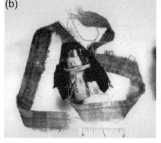 

Figure 11.2 These are examples of improvised incendiary devices. (a) This incendiary device, a light bulb with a small hole drilled into the base, filled with a medium petroleum distillate, and sealed with a putty-like material, was found in a light socket connected to a timer in a house under construction. The device probably would not have worked because too much liquid was in the bulb, which covered the filament. (b) A portion of a "Molotov cocktail" with a shot shell. (*Courtesy of Illinois State Police, Bureau of Forensic Sciences.*) (c) An improvised incendiary device consisting of a cigarette and matches can produce sufficient heat to cause the contents of the bag to burn. (*Courtesy of the Los Angeles County Sheriff's Department.*)

In cases in which a dead body is discovered in the investigation, a determination of the cause of death is necessary to ascertain whether the victim died as a result of the fire or the fire was set in order to conceal a homicide. The pathologist will be able to determine at the time of the autopsy whether the person died of smoke inhalation or was dead prior to the fire.

Case Review

A gas leak in a pizza-oven at a Turkish restaurant caused a huge explosion, killing 11 people and injuring dozens. The restaurant was closed at the time of explosion and all the casualties occurred at a nearby restaurant and among passersby (Figure 11.3a-c).

Figure 11.3 (a) A panoramic photograph showing the general scene of the explosion. (b) Photograph showing the impact of the explosion on adjacent shops. (c) the impact of the explosion on the walls and roof of the Turkish restaurant. (d) Photographs showing the gas lines (made of carbon steel) and the (e) ball valves of the gas distribution panel which were found disassembled, with all of the gas ball valves opened. The restaurant was not operating an automatic safety system for the gas supply. Instead, manually (f) connected gas pipes were used for the gas supply. (g) The pizza-oven, along with its two burners attached to a gas hose. (h, i) Photographs showing a match between the two parts of a broken gas hose nozzle, with one part attached to the gas ball valve and the other being inside the gas hose. (j) Leak testing which was conducted on the two burners, proving that one of the burners was leaking. (k) Finally, the LPG gas tank which was atop the roof of the restaurant. Traces of fire burns appear on the tank's external body as well as some damage which occurred after it crashed into the ground.

The restaurant usually opened at around noon and closed late in the night. The explosion occurred at 10:12 am, igniting a small fire and blowing out the windows of several adjacent buildings. The blast sprayed debris across a 50-meter radius.

Several badly damaged cars with shattered windshields and headlights dangling out of their casings were seen being towed away from the scene around noon.

The accident prompted an entire corner of the restaurant to collapse, and large portions of the exterior wall were missing. What appeared to be a section of a second-story floor was seen dangling toward the ground precariously, surrounded by piles of damaged concrete bricks and steel support beams. Wires hung out from corners of the wall, and knocked-over Pepsi machines could be seen inside the damaged building.

The preliminary investigation suggested a gas tank exploded, setting off a fire and causing part of the building to collapse, but this turned out to be groundless. The forensic experts, however, visited the site soon after the incident and samples from the debris were sent to the lab for examination.

The investigation concluded that there was no act of sabotage as no remnants of any explosives or other pieces of supportive evidence were found at the site. Moreover, the explosion was not centered in any particular area and if any explosives had been involved the impact would have been stronger.

It was later discovered that the gas had leaked from the oven gas ball valve, and as a result the restaurant was filled with flammable gas and that electric sparks from automatic operation and closure of electrical appliances such as the fridge then ignited the gas, causing the explosion (Figure 11.3d-i).

After the incident, measures were taken to ensure effective implementation of the law to protect citizens, residents, and property. As part of it, restaurants at fuel stations have been banned from using LPG cylinders and tanks and asked to replace them with electric stoves. A Civil Defence team has been conducting inspections to ensure all eateries abide by these safety procedures.

(*Case submitted courtesy of: Major General Hassan Ahmed Al-Obaidly, Director, Qatar Forensic Laboratory Dept., Doha, Qatar.*)

EXPLOSIVES

Explosives are useful tools by which people have accomplished some remarkable engineering feats. However, like many other things, explosives are used for criminal ends as well. Murder, burglary, extortion, terrorist activities, and similar activities involving explosives require the attention of the investigator. Bomb scene investigation is frequently treated as a specialty within some police agencies and is often associated with arson investigation. Although certain aspects of crime scene investigation of bombings differ from a common crime scene, the basics remain the same.

In broad terms, an explosive is a material capable of rapid conversion from either a solid or a liquid to a gas with resultant heat, pressure, and loud noise. Many chemicals, alone or in combination, possess the necessary properties for an explosive. Except for chemical compounds classed as explosives, the rest usually come to the investigator's attention only as the result of some accident. In such cases, consultation with a forensic chemist or criminalist will provide a satisfactory explanation for the explosion.

Explosives can be classed into two broad groups: low explosives and high explosives. High explosives consist of primary and secondary explosives; low explosives burn rather than explode. Damage by low explosives is caused by the force exerted by the rapid expansion of gases formed by burning. These types of explosives must be confined to explode. High explosives, in general, are detonated by shock and have much higher detonation velocities; they need not be confined to explode.

LOW EXPLOSIVES

Black powder is the most common type of low explosive. It is a mixture of potassium or sodium nitrate, sulfur, and charcoal. There has been wide variation in the formulation of this mixture over the years. Black powder is sensitive to heat, impact, friction, and sparks. When placed into a confined area, such as a pipe bomb, black powder can be a destructive explosive. Detonation can easily be accomplished by means of a safety fuse. If an unexploded pipe bomb is encountered, it is very important to exercise extreme care in opening the device because it can be set off by friction (Figure 11.4).

Figure 11.4 Debris from a pipe bomb packed with a low explosive. (*Courtesy of the Los Angeles County Sheriff's Department.*)

Safety fuses are used to initiate explosives non electrically; they are generally composed of black powder with a protective covering of cotton yarn or jute followed by an asphalt layer for water resistance. The asphalt covering is then covered with an insulating material such as a polyethylene plastic covering or a wax-impregnated yarn jacket. The color of the fuse is generally white, black, or orange.

Safety fuses should normally burn at a definite rate of speed but may burn faster or slower depending on several factors such as age, handling, altitude, and humidity. Usually, they burn at about 30 to 40 seconds per foot; however, the actual rate should be determined by testing a given length.

Smokeless powder is another low explosive encountered in bomb investigations. It is mainly used for small arms ammunition but is frequently used in pipe bombs. Two types of smokeless powder are marketed: single and double base. Single-base smokeless powder consists of nitrocellulose, while double-base is composed of nitrocellulose and nitroglycerine. Although smokeless powder is not as sensitive to friction as black powder, it should be handled with the same amount of care.

HIGH EXPLOSIVES

Primary explosives detonate when subjected to heat or shock. They are typically used as initiators of high explosives, to detonate main charges, and in blasting caps and firearm primers. For this type of explosive, the major interest in bomb investigation is in blasting caps. Blasting caps are of two types: electric and non-electric. They are small explosive devices, about one-quarter inch in diameter and from one to three inches in length. The case may be made of aluminum, copper, or bronze. The electric blasting caps have colored wires extending from them.

Secondary explosives detonate by shock from a suitable primary explosive. Their detonation velocities range from 3,300 feet per second in the case of ammonium nitrate to 29,900 feet per second in the case of HMX. Typically, high explosives are used to shatter or destroy objects.

Detonating cord is a cord-like explosive, similar in appearance to a safety fuse. It contains a central core of RDX or PETN covered with cotton or another textile, followed by a waterproof material or plastic covering.* The cord detonates at velocities from 18,000 to 23,000 feet per second. It is very insensitive to shock and heat and presents no special problems in handling. Detonating cord is used to set off charges of high explosives much in the same way as a safety fuse is used to set off multiple pyrotechnic devices. The detonating cord may be inserted, tied, or knotted inside the high explosive to initiate detonation. Detonating cord is used to set off simultaneous charges and is detonated by means of a blasting cap.

---

* HMX, RDX, and PETN are common names for high order secondary explosives.

Boosters or primer explosives are used to detonate very insensitive high explosives. The booster consists of a secondary explosive such as RDX, PETN, tetryl, or pentolite and is detonated by means of a blasting cap. Boosters are usually cylindrical in shape with a small opening to permit insertion of a blasting cap.

A large number of high explosives are used commercially and by the military. Next, some of the more common ones encountered in law enforcement work are detailed; however, the list is not intended to cover all of the many types.

Nitroglycerine was first developed in 1847, but it was not until 1867 that Alfred Nobel developed a method to desensitize this explosive sufficiently so that it could be used commercially. Nobel's invention, dynamite, was a mixture of nitroglycerine and diatomaceous earth. Today, dynamite contains EGDN (ethyleneglycoldinitrate) in addition to other materials used to desensitize nitroglycerine. Inert materials such as wood pulp or sawdust, cornmeal, sodium nitrate, and many other materials are found in dynamite, which is usually packaged in cylindrical sticks and wrapped in waxed paper. The sticks come in a variety of sizes; the most common is one and one-eighth to one and a half inches in diameter and eight inches in length. Other sizes may be as large as 12 inches in diameter and 4–36 inches long. There are four basic types of dynamite in use today: straight dynamite, ammonia dynamite, gelatin dynamite, and ammonia-gelatin dynamite.

1. *Straight dynamite*: Manufactured in strengths of 15% to 60% by weight of nitroglycerine. The nitroglycerine is generally absorbed onto a material such as wood pulp or ground meal (such as cornmeal, cornstarch, or the like). Dynamite has a sweet, pungent odor and frequently may cause headaches. Straight dynamite has an oily, slightly moist appearance and resembles a mixture of oil, sawdust, and clay. In older sticks of dynamite, the outer wrapper may often look oil-stained from the nitroglycerine seeping out of the mixture. Police should treat such dynamite with extreme caution because it is in a highly unstable form.
2. *Ammonia dynamite*: Some of the nitroglycerine is replaced with ammonium nitrate. Ammonia dynamite is less sensitive to shock than straight dynamite and has less of a shattering effect but is more suitable for "pushing." The color of ammonia dynamite is light brown, compared with a slight reddish tint in the case of straight dynamite.
3. *Gelatin dynamite*: A water-resistant form of dynamite manufactured by combining nitroglycerine with nitrocellulose. The resulting "gel" forms a thick, viscous liquid useful under wet conditions.
4. *Ammonia-gelatin dynamite*: A combination of the last two formulations. The addition of the ammonium nitrate is a cost-saving factor, and the gelatin allows the explosive to be used in wet conditions.

Ammonium nitrate is a readily available material used as an explosive and, in a less pure form, as a fertilizer. In its pure form, it is a white crystalline material but may be a light tan color in a less pure form. As an explosive, it is relatively insensitive and requires a booster charge to be detonated. Because of its easy availability as a fertilizer, although less pure than explosive grade ammonium nitrate, it is readily available for use in homemade bombs. A modification of ammonium nitrate sometimes used is a mixture of ammonium nitrate and fuel oil, also known as ANFO.

Water gels or slurries are classified as either blasting agents or explosives, depending upon what they contain and whether or not they are cap-sensitive. Water gels typically have an ammonium nitrate base, a sensitizer, a thickener, and 5%–40% water. The sensitizer may be an explosive such as trinitrotoluene (TNT), nitrostarch, or smokeless powder, or it may be a nonexplosive such as sugar, fuel oil, carbon, or a powdered metal. These explosives are rapidly gaining in popularity as substitutes for dynamite. Most slurries require a primer or booster for detonation; however, some manufacturers make cap-sensitive gels.

BLASTING AGENTS

Blasting agents, also known as nitrocarbonitrate (NCN), are insensitive chemicals and chemical mixtures that are detonated by means of a high-explosive primer or booster. In order to be classified as a blasting agent, the material must be unable to be detonated by a No. 8 blasting cap and contain no high explosives such as TNT or nitroglycerine. Blasting agents consist largely of ammonium nitrate. ANFO is considered a blasting agent and consists of 94% ammonium nitrate and 6% fuel oil. The advantage of blasting agents is that safety regulations governing shipping and storage are considerably less severe than those applicable to high explosives.

Binary explosives are two inert, nonexplosive chemicals that, when mixed, form a cap-sensitive high explosive. The materials are either both liquids or a powder and a liquid; in their unmixed states, they are very insensitive to shock or friction. One component is usually ammonium nitrate, while the other is a nonexplosive sensitizer.

MILITARY EXPLOSIVES

Sheet explosives are flexible, rubber-like sheets approximately one-quarter-inch thick that can be cut with a knife. These explosives are used in commercial and military circumstances. The high explosive used is either RDX or PETN. Sheet explosives are known as Flex-X, Datasheet, or M118 Demolition Block (the latter military sheet explosives). The most common type of military explosive is TNT. Military explosives differ somewhat from commercial explosives in that they must be used in combat conditions. Typically, they must be relatively insensitive to heat, shock, friction, and bullet impact, have high destruction power (brisance), be lightweight and convenient to use, be usable underwater, etc.

TNT is generally encountered in military explosives in quarter, half, and one-pound blocks. The blocks have metal ends with a threaded well at one end for a blasting cap. The container is cardboard, and the TNT is a light yellow to brown color although some newer formulations of TNT may be gray due to the addition of graphite.

RDX is used in so-called plastic explosives. Plastic explosives contain plasticizers in addition to RDX and are easy to mold in warm temperatures.

Composition C-3, containing 77% RDX, is a yellow putty-like material that has a distinctive heavy, sweet odor. When molded, it will stain the hands and clothing. The M3 block is enclosed in glazed paper that is perforated around the middle for ease in breaking open and weighs 2 1/4 pounds. The block does not have a cap well.

Composition C-4 is replacing C-3 in military use. C-4 contains 91% RDX, is white to light brown in color, has no odor, and does not stain the hands. The M5A1 block demolition charge contains C-4 in a clear white plastic container with a threaded cap recess at each end. It weighs two and a half pounds. Composition C-4 also comes in the M112 block demolition charge, an improvement of the M5A1 that replaces it as a standard issue. The M112 contains one and one-quarter pounds of composition C-4 with a pressure-sensitive adhesive tape on one surface, protected by a peelable paper cover. The C-4 in some blocks is colored dull gray and packed in a clear Mylar-film bag. In blocks of more recent manufacture, the C-4 is white and packed in an olive drab Mylar bag.

Military dynamite is not really dynamite, but a mixture of 75% RDX, 15% TNT, 5% SAE 10 motor oil, and 5% guar flour. It is packaged in waxed manila paper and marked M1, M2, or M3. Military dynamite is buff-colored granular material that crumbles easily and is slightly oily to the touch. It does not have the characteristic odor usually associated with dynamite because it contains no nitroglycerine.

The explosives discussed to this point are some of the more common ones encountered and represent explosives available through commercial and military sources. The explosives industry, however, is a rapidly changing one, and the reader should understand this when studying the subject. It is suggested that the investigator consult explosive manufacturers, law enforcement agencies that routinely deal with explosive cases, and forensic science laboratories for the latest information on the subject.

HOMEMADE EXPLOSIVES (HME)

If commercial or military explosives are not available, it is not particularly difficult for an individual to improvise from a large number of chemicals that, when mixed together, can produce highly destructive explosive devices. The investigator should recognize at least some of the more common materials that often find their way into homemade explosive devices.

Materials such as starch, flour, sugar, cellulose, etc., can be treated to become effective explosives. Powder from small arms ammunition and from firecrackers, match heads, and ammonium nitrate from fertilizers can be used in explosive devices. To detonate an improvised explosive device, several methods are available:

Blasting caps. Caps, especially electrical blasting caps, lend themselves to homemade bombs. Such devices may be set off by a timing mechanism, by movement, by wiring into an automobile ignition system, etc.

Percussion primers. Primers from shotgun, rifle, or pistol ammunition are sometimes used to detonate explosives that are heat sensitive.

Flashbulbs. Flashbulbs may be used to ignite heat-sensitive explosives such as black powder. If the bulb is placed in contact with the explosive, the resulting heat from the flashbulb will ignite materials such as black powder,

Match heads. Match heads are frequently found confined inside pipe bombs. They are sensitive to heat, friction, and shock, and when confined in this type of device, they can produce an effective explosion.

Smokeless powder. Powder from ammunition or for reloading purposes is frequently used as the main charge in pipe bombs.

Ammonium nitrate fertilizer. Ammonium nitrate mixed with fuel oil and an appropriate booster makes an extremely effective homemade explosives device.

Potassium or sodium chlorate. These compounds and sugar are used as incendiary and explosive materials.

Over the past several decades, two improved explosives, the peroxide-based explosive TATP* (triacetone triperoxide) and urea nitrate,[†] have been used by terrorist organizations.

Unfortunately, the internet and terrorist manifestos have become a source of recipes and easy instructions on how to manufacture homemade explosives. Generally, components are readily available and can be obtained at low cost. Investigators should familiarize themselves with these HMEs[‡] and be on the lookout for new types of explosive devices "advertised" on the Web. It would be wise for law enforcement to contact places of business in their jurisdictions that sell materials that could be used in homemade explosives and ask them to report any suspicious purchases.

The list of possible chemicals for improvised explosives is endless. Officers who come upon locations with large numbers of chemicals such as nitrates, chlorates, perchlorates, nitric acid, aluminum powder, magnesium, sodium, sulfur, charcoal, sugar, and sulfuric acid, to name just a few, should be aware that the location may be one where homemade explosives are made.

BOMB SCENE INVESTIGATION[§]

Physical evidence in bombing cases is useful in answering many questions. Some of the questions that the investigator will be interested in answering are

What materials were used to make the explosive device?

What was the level of skill or expertise of the suspect?

What was the target of the bomb?

Was the explosion accidental or was there criminal intent?

Where was the bomb made?

Where was the bomb placed?

Where did the suspect obtain the material to construct the device?

Who was the victim or intended victim?

Who made the bomb and who placed it?

How was the bomb detonated?

The nature of the target, whether or not the bomb exploded, the extent of damage, the location of the incident, and weather conditions are some of the factors that influence the action to be taken by the investigator. If a bomb is found that has not exploded, it is necessary to call in a bomb technician to render the device safe. The first priority of the technician is to disarm the bomb safely. If possible, the investigator should photograph the bomb prior to moving it and have the bomb technician note any changes made in the device when dismantling it. If the bomb must be exploded to be disarmed, it should be done in such a way as to avoid total destruction of the device.

---

* Used in the London metro bombing in 2005 and by the so-called "shoe bomber," Richard Reid, in 2001.
† Urea nitrate was used in the 1993 World Trade Center bombing and has been used in terrorist incidents in the Middle East.
‡ www.dni.gov/files/NCTC/documents/jcat/firstresponderstoolbox/78--NCTC-DHS-FBI---Triacetone-Triperoxide-(TATP)-.pdf.
§ The National Fire Protection Association has published NFPA 921 Guide for Fire and Explosion Investigations.

The scene should be thoroughly searched for evidence that may have been left by the suspect. Collection of evidence should include a search for forced entry and accompanying tool marks, fingerprints, footprints, and any other traces that may help link a suspect to the crime scene.

In cases in which the explosive device detonated, the work of the investigator is complicated considerably. The duties of the crime scene investigator are basically the same as outlined in other chapters, however, the investigator will have an additional consideration: safety will be a major area of concern. The scene of a bombing is generally very unsafe. The structure of the building where the bomb exploded may be seriously weakened and can collapse. Other unexploded secondary devices may still be in the area. Hazards such as broken gas mains and downed electrical lines are potential safety problems. Securing the crime scene is another problem. Unlike most crime scenes, bomb scenes frequently attract a large number of people such as police, fire department personnel, medical and ambulance personnel, HAZMAT teams, utility companies' personnel, property owners, the press, and sightseers. One of the first orders of business must be to coordinate the activities of the large number of people likely to be present and to remove individuals who are not needed.

Because of the nature of the crime, bomb scenes frequently contain a certain amount of confusion. It is necessary to restore order and control to the situation quickly to enable the investigators to accomplish the task of processing the scene. The first officers to arrive at the scene of a bombing will be concerned with emergency and safety-related activities such as rescue, evacuation, and assisting fire department personnel if required. Once the emergency phase is complete, efforts should be made to secure the crime scene and begin developing information on the circumstances of the case. Witnesses and victims should be interviewed and as much information as possible about what happened should be gathered.

Because of the number of persons present at the scene and the likelihood of several different investigative agencies being involved in the investigation, a team with representatives from each agency should be established to coordinate and control the investigation. Such a unit can act as a clearinghouse of information so that all information gathered from the investigative process can be integrated and studied.

Investigation of the actual scene of the bombing is a time-consuming task requiring a considerable amount of physical effort and attention to minute pieces of physical evidence. It is also dirty work requiring the investigator to sift through large quantities of debris to locate items of evidence. It is useful to have proper equipment to go through the scene. Coveralls/Tyvek suits, gloves, hard hats, goggles, work shoes, and other such items are useful for the investigator. Hand tools such as shovels, rakes, brooms, a heavy-duty magnet, and cutting tools are useful. Sifting screens of various sizes are needed for going through the debris. Wheelbarrows, trash cans to collect debris, portable lighting, ladders, and the like may be required as well.

An incident commander should be immediately designated to be responsible for processing and directing the bomb scene investigation. The leader also serves as a link between those coordinating the overall investigation and the crime scene investigation. The extent of the crime scene must be identified. The seat of the explosion can be a focal point, and the location furthest from the seat where fragments from the explosion are located will define the outer perimeter of the scene. A buffer area equal to approximately half the distance from the seat to the furthest point should be added. This represents the total area that should be secured and searched.

The bomb scene should be recorded. This may be accomplished in the standard way by means of photography, video, sketches, and aerial footage from a drone. Photographing, measuring, and sketching the crime scene may be done while the scene is searched.

Collecting physical evidence at the scene consists of the search for and recovery of items that may lead to information about the nature and type of explosive and the identity of the suspect. A search for the fusing mechanism of the bomb should be made. Items such as timing mechanisms, batteries, pieces of wire, safety fuses, blasting cap debris, and the like may yield information about the way in which the bomb was set to detonate. The scene should be searched for evidence to determine the type of explosive used. The seat of the explosion should be carefully examined for unexploded material and packaging material that may indicate the type of explosive used. If a portion of the container that held the device is found, laboratory tests may indicate the type of explosive. Similarly, the extent of damage to the container, for example, a pipe bomb, can indicate whether the explosive was a low-order or high explosive. In general, large fragments of a pipe bomb indicate a low explosive such as black powder, while small fragments indicate a high explosive.

The package that contained the explosive device may contain evidence to lead the investigator to a suspect. Fingerprints, DNA, names, addresses, and postmarks may be important information in the investigation. The investigator should not forget to search for other evidence besides the bomb debris. Items such as tire tracks, tool marks, and the like are valuable and must not be overlooked.

If a suspect is apprehended shortly after the explosion, the clothing should be collected and submitted to the laboratory for examination for trace evidence and explosive residue. The suspect's hands should be swabbed with cotton applicators moistened with acetone to test them for certain explosives. If the suspect's vehicle is located, it too should be carefully searched for tools, trace evidence, explosive residue, and materials that may have been used in the crime.

All evidence should be photographed where it was found, measured, and located on a crime scene sketch prior to being moved. The investigator should also remember to search high areas such as trees, roofs, ledges of buildings, and other places that may contain pieces of the exploded device.

Because of the large number of persons involved with the bomb scene search and the amount of evidence collected, it is helpful to keep an evidence log to detail each item of evidence collected, including the date, time, and name of the person collecting the material. The use of a log facilitates establishing a chain of evidence and makes inventory of all the evidence somewhat easier.

A word of caution: terrorists sometimes employ secondary explosive devices. Extreme care should be exercised when searching the crime scene, and consideration should be given to the possibility of other explosive devices!

The crime laboratory plays an important role in bomb scene investigation. Often the nature of the explosive used and information about the type of mechanism used to detonate it cannot be determined in the field. The laboratory will carefully and systematically examine all the items of evidence and attempt to answer some of the questions required by the investigator to assist in the solution of the case.

Bomb and arson scene investigations require much time and patience, and an extreme attention to detail by the crime scene investigating officer. The officer's willingness to carefully and painstakingly go through large amounts of debris and rubble in an attempt to locate pertinent physical evidence may result in a successful conclusion to the case.

OSAC FIRE & EXPLOSION INVESTIGATION SUBCOMMITTEE*

The Fire & Explosion Investigation Subcommittee focuses on standards and guidelines related to the investigation, analyses, and interpretation of crime scenes where arson or use of explosives is suspected. Two of the standards in this discipline that appear on the OSAC Registry are produced by the National Fire Protection Association (NFPA): *NFPA 921 Guide for Fire and Explosion Investigations* and *NFPA 1033 Standard for Professional Qualifications for Fire Investigator.*

Further Reading

Lentini, John J. *Scientific Protocols for Fire Investigation.* CRC Press, 2018.

Chapter Questions

1. (True or false) Arson is defined as the malicious burning of another's property or the burning of one's own property for some illegal purpose.
2. (True or false) A careful and thorough search at the fire scene does not produce much evidence due to the destructive nature of fires.
3. List the three questions that an arson investigator should focus on when conducting an investigation.

---

* www.nist.gov/osac/fire-explosion-investigation-subcommittee.

4. You are the investigator assigned to collect evidence from a suspected arson. Describe how you would collect evidence containing ignitable fluids.
5. Of the following items, which can be used as an igniter to start a fire?
    a) Matchbook.
    b) Black powder.
    c) Sodium and water.
    d) All of the above.
6. Which type of explosive is designed to be detonated by shock and has a high detonation velocity?
    a) Low.
    b) Medium.
    c) High.
    d) Black powder.
7. List several examples of high explosives.
8. Which of the following items can be used to ignite heat-sensitive explosives such as black powder?
    a) RDX.
    b) TNT.
    c) C-3.
    d) Flashbulbs.
9. List some of the questions you would be interested in answering while conducting a post-blast investigation.
10. During a post-blast investigation, which of the following is a main concern for the crime scene investigator?
    a) Collecting probative evidence.
    b) Bringing the guilty party to justice.
    c) Safety of crime scene personnel.
    d) Dealing with the media.

Chapter 12

Illicit Drugs and Toxicology

Drugs in bulk form or in blood or urine specimens are often involved as physical evidence in a wide variety of criminal cases. These substances are found in cases such as traffic accidents and fatalities, driving under the influence (DUI) of alcohol and/or drugs, public intoxication, possession or sale of controlled substances, illicit manufacture of controlled substances, and drug-facilitated sexual assaults. The purpose of this chapter is to describe the various types of drugs commonly encountered by police and to examine some of the crime scene investigation issues with regard to this class of evidence. To simplify the topic, a distinction is made between bulk drugs, that is, drugs in their usual solid or liquid form, and toxicological specimens, that is, blood or urine samples that are to be tested to determine whether a drug or its metabolites are present in a person's system.

The Drug Enforcement Administration[*] is charged with enforcing the controlled substance laws of the United States. Drugs are classified into five distinct schedules depending upon the drug's acceptable medical use and the drug's potential for abuse or dependency. Schedule I drugs have a high potential for abuse and the potential to create severe psychological and/or physical dependence. Schedule II, Schedule III, and subsequent schedules have a lower potential for abuse. Schedule V drugs represent the least potential for abuse.

Examples of drugs in the five different schedules may be found on the drug scheduling section of the DEA's website and is provided below:[†]

U.S. DEA DRUG SCHEDULE CLASSIFICATION

Schedule I

Schedule I drugs, substances, or chemicals are defined as drugs with no currently accepted medical use and a high potential for abuse. Some examples of Schedule I drugs are:

> Heroin, lysergic acid diethylamide (LSD), marijuana (cannabis),[‡] 3,4-methylenedioxymethamphetamine (ecstasy), methaqualone, and peyote

Schedule II

Schedule II drugs, substances, or chemicals are defined as drugs with a high potential for abuse, with use potentially leading to severe psychological or physical dependence. These drugs are also considered dangerous. Some examples of Schedule II drugs are:

---

[*] The Drug Enforcement Administration (www.dea.gov) publication *Drugs of Abuse* is an excellent resource guide for information on the most commonly abused drugs.
[†] www.dea.gov/drug-information/drug-scheduling.
[‡] Several states have decriminalized marijuana for personal use under state law. Marijuana remains a controlled drug, however, under Schedule I.

DOI: 10.4324/9780429272011-14

Combination products with less than 15 milligrams of hydrocodone per dosage unit (Vicodin), cocaine, methamphetamine, methadone, hydromorphone (Dilaudid), meperidine (Demerol), oxycodone (OxyContin), fentanyl, Dexedrine, Adderall, and Ritalin

Schedule III

Schedule III drugs, substances, or chemicals are defined as drugs with a moderate to low potential for physical and psychological dependence. Schedule III drugs abuse potential is less than Schedule I and Schedule II drugs but more than Schedule IV. Some examples of Schedule III drugs are:

Products containing less than 90 milligrams of codeine per dosage unit (Tylenol with codeine), ketamine, anabolic steroids, and testosterone

Schedule IV

Schedule IV drugs, substances, or chemicals are defined as drugs with a low potential for abuse and low risk of dependence. Some examples of Schedule IV drugs are:

Xanax, Soma, Darvon, Darvocet, Valium, Ativan, Talwin, Ambien, and Tramadol

Schedule V

Schedule V drugs, substances, or chemicals are defined as drugs with lower potential for abuse than Schedule IV and consist of preparations containing limited quantities of certain narcotics. Schedule V drugs are generally used for antidiarrheal, antitussive, and analgesic purposes. Some examples of Schedule V drugs are:

Cough preparations with less than 200 milligrams of codeine or per 100 milliliters (Robitussin AC), Lomotil, Motofen, Lyrica, and Parepectolin

PSYCHOACTIVE DRUGS

Drugs that find their way into police investigations are typically called psychoactive drugs. These drugs affect the user's psychological processes and change his or her mood, thinking, perception, and behavior. Psychoactive drugs may be illicit (e.g., lysergic acid diethylamide [LSD]) or lawful (e.g., barbiturates). They may be controlled (i.e., requiring a prescription) or uncontrolled (not requiring a prescription, e.g., alcohol or certain over-the-counter preparations). Drugs can be divided into several types based upon their effect on the user. The eight major categories discussed in this chapter are narcotics, depressants, stimulants, hallucinogens, cannabis, steroids, inhalants, and designer drugs.

Narcotics

Narcotics, also known as "opioids," produce a general sense of well-being by reducing tension, anxiety, and aggression. They are used medically for their analgesic (or painkilling) properties and have a high potential for abuse. There are several categories of narcotics: opium, opium derivatives, and semi-synthetic substitutes. Examples of narcotics include heroin and pharmaceutical drugs like OxyContin, Vicodin, codeine, morphine, methadone, and fentanyl.*
Opiate alkaloids are derived from the opium poppy, *Papaver somniferum* (Figure 12.1a-c).

Depressants

Depressants will induce sleep, relieve anxiety and muscle spasms, and prevent seizures. These are generally prescribed for the treatment of insomnia and tension and have a high potential for abuse and addiction. Drugs in this

---

* Fentanyl is a potent synthetic opioid that is used as an analgesic and anesthetic. It is approximately 100 times more potent than morphine and 50 times more potent than heroin as an analgesic.

Figure 12.1 (a) Heroin is a chemical derived from the resinous latex material extruded from the poppy. (*Photo credit: https://en.wikipedia.org/wiki/Opium.*) Heroin, which is synthesized from morphine, has a number of forms: (b) powder and (c) a tar-like material. (*Photo credit: US DOJ DEA.*)

Figure 12.2 Cocaine is seen in two forms (a) cocaine hydrochloride and (b) crack cocaine (*Photo credit: US DOJ DEA*). "Crack" cocaine is the free-base form of cocaine hydrochloride. Round pieces called "cookies," are in the shape of glass beakers used in the final processing. The "cookies" are broken into "rocks" for sale or individual use.

category include barbiturates like secobarbital, amobarbital, phenobarbital, and the like and nonbarbiturates such as glutethimide (Doriden), methaqualone (Quaalude), and chloral hydrate.

Another type of depressants are benzodiazepines. These drugs produce sedation and hypnosis, relieve anxiety, and reduce seizures. These drugs are only available through prescription and many users maintain their drug supply by getting prescriptions from several doctors. Alprazolam and clonazepam are the two most frequently encountered benzodiazepines on the illicit market. Another well known benzodiazepine is Rohypnol, or flunitrazepam. Rohypnol produces sedative-hypnotic and muscle relaxant effects and is known as a "date rape" drug.

Perhaps the most widely used and best-known central nervous system depressant today is ethyl alcohol or ethanol. Its usual short-term effects are sedation, euphoria, impaired judgment, slowed reaction time, decreased coordination, and decreased emotional control.

Stimulants

One of the few types of psychoactive drugs that have not become a law enforcement problem is the xanthine alkaloids, which contain such drugs as theophylline, theobromine, and caffeine. Cocaine is another class of central nervous system stimulant (Figure 12.2a and b). It is derived from the leaves of the *Erythroxylon coca* tree native to South America. The drug in its pure state is a white crystalline substance and is not generally used medicinally except as a local anesthetic in certain eye, nose, and throat surgical procedures (many in the medical community, however, dispute its legitimate use).

The third class of stimulants is amphetamines. Drugs in this group are amphetamine (Benzedrine), dextroamphetamine (Dexedrine), methamphetamine (Desoxyn), mixtures of Dexedrine, and amobarbital (Dexamyl), and non-amphetamine stimulants such as Ritalin and Preludin. These drugs are often prescribed for fatigue, narcolepsy, and attention deficit disorder (ADD) or attention deficit hyperactivity disorder (ADHD) in children, and in combination with barbiturates for treating obesity.

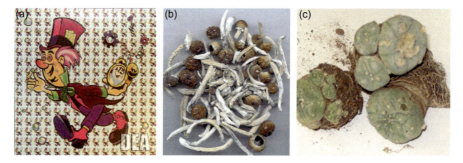

Figure 12.3 Some of the hallucinogenic drugs in this class include (a) LSD, (b) psilocybin, and (c) peyote (*Photo credit: US DOJ DEA*).

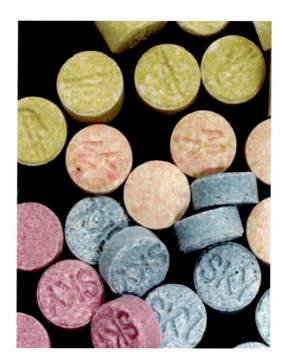

Figure 12.4 MDMA tablets, or Ecstasy (*Photo credit: US DOJ DEA*).

Hallucinogens

Hallucinogens are a group of drugs that currently have no accepted medical use. The drugs produce perceptual alterations, intense and varying emotional changes, ego distortions, and thought disruption. Drugs in this group include mescaline, which is derived from the *Lophophora* cactus, psilocybin, which occurs in several species of mushrooms (e.g., *Psilocybe Mexicana*); LSD, dimethyltryptamine (DMT); diethyltryptamine (DET); ketamine and PCP (Figure 12.3). Another popular illicit hallucinogen is MDMA (3,4-methylenedioxymethamphetamine). MDMA is known on the street by several names, for example, Adam, Ecstasy, X, and XTC (Figure 12.4).

Cannabis

Marijuana is defined legally as derivatives from the plant *Cannabis sativa* and is most often consumed by smoking the dried, crushed tops and leaves or resinous material known as hashish, which contains tetrahydrocannabinol (THC). Pharmacologically, marijuana is not classed in any of the preceding drug categories. Its usual short-term effects include relaxation, increased appetite, some alteration of time perception, and impairment of judgment and coordination (Figure 12.5).

Figure 12.5 Marijuana leaf with typical serrated leaves (*Photo credit: US DOJ DEA*).

Designer Drugs*

Every few years, new types of drugs become popular. These are the so-called "designer drugs." Designer drugs are a class of synthetic drugs synthesized by chemists working in clandestine drug laboratories. The motive is profit. Clandestine drugs present a serious problem for law enforcement and a danger to those who use them. Illicit chemists do what pharmaceutical researchers do to develop new active drugs. They synthesize drugs with similar structural features to known psychoactive substances. However, with designer drugs, neither quality control nor the testing of the substances is undertaken to determine if there are any harmful side effects. Designer drugs include drugs like fentanyl analogs and bath salts.

Synthetic cannabis is a psychoactive herbal and chemical product, which, when consumed, mimics the effects of cannabis. It is best known by the brand names K2 and Spice, both of which have largely become generic trademarks used to refer to any synthetic cannabis product. These drugs are chemically similar to cannabinoids but are not uniformly controlled.

These drugs are often marketed as "herbal incense"; however, some brands market their products as "herbal smoking blends" and are usually smoked by users. Although synthetic cannabis does not produce positive results in drug tests for cannabis, it is possible to detect its metabolites in human urine.

Steroids

Steroid abuse has long been a factor in professional sports and amateur athletic competition and bodybuilding. Anabolic steroids build muscle mass and thereby enhance performance. They are reported to cause liver and adrenal gland damage, infertility and impotence in men, and masculine characteristics in women. Steroids are scheduled, controlled substances. They have become a law enforcement problem as illicit sales of anabolic steroids have been noted. Many of the steroids sold to athletes through illicit channels are not manufactured for use in human beings but rather are veterinary drugs. Frequently, the drugs are manufactured outside the United States; packaging and labeling claiming the drugs to be specific steroids are usually incorrect. The drugs are available in a wide variety of forms and may be injectable solutions, capsules, transdermal patches, or pills (Figure 12.6).

---

* The Designer Drugs website (www.designer-drugs.de) is the most comprehensive mass spectra collection of designer drugs and covers the entire range of known designer drugs and related substances.

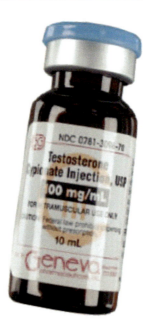

Figure 12.6 Steroids are a synthetic form of testosterone, a sex hormone naturally produced by men and women alike. By taking testosterone, its anabolic effects promote muscle building (*Photo credit: US DOJ DEA*).

Inhalants

The last group of psychoactive substances is chemicals that are inhaled. Such materials include glue, gasoline, paint, solvents, and the like. Juveniles frequently use these chemicals. The most common method involves placing the material into a plastic bag or onto a piece of cloth such as a sock and sniffing the material to obtain the intended result, intoxication or high. Another class of inhalants contains amyl nitrite, a vasodilator, used to relieve symptoms associated with angina pectoris.

Nonprescription Drugs

Nonprescription drugs rarely present law enforcement with major difficulties. They are included here as a reminder for officers investigating traffic accidents, fatalities, and cases of driving while under the influence. Over-the-counter drugs, particularly sleep aids, sedatives, and antihistamines, contain materials that make the user drowsy. The investigator who finds a subject who has taken these drugs alone or in combination with alcohol and is exhibiting unusual behavior can reasonably assume that the individual is likely to be under the influence.

CRIME SCENE SEARCH

Searching a crime scene for contraband drugs is somewhat different from other cases. In a contraband drug investigation, the CSI is looking for evidence that may have been hidden on the person, in a dwelling, or in a vehicle. The various rules of evidence including search and seizure and requirements for establishing a chain of custody hold in these cases as in others, and the investigator must be aware of current laws regulating search activities. Officer safety is also a concern. If hypodermic syringes were used, personnel need to be careful dealing with needles.

Searching a Suspect

Concerning personal search, the officer must be aware of unusual hiding places in which contraband may be hidden. Clothing and personal property should be carefully examined. Places such as cigarette packages, small cases, hollowed-out compartments in canes or umbrellas, lining of clothing, luggage, shoes, wallets, cellphones, and similar items may conceal evidence. Suspects have been known to swallow contraband or hide it in a body cavity such as the mouth, nose, rectum, or vagina. Thoroughness and experience will aid the officer in the search.

Searching a Dwelling

When searching a dwelling, the investigation should be done in a thorough, systematic manner. In addition to contraband, investigators should be alert for intelligence information such as telephone and address books, names and telephone numbers on loose pieces of paper, and so on. Sums of money and possibly stolen property should be documented and collected. Additionally, any damage to personal property or to the residence should be carefully noted and, if possible, photographed; the owner should be notified. One officer should be assigned to record the location and the name of the finder of each item of evidence.

To assist in the recording, a crime scene sketch should be made so that each piece of evidence can be charted. The officer should also make certain that each item of evidence is correctly marked for identification and properly preserved. If possible, two investigators should be assigned to a room. The search should begin at one wall, and everything hanging on that wall or resting against it should be carefully examined. Light switches and outlet boxes should be examined to determine whether paint on the screws or around the plate is chipped. The plates should be removed and searched. Molding around door frames should be examined for signs of stress to determine whether they conceal a hollow area. The tops of doors and doorframes should be examined for indentations. A plug on top of a door or hinges may conceal a hiding place. Walls should be checked to determine whether they were replastered. Wall pictures and the backs of televisions and radios should be examined. Curtain rods, the tops and bottoms of window blinds, and shades should be searched.

After the walls have been searched, furniture should be inspected. Items should be turned upside down and their bottoms examined. Throw pillows and cushions should be unzipped and the contents searched. Rugs should be rolled up. When searching the bathroom, the officer should look for waterproof containers inside toilet tanks, and containers under sinks, behind false tiles, or in laundry hampers. Prescription medicine bottles should be examined to determine whether they contain the drug listed on the container and for whom the prescription was intended. When evidence is located, it should be brought to the officer maintaining the evidence log and the search should be continued. It is a good practice to search each room a second time. Occasionally, evidence overlooked the first time will be noticed in the subsequent search. Drug detection dogs are also useful in searching a residence.

Searching a Vehicle

Automobiles are often used to hide contraband drugs. Searches involving motor vehicles should be conducted in a systematic and thorough manner. The vehicle can be divided into three areas for the search: the front end, interior, and rear. The front end of the vehicle offers many areas in which to hide contraband. A careful search should include the grille, bumper, radiator, inside surfaces of the fenders, air filter, and body frame. Using a hydraulic lift helps in the examination of the undercarriage of the vehicle. The interior of the vehicle is frequently used in concealing drugs. The seats should be removed from the car and carefully searched. The area behind the dashboard, the door side panels, headliner, and floor are possible areas where drugs may be hidden. Finally, the trunk and rear of the vehicle should be examined. Areas such as the spare tire well, spare tire, rear fender, and bumper area and undercarriage of the vehicle are all potential hiding places. Drug detection K9s can also be of very useful assistance when trying to locate drugs in a vehicle and can usually alert on a wide variety of known controlled substances.

CLANDESTINE DRUG LABORATORIES

An important source of illicit drugs today is the clandestine laboratory. Illicit drugs such as LSD, PCP, methamphetamine, and other illicit pharmaceuticals are manufactured in illicit laboratories. Police become involved in crime scene investigations involving illicit laboratories through intelligence gathering, complaints from neighbors, fires and explosions, unusually high utility bills, and often from detection of chemical odors while on routine patrol. Whatever the means of detection, the investigator must have an understanding of how such crime scenes are processed. The trained forensic chemist or criminalist should be an integral part of any such investigation. His or her training and experience in dealing with chemicals is extremely important from the standpoint of identifying drugs as finished and intermediate products and also from a safety consideration. In larger police agencies, specialized hazardous chemical response teams have been developed who handle chemical spills and disposal of toxic substances. These teams are especially helpful and should most certainly be included in any clandestine laboratory investigation.

The clandestine laboratory scene is a potentially dangerous and hazardous location. Chemicals present are often flammable, explosive, toxic, and corrosive. Proper precautions must be taken to ensure the safety of personnel at the scene. Scenes should be approached with extreme caution. It is not uncommon for chemicals to be unlabeled, and there are even reports of laboratories that were booby-trapped. As soon as the location has been secured, all windows and doors should be opened to ensure adequate ventilation and minimize the risk of fire. Light switches should not be turned on until the area is adequately ventilated; sparks can easily ignite highly flammable chemicals. Under no circumstances should anyone be allowed to smoke. The fire department should be notified and asked to stand by. Certain chemicals are especially dangerous if mixed with others. Chemicals such as lithium aluminum hydride are extremely explosive when combined with water, as is sodium. Cyanide salts will liberate hydrogen cyanide gas when in contact with acid. Most chemical solvents, such as ether, benzene, and the like, are highly flammable. Acids and alkaline materials are dangerous and can cause severe burns; others such as piperidine may cause headaches. Prolonged exposure to many volatile organic chemicals may be hazardous as well. Personal Protective Equipment (PPE), including a self-contained breathing apparatus (SCBA), is often used in clandestine lab investigations.

Extreme caution must be exercised in clandestine laboratory investigations! Before any evidence is collected, the laboratory should be photographed. Photographs of individual pieces of equipment, chemicals, laboratory glassware, finished product, and intermediates should be taken. The location should be searched for fingerprints and for laboratory notes, recipes, records, sales receipts from chemical supply companies, and other related items. Samples of chemicals from the final product, chemical precursors or intermediate products, and basic raw materials should be collected for crime laboratory analysis. A complete inventory of all chemicals, equipment, packaging material, and the like should be made. Such evidence will be very important if no final product is found. Laboratory notes, recipes, chemical precursors, and glassware will be important evidence at trial to prove conspiracy to manufacture controlled substances.

A further caution to be considered is that clandestine chemical labs may be homemade explosives laboratories rather than drug manufacturing labs. It is not unreasonable that chemicals are unlabeled; therefore, care should be taken when examination and collecting products.

COLLECTION AND PRESERVATION OF EVIDENCE

As with all physical evidence, the ultimate aim of collecting drug evidence is its legal admissibility as evidence in court and to determine the identity of the unknown substance. To assure this end, the investigating officer must be concerned with maintaining the integrity of the evidence from the time of seizure until its presentation in court. In addition to the usual requirements to maintain a chain of custody of the evidence, some other procedures are important. All drugs should be accurately weighed.* The gross weight of the package, including the drug and packaging material, should be determined and recorded. Individual pills, tablets, packets, balloons, etc., should be counted and the number written on the outer package and the report (Figure 12.7).

The packing material seized with the contraband should be kept with the evidence and properly marked for identification. Items should be placed in an appropriate evidence envelope and sealed and marked. Liquids should be placed in a clean, stoppered container or conical tube to minimize evaporation and then sealed and labeled. If the original container can be tightly sealed, it may be used to preserve the liquid.

FIELD TESTING

Because of the large amount of drug cases submitted to crime laboratories and the large amount of resources spent on unnecessary drug testing (many cases never make it to trial), the ability to train law enforcement to perform drug testing in possession cases is used by several jurisdictions throughout the United States. Field test results can help expedite the adjudication process by being a factor in obtaining an immediate plea agreement and helping reduce

---

* In some cases, especially in clandestine laboratory cases, products may be prone to drying. Some of the solvents associated with the evidence may evaporate during transportation resulting in a difference in the evidence weight from the time it is collected until it is examined in the laboratory. In such cases, packaging the evidence in airtight canisters or sealed glass jars may be used.

Illicit Drugs and Toxicology 187

Figure 12.7 In cases involving a large number of units, the total number of units can be weighed and the weight of the individual unit can be estimated by dividing the total weight by the number of individual units (*Photo credit: LASD*).

Figure 12.8 A color spot test for the presumptive testing of marijuana is the Duquenois-Levine test. In the presence of cannabis, this reagent turns purple (*Photo credit: LASD*).

the number of backlogged cases and improve the efficient use of resources. Drug evidence should still be submitted to the crime laboratory for complete analysis for cases to proceed to trial. Generally, field tests are color change tests and are only presumptive screening tests for one of the common controlled substances. In order to make a positive identification, a confirmatory test needs to be run in the laboratory using analytical instrumentation (Figure 12.8).

FORENSIC TOXICOLOGY*

Forensic toxicology deals with the application of toxicology to cases where adverse effects of the use of impairing, toxic, and lethal concentrations of drugs have medicolegal consequences. As used in this section, forensic toxicology describes the detection of drugs and alcohol in blood, urine, and tissue samples collected from suspects (or decedents) in criminal investigations. The presence or absence of drugs or alcohol in a person's body and the issue of whether the subject was under the influence is important in traffic investigations, DUI cases, the legal defense of diminished capacity, and public intoxication cases. The most common substance tested for in most police laboratories is alcohol in blood and urine specimens submitted in "drunk driving" cases.

Cases of DUI of alcohol represent a large percentage of all traffic fatalities and traffic accidents. Implied consent laws require a driver suspected of being under the influence of alcohol to submit to testing—blood or breath—to determine their blood alcohol level. The majority of states in the United States set a blood alcohol level at 0.08% (i.e., 0.08 g of ethyl alcohol per 100 mL of blood) as the level at which a person is presumed to be under the influence of alcohol to an extent that the driver is unable to operate a motor vehicle in a safe and prudent manner. The 0.08% level represents about 3 ounces of 100-proof alcoholic beverage in the body of a 150-pound individual. Blood and breath testing are routine procedures available in all jurisdictions to measure the blood alcohol level. Blood that is taken should be collected in a medically approved manner. The syringe used should not have been cleaned with alcohol, and nonalcoholic cleaning agents (e.g., aqueous zephiran) should be used to clean the area of skin from which the blood is to be drawn. Approximately 10–20 mL of blood should be collected in a container with an appropriate preservative and anticoagulant. If urine is collected, the subject should first be requested to void the bladder, wait approximately 20 minutes, and then urinate into a container into which an appropriate preservative has been placed. Approximately 25 mL of the sample should be collected. The officer should be present in each case to observe the collection procedure and to mark the evidence properly. The specimen should then be submitted to the laboratory for analysis.

Officers will find that some subjects, although exhibiting alcohol-like intoxication symptoms, have no or only a small amount of alcohol in their blood. The reason for this may be that the suspect has taken an additional central nervous system depressant which results in similar physiological effects. When questioning the suspect, the officer should try to determine whether the suspect has taken any other medication; when searching the individual during the booking process, it should be noted whether any solid dose drugs are found. This information is helpful to the forensic toxicologist when running tests on blood and urine specimens. A large number of depressant-type drugs are routinely encountered in traffic-related incidents today.

The type and quantity of sample required for analysis may vary from one jurisdiction to another, and the local crime laboratory should be contacted to determine the best sample for a specific drug analysis. In homicide cases in which a suspect is arrested, it is sometimes a useful practice to obtain blood and urine specimens from the suspect to be screened for the presence of drugs and alcohol. This strategy is particularly useful in those cases in which the suspect may raise the issue of diminished capacity at the time of trial.

Illicit drugs in bulk or in toxicological specimens are encountered in a large number of cases in criminal investigations. Investigators must be familiar with the hazards of various chemicals and the pharmacological effects of psychoactive substances as well as the usual considerations involved in the collection and preservation of physical evidence.

Death investigators are often interested to learn whether the victim or decedent had drugs, alcohol, or poison in their systems. Forensic toxicologists play a major role in such investigations and possess significant expertise in the effects of drugs on the body and particularly how to test for such drugs.

OSAC Seized Drugs Subcommittee†

The Seized Drugs Subcommittee focuses on standards and guidelines related to the examination of evidence to identify drugs and related substances. Several standards published by ASTM International are part of the OSAC Registry

---

* The Society of Forensic Toxicologists, (www.soft-tox.org/), and the International Association of Forensic Toxicologists, (www.tiaft.org/), are two organizations that can provide further information about forensic toxicology.
† www.nist.gov/osac/seized-drugs-subcommittee.

including *Standard Guide for Analysis of Clandestine Drugs*, *Standard Practice for Identification of Seized Drugs*, *Standard Guide for Sampling Seized Drugs for Qualitative and Quantitative Analysis*, and others.

SWGDRUG*

The Scientific Working Group for the Analysis of Seized Drugs (SWGDRUG) works to improve the quality of the forensic examination of seized drugs, to support the development of internationally accepted minimum standards, identifying best practices, and providing resources to help labs meet these standards. The SWGDRUG website also maintains drug monographs and searchable mass spectral (MS) and infrared (IR) libraries.

OSAC FORENSIC TOXICOLOGY SUBCOMMITTEE[†]

The Forensic Science Subcommittee focuses on standards and guidelines related to the analysis of biological samples for alcohol, drugs, poisons, and the interpretation of these results. Standards on the OSAC Registry include *Standard for Report Content in Forensic Toxicology and Best Practice Recommendation*, *Guidelines for Opinions and Testimony in Forensic Toxicology*.

SWGTOX

The Scientific Working Group for Forensic Toxicology (SWGTOX) was an organization established to develop and disseminate consensus standards for the practice of forensic toxicology. Its mission has since been absorbed by the OSAC Forensic Toxicology Subcommittee.

Further Reading

Bowden, Jan, and Vicky Manning. *Practical Drug Enforcement*. Routledge, 2006.

Christian Jr, Donnell R. *Forensic Investigation of Clandestine Laboratories*. CRC Press, 2003.

Jones, A. Wayne, Jorg Gustav Morland, and Ray H. Liu, eds. *Alcohol, Drugs, and Impaired Driving: Forensic Science and Law Enforcement Issues*. CRC Press, 2020.

King, Leslie A. *Forensic Chemistry of Substance Misuse: A Guide to Drug Control*. Royal Society of Chemistry, 2019.

Laing, Richard, et al., eds. *Hallucinogens: A Forensic Drug Handbook*. Academic Press, 2003.

Levine, B., and Sarah Kerrigan, eds. *Principles of Forensic Toxicology*, Springer, 2020.

Mills, Terry, and J. Conrad Roberson. *Instrumental Data for Drug Analysis*. CRC Press, 2018.

Moffat, Anthony C., et al. *Clarke's Analysis of Drugs and Poisons*. Vol. 3. Pharmaceutical Press, 2011.

Chapter Questions

1. Psychoactive drugs are defined as substances that affect the user's _____ process and change his or her mood, thinking, perception, and behavior.
   a) Physical.
   b) Psychological.
   c) Central nervous system.
   d) Coping.

---

* https://swgdrug.org/index.htm.
[†] www.nist.gov/osac/forensic-toxicology-subcommittee.

2. Which of the following would be an example of a central nervous system depressant?
   a) Ethanol.
   b) Caffeine.
   c) Cocaine.
   d) MDMA.
3. List several examples of central nervous system stimulants.
4. Describe the symptoms that a hallucinogen can produce and list several examples of specific drugs within this class.
5. Which of the following is not considered a narcotic?
   a) Fentanyl.
   b) Heroin.
   c) Opium.
   d) Benzodiazepines.
6. (True or false) LSD is considered to be a hallucinogen.
7. You are searching a person who was just arrested for selling crack to an undercover officer. Which of the following would you focus on during your search?
   a) Cigarette packs.
   b) Mouth.
   c) Shoes.
   d) All of the above.
8. During the search of a residence for contraband drugs, the investigators should also be concerned with searching for what?
   a) Legal documents.
   b) Intelligence information.
   c) Name of the resident's attorney.
   d) Documents showing ownership of the residence.
9. Which of the following is the blood alcohol level set by the majority of states in the United States at which a person is presumed to be under the influence?
   a) 0.08%.
   b) 0.10%.
   c) 0.15%.
   d) 0.25%.
10. Define what is meant by Schedule III drugs and list several examples.

CHAPTER 13

Document Evidence

Forensic Document Examination* is a forensic science discipline in which expert examiners evaluate disputed documents in the legal system. The forensic document examiner may establish that a document is genuine, can identify or exclude persons who wrote the documents, may identify the source of machine-produced documents, and can restore the legibility of documents. Documents such as fraudulent checks, counterfeit currency, ransom notes, bank robbery notes, suicide notes, contested wills, forged contracts, and fake passports are all examples of different types of evidence that may be collected at a crime scene and submitted to the forensic document examiner.

One characteristic of a document is the author's handwriting which may identify the source of the authorship. Handwriting is a means of establishing identity. Like fingerprints, it offers the investigator the ability to determine the identity of an individual. Handwriting characteristics are of two types: style characteristics and personal characteristics.

Style characteristics are the general type to which cursive writing belongs. This general type is learned in school and used by most people. Personal characteristics are changes made in the general style characteristics both intentionally and unconsciously by the writer. Individual characteristics are the ones used to establish the identity of a writer. Handwriting examination can be used to answer two questions: (1) Was a signature or document a forgery? (2) Were two writings made by the same person? To answer these questions, the document examiner makes a careful examination of the questioned writing and known exemplar writings. Factors such as the relative size of letters, their slope and spacing, the way in which they are formed, and other personal characteristics are used to make a determination.

Written documents occur in every facet of today's society. Daily business transactions include the use of checks, credit card receipts, money orders, purchase receipts, prescriptions, post-it notes, and so forth. Writings may occur on paper as letters and notes but may also be present on desks, tabletops, walls, floors, doors, and even dead bodies. Wherever they occur, they should never be overlooked. Once a document is discovered, it must be handled appropriately and preserved. Failure to do so may result in its inadmissibility as evidence.

Excessive handling may damage the document and smudge or obscure important writing characteristics, precluding any possibility of identification. The document should be preserved in the same condition in which it is found. Generally, this is best accomplished by placing it into a clear plastic envelope or sheet protector that keeps the document clean, preserves fingerprints, and prevents damage or destruction of minute identifying details. If the document is wet or soaked with blood, it should be allowed to air-dry at room temperature and then placed in a cardboard box for delivery to the laboratory. Documents should be handled with forceps so as not to leave prints or DNA that may confuse subsequent tests. Excessive handling may damage the document and smudge or obscure important writing characteristics. This may preclude any possibility of identification.

---

* The American Society of Questioned Document Examiners (www.asqde.org) is the oldest and largest organization in the world dedicated to the profession of forensic document examination.

DOI: 10.4324/9780429272011-15

Documents should not be altered in any way and should not be folded or creased. If the document is damaged or torn, no attempt should be made to repair it. The investigator should not write on the document to identify it. Documents should not be stapled together or to reports. If the document is stapled, the staple should be removed slowly and carefully so as not to tear the paper. A staple remover should not be used. Do not use a paper punch on a document. Documents should not be left under paper on which the investigator may be writing because indentations may damage the identifying characteristics on the questioned writing. The side of a lead pencil should not be rubbed across the document in order to observe indented writing. Stickers or gummed labels should not be affixed to the document.

The suspect should never handle the document during the course of the investigation. If chemical processing to develop fingerprints on documents is used, the document should first be photographed with a document scale present. After the chemical processing is completed, the paper should not come into contact with other papers because the stain can transfer. Paper should not be handled because additional fingerprints and smudges can easily be deposited onto it. Chemically processed documents should be kept in clear plastic envelopes or sheet protectors.

Burned papers and charred documents are sometimes found in arson investigations or in instances in which an attempt was made to destroy records by fire. Burned documents may be deciphered, provided they are reasonably intact. If the paper has been reduced to ashes it will not be possible to determine any writing. For this reason, it is particularly important to exercise the utmost care when collecting, preserving, and transporting this type of evidence.

If burned paper is found in a metal file box, it should not be removed from the box; rather, it should be transported in the container in which it was found. If the documents are found in the open, or if the files they are in cannot be taken to the laboratory, the paper should be carefully placed into rigid cardboard boxes. Charred papers can be picked up by gently sliding a flat piece of cardboard under them. Once picked up from the scene, they can gently be placed in boxes.

It is preferable to hand carry boxes to the laboratory because of the fragile nature of this evidence. If this is not possible, the paper must be packaged so that it will not break up in transit. Cotton or any other similar material that will preserve the evidence can be layered in the cardboard boxes.

If the paper is still burning when the investigator arrives at the scene, no attempt should be made to put out the fire, unless the air supply can be shut off without handling the document. If the burned material consists of a book, folded papers, or currency, no attempt should be made to separate the layers of paper. The debris should be kept together and submitted to the laboratory in that state.

Chemical treatment, photography, and examination under ultraviolet and infrared light often make the writing legible in charred documents. However, the documents must arrive intact in order for such examinations to be conducted.

If questioned writings are found on a wall or body in a homicide case, it is advisable to contact a document examiner for possible assistance at the crime scene (Figure 13.1). If this is not possible, photographs should be taken of the area. Writings on walls, desktops, mirrors, and other surfaces should be photographed with a scale present. If possible, the item containing the writing should be removed and submitted to the laboratory. If the writing is confined to a relatively small area, such as a wall, and circumstances justify it, the section should be cut out and taken to the laboratory.

It is necessary to mark documents that later may be entered into evidence during presentation of the court case. The best place to mark a document is usually on the back. This should be done inconspicuously with initials and date and as far away from other writings as possible. In the event this is not possible, the best solution is to use a pen with a different color ink so that the marking cannot be confused with the questioned writing. Red ink should be avoided because it does not survive well when ninhydrin is used to develop latent fingerprints. Extraneous markings and writings should never be placed on the document. If additional information beyond the investigator's initials and the date is necessary, it should be recorded in the CSI's notes. It is generally necessary to store documents for varying lengths of time, sometimes several years, pending final disposition of the case. The documents can be stored in protective plastic envelopes or sheet protectors and filed in folders or envelopes large enough to keep them flat. In this way, they will remain in good condition for long periods of time. Photographs can be kept in flat folders or envelopes. Documents processed for fingerprints with ninhydrin or other chemicals must be enclosed in clear plastic envelopes

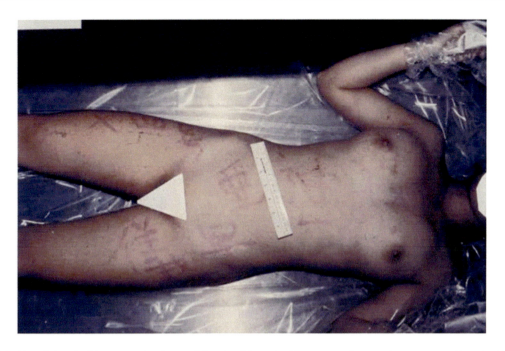

Figure 13.1 Not all handwriting cases involve traditional writings. In this case, a deceased woman was found with Chinese characters written in lipstick on her body. The Hong Kong Forensic Laboratory conducted chemical comparisons on the lipstick as well as writing comparisons in an effort to solve the case. (*Courtesy of SC Leung, Hong Kong, China.*)

or sheet protectors. Documents should be stored in an area with a relatively cool, dry temperature and away from excessive heat or direct sunlight.

Once the questioned documents have been discovered and received as evidence and have been properly handled and marked for identification, exemplar writings must be obtained. Exemplar writings are known specimens from the suspect and/or victim. They are extremely important and necessary to connect the suspect or victim to the document. Like the questioned document, exemplars must be properly identified and cared for. They should not be stapled, folded, rolled up, torn, punched, smeared with fingerprints, or otherwise damaged if they are to be acceptable as evidence. The purpose of exemplars is to give the examiner of the document in question a known specimen of the subject's writing, thus providing a source of the writer's individual writing habits and personal style characteristics.

There are two general types of handwriting exemplars: informal and formal. Informal exemplars are also referred to as nonrequest writing. These include the routine, normal course of business writings such as letters, application forms, business records, checks, etc. These documents are sometimes difficult to admit as evidence because their authenticity may be in question; however, they are the best examples of normal or natural handwriting. The subject prepares formal or "request writing" exemplars, usually at the request of the investigator. The format generally used is a handwriting exemplar card designated for that purpose. In addition to an exemplar card, fingerprint cards, booking slips, and, at times, tablet paper may be used to obtain miscellaneous or specific exemplar writing samples. The investigating officer will witness these writings.

The investigator should keep several helpful suggestions in mind when obtaining request exemplars. It is useful to study and become familiar with the questioned document, paying close attention to names, specific words, spellings, and other unusual features of the document. The writing instrument should be in good working order. Felt tip pens and pencils should be avoided unless they are the type of writing instrument used in the questioned writing.

The writer should be provided with a comfortable writing area. Generally, exemplars written in the backseat of a police car en route to the station are worthless. The investigator should be present to observe the writing because he or she will be called upon in court to testify to this fact. Only like materials can be compared; that is, cursive writing must be compared with cursive, printing with printing, block letters with block letters, etc.

Case Review (Figure 13.2)

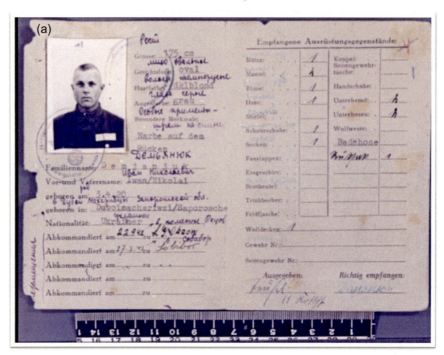

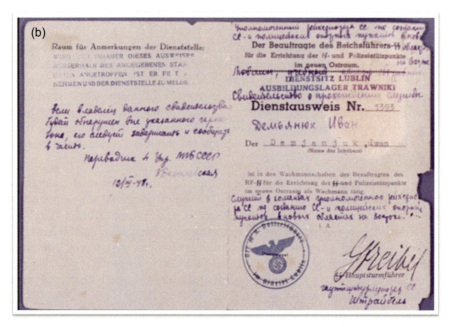

Figure 13.2 Known as "Ivan the Terrible," Ivan "John" Demjanjuk was a prison guard at German concentration camps during World War II. In this case, the question of identity was proven by forensic document examination. Through a series of legal proceedings in the United States, Israel, and Germany, Demjanjuk, age 91, was ultimately convicted in May 2011 in Germany of war crimes and of complicity in the murder of over 28,000 Jews while at Sobibor concentration camp. He died of natural causes on March 17, 2012. (a, b) The question of identity was resolved using the following techniques: the chemistry of photographic paper and emulsion; the chemistry of the writing inks; the chemistry of paper and stamp pad ink; the alignment of stamp impressions; and comparisons with ink and paper from known documents of the alleged period from the National Archives, German Archives and Russian Archives. (*Courtesy of Anthony Cantu, PhD, formerly with the US Secret Service Laboratory.*)

In addition to the exemplar card, specific writing specimens should be requested, including material contained in the questioned document. The wording of this questioned document should be dictated to the subject; the actual document should not be placed before the writer from which to copy. The writing instrument should be similar to the one used on the questioned document, and the paper should be similar with respect to size, style, plain, ruled, etc. Several specimens should be obtained as long as the subject is willing to cooperate. If the writer is trying to disguise the writing, it is best to interrupt the periods of writing with conversation and fresh paper from time to time.

This procedure makes it difficult for the subject to maintain a consistent alteration of natural writing habits. In the event of wide variation or difference in the questioned writing and the exemplar, it may be useful to have the writer provide additional exemplars with the other hand.

Because drug and alcohol use may show writing that varies, it may be necessary to obtain writing exemplars at various time intervals, sometimes several days apart. Handwriting reflects the effects of age, illness, injuries, and mental state. It is sometimes necessary for the investigator to obtain additional exemplars of the individual's writing by obtaining informal exemplars.

VIDEO SPECTRAL COMPARATOR

The video spectral comparator (VSC) can provide forensic document examiners an extensive toolbox for detecting irregularities on altered and counterfeit documents. Detection of alterations include: watermarks, different inks, tampering, photo-substitution, and others. The VSC uses filters to vary the light bombarding the document. The document is then viewed through the camera on a monitor (Figure 13.3).

GRAPHOLOGY

Graphology is the analysis of the characteristics and patterns of handwriting with the attempt to indicate the psychological state of the writer at the time of writing or evaluate their personality characteristics. Forensic Document Examination (FDE) does not attempt to create a personality profile of the writer. Moreover, graphology is not a foundational science for the practice of FDE in whole or in part.

OSAC FORENSIC DOCUMENT EXAMINATION SUBCOMMITTEE[*]

The Forensic Document Examination Subcommittee focuses on standards and guidelines related to the forensic analysis, comparison, and evaluation of documents. There have been three standards published by the AAFS Standards Board: *Standard for the Examination of Documents for Alterations*, *Standard for Examination of Documents for Indentations*, and *Standard for Examination of Stamping Devices and Stamp Impressions*. Other standards have been sent to a Standards Development Organization and are under development.

SWGDOC

Prior to the start of the OSACs, the Scientific Working Group for Forensic Document Examination (SWGDOC) developed standards and guidelines for the field of forensic document examination. All of their documents can be found on the SWGDOC website (www.swgdoc.org). While these documents contain a lot of good information for the FDE community, they are not endorsed by OSAC or NIST.

FORENSIC LINGUISTICS[†]

Written and spoken language may be characteristic of an individual. The use of words, syntax, spelling, and grammar may assist the investigator in establishing identity. Bank robbery demand notes, threatening letters, use of words in recorded phone messages, are examples of instances where forensic linguistics might provide assistance in a criminal or civil act.

---

[*] www.nist.gov/osac/forensic-document-examination-subcommittee.
[†] See, for example, the International Association of Forensic Linguistics, www.iafl.org.

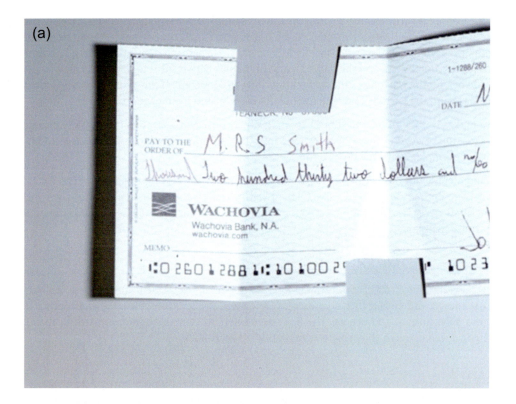

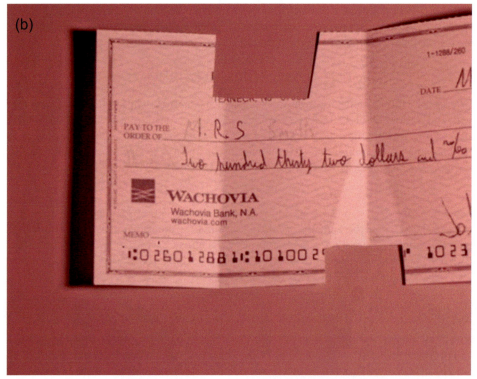

Figure 13.3 (a) A bank received a fraudulent check made out to "MRS Smith" for a "Thousand two hundred thirty two dollars." After viewing the check in the Video Spectral Comparator under infrared light (b) it was clear that the original check was made out to the "IRS" for "Two hundred thirty two dollars." Therefore, this nondestructive test shows that the check was altered with a different pen.

Forensic linguists are involved in many areas that relate to crime, both solving crime and absolving people wrongly accused of committing crimes. Some of these areas of research and expertise include:*

- voice identification (for instance, determining whether the voice on a threatening tape recording was that of the suspect; sometimes also called forensic phonetics)
- author identification (determining who wrote a particular text by comparing it to known writing samples of a suspect; sometimes also called forensic stylistics)
- discourse analysis (analyzing the structure of a writing or spoken utterance, often covertly recorded, to help determine issues such as who is introducing topics or whether a suspect is agreeing to engage in a criminal conspiracy)
- linguistic proficiency (did a suspect understand the Miranda warning or police caution?)
- dialectology (determining which dialect of a language a person speaks, usually to show that a defendant has a different dialect from that on an incriminating tape recording. As opposed to voice identification, which analyzes the acoustic qualities of the voice, dialectology uses linguistic features to accomplish similar goals.)
- "linguistic origin analysis" (the process of trying to determine what a person's native language is, often for purposes of granting or denying applications for political asylum. A more common term is "language analysis," but that term is overly broad.)
- "linguistic veracity analysis" (refers to various linguistically inspired methods for determining whether a speaker or writer was being truthful.)

Further Reading

Angel, Miriam, and Jan Seaman Kelly, eds. *Forensic Document Examination in the 21st Century*. CRC Press, 2020.

Coulthard, Malcolm, Alison Johnson, and David Wright. *An Introduction to Forensic Linguistics: Language in Evidence*. Routledge, 2016.

Ellen, David, Stephen Day, and Christopher Davies. *Scientific Examination of Documents: Methods and Techniques*. CRC Press, 2018.

Guillén-Nieto, Victoria, and Dieter Stein. "Introduction: Theory and practice in forensic linguistics." *Language as Evidence*. Palgrave Macmillan, Cham, 2022. 1–33.

Lewis, Jane. *Forensic Document Examination: Fundamentals and Current Trends*. Elsevier, 2014.

Mohammed, Linton A. *Forensic Examination of Signatures*. Academic Press, 2019.

Morris, Ron N. *Forensic Handwriting Identification: Fundamental Concepts and Principles*. Academic Press, 2020.

Chapter Questions

1. Document Evidence includes all of the following except:
    a. Contracts.
    b. Wills.
    c. Checks.
    d. Text messages.
2. (True or false) Known writings need not have words and letter combinations present in the questioned document.
3. Describe the differences between formal and informal handwriting exemplars.

---

* Peter Tiersma, *What is Forensic Linguistics?*, www.languageandlaw.org/FORENSIC.HTM.

4. Infrared light is used to:
   a. Detect if two different inks were used in a document.
   b. Determine the age of the document.
   c. Detect if human DNA is present on the document.
   d. All of the above.
5. (True or false) Graphology is an accepted forensic science that can determine the personality type of a suspect:
6. The Video Spectral Comparator (VSC) can:
   a. Determine who wrote a document.
   b. Determine handedness of the author.
   c. The chemical composition of the ink used to write the document.
   d. Detect alterations.
7. (True or false) Handwriting allows the investigator to determine the identity of the author of a document.
8. (True or false) It is impossible to read charred documents.
9. Indented writing can be viewed with:
   a. Oblique lighting.
   b. Perpendicular lighting.
   c. Thin layer chromatography.
   d. None of the above.
10. (True or false) Angle, slope, and speed of handwriting are examples of individual variations.

PART III

The Investigation and Special Considerations

Chapter 14

Ethics in Crime Scene Investigation

Forensic scientists, crime scene specialists, and investigators are the individuals whose jobs apply science and technology to the law. They shoulder an essential role in the criminal justice system and their skills and knowledge may establish the innocence or guilt of a defendant. Professional ethics and integrity are essential to their effort.*

Many forensic specialists work for law enforcement agencies responsible for the criminal investigation or the prosecution of cases. Some may argue that employment by police agencies creates the potential for bias; however, it is the integrity of the professional and steps the organization takes to minimize bias that is the deciding factor.

Forensic practitioners owe a duty to the truth. They may never favor a particular outcome in an investigation. The forensic practitioner's sole obligation is to serve the aims of justice. It makes no difference whether a defendant is ultimately found guilty of the crime or they are acquitted; forensic practitioners must investigate in a thorough, competent, and unbiased manner.

Forensic practitioners have an obligation not to overstate or understate scientific findings. As experts in the criminal justice system, they are in positions of authority and responsibility. Their education, training, experience, and skills give their opinions on technical matters considerable weight and importance to juries and courts.

Forensic science practitioners must exercise independence and integrity to perform their function within the legal system properly. They may not be prejudiced for or against an investigation in which they are involved. Their job is to champion their own expert opinions based on accepted and correctly performed scientific inquiry. Forensic scientists who understand their role in the criminal justice arena help protect individual rights and freedoms while ensuring justice is delivered.

Many professional societies maintain codes of ethics. Three examples are presented here to offer the reader an understanding of how these organizations view a practitioner's ethical responsibilities.

The International Association for Identification (IAI) is the oldest forensic science professional organization in the United States. Founded on August 4, 1915, in Oakland, California, it has a storied history in crime scene investigation and fingerprints and has branched out into many other forensic disciplines. The IAI's Code of Ethics and Standards of Professional Conduct states:

The ethical and professionally responsible International Association for Identification (IAI) member or certificant:

Professionalism

1.01 Is unbiased, and objective, approaching all assignments and examinations with due diligence and an open mind.

---

* In 2009, the National Academy of Sciences published a document, *Strengthening Forensic Science in the United States: A Path Forward*. The report found that, "oversight and enforcement of operating standards, certification, accreditation, and ethics are lacking in most local and state jurisdictions."

1.02 Conducts full and fair examinations in which conclusions are based on the evidence and reference material relevant to the evidence, not on extraneous information, political pressure, or other outside influences.

1.03 Is aware of his/her limitations and only renders conclusions that are within his/her area of expertise and about matters for which he/she has given careful consideration.

1.04 Truthfully communicates with all parties (i.e., the investigator, prosecutor, defense, and other expert witnesses) about information related to his/her analyses, when communications are permitted by law and agency practice.

1.05 Maintains confidentiality of restricted information obtained in the course of professional endeavors.

1.06 Reports to appropriate officials any conflicts between his/her ethical/professional responsibilities and applicable agency policy, law, regulation, or other legal authority.

1.07 Does not accept or participate in any case in which he/she has any personal interest or the appearance of such an interest and shall not be compensated based upon the results of the proceeding.

1.08 Conducts oneself personally and professionally within the laws of his/her respective jurisdiction and in a manner that does not violate public trust.

1.09 Reports to the appropriate legal or administrative authorities unethical, illegal, or scientifically questionable conduct of other practitioners of which he/she has knowledge.

1.10 Does not knowingly make, promote, or tolerate false accusations of a professional or criminal nature.

1.11 Supports sound scientific techniques and practices and does not use his/her position to pressure a practitioner to arrive at conclusions or results that are not supported by reliable scientific data.

Competency and Proficiency

2.01 Is committed to career-long learning in the forensic disciplines in which he/she practices, and stays abreast of new technology and techniques while guarding against the misuse of methods that have not been validated.

2.02 Expresses conclusions and opinions that are based on generally accepted protocols and procedures. New and novel techniques must be validated prior to implementation in case work.

2.03 Is properly trained and determined to be competent through relevant testing prior to undertaking the examination of the evidence.

2.04 Gives utmost care to the treatment of any samples or items of potential evidentiary value to avoid tampering, adulteration, loss or unnecessary consumption.

2.05 Uses controls and standards, including reviews and verifications appropriate to his/her discipline, when conducting examinations and analyses.

Clear Communications

3.01 Accurately represents his/her education, training, experience, and area of expertise.

3.02 Presents accurate and complete data in reports, testimony, publications and oral presentations.

3.03 Makes and retains full, contemporaneous, clear and accurate records of all examinations and tests conducted, and conclusions drawn, in sufficient detail to allow meaningful review and assessment of the conclusions by an independent person competent in the field.

3.04 Does not falsify or alter reports or other records, or withhold relevant information from reports for strategic or tactical litigation advantage.

3.05 Testifies to results obtained and conclusions reached only when he/she has confidence that the opinions are based on good scientific principles and methods. Opinions are to be stated so as to be clear in their meaning.

3.06 Attempts to qualify his/her responses while testifying when asked a question with the requirement that a simple "yes" or "no" answer be given, if answering " yes" or "no" would be misleading to the judge or the jury.

The ethical and professionally responsible International Association for Identification (IAI) member:

ORGANIZATIONAL RESPONSIBILITY

4.01 Does not misrepresent his/her affiliation with the IAI.

4.02 Does not issue any misleading or inaccurate statement that gives the appearance of representing the official position of the IAI.

4.03 Reports violations of this code of which he/she knows to the President of the IAI.

4.04 Cooperate fully with any official investigation by the IAI.

The California Association of Criminalists* (CAC) was founded in 1954 and is one of the earlier regional forensic science societies. The CAC has one of the most comprehensive codes of ethics of any professional science society and is presented here:

CODE OF ETHICS OF THE CALIFORNIA ASSOCIATION OF CRIMINALISTS

This Code is intended as a guide to the ethical conduct of individual workers in the field of criminalistics. It is not to be construed that these principles are immutable laws or that they are all-inclusive. Instead, they represent general standards that each worker should strive to meet. It is to be realized that each individual case may vary, just as does the evidence with which the criminalist is concerned, and no set of guidelines or rules will precisely fit every occasion. At the same time, the fundamentals set forth in this Code are to be regarded as indicating, to a considerable extent, the conduct requirements expected of members of the profession and of this Association. The failure to meet or maintain certain of these standards will justifiably cast doubt upon an individual's fitness for this type of work. Serious or repeated infractions of these principles may be regarded as inconsistent with membership in the Association.

Criminalistics is that professional occupation concerned with the scientific analysis and examination of physical evidence, its interpretation, and its presentation in court. It involves the application of principles, techniques, and methods of the physical sciences, and has, as its primary objective, a determination of physical facts which may be significant in legal cases.

It is the duty of any person practicing the profession of criminalistics to serve the interests of justice to the best of his or her ability at all times. In fulfilling this duty, he or she will use all of the scientific means at his or her command to ascertain all of the significant physical facts relative to the matters under investigation. Having made factual determinations, the criminalist must then interpret and evaluate their findings. In this they will be guided by experience and knowledge which, coupled with a serious consideration of the analytical findings and the application of sound judgment, may enable the criminalist to arrive at opinions and conclusions pertaining to the matters under study. These findings of fact, conclusions, and opinions should then be reported, with all the accuracy and skill of which the criminalist is capable, to the end that all may fully understand and be able to place the findings in their proper relationship to the problem at issue.

In carrying out these functions, the criminalist will be guided by those practices and procedures which are generally recognized within the profession to be consistent with a high level of professional ethics. The motives, methods, and actions of the criminalist shall at all times be above reproach, in good taste, and consistent with proper moral conduct.

I. **Ethics Relating to the Scientific Method:**
   A. The criminalist has a truly scientific spirit and should be inquiring, progressive, logical, and unbiased.
   B. The true scientist will make adequate examination of his or her materials, applying those tests essential to proof. The criminalist will not, merely for the sake of bolstering his or her conclusions, utilize unwarranted and superfluous tests in an attempt to give apparent Code of Ethics of the California Association of Criminalists greater weight to the results.
   C. The modern scientific mind is an open one, incompatible with secrecy of method. Scientific analyses will not be conducted by "secret processes," nor will conclusions in case work be based upon such tests and experiments as will not be revealed to the profession. This section is not intended to compel the issuance of a written report fully documenting all tests, experiments, and conclusions in every case.
   D. A proper scientific method demands reliability of validity in the materials analyzed. Conclusions will not be drawn from materials which themselves appear unrepresentative, atypical, or unreliable.
   E. A truly scientific method requires that no generally discredited or unreliable procedure be utilized in the analysis.

---

* www.cacnews.org.

F. The progressive worker will keep abreast of new developments in scientific methods and in all cases view them with an open mind. This is not to say that one need not be critical of untried or unproved methods, but will recognize superior methods, if and when they are introduced.

II. **Ethics Relating to Opinions and Conclusions:**
   A. Valid conclusions call for the application of proven methods. Where it is practical to do so, the competent criminalist will apply such methods throughout. This does not demand the application of "standard test procedures." But, where practical, use should be made of those methods developed and recognized by this or other professional societies.
   B. Tests are designed to disclose true facts and all interpretations shall be consistent with that purpose and will not be knowingly distorted.
   C. Where appropriate to the correct interpretation of a test, experimental controls shall be made for verification.
   D. Where possible, the conclusions reached as a result of analytical tests are properly verified by re-testing or by the application of additional techniques.
   E. Where test results are inconclusive or indefinite, any conclusions drawn shall be fully explained.
   F. The scientific mind is unbiased and refuses to be swayed by evidence or matters outside the specific materials under consideration. It is immune to suggestion, pressures, and coercions inconsistent with the evidence at hand, being interested only in ascertaining facts.
   G. The criminalist will be alert to recognize the significance of a test result as it may relate to the investigative aspects of a case. In this respect, however, the criminalist's interpretations will scrupulously avoid confusing scientific fact with investigative theory.
   H. Scientific method demands that the individual be aware of one's own limitations and refuse to extend one's self beyond them. It is both proper and advisable that the scientific worker should seek knowledge in new fields; he or she will not, however, be hasty to apply such knowledge before adequate training and experience has been achieved.
   I. Where test results are capable of being interpreted to the advantage of either side of a case, the criminalist will not choose that interpretation favoring the side by which he or she is employed merely as a means to justify his or her employment.
   J. It is both wise and proper that criminalists be aware of the various possible implications of their opinions and conclusions and be prepared to weigh them, if called upon to do so. In any such case, however, they will clearly distinguish between that which may be regarded as scientifically demonstrated fact and that which is speculative.

III. **Ethical Aspects of Court Presentations:**
   A. The expert witness is one who has substantially greater knowledge of a given subject or science than has the average person. An expert opinion is properly defined as "the formal opinion of an expert." Ordinary opinion consists of one's thoughts or beliefs on matters, generally unsupported by detailed analysis of the subject under consideration. Expert opinion is also defined as the considered opinion of an expert, or a formal judgment. It is to be understood that an "expert opinion" is an opinion derived only from a formal consideration of a subject within the expert's knowledge and experience.
   B. The ethical expert does not take advantage of the privilege to express opinions by offering opinions on matters within his or her field of qualification to which he or she has not given formal consideration.
   C. Regardless of legal definitions, the criminalist will realize that there are degrees of certainty represented under the single term of "expert opinion." He or she will not take advantage of the general privilege to assign greater significance to an interpretation than is justified by the available data.
   D. Where circumstances indicate it to be proper, the expert will not hesitate to indicate that, while he or she has an opinion, derived of study, and judgment within their field, the opinion may lack the certainty of other opinions he or she might offer. By this or other means, the expert takes care to leave no false impressions in the minds of the jurors or the court.
   E. In all respects, the criminalist will avoid the use of terms, and opinions which will be assigned greater weight than are due them. Where an opinion requires qualification or explanation, it is not only proper but incumbent upon the witness to offer such qualification.
   F. The expert witness should keep in mind that the lay juror is apt to assign greater or less significance to ordinary words of a scientist than to the same words when used by a lay witness. The criminalist, therefore, will avoid such terms as may be misconstrued or misunderstood.
   G. It is not the object of the criminalist's appearance in court to present only that evidence which supports the view of the side to which he or she is employed. The criminalist has a moral obligation to see to it that the court understands the evidence as it exists and to present it in an impartial manner.
   H. The criminalist will not by implication, knowingly or intentionally, assist the contestants in a case through such tactics as will implant a false impression in the minds of the jury or the court.

    I.   The criminalist, testifying as an expert witness, will make every effort to use understandable language while presenting explanations and demonstrations in order that the jury will obtain a true and valid concept of the testimony. The use of unclear, misleading, circuitous, or ambiguous language with a view of confusing an issue in the minds of the court or jury is unethical.

    J.   The criminalist will answer all questions in a clear, straight-forward manner and will refuse to extend his or her responses beyond their field of competence.

    K.   Where the expert must prepare photographs or offer oral "background information" to the jury or court in respect to a specific type of analytic method, this information shall be reliable and valid, typifying the usual or normal basis for the method. The instructional material shall be of a level that will provide the jury or the court with a proper basis for evaluating the subsequent evidence presentations, and not such as would provide them with a lower standard than the science demands.

    L.   Any and all photographic displays shall be made according to acceptable practice, and shall not be intentionally altered or distorted with a view to misleading court or jury.

    M.   By way of conveying information to the court, it is appropriate that any of a variety of demonstrative materials and methods be utilized by the expert witness. Such methods and materials shall not, however, be unduly sensational.

IV. **Ethics Relating to the General Practice of Criminalistics:**
    A.   Where the criminalist engages in private practice, it is appropriate that he or she set a reasonable fee for his or her services.

    B.   No services shall ever be rendered on a contingency fee basis.

    C.   It shall be regarded as ethical for one criminalist to re-examine evidence materials previously submitted to, or examined by, another. Where a difference of opinion arises, however, as to the significance of the evidence or to test results, it is in the interest of the profession that every effort be made by both analysts to resolve their conflict before the case goes to trial.

    D.   Generally, the principles of "attorney-client privilege" and "work product doctrine" are considered to apply to the work of a physical evidence consultant, except in a situation where a miscarriage of justice might occur. Justice should be the guiding principle. It is considered ethical for the discovery of work performed by a physical evidence consultant to be limited by legally allowed exceptions. Nothing in this code shall be intended to conflict with the California Evidence Code, the California Code of Civil Procedure, the Federal Rules of Evidence, the Federal Rules of Criminal Procedure, and/or the Federal Rules of Civil Procedure.

    E.   It shall be ethical for one of this profession to serve an attorney in an advisory capacity regarding the interrogation of another expert who may be presenting testimony. This service must be performed in good faith and not maliciously. Its purpose is to prevent incompetent testimony, not to thwart justice.

V. **Ethical Responsibilities to the Profession:**

In order to advance the profession of criminalistics, to promote the purposes for which the Association was formed, and encourage harmonious relationships between all criminalists of the State, each criminalist has an obligation to conduct himself or herself according to certain principles. These principles are no less matters of ethics than those outlined above. They differ primarily in being for the benefit of the profession rather than specific obligations to society. They, therefore, concern relationships between individuals and/or departments, business policies, and similar matters.

    A.   It is in the interest of the profession that information concerning any new discoveries, developments, or techniques applicable to the field of criminalistics be made available to criminalists generally. A reasonable attempt should be made by any criminalist having knowledge of such developments to publicize or otherwise inform the profession of them.

    B.   Consistent with this and like objectives, it is expected that the attention of the profession will be directed toward any tests or methods in use that appear invalid or unreliable so that they may be properly investigated.

    C.   In the interest of the profession, the individual criminalist should refrain from seeking individual publicity or publicity for his or her accomplishments on specific cases. The preparation of papers for publication in appropriate media, however, is considered proper.

    D.   The criminalist shall discourage the association of his or her name with developments, publications, or organizations in which he or she has played no significant part, merely as a means of gaining personal publicity or prestige.

    E.   The CAC has been organized primarily to encourage a free exchange of ideas and information between members. It is, therefore, incumbent upon each member to treat with due respect those statements and offerings made by his or her associates. It is appropriate that no member shall unnecessarily repeat statements or beliefs of another as expressed at CAC seminars.

F. It shall be ethical and proper for one criminalist to bring to the attention of the Association a violation of any of these ethical principles. Indeed, it shall be mandatory where it appears that a serious infraction or repeated violations have been committed and where other appropriate corrective measures (if pursued) have failed.

G. This Code may be used by any criminalist in justification of his or her conduct in a given case with the understanding that he or she will have the full support of this Association.

The American Society of Crime Laboratory Directors (ASCLD) is a professional society of crime laboratory directors and managers dedicated to providing excellence in forensic science through leadership and innovation. The organization's purpose is to foster professional interests, assist the development of laboratory management principles and techniques, acquire, preserve, and disseminate forensic based information; maintain and improve communications among crime laboratory directors; and promote, encourage and maintain the highest standards of practice in the field. ASCLD was founded in 1974 with the assistance of the FBI to bring local laboratories and the FBI Laboratory together. The ASCLD Code of Ethics is presented here:

ASCLD Code of Ethics*

Section 1: Policy

The American Society of Crime Laboratory Directors (ASCLD) recognizes that laboratory managers bear additional ethical responsibilities beyond those expected of forensic scientists involved in analytical casework. Ethical issues can arise from activities for which managers are accountable, such as: hiring, training, and supervising subordinates; establishing policies and procedures for evidence handling and analysis; providing quality assurance; budgeting and expenditure of authorized funds; and proper handling of agency property and supplies. While laboratory managers might not be involved directly in the analysis of evidence and presentation of courtroom testimony, their actions as managers can have a profound impact on the integrity and quality of the work product of a crime laboratory.

Section 2: Code

As members of ASCLD, we will strive to foster an atmosphere within our laboratories which will actively encourage our employees to understand and follow ethical practices. We shall report, to the extent permitted by law, to the Board of Directors any potential ethics violation committed by another member of ASCLD. Further, we shall endeavor to discharge our responsibilities toward the public, our employers, our employees, and the profession of forensic science in accordance with the following ASCLD Code of Conduct:

1. No member of ASCLD shall engage in any conduct that is harmful to the profession of forensic science, including, but not limited to, any proven illegal activity, any documented technical misrepresentation or distortion, any scholarly falsification as pertaining to membership requirements in ASCLD or their employment.
2. No member of ASCLD shall use their management position to develop or require the implementation of policies and procedures that would force or encourage an employee to arrive at a conclusion that is not supported by scientific data.
3. No member of ASCLD shall misrepresent their expertise or credentials in any professional capacity.
4. No member of ASCLD will knowingly fail to address or attempt to cover-up any misrepresentation and/or falsification of analytical work or testimonial presentations or the improper handling of evidentiary material by an employee of their laboratory.
5. No member of ASCLD will knowingly fail to notify customer(s), through proper laboratory management channels, of material nonconformities, or breaches of law, or professional standards that adversely affect a previously issued report or testimony from their laboratory.
6. No member of ASCLD shall make written or oral statements which imply that the member is speaking on behalf of ASCLD or the Board of Directors without the permission of the President.
7. No individual shall retain their membership in ASCLD if they have been convicted of a felony offense.

---

* www.ascld.org/wp-content/uploads/2020/02/ASCLD-Code-of-Ethics-2020.pdf.

Professional integrity and ethics are important elements of crime scene investigation and forensic science practice. While there are many "dos and don'ts" regarding ethical conduct, there is a simple test to use as a first step when you are faced with the question, "what is the right thing to do?" This is called the "Headline Test."

Ask yourself:

- How would the action or situation you are considering be viewed by others if it became headline news?
- Would you be comfortable reading a *New York Times* story that you were doing this or allowing a situation to happen?
- Would you be comfortable explaining to your spouse, children, or parents what you are about to do?

Finally, ethics can be summarized by the following quote from C.S. Lewis: "Integrity is doing the right thing, even when no one is watching."

Further Reading

Barnett, Peter D. *Ethics in Forensic Science: Professional Standards for the Practice of Criminalistics*. CRC Press, 2001.

Bowen, Robin T. *Ethics and the Practice of Forensic Science*. CRC Press, 2021.

Downs, J. C. Upshaw, and Anjali Ranadive Swienton, eds. *Ethics in Forensic Science*. Academic Press, 2012.

Franck, Harold, and Darren Franck. *Ethical Standards in Forensic Science*. CRC Press, 2020.

Passalacqua, Nicholas V., and Marin A. Pilloud. *Ethics and Professionalism in Forensic Anthropology*. Academic Press, 2018.

Chapter Questions

1. (True or false) An expert witness may accept payment for their testimony based on the outcome of the trial (contingency fee basis).
2. (True or false) An expert witness may give their opinion on the witness stand.
3. (True or false) An analyst may use a testing procedure on casework only if the method has been validated.
4. (True or false) One should attempt to qualify their response while testifying when asked a question with the requirement that a simple "yes" of "no" answer be given, if that simple answer would be misleading.
5. (True or false) If one does not complete their notes at the crime scene, they may fill them in the next day.
6. (True or false) It is okay to consume evidence during testing if one does not have enough sample to work with.
7. Which of the following is not considered an ethical violation:
    a. Dry-labbing.
    b. Claiming to have a master's degree if they are a week away from graduation.
    c. Disagreeing with another analyst's opinion in your lab.
    d. Not disclosing exculpatory information to the attorneys and/or court.
8. (True or false) It is okay to take an affirmation instead of an oath when testifying.
9. Ethical misconduct can result in:
    a. Arrest.
    b. Termination.
    c. Suspension.
    d. All of the above.
10. (True or false) A medical examiner may claim they are a member of a professional organization when they are only an associate member.

CHAPTER 15

Sexual Assault Investigation

SEXUAL ASSAULT

The #MeToo movement has shown just how widespread sex crimes are across the United States and the world. In no other type of crime is the testimony of the victim viewed with so much mistrust by juries, police, defense attorneys, and even prosecutors. It is for this very reason that physical evidence is so important to the investigation and prosecution of this crime.

Sexual assault investigation is different from any other major crime. Unlike homicide, robbery, or assault, a forensic nurse* plays the greatest role in the collection and preservation of physical evidence. In most crime scenes, CSIs are responsible for securing the crime scene, documenting the scene, and collecting evidence. This is not the case in a sexual assault investigation as the victim's body is generally seen as the primary crime scene. The sexual assault nurse examiner (SANE[†]) is required to make certain that fragile physical evidence from the victim's body and clothing is collected and preserved.

THE INTERVIEW

Depending on the jurisdiction of where the assault took place, either a SANE or a detective will interview the victim. Both must be knowledgeable about the types of evidence generally found in a sexual assault investigation. The detective must also be a skilled interviewer in order to elicit from the victim the painful details of the assault, and from these details determine what evidence may be available.

In addition to the forensic training, SANEs and Special Victim Unit detectives also undergo training in crisis counseling that will help them assist the victim in dealing with their trauma. Attitudes that women provoke rape or deserve it because they placed themselves in the situation have no place in modern police work. The victim should be treated nonjudgmentally and with sensitivity. Besides making observations about any of the victim's injuries, the psychological state of the victim may be significant. The interviewer should realize, however, that people in serious emotional crises might not immediately exhibit states of anguish and grief that might be expected. The victim might appear perfectly calm and in control of themselves when interviewed.

The interviewer should not assume that the victim is untruthful because they are not exhibiting extreme emotion. Statements in reports, such as "the victim appeared unusually calm, considering her complaint of rape," do nothing but confuse the investigation and raise doubt at the trial. The interviewer should ascertain whether the victim is sexually experienced and hence able to testify whether penetration and/or ejaculation took place. Another question that

---

* A Forensic Nurse is an RN who has received specialized education and training and provides care for patients experiencing health consequences associated with victimization or violence. Forensic nurses work in a variety of different fields, including sexual assault (as a Sexual Assault Nurse Examiner), domestic violence, child abuse and neglect, elder mistreatment, death investigation, and corrections.
[†] The SANE certification, given by the Commission for Forensic Nursing Certification (CFNC), designates that a nurse has achieved the highest standards of forensic nursing for sexual assault nurse examiners.

should be asked is whether the victim had consensual sex recently. In asking these types of questions, the investigator should be aware that many victims do not volunteer particularly sensitive details of the assault.

After a sexual assault, it is not uncommon that the victim may have an urge to wash, shower, douche, urinate, throw away her clothing, and clean up. During the interview, the SANE should determine which, if any, of these actions occurred. If any did, an attempt to collect evidence should still be made. A tissue or washcloth used by the victim to clean herself might still have semen present. Underwear, clothing, and/or condoms worn at the time of the crime, even if discarded or cleaned, should be collected for examination. The crime scene should be processed as outlined elsewhere in this book but several other aspects require attention.

- What was the M.O. of the suspect?
- Did he practice any unusual acts?
- Did he do or say anything unusual?
- Is there any physical evidence to substantiate these acts?
- Did he bite or lick the victim?
- Was the victim or suspect scratched or bruised? All of these details, together with any physical evidence, will greatly assist the investigation of the case.
- Does the victim recall drinking something which may have contained a "date rape" or drug facilitated rape substance?

MEDICAL EXAMINATION

Following the interview, a thorough examination is done. (In many cases, the victim goes directly to the emergency room; law enforcement is notified of the alleged sexual assault by hospital personnel and the interview is conducted in the hospital.) Because much of the evidence associated with rape is of a fragile nature, time is of the essence. A change of clothes should be obtained so that the clothing worn during the rape may be collected and vouchered as evidence. Many hospital emergency rooms have protocols established to deal with rape victims in which they are ranked in medical priority immediately after life-threatening cases. Hospitals are responsible for the victim's medical and psychological well-being, as well as the collection of physical evidence.

Once at the hospital, the detective should briefly go over the case with the attending physician and/or SANE. Pertinent information gleaned from the interview should be communicated to the examiner because it may facilitate the examination for physical evidence. The health care provider first takes a medical history from the victim and goes over the details of the assault. Doctors and nurses should be encouraged to take detailed notes and later couple the notes with medical findings during the examination phase. Details such as the date of the last menstruation, time of last consensual intercourse, presence of bruises not related to the assault, presence of bruises from the assault, and other related factors are important pieces of information.

Following the medical history, the SANE should conduct a thorough physical examination, including the genital area (Figure 15.1). Some hospitals only examine the genital area and miss a great deal of useful evidence. If the victim is wearing clothes from the assault, they should be collected and packaged in separate paper bags. The location of any cuts, bruises, lacerations, or contusions should be noted in the medical report. A helpful practice is the use of an anatomical diagram. The location of cuts, bruises, and the like can be charted on this diagram. Photographs of bruises or wounds should also be taken with an appropriate scale in the photo. Wounds on the body that are difficult to see can be enhanced with the help of UV photography. If the hospital does not have this capability, the police officer or CSI may provide a suitable camera. In some instances, the investigator may wish to wait a day or so until the bruises become black and blue and better show the location and extent of the assault.

Many hospitals, police departments, and medical examiner's offices have sexual assault evidence kits on hand to collect evidence from sexual assault victims. These kits greatly facilitate the collection and preservation of rape evidence. They also direct the examiner to look for certain types of evidence commonly found in rape cases (Figure 15.2).

The victim should next be carefully examined for trace evidence adhering to her body. Traces such as debris, grass, soil, vegetation, loose hair, fibers, and so on should be noted and collected. The presence of dried secretions such as

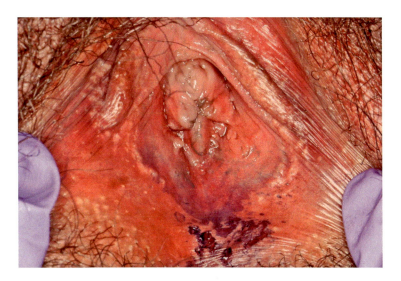

Figure 15.1 Toluidine Blue Dye highlights fresh injury. It adheres to the nuclei of the white blood cells that have been disrupted. (*Photo provided by Diana Faugno MSN, RN, Sexual Assault Nurse Examiner.*)

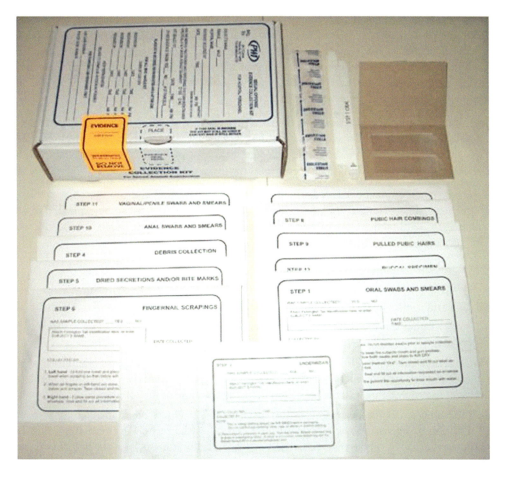

Figure 15.2 Example of the contents of a sexual assault evidence collection kit.

semen, blood, and saliva (from bite marks, licking, "hickies," etc.) are especially useful because such evidence may be typed using forensic DNA testing. Some facilities use a UV lamp or alternate light source to examine for the presence of seminal fluid as semen fluoresces under ultraviolet light. When these stains fluoresce, slightly moistened cotton swabs can be used to collect this evidence and preserve it.

Following examination of the extremities and torso, the genitalia are examined. Pubic hair combings are taken in an attempt to find foreign hairs, fibers, or other debris. The hairs, debris, and comb are all submitted for examination. As with all other evidence, these items should be appropriately documented in the medical report and labeled. A vaginal specimen is collected with cotton-tipped applicators and a portion is smeared onto microscope slides. This is done in order to test for the presence of spermatozoa. The slides should be air-dried and *not* stained when prepared. The slides should be placed in a slide protector, *not* in alcohol. Some locales also collect specimens from the cervix and vulva as well.

There are also separate sexual assault kits for suspects, acquaintances, and estranged partners. Oftentimes the collection of evidence from a suspect requires a court order. If a court order can be obtained expeditiously (these kits need to be collected within a shorter period of time than the kit for a victim), penile swabs can be collected to determine if the victim's DNA is present.

If anal or oral contact occurred, appropriate rectal and oral swabs should be collected. Sodomy is not limited to female victims. Male sexual assaults occur with some frequency in jail and prison environments, as well as elsewhere. Of particular importance in these cases is the physician's examination of the rectum as well as swab evidence taken for the examination of semen. Medical examination conclusively indicates if anal penetration has occurred. Beyond the medical examination and search for semen, other evidence is sometimes uncovered in such cases. A lubricant such as petroleum jelly may have been used and should be looked for. The container for these items can be examined for fingerprints and/or trace DNA. Additionally, any condoms and/or condom wrappers[*] found at the scene should also be collected. If oral sodomy is suspected, the oral cavity should be rinsed *after* the swab is taken prior to collection of a known buccal (cheek) swab from the victim.

Fingernails may also be examined and if sufficient debris is present, nail scrapings can be collected for trace evidence examination. The fingernails can also be clipped and submitted for DNA analysis if the victim scratched the perpetrator (Figure 15.3). Toxicology samples should be collected if the victim appears to be under the influence of some substance. Physical evidence collected in rape cases is used for three major purposes:

1. **To establish that sexual contact occurred.** The presence of seminal fluid and spermatozoa in the vaginal cavity is suggestive of vaginal penetration. The presence or absence of this evidence can be explained in any number of ways. The absence of seminal fluid in a case in which it was expected could be caused by the following reasons:
   - The time period between the rape and medical examination was too long.
   - The suspect wore a condom;[†] the suspect penetrated but did not ejaculate in the vagina.
   - The doctor or nurse examiner did not take an adequate sample.
   - Seminal fluid and spermatozoa may be present from a consensual intercourse and not from an alleged rape.
   - Seminal fluid, without spermatozoa, could be present from a male who underwent a vasectomy procedure, or is azoospermic.
2. **To establish that non-consensual intercourse occurred.** Physical evidence may substantiate that the victim did not consent to the intercourse. Evidence such as torn or soiled clothing, bruises, pulled-out hair, cuts, and other indications assist in proving that a struggle occurred during the time of the intercourse.
3. **To establish the identity of the perpetrator.** The suspect's identity may be established by a variety of means: eyewitness testimony, fingerprints, or bloodstains left behind at the scene. Additionally, it may be possible to determine the assailant's DNA type from semen left behind or cellular material at the hair root (especially prevalent with freshly pulled hairs) (Figure 15.4). The suspect may have left an article of clothing at the crime scene or unknowingly picked up some trace material such as fibers from a rug, clothing, or bedding. A cigarette butt,

---

[*] Condom wrappers are often opened with the teeth and can obtain DNA rich saliva.
[†] The Sexual Assault Lubricant Database maintained by the National Center for Forensic Science is a compilation of reference lubricants that can assist forensic scientists conducting lubricant analysis to help establish sexual contact occurred.

Figure 15.3 Clipped fingernails from a rape victim can be sent for DNA typing to determine the identity of a scratched suspect.

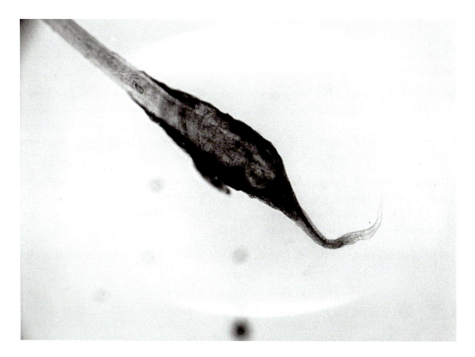

Figure 15.4 A pulled head hair with root. The abundance of epithelial cells from the scalp makes it ripe for DNA testing. In the absence of a root, a hair shaft can be typed with mitochondrial DNA testing. (*Courtesy of the Los Angeles County Sheriff's Department.*)

beer can, or piece of paper may yield fingerprint and/or DNA evidence. All are possible from a carefully and thoroughly conducted crime scene investigation. In order to obtain the best DNA results, known DNA samples from the parties involved in the investigation, including consensual partners need to be collected.

DATE-RAPE DRUGS

If during the course of an investigation, the victim makes a statement such as, "I was at a party, and this guy gave me a drink. Next thing I know, it's morning and I'm in someone's bed. I have no idea what happened," consider the possibility that the victim was drugged with Rohypnol or gamma-hydroxybutyrate (GHB).

Rohypnol, or flunitrazepam, known by various street names: Roachies, La Roche, Rope, Rib, Roche, Rophies, Roofies, and Ruffies, is the brand name of a sleeping pill marketed by Roche Pharmaceuticals in Mexico, South America, Europe and Asia, and first appeared in the U.S. in the early 1990s. Rohypnol belongs to the family of medications called nitro-benzodiazepines that includes Valium (diazepam) and Librium (chlordiazepoxide). Much of the Rohypnol abused in the U.S. is obtained by prescription in Mexico and transported across the border. Rohypnol is a fast-acting sedative that can render a victim unconscious within 20 to 30 minutes. Combined with alcohol, it can lead to coma and possibly death. It also produces complete or partial amnesia.

GHB has a number of street names such as "grievous bodily harm," "liquid ecstasy," and "easy lay," plus a host of other names depending on the region of the country. GHB is a depressant affecting the central nervous system and its effects are rapidly felt. Like "Ruffies," it can cause amnesia, unconsciousness, coma, and sometimes (when combined with alcohol) death. GHB generally comes in pure powder form or mixed with water. Body builders sometimes use it. In 1989, the FDA banned the sale of GHB and classified it as a Schedule I drug. A number of states have passed legislation outlawing the possession of GHB by making it a Schedule I drug under state law.

GHB is a liquid that can render a victim unconscious with as little as a teaspoonful mixed into a drink. The onset of symptoms comes within approximately 5 to 20 minutes. The victim has a feeling of extreme intoxication and impaired judgment. GHB does not produce the extreme muscle paralysis and memory loss associated with Rohypnol, but can cause unconsciousness and strong memory impairment.

The collection of a blood and urine specimen upon admission to the ER for analysis is key to the effective investigation of drug-facilitated sexual assault cases. The cooperation of the emergency room in the collection of specimens greatly helps law enforcement in such cases.

Victims who experience being drugged or are suspicious that they may have been drugged should refrain from voiding their bladders. If voiding is necessary, any clean container is suitable for a urine collection. GHB is eliminated rapidly from the blood (less than 6 hours), but it may be detected in urine. Samples collected from 12 to 24 hours post-dose will yield negative results. These samples should be submitted in a Drug Facilitated Sexual Assault Kit to the toxicology lab.

Investigators should collect any portion of the drink, if it is available, for laboratory examination. Also, if any powdery or crystalline material or pills are found, they too should be sent to the crime laboratory. It should also be mentioned that alcohol by itself is involved in many sexual assaults. Additionally, victims sometimes state that they have been drugged, when in reality they have had way too much to drink.

Finally for any and all evidence that is collected during a sexual assault investigation, a chain of custody needs to be started.

SEXUAL CHILD MOLESTATION AND INCEST

Child molestation and incest investigations have two related problem areas: difficulty in interviewing the victim and possible problems regarding the child's competency to testify in court. These difficulties, coupled with the family's reluctance to pursue or cooperate in the matter, make these cases a challenge. The key person in a sexual assault case involving children is the SANE. The SANE's ability to examine the victim and document findings of sexual assault is of major importance in this type of case. Because of the usual inability of the victim to testify, the physical evidence

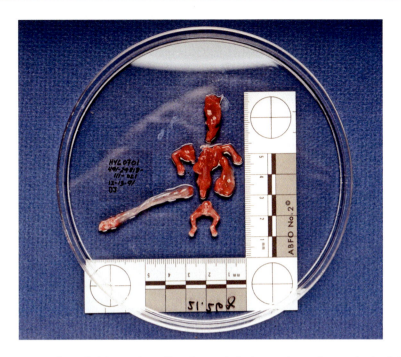

Figure 15.5 Some government forensic laboratories will perform criminal paternity testing on the fetal tissue from an aborted pregnancy after obtaining the alleged father's DNA sample. (*Courtesy of the Los Angeles County Sheriff's Department.*)

and medical testimony are particularly important. Child psychologists also play an important role in child abuse and child molestation cases. They help investigators by pointing out specific child behavior patterns generally associated with this type of crime. However, investigators should be aware that a child psychologist might inadvertently cause a young victim to color his or her story so as to tell the psychologist what he or she "wants to hear."

Physical evidence is often minimal in child molestation cases. The child's parents are often unaware of the crime. Telltale signs of child molestation such as nightmares, bed-wetting, urinary tract infections, and strange stories eventually lead parents or authorities to a suspicion of the cause. If molestation is suspected, the police are brought into the investigation. If clothing or bedding is available from a recent assault, they should be collected for DNA typing. In cases in which pregnancy results from a case of incest and the pregnancy is terminated, the fetus or products of conception can be used in DNA paternity testing to determine the identity of the sperm donor (Figure 15.5). If the product of conception is not morphologically well defined, the differences between fetal (chorionic villi) and maternal (decidua) parts of the placental tissue can be differentiated under the microscope. Beyond this, the police will need to rely heavily on medical findings. Child abuse cases also rely upon the findings of the pediatrician. Here, unexplained bruises, x-rays showing broken bones, and so forth will be important in the investigation. In addition to physical abuse, instances of malnutrition and poor hygienic conditions may occur. These types of cases are almost always emotionally charged and are difficult to prosecute and take to trial. To be sure, these crimes certainly do occur; however, investigators must be especially careful in these cases. Innocent people's names can be tarnished irrevocably if a careful investigation is not made. On occasion, children have been known to fabricate allegations of sexual abuse.

PUBLIC LEWDNESS/FORCIBLE TOUCHING

These types of crimes, often misdemeanors, include masturbating in public, or rubbing up against someone on a crowded bus or subway, and ejaculating on them. Swabs of semen or clothing should be submitted to the lab in these types of cases. In cases of groping or forcible touching, items of clothing can be submitted to the lab for trace DNA typing when a specific region of the clothing was touched by the perpetrator.

RAPE KIT BACKLOG

It is unknown exactly how many untested sexual assault kits remain in evidence lockers or on police department shelves. End The Backlog (www.endthebacklog.org) is a program of the Joyful Heart Foundation (www.joyfulheart foundation.org), a national non-profit founded by Mariska Hargitay with the mission to transform society's response to sexual assault and eliminate the backlog of cases around the country.

NATIONAL BEST PRACTICES

In 2016, NIJ published *National Best Practices for Sexual Assault Kits: A Multidisciplinary Approach*. In it are 35 recommendations to positively impact sexual assault practices and the experiences of victims and to ultimately result in safer communities.

CONCLUSION

Crimes referred to as "sexual assault" are improperly named. In reality, they have little to do with sex except that the genitals may be involved. They are in fact crimes of violence frequently involving suspects exhibiting "non-normal" psychological behavior. The investigator who understands the psychological as well as the physical evidence aspects of these crimes will likely be more effective in the investigation.

Further Reading

Chancellor, Arthur S. *Investigating Sexual Assault Cases*. Jones & Bartlett Publishers, 2012.

Hammer, Rita M., Barbara Moynihan, and Elaine M. Pagliaro, eds. *Forensic Nursing: A Handbook for Practice*. Jones & Bartlett Publishers, 2011.

Lynch, Virginia A., and Janet Barber Duval. *Forensic Nursing Science-e-book*. Elsevier Health Sciences, 2010.

National Institute of Justice. "National best practices for sexual assault kits: a multidisciplinary approach." August 7, 2017, https://www.ojp.gov/pdffiles1/nij/250384.pdf.

Chapter Questions

1. What is a SANE?
2. (True or false) The victim of a rape may appear perfectly calm and in control when being interviewed by the police.
3. Which of the following statements should not be included in the sexual assault report issued by the investigator?
    a) "The victim had several apparent bruises on her left shoulder."
    b) "The victim states that she had consensual sex 3 hours before the rape."
    c) "The victim appears unusually happy considering she was just raped."
    d) "Signs of forced entry were located on a rear window."
4. Of the following examples, which requires immediate attention from the lead investigator?
    a) The victim reports that she called her husband after the rape.
    b) The victim reports that the suspect kissed her on the cheek.
    c) The media is on scene and would like a statement.
    d) The victim has a criminal history.
5. A _____ should be immediately instituted when collecting evidence from the victim at the hospital.
    a) Photo log.
    b) Press release.

c) Crime scene log.
   d) Chain of custody.
6. List the three primary purposes of physical evidence in rape cases.
7. Which of the following is known as a date-rape drug?
   a) Rohypnol.
   b) Crack.
   c) Marijuana.
   d) LSD.
8. Which of the following can be a problem area when investigating a child molestation case?
   a) The child's ability to testify in court.
   b) The collection of probative evidence.
   c) Obtaining consent from the parents.
   d) Obtaining a search warrant.
9. Which of the following is an example of a crime classified as public lewdness?
   a) Rape.
   b) Elder abuse.
   c) Sexual imposition.
   d) Masturbating in public.
10. (True or false) It is possible for a sexual assault to have occurred without the presence of semen or saliva.

CHAPTER 16

Burglary Investigation

Burglary is one of the most commonly encountered crimes investigated by law enforcement. Because the nature of the crime is so varied, it is difficult to set down specific guidelines for its investigation. Many of the techniques and procedures outlined in earlier chapters of the text are pertinent to the burglary investigation. This chapter discusses some of the aspects of crime scene investigation that deal more specifically with the crime of burglary.

The first officer to arrive at the burglary scene must be concerned with the suspect's location as well as their own safety. In cases in which the burglary is in progress and the officer was called because of the presence of a prowler, silent alarm, or ringing burglar alarm, the first consideration must be to secure the scene. Once the suspect has been located or a determination has been made that the suspect is not at the scene, then the investigation can commence. Witnesses should also be located and separated for interviewing at a later time.

The officer conducting the crime scene investigation of a burglary should understand that most experienced burglars attempt to leave only a minimum amount of evidence at the location. The officer should also remember that it is impossible for the suspect not to change the crime scene in some small way by leaving traces behind or by picking up small items of evidence when leaving the scene. The officer, or evidence collection team, should try to identify and collect evidence left behind by the suspect, for example, fingerprints, DNA, shoe prints, hairs, tool marks, etc., and evidence from the suspect that may have been removed from the scene, for example, glass fragments, paint chips, wooden splinters, etc. The investigator should also be aware of the modus operandi, or M.O., of the burglar. Frequently, a suspect may be responsible for a large number of burglaries in an area and similarities in the cases may enable the investigator to concentrate on one rather than a number of suspects. Thus, in some instances it may be useful to examine tool marks left at different crime scenes to determine whether the same tool was used by a serial burglar.

POINTS OF ENTRY

The point of entry is an important starting point for the initial collection of physical evidence in burglary investigations. The experienced burglar attempts to gain entry by the easiest and safest available entrance.

ENTRY THROUGH WINDOWS

Window entry is usually accomplished by breaking a hole through a pane and removing the broken glass to reach the door latch or lock. To minimize the noise from falling glass, the burglar may press a rag against the window; sometimes adhesive tape may be used. In some cases, the burglar may remove the entire windowpane by removing the putty holding the glass in place. It has even happened that the burglar has replaced the glass intact and put in new putty. Where a screen covers a window, a careful examination of the edges for any cuts may show fibers from the suspect's sleeve where the arm was inserted to open or break the window. Glass fragments are a type of trace evidence often found on the suspect when a window was broken to gain entrance. When the window is broken, it is almost unavoidable that some pieces of the flying glass will adhere to the suspect's clothing. The investigator should

DOI: 10.4324/9780429272011-19

Figure 16.1 Dusting for fingerprints on glass of a broken window at the point of entry should also be done. (*Photo credit: Etan Tal,* https://commons.wikimedia.org/wiki/File:BurglaryIsrael2.jpg.)

collect specimens of the broken window for comparison with glass found on the burglar's clothes and also search for any fingerprints present on the windowpane, as well as prints present in the window putty. It is also possible for the suspect to have cut or scraped themselves on the broken glass. Any blood found on glass can be collected for DNA typing (Figure 16.1).

Searches for prints should be made in the dust on the window or ledge, if present. If entry is made by forcing in a tool to push back a window latch, tool marks should be searched for, documented, and photographed. Depending on the size of the item, a cast of the tool mark can be made at the crime scene, or the entire item can be brought back to the lab depending on agency policy. Samples of wood and paint should be collected for comparison if a tool is later found. A pry bar, screwdriver, or other tool is also sometimes used in forcing a window. In these cases, tool marks and specimens of building debris should be collected. Sometimes, the burglar may try to force several different windows to enter the building. The investigator should therefore examine all windows to determine if any "jimmy marks" are present and collect appropriate tool mark evidence. Paint chips are frequently dislodged while breaking in and the investigator should always collect samples for later comparison (Figure 16.2a and b). Later, examination of the suspect's clothing and tools may uncover paint that matches paint recovered at the crime scene.

ENTRY THROUGH DOORS

A burglar sometimes opens a door using a pry bar to attack the door and jamb around the lock until the bolt can be pushed back or is actually freed from the striker plate (Figure 16.3). A door jamb is sometimes so weak that it may be spread apart far enough to free the bolt. This can be done by mere pressure from the body or by inserting a jack

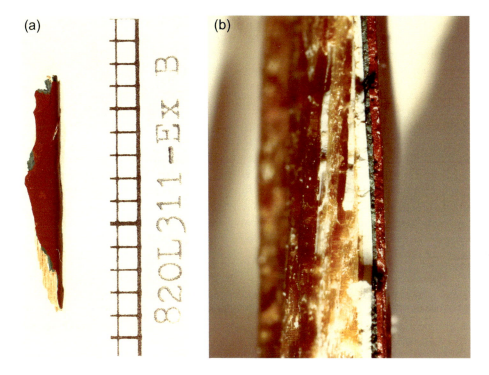

Figure 16.2 (a, b) A sliver of wood with multiple layers of paint can be compared to known samples at the point of entry and matched. (Courtesy of the Royal Canadian Mounted Police Forensic Laboratory Services.)

Figure 16.3 Using a pry bar to attack a lock and door jamb.

horizontally across the doorframe. The lock might also be made accessible through a hole that is drilled, sawed, or broken in a door panel. Many doors are fitted with glass that is simply broken so that the lock may be reached. Other weak points are mail slots, the frame of which may be removed, and transoms that may have been left open. A common method of entry is to push back spring-loaded bolts by means of a knife. The knife is inserted between the door and the jamb and the bolt is gradually worked back. The bolt is kept from springing back by outward pressure on the door. This method is easily detected by the series of scratches that run lengthwise along the bolt. Burglary by this method may be prevented by safety catches and deadbolt locks. Snap-lock bolts can also be opened by inserting a knife, spatula, or credit card pressed against the beveled face of the bolt and pushing it back. The instrument can be inserted between the door and the jamb or behind the molding on the jamb.

This method of entry is generally difficult to detect because a piece of plastic can be used without leaving any marks. It is, however, possible that pieces of plastic broke off and may be found in or near the lock. On locks on which the beveled face of the bolt faces inward, the bolt may be pushed back by a tool or a piece of wire that forces the bolt back by a pulling movement. This is usually discovered by scratch marks on the face of the bolt. Attention should be given to the opening for the bolt in the striker plate for the possibility that it may contain wadded paper or other material. A burglar might have surreptitiously stuffed something in the opening in the door jamb during an earlier visit to the premises. The effect of the wadding prevents the bolt from locking so that the burglar may later return and push the bolt back. If there is reason to suspect that the lock has been picked, the lock should be disassembled with great care. The investigator should avoid making new scratch marks inside the lock. If a pick has been used, it may have left marks in the coating of dust and oil usually found inside locks. Broken knife points, metal fragments from lock picks, and the like may also be found inside the lock.* Cases have been recorded in which mechanics who installed the lock made certain alterations to facilitate a later burglary.

Entry can also be made by cutting the hinge pins off with a bolt cutter. More commonly, the pins are simply knocked out with a hammer and chisel or screwdriver. With the pins out, the door can be lifted off the hinges. The door may then be replaced and the pins reinserted. This method of entry is readily revealed by the damage to the hinges and the chips of paint or metal on the floor below the hinges. Cylinder (pin-tumbler) locks may be picked by special picks, but usually the whole door is forced or the cylinder is removed. The cylinder may be pulled out by means of a special puller shaped from a pair of large nippers. To avoid detection of the removal, the lock cylinder is sometimes replaced or a similar cylinder put in its place. Sometimes, the retaining screw is removed surreptitiously during an earlier visit to the premises, which facilitates removing the cylinder. Still another means of gaining access through a door is by means of a wrench placed on the doorknob. The twisting motion exerted on the doorknob is sufficient to defeat the locking mechanism of inexpensive locks. Examination of the doorknob shows characteristic markings caused by the tool. The doorknob should be removed and submitted to the laboratory for comparison with tool marks made by the wrench and also for comparison of any metal shavings found in the teeth of the tool. In instances in which a padlock was used on a hinged hasp to lock a door, the padlock and cut shackle should be collected and sent to the laboratory. If a pair of bolt cutters or a similar cutting device is found, test cuts can be made and compared with tool marks left on the lock shackle.

ENTRY THROUGH BASEMENT WINDOWS AND SKYLIGHTS

Basement windows are forced in the same manner as ordinary windows. The investigator should pay special attention to the possibility that the burglar's clothes may have become torn and cloth fragments or fibers left behind. If any disturbed dust or dirt patterns are noted, the officer should collect samples of the dust and the dirt usually found in such places.

ENTRY THROUGH ROOFS

The presence of convenient utility poles, ladders, and other aids, makes entry through flat roofs a favorite M.O. Many otherwise well-protected stores have easy access roofs. Building material may contaminate the clothing of any burglar using this technique. A careful search will also show signs of ropes for entry and exit. Most stores are equipped with roof ventilators and exhaust fans. Entry through the ventilating system may result in tool marks, DNA, fingerprints, and dust contamination of clothing.

---

* Several YouTube channels such as LockPickingLawyer and Bosnianbill demonstrate numerous methods of attacks against locks and safes. Investigators should be aware of these channels to learn of different methods that burglars might have used to gain entry. Different lock types can also be searched and videos of how to open them can be viewed.

ENTRY THROUGH WALLS

Walls are broken by tools or by explosives. A brick wall is easily broken by a hammer and chisel or a sledgehammer. Burglars can be expected to become covered with dust during such an operation; samples of mortar and brick should be collected for comparisons. In blasting, a hole is usually chiseled between two bricks and the charge is inserted. Several small charges are normally used to avoid severe detonations and the possibility of the whole wall collapsing. Small hydraulic jacks may be used to force holes into a wall. In this operation, a narrow passageway is usually chosen where the base force can be distributed over a wide area by padding. After the initial hole is made, repeated thrusts are used to enlarge the hole sufficiently to gain entry. When an empty or infrequently occupied store is adjacent to the target, plaster walls may be cut to a thin supporting layer and the entire section removed at once. Entry into vaults is usually accomplished through the walls, which are easier to force than the door. The walls are often constructed of reinforced concrete that can be broken by repeated blasting or by hammer and chisel and acetylene torch.

ENTRY THROUGH FLOORS

This method of entry is often preferred in the case of warehouses or other buildings that have a crawl space underneath. The burglar usually drills or saws a hole in the floorboards large enough to crawl through. Entry through walls and floors is also made when the suspect knows that the premises are protected by burglar alarms on doors and windows.

Because many burglaries occur at night, the investigator should also check any outdoor lights to see whether the bulbs were unscrewed by the burglar to darken the area near the point of entry. These bulbs might contain fingerprints and/or trace DNA.

SIMULATED BURGLARIES

Simulated burglaries are often attempts at insurance fraud. To create a successful imitation of a burglary that will deceive the police, the perpetrator must strive to carry it out as naturally as possible, otherwise there will be gaps in the sequence of events. When windows are entered, the officer should therefore always check whether the window panes were broken from the outside, whether footprints are outside the window, whether broken glass has been trampled in these prints, whether the burglar could have reached the window, whether there are traces of actual entry (sand, dirt, etc.), whether objects inside the window are so placed that the window could be opened to permit entry, and so on. If the outside of the window glass is dirty, there may be marks from the object used to break it. If the glass is relatively clean, the side on which the force was applied might be revealed by dusting with fingerprint powder. In cases of forced doors, the damage should be examined to see whether it is only on the outside portions. Marks of prying may be present on the door as well as on the door jamb. If the tool marks are located high up so that the burglar probably had to stand on a box or a ladder, possible supports should be examined. If a burglary is suspected of being simulated, all tools belonging to the victim should be compared against any tool marks present and, if necessary, collected for further examination. Holes in floors, walls, and ceilings should be examined to determine the side from which the breach was started. The holes should also be examined to determine if any evidence of a person having crawled through is present. The CSI should further make an estimate of how long the burglar spent on the premises. The officer should also follow the burglar's actions in searching for valuables—were doors first opened and drawers emptied or did the burglar go directly to the location of the valuables? Also, was any food eaten at the crime scene? Unfinished food items may be a source of DNA evidence.

DETAILED EXAMINATION OF THE SCENE

Generally, a detailed examination of the crime scene proper should begin after the surrounding areas have been searched. Failure to search the surrounding areas initially may result in the inadvertent destruction of evidence by sightseers as well as by officers at the location. Approaches leading to and away from the scene should be examined for footprints, tire impressions, drag marks (such as those caused by a heavy object, e.g., a safe), and abandoned items such as tools, clothing, gloves, opened cash boxes, and so on. Obstacles leading to the building such as fences and gates should be examined for traces of blood, fabric, fibers, and tool marks. The number of suspects involved might be estimated from footprints. Areas where a suspect had to crawl or climb should be examined for traces of clothing. Samples of building material and soil should be collected for comparative purposes. The location from which the burglar "staked out" the location or where a "lookout" was standing should be examined for footprints, cigarette butts, cigarette package wrappers, matches, food items, and other such evidence. The point of entry should be examined for broken tools, tool marks, broken window glass, fibers, hair, blood, fingerprints, footprints, paint chips, wood, and other building materials. Known samples of materials should be collected. Photographs, measurements, and sketches should be made before any items are moved or collected. The examination of the interior of the burglarized business must sometimes be carried out while taking into account the wishes of the owner. The investigator may allow the owner or manager to specify which area of the premises is available for searching first.

The investigator should carry out the inside crime scene investigation in the normal detailed and systematic way. Attention should be given to evidence such as fingerprints, DNA, footprints, broken tools, tool marks, blood, and any other evidence that will aid in the solution of the case. (A burglar may have used the bathroom at a scene and will flush the toilet with an ungloved hand. Therefore, the flush handle should be examined for fingerprints.) Once the examination of areas of the location is completed, the proprietor should be notified. If evidence is found that requires time-consuming recovery, the owner and other personnel should be asked to stay out of the area until the examination is complete. A complete inventory of all items missing should be obtained from the owner, as well as a complete description of the items with any photos, including brand names, labels, markings, serial numbers, size, shape, color, and value. This facilitates identification of the stolen property later. The burglary victim should also be asked if anything seems out of place at the crime scene or if anything does not belong to them. Attention should be paid to these items.

An apprehended suspect should be thoroughly searched. Cuts and scratches should be noted and photographed. The clothing should be collected for examination for tears and building material that can place the suspect in contact with the crime scene. The suspect's vehicle should be searched for stolen property, burglary tools, and any other items of physical evidence. The investigator should remember that in some instances a search warrant might be necessary before the vehicle may be completely searched.

Video evidence should also be sought out, gathered, and viewed. Many homes now have video doorbells that can record any movement in front of the home. Neighbors to the burglary should be asked if they have any recording equipment that may have captured what happened (The Ring® and Nest® video doorbells are two examples of residential security equipment.) (Figure 16.4). Many retail establishments and businesses also use visible as well hidden recording equipment. Many times a picture or description of the suspect can be isolated from the video footage. If the suspect is wearing a mask or some other disguise, viewing the video can aid in determining what items the burglar may have touched. Further investigation can then be focused on those items.

The investigator should try to determine if the burglar was familiar with the premises. If the burglar removed valuables from an unlikely location without disturbing the rest of the scene or if keys that were hidden were used, the officer might infer that the suspect was familiar with the location. The investigator should try to make a determination about the type of person being sought. Was the burglary the work of a professional burglar? Was the crime simply a case of vandalism involving juveniles? Was anything unusual left at the scene? Answers to these questions, information obtained from interviews, and physical evidence examination will prove useful in the overall investigation.

SAFE BURGLARIES

Safes may be classified into two basic types: fire resistant and burglar resistant. Although providing a minimum resistance to attack by a professional burglar, fire-resistant safes are designed to withstand, resist, and retard the penetration of heat and to protect documents from destruction by fire. Such safes are constructed of metal and insulation consisting of a variety of materials such as vermiculite, cement, diatomaceous earth, sawdust, and the like. Burglar-resistant safes are specifically designed to resist the efforts of safe burglars and are constructed of steel that is resistant to forced entry by tools or torch. Burglar-resistant safes are not burglarproof but are designed to resist attack for a certain period of time.

Safes can be opened by a number of methods such as manipulation, punching, peeling, prying, ripping, chopping, drilling, burning, or by means of explosives. Manipulation is essentially a lost art that involves opening a safe by means of listening to and feeling the combination lock mechanism. Most safes today have manipulation-proof locks; the investigator should therefore assume that the suspect had knowledge of the combination if a safe in which the lock

Figure 16.4 The Nest® video doorbell is capable of sending an image to the homeowner as well as 24/7 streaming and HD video recording. The HDR video can also show sharp details even in bright and dark areas.

has been opened is found. The punching method involves knocking off the dial and punching the dial spindle into the safe. Newer safes have punch-proof spindles and relocking devices that automatically relock the safe when an attempt at a "punch job" is made. Peeling involves prying or peeling the faceplate from the safe door in such a way as to expose the locking mechanism. This is sometimes accomplished by first pounding the door with a sledgehammer until the door buckles and then inserting a pry bar. Entry by ripping or chopping is achieved by tearing a hole through a part of the safe other than the door such as the top, side, or bottom. Drilling is usually effective, but it is a time-consuming method and therefore only rarely used in safe burglaries. It is commonly done by perforating the door plate around the keyhole by a series of holes close together. A large portion of the lock mechanism is thereby bared so that the bolts can be manipulated. The front plate of some safes can also be peeled back if some of the screws or rivets in the edge are first removed. The paint covering the rivets is first scraped off so that the rivets are bared. The rivets are then drilled deeply enough for the plate to be separated. After a few rivets have been removed, the front plate is then forced up sufficiently to insert a chisel that is used to break the remaining rivets without drilling.

On some safes, the locking bolts can be reached by drilling through the side of the safe, directly against the face of the bolt. The bolt can then be driven back with a punch. The exact location of the bolts can be determined by the marks in the door frame that occur in daily use when the safe door is shut while the bolts are protruding. In cases of drilling, the burglar can be expected to have used some kind of lubricating oil for the bit. Samples of such oil and samples of metal shavings should be collected because the burglar's body or clothing may contain these materials. Simpler types of safes with combination locks may be opened by means of a thick, square steel plate provided with an opening at the center to be slipped over the dial knob. The corners of the plate are equipped with threaded bolts, the points of which touch the safe door. By tightening the bolts with a wrench, the knob and spindle are torn out. It also happens that safes are opened by a special bridge device screwed to the safe with bolts. The portion of the bridge over the door frame contains a threaded hole. A strong bolt is fitted into this hole and tightened far enough to force the door open.

Another method uses a circular cutter. Such devices are made in several different forms. Some are affixed to one or more holes that have been drilled into the safe, while others are strapped to the safe by long bolts and nuts or steel cable. Common to all types, however, is one or more hardened steel cutters held against the safe under tension and turned by means of a handle. The result is a round hole in the safe wall. These devices are normally not used on the safe door because the locking bars would interfere, but rather on the side or back of the safe. Cutting by acetylene torch is a very effective method against which only specially designed steel chests are completely resistant. A considerable disadvantage of this method lies in the fact that the apparatus required is heavy and difficult to transport. For this reason, the burning method is usually used only where complete welding equipment is available on the premises. Some burglars have used compact equipment that is large enough to do the job but light enough to be carried easily.

Burning is another method used by safe burglars using the so-called burning bar. The bar, a metal pipe, is packed with a mixture of powdered aluminum and iron oxide. The mixture is known as thermite and when ignited gives off an intense heat that can be directed to the safe. Burning is usually started around the dial hole. A sufficiently large hole is cut in the front plate of the door so that the lock mechanism is accessible. The operator may cut this hole in the form of a tongue that is folded back. Where the cutting is done on the sides or back of the safe, the inside plate must also be cut through. This method often ignites the contents of the safe, whereupon the burglar may use a soda pop bottle as a fire extinguisher. Sometimes, the burglar cuts off the safe door hinges, which reveals an ignorance of the construction of the safe. The manner of opening the safe by burning reveals the skill of the burglar. When the investigator is unable to estimate this skill, a specialist should be consulted. Samples to be collected at the scene are molten particles of metal (beads), slag, molten safe insulation, and the like. Such particles may be found on the clothing of a suspect.

The investigator should also keep in mind the possibility of minor burns in the burglar's clothes from flying particles. When the contents of the safe caught fire, the burglar may have been able to recover paper currency, some of which may be charred. Safe burglaries are often carried out by transporting the safe to an isolated location where it is opened by tools or explosives. In such cases, the burglars are usually less careful in their movements at the place of opening. Valuable footprints or tire tracks may be found at such places. The investigation should be carried out as soon as possible because inclement weather conditions may destroy the most valuable evidence.

SAFE BURGLARIES USING EXPLOSIVES

It is sometimes very difficult to gather physical evidence that will convict a safe burglar specializing in explosives. As a rule, the burglar is skilled at this method and takes pride in sweeping the crime scene clean of all traces that may be used as incriminating evidence. When examining such burglary scenes, the investigator should therefore proceed very thoroughly and take advantage of the mistakes sometimes made even by this type of burglar.

Experience has shown that these burglars usually make mistakes when disturbed or when fleeing the premises. The burglar may then leave behind or drop objects that have potential value as evidence. One weakness of these specialists is that they usually stick to one method in all their burglaries. The investigator thereby gets an opportunity to tie certain burglaries to a given criminal or to others whom they have trained. This fact may be valuable even when the burglars are not known. Explosives operators usually do not pick locks or make their way into the premises by other light-fingered methods. Their work is carried out with a great deal of noise and this is also characteristic of their method of entry. They generally use great force on doors and windows and may even use a charge on a door that could much more easily have been opened the usual way. On the other hand, they are very careful to protect themselves from surprises. They very rarely work alone and may have several helpers whose only duty is to act as lookouts.

Regarding the placing of the safe for the "blowing," three methods are normally found: it is left in place, it is pulled out from the wall, or it is laid on the floor. The first method is the most common. The second is used by burglars who do not want to have the safe blown against the wall and create vibrations in the building that may be more noticeable than the detonation. The third method is seldom used; its advantage is that it facilitates the placing of the charge.

In examining safes that have been moved or laid down, the investigator should be very careful in searching for latent finger and palm prints. Although explosives specialists will be sure to use gloves or other covering, it is still possible that they may leave identifiable fragments of palm prints on a safe that they have moved. The glove may slip during the heavy work, exposing a small piece of the palm, enough to produce a valuable print. In developing prints deposited under such conditions, great care must be exercised because they easily become smeared or even completely filled in because of the great pressure.

The charge is usually placed in the dial spindle hole after the dial is knocked off; it may be dynamite in powder or paste or other explosives. The hazard and the refined technique associated with the use of nitroglycerine usually limit its use to only the elite of the safe burglars. Round door safes have discouraged the use of explosives, however. Wrappers from explosives should be searched for and recovered, even though latent fingerprints are usually not found on waxed wrappers. In a favorable case, the wrapper may still be valuable as evidence. In general, the adhesive material used to affix the detonator that is found on the scene, such as clay, putty, plasticine, or soap, is brought in by the burglar. These substances must be soft and well kneaded to serve the purpose. Because the burglar may have kneaded these materials without wearing gloves before going to the scene, plastic fingerprints and/or DNA may be present. Such evidence should be searched for not only on the surface but also on inside layers of the kneaded material.

Prints and DNA may also be found on tape, but these are sometimes difficult to detect. The amount of safety fuse—when used—may vary in length. Explosives specialists usually cut these lengths before going to the scene and have widely varying ideas of the proper length—a fact that may have some value. Those using the longer fuses usually prefer to light the fuse and then retire to a safe distance from which they can observe the effect of the explosion and whether it was noticed. Safe burglars vary as to whether they use a dam or sound-absorbing blanket to contain the explosion. Those who do use a dam probably do so to muffle the detonation and to keep windows from bursting. Because the charge is mostly inside the door, the effect of the explosion is not enhanced by the use of a dam. When the burglar intends to demolish the door completely, the dam does have some effect, but it is usually an effect that the burglar wants to avoid. The burglar runs the risk that the inside door plate is blown into the safe with such force that new charges must be placed to dislodge it. Many explosives specialists make a habit of not using a dam at all. Instead, they open windows in the room in which the safe is located so that the shock wave will dissipate without breaking windows or attracting unwanted attention. Some burglars soak the dam with water, partly to make it denser and heavier and partly to prevent the possibility of fire. The materials used in dams are brought to or collected at the scene. The damage to the material gives an indication of how many separate charges were used.

Material that has been brought to the scene may sometimes give good leads for the investigation and the search for the suspect. The ideal explosion occurs when the charge is so well balanced that the locking bolts are pulled back and the door flies open. In such cases, the external damage to the safe may be limited to a slight bulge in the front plate around the dial hole. It does happen, however, that the locking bolts remain more or less closed, so new charges must be set off. To avoid this snag, some burglars put weight on the door handle in the direction in which the handle opens. A heavy cord is commonly tied to the handle and a heavy object is attached to the other end. Another method is to tie a heavy metal bar to the handle to act as a lever. At the detonation, the handle is turned by the weight of the heavy object so that the locking bolts are turned back. Locked drawers and compartments inside the safe are either forced open or blown. The investigator should keep in mind the possibility of finding parts of broken tools as well as tool marks at these places.

Fragments of tools may be searched for with a magnet because they are very difficult to find in the powdered insulation that usually pours from the broken safe. The search for fingerprints at scenes of safe blowing is usually complicated by the layer of finely divided safe insulation that settles on everything in the room. This dust should be removed, preferably by careful blowing, before developing with powder. To brush off the dust is wrong because the dust usually consists of gritty particles that will destroy the fingerprints. Visible prints that have been deposited by a dusty finger must be treated very carefully. Whenever an unexploded charge is found in the safe, it should be neutralized with great care. An apprehended suspect's clothes should be thoroughly searched for the presence of safe insulation or paint. Anyone who has been present in a room in which a safe has been blown can hardly avoid getting dust and safe insulation on his or her clothing. The dust may also adhere to the burglar's skin or in the hair, ears, nostrils, and under the fingernails. Such dust may be found on any part of the clothing, but particularly in the pant cuffs and on the shoes, mainly in the seams, in the lace holes, and on the soles.

In addition, paint chips are usually loosened in the explosion and the burglars run the risk of picking them up on their clothing when examining the safe after the detonation. In searching the scene, the investigator should therefore collect samples of the safe insulation and paint on the outside and inside of the safe for use in possible comparisons and also evaluate the possibility of wall paint loosened by the explosion falling on the burglar. The investigator should note the manufacturer of the safe so that the company may later be contacted for information on the composition of insulation and paint. If safe insulation or paint is not found on the suspect's clothes, the investigator should remember that the suspect might have done everything possible to eliminate such traces. The suspect's hands and clothing should also be examined for the presence of trace explosives. If the hands were not immediately washed, traces may be under the fingernails. In the clothing, such traces should primarily be searched for in the pockets—even the gloves may contain traces. If the burglar carried safety fuses in pockets, there may be characteristic stains on the pocket lining.

When a safe is blown, the burglar may be injured by sharp metal. The nose may start bleeding from the shock of the detonation. If blood is found at the scene, it should be recovered for later examination. The burglar may be so severely injured that immediate aid must be sought. Burglary is such a common crime that frequently a less than thorough investigation is conducted; however, a careful and detailed examination of the crime scene may result in developing evidence useful in an ultimate solution of the case.

Crime labs may not have the capacity to test for DNA in samples collected at burglary crime scenes. Backlogs from violent crimes as well as resource constraints are often the cause. Past cases have shown that when certain types of evidence are left behind at a burglary scene, such as articles of clothing, latex gloves, hats, cigarette butts, partially eaten food, eyeglasses, drink containers, cell phones, etc., a considerable number of crimes can be solved by DNA testing. Investigators should consult with the forensic science laboratory in their jurisdictions to determine under what qualifications property crime cases are accepted, and if there are a maximum number of items the laboratory will test. As state and national DNA databases continue to grow, more property crimes will be solved. In addition, if police agencies demand more forensic science services such as DNA in property crimes, forensic labs can make a stronger case for funding in these areas.

FORENSIC LOCKSMITHING*

> "Forensic locksmithing is the study and systematic examination of a lock or other device or associated equipment using scientific methods to determine if and how the device was opened, neutralized, or bypassed. These examinations include the use of various types of forensic techniques, [...] and includes microscopic examination, microphotography, regular photography, physical disassembly of the device or devices, and on occasion laboratory techniques, such as metallurgy and tool mark identification may be conducted."
>
> **—Don Shiles, Former President, Intl. Assoc. of Investigative Locksmiths**

Forensic locksmithing is a subdiscipline of criminalistics that combines the skills of locksmithing and forensic science. The forensic locksmith can be very instrumental in aiding a burglary investigation, insurance fraud investigation, or can identify the weaknesses of a security system.

The Forensic Institute of Physical Security (www.fiops.org) is an international organization that trains and certifies forensic locksmiths working in physical security (locks, keys, safes, and alarm systems).

Further Reading

Antrobus, Emma, and Andrew Pilotto. "Improving forensic responses to residential burglaries: Results of a randomized controlled field trial." *Journal of Experimental Criminology* 12.3 (2016): 319–345.

Tobias, Marc Weber. *Locks, Safes, and Security: An International Police Reference (Two Volumes)*. Charles C Thomas Publisher, 2000.

Chapter Questions

1. Which of the following things should be done by the officer at a burglary in progress call once the scene has been searched for possible suspects?
    a) Secure the scene.

---

* Lockpicking Forensics (Lockpickingforensics.com) is an excellent website that deals with this topic in depth. There are sections on normal wear, lockpicking, pick guns, key bumping, impressioning, decoding, bypass, destructive entry, key analysis, and lock disassembly, and more.

b) Identify any witnesses.
   c) Begin a crime scene search.
   d) All of the above.
2. Why is it important that the crime scene investigator find the point of entry at a burglary scene?
3. You are called in to process the scene of a residential burglary where a window was pried open. Which of the following pieces of evidence would you want to collect?
   a) Tool marks on the window frame.
   b) Paint samples from cans in the basement.
   c) Fingerprint standards from the workers who installed the window.
   d) Hairs found in the resident's bathroom.
4. Describe the various ways that a burglar can force entry through a door.
5. Which one of the following pieces of evidence would be the most useful in identifying the perpetrator of a residential burglary?
   a) Hair on a couch.
   b) Blood on broken glass at the point of entry.
   c) Mud on the floor inside the point of entry.
   d) Glass.
6. Describe what a simulated burglary is and list some of the things you should be looking for when dealing with such a scene.
7. You are conducting a burglary investigation and find a witness who reported seeing a suspicious male sitting in a car across from the scene before the burglary. Which of the following pieces of evidence would you want to collect when searching that area?
   a) Soil samples from the area.
   b) Cigarette butts on the ground.
   c) Tire impressions.
   d) All of the above.
8. Which of the following should be examined at a burglary scene In order to locate the suspect's fingerprints/DNA?
   a) Toilet flush handle.
   b) Exterior light bulbs that have been unscrewed.
   c) Drink containers in the refrigerator.
   d) All of the above.
9. Describe several ways that a safe can be opened by a burglar.
10. You stop a suspect on your way to a call of a burglary where a safe was opened by explosion. Which of the following pieces of evidence would you look for on the suspect's clothing?
    a) Hairs.
    b) Insulation material.
    c) Glass.
    d) Dirt.

Chapter 17

Motor Vehicle Investigation

The widespread use of motor vehicles in today's society has resulted in automobiles being associated with many different types of police investigations. Motor vehicles may be the instrument of crimes such as hit-and-run cases or traffic fatalities. A vehicle may also be the crime scene, for example, in cases in which a crime was committed in an automobile or in cases of auto theft. This chapter deals with evidence commonly associated with crimes in which a motor vehicle is involved.

GRAND THEFT AUTO

A vehicle may be stolen by juveniles for "joyriding," in connection with another crime as a means of fleeing, or for the purpose of stripping the vehicle of parts to be sold for profit. Unfortunately, vehicle theft is a high-frequency crime, and some police agencies do not have the personnel or resources with which to conduct thorough investigations. This often results in a search for physical evidence that consists of only dusting the vehicle for latent fingerprints. Stolen vehicles may be located in a variety of circumstances. Often uniformed officers while on patrol find them. The officer may make use of a "hot sheet" listing licenses of stolen vehicles, use a description from a police bulletin or broadcast, or notice some furtive movement on the part of the driver that results in a routine traffic stop and subsequent check for a stolen vehicle.

Once the vehicle has been identified as stolen, the examination for physical evidence begins. A preliminary investigation will determine whether a full search for physical evidence is needed. In instances in which the driver of the stolen vehicle is the thief, the need for identity determination by means of physical evidence is removed. It is still necessary to check the vehicle carefully and inventory any property inside. It is a good idea to look for evidence of other crimes as well.

Auto theft may be only one of other, more serious crimes with this in mind, the first officer to locate the stolen vehicle should take appropriate precautions. As with other crime scenes, the most fragile evidence should be collected first. This usually means fingerprints. It is recommended that the vehicle be moved to a special location such as a tow yard or police garage for the purpose of taking prints and looking for other evidence. Before any extensive search is undertaken, the need for a search warrant should be considered.

When the vehicle is moved, care should be taken not to destroy fingerprints or other evidence. If possible, the vehicle should be towed to the impound yard. Driving it might accidentally destroy certain evidence. Personnel at the tow yard should be reminded not to touch the vehicle until it has been processed for evidence. If the vehicle is wet from dew it should first be allowed to dry. In cold weather, the vehicle should be placed indoors and allowed to warm up to room temperature prior to searching for fingerprints. The examination for fingerprints should be conducted in a systematic manner. Areas most likely to have been handled by the suspect should be carefully fingerprinted. These include the rear-view mirror, steering wheel, shift lever, door handle, glove compartment, and windows. After prints have been lifted, the location, date, time, and other identifying information should be noted on the fingerprint card. Swabs of the vehicle should also be taken for trace DNA in case fingerprints do not produce any useful ridge detail.

DOI: 10.4324/9780429272011-20

Signs of forced entry should be noted. Known specimens of broken glass, chipped paint, and similar items should be collected for future comparison.

If the radio, entertainment system, navigation system, or any other electronics are missing, the electrical wires should be removed for possible comparison against recovered property. The wires should be marked in a way that clearly shows which ends were originally connected to the unit.

ABANDONED VEHICLES

Any officer who finds or investigates an ownerless vehicle not reported as stolen should not drive it away or subject it to more detailed examination until informed by the driver or owner of the reason why the vehicle was standing at that place. If it is known that a serious crime has been committed, the investigation of the vehicle must be done with the utmost care and thoroughness. The investigation must be planned carefully. The basic search for evidence in and on the vehicle should be carried out in a well-sheltered place, preferably in a garage or other suitable building, because rain or snow or even strong sunlight can destroy certain evidence. The vehicle should be towed from the place at which it was found as soon as possible, but only after certain preliminary investigations have been carried out.

The place where the vehicle is found should be photographed and sketched in the usual way. Photography is done while the vehicle is still on the spot, but sketching can wait until later. In sketches, the distance to the nearest occupied dwelling and to the nearest town or city should be noted. If necessary, a sketch may be made of the immediate surroundings, and another of neighboring districts, but suitable maps may replace the latter. The recording of the odometer should be noted; it is best to ask an expert whether anything of special importance from the car's computer in later models can be downloaded. The amount of gasoline should also be checked. The last routes taken in the navigation system or Global Positioning System (GPS) should be looked at to determine where the car might have come from and where it was headed. The account information from automatic toll collection devices, such as EZPass in the northeastern region of the United States, should be checked to establish when and where a vehicle might have been (Figure 17.1). An attempt is also made to determine whether the vehicle stopped at that point for some reason unforeseen by the driver, for example, engine trouble, depleted gasoline supply, inability to drive further, and so on. The floor in front of the driving seat is examined carefully. Preferably all dust and dirt at this place should be kept. The exterior is examined for the presence of any evidence that might fall off when the vehicle is driven or towed away.

An initial examination of the vehicle should be made for evidence that is easily collected or that might be damaged or destroyed when the vehicle is towed away. If possible, the detailed investigation of a vehicle should not be carried out

Figure 17.1 Electronic devices such as GPS navigation systems and/or EZPass toll collection transponders in cars can provide a wealth of information to investigators.

at the place where it is found. The examination site should be in the vicinity where the vehicle was found, if possible. A long tow can cause a deposit of dust or dirt that may completely destroy any possibilities of finding probative evidence.

After removing the vehicle to a sheltered place, a thorough investigation is made of the location where the vehicle was initially found and the surrounding area. It is possible that the suspect, after committing the crime, might have dropped or thrown away objects that show the route taken or supply incriminating evidence. The investigation should be done quickly, especially in highly traveled areas or if rain or snow is anticipated. If larger areas or stretches of road must be searched, it may be advisable to call for a search team; however, they must first be instructed in how to act if they find any evidence. A detailed investigation of the vehicle should be done only after it is completely dry.

The floor of the vehicle and seats should be examined first; only after this is done are any fingerprints developed and DNA swabs collected. It may be convenient first to examine the outside of the vehicle in order to avoid the risk of anyone heedlessly destroying evidence or leaving prints. Next, the contents of center consoles should be examined and documented. The contents of the glove compartment and any other storage spaces should be examined and noted in a similar way. In and under the seats, objects are sometimes found that the suspect has dropped. Any bloodstains in and on the vehicle should be examined for the direction of fall, the height of fall, the direction of movement, etc., after which they are photographed. The engine and trunk of the car should also be examined. In the investigation of a vehicle in which a crime of violence has been committed, it is advisable after collecting the evidence, to take measurements of the amount of room in the vehicle. A question may arise about the possibility of a suspect swinging an instrument, handling a firearm, and other such acts. Any evidence of the vehicle being used in any crime should be noted; safe paint and insulation in the trunk, outlines of boxes or tools, even bullet holes should be sought. The Vehicle Identification Numbers (VIN) should be checked in order to detect alterations in the identity of the vehicle. Any damage to the vehicle may indicate the abandonment and reported "theft" were to hide an accident. The exact condition of damage should be carefully noted and photographed.

Under suspicious circumstances, the temperature of the water in the radiator and the surrounding air temperature should be noted. From these data, it may be possible to establish the duration of time since the vehicle was abandoned. A careful search of the trunk is indicated in those cases in which it carried a dead body. If the victim was killed in one location, transported in the vehicle, and dropped at another site, minimal evidence may be found in the trunk. In some cases, the interior may have been cleaned to remove traces of blood. In such cases, it may be worthwhile to remove the liner to search for blood that might have seeped through and was not noticed by the suspect. Removal of the seats should also be considered for a thorough search. If noted, the smell of decomposition should be noted. Weapons, tools, and sometimes trace evidence that may link the victim to the vehicle should be searched for and collected. In cases of homicide, the seat covers or the entire seat can be submitted to the laboratory for testing for the presence of blood.

HOMICIDE IN A VEHICLE

Taxi cab, Uber, or Lyft drivers are sometimes the victims of robberies, often combined with an assault that may be fatal. For a desperate suspect, it is a simple matter to order the driver to a desolate area, assault the driver from behind without too great a personal danger, and then rob him. Because it would be dangerous to attack the driver while the vehicle is moving, the driver might be asked to stop under some pretext. After the robbery is completed it is not uncommon for the attacker to hide the victim and then drive the car as far away as possible from the scene.

In cases where the robbery victim dies, one can expect to find the vehicle and the victim in different locations; sometimes, the vehicle is found first. Therefore, there is a great risk that the examination of the vehicle is difficult or impossible because an overzealous officer has the vehicle removed, believing that it is only a case of "joyriding." For this reason, every officer who finds an abandoned vehicle should suspect the worst and exercise extreme care. After a license check has revealed that the car may have been at the scene of a crime, the procedure suggested in the section "Abandoned vehicles" should be followed and the procedure for the specific type of crime. The search of a vehicle in which a homicide was committed must be conducted with the same degree of care as would be used to search an indoor or outdoor crime scene involving a murder. Because of the cramped working area, it is essential to exercise care to not destroy any physical evidence in the vehicle. The procedures discussed elsewhere in the text for processing the crime scene are generally the same for a car.

Cases involving sabotage or acts of terrorism in which an explosive charge blew up the vehicle require a thorough investigation to recover as many parts of the device as possible. The debris from the explosion may cover a wide area, and a careful and systematic search is necessary to locate, chart, and recover as many pieces of the damaged vehicle and bomb as possible. Fragments of a timing mechanism, electrical devices, wires, and batteries, as well as explosive residue, may prove to be valuable evidence in the investigation. CAUTION: investigators should be extremely careful since secondary devices can be used to cause maximum casualties to first responders and investigators!

HIT-AND-RUN INVESTIGATION

Hit-and-run cases include two types: damage to other vehicles or property and death or injury to individuals. In both cases, physical evidence can assist in identifying the hit-and-run vehicle, establishing a connection between the vehicle and the victim or crime scene, and reconstructing the scene in general to determine the events surrounding the crime. Cases involving damage to other vehicles are often the result of driving under the influence or in a careless or reckless manner. The usual types of physical evidence found at the scene are paint chips or scrapings, glass, pieces of headlamps or plastic reflectors, and pieces from the grillwork of the vehicle. Most of these items are very small and therefore easily overlooked when searching the scene. Also, the impact from the crash may throw certain items some distance from the vehicle, and loose or broken parts still attached to the hit-and-run vehicle may subsequently fall off at a considerable distance from the scene. These considerations make a search of a greater area important in these cases (Figure 17.2).

The hit-and-run crime scene often has a factor not present at other scenes: traffic. If the fatality occurred in a busy intersection or on a well-traveled street, the officer may feel pressured to complete the investigation more quickly. Although time may be a consideration, it should not deter the investigator from doing a thorough and complete job of processing the scene. Overall crime scene photos should be taken as well as photographs from different views (Figure 17.3). Close-up photographs of the victim as well as of items of physical evidence must be taken. If the crime occurred at night, portable lighting should be brought in so that the area is adequately lit. The area should be examined for tire impressions and particularly for skid marks, which can be used to determine the direction and speed of the suspect vehicle.

Trace items of evidence present on the victim's body are also important. Care must be taken when moving the deceased so as not to lose valuable traces. When the deceased is brought to the morgue, clothing should be carefully searched for paint, glass, and other parts from the suspect's vehicle. These items should be packaged, tagged, and submitted to the crime laboratory for examination. If the victim was on a bicycle or motorcycle, it should be carefully examined. Various types of trace evidence, such as paint, may be present that can be used to tie the suspect vehicle to the crime. Lights from the victim's vehicle should be recovered and submitted to the laboratory to determine if they

Figure 17.2 This close-up of a physical match of broken pieces of a license plate holder proved a vehicle was associated with a hit-and-run accident. (*Courtesy of Los Angeles County Sheriff's Department.*)

Figure 17.3 In this busy street in New York City, officers, and CSIs must work expeditiously to process the scene so that the street can be opened back up to traffic.

were operational and whether they were on or off. Clumps of soil or dirt found at the scene should be documented and collected. These can be compared with dirt found on the undercarriage of the suspect's vehicle and may demonstrate a connection.

The scene should be examined for specific damage to the unknown vehicle. Broken parts of the vehicle should be collected for possible physical matching. In certain cases, the vehicle's make and sometimes the model can be determined by these parts. This information may be helpful if the investigator contacts automobile body shops or parts stores to determine if anyone recently came in to have a vehicle repaired. Occasionally, the force of impact is so great that impressions from the vehicle are made on the victim's body or clothing. Such evidence should be photographed and preserved for later comparison.

Paint chips are especially important items of physical evidence. If they are sufficiently large chips, it is possible to fit them physically into the vehicle in a jigsaw puzzle fashion. Paint will, at a minimum, be useful to determine the color of the hit-and-run vehicle, and in some instances, the make of the vehicle and year can be determined through laboratory examination. Further, physical and chemical comparisons of paint recovered at the scene can sometimes be made with that from the suspect's vehicle. Painted surfaces also tend to be repainted over time, building a characteristic layer structure that can also be used as a point of comparison. Tape should not be used to lift or collect the paint, as the adhesive may interfere with the paint analysis.

As part of the autopsy procedure, specimens of the victim's blood and hair should be collected for later testing. A toxicological sample of blood should be taken to determine whether the victim was under the influence of alcohol or other drugs. Clothing should be retained for fabric and fiber exemplars in addition to examining for patterns and other traces present. Once the suspected vehicle is found it should be taken off the road to a nearby place for examination.

When the vehicle is first found, if any evidence is noted that might be lost in moving the vehicle to a garage, it should be collected. If the owner of the vehicle claims that the car had been stolen, fingerprint examination is especially important to help prove or disprove this contention. The exterior of the vehicle should be thoroughly searched, including the undercarriage. The vehicle should be placed on a hydraulic lift to facilitate this examination. Evidence such as hair, blood, skin, and fabric and fiber evidence may be located there. Specimens of grease and dirt should be collected for comparison with debris found on the victim. The front area of the vehicle and the hood should be thoroughly examined. Occasionally, fabric impressions from the impact appear in the dust on the bumper. These should be carefully photographed with a scale and if possible the bumper or fender should be removed and submitted to the laboratory. All broken parts and damage to the vehicle are important items of evidence. Damage to the front end such as broken grills, headlights, scratched paint, and other damages are to be carefully noted and, if possible, removed and submitted to the laboratory. In some instances, evidence from the motorcycle or bicycle that the vehicle hit may be present; these items should be preserved.

Known specimens from the hit-and-run vehicle should be collected. These especially include paint that should be collected in the area of any damage to the vehicle. If scrapes containing other paint material are noted, these too should be collected to be compared with the victim's vehicle. In some cases, the victim may have been hit and thrown onto the vehicle hood or windshield. Fingerprints belonging to the victim as well as hairs, fibers, and blood should be searched for with this in mind. If the windshield is broken, glass should be collected and a search made for hairs and blood. Headlamps and taillights should be examined to determine whether they work and, if possible, they should be sent to the laboratory. Examination of the filament can determine if the lights were on or off at the time of impact. Broken headlamp lenses and signal light reflectors should be removed for comparison with evidence collected at the scene. Sometimes it is possible to make a physical match with these items.

Case Review

During a sailboat race on Lake Ontario, one boat was struck by lightning. The crew radioed to the race organizer that they were dropping out of the race and heading for Rochester, New York; this was the last contact with them. No SOS and no search for the boat were undertaken. Three days later, an American fisherman found two bodies (tied together) floating with a beacon light attached to one of them. The beacon was lit at the time of the discovery. When the beacon later came into possession of Canadian authorities, the bulb was burned out. At the inquest, there was apparently conflicting evidence: the type of light bulb (no.13) used can only last for approximately two hours with a set of new batteries. Thus, if the fisherman found the beacon lit, the boat must have capsized only hours before the bodies were discovered. The examining pathologist from the U.S. determined the bodies had been dead for approximately 70 hours. Scanning electron microscopic (SEM) examination of the filament discovered two breaks, both while the bulb was hot (ON)—an indication that the bulb had a "second life." The conflicting evidence can be explained with the bulb's "two lives" (although it is not proof). In the case of the very fine filament in the lamp, the SEM has a considerable advantage over conventional microscopes in demonstrating the breaks and re-established contact by providing a clear photograph with good depth of focus and a reflection-free image (Figure 17.4).

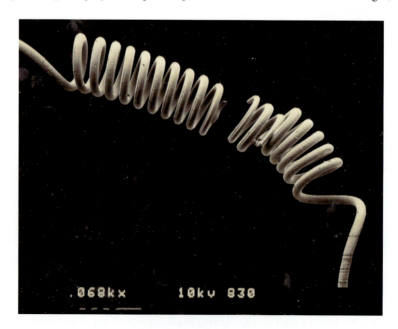

Figure 17.4 A scanning electron microscope (SEM) image of a lamp filament showing that there had been a break that reconnected and then a second break. (*Courtesy of the Centre of Forensic Science, Toronto, Canada.*)

If tire impressions were made at the scene, photographs containing a scale should be made of each tire. Inked tire impressions on paper can be made for comparison with tire impressions located at the crime scene. If the suspect driver is apprehended soon after the hit-and-run incident, a blood sample should be obtained. The sample should be submitted to the laboratory for testing for alcohol or other drugs to determine if the suspect was under the influence.

MARKS FROM VEHICLES

Vehicle marks are composed of tracks of wheels or runners. In a specific case, there may also be an indication of a particular type of load, for example, slipping branches in a load of wood or ends of logs in a load of lumber, the smell of fuel oil, or lubricating oil, etc.

WHEEL MARKS

With the aid of wheel marks, the direction of movement can be determined. When the ground is damp, the underlayer on which the wheel rolls forward is compressed and the bottom of the mark is formed as a series of steps. The compressed clods of earth in the mark are lifted in the same direction as the wheel is rolling. To assist the memory in this respect, it is easy to remember this rule: for the mark to become level again, the wheel must roll in the opposite direction. A vehicle that travels in a straight line actually leaves only the track of the rear wheels; to observe marks of the front wheels, it is necessary to find someplace where the vehicle has turned sharply or reversed.

In examining wheel marks, it is necessary to look for places showing defects or repairs in the tires. With the aid of successive marks of this type, the circumference of the tire can be determined. The track is measured between the center points of the two-wheel marks.

Preservation is achieved by photography and casting selected points showing characteristic marks or wear. When photographing, a scale is placed across the track and another along one side of it. Casting is done in the same way as for foot impressions (discussed in Chapter 9). In examining vehicle marks, it should be noted whether wheels that follow one another go in the same track or whether there is any deviation. If dual wheels are found, both tread marks should be recorded simultaneously because the relationship of one tread pattern to the other provides additional characteristics for the identification of the vehicle.

SKID MARKS

The speed of the suspect vehicle at the time of impact is sometimes at issue. If skid marks are present at the scene, a traffic officer with training in skid mark interpretation should be contacted and requested at the scene. Based upon factors such as the length of the mark and the coefficient of friction of the road surface, an approximation of the speed at which the suspect vehicle was traveling may be calculated.

AIRBAGS

The examination of deployed airbags can establish that a suspect was inside a vehicle at the time of vehicle impact and/or determine the position of the vehicle occupants prior to the crash. Airbags inflate when very hot gas is produced by a chemical reaction of solid propellant. This gas can leak through the seams of the airbag and singe the clothing of the occupants with a distinctive pattern. A particulate residue from the propellant can also be found on the hands and/or clothing of front-seat occupants. Airbags, if they have been deployed, can be cut out and sent to the lab for trace analysis and/or DNA typing. Make sure to mark the orientation of the airbag prior to removal. This can help determine who was driving the vehicle and the time of impact.

Investigations involving motor vehicles occur in many cases, such as vehicle thefts, abandoned vehicles, homicides, hit-and-run investigations, and so on. Physical evidence consisting of fingerprints, tool marks, glass, paint, fabric impressions, tire marks, physiological fluids, hairs, fibers, and the like should be carefully searched for, collected, and documented as in all crime scene investigations.

DIGITAL AUTOMOTIVE IMAGE SYSTEM (DAIS)

The Digital Automotive Image System (DAIS) is an investigative forensic program of automotive images. The system provides law enforcement personnel with a means of searching a database of vehicles to find a particular car. Multiple views of each car manufactured in the United States can be found by searching any combination of year, make, model, class, door number, and features. DAIS has been successfully used to assist in the investigation of bank robberies, child abductions, missing person cases, and others. This system is not available to the public and is restricted to members of law enforcement only.

Further Reading

Houck, Max M., ed. *Forensic Engineering.* Elsevier, 2017.

Stauffer, Eric, and Monica Bonfanti. *Forensic Investigation of Stolen-recovered and other Crime-related Vehicles.* Elsevier, 2006.

Struble, Donald E., and John D. Struble. *Automotive Accident Reconstruction: Practices and Principles.* CRC Press, 2020.

Chapter Questions

1. List the various types of criminal investigations that can be associated with a vehicle.
2. Which of the following motives would explain why a suspect stole a vehicle?
   a. Joyriding.
   b. To sell the parts for profit.
   c. To flee the scene of a crime.
   d. All of the above.
3. When processing a vehicle, why is it important to collect the most fragile evidence first?
4. Describe the proper procedure for examining an abandoned vehicle.
5. (True or false) The search of a vehicle in which a homicide was committed should be conducted with the same degree of care as would be used when conducting the search of an indoor or outdoor scene involving a murder.
6. When processing a scene involving the use of a vehicle as an improvised explosive device, which task is the most important?
   a. Finding out the exact time the bomb went off.
   b. Finding all metal parts of the vehicle.
   c. Finding as many parts of the explosive device as possible.
   d. Calling the FBI.
7. You are the lead CSI processing the scene of a hit-and-run accident. Which of the following pieces of evidence would you be most concerned about collecting?
   a. Fingerprints on the steering wheel.
   b. Mud samples from the tires.
   c. Tire standards from the victim's vehicle.
   d. Paint transfer on the victim's vehicle.
8. Which of the following can be used to determine the direction and speed of a suspect's vehicle in a hit-and-run?
   a. SEM analysis of the pieces of rubber from the tire.
   b. Skid marks.
   c. Glass debris.
   d. Location of vehicle parts.
9. How is the Digital Automotive Image System (DAIS) used?
10. How would you properly preserve wheel marks?

Chapter 18

Death Investigation

Of all major investigations, death investigation requires the greatest effort on the part of the CSI. The investigator is responsible for collecting an extensive amount of evidence and coordinating information from a variety of sources including witnesses, suspect(s), case detectives, forensic pathologists, criminalists, and district attorneys. Death investigation requires a team effort; only through the cooperation of persons from many disciplines, coordination of efforts, rigorous attention to detail, and adherence to protocols can a successful conclusion of an investigation be realized. This chapter brings together many of the concepts discussed previously in the text and examines areas unique to the investigation of death.

The finding of a dead body is usually the starting point and initial focus of the death investigation. (Occasionally, a death must be investigated even when a body has not been found, though this is far more difficult.) The rules for the first officer who arrives at the crime scene are the same as outlined in earlier chapters. The most important thing for the first officer to do upon arriving at the scene is to secure the area. The officer's main priority is to ensure their own personal safety first! This means making sure that no suspects are hiding at the crime scene that might be a threat. Once the scene is secure, the first officer can administer life saving measures to victims and summon EMS if needed. Once this task is accomplished. homicide investigators are notified if there is a suspicion of a murder. Determination of suspicious death at this point is critical. In some cases the first officer to arrive at the scene has erred and pronounced the death to be from natural causes, only to learn at a later time that the cause of death was the result of an unnoticed bullet wound. The point is that care and attention to detail are critical in these types of cases.

Once the investigation has begun, the CSI should attempt to find and identify all evidence that may be associated with the case. Even items that may seem unimportant and appear to be of no value should be considered potential evidence. In murder investigations, there is often an abundance of evidence even in cases in which the suspect has attempted to clean up after the crime. Even in a so-called "perfect murder," there will be much evidence to aid in the crime's solution. In fact, there is no perfect murder—only cases in which a deliberate killing could not be successfully prosecuted beyond a reasonable doubt.

In most cases, it is not difficult to determine that the suspicious death was the result of a murder rather than a suicide or accident. More difficult are those cases that are staged, so at first glance they seem to be an accident or suicide. In those cases, the first officer and/or investigator must be thoroughly familiar with all aspects of homicide investigation. The initial analysis of the situation and the evaluation of the case require at least as much knowledge as the subsequent investigation of the crime scene.

The officer should keep in mind that if a supposed suicide is judged to be a murder, a serious error has not been committed, even though the investigation may become more extensive than is necessary. If, on the other hand, a murder is judged a suicide, the officer has not only failed in the investigation but may also have made the solution of the crime and the apprehension of the killer more difficult, if not impossible.

MURDER, SUICIDE, OR ACCIDENT?

When evaluating whether the deceased died from an accident or suicide, or if death was caused by another person, it is generally best to suspect the worst—murder. Even if circumstances give the overwhelming appearance of suicide or accident, the investigation should be conducted in as much detail as possible. Murderers have been known to intentionally stage the death to appear to be an accident or suicide. The investigating officer must be aware of this possibility. Only through systematic and accurate investigation can a deception be revealed as that of homicide.

When investigating cases of sudden death, the officer should attempt to evaluate the circumstances revealed at the crime scene as quickly as possible. The following questions should try to be answered as soon as possible: What was the cause of death? Could the deceased have produced the injuries or brought about the circumstances that caused the death? Are there any signs of a struggle? Are there defensive wounds on the victim? Where is the weapon, instrument, or object that caused the injuries, or traces of the medium that caused death? Are there any witness statements? Although these are only some of the many questions that will arise in a death investigation, they are probably the most important ones for beginning the continued investigation.

Cause of Death

The first question the officer is required to answer is: what was the *cause of death*? It should be noted here that the determination of the cause of death at this time is the *apparent* cause of death and not the *actual* cause of death to be determined by the medical examiner through an autopsy. Determining the cause of death, whether it involves stabbing, shooting, strangulation, or other means, represents a starting point for the investigator and helps him/her to begin putting the facts and circumstances behind the death into focus.

In evaluating the cause of death, it is very useful for the investigating officer to have a good knowledge of the appearance of different types of injuries and wounds. The investigator is not expected to have the same expertise in this area as that of the forensic pathologist or medical examiner, but he or she must have at least a working knowledge of the subject in order to take the initial steps of the death investigation. An erroneous estimate of the cause of death may lead the investigation in the wrong direction and may even jeopardize the solution of the crime. For example, if an inexperienced officer mistakes a gunshot injury for a stab wound, the entire investigation may be sidetracked.

The officer should not confuse experience with expertise, for it is the province of the pathologist to determine the cause of death, no matter how much experience the investigator has. The officer's primary duty should be to keep in mind that success is usually the result of cooperation and teamwork between the medical examiner and the homicide investigator.

The Medicolegal Investigator (MLI)* can also play an important role at the death scene. In some jurisdictions, these professionals are physician assistants that have extensive training in medicine and death investigation. They respond to death scenes in order to assist the medical examiner in their determination of cause and manner of death. The cause of death coupled with other evidence at the death scene helps the medical examiner to determine the manner of death: homicide, suicide, accidental, natural, or undetermined.

SUICIDE

Could the deceased have produced the injuries or brought about the effect that caused death? A determination of whether death was the result of suicide or murder is extremely important in the initial phase of the investigation. Usually the decision is based upon an evaluation of the injuries that resulted in the death and other factors about the deceased's mental and emotional state prior to the death.

The common modes of death by suicide are drowning, hanging, shooting, poisoning/over dosing, jumping from heights, cutting arteries, stabbing, strangulation, and so-called "suicide by cop" (the intentional act of provoking a police officer to shoot). These factors must be considered along with the physical and psychological ability of the deceased to accomplish the act.

---

* The American Board of Medicolegal Death Investigators (www.abmdi.org) certifies individuals who have proven knowledge and skills necessary to perform medicolegal death investigations.

A detailed examination of the crime scene should be undertaken to determine if the facts are consistent with the theory of suicide. For example, it is reasonable to expect the means of death, such as a weapon or poison, to be close at hand and in proximity to the body. Failure to discover a weapon in the case of a suspected suicide makes that possibility unrealistic.

The nature and position of the injuries are useful considerations in drawing a conclusion. Hesitation marks are quite common in suicide cases involving slashing of the wrists. Similarly, gunpowder tattooing located around a gunshot wound is consistent with the firing of a weapon at close range. Such facts would be consistent with suicide. Defense wounds, however, are not expected to be found on the hands or arms of a suspected suicide (Figure 18.1a and b).

Wound location should be considered. The wound location should be within reach of the deceased, in the case of stabbing or cutting, generally on the wrists, neck, abdomen, or chest. A wound to the back of the head would raise suspicion. Also, wounds are generally grouped in one area, as in the case of hesitation marks on the wrist.

In suicides involving handguns, the victim usually drops the weapon or might throw it up to several feet away when the arms are flung outward. In such cases the floor or ground should be examined for dents or scratches resulting from the impact. Occasionally, the weapon is found in the victim's hand, but this is usually due to the gun or hand having been supported in some way at the moment of discharge.

No blood on the insides of the hands or on the corresponding parts of the gun grip is usually a good indication that the victim fired the shot if the rest of the hand is bloody. The same condition applies to knife handles when the victim causes the slashes. Bloodstains on the palm of the hand and the grip of the gun do not necessarily indicate murder. However, there is reason to be suspicious if the blood marks on the hand and grip do not match. In some cases a murderer has placed a gun in the victim's hand after rigor mortis has set in.

Someone found dead in a room in which the door is locked from the inside is usually considered to be a case of suicide or natural death. The crime scene investigator should not, however, be satisfied with this simple conclusion. Because there are methods by which doors, windows, or other openings can be "locked" from the outside, the investigator should pay particular attention to unusual traces and marks on doors, locks, latches, windows, etc.

Suicide by jumping from buildings or bridges is not uncommon in large cities. The body may land at some considerable distance from the perpendicular. For example, in a jump from an 80-foot vertical cliff, the body was found 42 feet from the base. This circumstance may seem suspicious, but it is explained by the fact that the force of an outward jump continues to act on the falling body.

A determination of suicide should also be based on interviews with the deceased's relatives and friends and on information from a physician or psychologist under whose care the victim may have been. Instances in which the individual had a history of suicide threats or suicidal tendencies are significant to the investigation. A thorough search for a suicide note at the crime scene, as well as at the victim's residence and workplace, is important. Although such notes are frequently found in plain view, usually near the body, the note may have been written earlier and left in another location. In some instances, several notes have been written and placed around the house or even mailed to friends or relatives. The note should be examined by a document examiner to verify its authenticity. A forensic linguist may also

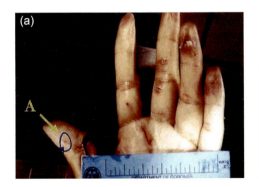
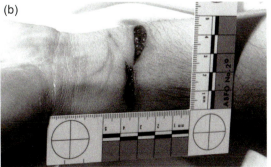

Figure 18.1 Investigators need to be able to distinguish between (a) defensive wounds and (b) hesitation marks. *Courtesy of the Los Angeles County Sheriff's Department and Coroner, respectively.*

be asked to determine authorship attribution. The investigator should collect known handwriting exemplars for this purpose and search for the writing instrument and paper used. The document and envelope should also be examined for latent fingerprints and/or DNA. In most jurisdictions the medical examiner takes custody of the suicide note and not law enforcement.

Motives for suicide should be considered. A terminal illness may prompt an individual to take his life so the investigator should gather information from the deceased's physician, prescriptions, medical records, etc. Poor financial situations may also be a cause and an investigation of the person's finances and debts should be undertaken. Other motives such as marital or family problems, high stress, and psychological problems should also be investigated. Cases of bullying have caused young people to take their life. Investigating a young person's social standing at their school, a review of their social media accounts, and interviewing teachers and classmates should be done if the suicide victim is a young person.

In cases of mental disorder, the killing of family members might precede a suicide. These cases must be investigated as thoroughly as other homicides. If the killer in such an instance survives an attempted suicide, it will be necessary to produce evidence about the mental state of the defendant. Psychiatric evaluation of the defendant may be influenced by the findings at the crime scene. Even if the suicide victim does not survive, the investigation must be conducted with care. Inheritance and insurance matters will be influenced by the order in which the victims died.

Case Review

On Thursday, May 14, 1998, at 03:48 a.m. the police at Haukiputaa municipality in northern Finland were informed about a dead man who lay on a bicycle lane on an Iijoki river bridge. In the crime scene investigation it was found out that the decedent, a man of 65 years of age, was shot. A bullet had hit his face on the right side, penetrated the skull and came out from behind the left ear. The autopsy revealed that it had been a close range shot with the barrel of the gun touching the skin. No weapon was found on the scene. The decedent was wearing standard outdoor gear, with a glove in his left hand. His wallet and some documents were found beside the body, as well as a bicycle which was found out to belong to the deceased. There were blood spots on the handrail of the bridge and on the bicycle. A car owned by the deceased was found at a cemetery gate half a kilometer from the scene. There were no eyewitnesses but a shot had been heard by people living nearby.

The investigators found out that the decedent had been returning from a trip with his old bicycle on the roof rack of his car and had some 50 km left to drive home. He had spent the previous night with a friend and had told him that he was seriously depressed.

Already at an early stage of the investigation the Haukiputaa police suspected that the case was in fact a carefully planned suicide. The police believed that the decedent had killed himself on the scene using his rifle and had supported it on the bridge handrail and his bicycle. It was believed that the gun had fallen into the river after the shot. Because of a very strong current in the river, it was not possible to search for the rifle by diving until that July. No gun was found.

On September 4, 1998, a wooden block, approximately 50 cm in length, was brought to Haukiputaa police (Figure 18.2a). Inside it there was a Tikka brand hunting rifle, shortened at both ends (Figure 18.2b). There was

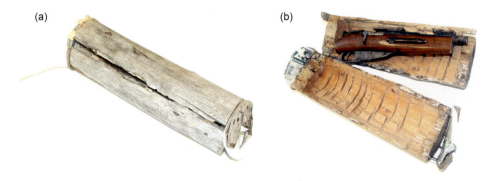

Figure 18.2 (a) Block of wood found at sea. (b) Shortened rifle found in wood. (*Courtesy of Kimmo Himberg, Finland Police, Finland.*)

a hole in both ends of the block and a string bound to the trigger and exiting out through the hole. The production number of the gun showed it to belong to the deceased. The wooden block had been found from the sea in the village of Olhava, approximately ten km from the Iijoki Bridge. The block had been washed to the shore. The person who found it took it to the nearest police station in the city of Oulu. Its origins were found through police databases.

Cases of suicide in which none of the commonly accepted motivations is apparent—even after some investigation—do occur. The opinions of relatives or friends of the deceased who are reluctant to accept the fact of suicide should not unduly influence the investigator. In many cases, the motivations for suicide are so deeply hidden that they may remain a mystery forever.

SIGNS OF STRUGGLE

If obvious signs of a struggle are found at the scene of a death, the case may be decided from the start as one of death by violence by the action of another person. In a room, the signs of a struggle generally consist of bloodstains, pulled-out hair, overturned or displaced articles of furniture, rumpled rugs, marks of weapons, and injuries caused by the deceased in self-defense.

Signs of a struggle show most clearly when an injured victim retreated or when an attempt was made to avoid the attack. From the visible signs, the course of events can often be reconstructed. Bloodstains can be considered the best clues for crime scene reconstruction. Generally, no bloodstains are produced during the first stage of the attack before bleeding has commenced. If victims do not immediately become unconscious at the first blow, stab, cut, or shot, it can nearly always be assumed that their hands will become covered with blood from touching the injured parts of their body. If victims attempt to escape or resist, their blood covered hands leave marks that often indicate their position in certain situations. After a struggle in a furnished room, a surprisingly large number of marks of bloodstained hands may be found on the legs of tables and chairs. A frequently occurring bloodstain is the typical one that comes from bloody hair. Bloody hair imprints are often found on the underside of tables and chairs.

The crime scene should be carefully searched for bloody prints on doors (and especially keys, door handles, and knobs), telephones, hung-up clothes, draperies, curtains, and the like. If blood spatter appears on a door, it is not sufficient to state on which side but it is also important to consider the position of the door when the blood spatter event occurred, and from what direction it came.

Blood spatter can indicate how far the drawer of a piece of furniture was pulled out or whether the door of a closet, kitchen cupboard, or another piece of furniture was open during a struggle. An important clue is a footprint in blood. Usually such prints are blurred and not suitable for identification. However, it may be possible to decide whether the footprint was made by the victim or the suspect. Don't forget to pull down any window shades to look for marks or stains on them. The parts of the legs of tables and chairs that touch the floor should also be examined. Any voids, or areas that show an absence of blood, may be important clues.

Pulled-out hair found in a case of death from violence is a clear indication that a struggle took place. When found, it should be collected immediately because it can easily disappear or alter its position from the results of a draft.

Overturned and displaced furniture gives a good idea of the direction in which a struggle moved or the route by which the victim attempted to escape. Chairs, pedestals, lamps, and other light pieces of furniture fall in the direction in which the struggling persons are moving. If there is reason to suspect that a criminal has righted overturned furniture, the articles should be examined for possible fingerprints or trace DNA. When a print is found on a piece of furniture, its position should be examined carefully; a firm grip on a chair may give rise to the suspicion that the chair was used as a weapon. When heavy furniture has been displaced, the amount of force required and the way in which this force acted should be considered. Furniture placed irregularly often gives the impression that it has been displaced from its position. Marks or scrapings indicate displacement, and the floor generally shows whether furniture has stood in the same place previously. Rumpled rugs often provide signs of a struggle, while marks of sliding on the floor sometimes form a useful guide.

A murder victim lying in a position of self-defense may kick against a wall, the floor, or furniture and the shoes then leave scuff marks, dirt, and rubber scraping from the shoe's heal.

Marks of weapons may occur, e.g., when an ax or other swinging weapon is swung and scrapes the ceiling or slips along a piece of furniture, or when the victim avoids the blow and the weapon hits the wall, floor, or furniture instead. In the case of murder with an ax, baseball bat, or similar weapon, a frequently occurring mark is one formed on walls or ceilings when the criminal swings the weapon up and back before striking. A bloodstained weapon may also leave cast-off patterns on the ceiling or drip patterns on the floor where blood dripped off the weapon. It could also produce a transfer stain on a surface where it was laid down or dropped, resulting from the contact between the bloody weapon and the other surface.

Defense injuries are a good indication that a fight took place. In cases of suicide and accidental death, marks are often found that at first sight appear to be marks of a struggle. Persons considering suicide may take a number of measures at various places to shorten their life. In a state of confusion, the individual may overturn or move furniture and also leave blood and other marks that at first cause suspicion. A careful investigation of the scene, however, can give a clear picture of the true course of events.

In outdoor homicide cases, signs of a struggle may not be as noticeable as those indoors. If a fight preceded the murder, the ground may be trampled. When shoe prints made with shoes of different sizes and appearances are found, or if the marks have the form that results from feet set down obliquely against the ground, these marks can be considered as evidence of a fight. At the scene of a suicide, especially in a case of hanging, the ground may be trampled, but as a rule the marks have the normal appearance of those of a person walking. Other signs of a struggle outdoors may be bloodstains, pulled-out tufts of hair, marks of weapons, and resistance injuries. Broken twigs, trampled leaves, torn-up moss and grass, footprints at places that a person would normally avoid, and other such indications can also be considered signs of a struggle.

LOCATION OF WEAPON

In cases of violent death, the cause of death must be decided as soon as possible so that a search for the weapon, tool, instrument, or other lethal objects can be conducted. The absence of a weapon or instrument at the scene sometimes indicates murder. If a weapon or instrument has been found, then the investigator may make a preliminary decision whether it is a murder or suicide. In searching for a weapon, nothing should be moved or altered at the crime scene. If evidence may be destroyed in the search, then the search should be postponed. If the weapon is found, it should be photographed and described in the position in which it is found. A pathologist should be consulted when it is necessary to determine what kind of object or weapon could have caused the injuries found on the victim.

EXAMINATION OF A DEAD BODY AT THE CRIME SCENE

Before examining a dead body, the police officer should consider all the precautions to be taken during the course of the work. A careless move—even one so slight as undoing a button or lifting a flap of a garment—may subsequently prove to be a mistake. In one case of an overzealous officer proceeded to examine a dead body and attempted to determine the track of a bullet and depth it had penetrated into the body by probing the wound with a pen. Such measures are entirely misguided.

When clothing is found on the body, it should only be removed and examined by the medical examiner at the time the body is examined. If a pathologist is not present the examination should include only the visible parts of the body. The clothing's position and state should be described in the report including, how clothes are buttoned, attached, creased and wrinkled, marked by injuries and stains, and so on. Any marks, cuts, or tears made by paramedics in life saving measures should be noted. Discarded gloves, gauze, bandages, and other medical equipment left at the scene by paramedics should not be confused with actual evidence (a good practice is to designate a place for paramedics to discard their medical waste and equipment outside of the crime scene area). Also, in cases where necessary, paramedics may be asked to provide fingerprint and/or DNA samples for elimination purposes.

The position of the clothes may be of importance. How far the pants are pulled up, for example, whether garments are twisted sideways or pulled down, backwards, or even inside-out, are important to photograph and record in one's notes. Any displacement from the normal position is measured. Buttons and other fastenings, e.g., zippers, safety pins and hooks, should be described. Unbuttoned or torn-off buttons should be indicated, along with any fabric defects. Shirts should be checked to determine if they button right to left or left to right. Sometimes, men wear women's clothes and vice versa.

Folds in the clothes should be examined, especially on the lower parts of the body. The report should indicate whether the folds go horizontally or vertically and if they have resulted from crumpling of the garment. When a body is dragged along, horizontal creases occur that are dirty on the outside but clean in the folds. When a body is lifted or moved by gripping the clothing, characteristic formations are produced. If the raised part of a fold is bloodstained but the inner part is free from blood, then the position of a part of the body when violence was exerted can be determined. If a garment is bloodstained and sharply delineated clean areas are on the inside of the bloodstain, then the fold formation can be reconstructed.

Damage to the clothes occurs from tearing, crushing, cutting, or penetration by edged weapons, ax blows, etc. The damage should be measured and the report should contain notations of the type, position, size, and manner of occurrence of the damage. In pertinent cases, the damage to the clothes should be compared during the autopsy with the position of corresponding wounds on the body. In this way, important information can be obtained regarding a particular body position when the injury was inflicted. Mannequins may be used for this purpose to examine trajectory and other reconstruction scenarios.

Stains may consist of blood, semen, saliva, phlegm, vomit, feces, urine, or other liquid, as well as dust, dirt, or other contamination. They are described with reference to type, location, size, degree of wetness, and, in pertinent cases, direction of flow. If liquid stains go through clothing material it is necessary to determine from which side the liquid has penetrated.

In describing bloodstains on a dead body or crime scene, the terminology generally used has been defined by the AAFS Standards Board (ASB). The recommended terminology along with standardized definitions can be found on their website.* This allows investigators to be on the same page when discussing, writing, or testifying about bloodstain pattern analysis.

Important information can be obtained from blood, saliva, phlegm, vomit, urine, or other liquid stains on a dead body if the direction of flow is observed. Streams of blood may be helpful in the reconstruction of events in a case of death by violence. All marks of blood flowing "in the wrong direction" or against gravity are examined and photographed. These suggest that the position of the body was moved (Figure 18.3).

A special form of bloodstain is expired blood. When a person continues to breathe or cough after blood has entered the air passages, expiration patterns can be found. These sometimes contain air bubbles in them and look similar to other spatter patterns. The presence of air bubbles does always indicate that the blood has been expirated, as air bubbles can also result from a transfer stain. Investigators should be very careful in not overstating opinions resulting from bloodstain pattern analysis.

Occasionally, a case of murder occurs in which the criminal wipes or washes the blood away from the victim. Such cleaning is generally easy to detect, especially when the skin is clean around the wound. Washing or wiping the hands generally leaves a thin rim of blood on the nails near the cuticles. When the blood has coagulated, small rolls of blood and dirt are often formed and penetrate cracks and hollows of the skin. If blood has been washed from the head, this fact is often easily detected by the traces of blood that remain in ears, nostrils, and hair. Moisture around the body may also reveal washing with water.

In connection with the occurrence of blood at the crime scene, some attempt should be made to estimate the amount. If blood has flowed out onto an absorbing layer, the depth of penetration should be noted. Floorboards should be lifted and carpets rolled back to check for pooled blood underneath these types of flooring (Figure 18.4).

---

* https://www.aafs.org/asb-standard/terms-and-definitions-bloodstain-pattern-analysis.

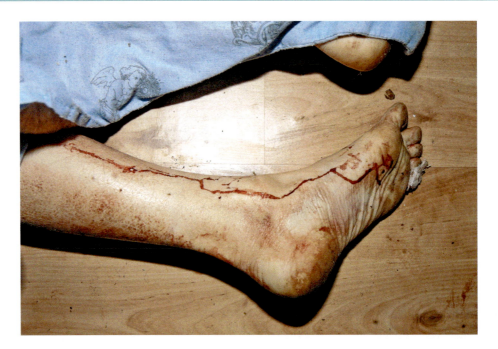

Figure 18.3 The blood on the victim's leg in this photo suggests that the victim had to have been standing at one point when bleeding as blood cannot flow sideways. *(Photo courtesy of Wendy van Hilst, Forensische Opsporing Amsterdam-Amstelland, Amsterdam, Holland.)*

Figure 18.4 Blood revealed under the linoleum floor at a crime scene. *(Photo courtesy of Wendy van Hilst, Forensische Opsporing Amsterdam-Amstelland, Amsterdam, Holland.)*

MURDER

In examining a dead body it is generally possible to take the necessary steps in a certain order, which is a guarantee that nothing will be forgotten or neglected. The various steps in an investigation when a pathologist is present are described next. If the pathologist or medicolegal investigator does not arrive in time, the investigation is carried out in the same way, but the CSI's moves must be evaluated so that clues that only a medical expert is capable of judging and investigating are protected as much as possible.

The first measure that should be taken without delay is to confirm the appearance of signs of certain death, of which the type and development and the time of their confirmation should be noted in the report. This is sometimes performed by paramedics if they are on scene when they fail to revive the victim.

The body is then photographed. Preferably, all photography should be completed before the position of the body is altered. If for some reason a change was made after it was discovered (e.g., when relatives cover the body or EMS performs life saving measures), the actual position should be photographed first, and then the original position may be reconstructed and photographed. The camera should be held in readiness for additional pictures during the course of the examination. In addition to digital photos, different types of digital panoramic recording systems should also be used to accurately document, measure, and map the crime scene. These types of systems are interactive and can be beneficial to quickly and accurately document the crime scene and create a permanent record that can be gone back to days, months, or years after the incident. The scans also serve as excellent courtroom exhibits for juries to show how the crime scene appeared. (Click on the following link using Google Chrome to view interactive panoramic scans of actual crime scenes: www.nytimes.com/interactive/2011/11/20/nyregion/nypd-crime-scene-panoramas.html?_r=0.)

A preliminary examination of the pockets of the dead person may precede the more detailed investigation if considered absolutely necessary. This is to be avoided if possible, but it may be necessary to confirm quickly whether there are any identification documents, wallet, purse, watch, or other valuable articles in the pockets. This examination must be done carefully so that the original position of the clothes can easily be restored later. It should be noted whether the pockets are turned inside out—this may reveal that they have been previously gone through, possibly by the perpetrator.

A written sketch of the position of the body is then made. The body's position in relation to the nearest article of furniture, object, or fixed point is measured and noted. Then the visible clothing is described. The next step is the detailed examination. Only visible details are examined and described. The original position must not be changed. It is preferable to describe the head, then the trunk, arms, and finally the legs.

The head is described and examined in relation to its position with respect to the body, whether the eyes and mouth are open, color of the skin, injuries, presence of blood, frothing at the mouth, state of the hair, presence of saliva, phlegm, vomit, and foreign bodies (soil, sand, vegetable matter, hair, etc.). The direction of flow of liquids is easily determined on the skin of the face and should therefore be noted.

In examining the trunk, notes should be made of its position, any bending or twisting, the position of visible clothing and condition, folds, injuries to the body and clothes, presence of blood, saliva, semen, phlegm, vomit, and foreign bodies.

Then the arms and, finally, the legs are examined in the same way as the trunk. The hands should be given special attention. The presence of rings, jewelry, or watches left by these objects should be noted. Electronic devices, such as Fitbits or iWatches, should also be noted as these electronics can contain information about when the victim was last alive and what they might have been doing. Foreign objects are also examined, especially fragments of hair or skin under the fingernails. The hands should be enclosed in clean paper bags tied securely at the wrists during transport of the body. Collection of fingernail scrapings and/or clippings should be taken during autopsy. When examining the legs, the distance between the knees and between the heels should be measured. Special attention should be given to the soles of the feet or shoes with respect to the presence of blood or other material in which the person may have stepped.

After examining the visible parts of the body, the police officer should attempt to visualize the course of events as deduced from observations. The officer's judgment should not be relied on solely; the opinions of others, especially the pathologist or MLI, should also be considered. From a number of opinions it is often possible to get a good reconstruction of the events.

The underside of the body and those portions covered by clothes should not be examined at the scene, unless it is done in the presence and at the request of the medical examiner or MLI. Normally, the body will not be turned over or undressed until the time of the autopsy. However, after the body has been photographed and described in all pertinent detail and has been lifted onto a stretcher, the area under the body should be examined. A critical piece of evidence may have been hidden under the body, perhaps in a large pool of blood. Bullets, or fragments of bullets, sometimes penetrate a body completely but are stopped by clothing. The projectile may thus roll out of the clothing of the victim and may even be overlooked, unless great care is exercised in lifting and transporting. The relationship between the location of injuries and bloodstains on the floor should also be established.

If possible, the body should be transported in the position in which it was found. If necessary, the clothing can be fixed in its original position by means of pins. In appropriate cases, the body should be moved on a clean sheet of cotton or plastic, body bag, or on an undertaker's impregnated paper sheet. This is partly to protect the body from contamination and partly to prevent minute evidence from being lost. An officer should accompany the body to the hospital, ME's office/morgue, or other place where the autopsy is to take place.

DETAILED EXAMINATION OF THE CRIME SCENE

After the preliminary investigation has shown that death was caused by the intent or agency of another person, or by suicide or accident, the detailed investigation can begin. How thoroughly this is to be done must be decided for each particular case. In suicide or accidental death, the detailed examination can be limited simply to those matters that appear to be directly related to events. If the death is caused by the intent or action of another person, everything should be investigated, even in cases where the criminal has been arrested immediately after the crime and has confessed. (There have been several cases where confessions have been thrown out or disallowed in court, so one should not rely on them exclusively.) In such cases, the investigation should decide whether the statements of the criminal are consistent. In a first statement, a criminal often makes consciously incorrect statements about personal actions in order to create extenuating circumstances. Those who investigate the scene of a crime have an opportunity of producing such an accurate reconstruction of the actual course of events that such an attempt by the criminal to evade cannot succeed.

Before the body is removed, the places at the scene where coroner personnel walked should be examined for evidence that might be destroyed, including the presence of blood. Even if the body is wrapped up well, drops of blood may fall from it as a result of unforeseen circumstances. Such marks can cause much unnecessary work for the investigators later. Those who carry away the body should be warned not to step in any blood.

As a rule, the investigation can then be continued with attention to such details or places where anything of significance might be expected. The CSI then follows a methodically planned examination of the crime scene, which will be the basis for the report of the investigation. It is started at a suitable point and everything is inspected in such a way and in such an order that nothing is forgotten. It may be useful to examine and describe the entrance, doors, and lock arrangements first. Then a description of the room as a whole follows. The length, width, height to ceiling windows, doors, floor covering, paint on walls and ceiling, color of wallpaper, lighting conditions, and other features should be described. Next, the room is described in detail and investigated in a certain order beginning from the entrance or from the place of death. Everything must be examined and described as a coherent whole. For example, if a writing desk is examined, then a description follows of the nearby parts of the floor and walls and also of the surface of the floor under the piece of furniture. As a rule, it is best for the ceiling to be described and examined last and as a whole. If for some reason a place has been examined in detail and described earlier, then a reference to it is put in the notes to facilitate writing of the final report.

In the investigation everything should be noted, even if it appears to have no significance in the case. Such unessential details are sorted out when the report is written, as are similar details that appeared to be important at first but were later found to be immaterial. The notes made at the scene of a crime must not under any circumstances be thrown away but should be placed in the file and kept with the records. Experience shows that such rough notes may be of great importance at some future date if the investigator is required to prove that the examination of certain details was not omitted. It is convenient to develop and preserve finger and palm prints at the same time as the final detailed investigation.

As far as possible, everything should be put back into its original position. When furniture is moved, it should be replaced with the greatest accuracy because the scene must be in its original state in case the suspect or witnesses are returned to the scene for questioning. Before any furniture is moved, a mark should be made around the legs or other suitable parts. Objects placed on furniture can be treated similarly.

A final important step after the sketching of the crime scene is measurement. It is desirable to do this early in the investigation, but this may not have been possible because of a risk that those who did the measuring might have destroyed evidence not yet discovered or produced fresh and misleading clues. One method that can be used is to have a preliminary sketch made as early as possible. Gradually, as the investigation proceeds and before each object is moved, measurements are made and recorded on the sketch. This method is somewhat inconvenient, however, because the measuring cannot be done as systematically as is desirable. Under such conditions, even experienced sketchers can easily forget important measurements. 3-D laser scanners and mapping tool programs, such as the SceneVision-3D®, are excellent tools that can record measurements quickly and accurately. The scanners rotate 360 degrees capturing thousands of laser data points that can be easily fashioned into a 3-D model. This allows for a permanent recording of everything at the crime scene and allows investigators to "return" to the crime scene long after the yellow tape is gone (Figure 18.5).

When there has been a shooting at the crime scene, it is necessary to look for weapons, cartridges, cartridge cases, and bullets. If a weapon is found, it is photographed at that spot, and a chalk line is drawn around it before it is moved. The weapon should always be made safe before sending it to the lab. In cases of presumed suicide, it is necessary to check whether the weapon lies in a place to which it might have dropped or slid. The base on which the weapon lies should always be examined. A dropped or thrown weapon generally leaves a scratch or dent in the furniture or floor, and the absence of such marks should be considered suspicious.

When cartridge cases are found, their position should be noted in the report, on the sketch, and on the envelope into which they are then placed. Bullets and bullet holes are also examined. The place from which the shot was fired can be determined quite accurately from the direction of the bullet penetration—a string is stretched along the calculated path of the bullet. The reconstruction is then photographed. Lasers and dowels can also be used, as well as sequential image burning to demonstrate the trajectory of a projectile using lasers. A bullet that has buried itself in a wall is cut out, but great care must be used so that the tool used does not touch the bullet. In cases of suicide, the shooter may fire one or more trial shots before firing the actual suicide shot. Chemical tests can also be performed to see if the suicide victim was actually the one holding the gun.

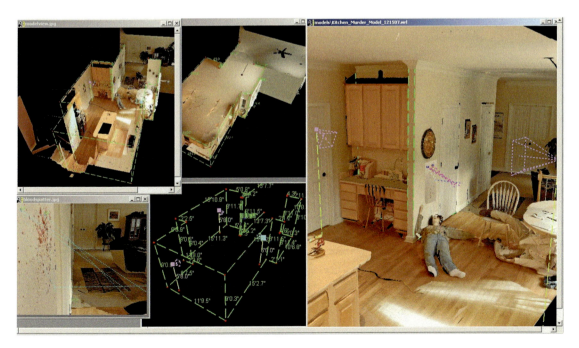

Figure 18.5 3-D models along with measurements of a mock crime scene. (*Photo courtesy of DeltaSphere,* www.deltasphere.com.)

Case Review

In a search after a young successful model and her boyfriend, the police arrived at their apartment where they had been living. The door was locked and the telephone went unanswered. The boyfriend's brother forced entry through a porch door and let the police in. They found the dead bodies of the couple. A loaded gun was found next to the girl's right hand. Her index finger was clutching the hammer of the gun (Figure 18.6a).

The man had two bullet holes in his chest, both fired from close range. The girl had one bullet entry wound in the lower section of her left breast and an exit wound on the right side of her back.

In his preliminary assessment, the medical examiner assumed that before committing suicide the woman killed her boyfriend, since he had been shot twice with heavy caliber bullets, and the gun was found next to her. This was also the message released to the media. After the medical team completed their examinations, Ferrotrace (manufactured by Ezra Technology, Jerusalem, Israel, and distributed by Arrowhead Forensics) was

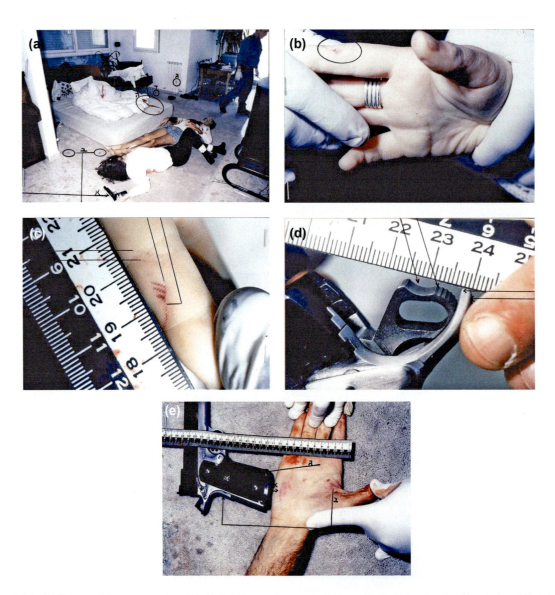

Figure 18.6 (a) The gun lying next to the girl initially led investigators to believe she had shot her boyfriend, then killed herself. (b–d) Further investigation, including testing with Ferrotrace, showed that the woman had never held the gun. (e) Testing of the boyfriend's hand, however, revealed he had held the gun both in the typical shooting position, and in the reverse position indicative of suicide. (*Courtesy of the Division of Identification and Forensic Science, Israel National Police*)

applied to the hands of the two bodies. (The appearance of a violet-magenta stain on the hand is the result of a chemical reaction between the reagent and iron found on the gun).

The reaction on the woman's index finger was exceptionally strong; its shape matched the upper back of the gun's hammer. There was one puzzling question, however, which had to be answered. The reaction on the finger that touched the gun was very intense, but there was no reaction on the palm of the hand (Figure 18.6b–d). The absence of a palm reaction raised the suspicion that the woman never really held the gun, and that it had been placed near her hand only after her death. The primary suspect in moving the gun became her boyfriend's brother, who had helped the police enter the apartment. Ferrotrace examination of the boyfriend's right hand indicated that he held the gun both in regular position (typical of shooting) and in reverse position (typical of suicide, with the thumb on the trigger, and the index and middle fingers on the safety) (Figure 18.6e). The fact that there were two bullet holes in the man's chest and only one in his girlfriend's did not change the police's conclusion that it was he who shot the girl, then committed suicide. Multiple shots as part of suicide are a known phenomenon when the first shot is not immediately fatal.

The following is a list of certain details that should be examined where appropriate. Because it consists partly of items of a changeable nature, they should be done immediately or as soon as possible, especially those easily forgotten or passed over even by an experienced investigator:

Stairs, passages, and entries to the scene, together with streets, passages, and yards in the immediate vicinity. Are there bloodstains or fingerprints on railings (mirrors can be used to help locate these on the underside of railings)? Are objects present that the criminal has dropped or thrown away? Is there illumination? Do trash cans contain evidence? If there is an elevator, the elevator shaft should be examined. Video surveillance footage should also be reviewed to determine possible probative pieces of evidence the suspect might have handled.

Outer doors. Are they bolted and/or locked? Are there marks of breaking in? Does the doorbell work?

Windows. Are they bolted? What is the position of the window-catch? Are there marks of breaking in or a possibility of seeing in? What is the position of curtains and blinds? Are there indications of marks outside the windows? Are there fingerprints present?

Mailbox. What is the date on mail or papers; are they in the right order of time?

Other papers and mail, newspapers, etc. at the crime scene. Are there date marks? Have letters been opened or do papers give the impression of having been read?

Inside doors. Are they bolted and/or locked; on which side is the key?

Hall, entrance. Are clothing and objects present that do not belong to the place and residents there, especially outer garments, headgear, scarves, gloves?

Lighting. Which lights were on when the crime was discovered? What are the electric meter readings?

Television, stereos, Amazon Echo®, Google Home®. Have they been left on or off? Could these electronics have recorded the last words spoken by the victim and/or suspect?

Heating conditions. Is there any fire or embers in fireplaces or any remaining heat? Do not forget to examine ash and burned residues and the setting on the thermostat.

Cooking conditions. Is the oven or stove on or is there any remaining heat? Was food or drink preparation in progress? In what condition is the food in the refrigerator?

Odors. Gas; gunpowder; strong tobacco fumes; alcohol; perfume; decomposition?

Clocks and watches. Are they running and showing the right time? When did they stop? Is there a time set on the alarm clock? What are the timestamps of texts and/or emails sent and received?

Signs of a party. How many bottles are present; are there labels on them and what are their contents (not always the same as label)? Are seals or corks on or in the bottles? How many glasses or cups of different kinds are present; what are their contents and is there a residue or odor in them? Has liquor been spilled or objects overturned? Have cigarette butts and match sticks been thrown on the table or floor? How many persons was the table set for and what dishes? Are there any fingerprints? Are the beverage containers suitable for DNA testing?

Contents of ashtrays. Are there remains of smoked tobacco or brand marks on cigarette butts? How were they extinguished? Are there marks of lipstick, burned matches? Remember that DNA and fingerprints may be present on cigarette butts.

Drawers and compartments in writing desks, cabinets, or other furniture. Are they shut and locked? In which drawer is the key? Have drawers been pulled out or taken away or have objects been taken out of them? Are there signs of disorder such as might result from a hurried search? Are cash, bank books, and objects of value exposed in a conspicuous or easily detected place?

Wastepaper baskets, trash cans. Has any object been thrown there by the criminal? Are there torn letters? Did the perpetrator throw out any latex gloves he might have been wearing?

Kitchen, bathroom, toilet. Are towels, rags, and like objects damp or do they show bloodstains? Are there bloodstains on the counter, bath, sink, toilet, or buckets? Are there objects or suspicious liquids in the water-trap or toilet? Are there fingerprints on any used paper? Is there evidence that the perpetrator tried to clean up?

Damage to ceiling, walls, and furniture. Investigate how it could have occurred in connection with the crime; marks of plaster or paint soon disappear from the floor due to trampling.

Garments taken off. At what places and in what order, beginning from top, were they taken off? Are they turned right side out or inside out? Are they properly hung up or in disorder? Are there clothes in the washing machine? Hamper?

General disorder. Is this typical of violent happenings or a struggle; can it result from lack of cleaning up over a long period, or incidentally, for example, in carrying out ordinary household operations, etc.

Shooting. The investigating officer should be able to account for the actual number of bullets fired together with a corresponding number of cartridge cases, or give a good explanation of why they are not found or cannot be found in the correct number (consider the possibility of a cartridge case getting caught up in the clothes of the dead person and not being found before the autopsy).

Hanging and strangling. Quickly confirm whether the cord used was taken from the scene or locality. Was it strong enough to support the weight of the deceased?

Suicide note. Is it in the handwriting of the victim? Has the writing instrument been found? Has indented writing come through onto the paper underneath? Is there more than one note? Are there fingerprints or DNA of persons other than the deceased?

Hiding places for weapons or objects that the criminal wished to conceal quickly. Some of the places most often forgotten by the investigator are locations above appliances and high furniture or between these and the wall, behind books in a bookcase, among bedclothes in a bed, behind heating elements, and on high shelves in wardrobe, pantry, and kitchen cupboards. Ordinary items with false bottoms sold in spy shops should also be considered, such as cans, books, and the like.

Compost heaps, manure heaps. These are very convenient for concealing objects without distinct signs of digging.

It is suggested in cases of serious crime that after the investigation has been concluded, the crime scene be kept intact until the final report has been written and read through by the superior officer and the prosecutor, recovered evidence has been examined, and the postmortem examination has been completed. It is not uncommon for a second or third visit to the crime scene to be made in order to collect additional evidence. When material recovered for examination has value as evidence, it should be preserved even after the criminal has been tried. There may be a review of the case, perhaps several years or decades later, and the evidence may then need to be produced.

OUTDOOR CRIME SCENES

The examination of a crime scene located outdoors must be planned quickly and carried out as soon as possible. The crime scene should be effectively roped off and the investigator must follow a definite plan of action. Changes in weather conditions may completely jeopardize the chances of finding evidence that is there. A number of different clues easily detected at first may disappear in a very short time, for example, by precipitation, drying, humidity, and animals. Ecological evidence must also be considered, such as soil, pollen, botany, and diatoms (Figure 18.7).

Figure 18.7 This outdoor crime scene from an assault can quickly be altered by weather, animals, etc. Items of evidence must be quickly documented and collected. (*Courtesy of Bode Technology and the Charles County, MD Sheriff's Office.*)

Because bloodstains on grass change color rapidly, they may be difficult to detect. A brief shower may completely wash away smaller stains. Other biological evidence, such as hair, seminal fluid, urine, feces, vomit, saliva, nasal secretions, skin fragments, brain substance, and so on, is quickly changed by drying or may be washed away. During the time of year when insects are particularly plentiful, biological evidence may be destroyed by their action. The path of a person through dewy grass may be discernible to the naked eye, but after an hour or so of direct sunlight the dew is dry and the grass has recovered its original shape. It may subsequently take hours before this track can be followed. Footprints and tire marks should therefore be protected and recorded as soon as possible.

When a shooting has taken place outdoors, the direction of firing must be determined quickly. Fresh twigs and leaves that have fallen to the ground usually mark a bullet's path through foliage, bushes, or hedges. After a few hours, these traces may have taken on the appearance of the surroundings. Evidence of a bullet striking the ground is usually found in the form of dirt or sand thrown over the surrounding vegetation. A passing shower may wash off these traces and make the location of the impact impossible to find. Cartridge cases may be trampled into the ground. A metal detector might then be the only way to find such evidence.

In cases of suspicious death, the officers can anticipate that the person, or persons, who discovered the body did not enter the scene with caution—which is to be expected. One of the first duties of the crime scene investigator is therefore to find out where those persons walked. The record of many cases has shown that clues created by these citizens have caused a tremendous amount of unnecessary work that could have been avoided if the person had been properly interviewed.

Case Review

On a winter day, a neighbor called the police to report the discovery of an apparently deceased female who was located behind his neighbor's residence. He informed the 911 operator that after noticing the body he had proceeded behind the house to confirm his observation. When the officers arrived at the scene, he met him at the front of his neighbor's residence and stated that he had walked around the right side of the home (as viewed from the front) to view the body and returned utilizing the same route. The officer and the caller then proceeded around the right side of the home to view the body together.

When other police officers arrived at the scene, the responding officer had secured the entire scene for protection. He had observed that fresh, undisturbed snow was located to the left and right prior to them walking around the home. The scene was processed with one key piece of evidence in mind; there were only 4 sets of tracks when there should have been 6. The caller had already locked himself into his story multiple times proceeding around the residence to double check on the status of the body therefore raising suspicion.

During the processing of the scene, crime lab personnel discovered additional tracks leading away from the decedent. These tracks did not lead to the front of the house but to the neighbor's backyard through an opening in the fence. Since the caller became the main suspect he was placed under surveillance. Soon after he was observed dumping several trash bags in a dumpster on a neighboring property. The crime lab personnel were called and the bags were retrieved and determined to contain bloody clothing. There was then significant evidence to obtain an arrest warrant for the suspect. (*Provided by Suffolk County Crime Laboratory, New York.*)

In making up a plan of action, officers should decide on a path to be used in going to and from the body. Because this path will be used frequently, it may be marked with stakes. The examination of the body then follows according to the outline given earlier in this chapter. Before too much attention is given to the body, the ground around it should be carefully examined. A second chance may not be available after a number of persons have looked at the body and trampled the area. The area surrounding the central scene should then be examined.

The investigators must try to remember their own tracks so that they can distinguish them from others that may be discovered. On snow-covered ground this is easily accomplished by investigators dragging their feet so that their own tracks become distinctive.

When possible, night time examination of outdoor crime scenes should be avoided. This rule should be followed even when suitable illumination is available. Most clues at outdoor scenes consist of minor changes in the ground cover, such as matted grass, torn moss, broken twigs, indistinct footprints, and the like. Such tracks may be visible from several yards away in daylight but are nearly impossible to detect at night even with powerful illumination. If a scene is viewed at night and an estimate made of the topography, daylight examination may be quite different. Because it is difficult to survey the scene and correctly interpret even gross evidence, it follows that it is even more difficult to find evidence as small as bloodstains, fragments of cloth, and fibers. Such evidence may be overlooked or destroyed if a thorough examination is attempted under poorly lit conditions. In these cases, an officer should be placed at the scene to guard the scene overnight until a proper search can be conducted in the morning.

Prevailing weather conditions or expected weather changes can be important in deciding whether to postpone the examination. If there is a chance of snow or rain, the examination must be started even if important evidence may be destroyed. Depending on the type of crime involved, other weather conditions may also have a certain influence. If snow falls before the examination is completed, some evidence may be covered and not retrieved until the snow has melted. In these situations tents can be set up over the crime scene during snow or rainfall.

Before the arrival of daylight, certain precautions should be taken. Some flash exposures should be taken of the body. The body should then be covered with a clean sheet over which is laid a tarpaulin in order to keep out dust, leaves, and other debris. If the body is suspended, the noose may break, and it is advisable to secure the body with a rope tied loosely around the chest. If the body is on the shoreline, it should be lifted far enough onto the beach so that swells will not make changes on the body.

In taking the photographs and the precautionary measures, the officers should not walk around aimlessly. As described earlier, a path should be selected and marked with stakes. The investigator should, of course, make note of changes that may take place on the body, such as signs of death, moisture on the clothing and under the body, and so on.

DISCOVERING A BODY HIDDEN AT ANOTHER LOCATION

When a homicide victim has been moved from the actual murder scene and hidden at a secondary location, conditions are somewhat different. Although the examination of such places is generally carried out in the same careful way as the primary crime scene, a reliable reconstruction of the crime is usually more difficult. Such locations normally do not yield as much evidence of the perpetrator as the primary scene.

The question often arises of how long the body has been lying at the place where it was found. The vegetation and other surrounding conditions may give some indications. The path over which the body was transported should be established at the outset. This detail should be attended to immediately, especially when there is risk of rain or snow. If the suspect's footprints are not clear enough, the path should be estimated as that most easily traversed if someone were carrying a body. Even when there are no footprints, other signs may be present, such as trampled grass, stains of dripping blood, marks from dragging, broken twigs, etc. If the criminal left the scene by another route, this path should also be examined at that time.

The body should be examined as described earlier in this chapter in the section "Examination of a Dead Body at the Crime Scene." Dust, dirt, and other traces on the skin and clothing that might fall off during transport should be recovered. A preliminary evaluation of such traces may suggest leads for the search for the actual scene. In removing the dead body from the place where it was found, it should be placed in a new body bag, clean plastic sheet or bed sheet that is then wrapped around the body. Blankets and tarpaulins should not be used because one can never be sure that they are absolutely clean. Because it is difficult to examine and recover trace evidence on the body properly, it should be transported intact to the place of autopsy where the detailed examination can take place.

After the body has been removed, the area underneath it should be examined. The amount of blood and body fluids should be estimated. It should also be determined how deeply into the ground such fluids have penetrated. If the murder weapon is expected to be found in the area, a search for it should be started. If branches, straw, and the like were used to cover the body, they should be examined for the possibility that the criminal may have dropped something while engaged in this activity.

INVESTIGATION OF A GREATLY ALTERED BODY OR SKELETON

Often difficulties arise in the identification of a dead body that has undergone such a great amount of alteration that only the skeletal parts remain. Important information can be obtained from a skeleton found whole or dismembered after a very long time or even after burning or other destruction of the body. Clothing or other objects found near the remains can also be used to help identify the deceased (Figure 18.8).

Such bodies or their remains are most frequently discovered outdoors; occasionally, they are found indoors in a cellar, attic, basement, furnace, freezer or other places. The remains may be those of a person who was murdered, run over by a vehicle, or committed suicide, was lost and became the victim of exhaustion or exposure, or was suddenly overcome by sickness and death.

The nature of the place where the discovery is made can vary considerably. Remains may be found under the ground or under a floor or the like; they may be lying in the open, covered with brush, moss, sacks, and so forth, or by overgrown vegetation. If the body was originally in the outdoors then the remains (both bones and clothing) are often dispersed over a large area by animals who have dragged parts away. It is not uncommon for remains and objects to be found several hundred yards away from the main site. This also applies to parts of a dismembered or burned body that have been buried or left on the ground because different parts may have been concealed or buried at different places, often far apart (Figure 18.9).

Foreign objects connected with the body or with transport of the body to the site (bags, sacks, duct tape, cords, etc.), which possibly form the sole proof of a crime and may even indicate how to trace the criminal, may also be found near the remains. A number of cases have occurred in which a correctly performed and accurate investigation of the place of discovery, combined with careful technical and forensic investigation of the remains of the body and other related objects, has led to the identification of the body. In order for the best result to be obtained, the investigator needs a good knowledge of the proper method of investigation and preservation of the remains and objects, and of the factors that affect distribution of the objects within a larger area.

The detective also needs to know the special methods used for further investigation of the discovery and how these methods can assist in determination of gender, age, and race of the deceased and of the time elapsed since the objects were first placed there. This knowledge is absolutely essential if the detective is to pay the necessary attention to the possibly small and apparently insignificant objects that are especially crucial in these respects. The precise determination of the characteristics necessary for establishing age, gender, stature, and so forth must be left to the forensic anthropologist. Likewise, the investigator must use the services of entomologists for the life cycles of insects, of

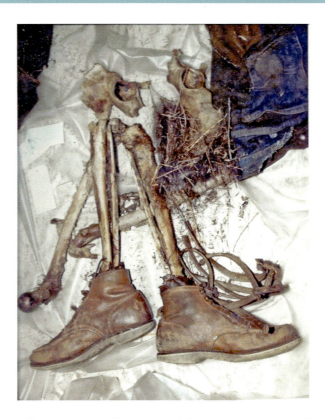

Figure 18.8 Skeletal remains found in remote areas offer a special challenge to the investigator. In this case, absent anything more than part of the pelvis, leg bones and shoes, a forensic anthropologist may only be able to provide the gender, height, and race of the decedent. DNA typing would then be needed to identify the remains using CODISmp (a separate version of CODIS used for missing persons) and the National Missing and Unidentified Persons System (NamUs) database. Missing person reports and debris scattered in the vicinity of the remains can offer additional information. (*Courtesy of Los Angeles County Sheriff's Department.*)

Figure 18.9 A body was dumped in a wooded area. By the time it was discovered about 24 hours after the killing, animals had already attacked and eaten a significant amount of it. (*Courtesy of Los Angeles County Sheriff's Department.*)

botanists for growth rates of roots, grasses, and other plants, of meteorologists for weather conditions that might suggest the time of repose of the body, as well as any other experts whose special knowledge will assist the investigation.

THE SCENE OF DISCOVERY

The task of investigating the scene of discovery includes searching for and recovering the remains of the body and all the objects in the area that may be of value for identification. As in all cases in which a body is found where a crime is suspected, the police officer should contact the medical examiner so that from the start the latter has an opportunity to become familiar with the case. For the purpose of identifying the body, the expertise of a forensic odontologist (dentist) may be needed to compare ante-mortem dental records to postmortem dental x-rays of the deceased. The forensic biologist can also help to identify the deceased by comparing the DNA type from a known sample (toothbrush, hairbrush, biopsy sample, Pap smear, etc.) to the DNA type developed from the remains. The procedure for the investigation is, of course, not always the same.

OUTDOORS

A discovery outdoors may be one of three different types according to whether the remains are found buried, lying exposed on the ground, or in water.

Remains that have been buried usually come to light during digging, construction, or other similar operations. There are also purely historical finds from old burial sites. (They can also be from more recent acts used to hide or dispose of a body.) The CSI called to such a scene should first photograph the remains in the state in which it was found, and then carefully expose the body. During this work, preferably done with assistants and in the presence of a forensic anthropologist or a forensic archeologist, detailed photographs should be taken in order to show the position of the body, and noteworthy details.

In exposing the body, special attention should be given to any filling material above the remains that differs from the surrounding earth, to any objects used as covering near it, and to any foreign material or bodies in the ground or near the body. In some instances, quicklime is placed on bodies to accelerate decomposition and make identification more difficult. If it is suspected, a sample of the earth should be taken so that it can be examined. Attention should also be given to the properties of the earth (type of soil, dampness, pH, etc.) because this is very important in deciding the length of time the body has been buried.

The color of bones can vary from light grayish-white to dark brownish-black, depending on the age of the find, kind, and properties of the soil, whether the parts are or were enclosed or covered in some way, or the measures that may have been taken with the body before burial, i.e., burning. It is often difficult to distinguish between small bones and stones, twigs, or other debris, therefore, the search should be carried out with great care and all remains, even if very small, should be kept and examined by an anthropologist. Certain very small bones and also the teeth are very important for determining the identity of the deceased. If the skeleton is much disintegrated, the earth should be sifted through a small mesh sieve. An alternate light source can also be used to help differentiate between fragmented human bones, rocks, and debris (Figure 18.10a and b).

Of great importance for investigation and identification are all remains of clothing and other objects that may be connected with the find, e.g., pocket contents, buttons, ornaments, rings, coins, etc., and objects that may be connected directly with the crime or transported to the crime scene, such as ropes, cords, sacks, bullets, duct tape, garbage bags, duffel bags, zip ties, or objects pushed into the mouth of the victim. Such loose objects are looked for and kept with great care because the risk of breaking into pieces may be great. Objects on or attached to the remains are not moved from their position before the discovery has been fully revealed or unearthed. The position of loose objects in relation to the remains of the body should be accurately marked, sketched, and photographed.

In taking possession of bones and especially of remains of clothing and the like, attention should be given to their association with any vegetation. Roots of trees or shrubs that have grown through them form a valuable aid in determining the length of time the object has been there. A determination of the age of a root of a tree that has grown through clothing gives a minimum value for the time the object has lain in the ground; this can be used as a starting

Figure 18.10 Bone fragments vs. rocks; (a) with white light and (b) CrimeScope LASER. (*Photo credit: SPEX Forensics,* www.spexforensics.com.)

point for further investigations and calculations. If possible such roots should be cut off and allowed to remain with the object; otherwise, they must be kept and labeled with the necessary information on their origin.

At the scene of the discovery attention should also be given to the occurrence of insect larvae and pupae or remains of them on the body. They are placed in a suitable container for examination by a forensic entomologist. For example, remains of fly larvae found on a buried body indicate that it was above ground for a certain period of time before being buried; the stage of development of the insect, larva, or pupa can give further valuable information. The amount and type of insect activity can also yield other clues about such things as the time of death.

If only a part of a body is found, then dismemberment may have been carried out before burial. In such a case a large area of the surroundings must be investigated carefully, with attention directed especially to all changes in the surface of the ground that give the impression of having been produced by human agency. The character of the ground, the possibility of burial at different places, etc. must then be used to guide the search. In some cases, police cadaver dogs can be used to help with the search. Ground-penetrating radar (GPR) is a tool that can be used to search for anomalies in the earth that could reveal evidence of a clandestine grave. Additional manpower should be brought in when large areas need to be searched. A sketch should be made of the terrain, giving the place where each object was found, and photographs taken. Using Google Maps® can be helpful in this process. In photography, each site is marked with a number or letter visible on the photograph and these are also shown on the sketches. The objects found at the different sites are placed in cartons or boxes marked with the number or letter given to the discovery location in the photographs and sketches.

A search for evidence in the vicinity of such a discovery, e.g., evidence of the criminal, vehicle tracks, or the like, usually has a low pay-off because of the long time that has generally elapsed since the crime was committed. However, marks on stems of trees or the like from vehicles, a bullet, and so on can be found after a comparatively long time, so a routine search should be made if the find is thought not to be too old. It should be remembered that trees and bushes might have grown considerably since the crime, so metal detectors can be helpful in these searches.

The discovery of a dead body found lying exposed on the ground is usually made in a forest, on a mountain slope, or at other remote places.

If dismembered body parts are discovered, the investigation of the scene must be extended to cover a large area. In this case it is quite normal for the parts of the body to be scattered over a number of places at some distance from one another. The same applies, however, to bodies that have not been dismembered because various animals and birds can drag the parts for a distance of up to several hundred yards from the original site.

Careful attention must be given to those cases that appear to be hiking, mountain climbing, or camping accidents. These may be the result of an attempt to cover up criminal assault or robbery. Lone hikers or naturalists can be easy prey for criminal attacks. Special attention must be paid to the absence of valuables, minor bruises from subduing blows, and evidence of soil or vegetation not found in the immediate vicinity. The investigation of a discovery of this kind is made in exactly the same way as for a body that has been buried. Special attention should be given to the relation of the vegetation to the find because this may be decisive in determining the length of time the body has lain there. Under the remains at the original site, smothered plants may be found or possibly no vegetation at all. Plants may have started to grow over the remains. If the body has lain there for several years, grass, undergrowth, moss, or other vegetation may have completely concealed part of the remains. The remains may have gradually become covered with a layer of soil or leaf mold from falling leaves and dead plants. Roots of trees and bushes may grow through parts of the find and especially remnants of clothing. The vegetative conditions should be described carefully, stating the type of vegetation and supplemented with photographs on which the different remains are marked in the manner described earlier. Any tree or other roots that have grown through the remains are kept for a determination of their age. If there is no risk of the roots falling out of the remains when they are collected, then the roots should be removed with them.

If remains of a body are found in water, it is generally much more difficult to investigate the place of discovery accurately, unless it is merely a small pool that can be drained. It must be remembered that currents, ice, floating timber, and other items may have carried parts of the body to places a long way from the place of discovery. Also, the find may be a body part that has been carried to the place of discovery in the same manner, possibly from a considerable distance.

If the discovery has been made in a harbor or river in which there are steamers and motorboats, propellers may have caused some of the injuries on the body. A propeller can cut off a leg or arm in such a way that it appears as if the body has been dismembered intentionally. Injuries to tissues and organs produced in this way often show clean cuts, as from an edged tool. Feeding by aquatic life can also be mistaken for injuries. Besides crime scene experience, investigators of underwater crime scenes need to be expert divers as well. The Professional Association of Diving Instructors (PADI) offers courses in underwater crime scenes.

Indoors

It is very rare for remains of a body found indoors to undergo as extensive a degree of change from decay or other causes as in the preceding cases. There have been cases of extensive change, however, where a body has been buried in a cellar or cut up and burned in the furnace, or when remains of a dismembered and/or burned body have been placed in a suitcase in an attic or garage. The procedure in such a case is the same as that described above.

If a body has been buried or if remains have been found in a suitcase, sack, or the like, then all objects that have been used to conceal the body or for wrapping are of special interest (Figure 18.11a and b). With such discoveries, the floor, walls, and ceiling of the place should be examined for bloodstains and objects should be looked for that might have been used in connection with the crime.

For example, if a furnace has been used to burn a body, it should be examined very carefully. After a cremation, the volume of the bones of an adult amounts to 2 to 3.5 liters (3.5 to 6 pints). In a freshly burnt state, the bones have a

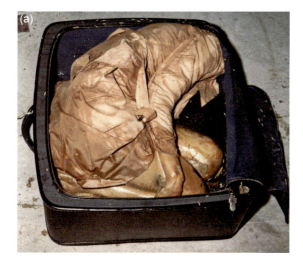

Figure 18.11 (a, b) Body discovered in a suitcase. (*Courtesy of Los Angeles County Sheriff's Department.*)

white to yellowish or grayish-white shade, which quickly changes to brown or brownish-black in the ground. At a certain state of burning the bones are soft and may assume peculiar twisted forms that depend to some extent on the underlayer.

The contents of the firebox and of the ash space should be sifted; every fragment of bone should be kept. Certain very small bones have been found to be very resistant to fire and may therefore be valuable for determining the age and gender of the deceased. Teeth are especially valuable. The crowns of teeth generally break up and split under the action of heat, but the roots often remain whole. On the other hand, teeth that have not erupted (e.g., with children) rarely break up and do not change in form or shrink to any appreciable extent; after burning, they have a whitish color and a chalky consistency. It is even possible to recover DNA from the pulp of a whole tooth because of the hard enamel that protects it.

In searching for and taking possession of burnt skeletal remains, great care should be observed due to their fragile nature. If remains that are especially brittle or liable to fall to pieces are found, they should be packed separately in test tubes, containers, or cartons according to size, with cotton, tissue paper, or the like as underlayer and filling for the container.

PACKING AND TRANSPORTING

Packing the remains of a body with any associated objects to be moved or sent to the morgue should be done to minimize any danger of destruction or falling apart of associated objects as the result of shaking or other movement. A skeleton with the long bones still connected together, with or without remains of soft tissues or organs, should be packed so that it will remain in that state during transport. Styrofoam, rags, tissue paper, or similar materials can be used as filling in the container and for the support of parts so that they do not rest on the bottom. Well-burnt remains should be transported in the custody of a police officer who keeps the package under control at all times to ensure that it is not exposed to shocks or jarring. Suitable packing materials are thin, soft paper, soft and flexible cloth, tissue paper, cotton, or foam packed in the container so that the object has a soft support and is also supported in a definite position.

EXAMINING REMAINS OF CLOTHING AND OTHER OBJECTS

The investigation of any remains of clothing and other objects is done in an effort to determine the original appearance of the garments, kind of cloth, color, and so on, and the detection of any manufacturer's or laundry marks. Shoes are examined for manufacturer's marks, size, repairs, and other identifying marks. Any object found in the clothes or at the scene is investigated. These objects may be characteristic of a particular trade or may provide some other way give information about the deceased or conditions in connection with the death (murder weapon, suicide weapon, objects used in transporting the body to the place, objects thrown away or forgotten by the suspect, etc.). In these investigations special attention should be given to everything that might assist in determining the length of time the remains have been there, e.g., alterations resulting from weather conditions, penetration of roots and other parts of plants into clothing, etc.

All information that is developed from this investigation is combined to form a description of the deceased and an explanation of the cause of death, time of death, and so on. This can subsequently be used to aid in identifying the body of someone reported as missing.

CLOTHING

Roots or other parts of plants that have penetrated portions of clothing should be kept and provided with a label showing type of garment and vegetation; afterwards the material is given to a botanist for determination of age. From tree and shrub roots that have penetrated the remains it is possible to determine the minimum period of time that the object has lain at the site. In the case of *unburied* remains this estimate must be increased by 1 or 2 years because the material must first "merge" into the soil before it can be penetrated by roots.

The type of textile, color, type of garment, and whether it is ready-made or tailor-made may be determined. Manufacturer's and laundry marks should be looked for, with the aid of an ultraviolet light. Buttons and the manner in which they are sewn on (by machine or hand) may be significant, as are any repairs in the garments. The remains of clothes are examined also for damage caused by edged tools, firearms, vehicles, and similar objects that may possibly correspond to marks and injuries on the body. The assistance of the pathologist is required for this. The nature of the damage can often be determined with certainty. Damage caused by animals may also occur on clothing, but this can generally be distinguished from other damage. The remains of underclothing and stockings or socks are also examined for color, textile material, manufacturer's marks, other marks, repairs, etc. Depending on the condition of the clothes, clothing can also be scraped near the collar, cuffs, underarm areas, headband, and the like for skin cells to be used in DNA typing.

BOOTS AND SHOES

The original color of boots and shoes may be difficult to determine because of changes to the leather by the action of soil, dampness, etc. The name of the maker, which is sometimes embossed, may be inside or at the back of the heel, or at other points on the inside; stamped marks may sometimes be a guide for identification. Any rubber soles or heels, their make, size, and types are also significant. The size of shoes can be determined from the length. Sometimes, a distinct impression of the sole of the foot and the toes can be observed on the inner sole of a shoe and this may be of value for comparison with shoes that may possibly be found in the house of a missing person. Shoe repairs may also help in identification.

ESTIMATING THE TIME OF DEATH

In cases of murder, suicide, or suspicious death, the determination of the time of death is very important. The most reliable estimate of the time of death comes from a variety of sources: postmortem changes such as body temperature, rigor mortis, lividity, and decomposition, and information developed during the investigation such as the last time the victim was seen alive. The correct estimate of the time of death is important when interviewing suspects in a homicide investigation. Such information can serve to eliminate a suspect who was elsewhere at the time of death or establish opportunity, i.e., the suspect could have been with the victim at the time of death. The investigator should realize that the estimate of the time of death is only an estimate. In some cases, a more precise determination can be made if the death occurred at or near the time of another event that was known.

POSTMORTEM SIGNS OF DEATH

After death a number of postmortem changes occur that are useful in determining, within limits, the approximate time of death. The various methods available are useful to make estimates, that is, ranges of times. The precise moment of death can be determined only in rare instances, such as when a bullet stops a clock. The amount of time between the death and discovery of the body also has a bearing on the time-of-death estimate. Generally, the shorter the time interval between death and the discovery of the body, the better is the estimate of the time of death.

CHANGES IN THE EYES

After death, changes become noticeable in the eyes. The cornea becomes dull and a film may appear over the eye. This may appear within several minutes to a few hours depending on whether the eyelid is open or closed, temperature, humidity, and air current. Because of these factors, clouding of the cornea is not considered a reliable indicator of the time of death.

TEMPERATURE OF THE BODY

Cooling of the body, or *algor mortis*, is another sign of death. The rate of cooling depends on several factors, including body temperature at the time of death, temperature of the environment, body covering and clothing, and relationship of the surface area to body weight. The body temperature will continue to fall or rise until it reaches ambient temperature, which usually occurs in about 18 to 20 hours.

Core body temperature is generally considered one of the more reliable indicators of the time of death up to approximately 18 hours. The usual way to determine core body temperature is to insert a thermometer into the liver. A comparison between that temperature and ambient temperature is used to determine the approximate time of death.

RIGIDITY OF THE BODY

Immediately after death, the body becomes flaccid. Biochemical changes in body muscles produce stiffening, known as *rigor mortis*, which usually appears within 2 to 6 hours after death. Rigor mortis is most notable first in the small muscles such as the jaw and fingers and is complete within 6 to 12 hours. The rigidity remains for 2 to 3 days and disappears gradually.

An examination of the body for rigor mortis can help indicate the time of death. If the rigidity is broken, it will generally not reappear unless the body is in the very early stages of rigor mortis. The victim's muscular development will affect the intensity of the rigidity. The very young and very old will likely develop less rigidity than adults with well-developed musculature.

LIVIDITY

After blood circulation stops, blood settles to the lowest portions of the body because of gravity. This is known as *livor mortis,* and is noted by the appearance of blue or reddish-violet marks on the skin (in cases of poisoning by carbon monoxide, cyanide or cold, the marks are "cherry red" and with potassium chlorate poisoning, light brown). The first indications of lividity occur in approximately 1 hour, with full development after 3 to 4 hours. Lividity can sometimes be confused with bruising or black-and-blue marks. The pathologist can differentiate between the two during the autopsy.

Under certain conditions lividity can move or change if the body is moved or the position of the body is changed. Postmortem lividity does not form on parts of the body exposed to pressure, e.g., parts that lie against the floor. If the position of the body or the position of articles of clothing pressing on the body is changed within 3 to 4 hours, the original lividity discoloration may partially disappear and a new pattern form. After this time, at least some of the original discoloration will remain. Even 9 to 12 hours after death, and sometimes later, new but successively weaker patterns are produced when the position of the body is changed, although the discoloration that was first formed is usually fixed by this time and does not change. If there was a large blood loss, livid stains will be weak. As a rule, fresh livid stains are not produced by a change in position more than 12 hours after death. Lividity discoloration may provide a limited indication of the time of death but can demonstrate a change of position or movement of the body several hours after death (Figure 18.12).

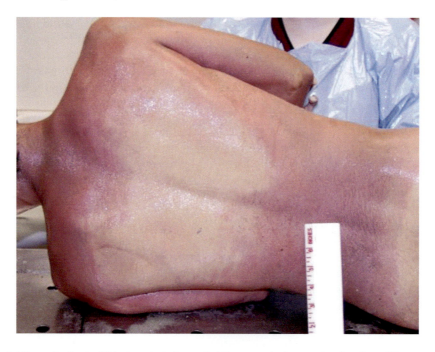

Figure 18.12 The lividity on the back of this decedent shows that they were laying on a hard surface. (*Photo credit:* www.pinterest.com/wen1304/shiban/.)

DECOMPOSITION OF THE BODY

The most certain sign of death, which cannot be misinterpreted by anyone, is the beginning of putrefaction. Decomposition, or putrefaction, is a combination of two processes: autolysis and bacterial action. Autolysis, the softening and liquefaction of tissue, occurs by means of chemical breakdown of the body. Bacterial action results in the conversion of soft tissues in the body to liquids and gases.

Putrefaction begins immediately upon death and generally first becomes noticeable within 24 hours by discoloration of the skin in the lower abdomen and groin. The discoloration has been described as greenish-red, blue-green, and even black and is pronounced within 36 hours. Bacterial action produces gases causing the body to swell up, while an unpleasant odor becomes quite noticeable. The swelling is particularly noticeable in the penis, scrotum, breasts, and other areas of loose skin attachment.

Blisters filled with watery fluid and gas appear on the skin, which gradually darkens in color. Material from tissue breakdown (purge) may exude through the mouth, nose, and anus. Within 3 days, the entire body shows signs of decomposition. The environment affects the rate of decomposition of the body. Colder temperatures tend to impede putrefaction while warmer temperatures increase it.

Similarly, if the body is placed in water containing a large number of bacteria, such as that from sewage effluent, decomposition is accelerated. A body in water generally decomposes more slowly because of colder temperatures and lack of oxygen. Because the body has a greater specific gravity than water, it sinks initially. Prolonged submersion in water causes a wrinkling effect around the skin of the hands and feet. The body orients itself in a head-down position that sometimes results in the scraping of the forehead when it comes into contact with the rough seafloor. After a period of 3 to 4 days in warmer water and about a week in cold, the body will surface owing to the formation of gas. Sometimes the skin and tissues burst and the body sinks again to the bottom. The process may repeat itself and the body floats to the surface again.

When a body is buried in a shallow grave with loose earth, it is destroyed fairly quickly; in 1 to 3 years all the soft tissue will disappear. The skeleton remains much longer. These time figures will vary greatly according to the type of soil, amount of water, acidity, drainage, and other such factors. In peat bogs, for example, the body will remain relatively well preserved for many years. Bodies buried in clay soil decompose at a slower rate than in other soils. In certain cases, bodies are relatively well preserved through mummification or the formation of adipocere, a wax-like substance caused by hydrolysis of body fat.

In very dry conditions, putrefaction is retarded and mummification may begin. It can become complete in warm, dry air or when a body is buried in dry, porous earth. Formation of adipocere occurs in bodies located in damp environments such as a swamp, wet soil, or even water. Adipocere is characterized by reasonably well-preserved external contours of the body; its formation is noticeable in about 6 to 8 weeks, with the complete formation in 18 months to 2 years. When a body lies in a cellar or other damp place it may become completely covered with mold, leaving black marks on the body. Buried embalmed bodies may also have mold present. (The Anthropological Research Facility, or "Body Farm," at the University of Tennessee at Knoxville conducts research on human decomposition in a variety of settings and conditions. More information can be seen on their website at http://fac.utk.edu/.)

ACTION OF INSECTS ON A DEAD BODY*

When a dead body lies above ground, it generally deteriorates quickly by the action of insects and their larvae. Different kinds of insects lay their eggs in the body and these rapidly develop into larvae (maggots) that can appear in such numbers that the dead body "teems with life." The body of an adult can be completely destroyed in less than 2 months, with only the skeleton remaining, that of a child in less than a month. The insects that appear on a body, to feed on it or to lay their eggs in it, always come in a certain definite order, depending on the state of decomposition of the body. This question has attained great importance in medicolegal practice because, by examining the insects found on a body at a particular time, it is possible to obtain a good idea of the postmortem interval (PMI).

---

* The following section is courtesy of Neal Haskell, PhD, BCE.

As a rule, the first insects that attack the body are flies. Even before death actually occurs the flies may begin to lay their eggs in the body, usually in the mucous membranes—e.g., in the eyes, nose, and mouth—but also in wounds and bloody parts of the body. The eggs are white and about 1/16 inch long, and are laid in clumps. On a body lying indoors they come especially from common houseflies (*Musca domestica*). This may be a significant point in the investigation because if eggs, larvae, or pupae of houseflies are found in a body lying outdoors or buried, it must be concluded that it has previously lain indoors. On bodies lying outdoors chiefly common bluebottles (*Calliphora erythrocephala*), greenbottles (*Lucilia caesar*), and sheep maggot flies (*Lucilia sericata*) lay their eggs. Flies can also lay their eggs in bodies buried in shallow graves. After only 1 to 2 days, the larvae of the fly come out of the eggs and immediately commence their work of destruction, changing into pupa after 10 to 14 days; after a further 12 to 14 days, the flies come out, to multiply again in their turn after a couple of weeks.

Among the beetles that live or multiply on a body, burying beetles and other kinds of carrion beetles appear on a dead body. Carrion beetles, as their name implies, are an important part of a vast host of scavengers responsible for recycling decaying materials. When a body is buried immediately after death, insects are not able to lay their eggs. Certain types of boring worms accelerate the decomposition process into the body. Some fly species can live and multiply for long time periods in a buried body.

When larvae, pupae, insect eggs, or fully developed insects are found on a body or in clothing, it is possible to estimate the postmortem interval. A forensic entomologist (FE) should perform these examinations from preserved specimens provided by the CSI and/or medical examiner.* The temperature of the scene should also be provided to the FE.

Initial insect activity (mainly maggots) should be collected from the body in hospital screw lid specimen cups. Maggots should be placed into either isopropyl or ethanol. If there are different sizes, include all the different sizes you see in one specimen container. If there are only a few specimens, collect as many as are present; if there are thousands, place whatever will fit into the container. This procedure should be repeated for different areas of maggot aggregations on the body and labeled with the necessary case information, including date/time, location, case #, sample #, and who collected the sample.

As the maggots feed and mature, they will complete feeding and move off the remains to search for a place to form the puparial stage (cocoon stage) of the life cycle. It is important to note that these maggots are not feeding on the remains and are crawling away from the body. Collect and label these in the same manner as the feeding maggots with the exception that the CSI will need to include the direction and approximate distance from the remains. This will ensure that documentation of this next stage (migrating maggots) of the life cycle has been recorded and will be included in the FE analysis. In outdoor settings the migrating maggots can crawl several yards from the remains and will usually take the route of least resistance.

The last life stage to search for is the puparial stage. They look like seeds or little footballs and will be found in loose soil up to 2 inches in depth when outside. When in houses, they will migrate to the walls and tuck down under the carpet edges or will be found under paper and other refuse on the floor. If you have this life stage present, do not place them in any solutions, but keep them alive and get them to a forensic entomologist without delay.

By following these few simple collection techniques used for insect collection at the scene or autopsy, the forensic entomologist can reliably and accurately evaluate the PMI of a case and estimate the time when the individual died. This information can then support or refute other pieces of evidence in the case.

OTHER INDICATIONS OF TIME OF DEATH

The forensic pathologist may be able to draw conclusions from the stomach contents and intestines regarding the time of the last meal, its quantity, and composition. The investigator can assist the pathologist by relaying any information found with regard to the composition of the last meal.

Watches and clocks may be valuable guides in determining the time of death. A clock may stop when it receives a blow during a struggle or is moved from its position by an explosion or shot. When investigating a suspicious death,

---

* A useful web page on forensic entomology can be found at: www.forensicentomology.com/.

the investigator should give careful attention to any clock found at the scene, including those on electronic devices. If clocks or watches are running, it should be noted whether they are showing the right time; the time at which they finally stopped should be determined. Older watches stop immediately upon contact with water, but a watch provided with a tight-fitting case and glass can run longer before stopping. Digital watches and clocks generally do not lend themselves to these techniques.

In investigating cases of a suspicious death, certain conditions can give a good indication for an approximate determination of the time of death. This may be obtained from papers and letters in a mailbox, dated receipts, food materials' state of decomposition, dampness of laundry, dust on furniture, cobwebs, evaporation of liquid in a glass, cup, or other vessel, flowers withering, drying in flowerpots, the date on a calendar or diary, food product dating codes, timestamps on sent or received emails, smartphone call logs, text messages, etc.

When a dead body is found outdoors, the growth of vegetation under and around it can be a guide in deciding the time when the body began lying there. Flowering plants may be buried and thus may indicate the time of burial. The colored matter of plant leaves under the body undergoes certain changes; chlorophyll generally disappears after a week. A good indication can also be obtained from a comparison between the stage of growth of plants under the body and of similar plants in the vicinity. When a body has been laid in one place for a considerable time, in favorable cases, the decaying vegetation underneath can indicate the time of year when the body was placed there. If the weather has changed, the amount of moisture under the body, compared with that in the surrounding area, may give some information. When a dead body is found in snow, its position in relation to layers produced by successive snowfalls should be determined accurately.

Some guidance may also be obtained from the degree of decay of clothing. Cotton fabrics decompose after 4 to 5 years; wool after 8 to 10 years; leather and silk only after 20 years or even longer.

THE AUTOPSY

The investigator present at the crime scene should also be present at the autopsy, or postmortem examination. The investigator's attendance is important so that the forensic pathologist can be briefed about pertinent findings at the crime scene, as well as other information that will be of value in the examination. Additionally, information uncovered at the autopsy and communicated verbally by the pathologist to the homicide investigator will be helpful in the criminal investigation.

Besides photographs taken at the crime scene, the victim should be photographed at the morgue clothed and unclothed. The pathologist and investigator should be present and carefully examine the victim prior to undressing the body. Color photographs should be taken of all pertinent details: the overall appearance of the body, close-ups of the face, injuries, ligatures and marks, and the like. A scale should be included in the photographs. X-rays are also taken of the body to locate foreign objects in the body and/or clothing.

Care should be taken in undressing the body. It should be undressed in the usual way; the clothing should not be cut, if possible. If cutting is required, care should be taken not to cut through bullet holes, knife cuts, tears, or stains. The garments should be packaged separately. If they are wet or blood-soaked they should be allowed to air-dry at room temperature, or in an evidence drying cabinet. Paper should be placed under the drying clothing to catch any trace material that might fall. It is important that bloodstained clothing be properly dried in order to obtain the most from forensic DNA testing.

After the clothes have been dried, they may be packaged for submission to the crime laboratory. The investigator and pathologist should be careful to establish a chain of custody of the evidence so it can be admissible in court. Trace evidence present on the victim and the clothing should not be overlooked. Body bags used to carry the body from the scene to the morgue should be carefully inspected for debris and trace material. Any trace evidence found on the body should be removed and properly packaged. Traces noted on the clothing should be removed and packaged only if the evidence might be lost in transit to the laboratory; otherwise the traces should remain and be packaged with the clothing. Investigators at the scene may wish to leave written instructions for the forensic pathologist or assistant responsible for collecting trace evidence from the body when it arrives at the morgue. Of course, it is strongly recommended that homicide investigators make every attempt to be present at the autopsy and to discuss the case with the pathologist.

Following photography, initial examination, and undressing, the fingers should be fingerprinted. There are several postmortem fingerprint techniques that work very well on bodies that are badly decomposed.* The skin of the body should be searched for bloody fingerprints as well. The techniques earlier described to obtain latent fingerprints from skin may be attempted on promising areas. An alternate light source can also be used to look for biological fluids on the body. UV light can also be used to look for ligature and strangulation marks, or other bruises that may not be visible to the naked eye. UV light can also be used to look for tattoos that have previously been removed to aid in the identification of the deceased. Fingernail scrapings and/or clippings should routinely be taken from all murder victims because DNA from the attacker is often present under the nails. A blood specimen should be collected during the actual postmortem examination as a known exemplar.

The body should next be washed and rephotographed. Identity photographs of the victim's face should be made at that time. The entire body, including injuries, should again be photographed. Photographs taken during the remainder of the autopsy may be of value in the subsequent investigation and should be encouraged. If the victim died as a result of a shooting, x-rays are necessary to identify and locate the bullet fragments, jacket, etc.

The purpose of the autopsy is to establish the cause and manner of death as well as the circumstances immediately surrounding the time of death. The homicide investigator uses this information together with information gathered from other sources in the solution of the crime. Two factors will have a significant bearing on the outcome of the case: the degree of care and skill in which the postmortem examination is conducted and the level of cooperation between the investigator and forensic pathologist.

The remainder of this chapter discusses the various types of injuries by different modes encountered in death investigations.

ABRASIONS

Abrasions generally result from violence applied obliquely, which scrapes off the top layer of the skin, but they can occur from violence directed straight against the body and may reproduce the shape of, say, the radiator of a car or the details of a weapon's surface. As a rule there is no bleeding. In a favorable case, it is possible to decide in which direction the body received the violence and, with some degree of certainty, what caused the injury. In general, it is very difficult to determine whether scraping of the epidermis was produced before or after death, although postmortem drying may leave a characteristic yellow parchment-like appearance. Removing or undressing the body must be carried out with care so that no injuries are produced.

CONTUSIONS OR BRUISES

Contusions or bruises are injuries to the tissues and organs produced by blunt external violence and result from compression, usually against the parts of the skeleton lying underneath. The most usual type of contusion is an extravasation of blood; when this is close to the skin it is commonly called a bruise or black-and-blue mark. In extravasation, the blood comes out into the surrounding tissues and remains there, unable to get away to the outside or to the body cavities. A bruise or black-and-blue mark initially shows swelling and has a reddish color; it then assumes a blackish-blue to bluish-red color, changing gradually to brownish with strong shades of green and yellow. In rare cases, a bruise resulting from a blow with a weapon will have the same form as the striking surface of the weapon. If a bruise is found on a dead body, it may be concluded with certainty that the injury was produced when the victim was alive. At the autopsy, it is usually possible to determine whether a contusion has been produced sometime before or in direct connection with the death. Only a pathologist can distinguish the livid patterns from bruises found on a dead body.

Contusions may occur at places other than those where violence was applied. For example, a blow against the back of the head can produce bruises around the eyes. Similarly, with an abnormal accumulation of blood in the blood vessels, as in cases of hanging or other forms of suffocation, bruises can appear in the face. Diffusion of blood may also appear in cases of poisoning and, in some diseases and infections of the blood, injury to the walls of the blood vessels.

---

* See Mulawka, M., *Postmortem Fingerprinting and Unidentified Human Remains*, Forensic Studies for Criminal Justice Series, Routledge, 2014.

CRUSHING WOUNDS

Crushing wounds occur most readily, with blunt violence, at those places where the skin is near the bones. They are characterized by irregular form, gaping and swollen edges to the wound, and often considerable bleeding into the surrounding tissues. The wound rarely takes the form of the object producing it, but an impression of the latter may be found. Sometimes a crushing wound is remarkably straight and even at the edges; this occurs when the skin breaks over the uniform edge of a bone or where it splits along a parallel fibered tissue structure. Such a wound may give the impression of having been produced by a sharp weapon. This type of wound can be detected with a degree of certainty because in deeper lying parts of it the walls of the wound are uneven and connected by bridges of tissue.

A crushing wound resulting from a blow on the head with a hammer or the head of an ax sometimes has the same form as the round or angular edge that produced it. If a blow of this type is so powerful that the weapon penetrates the cranium, the injury may have the same form.

When blunt violence is used against the body, it is possible for vital organs such as the brain, heart, lungs, liver, spleen, and kidneys to be damaged without any visible external injury. Bite wounds are a special form of crushing wounds.

BONE INJURIES

Bone injuries may result from blunt external violence, for example, directed against the head. If a bone injury has occurred during life, diffusion of blood is generally found near or around it. Blunt violence against the cranium may produce a fracture. The direction of the crack may make it possible to determine the direction from which the violence came.

CUTTING WOUNDS

Cutting wounds have even, sharp edges. When the direction of cutting is across the direction of the fibers of elastic tissue, the wound gapes; when the direction of cut is parallel to the fibers, the edges of the wound generally lie against one another. Often it is difficult to decide whether a cutting wound occurred during life or after death because contusion injuries, which may form a guide in such cases, are not found around the wound. As a rule a cutting wound is deepest at the place where the cutting object was first applied. The wound leaves hardly any detailed information about the instrument that caused it.

In cases of suicide, the cutting force is generally directed against the throat or insides of the wrists and, sometimes, against other parts of the body. The intent of the suicide is usually to produce bleeding by cutting the arteries. In cases of suicide there may be one or several cuts, generally not of a dangerous type, parallel or running into one another, known as "hesitation cuts." If it is established that such surface cuts were produced before the final fatal cut, it is quite certain that the case is one of suicide; the surface cuts were made because the suicide victim did not know how much force was required to produce the fatal cut or feared the pain anticipated from the act. The CSI should not, however, draw hasty conclusions from superficial cuts that give the impression of having been made before the fatal cut.

Nothing prevents a murderer who has knowledge of these circumstances from adding superficial cuts after making the fatal one in order to give the impression of suicide. Only a pathologist is competent to decide in what order the cuts were made. In some cases of suicide the individual has made a number of trial cuts at places other than the one where the fatal cut was made. Such trial cuts, which as a rule are superficial, may be situated on the temples, arms, or legs. With an active or desperate suicide, the first cut may be a fatal one, but that does not prevent the victim from adding a number of others before losing consciousness.

A suicidal person generally cuts in the direction where the cutting hand is placed. When a right-handed person cuts his or her throat, the position of the cut is generally on the left side of the throat; if the victim is left-handed the position is reversed. In connection with cuts in the throat, it should not be forgotten that a murderer might handle the weapon in exactly the same way as a suicide if the murderer overcomes the victim from the rear.

In cases of suicide by cutting the throat incisions made in the freehand can easily be confused with defense injuries. Such wounds may be produced when the suicide stretches the skin of the neck with the freehand so that the weapon can penetrate more easily. Wounds may also be produced from holding the blade in order to be able to put more force into the cut.

In cases of death from cutting the throat, there is reason to suspect murder when the position of the wound does not correspond with a natural hold on the weapon, or the direction of the wound does not correspond with the right- or left-handedness of the victim. Murder may be suspected if the wound is very deep or if it is irregular. Special attention should be given to the possible occurrence of fingernail marks and scratch injuries that would be produced if the murderer held the head of the victim fast, and also to the presence of defense injuries on the hands and arms. If cuts are on the clothing, it may be murder because suicides generally lay bare the part of the body that they intend to cut.

STAB WOUNDS

Stab wounds are generally produced by a knife, dagger, or scissors, but may also result from other weapons, e.g., an ice pick, awl, screwdriver, and similar items. If a stab wound has been produced by a sharp knife or dagger, it is not possible to determine the width of the blade from the size of the surface wound because the wound channel is generally wider than the weapon, especially if it is two-edged. When the weapon is stuck into the body, the edge has a cutting action, so the surface wound is considerably longer than the width of the blade; when the weapon is withdrawn, it usually assumes a different position, so the wound is enlarged still further. The weapon may also be turned when withdrawn, so the surface wound becomes curved or angular. A knife with a thick back produces a wedge-shaped wound.

When stab wounds are produced by a weapon with a blunt point, the outer wound is smaller than the cross-sectional width of the instrument. In such cases, when the weapon is driven into the body, the elastic skin is actually pressed inward and stretched until it breaks. When the weapon is withdrawn, the skin returns to its normal position, and the external wound contracts. If the weapon is cone-shaped and rough, the skin around the wound may break in radial cracks.

With a stab wound in the heart, death may not occur immediately. In some cases, people have survived a wound in the heart.

A suicide attempt by stabbing is generally in the region of the heart or, in some cases, in the stomach or other parts of the body. It is often found that a number of stab wounds are concentrated in a small, limited region, i.e., around the heart. In such a case the suicide has stabbed the body several times without result, in the same way described earlier in "Cutting Wounds." One fact that indicates suicide is clothes that are unbuttoned or have been taken off. In suicide the stab is generally directed into the body at right angles.

In cases of murder, the stab wounds are usually not concentrated in one place but scattered, especially when the victim has attempted self-defense. Knife stabs are, as a rule, directed in an oblique direction against the body, with the exception of cases in which the victim was lying down. A number of deep wounds and wounds in the back indicate murder. If the victim tried self-defense, the wound channel may be curved owing to the body being in a certain position when it received the stab. At the autopsy, it may be found that a wound channel does not go right through because the position of the body was such that the muscles were displaced from their normal position when they were penetrated. In such a case, the position of the dead person when he or she was stabbed can be reconstructed.

Case Review

The body of a dead woman was found by police in a house in Amsterdam, Holland in 2007. When the police arrived there were three people in the living room. Two of them pointed out the third and said that he stabbed the woman to death. The man was taken into custody. The job of the crime scene investigators was to determine whether the findings confirmed the alleged accusation.

The whole house was covered with bloodstains, varying from swipes, altered stains, flow patterns, and footprints made with and in blood. In the living room, 5 knives were found of which two were bloody. After the removal of all the clothing that was placed upon the body, the victim was found lying naked on her stomach (Figure 18.13a).

In a closet, in the living room female clothing was found that most probably belonged to the victim. The clothing was examined and in several pieces "perforations" were found. Considering the damage to the clothing it was very likely that the victim was wearing them during the stabbing. The Dutch Forensic Institute (NFI) in

Figure 18.13 Descriptions of photos (a–d) can be found in Case Review Summary on pages 268–269.

The Hague examined the clothing for blood of the victim and searched for a comparison between the damaged clothing and the knives.

Large amounts of blood on the mattress and bedding in the first and second bedrooms on the first floor was also found. (Figure 18.13b). In the first bedroom a rope tied to the central heating pipes was found. Next to the body similar pieces of rope were found, and in the bathroom a similar rope on a "roll" was found. It was surmised that the victim was tied to the central heating pipes next to the mattress.

Several bloody sponges, a cleaning mop and a bucket filled with bloody water were also recovered. Several bloody swipes and efforts taken to clean up the floor were also observed (Figure 18.13c).

Several blood transfers on the seat of the chair elevator indicated that there had been more than one instance of blood transfer made by a bloody person or bloody object. Looking at the blood pattern on the seat, the guard underneath the seat and on the footboard of the chair elevator it is probable that a bloody person was seated on the chair. This hypothesis is supported by the fact that several blood stained tissues on the chair elevator and also underneath the bare feet of the victim were found (Figure 18.13d).

Further investigation led to a partial visible shoeprint, made with/in blood. This became visible on the floor next to the bed in bedroom number two and in the living room next to the victim. The shoeprint was of the same kind as the shoes the suspect was wearing during his arrest.

The story according to the suspect and witness was that the man and woman had a relationship based upon friendship and drugs. They lived together in the house. She asked him to give her some drugs but he did not want to. She kept on asking and he got tired of it. When they were sitting on the sofa he stabbed her in the waist and they got into a fight. Blood fled and (also due to her physical condition) as she was not able to go upstairs he put her on the stair elevator and moved her to the bedroom. There he tied her with a rope to the central heating pipes. He left her and went downstairs. After a while she managed to get herself loose and went downstairs. There they had another fight which eventually led to her death. She was stabbed several times, her throat was cut, and she bled to death. The suspect did not really know what to do with the situation and covered her with clothing and made an effort to clean up the house.

(Courtesy of Senior Forensic Investigator Wendy Joan van Hilst, Forensische Opsporing Amsterdam-Amstelland, Holland.)

CHOPPING WOUNDS

Chopping wounds are generally produced by an ax or, more rarely, by a blow with some other edged tool, e.g., a heavy knife, sword, broadax, or the like. Usually, the wound is similar to a cutting wound, but is easily distinguished from the latter by a ring of contusion injury around the wound, and also by the crushing effect produced when the blow meets bony parts. If the edge of the weapon is deformed, tool marks may appear in these bony parts, which can, in favorable cases, lead to the identification of the weapon that was used.

When a blow from an ax or other edged weapon kills a person, murder can almost always be presumed. In cases of murder or other violent death from an ax, the wounds are generally in the head and in different directions. In certain cases, they may have the same direction, for example, when a sleeping person, or one who is held, is struck. Usually the criminal first delivers a few blows with the head of the weapon before completing the job with the edge.

Suicide with an ax has occurred but is rare. Generally, the suicide directs the weapon against the forehead and crown of the head. The first blow is relatively light and only produces superficial injuries that are not fatal; then the suicide continues by putting more force in the blows and possibly using the weapon with greater accuracy so that fatal injuries are produced. The wounds have a typical appearance that cannot be mistaken—they are directed from the forehead to the back of the head, approaching one another at the forehead.

Marks or Damage to Clothing

These can be very significant in the reconstruction of events. In cases of blunt violence, an impression of the weapon causing the injury may be found on the clothing, while headgear may show a clear mark of a hammer or other tool. In the case of a blow against the head, the tool used may even chip out a piece or corner of the headgear; this piece will have the same form as the striking surface of the weapon. An impression in the corresponding part of the outer clothing may show that a bruise on the body has resulted from a kick or from trampling. Impressions in clothing may be mixed with dust, dirt, or other contamination from the object producing the injury. Injuries to the clothes may be a good guide for the reconstruction of the course of events in the case of injury from cutting violence. In stabbing cases, the hole in the clothing may have a position different from that of the wound. A victim who has been stabbed may lift his arms in self-defense so that the clothing moves out of its usual position on the body; in such cases, the defensive position can be reconstructed. A garment perforated in several places by the same stab indicates creases in the clothes.

DEFENSE INJURIES

Self-defense wounds are generally found on the hands and arms of the murder victim. If a knife was used, the insides of the hands may be seriously gashed from gripping the blade of the knife. Stab and cut wounds may be produced on the arms and hands when a victim attempts to parry an attack. When a crushing weapon is used in a murder, the hands of the victim may be badly injured from putting them on the head to reduce the violence of the blow. Among defense injuries are also included those that occur when the victim attempts self-defense by attacking, e.g., knuckles injured from using fists against the criminal or nails broken from scratching.

FIREARM INJURIES

These must be considered as a special group of injuries because the investigation differs substantially in important respects from the investigation of other injuries. One might think that because a CSI should not touch a wound, it is not necessary to have a detailed knowledge of firearm injuries on a body. They are, however, so frequent and so important that whenever the pathologist cannot arrive in a reasonable time the CSI should be prepared to make personal observations and to take whatever measures are necessary. Because firearm injuries are frequently covered with blood, it is often impossible for an investigator to distinguish between a gunshot injury and one produced by other external mechanical violence. Under these circumstances it is necessary to wait patiently for the arrival of the pathologist or MLI; this holds even when it is important that the type of injury be determined at an early stage. The CSI should never probe in or around a gunshot wound because that may destroy or reduce the chance of the expert being able to determine the type of injury and to reconstruct the course of events.

BULLET INJURIES

When a bullet strikes the body, the skin is first pushed in and then perforated while in the stretched state. After the bullet has passed, the skin partially returns to its original position; the entry opening is drawn together and is smaller than the diameter of the bullet. Slower bullet velocities result in smaller entry openings. The bullet passing through the stretched skin forms the so-called "abrasion ring" around the entrance opening because the bullet slips against the skin that is pressed inward and scrapes the external epithelial layers. The skin in the abrasion ring becomes conspicuous by drying after some hours. In a favorable case, rifling marks on the bullet leave such a distinct mark in the abrasion ring that the number of grooves in the rifling can be counted. The combined section of the abrasion ring and entrance opening corresponds to or slightly exceeds the caliber of the bullet. When a bullet strikes the body squarely, the abrasion ring is round and when it strikes at an angle it is oval.

Along with the abrasion ring, another black-colored ring, the "smudge ring," often entirely covers the abrasion ring. This does not contain any powder residues or contamination from the bore of the firearm, but consists wholly of small particles originating from the surface of the bullet. The smudge ring, or "bullet wipe" may be absent in the case of clean-jacketed bullets or when the bullet has passed through clothing.

A bullet passing through the body forms a track that is usually straight, but can also be bent at an angle in an unpredictable manner if the bullet strikes or passes through a bone. Thus determining with certainty the direction of the weapon when the shot was fired is not possible from observation of the entrance and exit openings. The pathologist must calculate this direction by means of an autopsy. The velocity of the bullet has a great influence on the appearance of the track; straight tracks indicate a high-velocity, bent and angular ones a low velocity.

In gunshot injuries in soft tissue of the body, especially in the brain, the bullet can produce a considerable explosive effect, which is greatest with unjacketed or soft-nosed bullets from high-velocity firearms. Such a bullet may split into several parts, each of which forms its own track, and thus several exit wounds may be present. When such a bullet strikes the head, large parts of the cranium can be blown away and the brain scattered around. A soft-nosed bullet that, before hitting the body, is split by striking against a tree branch can produce a number of irregular entrance holes.

A shot through the head is not always fatal. To be immediately fatal the bullet must produce a bursting effect or injure a vital brain center. A shot through the brain that is not immediately fatal does not always produce unconsciousness. Even when a bullet has perforated the heart, the injured person can sometimes live for several hours, retaining some capacity for movement.

It is often difficult to distinguish an exit wound from an entrance wound, especially at long range with a metal-jacketed bullet, assuming that the bullet passes through the body intact. In a favorable case the exit wound may have a ragged appearance with flaps directed outward. To determine the direction of the shot with certainty in such a case, an autopsy is necessary. If the bullet has been damaged by its passage through the body or if there has been a bursting effect, then it is generally easy to determine the exit wound. This wound is often considerably larger than the entrance wound and shows a star-shaped, ragged character, with flaps directed outward. Note, however, that in contact shots the entrance wound may be ragged and star-shaped. A bullet that ricochets may strike with its side or obliquely and produce a large and uncharacteristic entrance wound.

CLOSE AND DISTANT SHOTS

It is very important to be able to estimate the distance from which a shot was fired. In many cases this fact is the only evidence available that can distinguish between suicide, a self-defense killing, manslaughter, or murder.

In practice, a distinction is made among contact, close, and distant shots. A *contact shot* is one in which the muzzle of the weapon is pressed against the body when the shot is fired. In a *close shot* the distance of the muzzle is less than about 18 inches from the body, while a *distant shot* is one fired at a distance greater than 18 inches.

In the case of a contact shot against an exposed part of the body, soot, metallic particles, and powder residues are driven into the body and can be found there during the autopsy. Blackening, caused by soot and powder, around the entry opening is often absent. A contact shot against a part of the body protected by clothing often produces a powder zone on the skin or in the clothes, while soot, powder residue, and fragments of clothing are driven into the track. With a contact discharge, the entrance wound differs considerably from an entrance wound in a close shot or distant shot. When the shot is fired, the gases of the explosion are driven into the track; however, they are forced out again and produce a bursting effect on the skin and clothes. The entrance wound is often star-shaped with flaps directed outward. It is also possible, in a contact shot, for the muzzle of the weapon to mark the skin, causing an impression that reproduces the shape of the muzzle of the weapon.

A close shot produces a zone of blackening around the entrance wound of the track, on the skin or also on the clothes. Sometimes, the flame from the muzzle has a singing action around this opening, with hair and textile fibers curled up. The zone of blackening is formed of substances carried along with the explosion gases.

When a cartridge is fired, the bullet is forced through the barrel of the weapon by the explosion gases. Only a small amount of this gas passes in front of the bullet. The combustion of the powder is never complete even with smokeless powder, still less with black powder, and the explosion gases therefore carry with them incompletely burned powder residues, the amount of which decreases as the distance increases. Thus, in a close shot, a considerable amount of incompletely burned powder residue is found on the target. Together with this residue, the gases also carry along impurities from the inside of the barrel consisting of rust (iron), oil, and particles rubbed off the bullet. Metallic residues from the percussion cap and cartridge case also occur in the gases of the explosion. If the shot is fired at right angles to the body, the zone of blackening is practically circular; if it is fired obliquely the zone is oval. The extent of the zone of blackening is often difficult to determine by direct observation, so it is often better to photograph it using an infrared camera. The zone of blackening gives valuable information for determining the distance from which a shot has been fired, which may be an important factor in deciding between murder and suicide. It is important that comparative test shots be fired with the *same weapon* and *same type of ammunition* as those used in the actual crime.

Close shots with black powder show marks of burning up to a distance of 4 to 6 inches and a distinct deposit of powder smoke up to 10 to 12 inches. Dispersed grains of powder embedded in the target may be detected even at a distance of 3 feet.

A *distant shot* is one in which none of the characteristics of a close shot can be detected (distance over about 18 inches). *Powder residues* occur on the object fired at in the form of incompletely and completely burned particles. A careful microscopic examination should precede any chemical examination because it is often possible to establish in this way the shape and color of unburned powder particles and to distinguish many kinds of powder (see Chapter 10).

Black powder, which consists of potassium nitrate, sulfur, and charcoal, is identified by the presence of potassium and nitrate in the entrance wound. Smokeless powder consists chiefly of nitrocellulose or of nitrocellulose with nitroglycerine and is identified by the presence of nitrite, which can be detected by various microchemical reactions. The grains of smokeless powder are generally coated with graphite and occur in many forms, e.g., round or angular discs, pellets, and cylinders.

MARKS FROM PRIMERS

At one time a primer generally contained a percussion composition of fulminate of mercury, stibnite (antimony sulfide), and potassium chlorate with a varying amount of powdered glass. Primers now have eliminated the mercury and the rust-forming products from the potassium chlorate. This has resulted in the replacement of the mercury fulminate by lead compounds, such as lead azide and lead styphnate, and in the replacement of the potassium chlorate by barium nitrate.

Thus in a chemical examination of a gunshot injury, the metals that first come into question are barium, lead, and antimony. For example, determining the lead content of a bullet wound and comparing it with that obtained from a test discharge against a similar object with the same ammunition from different distances, quite reliable information regarding the distance from which the actual shot was fired can be obtained in favorable cases.

TRACES FROM BULLETS

With injuries from plain lead bullets, such as those usually used in ordinary revolver ammunition, there is always a considerable amount of lead in the zone of blackening and in the smudge ring; in the latter it is even possible to detect lead from a distant shot. Lead traces from the surface of the bullet can also be found frequently in the exit hole. In some types of ammunition the bullet is greased; residues from these substances may be carried along with the bullet and found around the entrance opening. Metal-jacketed bullets consist of an inner lead core with an outer shell of some hard metal or alloy—the so-called jacket; the usual materials are copper, cupronickel, or brass. Traces of all these metals may be found in gunshot injuries.

TRACES FROM CARTRIDGE CASES

It is sometimes possible to detect copper in the track and in perforated clothing up to a range of 6 to 8 inches. This comes from the cartridge case, from which the expansion pressure wears off small particles of metal. Large amounts of copper found in the dirt ring are considered a characteristic indication of a close shot. If, however, a copper-coated bullet has been used, then naturally no conclusion can be drawn regarding the possibility of a close shot because, in this case, even a distant shot shows a distinct amount of copper.

TRACES FROM THE BARREL OF THE WEAPON

Iron can be found in and around the entrance wound in a case of shooting with a weapon that has not been used for a long time because the barrel may be rusty. With automatic hand weapons, traces of iron can be detected up to a distance of 8 to 12 inches.

INJURIES FROM SMALL SHOT

With shotguns, the shot column can have a very concentrated effect at distances up to 1 yard. With a distance of up to 4 to 8 inches, the wound is practically circular. The greater the distance is, the more irregular the wound is. At a distance of up to 2 to 3 yards there is generally a central entrance opening and around it are single small holes from the individual scattered shot. At a greater distance the shot spreads out more into small groups; at 10 yards the scattering can amount to 12 to 16 inches.

DAMAGE TO CLOTHES FROM SHOOTING

If a shot has passed through clothes, the position of the bullet hole should be compared with the direction of the wound track in the body in the same way as described previously in the section "Marks or Damage on Clothing."

MODES OF DEATH FROM SHOOTING

In suicide the weapon is usually directed against the forehead, temple, or heart; a shot fired upward and obliquely into the mouth is quite common. In deciding if a case is a suicide, an attempt should first be made to decide to what extent the victim could have fired the shot in the approximate direction given by the track. In the case of pistol or revolver shots against the temple, it is necessary to know whether the deceased was right- or left-handed; however, a person might fire a weapon with the left hand but be otherwise right-handed.

It is an essential condition for the assumption of suicide that the victim be wounded by a close discharge and that the weapon lies in the proper position with respect to the body. If these conditions indicate suicide the question should not be considered settled because nothing prevents some other person from firing the shot under the given conditions and then laying the weapon down in the proper position.

A more certain indication is if injuries produced when firing a shot are found on the hand of the dead person in the form of a mark on the thumb or forefinger or on the web of the thumb. Such marks may result from the recoil of the slide of an automatic pistol. The most certain proof of suicide is found in the form of fragments of tissue and blood-spattered from the wound onto the hand of the dead person. Although in cases of suicide, the hand of the deceased may be blackened by powder, this cannot be taken as proof because the weapon could have been pressed in the hand after the shot was fired. It is also necessary to decide whether the body is in a natural position under the circumstances. A fairly certain sign of suicide is when the person has taken off any hindering clothes or exposed some part of the body before firing. No weapon near the body is a very suspicious circumstance, but hasty conclusions should not be drawn from that fact alone. In some cases a fatally injured person has traveled a long way before finally expiring or has thrown the weapon into a body of water. It has also happened that members of the victim's family have removed the weapon deliberately in order to create an appearance of murder, sometimes in the hope of escaping what they consider to be the disgrace of a suicide in the family or to collect a life insurance policy.

It is a certain indication that a person died through the action of some other person when the discharge was beyond arm's reach. "Arm's reach" means the length of the arm plus possible assistance from an extension in the form of a stick or some other convenient means of reaching the trigger of a long-barreled weapon. It is true that it is possible to commit suicide by means of a distant shot, but this requires arrangements of such a type (string-pulls, etc.) that there should be no difficulty in revealing the truth. When the fatal shot was fired from behind, it is safe to assume that it is not suicide. A suicide *could* fire a shot at the back of the head, but such a possibility is very far-fetched. The fact that the deceased has more than one injury cannot always be taken as proof that death was from the action of some other person. Cases occur in which a suicide has fired two or possibly a number of shots, each of which produced a potentially lethal wound, before becoming incapable of continuing the firing.

It is quite common for a person to be fatally shot by accident or through personal fault. During hunting, it is possible to slip or stumble on uneven ground, fall when climbing over a gate or other obstacle, or drop the weapon, whereupon a fatal shot may be fired. In such cases, generally marks at the scene of the accident or marks on the weapon give a clear indication of what has happened. A fatal shot may also be fired accidentally when handling a firearm, e.g., when cleaning it. In such cases, the investigating officer should observe the greatest caution and not assume from the start that it was an accident. The victim may very well have committed suicide while giving the incident the appearance of an accident or a murderer may also simulate an accident.

The CSI who carries out the investigation of a fatal shooting should not attempt to carry out any experiments that impinge on the responsibilities of the pathologist or criminalist. However, it may be necessary to undertake precautionary measures in connection with evidence that may be lost or destroyed. It has been stated before that, in and around a gunshot wound, traces of incompletely burned powder residues, of metals from the primer, cartridge case, and bullet, grease, and dirt from the bullet and from the barrel of the weapon, as well as other such evidence, may be found. These marks may be of decisive significance in deciding, for example, the distance of the shooting; therefore, they must be protected as much as possible. In cases in which the bullet has gone through the clothes there is always the risk that evidence may be destroyed by rain or by moving the dead body. The CSI should therefore protect such evidence against destructive action by any suitable means, for example, by covering the actual place or, in suitable cases, by tying or pinning loose layers of clothing in a particular position. If there is any risk that the bullet hole in the clothes may become soaked with blood when the body is moved, the investigator must find some method of preventing it.

The hand that holds the firearm at the instant of firing can become blackened by powder in the area of the web of the thumb and on the thumb and forefinger. The deposit of powder smoke produced in this way can be identified chemically. Wrapping the deceased's hands in clean paper bags should protect them for later examination in the morgue.

EXPLOSION INJURIES

Explosion injuries are a variation of gunshot injuries. An explosive charge contains metal parts or is enclosed in a metal container that breaks up, e.g., a hand grenade; when it fractures metal objects, stones, ball bearings or the like in the immediate vicinity, the fragments thrown off have an exceptionally great force that quickly decreases. When such pieces from an explosion hit a nearby body they can produce very severe damage. A small splinter of only a few millimeters in diameter can perforate the brainpan. When it penetrates the body, it bores a wound channel that can easily be mistaken for a bullet track. The energy in a fragment from an explosion decreases so rapidly that generally it is not able to penetrate the body. At close quarters, air pressure alone can cause fatal injury.

The fatal effect of an explosive charge is limited to the immediate vicinity; at a greater distance air pressure may cause injury from falling. Another way of committing suicide is to detonate dynamite in the mouth. The effect of such an explosion is generally that the head is torn away, while the skin of the back of the neck, with adhering bone and soft parts, is left on the neck. Suicide by explosion in the mouth can be carried out with nothing more than a blasting cap. In this case the injuries are to the throat and breathing organs. Generally, no damage is visible in the face; the lips and the skin of the face remain uninjured. Suicide has also been achieved by an explosive vest placed on the torso, in which extensive lacerations are produced.

The CSI should remember that wounds should be photographed, even when they are on a living person. The investigator should therefore try to contact the doctor who has treated an injured person in order to discuss the possibility of photographing. This should not be delayed too long because a wound changes its appearance as it heals or is altered by therapy. Especially in the case of bite wounds and wounds of which the form reveals the character of the weapon or instrument, it is important that photographing should be done before a scab forms or an operation becomes necessary. A scale should always be laid next to the wound.

DEATH BY SUFFOCATION

The actual mode of death may be by hanging, strangulation, by hand, ligature, covering the mouth or nose, blocking the larynx or windpipe, crushing to death, or drowning.

HANGING

A mode of death in which a cord is placed around the neck and tightened by the weight of the body constitutes hanging. The effect of hanging is that the blood circulation to the brain ceases very quickly, which produces immediate unconsciousness; at the same time the air passages are closed up so that respiration ceases. The action of the heart may actually continue so that death occurs only after some minutes. With violent modes of hanging, injury may be produced to the vertebrae and spinal cord. The noose need not be very tight because only a small part of the weight of the body needs to be taken up for the hanging to be effective; the body does not need to hang free. The effect is the same if the hanging occurs with the body supported in a leaning, kneeling, sitting, or lying position. No one can escape from a tight-drawn noose once hanging in it because vagal inhibition occurs rapidly. This has been shown by a number of cases of persons who wished to try the effect of a hanging without any intention of completing it—they found themselves unable to recover from their situation. Thus children have been killed by hanging when, out of curiosity, they wanted to test a hangman's noose. Similarly, in some cases a hanging situation has been arranged in order to obtain a perverse sexual stimulation. The commonly held view that death by hanging may be preceded by an erotic sensation is, however, certainly incorrect.

In suicide by hanging, the rope may break and the suicide falls down, but subsequently repeats the hanging with another rope and possibly at another place. This may necessitate tedious investigations because the suicide may have received bleeding injuries caused by the fall or when, after the unsuccessful attempt, he or she wandered around in a daze. In such a case, wounds, marks of blood, and disorder at the scene might be incorrectly interpreted as signs of a struggle.

The rope used is often slender cord, but other objects may be used, for example, belts, suspenders, towels, scarves, thick shoelaces, etc. After hanging a typical mark on the neck is usually found: the so-called hanging groove. The broader and softer the noose, the less clearly the hanging groove shows. This is also the case when some part of the clothing comes between the noose and the neck. As a rule, however, the groove is distinct and full of detail, and it is often possible to distinguish marks of twisting, knots, and irregularities, while the width of the cord used can be calculated quite accurately.

The hanging groove generally has a typical appearance. The greatest pressure is exerted opposite the suspension point, i.e., if suspended from the back of the neck, the noose, if it is sufficiently thin or narrow, on the front side may have pressed in so deeply that it lies almost concealed by a roll of flesh. The groove then runs upward at an angle around the side of the neck, becomes less marked, and finally fades away as it approaches the back of the neck. The edges of the groove are generally puckered in the direction in which the cord slipped when the noose tightened. When hanging occurs in a lying or inclined position the groove may be more horizontal, which gives it a certain similarity with a strangulation groove, from which it can easily be distinguished because the hanging groove is less marked and disappears at the back of the neck. In cases of strangling in which the suspect's hands were held between the loop and the neck, the groove also disappears in the direction toward the hands. In general, however, the fingernails or knuckles produce such a great pressure against the neck that contusions appear in the skin. In rare cases, the noose may be applied at an angle on the neck or at the back of the neck, but the effect intended is still obtained because the large arteries of the neck are compressed effectively even when this method of hanging is used. Sometimes the noose may slip upward after the first tightening, whereby two or more hanging grooves are produced. This may give rise to suspicion of a crime, but generally the pathologist finds no difficulty in elucidating the actual circumstances. It can happen that a hanged person's fingers are found between the noose and the neck. This was not due to attempting to loosen the noose, but rather to the fingers not having been removed when the noose tightened.

On the skin of the neck, dead persons may show marks that can easily be confused with hanging grooves. Articles of clothing pressing against the neck can produce such marks. On bodies that have been in water for a long time or that are undergoing decomposition, the hanging groove may disappear.

Murder by hanging is rare. It could be used on children or persons who are unconscious and unable to defend themselves. In such cases, it is to be expected that the victim will show injuries other than those that occur from hanging. A murderer may attempt to give the appearance of suicide by hanging up the body after the onset of unconsciousness or death. If this is done by hoisting up the body, distinct clues may be present on the supporting object and on the rope. For example, a branch of a tree may show such a clear mark of rubbing on the bark that it is not difficult to elucidate the actual circumstances—especially when the rope has also slipped sideways. On the part of the rope that has lain on and slipped against the support, the fibers are always directed upward against the latter.

Persons who have committed suicide by hanging sometimes show other injuries, which alone could be fatal. In such cases hanging was employed after an unsuccessful attempt to commit suicide by other means. Such cases are easy to distinguish from those in which hanging is the final phase in a murder. Conditions generally give a clear picture of the course of events.

When a body is hanging free but there is no jumping-off point, such as a chair, table, step, stone, or stump in the vicinity, then there is every reason to suspect murder. In such cases, the scene must be examined carefully in order to determine whether it was possible for anyone to have climbed up to the point of attachment. With trees it is easy to find marks of climbing, e.g., twigs broken off or leaves, bark, or moss torn away, and similar traces should be found on the clothing of the dead person. An easily removable starting point, e.g., a chair, may actually have been removed by mistake before the arrival of the police.

In cases of hanging, livid stains are strongly marked on the feet, legs, and hands, and also immediately above the hanging groove. If such marks should be found on the back of a freely hanging body, for example, there is a question of the hanging having been done some time after death. The same question arises in a case when the arms or legs are bent because it is possible that the body may have been hung up after the onset of rigidity. After the rigidity has relaxed and the limbs have become straight, in some cases the wrinkles remaining in the clothes can indicate that the limbs were previously bent.

The presence of dirt on the clothes, e.g., leaves, parts of plants, soil, dust, or other material that is not present at the scene of the hanging should be noted especially, as should the presence of blood, saliva, or urine flowing in the wrong direction. Such observations may give rise to suspicion of a crime. If the knots and noose are formed in such a way that it is doubtful whether the dead person could have made them, this must be considered a suspicious circumstance.

In suicide by hanging, right-handed persons usually place the knot of the noose on the right-hand side of the neck and left-handed ones on the left; reversal of these positions is suspicious. When investigating a case of hanging, the CSI should always have in mind that the autopsy can rarely decide between murder and suicide. As a rule, the course of events can be determined only from examination of the scene and police investigation.

STRANGLING

This is usually done by hand or with a cord. In strangulation by hand, death sometimes occurs almost immediately from shock, but usually the squeezing of the neck arteries is incomplete, so death results from interruption of the supply of air to the lungs.

In manual strangulation, typical fingernail marks are on both sides of the throat—from the fingernails on one side and from the thumbnail on the other. If the criminal is right-handed, the mark of the thumbnail is generally on the right side of the throat and on the left side if left-handed. There are often marks of several grips with the hands and abrasion of the skin where the fingers slipped. When death has occurred from shock, marks of nails may be missing. Strangulation is generally preceded by a struggle, so other injuries may be found on the body, usually scratches or bleeding on the face, as well as marks on the clothes. Also present might be petechial hemorrhages in the white parts of the eyes (tiny red pinpoint marks on the eyes, resulting from blood leaking from the tiny capillaries) due to asphyxia.

Strangulation by hand has nearly always resulted from extraneous violence, i.e., from another person, although individual cases of suicide by strangulation by hand have occurred, with the suicide using a passive support for the hands so that the grip does not slip when unconsciousness occurs. In strangulation by ligature, death occurs in the same way as with hanging, but the strangulation groove generally has a course and appearance different from that of a hanging groove. Usually it goes around the neck in a horizontal direction or its back part may be situated somewhat lower down on the neck than the front part on the throat. In some cases it can, like the hanging groove, be directed back and upward. Usually the strangulation groove is located lower on the neck than the hanging groove.

Strangulation with a cord can generally be considered murder and defense injuries are usually found on the victim. Such injuries may be absent if the victim was overcome from behind or if a sleeping, unconscious, or defenseless person has been strangled. In a case in which the cord is left on the throat after the crime, it is generally fixed tightly by means of a number of turns and knots.

Strangulation with a cord is a rare form of suicide. In cases in which suicide can be presumed, the strangling has been carried out with a running noose or by a scarf, rope, or the like, laid around the neck and knotted with a half knot, which is drawn so tightly that the neck arteries are compressed and unconsciousness supervenes. In both cases, one can expect that the hands will hold the noose fast after death or that their position relative to it will give clear evidence of suicide.

In investigating the scene of a hanging or strangling, the procedure to be followed should be the same as described previously for the investigation of murder in general. It is important that the CSI learn something about how the knots and nooses that occur in hanging and strangling are made. The formation of knots and nooses of a certain type often indicates whether or not the person hanged could have made them. When a knot or noose is of a type that could not have been made by the victim, then this must cause suspicion. There is a reason for being suspicious when, in a case of hanging or strangling, skillfully made knots and nooses have been found.

In describing knots and nooses the usual names may be used, but it is not to be expected that everyone who reads the report will be familiar with them; therefore, their construction should be reproduced by a sketch or sketches and they should also be photographed.

The noose should be examined immediately and the origin of the material used should be determined as quickly as possible. If one or both ends of the cord have been recently cut and the corresponding pieces are not found at the scene, this circumstance must be elucidated. Cut-off portions of the material of the noose are often found at the scene and, in such a case, scissors or another edged tool should be found in a likely place.

The ground under or around a hanged person must be investigated as soon as possible so that any evidence will not be destroyed. If the individual was murdered and then hanged in order to give the appearance of suicide, it is to be expected that distinct evidence will be found because considerable effort is required to hang up a dead body.

It is not uncommon for a person to commit suicide by hanging or strangling but take measures to give it the appearance of murder. These measures may consist of binding the legs and attempts to bind the hands, but this, especially the attempt to bind the hands, is easily detected. The individual may also have used some kind of gag, for example, a handkerchief that is pushed in or bound around the mouth.

Knots in a hanging noose should not be undone or cut except in cases in which the victim's life may still be saved. Where it is possible, cut the rope or cord some distance above the head, loosen the noose, and pull it over the head.

Taking down a dead body must be done carefully so that no new injuries are produced. A convenient way is to raise the body a little so that the cord slackens and then cut the cord. The body is laid down and the noose is allowed to remain on the body. After the noose has been examined and photographed in its original condition, it is up to the pathologist to remove it during the autopsy.

The part remaining on the carrying object should be cut off at such a point that the knots are not altered or damaged, after which the cut-off parts are immediately bound together with string. If, for example, a cord is wound in several turns around the carrying object, a diagrammatic sketch of the arrangement is drawn as a reminder, after which the cord is cut and immediately wound around a similar object of the same diameter. When the line is composed of several parts (double or multiple), they are cut one by one and tied together in succession with cord or thread.

If it is suspected that a body has been hung up after death, the fibers in the cord must be protected, most conveniently by placing it stretched out in a long box so that it hangs freely. It can be held fast by loops attached by pins to the sides of the box.

What has been said about removing the hanging noose and strangling cord is the principal rule in cases in which it is to be expected that the life of the individual can be saved. If, however, the body has been dead for a long time (with certain signs of death present, e.g., putrefaction), the noose or cord is left in an untouched condition. The pathologist will examine it when making the postmortem examination. When, for any reason, the investigating officer must remove the noose or cord from such a body, the knots must not be deranged or loosened. A running noose can be loosened so far that it can be slipped over the head, but before that, the position of the knot on the fixed part should be marked in some way, e.g., with chalk or by sticking in a piece of wire or winding a thread around it. If the noose is tight and cannot be passed over the head, it is cut off at a convenient point, generally at one side of the neck, after which the ends are immediately tied together with string. The same method is used for conditions in which the cord cannot be loosened and drawn over the head. In such a case, the position of the knot on the fixed part is marked, after which the cutting is done.

In cases of strangulation the ligature should be removed in the same way as a noose in the case of hanging. Special care should be taken not to cut through knots that may not be visible from the outside. In general, the ligature should be removed in such a way that the manner of application may be reliably reconstructed. This may require photography and simple sketches to illustrate the various layers and knots.

Because the knots in a cord may be required as evidence, they must be sealed in a suitable manner and the circumference of the constructive loops should be measured and recorded.

BLOCKING OF THE MOUTH OR NOSE

This cause of death is rare and commonly occurs with newborn children. The stoppage may result either from a pillow or other soft object being pressed against the face or from a hand pressed against the mouth and nose. Death occurs from suffocation. Suffocation may also result from the mouth and nose being stopped with a handkerchief, piece of cloth, or cotton. When a pillow or other soft material is used there are no typical marks, but saliva or mucus may stick on the cushion and give some information about the course of events. It is possible that the suffocation may be accidental in cases in which a child turns onto his face. When suffocation or smothering is done by hand, scratches may be produced on the face. If the investigator suspects that the mouth and nose were stopped with cotton but later removed, an examination should be performed.

Elderly persons are sometimes murdered by blocking the mouth and nose with a soft covering such as a pillow. Murder can also result when a criminal, without intending to kill, has attempted to silence the cries of the victim in a case of rape.

BLOCKING OF THE LARYNX AND AIR PASSAGES

Blocking can occur, for example, when food goes down the "wrong way" or vomited stomach contents are unable to get out through the mouth. Infanticide can be committed by a finger pressed down in the throat of an infant causing suffocation. In this case there will be serious injuries in the mouth and throat.

SQUEEZING TO DEATH

This can occur, for example, with a panic in a crowd, where the victim is squeezed or trampled or when a person comes under a heavy falling object or is buried by a fall of earth. The external injuries are generally considerable and easily interpreted. Squeezing to death can generally be considered an accident, but the possibility should also be kept in mind that an earth slide was arranged with the intention of murder.

DROWNING

This is death due to liquid entering the breathing passages so that access of air to the lungs is prevented. The liquid need not necessarily be water; it may be mud, sludge, or other viscous material. Neither does the whole of the body need to be under the liquid. A person can drown when only the mouth and nose are under the surface. In a more general sense, the word "drowning" is used for every case of death in water, but this is incorrect because a death (for example, while bathing) may be due to heart failure, cerebral hemorrhage, or shock.

When a drowned person is drawn out of the water, white foam often comes out of the mouth and nostrils, where it forms white spongy puffs that can remain for quite a long time owing to the mucus contained in it.

When the cause of death is simply drowning, murder is comparatively rare and, as a rule, is committed only against children. If injuries are found on a drowned person that might have been produced by some other person, the drowning can generally be considered merely the final phase of a course of events involving murder or manslaughter. It can also happen that a criminal attempts to conceal the discovery of the crime by sinking the victim under water.

In cases of drowning, the question is generally whether it is suicide or accident. If the clothes have been removed or the place is chosen with the idea of avoiding the risk of bumping against a stony bottom, suicide is indicated. The opposite can indicate accident, as can marks of slipping found on stones at the edge of the water and injuries produced when the drowning person attempted a rescue, e.g., scraping of the skin of the hands and fingers or broken and torn nails.

The body of a drowned person may be tied in some way or heavy objects attached to it to make it sink and remain on the bottom. In such cases the investigator must proceed very cautiously with the investigation; it can be judged suicide, but suspicion of criminal acts should not be excluded.

A body lying in water is exposed to damage of many kinds. Propellers of boats may produce injuries. A body hit by a propeller can be cut in half. Bodies in water are also often damaged in the breakers offshore, against rocks, or when they bump against a stony and uneven bottom.

DEATH FROM ELECTRIC CURRENT

Death from electric currents can occur from the electricity supply or from lightning. Visible injuries may be present at the points of entry and exit of the current—the so-called "current marks." If electric sparks or an arc touches the skin, the burn often shows the same form as the object producing it. When the direct injury is slight, characteristically formed fissures and figures indicate the passage of the current. The current marks are often round, sharply delineated, and light in color, or they may consist of edges or surfaces with charred skin. In severe cases the injury penetrates the underlying tissues of the musculature and bones. The surface of the skin may be impregnated with fine metallic dust, which emanates from the current-carrying object; this can be so great that it appears as a discoloration, sometimes gray or black and sometimes blue or bluish green. The metallic dust can be determined spectrographically. Considerable changes in the skin may also be produced at the point of exit of the current. At the points of entry and exit of the current, the clothing may be torn or charred; sometimes the damage consists of a number of small holes with burned edges.

Death from electric current may be accident, suicide, or murder. In some cases a trap has been set using house current, with the intention of murder.

Death from lightning is rare. When injuries are present on the body of a person assumed to have been killed in this way, they may consist of current marks on the neck and soles of the feet; the clothes may be badly torn; metal objects in the clothes may be fused together, burned, or thrown away, even in cases where no injury is apparent on the body. So-called lightning figures on the skin are not burning injuries but result from changes in the blood vessels. These arboreal marks generally disappear very quickly after death.

DEATH FROM FIRES

Only a pathologist can determine the cause of death and injuries on a person who has been burned to death. Death may be due to suffocation by smoke, carbon monoxide poisoning, or injury from falling beams, overturned furniture, falling walls, and so on. Generally, the person is already dead from such causes before the fire begins to attack the body.

Burned bodies usually lie in a distorted position, the so-called "pugilistic attitude" caused by the contraction of the muscles under the action of heat. The skin and soft tissues crack gradually; the cracks sometimes have quite even edges that can easily be confused with cut and stab wounds. The bones become more or less brittle, so breakages occur. In the inner parts of the skull the pressure may become so great that the bones of the cranium may shatter. The limbs are destroyed first as heat gradually chars the body. A greatly charred body sometimes has the form of a torso.

For complete combustion, very intense heat for a comparatively long time is required. A newborn baby can be burned away in an ordinary stove in 2 hours, but in order to consume an adult in the same time, a temperature of 1250°C is needed, after which only certain bones remain.

Murder by burning does occur, but it can generally be assumed that the victim was subjected to other injuries before the fire was started. Disposing of a body by fire after murder is not uncommon. The criminal may in both cases have caused the fire with the objective of destroying evidence. The pathologist can easily decide whether the victim of a fire was alive or dead when the fire started. No signs of inhaled smoke or flakes of soot found in the respiratory organs suggest that the person was dead before the fire. Unburned skin may be found underneath a burned body that escaped burning. Tight-fitting clothing may also protect the skin from the fire. In such places signs of external violence may show clearly. Traces of blood may be found on unburned portions of clothing under the body. Uninjured parts of the skin around the wrists and ankles may indicate that the victim was bound before the start of the fire. A ligature around the neck, destroyed in the fire, may leave a distinct strangling groove.

DEATH BY FREEZING

Freezing to death does not as a rule produce any distinguishable injuries or changes in the body. At the autopsy, red spots may possibly be observed on those parts of the body where livid stains occur more rarely, e.g., the ears, tip of the nose, fingers, and toes. As a rule, only weak, helpless, insufficiently clothed, or drunken persons freeze to death.

Freezing to death can occur as the result of criminal actions, e.g., exposure of newborn or delicate children. A person who has been rendered helpless by an assault can also freeze to death. Persons who have died from freezing are occasionally found more or less undressed. This condition naturally gives rise to suspicions of murder. However, sometimes, at an advanced state of freezing, the victim gets a sensation of heat, which may explain this action.

DEATH BY POISONING

The determination of death by poisoning is frequently a joint effort on the part of the forensic pathologist and the forensic toxicologist. Only in certain instances will the CSI find the presence of physical evidence at the crime scene that indicates the death was caused by the ingestion of some poisonous substance.

Physical evidence located at the crime scene and noted upon gross examination of the deceased may sometimes be indicative of poisoning. Evidence such as drugs, narcotic paraphernalia, markings on the body, or the presence of acids or caustic substances may give an initial basis for forming an opinion about the case.

Corrosion around the mouth and face may be the result of consumption of acids or caustic chemicals such as hydrochloric acid, sulfuric acid, or lye. Odors of ammonia or burned almonds, or an odor associated with cyanides, can indicate certain poisons. In cyanide poisoning, lividity is a reddish color.

Certain drugs, such as opium alkaloids and nicotine, cause contraction of the pupils, while others such as atropine (belladonna) produce dilation.

In death from subacute and chronic arsenic poisoning a large quantity of thin stool resembling rice, often containing blood, may be found. Considerable excretion is also usual in the later stages of poisoning from corrosive sublimate or lead salts.

Strychnine causes convulsions; the corners of the mouth are drawn up and the face is fixed in a grin; the arms and legs are drawn together and the back is severely bent backward from contraction of the muscles.

Different colored materials in the vomit can give clues to the type of poisoning. Brown material resembling coffee grounds indicates poisoning with strong alkalis such as sodium or potassium hydroxide; yellow indicates nitric and chromic acids; blue-green, copper sulfate; black, sulfuric acid; and brown-green, hydrochloric acid. A sharp-smelling vomit indicates poisoning with ammonia or acetic acid.

Murders by using a poison that must be taken internally to be effective are not numerous. Generally murder by poison is committed only within a family or close group. In such cases, the criminal generally uses some poison that will not arouse suspicion from its color, odor, or taste. Murder or attempted murder by the use of poisonous gas occurs occasionally, e.g., carbon monoxide poisoning.

The investigator should know that, in a case of death from poisoning, only the investigation at the scene and examination of witnesses could decide whether a case is murder, suicide, or accident. The autopsy and toxicology report decides only the type and quantity of poison used.

It is not possible to go into a detailed description of different poisons and their actions. The boundary between poisonous and nonpoisonous substances is indefinite. A number of substances normally present in food can cause death by poisoning when they are taken in large amounts. Thus there is a case where the consumption of 13 ounces of table salt caused the death of an adult.

A number of poisons should be mentioned, including those with a powerful action and those responsible for most cases of poisoning:

Gaseous and liquid poisons. Some of the more common of the thousands of these types of poisons are carbon monoxide, hydrogen cyanide, freon, methanol, toluene, benzene, gasoline, and chloroform.

Heavy metals and other inorganic poisons. Compounds and salts of antimony, arsenic, barium, chromium, lead, mercury, and thallium; strong inorganic acids and bases such as hydrochloric acid, nitric acid, sulfuric acid, sodium hydroxide, potassium hydroxide, and ammonia.

Alcohol, over-the-counter, and illicit drugs. Ethyl alcohol; barbiturates; heroin; synthetically produced opiates, e.g., methadone; phencyclidine (PCP); minor tranquilizers such as Valium, Librium, meprobamate and over-the-counter medication when taken in excess. These drugs may be found in combination with each other and with alcohol.

Other vegetable and animal poisons. Atropine, cocaine, nicotine, scopolamine, strychnine, and snake poisons.

Bacterial poisons and food poisoning (botulism). Ricin, anthrax, and *E coli*.

The determination of poisoning as the cause of death can be made only by autopsy and toxicology testing. In a number of cases of poisoning, however, certain details in the appearance of the dead person or special circumstances in connection with the death may give some indication. The police officer that investigates the scene of a fatal poisoning can greatly assist the pathologist by recovering any evidence of poisoning.

The most usual indications are, first, residual poison in the form of tablets, powder, or residues in medicine bottles and, second, powder wrappings, boxes, tubes, ampoules, vials, and other containers. All such clues should be recovered and each one packed separately in a tube or envelope. When the dead person is lying in bed, the bedclothes must be examined very carefully because the poison may quite possibly have been in the form of powder and any that was spilled is difficult to detect.

All medicine bottles and tubes, including empty ones, should be kept, even if the stated contents are considered to be harmless. An apparently empty bottle may contain traces of powder, which can be identified by microchemical methods. The report of the investigation must state where such objects were found. Prescriptions can be useful guides for the pathologist.

Among the most important pieces of evidence in poisoning are cups, glasses, and other containers found in the immediate vicinity of the deceased, or in such places and under such conditions that they can be placed in direct relation to the death. If liquids left in a container are found, they should be transferred to clean bottles and then sealed. When a container holds merely sediment or undissolved residues, it should be wrapped in clean paper or, preferably, in a plastic bag. If finger or palm prints are on it, these must be preserved. Spilled liquids can be collected by means of a filter paper, which is then placed in a clean glass jar and well-sealed.

When food poisoning is suspected, or it is possible that dishes may have conveyed the poison, the dishes used should be collected and packed in a suitable manner. Food dishes and remains of food are packed in a clean, well-sealed glass jar. If such clues are not sent immediately to a public health laboratory, they should be kept in a refrigerator. If there is any suspicion of crime, remains of food should be looked for, also outdoors in garbage cans, compost heaps, the ground, and other such places.

Any hypodermic syringes found should be recovered and kept in such a way that they cannot become contaminated and the contents cannot run out or be pressed out. The needle of the syringe can be conveniently stuck in a cork to prevent its breaking. Finger or palm prints on the syringe must be preserved. When hypodermic syringes are found, ampoules and vials should be looked for in the vicinity.

Vomit, saliva, and mucus on or around the dead person may contain traces of poison and must be kept. Suspected stains on clothing and bed clothes are preserved by spreading each of the articles out on clean wrapping paper and rolling them separately in the paper. Stains of urine and feces can sometimes give the pathologist a guide in making a decision and should therefore be kept.

Cases of poisoning with methyl alcohol occur at times. It can usually be assumed that other persons are involved, so bottles and drinking vessels should be examined for possible finger and palm prints.

Chronic alcohol poisoning can give rise to sudden death, especially after bodily strain. In acute alcoholism, death occurs when the concentration of alcohol in the blood reaches 0.4 to 0.6%. However, the alcoholic subject can provoke sudden death through various strokes of misfortune in a number of ways (drowning, falling, traffic accidents, freezing, suffocation from vomit that cannot be ejected, and gagging from food in the windpipe). It has often happened that an alcoholic subject, while incapacitated, has died because of falling asleep in a position that made breathing difficult.

If the pathologist is present at an investigation, he or she will decide which evidence should be collected; otherwise the CSI should keep everything that might be suspected of being poison evidence and should subsequently submit it to the pathologist or toxicologist.

The presence of certain poisons in the human body can sometimes be confirmed a long time after death. Metallic poisons do not disappear with putrefaction. Arsenic can be detected in hair and bony parts hundreds of years after death; lead also remains for a long time in the bone tissues. Scopolamine, atropine, strychnine, and morphine can be detected after several years; carbon monoxide poisoning can be detected up to 6 months after death. Potassium cyanide is decomposed during putrefaction. Hydrocyanic acid and phosphorus remain for only a short time. Hypnotics are decomposed and disappear very quickly—some even in the time that elapses between administration and the occurrence of death. An exception is barbitone (veronal), which can be detected in the body 18 months after death. In cases of exhuming a body of a person suspected to have died through poisoning from metallic poisons (especially arsenic), samples of the soil from the grave should always be taken because the soil may contain the poison.

CARBON MONOXIDE POISONING

Carbon monoxide is always produced when the combustion of carbonaceous matter is incomplete. It is a normal constituent of smoke and explosion gases and also occurs in mine gases, natural gas, and the like.

Carbon monoxide is a colorless and very poisonous gas with no odor or taste. The minimum concentration that can be injurious to human beings is 0.01 vol%, while 0.2 vol% is dangerous to life. Continued exposure to such an atmosphere can produce death within 1 hour. If the concentration increases to 0.5 vol% or more, then unconsciousness ensues after a couple of minutes and death follows quickly. With higher concentrations, unconsciousness comes on like a blow. Chronic poisoning by carbon monoxide is quite common, often due to prolonged exposure in shops, garages, traffic tunnels, and streets with high buildings and very heavy motor traffic.

The danger from carbon monoxide is due to the fact that the senses do not give warning in time. With acute carbon monoxide poisoning there is a headache, faintness, and nausea, with flickers before the eyes. This usually is regarded as a temporary indisposition, so the individual in question may make the greatest mistake possible under the circumstances, that of lying down. Gradually, the person becomes sleepy and confused, and the limbs become numb. If the person finally begins to realize the danger, it is usually too late because the body is so weak that the poisoned victim cannot move to safety. In many cases of carbon monoxide poisoning, the victim is found close to a door or window, but was unable to open it or did not think to break the glass.

In cases of carbon monoxide poisoning, it is possible that the death was murder. The investigating officer should therefore not treat the investigation too casually. To decide on suicide or accident immediately is wrong. The case should be considered suspicious from the start and treated accordingly. The analysis of the situation and the result of the investigation must determine whether criminal action should be taken into account. At the autopsy the pathologist can determine only the cause of death.

Carbon monoxide poisoning from exhaust gases of internal combustion motors can occur when the engine of a vehicle is started up and allowed to run for a while in a garage with bad ventilation. Suicide may be committed in this way.

Because of the variety of chemical substances that can be fatal, the determination of the cause of death in suspected poisoning cases is no easy task. Toxicologists play a key role in these types of cases. In some instances the problem is compounded because the human body is able to metabolize the poison into another related substance, or metabolite. Other problems, e.g., the small concentration of the poison in the body or the metabolite being naturally present, sometimes make these tests difficult.

RAPE-HOMICIDE AND SEXUAL ASSAULT-RELATED MURDERS

Rape-homicides are murders committed in connection with rape and can be included with murders involving other sexual acts such as sodomy. The methods employed in the investigation of such murders are in general the same as those techniques used in the investigation of an "ordinary" murder or suspicious death. The injuries found on the victim are often similar to those encountered in rape investigations, such as bruises on the arms and shoulders caused by forcibly holding down the victim, ligature marks on the wrists if the victim was tied, bruises on the back and buttocks caused by forcing the victim on the ground, and marks on the insides of the thighs and knees, and around the genitalia. Physical evidence such as seminal fluid, hair, blood, skin and blood found under the victim's fingernails, etc. may also be present. Trace evidence found on the victim's clothing might also be noted. The presence of alcohol or drugs should be determined from toxicological analyses.

The investigator should understand that the sexual aspects of these types of murders might manifest themselves in different and sometimes bizarre ways. Thus, sadism and other forms of sexual perversion may lead the inexperienced investigator to assume that a crime other than a sex-related murder is being investigated. Indications such as feces or urine discovered at the scene of a murder may point to a sex-related murder. Sadistic acts such as mutilation of the body and, particularly, the sex organs and breasts, and violent injuries such as biting, strangulation, and multiple stab wounds are especially significant and strongly suggest this type of murder (Figure 18.14).

In investigating the crime scene, one should look for signs of a struggle. Evidence such as marks on the ground, pieces of torn clothing, fragments of textiles, torn-off buttons, blood, semen, and the like should be searched for and collected. Specimens of sand, soil, vegetation, and other materials should be collected for comparison with debris found on the suspect's clothing.

One type of accidental death that could appear to be a sex-related murder is autoerotic asphyxiation. In this type of accidental death the victim temporarily cuts off their air supply while usually masturbating to heighten their sexual arousal. When the victim is unable to free themself, they end up suffocating to death. Since oftentimes victims are found bound, these types of deaths can have the illusion of a sex-related murder.

When a suspect is apprehended, the clothing and body should be examined immediately. Scratch marks on the hands and arms, on the face, bite marks, torn clothing, soiled clothing, hair, and blood may be important evidence. Occasionally, these suspects are placed in a Tyvek® suit to preserve this evidence.

INFANTICIDE AND CHILD ABUSE

Homicide investigations of newborn and young children involve circumstances different from adult cases. The type of injuries causing death in infants and children are often nonfatal to adults. Often the abandoned child has no means of identification. In cases resulting in death in the home, the crime scene may show little or no physical evidence to associate the injuries with the victim. Finally, when the young victim of beating or neglect is brought to the emergency room for treatment, the child is almost always unable to communicate the cause of the injuries. These are some of the problems to be addressed in children's murder investigations.

In cases of newborn death, the pathologist is required to determine whether the child was viable, that is, capable of living. The infant is considered to be viable when it has attained a stage of development such that it would remain alive without any special care, e.g., in an incubator. Babies with a length of 10 to 16 inches can certainly be born alive, but as a rule are considered not to have reached such a stage of development that they can continue to live.

Infanticide, or killing a newborn child, can be committed in a variety of ways such as intentional neglect, killing with a weapon, suffocation, forcing objects into the nose or mouth, or by drowning.

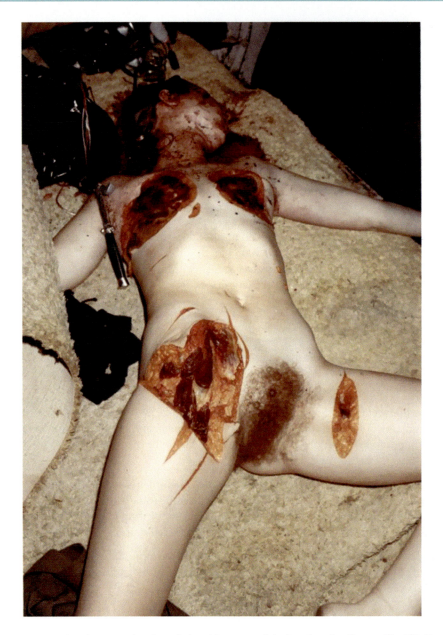

Figure 18.14 A murder case showing sex-related mutilation. (*Courtesy of the Los Angeles County Sheriff's Department.*)

Intentional neglect occurs when the parents fail to care for the child immediately after birth, in spite of being able to do so. Death may result from exposure, dehydration, or starvation. Heat regulation in the body of a newborn can be a significant factor in exposure-related deaths because the body temperature of a baby can drop rapidly.

Abandonment of the newborn child poses an additional problem. The child may be left without any means of identification. When an infant is left wrapped only in a blanket or even without any clothes, it is frequently impossible to discover evidence to determine the mother. Killing with a weapon may be carried out with blunt objects with the intent to injure the head or by striking the head against some hard object. Stabbing is another means sometimes used in infanticide.

Strangulation is another possible cause of death; manual strangling leaves injuries and sometimes scratch marks on the neck. Suffocation can be caused by placing a pillow on or using a hand to cover the mouth or nose. If the hand is used, scratch marks may be found on the face. It should be noted, however, that suffocation may be accidental and caused by the infant lying face down on soft bedding. Suffocation may also be caused by insertion of objects into the mouth. Items such as cotton inserted into the mouth may be the cause of death. Sudden infant death syndrome (SIDS) and sudden unexplained death syndrome (SUDS) must also be considered as possible causes of death.

The so-called battered child syndrome is another area in deaths of children. Frequent beatings and cruel treatment as a means of punishment or discipline sometimes result in deaths of children. Poisoning, starvation, severe beatings, and scalding in very hot water are all means of injury and often death.

Examination by a pediatrician is required in suspected child abuse cases. Often, the child is taken to the doctor or hospital emergency room and the parent may claim that the injury was the result of a fall or other unintentional injury. Careful examination of the injuries may show them to be inconsistent with the "accident" described. Also, x-rays may show several broken and healed bones characteristic of repeated and severe beating.

TRUNK MURDER, DISMEMBERMENT OF THE BODY

Trunk murder is the name commonly used to describe murders in which the criminal, in order to dispose of the body of the victim, places it in a trunk, chest, large suitcase, box, or similar container, which is then concealed or carried away. Even more commonly the victim is placed in a sack or covered with a blanket, clothing, or a tarpaulin. This crime is often associated with cutting up the body.

Dismemberment of a dead body may be offensive or defensive. The former is usually conditioned by passion and can be regarded as a form of sadism. A criminal who wants to conceal the body or to make it unrecognizable employs the latter. The method used may give information regarding occupational experience (butcher or person with anatomical knowledge), while the surfaces of the wounds can indicate the implements used (knife, ax, saw). Dust and dirt from the body can, in favorable cases, give information of local conditions where the dismemberment was carried out. The murderer may conceal parts of the body at different places over a considerable area, with the object of making identification of the victim difficult or impossible or may attempt to destroy the body, for example, in an acid bath or by burning.

Frequently, the place where the body was found is not the same as the crime scene. If the murdered person is unknown, success in the search for the crime scene depends largely on the possibility of being able to determine the origin of the containers or wrapping around the body or parts of the body. The first step is to determine if labels, stamps, or writing can throw any light on their origin. These examinations involve such delicate procedures that they should be entrusted to an expert from the beginning. The crime scene investigator's preliminary examination should therefore not become too extensive.

Dirt or dust present in the wrapping may give direct information regarding what had been in it before. Fingerprints, hair, and other traces of the criminal should be looked for. When looking for fingerprints, no development media should be used until the laboratory expert has completed the examination. Bodies or parts of bodies that are found enclosed in a package are generally wrapped in a large quantity of paper, scraps of clothing, plastic bags, etc.—obviously in order to prevent blood, other liquid, or odor from betraying the contents. The possibility that the fingerprints of the murderer will be found in blood or blood serum should be considered. Objects used to wrap the body or parts of the body can also be a useful guide in searching for the actual crime scene.

ACCIDENTAL DEATH

Occasionally an accidental death raises suspicion. The position of the body, injuries, appearance of the crime scene can all lead investigators into thinking the accidental death is a homicide. It is always better for an accidental death to be investigated as a homicide than vice versa (Figure 18.15).

SERIAL MURDERS

Serial murders are distinguished from multiple murders in that the latter are committed at about the same time and the victims are in some way connected with one another, e.g., through family ties, socially, or living close by. Serial murders occur over a period of time, sometimes years, and often over large geographic areas. Probably the most celebrated serial murderer in history was the infamous Jack the Ripper who terrorized London in the 1880s. Some

Figure 18.15 The unusual position of the body at this scene resulted from the deceased experiencing a heart attack after stepping from her bath tub. (*Courtesy of Western Maryland Regional Crime Lab.*)

infamous modern cases have occurred in New York, Los Angeles, Atlanta, Washington, and Florida. Serial murders are among the most difficult types of homicides to investigate because of their complexity and a component unique to this type of crime: public alarm.

Serial murders follow an almost predictable course. Investigators discover that the M. O. of a case they are working on has similarities to other cases. As the investigation progresses, investigators from a variety of police agencies may become involved in the investigation, as may others, i.e., criminalists, pathologists, and so on. Once it becomes clear that the case involves a serial murder, communication with all others in the total investigation is imperative. Principal investigators, forensic scientists and others who must take an active role in the case should be identified and should coordinate the investigation from this point on. All suspected future cases should be reviewed and, if possible, the crime scenes visited. Because of the delicate balance between the public's right to know and the possibility of public hysteria, all press contacts should be handled from a centralized source and specific details about the case should be withheld from the public so as not to hamper the investigation.

Once the news story breaks, enormous demands will be placed upon those responsible for the investigation. Here "cool heads" must reign. Doubtless, there will be tremendous public pressure to solve the case. Investigators will be inundated with telephone calls, yielding thousands of pieces of information (much of which will be of little value). "Copycat" cases, those with certain similarities to the serial murders, may develop.

Solving cases of the size and scope of a serial murder investigation usually involves little magic; hard work, long hours and attention to details solve these cases. The ability to sort through mountains of information, recognize behavioral patterns, and, above all, coordinate the efforts of scores of people associated with the various elements of the case makes for a successful investigator.

One final talent for the investigator to master is worth mentioning: leadership. This know-how plays a part in serial murder investigations and may also affect other types of police investigations. The detective is ultimately responsible for running a police investigation. He or she must rely on a host of professionals within the criminal justice system. Interpersonal skills really make a difference. Learning how to ask rather than demand, saying thank you for some extra effort, and establishing good, long-term cooperative working relationships distinguish the great investigator from the adequate one.

Death investigation brings together nearly all the skills and principles discussed throughout this text. It requires the coordination and cooperation of many disciplines and the capability of the investigator to assimilate large amounts of information. The skills needed to process the crime scene and the ability to recognize, collect, and preserve physical evidence are crucial. A mastery of the techniques of crime scene investigation is essential to modern law enforcement.

Further Reading

D'Michelle, P. DuPre. *Homicide Investigation Field Guide.* Academic Press, 2013.

Geberth, Vernon J. *Practical Homicide Investigation: Tactics, Procedures, and Forensic Techniques.* CRC Press, 2020.

Hanzlick, M. D. *Death Investigation: Systems and Procedures.* CRC Press, 2017.

Maloney, Michael S. *Death Scene Investigation: Procedural Guide.* CRC Press, 2017.

Chapter Questions

1. What are some of the initial questions that should be answered during a death investigation?
2. What is the difference between cause and manner of death?
3. Describe rigor mortis, algor mortis, and livor mortis.
4. In cases of violent death, why is it important to determine the apparent cause of death as soon as possible?
5. List some of the details a CSI should examine at a death scene.
6. What are the first types of insects to attack a dead body?
7. What are the similarities and differences between processing outdoor vs indoor death scenes?
8. What are the 5 categories of manner of death?
9. What are the signs of carbon monoxide poisoning?
10. What physical evidence is used to support a poisoning case?

Chapter 19

Digital Evidence and the Electronic Crime Scene

We live in a digital age. Much of our personal and business information is stored on computers, smart phones, tablet devices, portable USB "thumb" drives, off-line locations such as the "cloud," on audio and video digital storage devices, and so forth. In fact, the types and nature of digital storage devices keep growing. It should be no surprise that digital information becomes important in criminal investigations.

It is easy to lose important data when you do not know what you are doing. Therefore, a word to the wise: be certain to know what you are doing *before* you do anything when digital evidence is concerned or bring in a subject matter expert! Most agencies now have digital evidence or computer forensic units within their agencies. If your agency does not have one, state and federal agencies are available for that purpose. Regional Computer Forensics Laboratories (RCFL)* are located across the United States and can offer assistance. The RCFL program is a partnership between the FBI and other federal, state, and local law enforcement agencies. It provides forensic services and expertise in collecting and examining digital evidence for a wide range of investigations.

Like the types of digital devices discovered at crime scenes and criminal investigation in general, the types of crimes that may have pertinent digital evidence are equally considerable. A partial list follows; however, almost any crime may have a digital evidence component:

Child pornography.

Identity theft.

Gambling.

Fraud.

Terrorism.

Crimes of violence.

Trade secret theft.

Theft or destruction of intellectual property.

Financial crime.

Property crime.

Internet crimes.

Organized crime and drugs.

Public corruption.

Distribution of proceeds from other crimes.

White-collar crimes.

---

* For additional information, visit www.rcfl.gov/.

The FBI defines digital forensics as the application of science and engineering to the recovery of digital evidence in a legally acceptable method. Examiners use digital investigation and analysis techniques to determine potential legal evidence by applying their skills on a variety of software programs, different operating systems, varying hard drives sizes, and specific technologies. Examiners are capable of locating deleted, encrypted, or damaged file information that may serve as evidence in a criminal investigation.

The scope of digital evidence analysis is far too complex for this textbook, however, knowing what to do with digital evidence when encountered at a crime scene is crucial.

COMPUTER SEIZURE

With the massive amounts of electronic information being created and stored by individuals and companies, computer crimes are becoming more and more widespread. These computer crimes include a wide variety of crimes including child pornography, phishing scams, fraud, embezzlement, harassment, bullying, blackmail, and intellectual property theft, and identity theft.

When encountering a computer or any type of computer equipment or data devices (CDs, USB drives, portable hard drives, memory cards, smartphones, smartwatches, Internet of Things (IoT) devices, etc.) at a crime scene, the most important thing to remember is not to be in a hurry. Unless a suspect is destroying something in front of your eyes (which does happen), you can safely assume that the evidence is not going to be lost.

Digital devices like iPods, iPads, cameras, voice recorders, flash drives, and cell phones have become so commonplace that it is easy for CSIs to think that they are not related to a crime. All of these devices can hold both images and documents. Officers must, therefore, seize all types of electronic equipment because files can be stored on anything that a computer sees as a "drive."

The most common way computer evidence is destroyed is from mishandling the seized equipment. Some of the ways this happens are as follows:

Investigators become impatient and want to look at data by using the normal start-up and access procedures without considering the possibility of computer booby traps set by suspects, which may destroy data.

The nonexpert uses common software to start up the equipment. The software has properties that destroy the data.

Equipment (hardware and/or software) is mishandled at the crime scene or en route to the lab by improper evidence packaging or transportation.

Unauthorized persons get involved in looking at evidence through curiosity or a haphazard request—the "Hey Fred, do you know anything about computers?" syndrome.

You do not need to be an expert to seize a computer, but you should consult an expert. You will need experts to analyze and locate relevant computer data for your case properly and legally. Data and computer equipment must be treated like any other seized evidence. Chain of custody procedures and warrants also apply to digital evidence and specify what specifically is to be seized (i.e., CPU, peripheral devices, removable media, routers, etc.).

STEPS TO REMEMBER

- Consult your agency's computer crimes unit or other appropriate experts for advice prior to seizure.
- When approaching computer equipment at a crime scene, clear everyone away from the equipment and do not allow anyone to touch any of the equipment.
- With stand-alone computers (computers without network cables), pull the power cord to turn them off. Do not touch the keyboard or any of the switches! This ensures that no data is written to the hard drive. Depending on the type of alleged crime, a triage tool should sometimes be used to capture data from a live system. Once the power is pulled from the computer, potential probative data can be lost (i.e., whether an encryption application is running).
- If the system involves a network, do not unplug them. Call your agency's forensic computer expert before proceeding.
- If possible, take photos of the front and rear of all computers (where cables are attached).

- Before disconnecting any cables, label all connectors and computer connections with numbers or letters. Disconnect as few cables as possible. It may be necessary to disconnect some to avoid unsafe or heavy lifting; but usually one end of a cable can be disconnected, leaving the other end attached to a device. (Each cable should have two labels.)
- Attach an evidence tag to each individual piece of equipment and properly label it with the brand name, type, and model and serial numbers.
- Place all seized data CDs, memory cards, USB thumb drives, portable hard drives, etc., in labeled evidence envelopes. Keep magnetic storage media away from magnetic fields. Do not store in a hot area such as the trunk of a car.
- Document where all items were found at the location and who found them.
- Leave an inventory receipt form with persons at the location.
- Transport equipment in an enclosed vehicle. Avoid pickup beds and car trunks. If possible, use boxes and car seats or a van.
- Store equipment in a safe place where it is out of the way and will not be tripped over or stepped on.

In certain circumstances, it may be necessary to do an on-scene evidence preview to help determine what specific devices to look for. A preview of a suspect's hard drive can show whether an external device like a USB thumb drive or external hard drive was connected and when. An investigator should only perform this type of investigation in the field if they have the right training and equipment (Figure 19.1a and b).

Once the computer has been sent to the digital evidence laboratory, the following types of computer evidence can be examined for probative information: address books, diaries, email, financial records, images, internet activity logs, medical records, websites visited, internet searches, connection to other routers, and usernames and passwords.

COLLECTING VIDEO EVIDENCE

The utilization of video surveillance technology is a commonplace occurrence today. CCTV is used in banks, businesses, taxi cabs, government facilities, and many other places in order to deter robberies, shoplifting, and other crimes. It is also used for monitoring public areas in casinos, sports arenas, city streets, mass transit, and parking lots. Law enforcement uses include undercover operations, emergency and disaster responses, media releases, and crime scene recording, to mention just a few. Of course, the ubiquitous smartphone video camera plays a significant role not only in social media posts, but also in periodically recording unusual and occasionally provocative incidents. The

Figure 19.1 (a, b) A USB thumb drive disguised to look like a child's toy figure. Important electronic data can be easily hidden from investigators in this fashion.

following information is provided as a standard procedure for handling, securing, and protecting video information so that maximum investigative utility may be obtained and investigator's time and effort minimized.

DETERMINE IF THERE IS A VIDEO

One of the first questions asked by investigators responding to the crime scene should be, "Is there a video of the incident? Where are the cameras? Where are the recorders?"

STOP THE RECORDER

Often recorders continue after a crime has been committed; therefore, one of the first things to be done at the crime scene is to stop the recorders to avoid accidentally recording over the information captured.

CONFISCATE THE RECORDING MEDIUM IMMEDIATELY

When handling video evidence, note the time on the recorder and simultaneously note the actual time. Do this to the highest degree of accuracy possible, that is, to the second. Often the actual time and the time on the recorder will not be the same. Therefore, this time discrepancy may be needed and may be important in subsequent analysis. Also note any time differences with any other clocks in the vicinity that may have been noticed by witnesses. Next, note the position counter on the recorder and then write down the information about the recorder. Note the manufacturer, the model, the time-lapse mode, and any other recorder settings.

In addition to locating video equipment at the scene of a crime, look for additional videos that may have a view of a crime (perhaps down the street from the scene) and may contain, for instance, the car driving away. For example, when a crime occurs at a mall, convenience stores or bank ATM videos may record suspects entering or leaving the crime area. In addition, suspects may have been in other nearby locations, for instance, streets used for entry or exit routes. Also, it may be useful to look at recordings made earlier than when the crime occurred because sometimes suspects may have visited the location prior to the crime. If other tapes are located, the collection procedures mentioned previously also apply to them.

Many residential homes today contain video doorbells, such as the Ring* or Nest† systems. Contacting homeowners along the escape route a suspect may have taken can oftentimes yield video footage of the suspect's license plate or other investigative leads.

If the video is in digital format, make sure that the video collected is not compressed. Often uncompressed video will be in a format native to the manufacturer of the recording system. Uncompressed video ensures that no data is lost from the recording. It may be necessary to also obtain the software that plays the uncompressed video.

DOCUMENT THE VIDEO SYSTEM'S PHYSICAL RELATIONSHIP TO THE CRIME SCENE

Note the location of the cameras and their views in the report or diagram and photograph this data. Additionally, the size (height, depth, width) of reference objects in the scene should be measured so that they can be utilized to determine physical dimensions of other things such as the height of a suspect.

Protect the video! Make sure that the recording medium (tape, disc, computer, etc.) cannot be recorded over. More modern systems record directly onto a hard drive.

Once you have a video, what is the best procedure? Although it is often compelling, do not play it; remove the video and have it copied, thereby saving the original for laboratory examination. The reason this procedure is recommended is that in case something happens to the recording during the analysis and/or enhancement, the original can always be gone back to. If you go through the trouble to collect the video as evidence, it should be prudently handled.

---

* www.ring.com.
† www.nest.com.

From a CCTV analyst's perspective, the most common error is the following: only a portion of a recording is analyzed but additional or corroborating information appears in earlier parts of the recording.

Make certain that the original is secured as evidence and stored where it will not be damaged by any magnetic fields such as electric motors, solenoids, and magnetic metal detectors. Take care that the recording does not overheat; do not leave it in a hot car. Store it in a cool, dry location. Excessive heat and humidity will cause deterioration.

SEEK TECHNICAL ASSISTANCE IF PROBLEMS OCCUR

Any of the National Law Enforcement and Corrections Technology Centers (NLECTC)* may be contacted for advice and assistance if needed. Also, the FBI has the capability to perform video analysis and many of the larger criminalistics laboratories around the nation are available for consultation, guidance, and assistance.

What can be expected from the analysis of video recordings? They can show the crime scene; they often provide a synopsis of a crime and/or a description of a crime scene that would be hard to describe in words or testimony alone. The video is physical evidence similar to a photograph. It may provide images of actions, statements, or other physical evidence that may be part of a crime (handgun, rifle, knife, car) and it provides a format for which associative evidence may be used to establish a connection between a crime scene and an individual—for instance, the car at a crime scene compared with a car of a suspect or shoes observed on a person on the video of a crime compared with shoes of the suspect. Not only might it show a connection between a suspect and a crime, it might also provide an alibi for innocent individuals. In addition, video (even stop-action video) can be used to show action in a fashion from which intent may be inferred. For instance, motion video of a person can reveal vigor of actions (pace), emotions, or other outward indicators of his or her state of mind, not simply identity as a still photograph does. Newer technologies offer enhancements of faces and license plates depicted in video that can provide investigative leads. Video footage of a crime can also aid a criminalist in determining the most probative piece of evidence to collect and/or test. For example, video footage in the elevator of a residential apartment building showed the attacker of a rape victim touching certain areas of the elevator wall. These areas could then be focused on for fingerprinting and trace DNA collection. In addition, because of the high quality resolution of many videos today, ridge detail on the fingers can sometimes be seen; these video stills can be transformed into uploadable prints that can be searched in IAFIS to determine a person's identity when their face is not in the frame.

What is the difference between facial identification and facial recognition? Facial identification is the discipline of image-based comparisons of human facial features. Facial recognition is the automated searching of a facial image in a biometric database, typically resulting in a group of facial images ranked by computer-evaluated similarity. When performing facial image comparisons, an examiner performs a manual process to identify similarities between a facial image and a subject for the purposes of determining if they are the same person. The process of facial image comparison is similar to fingerprint comparisons in that it utilizes a morphological analysis of features of the face using the ACE-V method. (Photo or video anthropometry, or measurement of dimensions and angles of facial features, is not recommended!)

Despite what is seen on television, facial recognition systems present several limitations and are not as reliable as they claim to be. Some limitations are that the subject must be part of the database, the algorithms in these systems don't always recognize the same details that the human brain can perceive, and faces are not static like fingerprints and can change.

Preparation and planning are the keys to success in gathering digital evidence from digital media. Well-trained technicians knowledgeable in the procedure can make the best use of this powerful tool.

MOBILE DEVICE FORENSICS†

There are countless makes and models of mobile devices in use today and rapid changes in their technology present a unique forensic challenge. Before responding to a scene that might contain electronic evidence make sure that the

---

* www.iacpcybercenter.org/.
† The Scientific Working Group on Digital Evidence (SWGDE) has put together Best Practices for Mobile Device Evidence Collection & Preservation Handling and Acquisition.

Figure 19.2 A Faraday bag or box can block radio frequencies from reaching the mobile device and prevents usable wireless signals from going in or coming out. (*Photo Credit:* https://www.computerworld.com/article/3273491/easy-mobile-security-the-faraday-way.html.)

necessary equipment is taken to the scene. Documentation should occur according to agency SOPs similar to other items of evidence along with the description of the device state and unique identifiers (e.g., powered on/off, presence of a passcode, damage, make, model, and serial number, IMEI, MEID, ESN, and/or MAC address). If the device's display is viewable, it should be photographed. If the device is off, do not turn the device on.

If the device is on, and one can access the system settings, engage Airplane mode and disable WiFi and Bluetooth. Next, extend the display auto-lock so that the phone does not automatically lock or disable the lock code altogether. Keep the phone charged so that it does not run out of battery power and powers down. Volatile data, including encryption keys and data in the device's memory, can be lost if the device powers down. Therefore, make sure to seize the charging cable as well.

When collecting a mobile device at a crime scene or from a suspect, an attempt to block incoming and outgoing signals to the mobile device should be made by placing it in a **Faraday bag** (Figure 19.2). By utilizing a Faraday bag the device becomes isolated from all networks (cell carrier and WiFi) so that data cannot be destroyed remotely. Both the mobile device and the charging source should be placed inside the Faraday bag since the cable can act as an antenna and the device may be able to connect to the network.

All areas of the crime scene should be searched to identify peripherals and paired or linked devices. These devices may provide valuable information about the past location of a suspect (GPS device), vitals (a Fitbit device), what was said at a crime scene (Alexa Echo or Google Home devices), and other Internet of Things (IoT) devices.

If the mobile device is locked, too many failed attempts at guessing the password may cause the phone to erase its content. A more prudent method is to search for a backup stored on a computer or in an iCloud account. A backup stored on a computer may contain a pairing record between the phone and the computer which can be used to unlock a locked device.

DIGITAL/MULTIMEDIA SCIENTIFIC AREA COMMITTEE

The Digital/Multimedia Scientific Area Committee manages the activities of the following OSAC subcommittees: Digital Evidence, Facial Identification, Speaker Recognition, and Video/Imaging Technology and Analysis.

OSAC DIGITAL EVIDENCE SUBCOMMITTEE[*]

The Digital Evidence Subcommittee focuses on standards and guidelines related to information of probative value that is stored or transferred in binary form.

SWGDE[†]

The Scientific Working Group on Digital Evidence (SWGDE) brings together organizations actively engaged in the field of digital and multimedia evidence. Their published guidelines and best practices contain helpful information that can help CSIs investigating digital crime scenes.[‡]

OSAC FACIAL IDENTIFICATION SUBCOMMITTEE[§]

The mission of the Facial Identification Subcommittee is to develop consensus standards and guidelines for the image-based comparisons of human facial features and to provide recommendations for the research and development necessary to advance the state of the science.

FISWG

The Facial Identification Scientific Working Group (FISWG) works together with the OSAC FI Subcommittee on the development of additional standards and guidelines. The FISWG website[¶] has many other standards, guidelines, best practices, techniques, and use cases.

OSAC SPEAKER RECOGNITION SUBCOMMITTEE[**]

The Speaker Recognition Subcommittee focuses on standards and guidelines related to the practice of speaker recognition, voice data collection, measurement, transmission, and retrieval. The subcommittee has proposed the following standard to the Audio Engineering Society (www.aes.org): *Speech Collection Guideline for Speaker Recognition: Audio Collection at a Temporary Location*.

OSAC VIDEO/IMAGING TECHNOLOGY AND ANALYSIS SUBCOMMITTEE[††]

The Video/Imaging Technology and Analysis Subcommittee focuses on standards and guidelines related to the application of methods and technologies to analyze information related to forensic imagery from a variety of systems. The proposed standard, Standard Guide for Crime Scene Photography, to ASTM International (www.astm.org) provides very useful information for CSIs performing crime scene photography: equipment, deletion of photographs, storage, general crime scene documentation, photographing living persons, photographing deceased persons, and photographing vehicles.

SWGIT

The Scientific Working Group on Imaging Technology (SWGIT) has terminated operations with the formation of the OSACs.

Further Reading

Årnes, André, ed. *Digital Forensics*. Wiley, 2017.

---

[*] www.nist.gov/osac/digital-evidence-subcommittee.
[†] www.swgde.org/home.
[‡] www.swgde.org/documents/published.
[§] www.nist.gov/osac/facial-identification-subcommittee.
[¶] https://fiswg.org/documents.html.
[**] www.nist.gov/osac/speaker-recognition-subcommittee.
[††] www.nist.gov/osac/videoimaging-technology-and-analysis-subcommittee.

Hassan, Nihad A. *Digital Forensics Basics: A Practical Guide Using Windows OS*. Apress, 2019.

Johansen, Gerard. *Digital Forensics and Incident Response: Incident Response Techniques and Procedures to Respond to Modern Cyber Threats*. Packt Publishing Ltd, 2020.

Johnson, Thomas A. *Forensic Computer Crime Investigation*. CRC Press, 2005.

Kävrestad, Joakim. *Fundamentals of Digital Forensics*. Springer International Publishing, 2020.

Oettinger, William. *Learn Computer Forensics: A Beginner's Guide to Searching, Analyzing, and Securing Digital Evidence*. Packt Publishing Ltd, 2020.

Valentine, Tim, and Josh P. Davis. *Forensic Facial Identification: Theory and Practice of Identification from Eyewitnesses, Composites and CCTV*. Wiley, 2015.

Chapter Questions

1. List some of the most common ways that computer evidence is destroyed.
2. What are some of the types of crimes associated with digital evidence?
3. Define digital evidence.
4. What is a Faraday bag?
5. What should be done if a mobile device is locked?
6. What is the difference between facial identification and facial recognition?
7. How should one calibrate the time stamp on video evidence?
8. Why is it important to label all cords and wires before seizing a computer at a crime scene?
9. (True or false) Facial identification comparison uses the same ACE-V method as fingerprint comparison.
10. What are some of the limitations of facial recognition software?

Chapter 20

Report Writing, Courtroom Testimony, and the Future

Communicating scientific and technical information to laypersons, whether police investigators, lawyers, judges, juries, or the public, is the hallmark of effective forensic science and, by extension, crime scene investigation. If consumers of scientific and technical material are generally unable to understand the meaning of the information, the whole exercise of crime scene investigation becomes meaningless. You may be the world's greatest CSI or forensic scientist, but if you can't explain what your science is about to laypeople, your abilities are pointless.

There are two types of communication to be discussed in this chapter: written communication and oral communication. Each requires above average skills in communicating information. Experts often fall back to technical jargon which is perfectly understandable to other experts but often is not readily understood by the layperson. With forensic science material, information more easily understood by non-scientists is the appropriate manner in which to proceed.

In addition to detailing the steps taken in an investigation, the crime scene investigator and forensic scientist will also have to explain how the information gleaned from a case and the resulting laboratory work informs the investigation. Stated simply: what does the evidence mean?

Lawyers and scientists not generally associated with law enforcement have asserted that some of the findings provided by experts are overstated and, in some cases, invalid. This is especially the case with comparative testing such as with footwear evidence, tire impression evidence, tool marks, bite marks, firearms evidence, and even fingerprints. Experts can expect to be challenged when offering their opinions that two items of evidence are unique and come from the same source.

REPORT WRITING*

In the past, prosecution expert witnesses were trained to provide minimal information about a test which was performed on evidence. Often, a statement about how the examiner came to receive the evidence and a conclusion represented the totality of a laboratory report.

Defense lawyers have learned over the years to demand more. Often this is accomplished by discovery, where defense attorneys subpoena any and all relevant information about how tests were conducted as well as records about the training and expertise of the examiner. In short, if an attorney wishes to have information about evidence related to a case, they can obtain it.

In 2009, a National Academy of Sciences[†] report made the following statement about reports and testimony:

> There is a critical need in most fields of forensic science to raise the standards for reporting and testifying about the results of investigations. For example, many terms are used by forensic examiners in reports and in court testimony to describe

---

* The Dept of Justice (DOJ) has issued documents to provide guidance to the Department's forensic examiners on uniform language when writing reports and testifying: www.justice.gov/olp/uniform-language-testimony-and-reports.
[†] www.ojp.gov/pdffiles1/nij/grants/228091.pdf. See Chapter 6, page 185.

findings, conclusions, and the degrees of association between evidentiary material (e.g., hairs, fingerprints, fibers) and particular people or objects. Such terms include but are not limited to "match," "consistent with," "identical," "similar in all respects tested," and "cannot be excluded as the source of." ... Yet the forensic science disciplines have not reached agreement or consensus on the precise meaning of any of these terms. Although some disciplines have developed vocabulary and scales to be used in reporting results, they have not become standard practice. This imprecision in vocabulary stems in part from the paucity of research in forensic science and the corresponding limitations in interpreting the results of forensic analyses. As a general matter, laboratory reports generated as the result of a scientific analysis should be complete and thorough. They should describe, at a minimum, methods and materials, procedures, results, and conclusions, and they should identify, as appropriate, the sources of uncertainty in the procedures and conclusions along with estimates of their scale (to indicate the level of confidence in the results). Although it is not appropriate and practicable to provide as much detail as might be expected in a research paper, sufficient content should be provided to allow the nonscientist reader to understand what has been done and permit informed, unbiased scrutiny of the conclusion.

Some forensic laboratory reports meet this standard of reporting, but most do not. Some reports contain only identifying and agency information, a brief description of the evidence being submitted, a brief description of the types of analysis requested, and a short statement of the results (e.g., "The green, brown plant material in item #1 was identified as marijuana"). The norm is to have no description of the methods or procedures used, and most reports do not discuss measurement uncertainties or confidence limits. Many disciplines outside the forensic science disciplines have standards, templates, and protocols for data reporting. Although some of the Scientific Working Groups have a scoring system for reporting findings, they are not uniformly or consistently used.

Forensic science reports, and any courtroom testimony stemming from them, must include clear characterizations of the limitations of the analyses, including associated probabilities where possible. Courtroom testimony should be given in lay terms so that all trial participants can understand how to weigh and interpret the testimony. In order to enable this, research must be undertaken to evaluate the reliability of the steps of the various identification methods and the confidence intervals associated with the overall conclusions.

The amount of information presented in a report is often determined by a laboratory's policies and practices. However, over time, it is likely that examiners will be expected to prepare more detailed reports and provide information about the nature of the testing performed and what was the basis of the examiner's conclusions. If these details are not part of a report, they will certainly be asked in court.

COURTROOM TESTIMONY

Forensic practitioners are often called to court to testify as expert witnesses. Testifying in court is a challenge, particularly, for an inexperienced person. Training and experience eventually make it easier.* The following are some pointers for effective expert witness testimony:

Before going to Court

- Carefully prepare your reports and consider appropriate language, completeness, and opinions.
- Schedule a pretrial conference with the prosecutor and/or defense attorney to go over the findings in your lab report.
- Review the case before you arrive in court.
- Never allow a prosecutor or defense attorney to push you beyond your area of expertise or opinion. Ask yourself, can my testimony withstand the evaluation of a competent opposing expert?

Giving Expert Testimony

- Dress the part of an expert. Wear conservative clothing. Remove any piercings on the face other than earrings. Avoid wearing lapel pins or jewelry that designates membership in a club or group. Your appearance carries a tremendous amount of weight in how well juries are willing to believe what you say.
- When answering questions, respond to the jury, not the lawyer. Talk to the jury and make eye contact. Look at the individual jurors. (In a bench trial without a jury, make eye contact with the judge.)
- Sit up straight. Do not slouch or look too comfortable. Don't swivel in your chair.

---

* For those who find public speaking to be a challenge, Toastmasters International (www.toastmasters.org) is an excellent way to improve your skills.

- Turn off your cell phone.
- Pause before giving your answer. Give the opposing counsel a chance to object. Also, consider what you are going to say.
- Try to avoid "ums" and "ahs" when speaking.
- Present a professional demeanor. Not only what you say is important, but also how you say it and how you look saying it.
- Be aware of your physical presence—how you sit, and your body language. Do not fumble with exhibits or props.
- Do not fidget or sway when standing.
- Watch your demeanor. Do not appear too confident (it may be construed as arrogance).
- Avoid animosity. Appear sincere, objective, polite, and fair. Concede, if you do not know the answer.
- Listen to your speech, volume, and pace. Be deliberate, but not slow.
- Present your opinions with emphasis. Educate using nontechnical language. Use analogies. Make your testimony interesting!
- Concentrate: listen to every word of counsel. Do not jump the gun with your replies.
- Pause to clarify concepts.
- REMEMBER: A court reporter is recording everything you say. Be specific when giving your testimony. Consider bringing a spelling sheet for the court reporter of any technical words you might use in your testimony.
- Respond directly to the question.

Cross-examination
- The witness dictates the pace. You do not need to answer any question yes or no. Explain your rationale.
- Be careful with questions such as "Is it possible that …?" or "Is it fair to say?"
- It is acceptable to say, "I don't believe I am qualified to answer that question."
- Listen to all aspects of the hypothetical question. If you are unsure what the question is, ask for clarification.
- If you are not given a chance to explain your answer, ask if you can respond to clarify your statement.
- Remember your demeanor and attitude. You are not supposed to take sides.
- The louder and more belligerent the lawyer becomes, the more composed and polite you should become. Do not lose your temper.
- If you are asked a particularly lengthy, confusing question simply say, "I don't understand your question. Could you rephrase it?"

Other Points
- Speak in a manner that lay people can understand. Avoid jargon, especially scientific jargon.
- Go over prior testimony, reports, and exhibits before the trial. Try to have a pretrial conference with the prosecutor.
- Remember the "KISS" Principle and keep it simple!
- Be objective. You are not an advocate. It should not matter to you whether the case results in a guilty or not guilty verdict. Your salary will stay the same. Your job is to be an advocate for your opinion.
- Use visual aids, analogies, illustrations from everyday life, the overhead projector, and/or PowerPoint presentations.
- Pay attention to the judge. Wait for the judge to rule on an objection before answering. Objection sustained means you cannot answer the previous question. Objection overruled means that you can answer.
- Do not box yourself into a corner. Beware of questions like, "Have you ever made a mistake" and "Isn't it possible?"
- Do not try to avoid a difficult question. Juries are suspicious of evasive answers.

- Be aware of the cross-examination trick of taking an excerpt from a publication out of context or an excerpt from a nonexistent article. You can always ask the lawyer to show you the article to refresh your memory or even to read.
- Be able to say, "I don't know" or "I was wrong."
- Take the lead to meet with and talk with counsel.
- Practice deep breathing.
- Be an active listener.
- Mentor new, inexperienced prosecutors. If he or she is new or inexperienced in a given area, be patient and offer your assistance as an expert. Try to remember how you felt the first few times you appeared in court.

It's important for experts to stay abreast of court decisions affecting forensic science as well as challenges prosecution expert witnesses are facing. The defense bar makes it a point in keeping up with the latest trend in forensic science and their questions can be pointed. One topic which seems to come up is your knowledge in a particular area. Stated simply, how do you know what you claim to know? To be able to demonstrate your expertise, publications in peer reviewed journals are helpful as is membership and attendance in professional societies. Knowledge gained while in school becomes stale in a few years and it is imperative to keep up with your area of expertise with continuing education.

Don't allow yourself to be pushed too far by either the prosecutor or defense attorney. If you don't know, simply say, "I don't know. It's beyond my area of expertise." Unfortunately, it's easy to stretch your expertise to the breaking point and be made to look foolish to the jury or court.

STATISTICS*

The focus on statistics both in report writing and courtroom testimony has grown in recent years. Defense lawyers want a way for expert witnesses to quantify their opinion. When an expert states that two items of evidence have common features and could have come from a common source, what does that mean? How certain is the expert that the items of evidence came from the same source or person? DNA evidence routinely uses statistics to explain to the jury the weight of the evidence in the form of random match probabilities and likelihood ratios. These statistics are more difficult to calculate for other types of pattern physical evidence because there is no statistic to express that two bullets or two fingerprints came from the same source. How can an expert testify about a confidence level in such cases? The only approach an expert may take is to explain to the jury the extent of the training and experience he or she has and that based on that, the expert can state that he or she has a high level of confidence that the evidence had a common source. A statement that it is not possible to state with complete certainty that the evidence shares a unique source should be made.

In cases involving evidence having similar class characteristics, such as a fiber, glass sample, or other similar types of evidence such as mass produced materials, an expert can testify that the material comes from a common source but cannot be differentiated from any other similar sample. This may beg the question, and the expert might be asked about how often they would expect to see such an item in the general vicinity of the crime scene. If a shoe print, for example, is located at a burglary scene and is similar to a suspect's shoe, the question becomes, how often would you expect to find this shoe in a given area. Naturally, such a question is difficult to answer unless a major study were conducted.

Forensic scientists have long had a difficult time expressing conclusions about the similarity of certain types of physical evidence. Terms such as similar, consistent with, unique, convey different meanings to different people. Laypersons might believe that such expressions connote that two pieces of evidence came from one source when closer examination of an expert witness might well show absolute identification is not what the witness meant to imply.

---

* The Center for Statistics and Applications in Forensic Science (www.forensicstats.org) serves as a research center to apply proven statistical and scientific methods to improve the accuracy of the analysis and interpretation of forensic science.

DNA testing in forensic cases saw the beginning of statistics being used as a way to quantify the weight of an examiner's conclusion. Rather than simply saying that the two biological samples were similar, experts would testify about the rarity of the DNA profile in terms of the random match probability. In other words, what is the probability of finding this same DNA profile in the population? Examiner's could also report a likelihood ratio about the likelihood of a suspect being included in a mixture vs. some other random person being included.

In 2016, a report was issued entitled, *REPORT TO THE PRESIDENT. Forensic Science in Criminal Courts: Ensuring Scientific Validity of Feature-Comparison Methods.* In part, the report noted:

> Examiners have sometimes testified, for example, that their conclusions are "100 percent certain;" or have "zero," "essentially zero," or "negligible," error rate. As many reviews—including the highly regarded 2009 National Research Council study—have noted, however, such statements are not scientifically defensible: all laboratory tests and feature-comparison analyses have non-zero error rates.

The report correctly notes that many of the comparative analysis results are based on subjective rather than objective test results. DNA testing which uses statistics to express to the courts a value of the conclusions reported by the examiner is unique. The majority of forensic testing of a comparative nature relies on the examiner's experience. Statistical information for firearms testing, fingerprints, footwear evidence, tire impressions, and other pattern forensic evidence is still in its infancy.

The difficulty in this approach is that many other disciplines which frequently are used in civil and criminal cases, such as medicine, engineering, psychiatry, to name but a few, similarly do not have objective data to support the expert's opinion. Judges who are the "gatekeepers" of the admissibility of these cases have to have a means to determine whether the opinion proffered is admissible.

Experts giving opinion testimony must have the ability to explain their findings in a nuanced way for juries and courts to determine the value of such information offered to the trier of fact. If the expert does not have objective data to support his or her conclusions, experience and training have to be used to explain how a conclusion was reached.

Courtroom testimony is by far the most challenging of all the duties of an expert. Few things can prepare someone for an aggressive cross-examination. The one piece of advice that can be given to novices is that with practice it becomes easier. However, one should always be prepared and study the case, notes, laboratory reports, conclusions, and possible alternative opinions before taking the witness stand.

FUTURE ISSUES IN FORENSIC SCIENCE

Predicting the future is difficult especially since human knowledge doubles at an astounding rate and change is inevitable. Forensic science is no different from any other area of knowledge. As stated elsewhere, crime scene investigators and forensic practitioners must stay abreast of their fields of study. Not staying current can only lead to obsolescence.

Given that the field of forensic science is evolving rapidly, what changes might we see in the future? The following topics are some of the areas we expect to see major changes in the practice of crime scene investigation and forensic science.

THE HUMAN BIOME AND MICROBIAL FORENSICS*,†,‡

The human biome consists of a vast assortment of microorganisms made up of flora, fauna, viruses, and fungi that live on and in humans. Theoretically, these should be unique to an individual and may be able to differentiate one person from another. Numerous questions need to be answered before forensic microbial analysis can be used to identify specific persons. How stable is the human biome, i.e., does it change over time, how long can samples be kept and later

---

* https://pubmed.ncbi.nlm.nih.gov/30302518/.
† www.ncbi.nlm.nih.gov/pmc/articles/PMC7080133/.
‡ https://link.springer.com/article/10.1007%2Fs00253-018-9414-6.

compared with microorganisms of a subject and how different are assays from one individual to another? These and other questions must be determined before procedures enter mainstream forensic science testing.

ROBOTICS

Laboratory automation is becoming more and more used in laboratory settings, particularly in routine testing processes. Aspects of DNA testing and toxicology, for example, have already been aided by robots. As the forensic community matures, it is likely that more robotic platforms will enter into the lab space. Laboratory robotics can remove a large portion of human error and can ensure that samples are processed in a standardized way. Electronic barcodes on individual samples can also help alleviate the possibility of sample mix ups.

ARTIFICIAL INTELLIGENCE

Artificial intelligence or "AI" is expected to become an important technology for forensic science and crime scene investigation. Computer software is already used to scan digital fingerprint files to select possible candidates for human comparisons. There are a host of other types of physical evidence that could be aided by AI. Blood stain patterns, footwear evidence, firearms evidence are likely applications.

With miniaturization, portable equipment could be ready for field use. An example of this might be fingerprint readers used by uniformed personnel in the field to identify arrestees before removing the person to the police station. Elements of this technology already exist and a field device could be a welcome addition to the CSI's toolbox.

GENERATIVE ADVERSARIAL NETWORK (GAN)

Generative Adversarial Networks (GAN) are a class of machine learning where the network learns to generate new data from training data in a two-player game. The two "players" are the generator and the discriminator. The two adversaries are in constant battle throughout the training process, each one "learning" from the other and becoming a better generator and a better discriminator. GANs trained on photographs, for example, can generate new realistic photographs that look entirely authentic to human observers, with many realistic characteristics. These photographs, however, are of people that do not exist!

GANs can also reconstruct 3D models of objects from images, generate novel objects as 3D point clouds, and produce motion pattern video. GANs can be used to age face photographs to show how an individual's appearance might change with age.

A serious concern is the potential use of GAN-based human image synthesis for malicious purposes.* The production of deep fakes (i.e., incriminating photographs and videos) can be used to generate unique, realistic profile photos of people who do not exist, create fake social media profiles, and make politicians appear to say things when in fact they said nothing of the kind. Being able to detect deep fake images and video is a goal of the digital forensic community.

VIRTUAL REALITY/AUGMENTED REALITY†

The distinctions between Virtual Reality (VR) and Augmented Reality (AR) amounts to the devices required and the experience itself: AR uses real-world settings while VR is completely virtual. VR requires a headset device, but AR can be accessed with a smartphone or similar device. AR enhances both the virtual and real world while VR only enhances a fictional reality. Virtual reality (VR) implies a complete immersion experience that shuts out the physical world.

This technology may aid in describing the events at a crime scene and may prove helpful to juries to better understand the events which transpired. The problem with this type of technology is that it relies on a technician to program the scene. It may be argued that such depictions are biased to a particular scenario of events which might not accurately predict what actually occurred.

---

* See for example, www.businessinsider.com/what-is-deepfake.
† www.forensicscolleges.com/blog/resources/forensics-and-vr.

VIRTOPSY*

Virtopsy is a virtual alternative to a traditional autopsy and is conducted by means of scanning and imaging technology. The idea to conduct virtual autopsies is not entirely new and has been used on mummies. Virtopsy methods are ground breaking. It is a new high-tech tool for research and practical death investigation in modern forensic pathology. Cost of the technology is a factor and is a reason that virtopsy has not gained wider usage. The procedure is non-invasive, less traumatic for surviving family members and may be acceptable to religious communities who are generally against autopsies. The downside is that not every pathological finding can be viewed by the medical examiner with the absence of a traditional autopsy and only a Virtopsy. Many forensic pathologists are of the opinion that virtopsies are a great tool to supplement, not replace, the traditional autopsy.

TIME-TRACING FINGERPRINTING[†,‡,§]

The time a fingerprint was left at the crime scene has long been a question facing fingerprint examiners and police investigators. It is well known that prints left on items of evidence can be present for lengthy periods of time. In the past few years there has been research to attempt to determine the length of time a print was left at the scene. Experimental results show that certain chemicals present in fingerprints migrate away from the substrate in a few days. The studies suggested that it might be possible to determine if a print was deposited recently, within a few days, or longer.

These and other technologies offer a promising and fascinating future for the forensic science field. It is up to practitioners to learn about these methods and new discoveries and to stay current in emerging technologies.

Further Reading

Airlie, Melissa, et al. "Contemporary issues in forensic science—Worldwide survey results." *Forensic Science International* 320 (2021): 110704.

Dowdeswell, Tracey Leigh. "Forensic genetic genealogy: A profile of cases solved." *Forensic Science International: Genetics* 58 (2022): 102679.

Kukucka, Jeff, and Itiel, Dror. "Human factors in forensic science: psychological causes of bias and error." (2022).

Oosthuizen, Tersia, Loene, M. Howes, and Rob, White. "Forensic science and environmental offences: Litter, DNA analysis and surveillance." *Forensic Science International: Animals and Environments* (2022): 100042.

Pylant, Mackenzie, and Melanie, Ponce. "A review on the field of forensic science and different techniques that can be applied to identify the pathogen and perpetrator of a bio crime." *The Cougar Journal of Undergraduate Research* 1.1 (2022): 1–7.

Varga, Z., et al. "Trends and perspectives in Nuclear Forensic Science." *TrAC Trends in Analytical Chemistry* 146 (2022): 116503.

Wani, Atif Khurshid, Nahid Akhtar, and Saurabh, Shukla. "CRISPR/Cas9: Regulations and Challenges for law enforcement to Combat its Dual-use." *Forensic Science International* (2022): 111274.

---

* Youtube video depicting a virtopsy: www.youtube.com/watch?v=3nd9W5rjepo.
† www.nist.gov/news-events/news/2015/08/who-what-when-determining-age-fingerprints.
‡ https://pubs.acs.org/doi/abs/10.1021/acs.analchem.5b02018.
§ De Alcaraz-Fossoul, Josep, ed. Technologies for Fingermark Age Estimations: A Step Forward. Springer International Publishing, 2021.

Appendix A: Equipment for Crime Scene Investigations

The crime scene investigator needs special equipment to aid in collection and preservation of evidence, photography, and sketching. Equipment should be flexible, portable, and arranged in suitable carrying cases. The following list of supplies and equipment suggests many items generally useful to have on hand at a crime scene investigation. Experience will suggest additional materials that the investigator will find helpful.

BASIC EQUIPMENT

Flashlight and spare batteries
Laptop computer or tablet
Disposable latex/nitrile examination gloves
Coveralls or disposable clothing (Tyvek® suits)
50-foot steel surveyor's tape
12-foot steel tape measures
12-inch rulers
6-inch rulers
Writing paper and report forms
Graph paper
Clipboard
Writing and marking pens, pencils
Metal scribe
Chalk and crayons
Evidence tags
Evidence sealing tape
Stapler and staples
Adhesive and cellophane tape
Rubber bands
Scissors
Scalpel and replacement blades
Assorted large and small forceps
Spatulas
Paper towels
Hand magnifier
Disposable pipettes and rubber bulbs
Cotton-tipped applicators
Test tubes and corks
Plastic conical tubes
Compass
Magnet

pH paper
Anti-putrefaction masks
Odor eliminators
Thumbtacks

EVIDENCE PACKAGING SUPPLIES

Envelopes of various sizes
Paper bags
Plastic bags
Pillboxes
Metal paint cans and lids
Cardboard boxes
Zip-ties
Screw-cap glass vials of various sizes
Plastic screw cap specimen cups
Paper

PHOTOGRAPHIC EQUIPMENT

Digital SLR camera
Lenses—normal, wide angle, and macro
Filters (polarizing, UV, contrast, etc.)
Electronic media storage devices
Flash unit and fresh batteries
Tripod
Level
Rulers and other devices to show scale of items
Light meter
Carrying case
3D scanner and software (FARO)
Lens brush and lens tissue
Video camera
Smartphone if all other recording devices are unavailable

FINGERPRINT EQUIPMENT

Fingerprint brushes
Magna-Brush
Lift cards
Magnifier
Fingerprint powders
Lifting tape
Rubber lifters

HAND TOOLS

Hammers
Hand or power saw
Screwdrivers
Wrench
Vise-Grips
Pliers
Knife
Shovels
Sifters
Rake
Bolt cutters
Power drill
Electrical extension cords
Wire cutters
Hacksaw
Socket wrench set
Rope
Wood chisel
Ax
Cotton work gloves
Pry bar
Spatula

DNA/BLOOD COLLECTION SUPPLIES

K–M reagent, or other presumptive blood tests
3% Hydrogen peroxide
Saline
Distilled water
Luminol/Bluestar® reagent
Spray bottle
Cotton cloth
Rubber gloves
Spot plates
Sterile cotton-tipped applicators/swabs
10% Bleach
70% Ethanol
Disposable pipettes and rubber bulbs
Vacuum blood collection tubes
Syringes
Toothpicks
Labels

CASTING MATERIALS

Dental stone
Rubber or plastic mixing bowls
Wooden spatula
Metal retaining bands
Wire or wooden splints for support
Baffle
Cardboard boxes to hold finished cast
Silicone rubber or dental impression material
Modeling clay for dam
Ziploc® plastic baggies for mixing

OTHER EQUIPMENT

Ladder
Portable vacuum and filters
Portable generator
Handheld tape recorder
Metal detector
Portable floodlights
Gunshot residue testing kits
Thermometer
Insect net for live flying insect specimens

SAFETY EQUIPMENT

Hard hat
Hazardous chemical reference material
Access to breathing devices (i.e., SCBAs) for clandestine drug labs
Coveralls
Heavy gloves
Masks
Crime scene tape

GENERAL CRIME SCENE SUPPLY COMPANIES

ACE Fingerprint Equipment Laboratories
Arrowhead Forensics
CrimeTech, Inc.
Doje's Forensic Supplies
ECPI
Evident
EVI-PAQ

Fitzco
Forensics Source
The Lynn Peavey Company
ORC Forensics
Safariland Group
Sirchie
Spex Forensics

Appendix B: Forensic Science Websites

Literally, thousands of sites on the internet offer valuable information on forensic science, crime scene investigation, and related information. The following are some of the most popular.

FORENSIC SCIENCE ORGANIZATIONS BY REGION

International

International Association of Forensic Sciences
- www.iafs2023.com.au

International Association for Identification
- www.theiai.org

Canadian Society of Forensic Science
- www.csfs.ca

The Chartered Society of Forensic Sciences
- www.csofs.org

European Network of Forensic Science Institutes
- www.enfsi.eu

Asian Forensic Sciences Network
- www.asianforensic.net

Australian and New Zealand Forensic Science Society
- www.anzfss.org

Canadian Identification Society
- www.cis-sci.ca

The British Academy of Forensic Sciences
- www.bafs.org.uk

South African Academy of Forensic Sciences
- www.saafs.org.za/

United States

American Academy of Forensic Sciences
- www.aafs.org

American Board of Criminalistics (ABC)
- www.criminalistics.com

American Society of Crime Lab Directors
- www.ascld.org

American Society for Testing and Materials
- www.astm.org

National Forensic Science Technology Center
- www.nfstc.org

The Consortium of Forensic Science Organizations
- www.thecfso.org

Organization of Scientific Area Committees
- www.nist.gov/osac

National Clearinghouse for Science, Technology, and the Law
- www.ncstl.org

Regional

California Association of Criminalistics
- www.cacnews.org

Northwest Association of Forensic Scientists
- www.nwafs.org

Northeastern Association of Forensic Scientists
- www.neafs.org

Mid-Atlantic Association of Forensic Scientists
- www.maafs.org

Midwestern Association of Forensic Scientists
- www.mafs.net

Southern Association of Forensic Scientists
- www.safs1966.org

FORENSIC SCIENCE ORGANIZATIONS BY DISCIPLINE

Accreditation

ANSI-ASQ National Accreditation Board
- www.anab.org

American Association for Laboratory Accreditation
- www.a2la.org

International Laboratory Accreditation Cooperation
- www.ilac.org

International Organization for Standardization
- www.iso.org

Anthropology
American Board of Forensic Anthropology
- www.theabfa.org

Bloodstain Pattern Analysis (BPA)
International Association of Bloodstain Pattern Analysts
- www.iabpa.org

Crime Scene
Crime Scene Investigator Network
- www.crime-scene-investigator.net

Crime Scene Investigator
- www.crimesceneinvestigatoredu.org

Association for Crime Scene Reconstruction
- www.acsr.org

International Association of Forensic & Security Metrology
- www.iafsm.org

International Crime Scene Investigators Association
- www.icsia.org

Underwater Criminal Investigators
- www.ucidiver.com

Digital Evidence
Association of Digital Forensics, Security and Law
- www.adfsl.org/

DNA
Short Tandem Repeat DNA Internet Database
- strbase.nist.gov/

Scientific Working Group on DNA Analysis Methods
- www.swgdam.org

Drugs
Office of National Drug Control Policy
- www.whitehouse.gov/ondcp

Entomology

Entomological Society of America
- www.entsoc.org

North American Forensic Entomology Association
- www.nafea.net

Forensic Entomology
- www.forensicentomology.com

Evidence Procedures

International Association for Property & Evidence
- www.iape.org

Fire Science

NIST Fire Research Division
- www.nist.gov/el/fire_research/index.cfm

International Association of Arson Investigators
- www.firearson.com

Firearms Identification

Association of Firearm and Tool Mark Examiners
- www.afte.org

Impressions

Tread Forensics
- treadforensics.com

Medicolegal Death Investigation

American Board of Medicolegal Death Investigators
- www.abmdi.org

International Homicide Investigators Association
- www.ihia.org

Microscopy

McCrone Research Institute
- www.mccroneinstitute.org

Missing Persons

National Missing and Unidentified Persons System
- www.namus.gov

International Commission on Missing Persons
- www.icmp.int

Nursing

Sexual Assault Forensic Examiner Technical Assistance
- www.safeta.org

International Association of Forensic Nurses
- www.forensicnurses.org/

Odontology

American Society of Forensic Odontology
- www.asfo.org

American Board of Forensic Odontology
- www.abfo.org

Pathology

National Association of Medical Examiners
- www.thename.org

International Association of Coroners & Medical Examiners
- theiacme.com

Psychiatry/Psychology

American Academy of Psychiatry and the Law
- www.aapl.org

American Board of Forensic Psychology
- www.abfp.com/

Quality Assurance

Association of Forensic Quality Assurance Managers
- www.afqam.org

American Standards Board
- www.asbstandardsboard.org

Questioned Documents

American Society of Questioned Document Examiners
- www.asqde.org

American Board of Forensic Document Examiners
- www.abfde.org

Board of Forensic Document Examiners
- www.bfde.org/

Radiology

International Society of Forensic Radiology and Imaging
- www.isfri.org

International Association of Forensic Radiographers
- www.afr.org.uk

Toxicology

American Board of Forensic Toxicologists
- www.abft.org

Society of Forensic Toxicologists, Inc.
- www.soft-tox.org

The International Association of Forensic Toxicologists
- www.tiaft.org/

Trace Evidence

American Society of Trace Evidence Examiners
- www.asteetrace.org/

Wildlife Forensics

Society for Wildlife Forensic Science
- www.wildlifeforensicscience.org

Federal Forensic Laboratories

Bureau of Alcohol, Tobacco, Firearms and Explosives (ATF)
- www.atf.gov

Federal Bureau of Investigation (FBI)
- www.fbi.gov

Drug Enforcement Administration (DEA)
- www.dea.gov

US Postal Inspection Service
- www.postalinspectors.uspis.gov

US Fish & Wildlife Service
- www.fws.gov

US Postal Inspection Service (USPIS)
- www.uspis.gov/

US Dept of Defense - Naval Criminal Investigative Service
- www.ncis.navy.mil/

Army Criminal Investigation Lab - Defense Forensic Science Ctr
- www.cid.army.mil/dfsc-usacil.html

Forensic Science Lexicon

Forensic Science contains dozens of disciplines, each with its own jargon and vocabulary. As a result, a word might mean one thing to some, but something else to others. To help facilitate clear communication across the many forensic disciplines, the Organization of Scientific Area Committees for Forensic Science (OSAC) has created a Lexicon of Forensic Science Terminology, which can be accessed from the OSAC website (www.nist.gov/osac/osac-lexicon). This lexicon contains over 4,000 terms and their definitions.

Bibliography

The following bibliography provides sources relevant to many of the areas covered in the text. These references serve as a starting point from which the reader wishing additional information may begin, but by no means represents an exhaustive bibliography on forensic science. The reader is also directed to the FIU Research Forensic Library (www.forensiclibrary.org) to search the forensic science literature, and to the Registry of the Organization of Scientific Area Committees for Forensic Science (nist.gov/osac/osac-registry) for information on forensic science standards and best practices.

CHAPTER 1

Bell, Suzanne. *Encyclopedia of Forensic Science*. Infobase Publishing, 2008.

Bergman, R. A. "The impact of technological advancement on forensic science practice." *Canadian Society of Forensic Science Journal* 21.4 (1988): 169–175.

Fisher, David, Barry Fisher, and Jason Kolowski. *Forensics Demystified*. McGraw Hill Professional, 2006.

Girard, James E. *Criminalistics: Forensic Science, Crime, and Terrorism: Forensic Science, Crime, and Terrorism*. Jones & Bartlett Learning, 2021.

Nordby, Jon J. *Dead Reckoning: The Art of Forensic Detection*. 2000.

Robbers, Monica LP. "Blinded by science: The social construction of reality in forensic television shows and its effect on criminal jury trials." *Criminal Justice Policy Review* 19.1 (2008): 84–102.

CHAPTER 2

Bradford, L. W., and A. A. Biasotti. "Teamwork in the forensic sciences: Report of a case." *Journal of Forensic Science* 18.1 (1973): 31–39.

Collinson, J. G. "The Role of the Investigating Officer." *Journal of the Forensic Science Society* 10.4 (1970): 199–203.

Gardner, Ross M., and Donna Krouskup. *Practical Crime Scene Processing and Investigation*. CRC Press, 2018.

Hawthorne, Mark R. *First Unit Responder: A Guide to Physical Evidence Collection for Patrol Officers*. CRC Press, 2021.

Horvath, Frank, and Robert Meesig. "The criminal investigation process and the role of forensic evidence: A review of empirical findings." *Journal of Forensic Science* 41.6 (1996): 963–969.

CHAPTER 3

Berg, Erik. "Evolution of the crime scene diagram." *Journal of Forensic Identification* 45.1 (1995): 25–29.

Duncan, Christopher D. *Advanced Crime Scene Photography*. CRC Press, 2015.

Miranda, Michelle D. *Forensic Analysis of Tattoos and Tattoo Inks*. CRC Press, 2015.

Moreau, Dale M. *Fundamental Principles and Theory of Crime Scene Photography*. Forensic Science Training Unit, FBI Laboratory (undated), 2013.

Penalver, J., T. Kahana, and J. Hiss. Prosthetic devices in positive identification of human remains. *Journal of Forensic Identification* 47 (1997): 400.

Porter, Glenn, and Michael Kennedy. "Photographic truth and evidence." *Australian Journal of Forensic Sciences* 44.2 (2012): 183–192.

Scott, Harry. "The role of the photographer." *Journal of the Forensic Science Society* 10.4 (1970): 205–212.

Siljander, Raymond P., and Darin D. Fredrickson. *Applied Police and Fire Photography*. Charles C. Thomas, 1976.

Warlen, S. C. "Crime scene photography: The silent witness." *Journal of Forensic Identification* 45.3 (1995): 261–265.

Wertheim, P. A. "Crime scene note taking." *Journal of Forensic Identification* 42.3 (1992): 230–236.

CHAPTER 4

Becker, Ronald F., Stuart H. Nordby, and J. Jon. *Underwater Forensic Investigation*. CRC Press, 2013.

Dror, Itiel E., and Jeff Kukucka. "Linear sequential unmasking–expanded (LSU-E): A general approach for improving decision making as well as minimizing noise and bias." *Forensic Science International: Synergy* 3 (2021).

Fish, Jacqueline T., Robert N. Stout, and Edward Wallace. *Practical Crime Scene Investigations for Hot Zones*. CRC Press, 2010.

Hawthorne, Mark R. *First Unit Responder: A Guide to Physical Evidence Collection for Patrol Officers*. CRC Press, 2021.

Shelef, R., and R. Elkayam. "Collecting and packaging exhibits from the scene of the crime for transfer to the forensic laboratory." *Occupational Health and Industrial Medicine* 1.37 (1997): 9.

Wallace, Edward, Michael Cunningham, and Daniel Boggiano. *Crime Scene Unit Management: A Path Forward*. Routledge, 2015.

CHAPTER 5

Damelio, Robert, and Ross M. Gardner. *Bloodstain Pattern Analysis: With an Introduction to Crime Scene Reconstruction*. CRC Press, 2001.

Gardner, Ross M., and Tom Bevel. *Practical Crime Scene Analysis and Reconstruction*. CRC Press, 2009.

Haag, Michael G., and Lucien C. Haag. *Shooting Incident Reconstruction*. Academic Press, 2020.

Hall, Adam B., and Richard Saferstein. *Forensic Science Handbook* (Vol. I). CRC Press, 2020.

Macdonell, Herbert Leon. "Bloodstain pattern interpretation." *Wiley Encyclopedia of Forensic Science* (2009).

MacDonell, Herbert Leon, and Lorraine Fiske Bialousz. *Flight Characteristics and Stain Patterns of Human Blood*. National Institute of Law Enforcement and Criminal Justice, 1971.

Noon, Randall. *Introduction to Forensic Engineering*. CRC Press, 2020.

Petty, Stephen E. *Forensic Engineering* (Vol. 806). CRC Press, 2017.

Pizzola, Peter A., Steven Roth, and P. R. De Forest. "Blood droplet dynamics: I." *Journal of Forensic Science* 31.1 (1986a): 36–49.

Pizzola, Peter A., Steven Roth, and P. R. De Forest. "Blood droplet dynamics: II." *Journal of Forensic Science* 31.1 (1986b): 50–64.

Raymond, M. A., E. R. Smith, and J. Liesegang. "The physical properties of blood--forensic considerations." *Science & Justice: Journal of the Forensic Science Society* 36.3 (1996): 153–160.

CHAPTER 6

Bentsen, R. K., et al. "Post firing visualisation of fingerprint on spent cartridge cases." *Science & Justice* 36.1 (1996): 3–8.

Bettencourt, D. S. "A compilation of techniques for processing deceased human skin for latent prints." *Journal of Forensic Identification* 41.2 (1991): 111–120.

Bobev, Kostadin. "Fingerprints and factors affecting their condition." *Journal of Forensic Identification* 45.2 (1995): 176–183.

Campbell, B. M. "Separation of adhesive tapes." *Journal of Forensic Identification* 41.2 (1991): 102–106.

Campbell, Grace. *Fingerprints.* Lerner Digital™, 2021.

Cole, Simon A. *Suspect Identities: A History of Fingerprinting and Criminal Identification.* Harvard University Press, 2009.

Creighton, J. 1997. Visualization of latent impressions after incidental or direct contact with human blood. *Journal of Forensic Identification* 47: 534.

Datta, Ashim K., et al. *Advances in Fingerprint Technology.* CRC Press, 2001.

Friesen, J. Brent. "Forensic chemistry: The revelation of latent fingerprints." *Journal of Chemical Education* 92.3 (2015): 497–504.

Geng, Q. "Recovery of super glue over-fumed fingerprints." *Journal of Forensic Identification* 48 (1998): 17–21.

Goetz, M. "Cyanoacrylate fuming precautions." *Journal of Forensic Identification* 46 (1996): 409–411.

Hawthorne, Mark R., Sharon L. Plotkin, and Bracey-Ann Douglas. *Fingerprints: Analysis and Understanding the Science.* CRC Press, 2021.

James, J. D., C. A. Pounds, and B. Wilshire. "Obliteration of latent fingerprints." *Journal Forensic Science* 36.5 (1991): 1376–1386.

Kahana, T., et al. "Fingerprinting the deceased: Traditional and new techniques." *Journal of Forensic Science* 46.4 (2001): 908–912.

Keating, D. M., and J. J. Miller. "A technique for developing and photographing ridge impressions on decomposed water-soaked fingers." *Journal of Forensic Science* 38.1 (1993): 197–202.

Lee, Henry C., et al. "The effect of presumptive test, latent fingerprint and some other reagents and materials on subsequent serological identification, genetic marker and DNA testing in bloodstains." *J Forensic Ident* 39.6 (1989): 339–358.

Lennard, Christopher J., and Pierre A. Margot. "Sequencing of reagents for the improved visualization of latent fingerprints." *Journal of Forensic Identification* 38.5 (1988): 197–210.

Masters, N., and J. DeHaan. "Vacuum metal deposition and cyanoacrylate detection of older latent prints." *Journal of Forensic Identification* 46 (1996): 32–48.

McCarthy, Mary M., and David L. Grieve. "Preprocessing with cyanoacrylate ester fuming for fingerprint impressions in blood." *Journal of Forensic Identification* 39.1 (1989): 23–32.

Menzel, E. Roland, Richard A. Bartsch, and J. L. Hallman. "Fluorescent metal-Ruhemann's Purple coordination compounds: Applications to latent fingerprint detection." *Journal of Forensic Science* 35.1 (1990): 25–34.

Onstwedder, J., and T. E. Gamboe. "Small particle reagent: Developing latent prints on water-soaked firearms and effect on firearms analysis." *Journal of Forensic Science* 34.2 (1989): 321–327.

Phillips, Clarence E., Douglass O. Cole, and Gary W. Jones. "Physical developer: A practical and productive latent print developer." *Journal of Forensic Identification* 40.3 (1990): 135–147.

Pierce, D. S. "Tonally reversed friction ridge prints on plastics." *Journal of Forensic Identification* 39.1 (1989): 11–22.

Saunders, J. C. "Macroscopic examination of overlapping latent prints on non-porous items." *Journal of Forensic Identification* 43.2 (1993): 138–143.

Shelef, R., et al. "Development of latent fingerprints from incendiary bottles: Development of latent fingerprints from unignited incendiary bottles; optimization of small particle reagent for the development of latent fingerprints from glass surfaces washed in accelerant fluids; recovery of latent fingerprints from so." *Journal of Forensic Identification* 46.5 (1996a): 556–569.

Shelef, R., et al. "Recovery of latent fingerprints from soot-covered incendiarized glass surfaces." *Journal of Forensic Identification* 46 (1996b): 565–572.

Tucker, G. "A modified crystal violet application technique for black electrical tape." *Journal of Forensic Identification* 40 (1990): 148–50.

Upadhyay, S., and B. Yadav. "Latent Fingerprint on Human Skin: A Silent Diagnosis." *Journal of Forensic Science & Criminology* 7.2 (2019): 205.

Weaver, D. E., and D. C. Fullerton. "Large scale cyanoacrylate fuming." *Journal of Forensic Identification* 43.2 (1993): 135–137.

West, Michael H., et al. "Reflective ultraviolet imaging system (RUVIS) and the detection of trace evidence and wounds on human skin." *Journal of Forensic Identification* 40.5 (1990): 249–255.

Wiesner, S., and E. Springer. "Improved technique for recovering fingerprints on aluminum foil." *Journal of Forensic Identification* 47 (1997): 138–140.

CHAPTER 7

Barbaro, Anna. "DNA databases." *Forensic DNA Typing: Principles, Applications and Advancements*. Springer, 2020. 629–638.

Burrill, Julia, Barbara Daniel, and Nunzianda Frascione. "A review of trace 'Touch DNA' deposits: Variability factors and an exploration of cellular composition." *Forensic Science International: Genetics* 39 (2019): 8–18.

Butler, John M. *Fundamentals of Forensic DNA Typing*. Academic Press, 2009.

Butler, John M. *Advanced Topics in Forensic DNA Typing: Interpretation*. Academic Press, 2014.

Dash, Hirak Ranjan, Pankaj Shrivastava, and Surajit Das. *Principles and Practices of DNA Analysis: A Laboratory Manual for Forensic DNA Typing*. Springer, 2020.

Elkins, Kelly M., and Cynthia B. Zeller. *Next Generation Sequencing in Forensic Science: A Primer*. CRC Press, 2021.

Fonneløp, Ane Elida, Thore Egeland, and Peter Gill. "Secondary and subsequent DNA transfer during criminal investigation." *Forensic Science International: Genetics* 17 (2015): 155–162.

Gosch, Annica, and Cornelius Courts. "On DNA transfer: The lack and difficulty of systematic research and how to do it better." *Forensic Science International: Genetics* 40 (2019): 24–36.

Gosch, Annica, et al. "DNA transfer to firearms in alternative realistic handling scenarios." *Forensic Science International: Genetics* 48 (2020): 102355.

Gunn, Alan. *Essential Forensic Biology*. John Wiley & Sons, 2019.

Matte, Melinda, et al. "Prevalence and persistence of foreign DNA beneath fingernails." *Forensic Science International: Genetics* 6.2 (2012): 236–243.

Srivastava, Ankit, Abhimanyu Harshey, and Pankaj Shrivastava. "Legal Aspects of Forensic DNA Typing." *Forensic DNA Typing: Principles, Applications and Advancements*. Springer, 2020. 607–628.

Turow, Scott. *Silent Witness: Forensic DNA Evidence in Criminal Investigations and Humanitarian Disasters*. Oxford University Press, 2020.

CHAPTER 8

Antoci, P. R., and N. Petraco. "A technique for comparing soil colors in the forensic laboratory." *Journal of Forensic Science* 38.2 (1993): 437–441.

Blackledge, Robert D., ed. *Forensic Analysis on the Cutting Edge: New Methods for Trace Evidence Analysis*. John Wiley & Sons, 2007.

Blackledge, Robert D. *Tapes with Adhesive Backings: Their Characterization in the Forensic Science Laboratory*. Carl Hanser Verlag, 1987.

Bock, Jane H., and David O. Norris. "Forensic botany: An under-utilized resource." *Journal of Forensic Science* 42.3 (1997): 364–367.

Bresee, R. R. "Evaluation of textile fiber evidence: A review." *Journal of Forensic Science* 32.2 (1987): 510–521.

Brooks, Evie, et al. "Forensic physical fits in the trace evidence discipline: A review." *Forensic Science International* 313 (2020): 110349.

Budworth, Geoffrey. "Identification of knots." *Journal of the Forensic Science Society* 22.4 (1982): 327–331.

Chable, Julien, Claude Roux, and C. Lennard. "Collection of fiber evidence using water-soluble cellophane tape." *Journal of Forensic Science* 39.6 (1994): 1520–1527.

Chauhan, Rohini, Raj Kumar, and Vishal Sharma. "Soil forensics: A spectroscopic examination of trace evidence." *Microchemical Journal* 139 (2018): 74–84.

Dixon, K. C. "Positive identification of torn burned matches with emphasis on crosscut and torn fiber comparisons." *Journal of Forensic Science* 28.2 (1983): 351–359.

Duncan, Christopher D. *Processing Vehicles Used in Violent Crimes for Forensic Evidence*. CRC Press, 2021.

Grieve, M. C. "The role of fibers in forensic science examinations." *Journal of Forensic Science* 28.4 (1983): 877–887.

Mistek, Ewelina, et al. "Toward locard's exchange principle: Recent developments in forensic trace evidence analysis." *Analytical Chemistry* 91.1 (2018): 637–654.

Petraco, N. "Trace evidence: The invisible witness." *Journal of Forensic Science* 31.1 (1986): 321–328.

Petraco, N. "A simple trace evidence trap for the collection of vacuum sweepings." *Journal of Forensic Science* 32.5 (1987): 1422–1425.

Stoney, David A., and Paul L. Stoney. "Critical review of forensic trace evidence analysis and the need for a new approach." *Forensic Science International* 251 (2015): 159–170.

Suzanski, Thomas William. "Dog hair comparison: A preliminary study." *Canadian Society of Forensic Science Journal* 21.1–2 (1988): 19–28.

Vanderkolk, J. R. "Identifying consecutively made garbage bags through manufactured characteristics." *Journal of Forensic Identification* 45 (1995): 38–50.

Walsh, K. A. J., J. S. Buckleton, and C. M. Triggs. "A practical example of the interpretation of glass evidence." *Science & Justice* 36.4 (1996): 213–218.

Woodman, Peter A., et al. "To trace or not to trace: A survey of how police use and perceive chemical trace evidence." *Forensic Science International* 309 (2020): 110178.

CHAPTER 9

Cassidy, Michael J. *Footwear Identification*. Public Relations Branch of the Royal Canadian Mounted Police, 1980.

Davis, Roger J. "A systematic approach to the enhancement of footwear marks." *Canadian Society of Forensic Science Journal* 21.3 (1988): 98–105.

Ellen, D. M., D. J. Foster, and D. J. Morantz. "The use of electrostatic imaging in the detection of indented impressions." *Forensic Science International* 15.1 (1980): 53–60.

Facey, O. E., I. D. Hannah, and D. Rosen. "Shoe wear patterns and pressure distribution under feet and shoes, determined by image analysis." *Journal of the Forensic Science Society* 32.1 (1992): 15–25.

Hilderbrand, D. S., and M. Miller. "Casting materials: Which one to use." *Journal of Forensic Identification* 45.6 (1995): 618–630.

Hueske, E. "Photographing and casting footwear/tiretrack impressions in snow." *Journal of Forensic Identification* 41.2 (1991): 92–95.

Mankevich, A. "Determination of shoe size in out-of-scale photographs." *Journal of Forensic Identification* 40.1 (1990): 1–13.

Ojena, S. M. "A new improved technique for casting impressions in snow." *Journal of Forensic Science* 29.1 (1984): 322–325.

Petraco, Nicholas. *Color Atlas of Forensic Toolmark Identification*. CRC Press, 2010.

Pierce, D. S. "Identifiable markings on plastics." *Journal of Forensic Identification* 40.2 (1990): 51–59.

Shor, Yaron, et al. "Physical match: Insole and shoe." *Journal of Forensic Sciences* 48.4 (2003): 808–810.

Springer, Eliot. "Toolmark examinations: A review of its developments in the literature." *Journal of Forensic Sciences* 40 (1995): 964–968.

VanHoven, H. "A correlation between shoeprint measurements and actual sneaker size." *Journal of Forensic Science* 30.4 (1985): 1233–1237.

CHAPTER 10

Andrasko, Jan. "Characterization of smokeless powder flakes from fired cartridge cases and from discharge patterns on clothing." *Journal of Forensic Science* 37.4 (1992): 1030–1047.

Andrasko, J., and S. Pettersson. "A simple method for collection of gunshot residues from clothing." *Journal of the Forensic Science Society* 31.3 (1991): 321–330.

Barnum, C., and D. Klasey. "Factors affecting the recovery of latent prints on firearms." *Journal of Forensic Identification* 47 (1997): 141–149.

Basu, Samarendra. "Formation of gunshot residues." *Journal of Forensic Science* 27.1 (1982): 72–91.

Boyce, Arthur Robert, and Keith Simpson. "Identification of a Firearm in Murder without the Weapon." *The Police Journal* 22.1 (1949): 32–36.

Burke, T. W., and W. F. Rowe. "Bullet ricochet: A comprehensive review." *Journal of Forensic Science* 37.5 (1992): 1254–1260.

Burnett, Bryan. "The form of gunshot residue is modified by target impact." *Journal of Forensic Science* 34.4 (1989): 808–822.

Burnett, B. R. "Detection of bone and bone-plus-bullet particles in backspatter from close-range shots to heads." *Journal of Forensic Science* 36.6 (1991): 1745–1752.

Collins, K. A., and P. E. Lantz. "Interpretation of fatal, multiple, and exiting gunshot wounds by trauma specialists." *Journal of Forensic Science* 39.1 (1994): 94–99.

DeGaetano, D., and J. A. Siegel. "Survey of gunshot residue analysis in forensic science laboratories." *Journal of Forensic Science* 35.5 (1990): 1087–1095.

DiMaio, Vincent JM. *Gunshot Wounds: Practical Aspects of Firearms, Ballistics, and Forensic Techniques.* CRC Press, 2015.

Fackler, Martin L. "Wound ballistics: A review of common misconceptions." *JAMA* 259.18 (1988): 2730–2736.

Harruff, Richard C. "Comparison of contact shotgun wounds of the head produced by different gauge shotguns." *Journal of Forensic Science* 40.5 (1995): 801–804.

Havekost, D. G., C. A. Peters, and R. D. Koons. "Barium and antimony distributions on the hands of nonshooters." *Journal of Forensic Science* 35.5 (1990): 1096–1114.

Heard, Brian J. *Handbook of Firearms and Ballistics: Examining and Interpreting Forensic Evidence.* John Wiley & Sons, 2011.

Klatt, E. C., D. L. Tschirhart, and T. T. Noguchi. "Wounding characteristics of. 38 caliber revolver cartridges." *Journal of Forensic Science* 34.6 (1989): 1387–1394.

Medich, M. G., et al. "Single wound produced by simultaneous discharge of both shells from a double-barrel shotgun." *Journal of Forensic Science* 35.2 (1990): 473–476.

Meng, H. H., and B. Caddy. "Gunshot residue analysis: A review." *Journal of Forensic Science* 42.4 (1997): 553–570.

Missliwetz, J., W. Denk, and I. Wieser. "Shots fired with silencers: A report on four cases and experimental testing." *Journal of Forensic Science* 36.5 (1991): 1387–1394.

Nichols, Clay A., and Mary Ann Sens. "Recovery and evaluation by cytologic techniques of trace material retained on bullets." *The American Journal of Forensic Medicine and Pathology* 11.1 (1990): 17–34.

Nichols, Ronald G. "Firearm and toolmark identification criteria: A review of the literature." *Journal of Forensic Science* 42.3 (1997): 466–474.

Petraco, N., and P. R. De Forest. "Trajectory reconstructions I: Trace evidence in flight." *Journal of Forensic Science* 35.6 (1990): 1284–1296.

Singer, Ronald L., Dusty Davis, and Max M. Houck. "A survey of gunshot residue analysis methods." *Journal of Forensic Science* 41.2 (1996): 195–198.

Smith, O. C., et al. "Characteristic features of entrance wounds from hollow-point bullets." *Journal of Forensic Science* 38.2 (1993): 323–326.

Stone, I. C., and C. S. Petty. "Interpretation of unusual wounds caused by firearms." *Journal of Forensic Science* 36.3 (1991): 736–740.

Thompson, Robert M. *Firearm Identification in the Forensic Science Laboratory*. National District Attorneys Association, 2010.

Walker, Robert E. *A Field Guide to Ghost Guns: For Police and Forensic Investigations*. CRC Press, 2021.

CHAPTER 11

Beveridge, Alexander. *Forensic Investigation of Explosions*. CRC Press, 1998.

Davis, Tenney L. *The Chemistry of Powder and Explosives*. Pickle Partners Publishing, 2016.

Dhole, V. R., M. P. Kurhekar, and K. A. Ambade. "Detection of petroleum accelerant residues on partially burnt objects in burning/arson offences." *Science & Justice* 35.3 (1995): 217–221.

Dietz, William R. "Improved charcoal packaging for accelerant recovery by passive diffusion." *Journal of Forensic Science* 36.1 (1991): 111–121.

Evans, Hiram K., et al. "An unusual explosive, triacetonetriperoxide (TATP)." *Journal of Forensic Science* 31.3 (1986): 1119–1125.

Furton, Kenneth G., Jose R. Almirall, and Juan C. Bruna. "A novel method for the analysis of gasoline from fire debris using headspace solid-phase microextraction." *Journal of Forensic Science* 41.1 (1996): 12–22.

Garner, Daniel D., Mary Lou Fultz, and Elliott B. Byall. "The ATF approach to post-blast explosives detection and identification." *Journal of Energetic Materials* 4.1–4 (1986): 133–148.

Icove, David J., Carolyn M. Blocher, and John David DeHaan. *Instructor's Manual: Kirk's Fire Investigation*. Prentice Hall, 2002.

Keto, R. O. "Improved method for the analysis of the military explosive composition C-4." *Journal of Forensic Science* 31.1 (1986): 241–249.

Kolla, P. "Trace analysis of explosives from complex mixtures with sample pretreatment and selective detection." *Journal of Forensic Science* 36.5 (1991): 1342–1359.

Lentini, John J. "The evolution of fire investigation and its impact on Arson cases." *Criminal Justice* 27 (2012): 12.

Lentini, John J. "Fire investigation: Historical perspective and recent developments." *Forensic Science Review* 31 (2019): 37–44.

Loscalzo, P. J., P. R. DeForest, and J. M. Chao. "A study to determine the limit of detectability of gasoline vapor from simulated arson residues." *Journal of Forensic Science* 25.1 (1980): 162–167.

Madrzykowski, Daniel M. "Future of Fire Investigation." (2000): 44–45.

Mealy, Christopher, Matthew Benfer, and Dan Gottuk. "Liquid fuel spill fire dynamics." *Fire Technology* 50.2 (2014): 419–436.

O'donnell, J. F. "Interferences from backgrounds in accelerant residue analysis." *Fire and Arson Investigator* 39.4 (1989): 25–27.

Pinorini, M. T., et al. "Soot as an indicator in fire investigations: Physical and chemical analyses." *Journal of Forensic Science* 39.4 (1994): 933–973.

Stauffer, Éric. "Interpol review of fire investigation 2016–2019." *Forensic Science International: Synergy* 2 (2020): 368–381.

Tindall, Reta, and Kevin Lothridge. "An evaluation of 42 accelerant detection canine teams." *Journal of Forensic Science* 40.4 (1995): 561–564.

Tsaroom, Shalom. "Investigation of a murder case involving arson." *Journal of Forensic Science* 41.6 (1996): 1064–1067.

Twibell, J. D., and S. C. Lomas. "The examination of fire-damaged electrical switches." *Science & Justice* 35.2 (1995): 113–116.

CHAPTER 12

Bell, Suzanne. *Forensic Chemistry*. CRC Press, 2022.

Cooper, Gail, and Adam Negrusz, eds. *Clarke's Analytical Forensic Toxicology*. Pharmaceutical Press, 2013.

King, Leslie A. *Forensic Chemistry of Substance Misuse: A Guide to Drug Control*. Royal Society of Chemistry, 2019.

Kobilinsky, Lawrence, ed. *Forensic Chemistry Handbook*. John Wiley & Sons, 2011.

Lappas, Nicholas T., and Courtney M. Lappas. *Forensic Toxicology: Principles and Concepts*. Academic Press, 2021.

LeBeau, Marc A., and Ashraf Mozayani, eds. *Drug-facilitated Sexual Assault: A Forensic Handbook*. Academic Press, 2001.

Molina, D. Kimberley, and Veronica M. Hargrove. *Handbook of Forensic Toxicology for Medical Examiners*. CRC Press, 2018.

Smith, Fred. *Handbook of Forensic Drug Analysis*. Elsevier, 2004.

CHAPTER 13

Allen, Michael J. *Foundations of Forensic Document Analysis: Theory and Practice*. John Wiley & Sons, 2015.

Barton, B. C. "The use of an electrostatic detection apparatus to demonstrate the matching of torn paper edges." *Journal of the Forensic Science Society* 29.1 (1989): 35–38.

Beck, Jan. "Sources of error in forensic handwriting evaluation." *Journal of Forensic Science* 40.1 (1995): 78–82.

Bisesi, Michael S. *Scientific Examination of Questioned Documents*. CRC Press, 2006.

Breedlove, C. H. "The analysis of ball-point inks for forensic purposes." *Journal of Chemical Education* 66.2 (1989): 170.

Brunelle, Richard L. "Ink dating: The state of the art." *Journal of Forensic Science* 37.1 (1992): 113–124.

Gilmour, C., and J. Bradford. "The effect of medication on handwriting." *Canadian Society of Forensic Science Journal* 20.4 (1987): 119–138.

Harris, Joel. "Developments in the analysis of writing inks on questioned documents." *Journal of Forensic Science* 37.2 (1992): 612–619.

Hilton, Ordway. "History of questioned document examination in the United States." *Journal of Forensic Science* 24.4 (1979): 890–897.

Hilton, Ordway. *Scientific Examination of Questioned Documents*. CRC Press, 1992.

Hilton, Ordway. *Scientific Examination of Questioned Documents*. Elsevier North-Holland, 1981.

Hilton, Ordway. "Signatures: Review and a new view." *Journal of Forensic Science* 37.1 (1992): 125–129.

Horan, George J., and James J. Horan. "How long after writing can an ESDA image be developed?" *Forensic Science International* 39.2 (1988): 119–125.

Kam, Moshe, Gabriel Fielding, and Robert Conn. "Writer identification by professional document examiners." *Journal of Forensic Sciences* 42.5 (1997).

Mittal, S. C., and V. N. Sehgal. "The forensic examination of unfamiliar scripts." *International Criminal Police Review* 418 (1989): 11–15.

Plamondon, Rejean, and Guy Lorette. "Automatic signature verification and writer identification: The state of the art." *Pattern Recognition* 22.2 (1989): 107–131.

Sharf, Sara, Rachel Gabbay, and Sharon Brown. "Infrared luminescence of indented writing as evidence of document alteration." *Journal of Forensic Science* 42.4 (1997): 729–732.

Tolliver, Diane K. "The electrostatic detection apparatus (ESDA): Is it really non-destructive to documents?." *Forensic Science International* 44.1 (1990): 7–21.

West, M. H., R. E. Barsley, J. Frair, and F. Hall. 1990. Reflective ultraviolet imaging system (RUVIS) and the detection of trace evidence on human skin. *Journa; of Forensic Identification* 40: 249.

CHAPTER 14

Knight, Bernard. "Ethics and discipline in forensic science." *Journal of the Forensic Science Society* 29.1 (1989): 53–59.

Peterson, Joseph L., and John E. Murdock. "Forensic science ethics: Developing an integrated system of support and enforcement." *Journal of Forensic Science* 34.3 (1989): 749–762.

Rosner, Richard. "Ethical practice in the forensic sciences and justification of ethical codes." *Journal of Forensic Science* 41.6 (1996): 913–915.

Saks, Michael J. "Prevalence and impact of ethical problems in forensic science." *Journal of Forensic Science* 34.3 (1989): 772–793.

CHAPTER 15

Brauner, Paul, and Nira Gallili. "A condom: The critical link in a rape." *Journal of Forensic Science* 38.5 (1993): 1233–1236.

Burnier, Céline, et al. "Investigation of condom evidence in cases of sexual assault: Case studies." *Forensic Science International: Reports* 4 (2021): 100221.

Campbell, Bradley A., and David S. Lapsey Jr. "Do impulsivity and education moderate the effectiveness of police sexual assault investigations training? Findings from a Solomon four-group quasi-experiment." *Criminal Justice and Behavior* 48.10 (2021): 1411–1430.

Campbell, Rebecca, et al. "Why do sexual assault survivors seek medical forensic exams and forensic evidence collection? Exploring patterns of service needs in a state-wide study." *Psychology of Violence* 11.3 (2021): 264.

Colbert, Alison M., Cindy Peternelj-Taylor, and Carolyn M. Porta. "2020: Forensic nursing: The state of the specialty." *Journal of Forensic Nursing* 16.4 (2020): 183–185.

Davis, Robert C., et al. "Investigative outcomes of CODIS matches in previously untested sexual assault kits." *Criminal Justice Policy Review* 32.8 (2021): 841–864.

García, M. G., et al. "Drug-facilitated sexual assault and other crimes: A systematic review by countries." *Journal of Forensic and Legal Medicine* 79 (2021): 102151.

Hazelwood, Robert R., and Janet Warren. "The serial rapist: His characteristics and victims (Part I)." *FBI Law Enforcement Bulletin* 58 (1989): 10.

Markey, James, et al. "Sexual assault investigations and the factors that contribute to a suspect's arrest." *Policing: An International Journal* (2021).

Valentine, Julie L., et al. "Evidence collection and analysis for touch deoxyribonucleic acid in groping and sexual assault cases." *Journal of Forensic Nursing* 17.2 (2021): 67.

CHAPTER 16

Baskin, Deborah, and Ira Sommers. "Solving residential burglaries in the United States: The impact of forensic evidence on case outcomes." *International Journal of Police Science & Management* 13.1 (2011): 70–86.

Bradbury, Sarah-Anne, and Andy Feist. *The Use of Forensic Science in Volume Crime Investigations: A Review of the Research Literature*. Research Development and Statistics Directorate, Home Office, 2005.

Burrows, J., and R. Tarling. "Measuring the impact of forensic science in detecting burglary and autocrime offences." *Science & Justice: Journal of the Forensic Science Society* 44.4 (2004): 217–222.

Fullár, Alexandra, Vera Kutnyánszky, and Norbert Leiner. "Identification of burglars using foil impressioning based on tool marks and DNA evidence." *Forensic Science International* 316 (2020): 110524.

Mildenhall, D. C. "Hypericum pollen determines the presence of burglars at the scene of a crime: An example of forensic palynology." *Forensic Science International* 163.3 (2006): 231–235.

Pfeifer, Céline M., and Peter Wiegand. "Persistence of touch DNA on burglary-related tools." *International Journal of Legal Medicine* 131.4 (2017): 941–953.

Tièche, Colin Charles, Markus Dubach, and Martin Zieger. "Efficient DNA Sampling in Burglary Investigations." *Genes* 13.1 (2021): 26.

Wang, Zhen, et al. "Study on traces left on a mechanical lock picked by a 3D printed key in toolmarks examination." *Forensic Science International* 317 (2020): 110514.

Wüllenweber, Sarah, and Stephanie Giles. "The effectiveness of forensic evidence in the investigation of volume crime scenes." *Science & Justice* 61.5 (2021): 542–554.

CHAPTER 17

Bates, Eoin A. "Digital vehicle forensics." [online].[cit, 2019-11-17]. Available at https://abforensics. com/wp-content/uploads/2019/02/INTERP OL-4N6-PULSE-IssueIV-BATES. pdf (2019).

Burke, Michael P. *Forensic Medical Investigation of Motor Vehicle Incidents*. CRC Press, 2006.

Clark, Warren E. *Traffic Management and Collision Investigation*. Prentice-Hall, 1982.

Drummond, F. C., and P. A. Pizzola. "An unusual case involving the individualization of a clothing impression on a motor vehicle." *Journal of Forensic Science* 35.3 (1990): 746–752.

Hamm, E. D. "Locating an area on a suspect tire for comparative examination to a questioned track." *Journal of Forensic Identification* 38.4 (1988): 143–151.

Lambourn, Richard F. "The calculation of motor car speeds from curved tyre marks." *Journal of the Forensic Science Society* 29.6 (1989): 371–386.

Nogayeva, Saule, James Gooch, and Nunzianda Frascione. "The forensic investigation of vehicle–pedestrian collisions: A review." *Science & Justice* 61.2 (2021): 112–118.

Ryland, S. G., and R. J. Kopec. "The evidential value of automobile paint chips." *Journal of Forensic Science* 24.1 (1979): 140–147.

Stoner, Dale, and Ilya Zeldes. "Speedometer examination: An aid in accident investigation." *FBI L. Enforcement Bulletin* 49 (1980): 11.

Taylor, M. C., et al. "A data collection of vehicle topcoat colours. 3. Practical considerations for using a national database." *Forensic Science International* 40.2 (1989): 131–141.

CHAPTER 18

Anderson, G. S. "The use of insects to determine time of decapitation: A case-study from British Columbia." *Journal of Forensic Science* 42.5 (1997): 947–950.

Byrd, Jason H., and Jeffery K. Tomberlin, eds. *Forensic Entomology: The Utility of Arthropods in Legal Investigations*. CRC Press, 2019.

Danto, Bruce L., and Thomas Streed. "Death investigation after the destruction of evidence." *Journal of Forensic Science* 39.3 (1994): 863–870.

DiMaio, Vincent JM. *Gunshot Wounds: Practical Aspects of Firearms, Ballistics, and Forensic Techniques*. CRC Press, 2015.

DiMaio, Vincent JM, and D. Kimberley Molina. *DiMaio's Forensic Pathology*. CRC Press, 2021.

Eisele, J. W., D. T. Reay, and Angus Cook. "Sites of suicidal gunshot wounds." *Journal of Forensic Science* 26.3 (1981): 480–485.

Erskine, Kevin L., and Erica J. Armstrong. *Water-related Death Investigation: Practical Methods and Forensic Applications*. CRC Press, 2021.

Felthous, Alan R., and Anthony Hempel. "Combined homicide-suicides: A review." *Journal of Forensic Sciences* (1995).

Gee, David John. "A pathologist's view of multiple murder." *Forensic Science International* 38.1–2 (1988): 53–65.

Geberth, Vernon J. "Sex-related homicide investigations." *Routledge International Handbook of Sexual Homicide Studies*. Routledge, 2018. 448–470.

Henssge, C. "Death time estimation in case work. I. The rectal temperature time of death nomogram." *Forensic Science International* 38.3–4 (1988): 209–236.

Henssge, Claus, Burkhard Madea, and Elisabeth Gallenkemper. "Death time estimation in case work. II. Integration of different methods." *Forensic Science International* 39.1 (1988): 77–87.

Howard, John D., et al. "Processing of skeletal remains: A medical examiner's perspective." *The American Journal of Forensic Medicine and Pathology* 9.3 (1988): 258–264.

Kintz, Pascal, et al. "Fly larvae: A new toxicological method of investigation in forensic medicine." *Journal of Forensic Science* 35.1 (1990): 204–207.

Mack Jr, Huey A. "Identification of victims: The beginning of a homicide investigation." *Journal of Forensic Identification* 45.5 (1995): 510–512.

Mann, Robert W., William M. Bass, and Lee Meadows. "Time since death and decomposition of the human body: Variables and observations in case and experimental field studies." *Journal of Forensic Science* 35.1 (1990): 103–111.

Owsley, Douglas W. "Techniques for locating burials, with emphasis on the probe." *Journal of Forensic Science* 40.5 (1995): 735–740.

Payne-James, Jason, and Richard Martin Jones, eds. *Simpson's Forensic Medicine*. CRC Press, 2019.

Pittner, Stefan, et al. "The applicability of forensic time since death estimation methods for buried bodies in advanced decomposition stages." *PloS one* 15.12 (2020): E0243395.

Pollanen, Michael S., and David A. Chiasson. "Fracture of the hyoid bone in strangulation: Comparison of fractured and unfractured hyoids from victims of strangulation." *Journal of Forensic Science* 41.1 (1996): 110–113.

Re, Giuseppe Lo, et al., eds. *Radiology in Forensic Medicine: From Identification to Post-mortem Imaging*. Springer, 2019.

Rhine, J. Stanley, and B. K. Curran. "Multiple gunshot wounds of the head: An anthropological view." *Journal of Forensic Science* 35.5 (1990): 1236–1245.

Rodriguez, William C., and William M. Bass. "Decomposition of buried bodies and methods that may aid in their location." *Journal of Forensic Science* 30.3 (1985): 836–852.

Spitz, Werner U., Daniel J. Spitz, and Russell S. Fisher, eds. *Spitz and Fisher's Medicolegal Investigation of Death: Guidelines for the Application of Pathology to Crime Investigation*. Charles C Thomas Publisher, 2006.

Thali, Michael, Richard Dirnhofer, and Peter Vock. *The Virtopsy Approach: 3D Optical and Radiological Scanning and Reconstruction in Forensic Medicine*. CRC Press, 2009.

Ubelaker, Douglas H. "Hyoid fracture and strangulation." *Journal of Forensic Science* 37.5 (1992): 1216–1222.

Vass, Arpad A., et al. "Time since death determinations of human cadavers using soil solution." *Journal of Forensic Science* 37.5 (1992): 1236–1253.

Viero, A., et al. "Crime scene and body alterations caused by arthropods: Implications in death investigation." *International Journal of Legal Medicine* 133.1 (2019): 307–316.

CHAPTER 19

Bernardo, Bruno, and Vitor Santos. "Mobile device forensics investigation process: A systematic review." *Handbook of Research on Cyber Crime and Information Privacy*, 2021. 256–288.

Casey, Eoghan. *Handbook of Digital Forensics and Investigation*. Academic Press, 2009.

Easttom, Chuck. *An In-Depth Guide to Mobile Device Forensics*. CRC Press, 2021.

Hou, Jianwei, et al. "A survey on digital forensics in Internet of Things." *IEEE Internet of Things Journal* 7.1 (2019): 1–15.

Hrenak, Andrew. "Mobile device forensics: An introduction." *Cyber Forensics*. CRC Press, 2021. 291–322.

Jones, G. Maria, S. Godfrey Winster, and L. Ancy Geoferla. "A role of digital evidence: Mobile forensics data." *Advanced Smart Computing Technologies in Cybersecurity and Forensics*. CRC Press, 2021. 47–63.

Kävrestad, Joakim. *Fundamentals of Digital Forensics*. Springer International Publishing, 2020.

van Beek, Harm MA, et al. "Digital forensics as a service: Stepping up the game." *Forensic Science International: Digital Investigation* 35 (2020): 301021.

CHAPTER 20

Bohan, Thomas L., and E. J. Heels. "The case against Daubert: The new scientific evidence "standard" and the standards of the several states." *Journal of Forensic Science* 40.6 (1995): 1030–1044.

Faigman, David L., et al. *Modern Scientific Evidence: The Law and Science of Expert Testimony* (Vol. 1). West Publishing, 2002.

Giannelli, Paul C. "Evidentiary and procedural rules governing expert testimony." *Journal of Forensic Science* 34.3 (1989): 730–748.

Havard, John DJ. "Expert scientific evidence under the adversarial system. A travesty of justice?" *Journal of the Forensic Science Society* 32.3 (1992): 225–235.

Hollien, Harry. "The expert witness: Ethics and responsibilities." *Journal of Forensic Science* 35.6 (1990): 1414–1423.

Roux, Claude, Sheila Willis, and Céline Weyermann. "Shifting forensic science focus from means to purpose: A path forward for the discipline?" *Science & Justice* 61.6 (2021): 678–686.

Index

Note: Page numbers followed by f and t indicate figures and tables respectively.

AAFS Standards Board (ASB), 245
Abandoned vehicles, 232–233
Abrasion ring, 270
Abrasions, 266
Accidental death, 285, 286f
Accident reconstruction, 62–64
    case review, 62–64
    CSIs and forensic engineers, 62
    facial trauma to victim, 63f
    used in civil cases, 62
ACE-V, four-step process, 86
Advanced crime scene investigation, 53
Advanced Fingerprint Identification Technology (AFIT), 76
Airbags, 237
Altered stains, 60
American National Standards Institute (ANSI), 60
American Society for Testing Materials (ASTM), 126
American Society of Crime Laboratory Directors (ASCLD)
        Code of Ethics
    section 1: policy, 206
    section 2: code, 206–207
Amido Black, 73
Ammonia dynamite, 172
Ammonia-gelatin dynamite, 172
Ammonium nitrate and fuel oil (ANFO), 172
Ammunition, 145–146
    caliber of rifled weapon, 146f
    description of firearms, 25
    gunpowder or smokeless powder, 146, 147f
    inside of shotgun shell, 146f
    moving gun, 25
    rifling, consisting of lands and grooves, 147f
Amped software, detecting photo tampering, 36
Amphetamines, 181
Ancestry determinations, 99
ANDE's 6C Rapid DNA Instrument, 101f
Antemortem x-rays of metal rod placement, 36f
Arrestee index, 100
Arson
    Cameron Todd Willingham case, 165–167
    crime scenes, 166
    defined, 165
    investigations, 166–167
    physical evidence, 167–170
        case review, 169–170, 169f
        collection and preservation, 167, 167f
        ignitable fluids or accelerants, 167–168
        laboratory analysis, 167–168
        M.O. (modus operandi), 168, 168f
Artificial intelligence (AI), 302
Asbestos, 110
Ash, 116

Association for Crime Scene Reconstruction, 11, 53
Assortment of materials, 44
Augmented Reality (AR), 302
Autopsy, 265–266
Autosomal STR, 100–101

Backspatter, 152
Ballistics, 143
Barricade, 22
Battered child syndrome, 285
Benzodiazepines, 181
Binary explosives, 172
Biogeographical ancestry markers, 100
Biological evidence, 44
Biological stains
    removal of, 94–95
    sterile cotton-tipped swabs, 94–95, 94f
Black fingerprint powder, 72
Black powder, 170–171
Blank samples, 44
Blasting agents, 172
Blood samples or buccal (cheek) swabs, 44
Bloodstain pattern analysis (BPA)
    American National Standards Institute (ANSI), 60
    basic types of bloodstains, 60
    bloodstain pattern evidence, 59
    case review, 60–62
    Quality Assurance Program in Bloodstain Pattern Analysis, 60
    Standard for Report Writing in Bloodstain Pattern Analysis, 60
    Standard for the Validation of Procedures in Bloodstain Pattern Analysis, 60
    Standards for a Bloodstain Pattern Analyst's Training Program, 60
Bloodstains; *see also* Presumptive blood tests
    bloodstained objects, 95
    collection and preservation of
        air-dried sample, stored in paper bag, 94
        biological evidence, 94
        DNA, source of, 94
    description and recording of photographs, 93
    pattern evidence, 59
    searching for
        chart from SPEX Forensics, 92f
        lasers, 91
        M-Vac system is a wet-vacuum DNA collection tool, 94f
        objects, bloodstains on, 93
        sterile razor blade, to scrape an article of clothing, 93, 93f
    types of
        altered stains, 60

case review, 60
passive stains, 60
spatter, 60
Bluestar® reagent, 91
Board Certified Latent Print Examiner (CLPE), 86, 86f
Body removal, 24
Bomb scene investigation, 174–176
Bomb technician, 26
Bone injuries, 267
Boosters or primer explosives, 172
Botanist, 26
Brushing powder over latent print, 71
Building materials, 109
Bullets, 157
    fragments, 151f
    fully jacketed (solid nose) bullets, 157
    glass perforated by bullet, 119–120, 120f
    injuries, 270–271
    lead bullets, 158
    marking, 157–159, 159f
    semi-jacketed bullets, 158
    severely mutilated bullets, 157f
    traces, 272
    types, 158f
Burglary investigation
    detailed examination of scene, 223–224
    entry through basement windows and skylights, 222
    entry through doors, 220–222, 221f
    entry through floors, 223
    entry through roofs, 222
    entry through walls, 223
    entry through windows, 219–220, 220f
    forensic locksmithing, 228
    points of entry, 219
    safe burglaries, 224–226
    safe burglaries using explosives, 226–228
    simulated burglaries, 223
Burned papers and charred documents, 192
Burning bar, 226
Buttons, 114

Cadaver dog handler, 26
CAD software
    computer-animated graphics, 40
    3D pictorial form, 40
Caliber of rifled weapon, 146f
California Association of Criminalists (CAC), 203
Cannabis, 182–183
Capillary electrophoresis, 98
Carbon monoxide poisoning, 282
Cartridge cases, 154–157
    extractor marks on a cartridge casing, 156f
    fired cartridge cases, 155
    primer face of cartridge, 156f
    revolver cartridge cases, 155
    severely mutilated bullets, 157f
    smaller caliber projectiles, 155
Casting
    with dental stone, 132–133
    impressions in snow, 133
    tool marks, 137, 138f
    water-filled impressions, 133

Catalytic tests, *see* Presumptive blood tests
Cell phone, use of, 23
Certified latent print examiner, 86f
Chain of custody, 48–50
Changing or contaminating the scene, 20
Chemical, Biological, Radiological, Nuclear, and Explosive (CBRNE), 51
Chemical kits, 90
Chemical messenger, 97
Chemicals, 90
Chemiluminescence, 91
Chips and splinters of wood, 117
Chopping wounds, 269–270
Chromosomes, 97
Cigarettes and tobacco, 115, 115f
Civilian emergency medical personnel, 21
Cleaning, 22
Clean paint cans, 45f
Clear storage cases, 46f
Close and distant shots, 271–272
Close-up pictures, 32
Clothing
    clothes from murder and assault victims, 106
    on deceased victims, 106
    wet cloths, air-dry before packaging, 105
Cocaine, 181, 181f
Cognitive bias, 15
    avoidance of cognitive dissonance, 15
    confirmation bias, 15
    contextual bias, 15
    Dror, Itiel, 15
Collection of evidence
    assortment of materials, 44
    biological evidence, 44
    blank samples, 44
    blood samples or buccal (cheek) swabs, 44
    chain of custody, 48–50
    Chemical, Biological, Radiological, Nuclear, and Explosive (CBRNE), 51
    clean paint cans, 45f
    clear storage cases, 46f
    contamination, 45
    double-wrap very small objects, 45
    druggist's fold, 45
    HAZMAT crime scenes, 51
    International Association for Property and Evidence (IAPE), 48
    known samples, or exemplars, 44
    Laboratory Information Management Systems (LIMS), 49
    microscopic or trace evidence, 45
    paper bags with chain of custody markings, 44f
    preservation
        packaging instructions, 49–50
        voucher with complete inventory, 49
        written request to laboratory, 49
    Professional Association of Diving Instructors (PADI), 50
    safe package, 45
    set priorities, 48
    trace evidence, collection, 45
    underwater crime scene, 50
COmbined DNA Index System (CODIS), 99
    arrestee index, 100

convicted offender index, 100
detainee index, 100
forensic partial and forensic mixture indexes, 100
forensic unknown index, 99
legal index, 100
missing person index, 100
relatives of missing person index, 100
unidentified human remains index, 100
Command officers, 26
Commingled items, 89
Comparative examination, 129
Comparison footprints
    case review, 135, 136f
    identification, 135
    from suspect, 134, 134f
Comparison microscope, 144f, 145f, 148f
Composition C-3, 173
Composition C-4, 173
Compression marks, 129
Consortium of Forensic Science Organizations (CFSO), 3
Contamination, 45
    commingled items, 89
    definition, 89
    of fingers, 78
Continued protection of scene
    command officers, 26
    News reporters, dealing with, 26
Control or known trace samples, 109
Contusions or bruises, 266
Convicted offender index, 100
Cordage and rope, 115
Cosmetics, 123
Courtroom testimony, 298–300
    cross-examination, 299
    giving expert testimony, 298–299
    before going to court, 298
    other points, 299–300
Cracked or burst panes of glass, 120–121
Crime scene, 166
    case review, 26–27, 27f
    continued protection
        command officers, 26
        news reporters, dealing with, 26
    dead person on scene
        officer's cell phone, use of, 23
        signs of death, 23
    dos and don'ts, 20t
    entering scene
        to avoid cleaning, 22
        cleaning, 22
        location of objects, 21
        notes, 21
    firearms and ammunition, 25
    first officer at scene, 17–20
    injured person
        civilian emergency medical personnel, 21
        proper removal and custody of victim's clothing, 21
    investigating till personnel arrival
        first officer's duty, 25
    personnel, 26–27
        cross-train all personnel, 26
        specialty personnel, 26

press, at crime scenes, 23f
protecting integrity
    barricade, 22
    limiting movements, 22, 23
    protective measures, 23
    remote video camera, 22
    temporary tent to protect outdoor crime scene, 22
recording time
    time of arrival at scene, 20
    time spent at scene, 20
summoning medical examiner, 23–24
    body removal, 24
    cases of strangulation or hanging, 24
    medicolegal death investigator (MLI), 24
    postmortem lividity or livor mortis, 24
    rigor mortis, 24
suspect at scene, 20
    changing or contaminating scene, 20
    safety, 20
Crime scene photography
    cameras, types of
        digital single lens reflex (DSLR) camera, 31
        save and storing of images, 32
    detailed photographs, 30
    Forenscope, 31f
    FujiFilm X-T1 Forensic IR Kit, 31f
    number of photographs
        close-up pictures, 32
        360-degree photographs, 33
        evidence photographs, 32
        examination quality photographs, 32
        location, 32
        L-Tron Corporation's OSCR360 Capture Kit, 33
        photo log, 33
        posed photographs, 33
        purposes, 32
        using a flash, 33
        witness photographs, 32
Crime scene reconstruction
    accident reconstruction, 62–64
    advanced crime scene investigation, 53
    assistance of associated persons, 58
    Association for Crime Scene Reconstruction, 53
    blood, 59f
    bloodstain pattern analysis (BPA), 59–62
    case review, 53–58
        pictures of evidence, 54f
        still photos, 55f
    forensic shooting reconstructions, 64–65
    International Association for Identification, 53
    International Association of Bloodstain Pattern
        Analysts, 53
    Locard's Exchange Principle, 57
    order of clothing fragments, 58f
    process of reconstruction, 58
Criminal Investigation: A Practical Handbook for Magistrates, Police Officers, and Lawyers (Gross), 57
Cross-training the personnel, 26
Crushing wounds, 267
CSI: Crime Scene Investigation, TV show, 3
CSI effect, 8–9, 40
    negative evidence, 9

Index

Current marks, 279
Curved lines, edge of glass in concentric fracture, 118f
Curved surfaces with latent fingerprints, 77
Cut-resistant gloves, 89
Cutting wounds, 267–268
Cyanoacrylate fuming of credit card, 74f

Damp objects, 78
Data-driven documentation, 40
Datasheet, 173
Date rape, 181
Date-rape drugs, 214
    gamma-hydroxybutyrate (GHB), 214
    Rohypnol or flunitrazepam, 214
Dead person on scene
    officer's cell phone, use of, 23
    signs of death, 23
Death by Fire (2010), 165
Death investigation
    abrasions, 266
    accidental death, 285, 286f
    action of insects on dead body, 263–264
    autopsy, 265–266
    blocking of larynx and air passages, 278
    blocking of mouth or nose, 278
    bone injuries, 267
    boots and shoes, 261
    bullet injuries, 270–271
    carbon monoxide poisoning, 282
    cause of death, 240
    changes in eyes, 261
    chopping wounds, 269–270
    close and distant shots, 271–272
    clothing, 260–261
    contusions or bruises, 266
    crushing wounds, 267
    cutting wounds, 267–268
    damage to clothes from shooting, 273
    death by freezing, 280
    death by poisoning, 280–282
    death by suffocation, 274
    death from electric current, 279
    death from fires, 279–280
    decomposition of body, 263
    defense injuries, 270
    detailed examination of crime scene, 248–252, 249f
        case review, 250–252, 250f
    discovering body hidden at another location, 254–255
    drowning, 278–279
    estimating time of death, 261
    examination of dead body at crime scene, 244–245, 246f
    examining remains of clothing and other objects, 260
    explosion injuries, 274
    firearm injuries, 270
    hanging, 275–276
    infanticide and child abuse, 283–285
    injuries from small shot, 273
    investigation of greatly altered body or skeleton, 255, 256f, 257
    lividity, 262, 262f
    location of weapon, 244
    marks from primers, 272
    modes of death from shooting, 273–274
    murder, 246–248
    other indications of time of death, 264–265
    outdoors, 257–260, 258f
        case review, 253–254
        crime scenes, 252–254, 253f
        indoors, 259–260, 259f
    packing and transporting, 260
    postmortem signs of death, 261
    rape-homicide and sexual assault-related murders, 283, 284f
    rigidity of body, 262
    scene of discovery, 257
    serial murders, 285–287
    signs of struggle, 243–244
    squeezing to death, 278
    stab wounds, 268–269
        case review, 268–269, 269f
    strangling, 276–278
    suicide, 240–243, 241f
        case review, 242–243, 242f
    temperature of body, 261
    traces from barrel of weapon, 273
    traces from bullets, 272
    traces from cartridge cases, 272
    trunk murder, dismemberment of body, 285
Decedent, fingerprints from, 82–84
    difficulty in decomposed body, 82
    diluted liquid fabric softener, 83
    fingerprints from corpse removed from water, 83
    number of prints of same finger, 82
    palm print from dead body, 84
    photography, 83
    printing ink, 83
    scraping of attached tissues, 84
    softening dried fingers, 83
Defense injuries, 270
360-Degree photographs, 33
Dental and body x-rays, 34
Department of Justice (DOJ), 4
Depressants, 180–181
Designer drugs, 183
    fentanyl analogs and bath salts, 183
    herbal incense, 183
    synthetic cannabis, 183
Detailed photographs, 30
Detailed search, 43
Detainee index, 100
DFO (1,8-diazafluoren-9-one), 73
Dialectology, 195
Difficulty in decomposed body, 82
Digital audio recorders, 29–30
Digital automotive image system (DAIS), 238
Digital evidence and electronic crime scene, 289–290
    collecting video evidence, 291–292, 291f
    computer seizure, 290
    confiscating recording medium, 292
    Digital/Multimedia Scientific Area Committee, 294
    document video system's physical relationship, 292–293
    Facial Identification Scientific Working Group (FISWG), 295
    mobile device forensics, 293–294
    OSAC Digital Evidence Subcommittee, 295

OSAC Facial Identification Subcommittee, 295
OSAC Speaker Recognition Subcommittee, 295
OSAC video/imaging technology and analysis subcommittee, 295
Scientific Working Group on Digital Evidence (SWGDE), 295
Scientific Working Group on Imaging Technology (SWGIT), 295
stop recorder, 292
technical assistance, 293
video, 292
Digital forensics, 290
Digital/Multimedia Scientific Area Committee, 294
Digital single lens reflex (DSLR) camera, 31
Diluted liquid fabric softener, 83
Divers, 26
DNA reference samples for identification, 100
DNA technology, 72
Document evidence
    author's handwriting, 191
    burned papers and charred documents, 192
    case review, 194f
    chemical treatment, 192
    damages, excessive handling, 191
    documents processed for fingerprints, 192
    examination under ultraviolet and infrared light, 192
    Forensic Document Examination, 191
    forensic linguistics, 195–197
    formal exemplars, 193
    graphology, 195
    handling, 192
    handwriting examination, 191
    informal exemplars, 193
    OSAC Forensic Document Examination Subcommittee, 195
    photography, 192
    style characteristics, 191
    SWGDOC, 195
    video spectral comparator (VSC), 195, 196f
    writings, on wall or body, 193f
    written documents, 191
Documenting crime scene
    case-specific requirements, 29
    dead body, photographing (*see* Photographing a dead body)
    "L" shaped ruler, 33f
    note-taking, 29–30
    photography (*see* Crime scene photography)
    sketching (*see* Sketching crime scene)
    Standard Operating Procedures (SOPs), 29
    3D scanning, 40, 41f
    videography (*see* Videography)
Double-based powder, 146
Double packaging, 109
Drones, 37–38
    Federal Aviation Administration (FAA), 37
    Light Detection and Ranging (LiDAR), 37
    mission creep, 38
    technology, 22
    Unmanned Aerial Vehicles (UAVs), 37
Drowning, 278–279
Drug Enforcement Administration (DEA), 179
Druggist's fold, 45
Dust prints, 133–134
    lifting by photographic paper, 134
    lifting by special lifter, 134
    lifting by static electricity, 134
    recovering object with footprint, 133
Dynamite, 172
    ammonia dynamite, 172
    ammonia-gelatin dynamite, 172
    gelatin dynamite, 172
    straight dynamite, 172

Ear prints (auricle morphometry), 80
Electrical wire, 125–126
Electrostatic dust lifters, 134
Elevation drawing, 39
Elimination palm prints, 80
Enlargements or enhancements, 36
Equipment
    basic equipment, 305–306
    casting materials, 308
    colored pencils, 38
    DNA/BLOOD collection supplies, 307
    evidence packaging supplies, 306
    fingerprint equipment, 306
    general crime scene supply companies, 308–309
    graph paper, 38
    hand tools, 307
    other equipment, 308
    photographic equipment, 306
    safety equipment, 308
    total station, 38, 39f
Ethics
    ASCLD Code of Ethics
        section 1: policy, 206
        section 2: code, 206–207
    Code of Ethics of the California Association of Criminalists, 203–206
        ethical aspects of court presentations, 204–205
        ethical responsibilities to profession, 205–206
        ethics relating to opinions and conclusions, 204
        ethics relating to general practice of criminalistics, 205
        ethics relating to scientific method, 203–204
    organizational responsibility, 203
    professionalism, 201–202
        clear communications, 202
        competency and proficiency, 202
Evidence
    biological evidence, 44
    definition, 6
    digital (*see* Digital evidence and electronic crime scene)
    fingerprint (*see* Fingerprint evidence)
    impression (*see* Impression evidence)
    photographs, 32
    physical (*see* Physical evidence)
    real, 6
    testimonial evidence, 6
Evidence collection teams, 18
Examination
    comparative examination, 129
    of dead body at crime scene, 244–245, 246f
    of developed fingerprints, 78
    firearms (*see* Firearms examination)

handwriting examination, 191
quality photographs, 32
under ultraviolet and infrared light, 192
Exculpatory evidence, 14
Exemplars or known samples, 44
Explosion injuries, 274
Explosives, 170
    binary explosives, 172
    blasting agents, 172
    bomb scene investigation, 174–176
    high explosives, 171–172
        ammonium nitrate, 172
        boosters or primer explosives, 172
        detonating cord, 171
        dynamite, 172
        nitroglycerine, 172
        primary explosives, 171
        secondary explosives, 171
        water gels or slurries, 172
    homemade (see Homemade explosives (HME))
    low explosives, 170–171, 171f
        black powder, 170–171
        smokeless powder, 171
    military (see Military explosives)
    OSAC Fire & Explosion Investigation Subcommittee, 176

Fabric marks, 135
Facial Identification Scientific Working Group (FISWG), 295
Fake fingerprints, 87
Faraday bag or box, 294, 294f
FARO 3D digital scanner, 41f
FBI's Quality Assurance Standards (QAS) for DNA analysis, 102
Feathers (plumology), 124
Federal Aviation Administration (FAA), 37
Fiber brushes, 72
Fiberglass filament brush, 82
Fiber match confirmatory tests, 48f
Final survey, checklist, 51
Fingerprint evidence
    ACE-V, 86
    case review, 70, 79
    collaboration, 71
    contamination of fingers, 78
    from decedent (see Decedent, fingerprints from)
    development with powders (see Powders, development with)
    ear prints (auricle morphometry), 80
    elimination palm prints, 80
    enhancement using adobe photoshop, 84
    examination of developed fingerprints, 78
    examiner conclusions (see Fingerprint examiner conclusions)
    fake fingerprints, 87
    flashlight, 70
    forensic chemists, 71
    friction ridges, 80
    IAFIS, 75–76
    IAI certification, 86
    identification specialists, 71
    lasers and alternative light sources, 75
    latent (see Latent fingerprints)
    legitimate fingerprints, 80
    lip prints (cheiloscopy), 80
    longevity of, 78
    oblique illumination, 70
    from online photos, 87
    OSAC friction ridge subcommittee, 86–87
    of other coverings, 81–82
    palm prints, 69, 78–79
    on paper, 78
    patent fingerprints, 71
    places, 70
    plastic fingerprints, 71, 78
    preservation with (see Preservation)
    principles of uses in CSI, 69
    prints of gloves (see Gloves, prints of)
    RUVIS, 75
    from sole of foot, 80
    temperature conditions, 78
    transporting objects, 80
Fingerprint examiner conclusions
    certified latent print examiner, 86f
    fingerprint ridge detail, 85f
    inconclusive/lacking support, 85
    qualifications, 85–86
    source exclusion, 84
    source identification, 85
    support for different sources, 84
    support for same source, 85
Firearms examination, 25
    and ammunition at scene (see Ammunition)
    ballistics, 143
    bullets, 157
    cartridge cases, 154–157
    characteristics
        caliber designation, 145
        homemade weapons, 143
        obsolete weapons, 143
        revolver, 143
        revolver-type firearms, 145
        semi-automatic pistol, 145
        single shot-firearm, 145
        single-shot pistol, 143
        St. Valentine's Day Massacre, 144f
        3-D printed guns, 143
        zip guns, 143
    comparison microscope, 144f, 145f, 148f
    evidence, 147–148
        bullet fragments, 151f
        contamination, 152
        location and position of cartridges and bullets, 150–151
        shotgun wads, 152f
    gunshot residue (GSR) analysis, 148–150, 149f
    handling of
        fingerprint impressions, 153
        loose objects or particles, 153
        precautions, 154
        revolver, 153
        semi-automatic pistol, 153
        serial number restoration, 154f
        weapons of single-shot or repeating types, 153
    injuries, 270
    Integrated Ballistic Identification System (IBIS), 162

marking bullets (*see* Bullets)
NIBIN workstation, 162, 162f
OSAC Firearms & Toolmarks Subcommittee, 163
powder pattern examination, 161–162
reference library, 160f
small shot, 159–160
SWGGUN, 163
TEST FIRING, 160–161
test firing, 160–161
3D printed ghost guns, 162, 163
Fired cartridge cases, 155
First officer
    duty, 25
    at scene, 17–20
        every contact leaves trace, 18
        evidence collection teams, 18
        guidelines, 19
        Locard Exchange Principle, 18
        ongoing training and continuing education, 18
        physical evidence, 17
        preventative and preliminary measures, 19
        resources of crime scene unit, 18
        uniformed personnel, 17
Flashlight, 33, 70
Flex-X, 173
Floor plan, or bird's-eye-view sketch, 39
Foodstuffs, 123
Footprints, 129–130
    on floors, 130–131, 131f
    individual's style of running, 130
    preservation of, 133–134
        lifting by photographic paper, 134
        lifting by special lifter, 134
        lifting by static electricity, 134
        recovering object with footprint, 133
    value of, 130
Footwear, 106; *see also* Impression evidence
    casting impressions, 132
    evidence, preservation of, 131
    OSAC footwear and tire subcommittee, 140
    photographing impressions, 131–132, 131f
    preservation of, 130
    and tire impressions, 130
Forenscope, 31f
Forensic anthropologist, 26
Forensic ballistics, 163
Forensic DNA grade standard, 90
Forensic DNA typing, 97
    buccal swabs, 97
    chromosomes, 97
    STR analysis, 97
Forensic document examination, 191
Forensic engineer, 26
Forensic entomologist, 26
Forensic Genetic Genealogy (FGG)
    case review, 101–102
    genetic association to shared common ancestor, 101
    OSAC Human Forensic Biology Subcommittee, 102
    STR DNA typing, difference, 101
Forensic linguistics, 195–197
    author identification, 195
    dialectology, 195
    discourse analysis, 195
    linguistic origin analysis, 195
    linguistic proficiency, 195
    linguistic veracity analysis, 195
    voice identification, 195
Forensic partial and forensic mixture indexes, 100
Forensic phonetics, 197
Forensic science
    organizations by discipline, 312–316
    organizations by region, 311–312
    role in investigation and adjudication of crimes, 6
    websites, 311–316
Forensic shooting reconstructions, 64–65
    entrance holes of three bullets, 64f
    stringing, 65f
Forensic stylistics, 197
Forensic toxicology, 188–189
Forensic traces
    ASTM, 126
    collection and preservation, 109
    examples of, 109–122
    NIST, 126
    objects left at crime scene (*see* Objects)
    OSAC trace materials subcommittee, 126
    sources of traces, 105–106
    SWGMAT, 126
Forensic unknown index, 99
Formal exemplars, 193
Fracture match, 140
Fractures, radial and concentric, 118
Friction ridges, 80
Fruit of the poisonous tree, 43
FujiFilm X-T1 Forensic IR Kit, 31f
Full-face and right-profile face photos, 36
Fully jacketed (solid nose) bullets, 157
Funding, 14

Gelatin dynamite, 172
Genealogy research, 99
Generation Identification (NGI), 76
Generative Adversarial Networks (GAN), 302
Gentian violet or crystal violet, 73
Geologist, 26
Glass, 118
    broken panes, 118–119
    perforated by bullet, 119–120, 120f
    splinters, 121–122, 122f
Global Positioning System (GPS), 40, 232, 232f
Gloves, prints of
    comparison prints, 81
    on smooth surfaces, 81
    white or black powder, 81
    wrinkled or textured surface pattern, 81
Graphology, 195
Gun(s)
    ghost guns, 163
    moving gun, 25
Gunpowder
    or smokeless powder, 146
    photomicrograph example, 147f
Gunshot residue (GSR) analysis, 106, 148–150, 149f
    handcuffing, 149

negative GSR results, 149
primers, 149
SEM/EDX analysis, 149

Hairs, 106, 123–124
Hallucinogens, 182, 182f
Handcuffing, 149
Handwriting examination, 191
Hanging, 275–276
Hashish, 182
HAZMAT team, 26, 51, 175
Headlamps, 125
Headline Test, 207
Heinrich, Edward Oscar (Wizard of Berkeley), 58
Heroin, 181f
Hesitation cuts, 267
Hit-and-run investigation, 234–237, 234f, 235f
  case review, 236–237, 236f
Homemade explosives (HME), 173–174
  improvised explosive device, methods
    ammonium nitrate fertilizer, 174
    blasting caps, 174
    flashbulbs, 173–174
    match heads, 174
    percussion primers, 174
    potassium or sodium chlorate, 174
    smokeless powder, 174
  peroxide-based explosive TATP (triacetone triperoxide), 174
  urea nitrate, 174
Homemade weapons, 143
Homicide, 233–234
Human biome and microbial forensics, 301–302

IAI certification, 86
  Board Certified Latent Print Examiner (CLPE), 86, 86f
  program in Latent Certification, 86
Identification photographs, 36
Identity markers, 100
Illicit drugs and toxicology
  clandestine drug laboratories, 185–186
  collection and preservation of evidence, 186, 187f
  crime scene search, 184–185
    searching a dwelling, 185
    searching a suspect, 184
    searching a vehicle, 185
  field testing, 186–187, 187f
  forensic toxicology, 188–189
    OSAC Seized Drugs Subcommittee, 188–189
  OSAC forensic toxicology subcommittee, 189
  psychoactive drugs, 180–184
  SWGDRUG, 189
  SWGTOX, 189
  U.S. DEA drug schedule classification, 179–180
Illustrative diagram or drawing, 38
Impeachment evidence, 14
Impression evidence
  casting impressions in snow, 133
  casting tool marks, 137, 138f
  casting water-filled impressions, 133
  casting with dental stone, 132–133
  comparative examination, 129
  comparison of footprints (see Footprints)
  compression marks, 129
  fabric marks, 135
  fragments of tools, 139–140
  marks on clothes and parts of body, 135
  mikrosil, 137, 138f
  OSAC footwear and tire subcommittee, 140
  preservation of footprints (see Dust prints)
  preservation of footwear (see Footwear)
  preservation of tool marks, 137
  preserving a tool, 139
    manufacturing marks, 139
  scraping marks, 129
  SWGTREAD standards, 140–141
  taking comparison footprints from suspect, 134, 134f
  tire tread and tire track evidence, 140, 141f
    noise treatment, 140
    random individual characteristics, 140
    tread design, 140
    tread wear features, 140
  tool marks, 135–136
  on tools, 137–139
    hacksaw marks, 139
    mikrosil, 138f
    saw marks, 139
  value of footprints, 130
Inconclusive/lacking support, 85
Infanticide and child abuse, 283–285
Informal exemplars, 193
Information included in crime scene sketches, 38
Infrared (IR) photography, 34, 162
Inhalants, 184
Injured person on scene
  civilian emergency medical personnel, 21
  proper removal and custody of victim's clothing, 21
Integrated automated fingerprint identification system (IAFIS), 75–76
  Advanced Fingerprint Identification Technology (AFIT), 76
  Generation Identification (NGI), 76
  Livescan technology, 76
  manual searches, 76f
Integrated Ballistic Identification System (IBIS), 162
International Association for Identification (IAI), 11, 35, 53, 201
  certification in Forensic Photography and Imaging, 35
International Association for Property and Evidence (IAPE), 48
International Association of Bloodstain Pattern Analysts, 53
Interpretation Guidelines, 102
Iodine, 73
ISO 18385—forensic DNA grade, 90
  forensic DNA grade standard, 90
ISO/IEC 17020 accreditation, 12
  accreditation for forensic inspection services, 12
  ANSI National Accreditation Board (ANAB), 12
ISO/IEC 17043 accreditation, 12
"Ivan the Terrible," 194f

Jacket, 272

Kastle–Mayer test, 90, 91f
Kinship analysis, 99
Kirk, Paul L., 18f
Kromekote® Lift Technique, 82

Laboratory Information Management Systems (LIMS), 49
Latent fingerprints, 71, 78
    examiners, 71
    on human skin, 82
        fiberglass filament brush, 82
        Kromekote cards, 82
        Kromekote® Lift Technique, 82
        Magna-Brush, 82
    partial print, using ninhydrin, 74f
Lead bullets, 158
Legal cases regarding forensic science, 12–14
    Brady v. Maryland, 373 U.S. 83 (1963), 13–14
    Bullcoming v. New Mexico, 131 S. Ct. 62 (2010), 13
    Daubert v. Merrell Dow Pharmaceuticals, 509 U.S. 579 (1993), 13
    Federal Rules of Evidence Rule 702, 13
    Frye v. United States, 293 F. 1013 (D.C. Cir. 1923), 12
    Kumho Tire Co. v. Carmichael, 526 U.S. 137 (1999), 13
    Maryland v. King, 569 U.S. (2013), 14
    Melendez-Diaz v. Massachusetts, 129 S.Ct. 2527 (2009), 13
Legal index, 100
Legitimate fingerprints, 80
Leucomalachite green, 90
Lifter, 77
Light Amplification by Stimulated Emission of Radiation (laser), 75
Light Detection and Ranging (LiDAR), 37
Lightweight, portable, low-light video cameras, 36
Limiting movements, 22, 23
Linguistic origin analysis, 195
Linguistic proficiency, 195
Linguistic veracity analysis, 195
Lip prints (cheiloscopy), 80
Livescan technology, 76
Lividity, 262, 262f
Livor mortis, 24, 262
Locard, Edmond, 19f
Locard Exchange Principle, 18, 57, 105
Location, 32
    of cartridges and bullets, 150–151
    measurement to show, 39
    of objects, crime scene, 21
    objects in sketch, 39
    photographs, 32
    of weapon, 244
Locksmith, 26
Low explosives, 170–171, 171f
"L" shaped ruler, 33f
L-Tron Corporation's OSCR360 Capture Kit, 33, 33f
Luminol test, 90

Magna-Brush, 82
Magnetic fingerprint powders, 72, 72f
Marijuana, 182, 183f
Massively parallel sequencing/next generation sequencing
    ANDE's 6C Rapid DNA Instrument, 101f
    autosomal STR, Y-STR, and X-STR allele calls, 100–101
    biogeographical ancestry markers, 100
    identity markers, 100
    phenotypic markers, 100
    Rapid DNA, 101
    ThermoFisher's RapidHIT ID, 101f

Matches, 115–116
Material evidence, 14
M118 Demolition Block, 173
MDMA tablets, 182f
Medical examiner, summoning, 23–24
    body removal, 24
    cases of strangulation or hanging, 24
    livor mortis, 24
    Medicolegal Death Investigator, 24
    postmortem lividity or livor mortis, 24
    rigor mortis, 24
Medicolegal Death Investigator (MLI), 24, 240
Mental health, 14–15
Metals, 111
Microscopic or trace evidence, 45, 107
Mikrosil, 137, 138f
Military dynamite, 173
Military explosives, 173
Missing person index, 100
Missing persons
    DNA reference samples for identification, 100
    National Institute of Justice (NIJ), 100
    National Missing and Unidentified Persons System (NamUs), 100
Mission creep, 38
Mitochondrial DNA (mtDNA), 99
    applications in criminal investigations, 99
    nuclear DNA, 99
Motor vehicle investigation
    abandoned vehicles, 232–233
    airbags, 237
    digital automotive image system, 238
    grand theft auto, 231–232
    hit-and-run investigation, 234–237, 234f, 235f
        case review, 236–237, 236f
    homicide in a vehicle, 233–234
    marks from vehicles, 237
    skid marks, 237
    wheel marks, 237
Murder, 246–248

Narcotics, 180
NAS Report, recommendations, 3–4
National Academy of Science report "Strengthening Forensic Science in the United States: A Path Forward," 10
National Academy of Sciences (NAS), 3
National Commission on Forensic Science (NCFS), 10
National Fire Protection Association (NFPA), 176
National Institute of Forensic Science (NIFS), 3
National Institute of Justice (NIJ), 100
National Institute of Science and Technology (NIST), 4
National Institute of Standards and Technology (NIST), 126
National Integrated Ballistic Information Network (NIBIN) workstation, 162, 162f
National Law Enforcement and Corrections Technology Centers (NLECTC), 293
National Missing and Unidentified Persons System (NamUs), 100
News reporters, dealing with, 26
"Night Stalker," 27f
Ninhydrin solution, 73
Nitro-benzodiazepines, 214

Nitrocarbonitrate (NCN), *see* Blasting agents
Nitroglycerine, 172
Nonprescription drugs, 184
Nonrequest writing, 193
Note-taking, 21
    digital audio recorders, 29–30
    general points, 29–30
    information to be covered, 30
Nuclear DNA, 99

Objects
    bloodstained objects, 95
    damp objects, 78
    double-wrap very small objects, 45
    left at crime scene, 122–126
        articles of clothing, 122
        case review, 122, 123f
        cosmetics, 123
        electrical wire, 125–126
        feathers (plumology), 124
        foodstuffs, 123
        hair, 123–124
        headlamps, 125
        paper, 122
        physical fit, 126
        product markings, 122
        tape, 125, 125f
    as sources of trace evidence
        case review, 107–108, 108f
        microscopic items, 107
        tools used in burglaries, 107, 107f
    transporting objects with fingerprints, 80
        wrapping, 80
Oblique illumination, 70
Ongoing training and continuing education, 18
Opioids, *see* Narcotics
Order of clothing fragments, 58f
Organization of Scientific Area Committees (OSAC), 4, 5f
Ortho-tolidine, 90
OSAC Digital Evidence Subcommittee, 295
OSAC Facial Identification Subcommittee, 295
OSAC Fire & Explosion Investigation Subcommittee, 176
OSAC Firearms & Toolmarks Subcommittee, 163
OSAC footwear and tire subcommittee, 140
OSAC Forensic Document Examination Subcommittee, 195
OSAC friction ridge subcommittee, 86–87
OSAC Human Forensic Biology Subcommittee, 102
OSAC Seized Drugs Subcommittee, 188–189
OSAC Speaker Recognition Subcommittee, 295
OSAC trace materials subcommittee, 126
OSAC video/imaging technology and analysis subcommittee, 295
Outdoor crime scenes, 252–254, 253f, 257–260, 258f
    case review, 253–254
    indoors, 259–260, 259f
Outdoors in ice or snow, 78

Packaging instructions, 49–50
    arson evidence, 50
    cartridge cases and bullets, 50
    charred paper, 50
    controlled substances, 50
    DNA swabs, 50
    firearms, 50
    live and preserved samples for entomological evidence, 50
    live-cartridges, 50
    sharp objects, 50
    stomach contents and organs, 50
    strands of hair on garments, 49
    tool marks on objects, 49
    victim's clothing, 49
Paint, 110–111
Palm prints, 69, 78–79
    case review, 79–80
    from dead body, 84
    developed on car door window, 79f
    online training course, 78
    principles of uses in CSI, 69
Paper, 44f, 122
Passive stains, 60
Patent fingerprints, 71
Paternity testing, 99
Paul L. Kirk Award, 18f
PCAST report, 5f
Perfect murder, 239
Permanent record of relationship of evidence, 38
Peroxide-based explosive TATP (triacetone triperoxide), 174
Personal protective equipment (PPE), 89, 186
Perspective drawing, 39
Phenolphthalin, 90
Phenotypic markers, 100
Photography, 83, 109, 192
    admissibility of photographs
        Amped software, detecting photo tampering, 36
        enlargements or enhancements, 36
    antemortem x-rays of metal rod placement, 36f
    black and white or IR photography, 34
    dental and body x-rays, 34
    of fingerprints, 76, 77
    full-face and right-profile face photos, 36
    identification photographs, 36
    International Association for Identification, 35
        certification in Forensic Photography and Imaging, 35
    strangulation marks, ultraviolet photography, 35
    tattoos, identification of victims and suspects, 34
    ultraviolet (UV) and infrared (IR) photography, 34
    whole-face pictures, 36
Photo log, 33
Physical developer (PD), 73
Physical evidence, 17
    4th Amendment, protection from unreasonable searches/seizures, 43
    can corroborate victim's testimony, 7
    can establish identity of associated persons, 7
    can exonerate innocent, 7
    can place suspect in contact with victim or scene, 6, 7
    case review, 46–48, 48f
    classification and individualization, 9–10
        calculation, fingerprints or firearms evidence, 9
        difference, 9
        fibers identification, 9
    collection of (*see* Collection of evidence)
    corroborate testimony, 9
    detailed search, 43

exceptions to warrant requirement, 43
final survey checklist, 51
latex gloves, 8f
patent fingerprint in blood, 7f
physical match or jigsaw match, example, 10f
releasing scene, 51
reliable than eyewitnesses, 8
scientific certainty, 10
suspect, admissions or even confess, 8
Physical fit, 126
Places, 70
Plant material, 118
Plastic explosives, see RDX
Plastic fingerprints, 71
Plastic prints, 78
Poisons
    alcohol, over-the-counter, and illicit drugs, 281
    bacterial poisons and food poisoning (botulism), 281
    gaseous and liquid poisons, 281
    heavy metals and other inorganic poisons, 281
    other vegetable and animal poisons, 281
Polymerase chain reaction (PCR)
    based technology, 97–98
    thermal cycler, 98f
    ThermoFisher 3500xl Genetic Analyzer, 98f
Posed photographs, 33
Postmortem lividity or livor mortis, 24
Postmortem signs of death, 261
Post-traumatic stress disorder (PTSD), 15
Powder pattern deposit, 161
Powder pattern examination, 161–162
    distribution of particles, 161
    infrared photography, 162
Powders, development with, 71–74
    amido black, 73
    black fingerprint powder, 72
    brushing powder over latent print, 71
    cyanoacrylate fuming of credit card, 74f
    DFO (1,8-diazafluoren-9-one), 73
    DNA technology, 72
    fiber brushes, 72
    gentian violet or crystal violet, 73
    iodine, 73
    magnetic fingerprint powders, 72, 72f
    ninhydrin solution, 73, 74f
    PD or SPD, 73
    Safety Data Sheets (SDSs), 72
    silver nitrate solution, 73
    small particle reagent, 73
    Sudan black, 73
    superglue or cyanoacrylate fuming, 74
    vacuum metal deposition (VMD), 74
Preservation
    of evidence
        footwear evidence, 131
        packaging instructions, 49–50
        voucher with complete inventory, 49
        written request to laboratory, 49
    with fingerprint-lifting tape, 78–79
    of footprints (see Dust prints)
    of footwear and tire impressions, 130
    by photography of fingerprints, 76, 77
    of plastic fingerprints
        curved surfaces with latent fingerprints, 77
        lifter, 77
    tool, 139
        manufacturing marks, 139
    of tool marks, 137
President's Council of Advisors on Science and Technology (PCAST), 4
Press, at crime scenes, 23f
Presumptive blood tests, 90–91
    bloodstains, collection and preservation of (see Bloodstains)
    Bluestar® reagent, 91
    chemical kits, 90
    chemicals, 90
    chemiluminescence, 91
    forensic DNA typing, 97
    Kastle–Mayer test, 90, 91f
    luminol test, 90
    PCR (see Polymerase chain reaction (PCR))
    species testing, 95–96, 96f
Preventative and preliminary measures, 19
Primary explosives, 171
Primers, 149
Printing ink, 83
Product markings, 122
Professional Association of Diving Instructors (PADI), 50, 259
Professional development, 11–12
    Association for Crime Scene Reconstruction, 11
    continuing education and attendance, seminars and workshops, 11
    International Association for Identification (IAI), 11
    certification, 11
    Journal of Forensic Identification, 11
    law enforcement agencies, 11
Protective measures, 23
    integrity of scene
        barricade, 22
        limiting movements, 22, 23
        protective measures, 23
        remote video camera, 22
        temporary tent, 22
    protected insides, 81–82
Psychoactive drugs, 180–184
    cannabis, 182–183
    depressants, 180–181
    designer drugs, 183
    hallucinogens, 182
    inhalants, 184
    narcotics, 180
    nonprescription drugs, 184
    steroids, 183–184
    stimulants, 181
Pugilistic attitude, 279

Quality Assurance Program in Bloodstain Pattern Analysis, 60

Rape
    date-rape drugs, 214
    homicide, 283, 284f
    rape kit backlog, 216
Rapid DNA, 101

RDX, 173
Recommendations for the Efficient DNA Processing of Sexual Assault Evidence Kits, 102
Reconstruction process, *see* Accident reconstruction; Crime scene reconstruction
Recording time
    of arrival at scene, 20
    spent at scene, 20
Record of conditions, 38
Reflective Ultra Violet Imaging Systems (RUVIS), 75
Releasing scene, 51
Remote video camera, 22
Report writing, 297–298
Revolver, 143, 153
    cartridge cases, 155
    type firearms, 145
Rib markings, 118
Rifling, consisting of lands and grooves, 147f
"Right to Know" training, 89
Rigor mortis, 24, 262
Ring® and Nest® video doorbells, 224, 225f
Robotics, 302
Ron Smith & Associates, 78
"Ruhemann's Purple," 73
Rust, 111

Safe insulation, 110
Safe package, 45
Safety, 20
Safety Data Sheets (SDSs), 72
Sawdust, wood meal, or particles of finely powdered wood, 117
Scanning Electron Microscopy/Energy Dispersive X-ray (SEM/EDX) analysis, 149
Scientific certainty, 10
Scientific Working Group for Firearms and Toolmarks (SWGGUN), 163
Scientific Working Group for Forensic Document Examination (SWGDOC), 195
Scientific Working Group for Forensic Toxicology (SWGTOX), 189
Scientific Working Group for Materials Analysis (SWGMAT), 126
Scientific Working Group for the Analysis of Seized Drugs (SWGDRUG), 189
Scientific Working Group on Digital Evidence (SWGDE), 295
Scientific Working Group on DNA Analysis Methods (SWGDAM), 102
    FBI's QAS for DNA analysis, 102
    Interpretation Guidelines, 102
    Recommendations for the Efficient DNA Processing of Sexual Assault Evidence Kits, 102
    Training Guidelines, 102
    Validation Guidelines, 102
Scientific Working Group on Friction Ridge Analysis, Study and Technology (SWGFAST), 87
Scientific Working Group on Imaging Technology (SWGIT), 295
Scraping marks, 129
Scraping of attached tissues, 84
Secondary explosives, 171
Self-contained breathing apparatus (SCBA), 186
Semi-automatic pistol, 145, 153
Semi-jacketed bullets, 158
Serial murders, 285–287
Serial numbers, restoration, 154f
Set priorities, 48
Sexual assault investigation, 216
    date-rape drugs, 214
    evidence collection kit, 210, 211f
    interview, 209–210
    medical examination, 210–214
    national best practices, 216
    physical evidence
        to establish identity of perpetrator, 212, 213f, 214
        to establish non-consensual intercourse occurred, 212
        to establish sexual contact occurred, 212
    physical examination, 210, 211f
    public lewdness/forcible touching, 215
    rape kit backlog, 216
    sexual assault, 209
    sexual child molestation and incest, 214–215, 215f
    trace evidence, 212, 213f
Sexual assault nurse examiner (SANE), 209
Sexual assault-related murders, 283, 284f
Sheet explosives, 173
Sherlock Holmes, 57
Short tandem repeat (STR), 97
Shotgun wads, 152f
Signs of death, 23
Silver nitrate solution, 73
Single shot-firearm, 145
Single-shot pistol, 143
Sketches, types of, 39
Sketching crime scene, 38–40
    CAD software
        computer-animated graphics, 40
        3D pictorial form, 40
    equipment
        colored pencils, 38
        graph paper, 38
        total station, 38, 39f
    illustrative diagram or drawing, 38
    information, 38
    locating objects
        GPS, 40
        measurement, 39
    permanent record of relationship of evidence, 38
    record of conditions, 38
    types of sketches, 39
        ceiling, 39
        elevation drawing, 39
        floor plan, or bird's-eye-view sketch, 39
        perspective drawing, 39
Smaller caliber projectiles, 155
Small particle reagent, 73
Small shot, 159–160
Smartphones, 36
Smokeless powder, 171
Softening dried fingers, 83
Soil, 116
Source exclusion, 84
Source identification, 85
Sources of traces
    clothing

clothes from murder and assault victims, 106
   on deceased victims, 106
   wet cloths, air-dry before packaging, 105
 evidence from body
   gunshot residue (GSR), 106
   hairs, 106
 footwear, 106
Spatter, 60
Specialty personnel, 26
Special Victim Unit detectives, 209
Species testing
 crime-lite 80s, 96f
  positive presumptive test, presence of acid phosphatase, 96f
 semen-stained evidence, 95–96
Squeezing to death, 278
Stabilized physical developer (SPD), 73
Stab wounds, 268–269
 case review, 268–269, 269f
Standard for Forensic DNA Interpretation and Comparison Protocols, 102
Standard for Report Writing in Bloodstain Pattern Analysis, 60
Standard for the Validation of Procedures in Bloodstain Pattern Analysis, 60
Standard for Validation of Probabilistic Genotyping Systems, 102
Standard Operating Procedures (SOPs), 29
Standards for a Bloodstain Pattern Analyst's Training Program, 60
Standards for Training in Forensic Serological Methods, 102
Statistics, 300–301
Steroids, 183, 184f
Stimulants, 181
Straight dynamite, 172
Strangling, 276–278
Strangulation
 cases of hanging, 24
 marks, ultraviolet photography, 35
STR DNA typing, difference, 101
Strengthening Forensic Science in the United States: A Path Forward, 3
Stringing, 65f
Style characteristics, 191
Sudan black, 73
Sudden infant death syndrome (SIDS), 285
Sudden unexplained death syndrome (SUDS), 285
Suicide, 240–243, 241f
 case review, 242–243, 242f
Superglue or cyanoacrylate fuming, 74
Surgical gloves, 89
Suspect, found at scene, 20
SWGTREAD standards, 140–141

Tape, 125, 125f
Tattoos, identification of victims and suspects, 34
Teamwork, 10–11
 importance of, 11
 role of each member, 11
Temperature conditions, developing fingerprints, 78
 damp objects, 78
 outdoors in ice or snow, 78

Test firing, 160–161
 degree of stippling and spread out, 161f
 recovering a test shot, 161f
Tetramethylbenzidine, 90
Textiles and fibers, 112–113
Thermal cycler, 98
ThermoFisher's RapidHIT ID, 101f
3-D printed guns, 143, 163
3D scanning
 CSIs, 40
 data-driven documentation, 40
 FARO 3D digital scanner, 41f
Time of arrival at the scene, 20
Time spent at the scene, 20
Time-tracing fingerprinting, 303
Tire tread and tire track evidence, 140, 141f
 noise treatment, 140
 random individual characteristics, 140
 tread design, 140
 tread wear features, 140
Tool(s)
 casting, tool marks, 137, 138f
 fragments of, 139–140
 marks, 135–136
  preservation of, 137
 preserving, 139
 trace evidence on, 137–139
   hacksaw marks, 139
   mikrosil, 138f
   saw marks, 139
 used in burglaries, 107, 107f
Trace evidence; *see also* Forensic traces
 collection and preservation, 45
  control or known trace samples, 109
  double packaging, 109
  photographs, 109
 examples of, 109–122
   asbestos, 110
   ash, 116
   broken panes, glass, 118–119
   building materials, 109
   buttons, 114
   case review, 111–114, 112f, 114f
   chips and splinters, wood, 117
   cigarettes and tobacco, 115, 115f
   cordage and rope, 115
   cracked or burst panes of glass, 120–121
   curved lines, edge of glass in concentric fracture, 118f
   glass, 118
   glass perforated by bullet, 119–120, 120f
   glass splinters, 121–122, 122f
   matches, 115–116
   metals, 111
   paint, 110–111
   plant material, 118
   rust, 111
   safe insulation, 110
   sawdust, wood meal, or particles of finely powdered wood, 117
   soil, 116
   textiles and fibers, 112–113
   wood, 116–117

Training Guidelines, 102
Trinitrotoluene (TNT), 172, 173
Trunk murder, dismemberment of body, 285
Twilight zone, 13
Tyvek™, 89

Ultraviolet (UV) photography, 34
Underwater crime scene, 50
Unidentified human remains index, 100
Uniformed personnel, 17
Unmanned Aerial Vehicles (UAVs), 37, 37f
Urea nitrate, 174
USB thumb drive or external hard drive, 291
U.S. DEA drug schedule classification
    schedule I drugs, 179
    schedule II drugs, 179–180
    schedule III drugs, 180
    schedule IV drugs, 180
    schedule V drugs, 180

Vacuum metal deposition (VMD), 74
Validation Guidelines, 102
Vehicle Identification Numbers (VIN), 233
Video evidence, 224, 225f
Videography
    drones, 37–38
        Federal Aviation Administration (FAA), 37
        Light Detection and Ranging (LiDAR), 37
        mission creep, 38
        Unmanned Aerial Vehicles (UAVs), 37
    lightweight, portable, low-light video cameras, 36
    Smartphones, 36
    Unmanned Aerial Vehicle (UAV), 37f
Video spectral comparator (VSC), 195, 196f
Virtopsy, 303
Virtual reality (VR), 302
Voice identification, 195
Voucher with complete inventory, 49

Water gels or slurries, 172
Whole-face pictures, 36
Witness photographs, 32
Wood, 116–117
Wrapping, 80
Writings, on wall or body, 193f
Written documents, 191

X-STR allele calls, 100–101

Y-STRS, 100–101
    ancestry determinations, 99
    found in males, 99
    genealogy research, 99
    paternity testing, 99

Zip guns, 143